D-DAY

Also by Stephen E. Ambrose

Band of Brothers
Citizen Soldiers
The Victors
Nothing Like It In The World
Comrades
The Wild Blue

D-DAY

June 6, 1944

The Climactic Battle
of World War II

Stephen E. Ambrose

POCKET
BOOKS

Acknowledgments

Dr. Forrest Pogue began the process of collecting the oral histories of the men of D-Day on June 6, 1944. He was a sergeant (with a Ph.D. in history) serving with S. L. A. Marshall's team of historians in the Army's Historical Section, charged by Gen. George C. Marshall with collecting data from men of all ranks for an official history of the war. The team ultimately produced *The U.S. Army in World War II* (known as the Green Books from the color of the bindings), a series of scores of volumes known worldwide for accuracy and thoroughness. In 1954, Dr. Pogue published the penultimate volume in the ETO series, *The Supreme Command*, based on the documents generated by SHAEF and on interviews Pogue conducted with Eisenhower, Montgomery, and their principal subordinates. *The Supreme Command* is a genuinely great work, still the authoritative account.

But on D-Day, Dr. Pogue was working at the other end of the chain of command. He was on an LST serving as a hospital ship off Omaha Beach, interviewing wounded men about their experiences that morning. This was pioneering work in oral history; later Dr. Pogue was one of the founders of the Oral History Association.

Since I first began working for General Eisenhower as one of the editors of his wartime papers, Dr. Pogue has been my model, guide, and inspiration. He is important to my life, and to this book, in ways that go far beyond his publications (which include his four-volume, classic biography of Gen. George C. Marshall). For three decades he has been marvelously generous with his time and wisdom. At historical conferences, on eight long trips to Normandy and the other European battlefields, by correspondence and over the telephone, he has taught me and encouraged me in more ways than could ever be counted.

There are hundreds of young, and not so young, historians of World War II and of American foreign policy who are beholden to Dr. Pogue. He has brought up an entire generation of historians. His generosity with his time and knowledge goes far beyond the call of duty. To see him at a conference, surrounded by young historians and graduate students eager to hear and learn from him, is to see a great man doing great service. None of us can ever repay our debt to him, nor fully express our gratitude. He has touched our lives as a person and made us better at our craft. He is the first and the best historian of D-Day. That he has allowed me to dedicate this book to him fills me with pride and pleasure.

My interest in D-Day, first inspired by Dr. Pogue's writing, was strengthened in 1959 when I read Cornelius Ryan's *The Longest Day*. I thought then, and still do, that it was a superb account of the battle. Although I have developed some disagreements with Ryan over what happened on June 6, 1944, and have come to some different conclusions, I would be remiss if I failed to acknowledge my debt to his great work.

This book is based overwhelmingly on oral and written histories collected from the men of D-Day by the Eisenhower Center at the University of New Orleans over the past eleven years. The Center now has more than 1,380 accounts of personal experiences. This is the most extensive first-person, I-was-there collection of memoirs of a single battle in existence. Although space limitations made it impossible for me to quote directly from each oral history or written memoir, all the accounts contributed to my understanding of what happened. The contributors are listed in alphabetical order in Appendix A. To every man who contributed, I offer my deeply felt thanks.

Russell Miller of London has done extensive interviewing with British D-Day veterans. Student workers at the Eisenhower Center have transcribed some of his tapes, which he has graciously allowed me to use in this book. The Imperial War Museum in London has also provided tapes of the interviews the staff has done over the years, which have been transcribed by the Eisenhower Center. Andre Heintz has done interviews over the years with residents of the Calvados Coast; they are today in the Battle of Normandy Museum in Caen; he has kindly allowed me to use them for this book. The United States Army Military Institute at Carlisle Barracks, Pennsylvania, allowed me to use its extensive collection of interviews done by Forrest Pogue, Ken Heckler, and others, and its extensive manuscript holdings.

Phil Jutras, an American paratrooper who settled in Ste.-Mère-Église and who is the director of the Parachute Museum there, also collected oral histories from American veterans and from residents of Ste.-

Mère-Église, which he has most generously donated to the Eisenhower Center and allowed me to use for this book.

Capt. Ron Drez, USMC, a rifle-company commander at Khe Sahn in 1968, is the assistant director of the Eisenhower Center. For nearly ten years he has been doing group and individual interviews at veterans reunions, in New Orleans and around the country. Because of his own distinguished combat record, he has excellent rapport with the D-Day veterans. He gets them to talking and reminiscing as few others can do. His contribution to this book is invaluable. Dr. Günter Bischof, a native of Austria whose father was a Wehrmacht soldier and eventually a POW in America, is the associate director of the Center. He has done and is doing interviews with German veterans. His contribution is also invaluable. The Center is exceedingly lucky to have Drez and Bischof on the team.

Ms. Kathi Jones is the major force of the Eisenhower Center. Without her, none of us could do our work. She handles our correspondence, keeps the books, maintains our schedules, makes our appointments, runs our annual conferences, directs our student workers on their transcribing tasks, organizes the oral histories and memoirs, reaches out to the veterans, soothes damaged egos, and in general serves as our chief of staff. Her dedication to her work and her ability to keep our myriad of activities running smoothly are exemplary. She does all this, and more, without ever losing her temper or her good humor. Dwight Eisenhower once called Beetle Smith "the perfect chief of staff." So say we of Kathi Jones.

Mrs. Carolyn Smith, secretary of the Eisenhower Center, along with student workers Marissa Ahmed, Maria Andara Romain, Tracy Hernandez, Jerri Bland, Scott Peebles, Peggy Iheme, Jogen Shukla, and Elena Marina, graduate students Jerry Strahan, Olga Ivanova, and Gunther Breaux, and volunteers Col. James Moulis, Mark Swango, C. W. Unangst, John Daniel, Joe Flynn, John Niskoch, Joe Molyson, Stephenie Ambrose Tubbs, and Edie Ambrose are all underpaid (or not paid at all) and overworked. They have stayed with it; without them there would be no Eisenhower Center, no oral history collection. The transcribers have had a terrible time with the names of French villages (as pronounced by American GIs) but they have persevered and triumphed. My debt to them is very great.

The Eisenhower Center will continue to collect oral histories and written memoirs, artifacts and wartime letters, from the men of D-Day, from all services and nations, so long as there are survivors. We urge all veterans to write us at the University of New Orleans, New Orleans, La. 70148, for instructions on preparing their histories.

In 1979 my dearest friend, Dr. Gordon Mueller, persuaded me to lead a battlefield tour, "From D-Day to the Rhine in Ike's Footsteps." Mr. Peter McLean of Peter McLean, Ltd., in New Orleans organized the tour. Mr. Richard Salaman of London served as courier for the tour. It was a great experience for me, primarily because more than two dozen D-Day veterans joined the tour—ranging in rank from general officer to private—and gave me on-site accounts of their D-Day experiences. We repeated the tour eight times. McLean and Salaman are great guys to work with and dear friends who have contributed mightily to my knowledge and understanding of D-Day.

So have many others, scholars, authors, documentary makers, and veterans, far too many to list here—they know who they are.

Alice Mayhew, as always, was an outstanding editor. Her staff at Simon & Schuster, especially Elizabeth Stein, as always did an excellent job of production. My agent, John Ware, was a fine source of encouragement and support.

My wife, Moira, has been my partner in this enterprise, flying back and forth across the Atlantic and to veterans' reunions in the States. Every one of the hundreds of veterans she has met will attest that she has a wonderful way with them, putting them at their ease, making them comfortable, enjoying being with them, fascinated by their stories, providing a soft, sensitive woman's touch to our meals, meetings, tramps over the battlefields, and airplane hassles. In addition, as with all my writing, she is my first and most critical reader. Her contribution to my work and my life is beyond measure; indeed, she is as dear to me as life itself.

As I've tried to make clear in the preceding paragraphs, this book is very much a team effort. I like to think that General Eisenhower would have approved. From the moment he took up his responsibilities as Supreme Commander Allied Expeditionary Force until the German surrender, he insisted on teamwork. Of all his outstanding characteristics as leader of the multination, multiservice Crusade in Europe, his insistence on teamwork was the key to victory.

General Eisenhower liked to speak of the fury of an aroused democracy. It was in Normandy on June 6, 1944, and in the campaign that followed, that the Western democracies made their fury manifest. The success of this great and noble undertaking was a triumph of democracy over totalitarianism. As president, Eisenhower said he wanted democracy to survive for all ages to come. So do I. It is my fondest hope that this book, which in its essence is a love song to democracy, will make a small contribution to that great goal.

STEPHEN E. AMBROSE
Director, The Eisenhower Center
University of New Orleans

FOR FORREST POGUE, THE FIRST HISTORIAN OF D-DAY

"The most difficult and complicated operation ever to take place."

WINSTON CHURCHILL

"The destruction of the enemy's landing is the sole decisive factor in the whole conduct of the war and hence in its final results."

ADOLF HITLER

"The history of war does not know of an undertaking comparable to it for breadth of conception, grandeur of scale, and mastery of execution."

JOSEPH STALIN

"Good Luck! And let us all beseech the blessing of Almighty God upon this great and noble undertaking."

DWIGHT D. EISENHOWER,
Order of the Day, June 4, 1944

"In this column I want to tell you what the opening of the second front entailed, so that you can know and appreciate and forever be humbly grateful to those both dead and alive who did it for you."

ERNIE PYLE, June 12, 1944

Airborne and infantry divisions in World War II armies were made
   up of:
            Squads (usually nine to twelve men)
            Three squads to a platoon
            Three or four platoons to a company
            Three or four companies to a battalion
            Three or four battalions to a regiment
            Three or four regiments to a division
            plus attached engineers, artillery, medical, and other
            support personnel.

U.S., British, and Canadian infantry divisions were from 15,000 to
   20,000 strong on D-Day.
Allied airborne divisions were about one-half that size.
Most German divisions were less than 10,000.

Contents

Maps

PROLOGUE

At 0016 HOURS, June 6, 1944,* the Horsa glider crash-landed along-side the Caen Canal, some fifty meters from the swing bridge crossing the canal. Lt. Den Brotheridge, leading the twenty-eight men of the first platoon, D Company, the Oxfordshire and Buckinghamshire Light Infantry Regiment, British 6th Airborne Division, worked his way out of the glider. He grabbed Sgt. Jack "Bill" Bailey, a section leader, and whispered in his ear, "Get your chaps moving." Bailey set off with his group to pitch grenades into the machine-gun pillbox known to be beside the bridge. Lieutenant Brotheridge gathered the remainder of his platoon, whispered "Come on, lads," and began running for the bridge. The German defenders of the bridge, about fifty strong, were not aware that the long-awaited invasion had just begun.

As Brotheridge led his men at a fast trot up the embankment and onto the bridge, seventeen-year-old Pvt. Helmut Romer, one of the two German sentries on the bridge, saw the twenty-one British paratroopers—appearing, so far as he was concerned, literally out of nowhere—coming at him, their weapons carried at their

---

* British double-daylight savings time. French time was one hour earlier. Throughout Nazi-occupied Europe, clocks were set at Berlin time, and the Germans did not use daylight savings time, while the British set their clocks two hours ahead.

hips, prepared to fire. Romer turned and ran across the bridge, shouting "Paratroopers!" at the other sentry as he passed him. That sentry pulled out his *Leuchtpistole* and fired a flare; Brotheridge fired a full clip of thirty-two rounds from his Sten gun.

Those were the first shots fired by the 175,000 British, American, Canadian, Free French, Polish, Norwegian, and other nationalities in the Allied Expeditionary Force set to invade Normandy in the next twenty-four hours. The shots killed the sentry, who thus became the first German to die in defense of Hitler's Fortress Europe.

Brotheridge, twenty-six years old, had been training for this moment for two years, and for the specific task of seizing the bridge by a *coup de main* operation for six months. He had come up from the ranks; his company commander, Maj. John Howard, had recommended him for the OCTU—Officer Cadet Training Unit—back in 1942. His fellow platoon officers were university graduates, if not rich at least well-to-do, if not aristocrats at least upper class, and at first they were a bit uneasy when Brotheridge returned as an officer because "He wasn't one of us, you know."

Brotheridge played soccer, not cricket. He was a first-class athlete, good enough that it was freely predicted he would become a professional soccer player after the war. He got on easily with the men and had no sense at all of that vast gulf that so often separates British subalterns from the enlisted men.

Brotheridge would go into the barracks at night, sit on the bed of his batman, Billy Gray, and talk soccer with the lads. He would bring his boots along and shine them as he talked. Pvt. Wally Parr never got over the sight of a British lieutenant polishing his boots while his batman lay back on his bed, gassing on about Manchester United and West Ham and other soccer teams.

Den Brotheridge was a lanky, laughing, likable sort of chap, and his fellow officers warmed to him. Everyone admired him; he was fair, conscientious, hard-driving, quick to learn, a master at all the weapons in the company, an able teacher and an apt pupil, a natural leader. When Major Howard selected Brotheridge as leader of 1st Platoon, the other lieutenants in the company agreed that Den was the right man to lead the first troops to go into action on D- Day. Brotheridge was as good as any junior officer in the British army, among the best the country had produced to fight for its freedom in the life-and-death struggle.

Brotheridge had more at stake in the struggle than most, for he was one of the few married men in D Company, and his wife, Margaret, was eight months pregnant. So he had had an unborn child's future on his mind during the flight over the English Channel.

Romer's shout, the *Leuchtpistole* flare, and Brotheridge's Sten gun combined to pull the German troops manning the machine-gun pits and the slit trenches on both sides of the bridge into full alert. They began opening fire from their *Maschinengewehr* (MG-34) and their *Gewehrs* and *Karabiners* (rifles and carbines).

Brotheridge, almost across the bridge, his platoon following, the men firing from their hips, pulled a grenade out of his pouch and threw it at the machine-gun pit to his right. As he did so, he was knocked over by the impact of a bullet in his neck. He fell forward. His platoon ran past him, with two other platoons from two other gliders close behind. The men of D Company cleared out the machine-gun pits and slit trenches in short order; by 0021 the enemy in the immediate vicinity of the bridge had either been killed or had run off.

Private Parr went looking for Brotheridge, who was supposed to set up his command post at a café beside the bridge. "Where's Danny?" Parr asked another private. (To his face, the men all called him "Mr. Brotheridge." The officers called him "Den." But the men thought of him and referred to him as "Danny.")

"Where's Danny?" Parr repeated. The private did not know. Parr ran to the front of the café. He found Brotheridge lying on the ground in the road opposite the café. His eyes were open and his lips were moving, but Parr could not make out what he was saying. Parr thought, What a waste! All the years of training we put in to do this job—it lasted only seconds and there he lies.

Stretcher-bearers carried Brotheridge back across the bridge to an aid station. The company doctor, John Vaughan, found the wounded lieutenant "lying on his back looking up at the stars and looking terribly surprised, just surprised." Vaughan gave him a shot of morphine and began to dress the bullet hole in the middle of his neck. Before he could complete the first aid, Brotheridge died. He was the first Allied soldier to be killed by enemy fire on D-Day.

• •

Lt. Robert Mason Mathias was the leader of the second platoon, E Company, 508th Parachute Infantry Regiment, U.S. 82nd Airborne Division. At midnight, June 5/6, 1944, he was riding in a C-47 Dakota over the English Channel, headed toward the Cotentin Peninsula of Normandy. Two hours later, the plane was over France and starting to take some flak from German guns. At 0227 hours, Lieutenant Mathias saw the red light go on over the open door of the plane, the signal to get ready.

"Stand up and hook up!" Lieutenant Mathias called out to the sixteen men behind him as he hooked the clip from his parachute to the static line running down the middle of the roof of the aircraft. He stepped to the open door, ready to jump the instant the pilot decided the plane was over the drop zone and turned on the green light.

The Germans below were firing furiously at the air armada of 822 C-47s carrying the 82nd and 101st Airborne divisions into battle. *Flakvierling-38s* (20mm four-barreled antiaircraft guns) filled the sky with explosions; machine-gun tracers—green, yellow, red, blue, white—arched through the sky. The sight was at once awesome (nearly every paratrooper thought this was the grandest Fourth of July fireworks display he had ever seen) and terrifying. For every visible tracer, there were five unseen bullets. Unseen, but not unheard—the bullets rattled against the wings of the C-47s, sounding like rocks being shaken in a tin can. Flying at less than 1,000 feet and slower than 120 miles per hour, the planes made easy targets.

Looking out the door, Lieutenant Mathias could see an intense fire raging. A hay barn on the edge of the village of Ste.-Mère-Église had caught fire, probably from a spent tracer, and was burning fiercely, illuminating the horizon. As the C-47 lurched this way and that, a consequence of the pilot's futile attempts to escape the flak, the men behind Mathias were calling out "Let's go," "For Christ's sake let's go," or "Jump, damn it, jump." As machine-gun bullets came up through the fuselage, the men instinctively put their hands over their crotches. They had made a dozen or more practice jumps; never had it occurred to them they would be so eager to get out of an airplane in flight.

Mathias had his hands on the outside of the doorway, ready to propel himself into the night the instant the green light went on. A shell burst just beside him. Red-hot flak ripped through his reserve chute into his chest, knocking him off his feet. With a mighty effort, he began to pull himself back up. The green light went on.

At twenty-eight years of age, Mathias was five or so years older than the other lieutenants in the 508th, but he did not look it. He had reddish blond hair and an Irishman's freckles, which gave him a boyish appearance. Long and lanky (six foot one, 175 pounds), he was in superb condition, all raw bone and muscle, strong enough to survive a blow that would have felled an ox and recover almost instantly. He regained his feet and resumed his post at the door.

It was the kind of action his men had learned to expect from Bob Mathias. He was immensely popular with his platoon and fellow officers. For two years he had been preparing himself and his platoon for this moment. He was known to be absolutely fair, totally dedicated. He was the best boxer in the regiment, and the best marcher. On one twenty-five-mile march, an intraplatoon competitive hike, when everyone was pushing to the limit, one of his men gave out. Mathias picked him up and carried him the last three-quarters of a mile home.

When he censored the mail, one of his privates, Harold Cavanaugh, related, "He took extreme pains so that all that he would see were the contents. If something were written that should not have been, then and only then would he look to see the author's name. He personally would take it back to the writer to explain why certain sections had to be deleted. After the required correction, the letter was on its way. The least time possible was lost and the author always knew what would be read by the addressee."

Mathias was a devout Catholic. He went to Mass as often as possible and did all he could to make church attendance convenient for his men. He never swore. His company commander said of him, "He can hold more than his own with the toughest man alive; yet you won't ever hear him use hell or damn."

When a man in the second platoon had a problem, Mathias could sense it. He would discreetly offer his counsel, but he never intruded. One of his privates recalled, "He made allowances, but never compromised his standards. He seemed deeply hurt on the few occasions we failed to meet his expectations, but he never lost his temper."

He had prepared himself in every way possible for the upcoming struggle. He was a student of military history. He had mastered every weapon and skill necessary to a rifle company. He had studied German weapons, organization, and tactics. He had learned the German language well enough to speak it fluently, and French well enough to ask directions. He had taught his men German commands and French phrases. "Valuable lessons," Cavanaugh remarked. Afraid the Germans would use gas, Mathias had given his platoon schooling in vesicants, lacrimators, sternutators, and the like. "This knowledge later proved useless," Cavanaugh remarked, "but he wasn't overlooking a single phase of warfare."

Col. Roy E. Lindquist, commanding the 508th, said of Mathias, "He will either earn the Medal of Honor or be the first 508th man killed in action."

At the airfield on the evening of June 5, as the 508th loaded up, Mathias had shaken hands with each member of his platoon. The platoon was being carried in two planes; Private Cavanaugh, who was in the other stick, recalled, "There was an air of deserved confidence about this grand fellow. We shook hands and he said: 'We'll show 'em, won't we, Irish?' "

When Lieutenant Mathias was wounded from the shell burst and the green light went on, he had enough strength to push himself out of the way, so that the men behind him could jump. Had he done so, the crew of the C-47 could have applied first aid and—perhaps—gotten him back to England in time for a life-saving operation. Later, every man in his stick was certain that Mathias must have had that thought.

Instead, Mathias raised his right arm, called out "Follow me!" and leaped into the night. Whether the shock from the opening parachute, or the shock of hitting the ground, or excessive bleeding from his multiple wounds was the cause, no one knows, but when he was located a half hour or so later, he was still in his chute, dead. He was the first American officer killed by German fire on D-Day.

Operation Overlord, the invasion of German-occupied France in June 1944, was staggering in its scope. In one night and day, 175,000 fighting men and their equipment, including 50,000 vehicles of all types, ranging from motorcycles to tanks and armored bulldozers, were transported across sixty to a hundred miles of open water and landed on a hostile shore against intense opposition. They were either carried by or supported by 5,333 ships and craft of all types and almost 11,000 airplanes. They came from southwestern England, southern England, the east coast of England. It was as if the cities of Green Bay, Racine, and Kenosha, Wisconsin, were picked up and moved—every man, woman and child, every automobile and truck—to the east side of Lake Michigan, in one night.

The effort behind this unique movement—which British prime minister Winston S. Churchill rightly called "the most difficult and complicated operation ever to take place"—stretched back two years in time and involved the efforts of literally millions of people. The production figures from the United States, in landing craft, ships of war, airplanes of all types, weapons, medicine, and so much more, were fantastic. The figures in the United Kingdom and Canada were roughly similar.

But for all that American industrial brawn and organizational ability could do, for all that the British and Canadians and other allies could contribute, for all the plans and preparations, for all the brilliance of the deception scheme, for all the inspired leadership, in the end success or failure in Operation Overlord came down to a relatively small number of junior officers, noncoms, and privates or seamen in the American, British, and Canadian armies, navies, air forces, and coast guards. If the paratroopers and gliderborne troops cowered behind hedgerows or hid out in barns rather than actively seek out the enemy; if the coxswains did not drive their landing craft ashore but instead, out of fear of enemy fire, dropped the ramps in too-deep water; if the men at the beaches dug in behind the seawall; if the noncoms and junior officers failed to lead their men up and over the seawall to move inland in the face of enemy fire—why, then, the most thoroughly planned offensive in military history, an offensive supported by incredible amounts of naval firepower, bombs, and rockets, would fail.

It all came down to a bunch of eighteen-to-twenty-eight-year-olds. They were magnificently trained and equipped and supported, but only a few of them had ever been in combat. Only a few had ever killed or seen a buddy killed. Most were like Den Brotheridge and Bob Mathias—they had never heard a shot fired in anger. They were citizen-soldiers, not professionals.

It was an open question, toward the end of spring 1944, as to whether a democracy could produce young soldiers capable of fighting effectively against the best that Nazi Germany could produce. Hitler was certain the answer was no. Nothing that he had learned of the British army's performance in France in 1940, or again in North Africa and the Mediterranean in 1942–44, or what he had learned of the American army in North Africa and the Mediterranean in 1942–44, caused him to doubt that, on anything approaching equality in numbers, the Wehrmacht would prevail. Totalitarian fanaticism and discipline would always conquer democratic liberalism and softness. Of that Hitler was sure.

If Hitler had seen Den Brotheridge and Bob Mathias in action at the beginning of D-Day, he might have had second thoughts. It is Brotheridge and Mathias and their buddies, the young men born into the false prosperity of the 1920s and brought up in the bitter realities of the Depression of the 1930s, that this book is about. The literature they read as youngsters was antiwar, cynical, portraying patriots as suckers, slackers as heroes. None of them wanted to be part of another war. They wanted to be throwing baseballs, not hand grenades, shooting .22s at rabbits, not M-1s at other young men. But when the test came, when freedom had to be fought for or abandoned, they fought. They were soldiers of democracy. They were the men of D-Day, and to them we owe our freedom.

Before we can understand what they accomplished, however, and how they did it, and appreciate their achievement, we must look at the big picture.

I

THE DEFENDERS

AT THE BEGINNING OF 1944, Nazi Germany's fundamental problem was that she had conquered more territory than she could defend, but Hitler had a conqueror's mentality and he insisted on defending every inch of occupied soil. To carry out such orders, the Wehrmacht relied on improvisations, of which the most important were conscripted foreign troops, school-age German youths and old men, and fixed defensive positions. It also changed its tactical doctrine and weapons design, transforming itself from the highly mobile blitzkrieg army of 1940–41 that had featured light, fast tanks and hard-marching infantry into the ponderous, all-but-immobile army of 1944 that featured heavy, slow tanks and dug-in infantry.

Like everything else that happened in Nazi Germany, this was Hitler's doing. He had learned the lesson of World War I—that Germany could not win a war of attrition—and his policy in the first two years of World War II had been blitzkrieg. But in the late fall of 1941 his lightning war came a cropper in Russia. He then made the most incomprehensible of his many mistakes when he declared war on the United States—in the same week that the Red Army launched its counteroffensive outside Moscow![1]

In the summer of 1942, the Wehrmacht tried blitzkrieg against the Red Army again, but on a much reduced scale (one army group on one front rather than three army groups on three fronts), only to come a cropper once more when the snow began to fall. At the end of January 1943, nearly a quarter of a million German troops at Stalingrad surrendered. In July 1943, the Wehrmacht launched its last offensive on the Eastern Front, at Kursk. The Red Army stopped it cold, inflicting horrendous casualties.

From Kursk on, Hitler had no hope of winning a military victory against the Soviet Union. That did not mean his cause was hopeless. He had a lot of space to trade for time on the Eastern Front, and in time it was inevitable that the strange alliance—Great Britain, the Soviet Union, and the United States—that only he could have brought together would split asunder.

His death and the total defeat of Nazi Germany would for certain lead to the breakup of the alliance, but Hitler wanted the breakup to take place while it would still benefit him, and he had good reason to believe that might happen—if he could convince Stalin that he couldn't depend on the United States and Britain. In that event, Stalin could well conclude that the cost of victory to the Red Army fighting alone was too high. Once the Red Army had returned to the start line of June 1941—that is, in occupation of eastern Poland—Stalin might be willing to negotiate a peace based on a division of Eastern Europe between the Nazis and Soviets.

Between August 1939 and June 1941 the Nazi and Soviet empires had been partners, joined together in an alliance based on a division of Eastern Europe between them. To return to that situation, Hitler had to persuade Stalin that the Wehrmacht was still capable of inflicting unacceptable casualties on the Red Army. To do that, Hitler needed more fighting men and machines. To get them, he had to strip his Western Front. To do that, he had to hurl the forthcoming invasion back into the sea.

That is why D-Day was critical. In a November 3, 1943, Führer Directive (No. 51), Hitler explained it all with crystal clarity: "For the last two and one-half years the bitter and costly struggle against Bolshevism has made the utmost demands upon the bulk of our military resources and energies. . . . The situation has since changed. The threat from the East remains, but an even greater danger looms in the West: the Anglo-American landing! In the East, the vastness of the space will, as a last resort, permit a loss of territory even on a major scale, without suffering a mortal blow to Germany's chance for survival.

"Not so in the West! If the enemy here succeeds in penetrating our defense on a wide front, consequences of staggering proportions will follow within a short time." (What he meant was that a successful Anglo-American offensive in 1944 would pose a direct threat to Germany's industrial heartland, the Rhine-Ruhr region. Southeastern England is closer to Cologne, Düsseldorf, and Essen than they are to Berlin; put another way, in the fall of 1943 the front line in the East was more than 2,000 kilometers from Berlin, while in the West the front line was 500 kilometers from the Rhine-Ruhr, 1,000 kilometers from Berlin. A successful 1944 Red Army offensive would overrun parts of Ukraine and White Russia, areas important but not critical to Germany's war-making capability. A successful 1944 Anglo-American offensive would overrun the Rhine-Ruhr, areas that were indispensable to Germany's war-making capability.)

Thus, Hitler declared, it was on the French coast that the decisive battle would be fought. "For that reason, I can no longer justify the further weakening of the West in favor of other theaters of war. I have therefore decided to strengthen the defenses in the West. . . ."[2]

This reversed a policy established in the fall of 1940, with the abandonment of preparations for Operation *Seelöwe* (Sea Lion), the invasion of England. Since that time, the Wehrmacht had stripped down its forces in France, transferring men and equipment to the Eastern Front on an ever-increasing scale.

Hitler's reasons for shifting priority to the West in 1944 were more political than military. On March 20, he told his principal commanders in the West, "The destruction of the enemy's landing attempt means more than a purely local decision on the Western Front. It is the sole decisive factor in the whole conduct of the war and hence in its final result."[3] He went on to explain, "Once defeated, the enemy will never again try to invade. Quite apart from their heavy losses, they would need months to organize a fresh attempt. And an invasion failure would also deliver a crushing blow to British and American morale. For one thing, it would prevent Roosevelt from being reelected—with any luck he'd finish up in jail somewhere! For another, war weariness would grip Britain even faster and Churchill, already a sick old man with his influence waning, wouldn't be able to carry through a new invasion operation." At that point, the Wehrmacht could transfer forty-five divisions from the West to the East to "revolutionize the situation there. . . . So the whole outcome of the war depends on each man fighting in the West, and that means the fate of the Reich as well!"[4]

This was Germany's only hope. More correctly, it was Hitler's and the Nazis' only hope; for the German people and nation, the decision to continue the struggle spelled catastrophe. In any case, had Hitler's scenario worked out, in the summer of 1945 the U.S. Army Air Force, secure in its bases in England, would have started dropping atomic bombs on Berlin and other German cities. But of course in early 1944 no one knew when, or even if, the American Manhattan Project would be able to produce such a bomb.

Hitler's problem was not his priorities, it was how to hurl the coming invasion back into the sea. That problem was compounded by many factors, summed up in one word—shortages. Shortages of ships, planes, men, guns, tanks. Germany was overextended far worse than she had been in World War I. Hitler had criticized the Kaiser for getting into a two-front war, but at the end of 1943 Hitler was fighting a three-front war. On the Eastern Front, his troops were stretched over more than 2,000 kilometers; on the Mediterranean Front, which ran from southern Greece through Yugoslavia, then across Italy and southern France, his troops were defending a line of some 3,000 kilometers; on the Western Front, his troops were called on to defend 6,000 kilometers of coastline, running from Holland to the southern end of the Bay of Biscay.

Actually, there was a fourth front—at home. The Allied air offensive against German cities had driven the Luftwaffe out of France, forcing it to fight over German skies to defend German cities. The bombing had not had a decisive effect on German war production—not even close, as Germany was increasing its output of tanks and guns through 1943, although not fast enough to make up the losses—but it had put the Luftwaffe on the defensive.

Hitler hated that. Everything in his own psychology, everything in German military tradition, cried out for taking the offensive. But Hitler could not attack his enemies, at least not until his secret weapons came on line. It was gall and wormwood to him, but he had to stay on the defensive.

That necessity so stuck in his craw that it led him to make strategic and technological blunders of the greatest magnitude. When German physicists told him in 1940 that it might be possible to build an atomic bomb by 1945, he ordered them to abandon the project on the grounds that by then the war would have been won or lost. That was almost certainly a wise decision, not because his prediction was accurate but because Germany did not have the industrial or natural resources to produce an atomic bomb. German scientists went to work instead on other weapons; at Hitler's insistence, these were offensive weapons such as diesel submarines, pilotless aircraft, and rockets. The *Vergeltungswaffen* (vengeance weapons) were designed and used, eventually, but in no way were they decisive. The V-2, the world's first medium-range ballistic missile, was not a military weapon at all but a terrorist device. (The Scud missiles used by Iraq in 1991 in the Gulf War were only slightly improved versions of the V-2; like the V-2, they were inaccurate and carried only a small explosive load.)

Hitler's passion for bombing London and his indifference to defending German cities led to a monstrous, history-changing misjudgment. In May 1943, Professor Willy Messerschmitt had an ME-262 twin-jet fighter ready for serial production. Its cruise speed was 520 miles per hour, more than 120 miles an hour faster than any plane the Allies could send against it, and it mounted four 30mm cannon. *Reichsmarschall* Hermann Goering wanted the plane, but he had to clear it with Hitler. Hitler had been burned by Goering's promises too many times, and not until December 1943 did Hitler witness a demonstration of the 262's capabilities. Hitler was impressed, but he wanted a bomber to hit London, not a fighter to defend Germany. Goering assured him that the 262 could be modified to carry bombs, whereupon Hitler went into great raptures about what the jet bomber would do to London and to the anticipated Allied landings in France.

Goering, typically, had not known what he was talking about. Messerschmitt could not make a fighter into a bomber, and a larger jet airplane was pushing the technology too hard. So he ignored Hitler's order and the Messerschmitt works started turning out 262s, a total of about 120 by April 1944. When Hitler got this news, he braced Goering and gave him strict orders that not only was the 262 *not* to be built as a fighter but that nobody should even refer to it as a fighter—it was to be known as the *Blitz*-bomber.

For the next six months, Messerschmitt tried manfully to make a bomber out of a fighter. He got nowhere. Finally, in November 1944 Hitler authorized the formation of the first jet-fighter wing. But by then the transportation system was a shambles, the fighter-pilot force was decimated, and the fuel sources all but dried up.* The Luftwaffe never got more than a token force into the air before things fell apart.

The Germans built more than 1,000 ME-262s, but only in the last six weeks of the war did they get as many as 100 in the air at one time. But as a secret report in 1960 to President Dwight Eisenhower pointed out, "During that time the Germans literally flew rings around our fighters and bored holes in our bomber formations with complete impunity. . . . For example, 14 fighter groups escorted the 1,250 B-17 raid on Berlin March 18 [1945]— almost a one-for-one escort ratio. They were set upon by a single squadron of ME 262's which knocked down 25 bombers and five fighters, although outnumbered roughly 100 to 1. The Germans lost not a single plane."

The report (which Eisenhower had asked to have prepared for his personal use only) was written by White House staff officer Ralph Williams. He said he had talked to Gen. Carl Spaatz, commander of the Eighth Air Force in World War II. Spaatz "freely conceded that none of our fighters was any match for the German jets, and . . . added that if the Germans had been able to get them deployed in force to the French coast they could have denied us air superiority and frustrated the Normandy landings and might even have compelled us to work our way up into Europe via the Italian route."[5]

But what might have been wasn't; there were no German jets over France or the English Channel in June 1944, and precious few prop airplanes.

There were also precious few ships of war, and those that were there were E-boats, an oversize German version of the American patrol boat (PT boat), almost as big as a destroyer escort (the E stood for "enemy"). They were capable of laying mines and firing torpedoes and running away at high speed. Other than the E-boats, the only contribution the German navy could make to the defense of Fortress Europe was minelaying.

With no air force and no navy, the German defenders of Fortress Europe were blind and forced to stretch out to cover every conceivable landing site. Control of the air and sea gave the Allies unprecedented mobility and almost certain surprise—in briefest form, they would know where and when the battle would be fought, and the Germans would not.

* The jets were powered by synthetic fuel, one source of which was the German 1944 potato crop made into alcohol. The German people paid a terrible price in 1945 for this madness.

In World War I, preparations for a massive offensive could not be hidden. The buildup of troops took weeks; the artillery preparation took days; by the time the offensive began, the defenders knew where and when it would hit and could strengthen their positions at the point of attack. But in the spring of 1944, the Germans could only guess.

Hitler's spiritual mentor, Frederick the Great, had warned, "He who defends everything, defends nothing."[6]

It was the human and material wastage of the war on the Eastern Front that forced Hitler to ignore Frederick's warning and adopt a policy on the Western Front of fixed fortifications. Wehrmacht losses had been staggering. In June 1941, the Wehrmacht went into Russia with 3.3 million men. By the end of 1943 it had suffered nearly 3 million casualties, about one-third of which were permanent (killed, missing, captured, or unfit for combat due to wounds). Despite heroic efforts to make up the deficit by drawing down in France and calling up fresh conscripts from within Germany, after the Kursk battle (next to Verdun, the greatest battle ever fought, with more than 2 million men engaged) the Wehrmacht on the Eastern Front was down to 2.5 million, attempting to hold a line that stretched from Leningrad in the north to the Black Sea in the south, nearly 2,000 kilometers.

When the Wehrmacht invaded the Soviet Union, it prided itself on its "racial purity." The desperate need for replacements forced it to drastically modify and eventually abandon that policy. Initially, so-called Volksdeutsche ("racial Germans") from Poland and the Balkan countries were required to "volunteer." They were classified as Abteilung 3 der Deutschen Volkslists (Section 3 of the German Racial List); this meant that they were vested with German citizenship for a probationary period of ten years and were liable to military service but could not rise above the rank of private first class. In 1942–43 recruiting in the occupied territories of the Soviet Union was aggressively pursued for the struggle against communism; initially there was some truth to the designation of these recruits as Freiwilligen (volunteers), as men from the western republics of the Soviet empire signed up for the fight against Stalin. When the German retreat began, there were fewer Freiwilligen, more Hilfswilligen (auxiliaries) conscripted from the occupied territories and from Red Army prisoners of war. By the beginning of 1944 the Wehrmacht had "volunteers" from France, Italy, Croatia, Hungary, Romania, Poland, Finland, Estonia, Latvia, Lithuania,

Asian Russia, North Africa, Russia, Ukraine, Ruthenia, the Muslim republics of the Soviet Union, as well as Volga-Tatars, Volga-Finns, Crimean Tatars, and even Indians.

The so-called *Ost* (east) battalions became increasingly unreliable after the German defeat at Kursk; they were, therefore, sent to France in exchange for German troops. At the beach called Utah on the day of the invasion, Lt. Robert Brewer of the 506th Parachute Infantry Regiment, 101st Airborne Division, U.S. Army, captured four Asians in Wehrmacht uniforms. No one could speak their language; eventually it was learned that they were Koreans. How on earth did Koreans end up fighting for Hitler to defend France against Americans? It seems they had been conscripted into the Japanese army in 1938—Korea was then a Japanese colony—captured by the Red Army in the border battles with Japan in 1939, forced into the Red Army, captured by the Wehrmacht in December 1941 outside Moscow, forced into the German army, and sent to France.[7] (What happened to them, Lieutenant Brewer never found out, but presumably they were sent back to Korea. If so, they would almost certainly have been conscripted again, either into the South or the North Korean army. It is possible that in 1950 they ended up fighting once again, either against the U.S. Army, or with it, depending on what part of Korea they came from. Such are the vagaries of politics in the twentieth century.) By June 1944, one in six German riflemen in France was from an *Ost* battalion.

Furthermore, the Wehrmacht sharply relaxed its physical standards to bring more genuine Germans into the line. Men with stomach and lung ailments were sent to the front. Convalescence time was cut, as was training time for recruits. Younger and older men were called up; of an army of 4,270,000 men in December 1943, more than a million and a half were over thirty-four years old; in the 709th Division, on the Cotentin Peninsula, the average age was thirty-six; in the Wehrmacht as a whole the average age was thirty-one and a half (in the U.S. Army the average age was twenty-five and a half). Meanwhile, the classes of 1925 and 1926 were called up.[8]

As a consequence of these desperate measures, the Wehrmacht did not have the resources to conduct a defense in depth, based on counterattacks and counteroffensives. It lacked sufficient high-quality troops, it lacked sufficient mobility, it lacked sufficient armor. The old men, boys, and foreign troops were of value only if they were put into trenches or cement fortifications, with German NCOs standing behind them, pistol in hand, ready to shoot any man who left his post.

In 1939 Hitler had characterized the Wehrmacht as "an army such as the world has never seen." It was far from that at the end of 1943. The U.S. War Department described the German soldier as "one of several different types. . . . The veteran of many fronts and many retreats is a prematurely aged, war weary cynic, either discouraged and disillusioned or too stupefied to have any thought of his own. Yet he is a seasoned campaigner, most likely a noncommissioned officer, and performs his duties with the highest degree of efficiency.

"The new recruit, except in some crack SS [*Schutzstaffel*, or Protection Detachment] units, is either too young or too old and often in poor health.

"He has been poorly trained for lack of time but, if too young, he makes up for this by a fanaticism bordering on madness. If too old, he is driven by the fear of what his propagandists have told him will happen to the Fatherland in case of an Allied victory, and even more by the fear of what he has been told will happen to him and his family if he does not carry out orders exactly as given. Thus even the old and sick perform, to a certain point, with the courage of despair.

"The German high command has been particularly successful in placing the various types of men where they best fit, and in selecting those to serve as cannon fodder, who are told to hold out to the last man, while every effort is made to preserve the elite units, which now are almost entirely part of the Waffen-SS [combat troops of the SS]. The German soldier in these units is in a preferred category and is the backbone of the German Armed Forces. He is pledged never to surrender and has no moral code except allegiance to his organization. There is no limit to his ruthlessness."[9]

Beyond the Waffen-SS, the best of the young recruits went into the *Fallschirmjäger* (paratroop) or panzer (armored) units. These elite troops had been carefully brought up in Nazi Germany for just this challenge. Born between 1920 and 1925, they had grown up in Hitler's Germany, subject to constant and massive propaganda, members of the Nazi Youth. Given good equipment— and they got the best Germany could produce, which in small arms, armored vehicles, and artillery was among the best in the world—they made first-class fighting outfits.

In naturally strong coastal defenses made stronger by the skill of German engineers, even second- and third-class troops could inflict heavy casualties on an attacking force. Hitler roundly declared that it was a soldier's duty "to stand and die in his defenses."[10] That was a World War I mentality, a far cry from blitzkrieg, inappropriate to the age of tanks and other armored vehicles, but, given the situation, inevitable. What gave the concept some believability was the plan to use the crack Waffen-SS, paratroops, and armored troops in an immediate counterattack. At the end of 1943 those troops and tanks were still on the Eastern Front, or forming up inside Germany, but Hitler's directive of November 3, 1943, meant that many of them, perhaps enough, would be standing just behind the Atlantic Wall when the assault began.

As early as March 1942, Hitler laid down the basic principle in Directive No. 40. He ordered that the Atlantic coast defenses should be so organized and troops so deployed that any invasion attempt be smashed before the landing or immediately thereafter.[11] In August 1942, he decreed that fortress construction in France proceed with *Fanatismus* (fanatic energy), to create a continuous belt of interlocking fire emanating from bombproof concrete structures. In the words of the official American historian, Gordon Harrison, "Hitler was not then, and never would be, convinced that defense could not be made invulnerable if enough concrete and resolution could be poured into it."[12]

In September 1942, at a three-hour conference with Goering, Reich Minister Albert Speer (chief of Organization Todt, the German construction organization), Field Marshal Gerd von Rundstedt, commander in the West, Gen. Guenther Blumenstedt (chief of staff, *Oberbefehlshaber West*—OB West, the German ground headquarters of the Western Front), and others, Hitler reiterated his orders to prepare the strongest possible fixed fortifications along the Atlantic Wall. They must be built, he said, on the assumption that the Anglo-Americans would enjoy air and naval supremacy. Only concrete could stand up to the crushing weight of bombs and shells. He therefore wanted 15,000 concrete strong points to be occupied by 300,000 men. As no portion of the coast was safe, the whole would have to be walled up. He wanted the fortifications completed by May 1, 1943.[13]

Most of this was pure fantasy and, aside from the top-priority positions, almost none of it was accomplished at the end of 1943. But the policy had been set, the commitment made.

Rundstedt was unhappy with the idea of fixed fortifications. He argued that the Germans should hold their armored units well back from the coast, out of range of Allied naval gunfire, capable of mounting a genuine counteroffensive. But shortages of armor, men, fuel, and air coverage made that questionable.

What Hitler could do was attempt to anticipate the landing site, keep what armor was available for the West near that place, and use it for local counterattacks while the Atlantic Wall held up the invaders. Tanks could seal off any penetration; tanks could drive the lightly armed and unarmored first wave of invaders back into the sea, if the fortifications were strong enough to keep the Allies from establishing momentum. The trick was to pick the place to make the fortifications that strong.

The Pas-de-Calais was the logical place for the invasion for two overwhelming reasons: between Dover and Calais is where the English Channel is narrowest, and the straight line from London to the Rhine-Ruhr and on to Berlin runs London-Dover-Calais-Belgium.

Hitler had to make a bet, and in 1943 he bet the invasion would come at the Pas-de-Calais. In a way, he tried to force the Allies to invade there. In the summer of 1943, he decided to install the launching sites for the V-1 and V-2 *Vergeltungs* weapons in that area. He believed that whatever the Allies' previous plans might have been, the V weapons would be so dangerous as to force them to attack directly in the Pas-de-Calais in order to overrun the launching sites.

Thus the area around Calais became by far the strongest fortified portion of the *Kanalküste* (Channel coast), and in 1944 the location of by far the greatest concentration of German armor in the West. It was there that the Atlantic Wall came closest to what German propaganda claimed it was, an impregnable fortress.

He was a strange man, the German führer. In the view of the deputy chief of operations at *Oberkommando der Wehrmacht* (OKW), Gen. Walter Warlimont, "He knew the location of the defenses in detail better than any single army officer." Hitler's passion for detail was astonishing. On one occasion, he pointed out that there were two fewer antiaircraft guns on the Channel Islands than had been there the previous week. The officer responsible for this supposed reduction was punished. It turned out to have been a miscount.

Hitler spent hours studying the maps showing German installations along the Atlantic Wall. He demanded reports on building progress, the thickness of the concrete, the kind of concrete used, the system used to put in the steel reinforcement—these reports often ran to more than ten pages.[14] But, after ordering the creation of the greatest fortification in history, he never bothered to inspect any part of it. After leaving Paris in triumph in the summer of 1940, he did not set foot on French soil again until mid-June 1944. Yet he declared this was the decisive theater!

2

THE ATTACKERS

THE ALLIED PROBLEM was to land, penetrate the Atlantic Wall, and secure a lodgment in an area suitable for reinforcement and expansion. The sine qua non of the operation was to achieve surprise. If the Germans knew where and when the attack was coming they could surely concentrate enough men, concrete, tanks, and artillery at the spot to defeat the assault.

It was going to be difficult enough even with surprise. Amphibious operations are inherently the most complicated in war; few have ever been successful. Julius Caesar and William the Conqueror had managed it, but nearly every other invasion attempted against organized opposition had failed. Napoleon had not been able to cross the English Channel, nor had Hitler. The Mongols were defeated by the weather when they tried to invade Japan, as were the Spanish when they tried to invade England. The British were frustrated in the Crimea in the nineteenth century and defeated at Gallipoli in World War I.

In World War II, the record got better. By the end of 1943 the Allies had launched three successful amphibious attacks—North Africa (November 8, 1942), Sicily (July 10, 1943), and Salerno (September 9, 1943), all involving British and American land, sea, and air forces under the command of Gen. Dwight D. Eisenhower. None of the coastlines, however, had been fortified. (The only attack against a fortified coast, by the Canadians at Dieppe in northern France in August 1942, had been decisively defeated.) In North Africa, the Allies had achieved surprise when they attacked a French colonial army without a declaration of war, and even then they encountered many difficulties. At Sicily the opposition had been mainly dispirited Italian troops; nevertheless, there were some horrendous foul-ups, including the shooting down by Allied naval craft of Allied transport planes carrying the U.S. 82nd Airborne Division into battle. At Salerno, the Germans had quickly recovered from the twin surprises of the Italian double cross and the seaborne landings and come awfully close to driving the Anglo-American troops back into the sea, despite being outnumbered and outgunned.

Going into 1944, in short, there was precious little in the way of precedent or historic example the Allies could look to for inspiration. What they were about to attempt had not been done before.

But it had to be done. U.S. Army chief of staff George C. Marshall had wanted to invade France in late 1942, and even more in mid-1943. British hesitation and political necessity had forced a diversion to the Mediterranean. At the end of 1943, however, the British overcame their doubts and the Allies committed themselves to a cross-Channel attack as the decisive effort for 1944.

There were manifold reasons, of which the overriding one was the obvious point that wars are won by offensive action. For all his hesitation about when the offensive should begin, British prime minister Winston Churchill always knew that it must happen. As early as October 1941, he had told Capt. Lord Louis Mountbatten, head of Combined Operations, "You are to prepare for the invasion of Europe, for unless we can go and land and fight Hitler and beat his forces on land, we shall never win this war."[1]

To precisely that end, Marshall had transformed the U.S. Army from a cadre of 170,000 men in 1940 to an army three years later that numbered 7.2 million (2.3 million in the Army Air Force). It was the best equipped, most mobile, with the most firepower, of any army on earth. This achievement was one of the greatest accomplishments in the history of the Republic.

To use that army only in Italy was unacceptable. Failure to mount an assault to create a second front would be a double cross to Stalin and might lead to precisely the political consequence—a separate Nazi-Soviet armistice—Hitler was counting on. Or, perhaps worse, a Red Army liberation (and thus postwar occupation) of Western Europe. At a minimum, no cross-Channel attack in 1944 would put off victory against the Nazis until at least late 1945, possibly until 1946. Meanwhile, the political pressure to say to the British "To hell with it, if you won't fight in France, we will take our army to the Pacific" would become all but irresistible.

So there had to be an assault. And for all the difficulties, for all the German advantages—land lines of communication, fighting on the defensive, fixed fortifications—the Allies had the decisive edge. Thanks to their control of the sea and air, and to the mass production of a bewildering variety of landing craft, the Allies had unprecedented mobility. They would choose the time and place the battle would be fought.

As soon as the battle began, however, the advantage would shift to the Germans. Once in France, the Allied paratroops and seaborne troops would be relatively immobile. Until the beachhead had been expanded to allow self-propelled artillery and trucks to come ashore, movement would be by legs rather than half-tracks or tires. The Germans, meanwhile, could move to the sound of the guns by road and rail—and by spring 1944 they would have fifty infantry and eleven armored divisions in France. The Allies could hardly hope to put much more than five divisions into the attack on the first day, enough to give them local superiority to be sure, but all reinforcements, plus every bullet, every bandage, every K ration, would have to cross the English Channel to get into the battle.

So the Allies really had two problems—getting ashore, and winning the battle of the buildup. Once they had established a secure beachhead and won room to deploy inland, the weapons being produced in massive quantity in the United States could be brought into France, sealing the German fate. It would then be only a question of when and at what cost unconditional surrender was achieved. But if the Wehrmacht could bring ten divisions of infantry and armor into the battle by the end of the first week to launch a coordinated counterattack, its local manpower and firepower advantages could be decisive. Long-term, the Allied problem appeared to be even greater, for there would be sixty-plus German divisions in France in the spring of 1944 while the Allies would need seven weeks after D-Day to complete the commitment of the forty-odd divisions they would gather in Britain.

To win the battle of the buildup, the Allies could count on

their vast air fleets to hamper German movement—but interdiction would be effective only in daylight and good weather. Far more effective would be to immobilize the panzer divisions through trickery—fooling the Germans not only in advance of the attack, but making them believe that the real thing was a feint. That requirement would be *the* key factor in selecting the invasion site.

Whatever site was selected, the assault would be a direct frontal attack against prepared positions. How to do that successfully at an acceptable cost was a problem that had stumped generals on all sides between 1914 and 1918 and had not been solved by the end of 1943. The Wehrmacht had outflanked and outmaneuvered its opponents in Poland in 1939, in France in 1940, and in Russia in 1941. Direct frontal attacks by the Red Army against the Wehrmacht in 1943, and by the British and Americans in Italy that same year, had been costly and relatively ineffective. And the frontal attack on D-Day would be from sea to land.

In World War I, all frontal attacks had been preceded by tremendous artillery bombardments, sometimes a week or more long. Thanks to their enormous fleet, the Allies had the firepower to duplicate such artillery preparation. But the Allied planners decided that surprise was more important than a lengthy bombardment, so they limited the pre-assault bombardment to a half hour or so, in order to ensure surprise.

(Later, critics charged that the heavy losses suffered at the beach called Omaha would have been less had there been a pre-invasion air and sea bombardment of several days, as was done later in the Pacific at Iwo Jima and Okinawa. What the criticism missed was the central point. As Samuel Eliot Morison wrote in his official history of the U.S. Navy, "The Allies were invading a continent where the enemy had immense capabilities for reinforcement and counterattack, not a small island cut off by sea power from sources of supply. . . . Even a complete pulverizing of the Atlantic Wall at Omaha would have availed us nothing, if the German command had been given 24 hours' notice to move up reserves for counterattack. We had to accept the risk of heavy casualties on the beaches to prevent far heavier ones on the plateau and among the hedgerows."[2])

In World War I, when the artillery barrage lifted the infantry would climb out of the trenches and attempt to cross no-man's-land. In an amphibious assault, the attacking infantry would not have jump-off trenches close to the enemy line; rather they would have to struggle up out of the water and across wet sand, which would hamper their equipment and agility.

And how would they get from transport ships suitable for bringing them across the Channel to the shore? At the beginning of World War II, no one knew. In the late 1930s, the U.S. Marines, anticipating that a war against Japan in the Pacific would involve island attacks, had pressed the Navy to build landing craft, but the Navy was interested in aircraft carriers and battleships, not small boats, so little was done. The Wehrmacht had planned to cross the Channel to attack England in 1940 using towed barges to transport its infantry assault units. Those barges had been built for Europe's canal and river systems; on the open Channel, with anything other than an absolute calm, they would have been worse than useless.

The British got started on a solution in 1941, with the landing ship, tank (LST) and the landing craft, tank (LCT). The LST was a big ship, as big as a light cruiser, 327 feet long, displacing 4,000 tons, but it was flat bottomed and thus hard to control in any kind of sea. It was capable of grounding and discharging tanks or trucks on shallow-gradient beaches; when it beached, two bow doors opened to the sides and a ramp was lowered to allow the vehicles to drive ashore. It could carry dozens of tanks and trucks in its cavernous hold, along with small landing craft on its deck.

The LCT (in U.S. Navy parlance, a "ship" was over 200 feet in length, a "craft" less than that) was a flat-bottomed craft 110 feet long, capable of carrying from four to eight tanks (eventually there were four types of LCTs) across relatively wide bodies of water, such as the Channel, even in relatively rough seas, and discharging its cargo over a ramp. When America came into the war, it took on the task of all LST and most LCT production, in the process considerably improving the designs.

The LSTs and the LCTs became the workhorses of the Allies. They were the basic vehicle-carrying landing craft, used successfully in the Mediterranean in 1942 and 1943. But they had significant shortcomings. They were slow, cumbersome, easy targets (those who sailed LSTs insisted the initials stood for Long Slow Target). They were not suitable for landing platoons of fighting men, the skirmishers who would have to lead the way in the first wave. For that job, what was needed was a small boat of shallow draft with a protected propeller that could beach by the bow, extract itself quickly, and have a small turning circle to enable it to turn out to open water without danger of broaching in a heavy surf. It would also require a ramp so that the riflemen could move onto the beach in a rush (rather than jumping over the sides).

Various designers in America, both in and out of the Navy, took up the problem. They came up with a variety of answers, some of which worked. The best were the LCIs (landing craft, infantry, a seagoing troop-landing craft of 160-foot length capable of carrying a reinforced company of infantry—nearly 200 men—and discharging the men down ramps on each side of the bow), the LCMs (landing craft, medium), and the LCVPs (landing craft, vehicle and personnel).[3]

There were many other types, including the oddest of all, a floating two-and-a-half-ton truck. It was designed by a civilian employee at the Office of Scientific Research and Development, Palmer C. Putnam. He took a deuce-and-a-half truck—the U.S. Army's basic (and much loved) truck—and turned it into an amphibian by providing buoyancy through a body made up largely of sealed, empty tanks and by giving it a pair of small propellers to provide forward motion in water. Once it hit the sand, it would operate as a truck. The vehicle was capable of making five and a half knots in a moderate sea, fifty miles per hour on land. It could carry artillery pieces, fighting men, or general cargo.

Most everyone laughed at this hybrid at first, but it soon showed its stuff and was adopted. The Army called it a DUKW: D for 1942, the year of design; U for amphibian; K for all-wheel drive; W for dual rear axles. The users called it a Duck.[4]

Production was as great a problem as design. The difficulties involved in building a landing-craft fleet big enough to carry three to five divisions ashore in one day were enormous. Neither the Navy nor the shipyards had any experience in such matters. There were competing priorities. In 1942 escort vessels and merchant shipping were more immediate necessities, and they got the available steel and marine engines.

As a result, there were severe shortages, so severe that the chief limiting factor in planning the invasion was lack of sufficient landing ships and craft. Indeed, that was the single most important factor in shaping the whole strategy of the war, in the Pacific, in the Mediterranean, in the Atlantic. Churchill complained with some bitterness that "the destinies of two great empires . . .

seemed to be tied up in some goddamned things called LSTs."[5]

That these shortages were overcome was a miracle of production and a triumph of the American economic system. The Navy did not want to mess around with small boats, and their big contractors, the large shipyards, felt the same. Perforce, the job fell to small businessmen, entrepreneurs, high-risk takers with little boatyards, designing boats on speculation, producing them on the basis of a handshake contract.

There were many such men, but the greatest designer and builder of landing craft was Andrew Jackson Higgins of New Orleans.

The first time I met General Eisenhower, in 1964 in his office in Gettysburg, where he had called me to discuss the possibility of my becoming one of the editors of his official papers, he said at the end of the conversation, "I notice you are teaching in New Orleans. Did you ever know Andrew Higgins?"

"No, sir," I replied. "He died before I moved to the city."

"That's too bad," Eisenhower said. "He is the man who won the war for us."

My face must have shown the astonishment I felt at hearing such a strong statement from such a source. Eisenhower went on to explain, "If Higgins had not designed and built those LCVPs, we never could have landed over an open beach. The whole strategy of the war would have been different."

Andrew Higgins was a self-taught genius in small-boat design. In the 1930s he had been building boats for the oil industry, which was exploring in the swamps of south Louisiana and needed a shallow-draft vessel that could run up on a bank and extract itself. His "Eureka" boat, made of wood, filled the need perfectly. He was so confident there would be a war and a need for thousands of small boats, and so certain that steel would be in short supply, that he bought the entire 1939 crop of mahogany from the Philippines and stored it for future use.

When the Marines forced the Navy to begin experimenting with landing craft, Higgins entered the competition. The Navy Bureau of Ships wanted to do the design itself and wanted no part of this hot-tempered, loud-mouthed Irishman who drank a bottle of whiskey a day, who built his boats out of wood instead of metal, whose firm (Higgins Industries) was a fly-by-night outfit on the Gulf Coast rather than an established firm on the East Coast, and who insisted that the "Navy doesn't know one damn thing about small boats."

The struggle between the bureaucracy and the lonely inventor lasted for a couple of years, but one way or another Higgins managed to force the Navy to let him compete for contracts—and the Marines loved what he produced, the LCVP. It was so far superior to anything the Navy designers, or the private competitors, could build that excellence won out over blind, stupid, stuck-in-the-mud bureaucracy.

Once he got the initial contract, Higgins showed that he was as much a genius at mass production as he was at design. He had assembly lines scattered throughout New Orleans (some under canvas). He employed, at the peak, 30,000 workers. It was an integrated work force of blacks, women, and men, the first ever in New Orleans. Higgins inspired his workers the way a general tries to inspire his troops. A huge sign hung over one of his assembly lines: "The Man Who Relaxes Is Helping the Axis." He put pictures of Hitler, Mussolini, and Hirohito sitting on toilets in his factories' bathrooms. "Come on in, brother," the caption read. "Take it easy. Every minute you loaf here helps us plenty." He paid top wages regardless of sex or race.[6]

Higgins improved the design of the LCTs and produced hundreds of them; he helped design the patrol boats (PT boats) and built dozens of them; he had an important subcontractor role in the Manhattan Project; he made other contributions to the war effort as well.

Mostly, however, Higgins Industries built LCVPs. It was based on the Eureka design, but substituted a square bow that was actually a ramp for the spoonbill bow of the Eureka. At thirty-six feet long and ten and a half feet wide, it was a floating cigar box propelled by a protected propeller powered by a diesel engine. It could carry a platoon of thirty-six men or a jeep and a squad of a dozen men. The ramp was metal but the sides and square stern were plywood. Even in a moderate sea it would bounce and shake while swells broke over the ramp and sides. But it could bring a rifle platoon to the shoreline and discharge the men in a matter of seconds, then extract itself and go back to the mother ship for another load. It fit the need perfectly.

By the end of the war, Higgins Industries had produced over 20,000 LCVPs. They were dubbed "Higgins boats," and they carried infantry ashore in the Mediterranean, in France, at Iwo Jima and Okinawa, and at other Pacific islands. More American fighting men went ashore in Higgins boats than in all other types of landing craft combined.*

The Higgins boats were carried across the Atlantic—and later across the Channel—on the decks of LSTs. They were lowered by davits. (One of Higgins's arguments with the Bureau of Ships had been about length; he insisted that a thirty-six-foot boat was the right length to meet the requirements, while the Navy said it had to be a thirty-foot boat because the davits on the LSTs were designed for a boat of that length. "Change the davits," Higgins thundered, and eventually that commonsense solution was adopted.) Together with the LCTs and other craft, they gave the Allies unprecedented mobility.

The Allies had other advantages to help solve their problems. The Germans, who had been pioneers in creating a paratroop force, had given up on airborne operations after suffering disastrous losses in the 1941 capture of Crete, and in any case they did not have the transport capacity to mount much more than a small raiding party. But the American, British, and Canadian armies had airborne divisions, and they had the planes to carry them behind enemy lines. Those planes were designated C-47s and dubbed Dakotas. Each could carry a stick of eighteen paratroopers. The Dakota was the military version of the DC-3, a twin-engine plane built by Douglas Aircraft in the 1930s. It was unarmed and unarmored, but it was versatile. It was slow (230 miles per hour top speed) but the most dependable, most rugged, best designed airplane ever built. (A half century and more later, most of the DC-3s built in the thirties were still in service, primarily flying as commercial transports over the mountains of South and Central America.)

The men the Dakotas carried were elite troops. There were two British airborne divisions, the 1st and 6th, and two American, the 82nd and 101st. Every paratrooper was a volunteer. (Glider-borne infantry were *not* volunteers.) Each paratrooper had gone

---

* After the war, Higgins was beset by problems, some of his own making. He was not a good businessman. He could not bring himself to cut back because he hated to put his work force on unemployment. He fought the labor unions and lost. He was ahead of his time as he tried to move into helicopters and pleasure motor and sailing craft, pop-up tent trailers, and other leisure-time items that would eventually take off but not in 1946–47. He was brilliant at design but lousy at marketing, a master of production but a terrible bookkeeper. He went bust. Higgins Industries went under.

But he was the man who won the war for us, and it is a shame that he has been forgotten by the nation and by the city of New Orleans.

through a rigorous training course, as tough as any in the world. The experience had bonded them together. Their unit cohesion was outstanding. The men were superbly conditioned, highly motivated, experts in small arms. The rifle companies in the Allied airborne divisions were as good as any in the world. So were the other elite Allied formations, such as the American Rangers and the British Commandos.

The U.S. Army's infantry divisions were not elite, by definition, but they had some outstanding characteristics. Although they were made up, primarily, of conscripted troops, there was a vast difference between American draftees and their German counterparts (not to mention the *Ost* battalions). The American Selective Service System was just that, selective. One-third of the men called to service were rejected after physical examinations, making the average draftee brighter, healthier, and better educated than the average American. He was twenty-six years old, five feet eight inches tall, weighed 144 pounds, had a thirty-three-and-a-half-inch chest, and a thirty-one-inch waist. After thirteen weeks of basic training, he'd gained seven pounds (and converted many of his original pounds from fat to muscle) and added at least an inch to his chest. Nearly half the draftees were high-school graduates; one in ten had some college. As Geoffrey Perret puts it in his history of the U.S. Army in World War II, "These were the best-educated enlisted men of any army in history."[7]

At the end of 1943 the U.S. Army was the greenest army in the world. Of the nearly fifty infantry, armored, and airborne divisions selected for participation in the campaign in northwest Europe, only two—the 1st Infantry and the 82nd Airborne—had been in combat.

Nor had the bulk of the British army seen action. Although Britain had been at war with Germany for four years, only a small number of divisions had been in combat, and none of those designated for the assault had more than a handful of veterans.

This posed problems and caused apprehension, but it had a certain advantage. According to Pvt. Carl Weast of the U.S. 5th Ranger Battalion, "A veteran infantryman is a terrified infantryman."[8] Sgt. Carwood Lipton of the 506th Parachute Infantry Regiment (PIR) of the 101st Airborne commented, "I took chances on D-Day I would never have taken later in the war."[9]

In *Wartime*, Paul Fussell writes that men in combat go

through two stages of rationalization followed by one of perception. Considering the possibility of a severe wound or death, the average soldier's first rationalization is: "It *can't* happen to me. I am too clever/agile/well-trained/good-looking/beloved/tightly laced, etc." The second rationalization is: "It *can* happen to me, and I'd better be more careful. I can avoid the danger by watching more prudently the way I take cover/dig in/expose my position by firing my weapon/keep extra alert at all times, etc." Finally, the realization is "It *is going to* happen to me, and only my not being there is going to prevent it."[10]

For a direct frontal assault on a prepared enemy position, men who have not seen what a bullet or a land mine or an exploding mortar round can do to a human body are preferable to men who have seen the carnage. Men in their late teens or early twenties have a feeling of invulnerability, as seen in the remark of Charles East of the 29th Division. Told by his commanding officer on the eve of D-Day that nine out of ten would become casualties in the ensuing campaign, East looked at the man to his left, then at the man to his right, and thought to himself, You poor bastards.[11]

Men like Sergeant Lipton and Private East—and there were thousands of them in the American army—could overcome the problem of inexperience with their zeal and daredevil attitude.

The ordinary infantry divisions of the British army were another matter. They had been in barracks since the British Expeditionary Force retreated from the Continent in June 1940. The ordinary soldier was not as well educated or as physically fit as his American counterpart. Superficial discipline—dress, saluting, etc.—was much better than among the GIs, but real discipline, taking and executing orders, was slack. The British War Office had been afraid to impose discipline too strictly in a democratic army on the odd notion that it might dampen the fighting spirit of the men in the ranks.

Those British soldiers who were veterans had been badly beaten by the Wehrmacht in 1940; their overseas mates had surrendered to an inferior Japanese army in Singapore in February 1941, to an inferior German army in Tobruk, Libya, in June 1942, and again to an inferior German force on the Greek island of Leros in November 1943. The one British victory in the war, at El Alamein in November 1942, had been won over an undersupplied, outgunned, and outmanned Afrika Korps. In pursuing the defeated Afrika Korps into Tunisia, as in the ensuing campaigns in Sicily and Italy, the British Eighth Army had not displayed much of a killer instinct.

The Germans who fought against the British often expressed their surprise at the way in which British troops would do only what was expected of them, no more. They found it remarkable that the British would abandon a pursuit to brew up their tea, and even more remarkable that British troops would surrender when their ammunition ran low, when their fuel ran out, or when they were encircled. Gen. Bernard Law Montgomery, commander of the Eighth Army, wrote his superior, Chief of the Imperial General Staff Field Marshal Alan Brooke: "The trouble with our British lads is that they are not killers by nature."[12]

One reason for the shortcomings of the World War II British army was inferior weaponry. British tanks, trucks, artillery, and small arms were not as good as those of their enemies, or of their American partners. Another reason was the way in which the poison of pacifism had eaten into the souls of British youth after the catastrophes of the Somme, Flanders, and elsewhere in World War I. In addition, senior officers were survivors of the trenches. They had nightmares from the experience. They mistrusted offensive action in general, direct frontal assaults even more. What their generals had ordered them to do, charge across no-man's-land, they would not. They knew it was stupid, futile, suicidal. Their mistake was in thinking that the lessons of World War I applied to all offensive action.

On the eve of the invasion, General Montgomery visited D Company, the Oxfordshire and Buckinghamshire Light Infantry, a gliderborne outfit in the 6th Airborne Division. Its commanding officer was Maj. John Howard. D Company had a special mission. It was composed of volunteers, had excellent junior officers, was well trained and primed to go. It was an outstanding rifle company. Montgomery's parting words to Howard were, "Bring back as many of the chaps as you can."[13]

Montgomery's approach to the launching of an offensive was markedly different from that of Field Marshal Douglas Haig in World War I, and certainly far more commendable. And yet those were strange words to say to the commander of an elite force undertaking an absolutely critical task. One might have thought something like "John, whatever else, get the job done" would have been more appropriate.

In part, Montgomery's caution was simple realism. Britain

had reached her manpower limits. The British army could not afford heavy losses; there was no way to make them up. But it was precisely this point that infuriated Americans. In their view, the way to minimize casualties was to take risks to win the war as soon as possible, not to exercise caution in an offensive action.

Something else irritated the Americans—the supercilious contempt for all things American that some British officers could not help displaying, and the assumed superiority of British techniques, methods, tactics, and leadership that almost all British officers shared and many of them displayed. Put directly, most British officers regarded the Americans as neophytes in war who were blessed with great equipment in massive quantities and superbly conditioned but inexperienced enlisted men. Such officers felt it was their duty, their destiny, to train and teach the Yanks. Field Marshal Sir Harold Alexander wrote to Brooke from Tunisia about the Americans: "They simply do not know their job as soldiers and this is the case from the highest to the lowest, from the general to the private soldier. Perhaps the weakest link of all is the junior leader, who just does not lead, with the result that their men don't really fight."[14]

Another major problem the Allies faced at the end of 1943 was precisely the fact that they were allies. "Give me allies to fight against," said Napoleon, pointing to an obvious truth. The Yanks got on British nerves; the Limeys got on American nerves. This was exacerbated by proximity; as the American army in Britain began to grow in anticipation of the invasion, the friction increased. According to the British, the trouble with the Yanks was that they were "overpaid, oversexed, and over here." The GIs responded that the trouble with the Limeys was they were underpaid (which was true) and undersexed, which tended to be true as British girls naturally gravitated to the GIs, who had money to throw around and were billeted in villages rather than segregated in isolated barracks.

In Tunisia, Sicily, and Italy the Tommies and the GIs had fought side by side, but there had been too much friction, too little functioning as a team. If they were going to penetrate the Atlantic Wall, they were going to have to learn to work together. One indication that they could do so was the designation of the force. Back in 1917, when members of the American Expeditionary Force were asked what AEF stood for, the Yanks replied, "After England Failed." But in 1943 AEF stood for Allied Expeditionary Force.

• •

As against the untested, cocky, "damn the torpedoes, full steam ahead" American army and the war-weary, too cautious British army, the Germans could put into the battle troops who (as described by Max Hastings) "possessed an historic reputation as formidable soldiers. Under Hitler their army attained its zenith." Hastings asserts: "Throughout the Second World War, wherever British or American troops met the Germans in anything like equal strength, the Germans prevailed."[15]

Hastings's judgment has become popular among military historians a half-century after the war. The German soldier in World War II has assumed a mythical quality as the best fighting man not only in that war but in almost any war ever fought.

The judgment is wrong. The Wehrmacht had many fine units, and many outstanding soldiers, but they were not supermen. Not even the Waffen-SS elite troops of 1944–45 were much, if any, better than ordinary Allied troops. And the Allied elite units, the airborne and Rangers and Commandos, were better than anything the Germans put into the field.

What made the Germans look so good, what so impressed Hastings and others, was the kill ratio. It was almost two-to-one in favor of the Wehrmacht, sometimes higher. But that criterion ignores a basic fact: the Wehrmacht vs. the Anglo-American armies was almost always fighting on the defensive behind prepared positions or fixed fortifications, such as the Mareth Line in Tunisia, the Winter Line in Italy, the Atlantic Wall in France, the West Wall in the final defense of Germany's borders. Even then, the Germans never did manage to hold a position—they were always driven back. Of course, the argument is that they were driven back by overwhelming firepower, that the Allies won because they outproduced the Germans, not because they outfought them. There is truth to that.

But the only time in World War II that the Wehrmacht undertook a genuine offensive against American troops, it was soundly whipped. In the Ardennes, in December 1944, the Germans had the manpower and firepower advantage. At Bastogne, where the 101st Airborne was encircled, it was almost a ten-to-one advantage. Allied control of the air was useless for the first week of the battle, due to miserable weather. The Germans were close to their supply dumps, even to their manufacturing sites— tanks rolling out of factories in the Rhine-Ruhr region could start firing almost as they left the factory gate. The Germans had some of their best Waffen-SS and panzer divisions in the attack. They had ample artillery support. But the lightly armed 101st, cut off from its supplies, cold, hungry, unable to properly care for its wounded, running low on or even out of ammunition, with little artillery support, held off desperate German attacks for more than a week.

The American elite unit prevailed over the elite German units. Elsewhere in the Ardennes the same pattern prevailed. Once they had recovered from their surprise, the American regular infantry units gave an excellent account of themselves.

In 1980, *Time* magazine columnist Hugh Sidey asked Gen. Maxwell Taylor, the wartime commander of the 101st Airborne, to assess the performance of the American soldiers under his command in World War II. There were many problems at first, Taylor said, but by December 1944 there were companies in his division "that were better than anything anywhere. The men were hardened, the officers tested, their equipment upgraded and they had that wonderful flexibility and self-confidence imparted by a democratic society. No other system could produce soldiers like that, but it did take some time."[16]

So although the German army contained some very good units, it just won't do to call that army as a whole the best in the war. It would be more accurate to say that after 1941 the side on the defensive almost always gave a better account of itself.

Neither were the Germans superior to the Allies on the technological front. True, their infantry weapons tended to be better, and they had some innovative gadgets, such as the V-1 pilotless bomber, and some genuine breakthroughs, such as the snorkel submarine and the V-2 ballistic missile. But they had fallen badly behind in the quality and design of fighter and bomber aircraft (except for the too-late ME 262), they were not even in the atomic-bomb race, their encoding system, the Enigma machine, had been hopelessly compromised, and—strangely enough for a country that had Mercedes and Volkswagen—they were badly outclassed in motor transport.

The British were outstanding in science and technology. The proximity fuse, radar, and sonar were British innovations, as was penicillin. Much of the basic work on the atomic bomb was done by British physicists. The British were inventive. For example, they were working on special tanks, called "Hobart's Funnies" after Gen. Percy Hobart of the 79th Armoured Division. In March 1943, Hobart had been given the job of figuring out how to get armored support onto and over the beaches, to breach the concrete and minefields of the Atlantic Wall. He came up with swimming tanks. Duplex drive (DD), they were called, after their twin propellers working off the main engine. They had a waterproof, air-filled canvas screen all round the hull, giving the DD the appearance of a baby carriage. The inflatable screen was dropped when the tank reached the shore.

Another of Hobart's Funnies carried a forty-foot box-girder bridge for crossing antitank ditches. The "Crab" had a rotating drum in front of the tank; as it turned it thrashed the ground in front with steel chains, safely detonating mines in its path. There were others.

Even more astonishing than swimming tanks was the idea of towing prefabricated ports across the Channel. By the end of 1943 thousands of British workers were helping to construct the artificial ports (code name Mulberries) and the breakwaters to shelter them. The "docks" consisted of floating piers connected by treadway to the beach. The piers were devised so that the platform, or roadway, could slide up and down with the tide on four posts that rested on the sea bottom. The breakwater (code name Phoenix) combined hollow, floating concrete caissons about six stories high with old merchant ships. Lined up end to end off the French coast, the ships and Phoenixes were sunk by opening their sea cocks. The result: an instant breakwater protecting instant port facilities, in place and ready to go on D-Day plus one.*

There were many other British triumphs. One of the most important was Ultra. Ultra was the code name for the system of breaking the German Enigma encoding machine. From 1941 onward, the British were reading significant portions of German radio

---

* The Mulberries were not in operation long; a great storm two weeks after D-Day knocked out the American Mulberry and badly damaged the British one. But the great LST fleet more than made up the difference, raising the question: Was the expenditure of so much material and manpower on building the Mulberries wise? Russell Weigley's answer is yes. He writes: "Without the prospect of the Mulberries to permit the beaches to function as ports, Churchill and his government would probably have backed away from Overlord after all" (Russell Weigley, *Eisenhower's Lieutenants: The Campaigns of France and Germany, 1944–45* [Bloomington: Indiana University Press, 1981], p. 103).

traffic, giving the Allies a generally accurate, and occasionally exact and total, picture of the enemy order of battle. As that is the most basic and priceless of all intelligence in war—where are the enemy units? in what strength? with what capabilities?—Ultra gave the Allies an immense advantage.

When the Ultra secret was finally revealed in the early 1970s, people asked, "If we were reading German radio traffic right through the war, how come we didn't win the war sooner?" The answer is, we did.

The intelligence advantage was even greater thanks to the British Double Cross System and to German conceit. In 1940, the British had managed to arrest all German spies in the United Kingdom. They were "turned," persuaded at the point of a gun to operate as double agents. For the next three years they sent information to their controllers in Hamburg via Morse code, information carefully selected by the British. It was always accurate, as the aim of the operation was to build Abwehr (the German security service) trust in the agents, but was always either insignificant or too late to be of any use.[17]

Sometimes the information passed on could prove disconcerting to the Allied forces preparing for the invasion. Sgt. Gordon Carson of the U.S. 101st was stationed in Aldbourne, west of London, late in 1943. He liked to listen to "Axis Sally" on the radio. Sally, known to the men as the "Bitch of Berlin," was Midge Gillars, an Ohio girl who had wanted to be an actress but had become a Parisian fashion model. There she met Max Otto Koischwitz, married him, and moved to Berlin. When the war came, she became a disc jockey. She was popular with the American troops because of her accent and her sweet, sexy voice and because she played the latest hits, interspersed with crude propaganda (Why fight for the communists? Why fight for the Jews? etc.) that gave the men a laugh.

But they did not laugh when Sally interspersed her commentary with remarks that sent chills up the spines of her listeners, such as: "Hello to the men of Company E, 506th PIR, 101st A/B in Aldbourne. Hope you boys enjoyed your passes to London last weekend. Oh, by the way, please tell the town officials that the clock on the church is three minutes slow."[18]

Axis Sally had her facts straight and hundreds of GIs and Tommies tell stories similar to Carson's about the clock. Fifty years later, the veterans still shake their heads and wonder, "How the hell did she know that?" She knew because the Double Cross System had given her the information.*

The receipt of so much information from their agents reinforced the German conceit that they had the best set of spies in the world. That added to their conviction that Enigma was the best encoding machine, absolutely unbreakable, and made them think that they had the best intelligence and counterintelligence systems in the world.

Fooling the Germans about Allied capabilities and intentions was the negative side of the espionage struggle. The positive side was gathering information on the German order of battle. Of course, Ultra was making a priceless contribution here; to supplement Ultra, the Allies had two sources that, at the end of 1943, they were ready to put into full action. The first was air reconnaissance. With the Luftwaffe fighting on the defensive, mostly inside Germany, the Americans and British were free to fly over France and take all the photographs they wished.

But tank and artillery parks could be hidden in woods, field emplacements camouflaged, which brought into play the second Allied source, the French Resistance. Partly to keep the economy producing at full capacity, partly because in France the German occupiers tried to act in a decent fashion in order to make friends, French civilians were not evacuated from the coastal areas. They could see where the Germans were positioning their guns, hiding their tanks, placing their mines. When the time came, they had ways of getting that information over to England, primarily by working with the Special Operations Executive (SOE), a part of the vast British intelligence gathering/covert operations network that was one of the great British accomplishments in the war.

It is far too simple to say that the marriage of British brains and American brawn sealed the fate of Nazi Germany in the West. The British contributed considerable brawn, for one thing, and the Americans contributed considerable brains. Still, there is some truth in it. If the British miracles of World War II included Hobart's Funnies, Mulberries, Ultra, and the Double Cross System, the American miracles included production of war matériel such as the world had never seen.

* After the war, Ms. Gillars was tried and convicted of treason. She served a dozen years in a federal reformatory. Released in 1961, she taught music in Columbus, Ohio. She died at age eighty-seven in 1988.

At the beginning of 1939, American industry was still flat on its back. Factory output was less than one-half of capacity. Unemployment was above 20 percent. Five years later unemployment was 1 percent while factory capacity had doubled, then doubled again and yet again. In 1939, the United States produced 800 military airplanes. When President Franklin Roosevelt called for the production of 4,000 airplanes *per month*, people thought he was crazy. But in 1942, the United States was producing 4,000 a month, and by the end of 1943 8,000 per month. There were similar, all-but-unbelievable great leaps forward in the production of tanks, ships, landing craft, rifles, and other weapons. And all this took place while the United States put a major effort into the greatest industrial feat to that time, the production of atomic weapons (hardly begun in 1942, completed by mid-1945).

That a cross-Channel attack against the Atlantic Wall could even be contemplated was a tribute to what Dwight Eisenhower called "the fury of an aroused democracy." What made D-Day possible was the never-ending flow of weapons from American factories, the Ultra and the Double Cross System, victory in the Battle of the Atlantic, control of the air and sea, British inventiveness, the French Resistance, the creation of citizen armies in the Western democracies, the persistence and genius of Andrew Higgins and other inventors and entrepreneurs, the cooperation of business, government, and labor in the United States and the United Kingdom, and more—all summed up in the single word "teamwork."

3

THE COMMANDERS

THE TWO MEN had much in common. Born in 1890, Dwight Eisenhower was one year older than Erwin Rommel. They grew up in small towns, Eisenhower in Abilene, Kansas; Rommel in Gmünd, Swabia. Eisenhower's father was a mechanic, Rommel's a schoolteacher. Both fathers were classic Germanic parents who imposed a harsh discipline on their sons, enforced by physical punishment. Both boys were avid athletes. Eisenhower's sports were football and baseball, Rommel's cycling, tennis, skating, rowing, and skiing. Although neither family had a military tradition, each boy went off to military school; in 1910 Rommel entered the Royal Officer Cadet School in Danzig, while Eisenhower in 1911 went to the U.S. Military Academy at West Point.

As cadets, neither was an outstanding student, but both were competent and they shared a proclivity for breaking the rules. Rommel wore a forbidden monocle, while Eisenhower smoked forbidden cigarettes. They were dashingly good-looking in their uniforms; each courted and won the hand of a vivacious, young, and much-sought-after beauty—in 1916 Rommel married Lucie Mollin; the next year, Eisenhower married Mamie Doud.[1]

Their careers diverged in World War I. Rommel was a combat leader in France and Italy, highly decorated (Iron Cross, first and second class, and the coveted *Pour le Merite*). Eisenhower was stuck in the States as a training commander, a bitter blow to him from which he feared he would never recover. Still, as junior officers, both showed remarkable leadership ability.

Theodor Werner, one of Rommel's platoon leaders, recalled: "When I first saw him [in 1915] he was slightly built, almost schoolboyish, inspired by a holy zeal, always eager and anxious to act. In some curious way his spirit permeated the entire regiment right from the start, at first barely perceptibly to most but then increasingly dramatically until everybody was inspired by his initiative, his courage, his dazzling acts of gallantry. . . . His men idolized him and had boundless faith in him."[2]

Sgt. Maj. Claude Harris recalled of Eisenhower: "[He] was a strict disciplinarian, an inborn soldier, but most human, considerate. . . . Despite his youth, he possessed a high understanding of organization. . . . This principle built for him high admiration and loyalty from his officers perhaps unequaled by few commanding officers."[3] Lt. Ed Thayer, one of Eisenhower's subordinates, wrote of him: "Our new Captain, Eisenhower by name, is, I believe, one of the most efficient and best Army officers in the country. . . . He has given us wonderful bayonet drills. He gets the fellows' imaginations worked up and hollers and yells and makes us shout and stomp until we go tearing into the air as if we meant business."[4]

In the interwar years, Rommel remained a line officer, while Eisenhower was a staff officer. Promotions were slow at best, but neither ever thought of any life other than that of a soldier, even though each was ambitious and could have been a success at any number of civilian occupations. They impressed their superiors. Rommel's regimental commander wrote of him in 1934: "Head and shoulders above the average battalion commander in every respect."[5] That same year Eisenhower's superior, Chief of Staff Douglas MacArthur, wrote of him: "This is the best officer in the Army. When the next war comes, he should go right to the top."[6]

The war brought both men out of obscurity. Rommel made his reputation first as commander of the panzer division that led the way through France in 1940; he added enormous luster to it and became a world figure as commander of the Afrika Korps in the eastern North African desert in 1941–42. Eisenhower became a world figure in November 1942 in the western North African desert as commander of the Allied forces.

Despite his spectacular victories in the desert, after Rommel lost the Battle of El Alamein in the late fall of 1942 he became what

Hitler called a defeatist, what others would call a realist. On November 20, when he learned that of fifty transport airplanes bringing fuel for his tanks forty-five had been shot down (thanks to an Ultra intercept), Rommel went for a walk in the desert with one of his young battalion commanders, Maj. Baron Hans von Luck.

"Luck, that's the end!" the major recalled Rommel saying. "We can't even hold Tripolitania, but must fall back on Tunisia. There, in addition, we shall come upon the Americans. . . . Our proud Africa army, and the new divisions that have landed in northern Tunisia, will be lost. . . ."

Major Luck protested that they still had a chance.

Rommel said no. As Luck recalled the conversation, Rommel said, "Supplies will not be forthcoming. Hitler's HQ has already written off this theater of war. All he requires now is that 'the German soldier stands or dies!' . . . Luck, the war is lost!"[7]

Despite his misgivings, Rommel fought on. The Americans, coming from the west, were waiting for the Afrika Korps in Tunisia. There, in February 1943, Rommel and Eisenhower first clashed, in the Battle of Kasserine Pass. Through surprise and audacity, Rommel scored impressive initial gains against the untried and inadequately trained American troops, who were led by untried and ill-prepared American generals—including Eisenhower, who was fighting his first real battle. Eisenhower made many mistakes but recovered from them, used his logistical and fire power superiority effectively, and eventually won the battle.

By this time Rommel was suffering from high blood pressure (so was Eisenhower), violent headaches, nervous exhaustion, and rheumatism. Partly to preserve Rommel's health, partly to preserve his reputation (surrender in North Africa was imminent), partly to save himself from daily demands for more supplies for North Africa, Hitler ordered Rommel home, after promoting him to field marshal. He spent most of the remainder of 1943 without a command.

Eisenhower spent the remainder of 1943 commanding the assaults on Sicily and Italy. Both attacks were successful, but the campaigns that followed were disappointing. In Sicily, the American Seventh Army (five divisions strong) and the British Eighth Army (four divisions strong) took five weeks to drive two German divisions from the island; in Italy, progress was excruciatingly slow, and the Germans managed to impose a stalemate far south of Rome.

Despite the disappointments and personal exhaustion, Eisenhower was consistently optimistic. He wrote his wife, "When pressure mounts and strain increases everyone begins to show the weaknesses in his makeup. It is up to the Commander to conceal his: above all to conceal doubt, fear and distrust." How well he was able to do so was indicated by a member of his staff, who wrote from North Africa, "[Eisenhower] was a living dynamo of energy, good humor, amazing memory for details, and amazing courage for the future."[8]

He made a study of leadership, which in his view was not an art but a skill to be learned. "The one quality that can be developed by studious reflection and practice is the leadership of men," he declared. He wrote that it was at his first command post, in Gibraltar in early November 1942, "that I first realized how inexorably and inescapably strain and tension wear away at the leader's endurance, his judgment and his confidence." No matter how bad things got, no matter how anxious the staff became, the commander had to "preserve optimism in himself and in his command. Without confidence, enthusiasm and optimism in the command, victory is scarcely obtainable."

Eisenhower realized that "optimism and pessimism are infectious and they spread more rapidly from the head downward than in any other direction." He learned that a commander's optimism "has a most extraordinary effect upon all with whom he comes in contact. With this clear realization, I firmly determined that my mannerisms and speech in public would always reflect the cheerful certainty of victory—that any pessimism and discouragement I might ever feel would be reserved for my pillow."[9]

Eisenhower never talked to a subordinate the way Rommel talked to Major Luck. (Of course, Eisenhower had much more to be optimistic about.) But there were other striking differences between the two men, based as much on personality as on their positions. Rommel was impatient with the difficulties of logistics and administration while Eisenhower, for almost two decades a staff officer, was a master at both. Rommel tended toward arrogance while Eisenhower carefully cultivated an image of himself as a simple Kansas farm boy trying to do his best. Rommel did not like his Italian allies, indeed hardly tried to hide his contempt for them, while Eisenhower had a genuine liking for his British allies and did all he could to ensure smooth cooperation with them. Rommel often allowed his temper to flare with his staff (as did Eisenhower) and found it hard to delegate authority, an area in which Eisenhower was his exact opposite. Rommel was a loner, a solitary genius, a general who led by inspiration and intuition; Eisenhower was a team player, a manager of vast enterprises, a general who led by deciding what was the best plan after careful consultation with his staff and field commanders, then getting everyone behind the plan.

On the battlefield, Rommel was an aggressive risk taker, Eisenhower a cautious calculator. Rommel won battles through brilliant maneuvering, Eisenhower by overwhelming the enemy. As Rommel always commanded forces that were inferior in numbers and firepower, his method was appropriate to his situation; as Eisenhower always commanded forces that were superior, so was his. Perhaps they would have acted differently had their situations been reversed, but that can be doubted—the way they exercised leadership fit their personalities.

For all these differences, they had some remarkable similarities. Historian Martin Blumenson has written of Rommel, "If he demanded much from his men, he gave no less of himself. He worked hard, fought hard, lived simply, talked easily with his troops, and was devoted to his wife and son."[10] Exactly those same words could be written about Eisenhower.

Each general had a strong, happy marriage. Through the war years, each man wrote regularly to his wife. In the letters, they said things they said to no other person, revealed their hopes and apprehensions, complained about the small irritations of life, expressed a constant desire to get back together to enjoy a quiet domestic life, recalled incidents from the early years of their marriages and, in short, used the letter-writing moments as an opportunity to find some peace and quiet in the midst of the war raging all around them.[11]

Each general had one son. Manfred Rommel joined the Luftwaffe as an antiaircraft gunner in early 1944, immediately after his fifteenth birthday. John Eisenhower was a cadet at West Point who graduated on June 6, 1944, and went straight into the army. Each son has had a successful career in a field different from his father's, Manfred as a politician, John as a writer of military history.

Rommel and Eisenhower shared another fundamental trait: each hated what the war made him do. They wanted to build, not destroy, to nurture life, not snuff it out. Destruction appalled them; construction delighted them. Rommel once said that, when the war ended, he wanted to go to work as a hydraulic engineer, building water-powered generators all across Europe. (His son, as mayor of Stuttgart, sponsored tremendous construction projects in that booming city in the '70s, '80s, and '90s.) With the St. Lawrence Seaway and the Interstate Highway System, Eisenhower the president became one of the great constructors in American history. Had he lived, Rommel might have played a similar role as chancellor of West Germany. What we know about him leads to the thought that he might have been as popular a politician as Eisenhower proved to be.

In late October 1943, Gen. Alfred Jodl, chief of operations at *Oberkommando der Wehrmacht* (OKW), suggested to Hitler that Rommel be given tactical command in the West, under Field Marshal Gerd von Rundstedt, who was Commander in Chief West. Rundstedt was Germany's senior serving field marshal, at sixty-nine much too old to command in battle. He was short of energy and short of supplies, so although he had been charged with building an impregnable Atlantic Wall, outside of the Pas-de-Calais little had been done. Jodl's idea was that Rommel would provide the badly needed drive to get on with the work.

Typically, Hitler temporized. He did not give Rommel tactical command for the invasion battle, but he did order him to make an inspection of the Atlantic Wall and report back to him. When he gave Rommel this news on November 5, Hitler stressed the significance of the assignment: "When the enemy invades in the west it will be the moment of decision in this war, and the moment must turn to our advantage. We must ruthlessly extract every ounce of effort from Germany."[12]

Rommel spent the middle two weeks of December on his inspection tour, traveling from the North Sea to the Pyrenees Mountains. He was shocked by what he saw. He denounced the Atlantic Wall as a farce, "a figment of Hitler's *Wolkenkuckucksheim* [cloud-cuckoo-land] . . . an enormous bluff . . . more for the German people than for the enemy . . . and the enemy, through his agents, knows more about it than we do."

Drawing on his experience in North Africa, Rommel told his chief engineer officer, Gen. Wilhelm Meise, that Allied control of the air would prevent the movement of German reinforcements to the battle area, so "Our only possible chance will be at the beaches—that's where the enemy is always weakest." As a start on building a genuine Atlantic Wall, he said, "I want antipersonnel mines, antitank mines, antiparatroops mines. I want mines to sink ships and mines to sink landing craft. I want some minefields designed so that our infantry can cross them, but no enemy tanks. I want mines that detonate when a wire is tripped; mines that explode when a wire is cut; mines that can be remote controlled, and mines that will blow up when a beam of light is interrupted."[13]

Rommel predicted that the Allies would launch their invasion with aerial bombings, naval bombardments, and airborne assaults, followed by seaborne landings. No matter how many millions of mines were laid, he felt that the fixed defenses could only hold up the assault, not turn it back; it would take a rapid counterattack on D-Day itself by mobile infantry and panzer divisions to do that. So those units had to be moved close to the coast to be in position to deliver the decisive counterattack.

On this critical issue, Rundstedt disagreed. Rundstedt wanted to let the Allies move inland, then fight the decisive battle in the interior of France, well out of range of the heavy guns of the British and American battleships and cruisers.

This fundamental disagreement would plague the German high command right through to D-Day and beyond. Rundstedt and Rommel were offensive-minded generals, as were all Wehrmacht-trained officers. But they were on the defensive now. German generals never learned to like it, although in a tactical sense they became proficient at it—as the Red Army could attest. In the strategic sense, they never learned the plain lesson the Red Army could have taught them, had they studied Red Army strategy—that a flexible defense that can give under pressure and strike back when the attacker was overextended best suited the conditions of World War II.

Rommel's riposte, that Allied air power would make movement inland difficult if not impossible, ignored Rundstedt's point, that by fighting on the beach the Germans would be putting themselves under the guns of the Allied fleet.

Despite their disagreement, Rommel and Rundstedt got on well together, and in any case they were agreed that the attack would most likely come at the Pas-de-Calais. Rundstedt recommended that Rommel's Army Group B headquarters be given command of the Fifteenth and Seventh armies, stretching from Holland to the Loire River in southern Brittany. Hitler agreed. On January 15, 1944, Rommel took up his new command.

•   •

At the end of November 1943, Roosevelt and Churchill and their staffs went to Teheran, Iran, for a meeting with Stalin. The Soviet leader wanted to know about the second front. Roosevelt assured him that the invasion was definitely on for the spring of 1944. It had a code name, selected by Churchill from a list kept by the British chiefs of staff—Overlord. Stalin demanded to know who was in command. Roosevelt replied that the appointment had not yet been made. Stalin said in that case he did not believe the Western Allies were serious about the operation. Roosevelt promised to make the selection in three or four days.

Despite his promise, Roosevelt shrank from the distasteful task of making the decision. His preferred solution—Chief of Staff George Marshall for Overlord, with Eisenhower returning to Washington to become chief of staff of the Army—had little to recommend it. It would make Eisenhower Marshall's boss, an absurd situation, and—worse—put Eisenhower in a position of giving orders to his old boss, MacArthur, now commander in the Southwest Pacific Theater. Nevertheless, Roosevelt desperately wanted to give Marshall his opportunity to command in the field the army he had raised, equipped, and trained. When the entourage arrived in Cairo, Egypt, in early December, Roosevelt asked Marshall to express his personal preference and thus, the president hoped, make the decision for him. But Marshall replied that while he would gladly serve wherever the president told him to, he would not be the judge in his own case.

Roosevelt reluctantly made his decision. As the last meeting at Cairo was breaking up, Roosevelt asked Marshall to write a message to Stalin for him. As Roosevelt dictated, Marshall wrote, "The immediate appointment of General Eisenhower to command of Overlord operation has been decided upon."[14]

Eisenhower got the most coveted command in the war by default, or so it seemed. In explaining his reasoning afterward, Roosevelt said that he just could not sleep at night with Marshall out of the country. Since the commander had to be an American (because the Americans were contributing three-fourths of the total force committed to Overlord), a process of elimination brought it down to Eisenhower.

But there were manifold positive reasons for Eisenhower's selection. He had commanded three successful invasions, all of them joint operations involving the British and American air, sea, and land forces. He got on well with the British, and they with him. General Montgomery, already selected as commander of the ground forces committed to Overlord, said of Eisenhower, "His real strength lies in his human qualities. . . . He has the power of drawing the hearts of men towards him as a magnet attracts the bit of metal. He merely has to smile at you, and you trust him at once."[15]

Adm. Sir Andrew Cunningham, the first sea lord, told Eisenhower it had been a great experience to serve under him in the Mediterranean. He had watched Eisenhower bring together the forces of two nations, made up of men with different upbringings, conflicting ideas on staff work, and basic, "apparently irreconcilable ideas," and forge them into a team. "I do not believe," Cunningham said, "that any other man than yourself could have done it."[16]

The key word was "team." Eisenhower's emphasis on teamwork, his never-flagging insistence on working together, was the single most important reason for his selection.

On December 7, 1943, Eisenhower met Roosevelt in Tunis, where the president was stopping on his way back to Washington. Roosevelt was taken off his plane and put in Eisenhower's car. As the automobile began to drive off, the president turned to the general and said, almost casually, "Well, Ike, you are going to command Overlord."[17] His title was Supreme Commander Allied Expeditionary Force.

At Marshall's insistence, Eisenhower returned to the States for a two-week furlough, followed by a series of briefings and meetings. He flew to Britain in mid-January, landing in Scotland and taking a train to London. On January 15, 1944, he took up his new command.

When Eisenhower had first visited London, in June 1942, there was a suite waiting for him at Claridge's, then London's best and most expensive hotel. But the liveried footmen were not to his taste, nor was the ornate lobby, and he found his suite, with its black-and-gold sitting room and pink bedroom, appalling. He moved to a less elegant hotel and had aides secure for him a quiet place in the country where he could relax. It was a small, modest, two-bedroom house in Kingston, Surrey, called Telegraph Cottage.

When Eisenhower returned to London in January 1944, he

immediately complained that having Overlord headquarters in the city was distracting. Churchill, the American ambassador, and other VIPs felt free to call on him at any hour, and the staff found the temptations of London night life too much to pass up. Within two weeks he moved the headquarters to Bushy Park, outside the city. There the staff, with considerable grumbling, moved into tents. Aides found a nearby mansion in Kingston Hill for his residence; he found it much too grand. He asked about Telegraph Cottage and found that Air Marshal Arthur Tedder, his deputy supreme commander, was living there. He persuaded Tedder to switch residences. The supreme commander thus had the least pretentious home of any general officer in England.

When Rommel went to Paris at the beginning of January 1944 to meet with Rundstedt (who was living in considerable splendor in the Hotel George V), the city seemed to him like a Babel. He wanted to establish his headquarters somewhere else. His naval aide, Vice Adm. Friedrich Ruge, said he had just the place. On a trip back to Paris from the coast, Ruge had stopped in at the Chateau La Roche-Guyon, located on the Seine River in a village of 543 residents some sixty kilometers downstream from Paris. The chateau had been the seat of the dukes de La Rochefoucauld for centuries. Thomas Jefferson had been a guest there in the late eighteenth century, when he was American ambassador to France and a friend of the most famous of the dukes, the writer François.

Ruge was an avid reader of La Rochefoucauld's maxims and had called on the duchess to pay his respects. Ruge told Rommel the location was perfect, out of Paris, within equal distance of the Seventh and Fifteenth armies' headquarters, and the chateau was large enough to hold the staff. So the staff, with much grumbling, left Paris to set up headquarters in the sleepy village of La Roche-Guyon.

Eisenhower wanted a dog for a companion. Aides found him a Scottie puppy. He named it Telek, a shortened form of Telegraph Cottage. Rommel wanted a dog for a companion. Aides found him a dachshund puppy. The dogs slept in their respective masters' bedrooms.

There were more meaningful comparisons. Each general jammed his feet into the stirrups, took hold of the reins, and galloped into action. Where there had been hesitation and drift, there was now conviction and movement. Their resolution was absolute. "I'm going to throw myself into this new job with everything I've got," Rommel wrote his wife, "and I'm going to see it turns out a success."[18] Eisenhower said on arrival, "We are approaching a tremendous crisis with stakes incalculable."[19]

The generals set a pace that left other men in their early fifties panting and exhausted. They were typically on the road by 6:00 A.M. each day, inspecting, driving, training, preparing their men. They ate on the run, field rations or a sandwich and a cup of coffee. They did not return to their quarters until well after dark. Eisenhower averaged four hours sleep per night, Rommel hardly more. One difference: Eisenhower smoked four packs of cigarettes a day, while Rommel never smoked.

There were other, significant differences. Although both men were full of resolve, the defender could not keep his doubts out of his mind, while the attacker refused to entertain any doubts. On January 17, Rommel wrote his wife, "I think we're going to win the battle for the defense of the west for certain—provided we get enough time to set things up."[20] For Eisenhower, there were no "provideds," only challenges. On January 23, he told his superiors on the Combined Chiefs of Staff (CCS), "Every obstacle must be overcome, every inconvenience suffered and every risk run to ensure that our blow is decisive. We cannot afford to fail."[21]

One factor in Rommel's pessimism was the confused command structure. For all their prattling about the "führer" principle of "ein Volk, ein Reich, ein Führer" (one people, one state, one leader), the Nazis ran the armed services as they ran the government, by the principle of divide and rule. Hitler deliberately mixed the lines of authority so that no one ever knew precisely who was in command of what. This characteristic of the führer's was exacerbated by the natural and universal tendency of air, sea, and ground forces to indulge in interservice rivalry. So, in Rommel's case, he did not have control over the Luftwaffe in France, nor of the navy, nor of the administrative governors in the occupied territories. He did not have administrative control of the Waffen-SS units in France, nor of the paratroop or antiaircraft units (they belonged to the Luftwaffe).

The fragmentation of command reached ridiculous proportions. For example, the naval coastal guns along the Channel would remain under naval control as the Allied fleets approached the coast. But the moment Allied troops began to land, command of the coastal batteries would revert to the Wehrmacht.

Bad enough for Rommel, it was never clear whether he or Rundstedt would control the battle. Worst of all, Hitler wanted to command himself. Hitler kept control of the panzer divisions in his hands. They could be committed to the battle only on his orders—and his headquarters was a thousand kilometers from the scene, and those were the divisions Rommel was depending on for a first-day counterattack. It was madness.

Eisenhower had no such problems. His command was clear-cut, absolute. Initially, he had not been given command of the Allied bomber forces (U.S. Eighth Air Force, British Bomber Command), but when he threatened to resign if not allowed to use the bombers as he saw fit, the CCS gave him what he wanted. Every soldier, every airman, every sailor, every unit in the United Kingdom in the spring of 1944 took orders from Eisenhower. Thus did the democracies put the lie to the Nazi claim that democracies are inherently inefficient, dictatorships inherently efficient.

Thanks to the clear-cut command authority, a single-minded clarity of purpose pervaded Supreme Headquarters Allied Expeditionary Force (SHAEF), in contrast to the situation at OB West and Army Group B. A factor in creating unity at SHAEF was Eisenhower's relationship with his immediate subordinates, which contrasted sharply with Rommel's command structure. Eisenhower had worked with most of his team in the Mediterranean and had played a role in the selection of most of the army, corps, and division commanders, while Rommel hardly knew the generals commanding his armies, corps, and divisions.

This is not to say that Eisenhower liked, or even wanted, all his subordinates. He did not like General Montgomery and feared that he would be too cautious in battle. But Eisenhower knew that Monty, Britain's only hero thus far in the war, absolutely had to have a major role and so he was determined to work as effectively with Monty as possible—as he had done in the Mediterranean. He thought the tactical air commander, Air Vice Marshal Sir Trafford Leigh-Mallory, too cautious and pessimistic, but he determined to get the most out of him. He liked and admired his deputy, Air Marshal Tedder, enormously; so too the naval commander in chief, Adm. Bertram Ramsay. Eisenhower had worked closely and well with Tedder and Ramsay in the Mediterranean.

His principal American ground commander, Gen. Omar N. Bradley, was a West Point classmate, an old and close friend, a man whose judgments Eisenhower trusted implicitly. His chief of staff,

Gen. Walter B. Smith, had been with him since mid-1942. Eisenhower characterized Smith as "the perfect chief of staff," a crutch to a one-legged man. "I wish I had a dozen like him," Eisenhower told a friend. "If I did, I would simply buy a fishing rod and write home every week about my wonderful accomplishments in winning the war."[22]

Rommel had never worked with his army commanders, Gen. Hans von Salmuth of the Fifteenth and Gen. Friedrich Dollmann of the Seventh. With Salmuth, he would have shouting arguments. Dollmann had little field experience, was in poor health, and did not much like Rommel. Neither Salmuth nor Dollman were ardent Nazis. Gen. Baron Leo Geyr von Schweppenburg commanded the panzer group in the West. A veteran of the Eastern Front, Schweppenburg was horrified at Rommel's proposal to use the tanks close up; in his view, that was to misuse the tanks as fixed artillery. Their controversy was never resolved, but it hardly mattered, as Rommel did not command the panzer group.

Rommel fired his first chief of staff. The successor was Gen. Hans Speidel, a Swabian from the Württemberg district who had fought with Rommel in World War I and had served with him in the twenties. Speidel was an active plotter against Hitler, more politically adroit and aware than his chief. Eventually he was able to persuade Rommel to support the conspiracy against Hitler, which was growing through the early months of 1944.

Here was a profound difference between Rommel and Eisenhower. Eisenhower believed with all his heart in the cause he was fighting for. To him, the invasion was a crusade designed to end the Nazi occupation of Europe and destroy the scourge of Nazism forever. He hated the Nazis and all they represented. Although a patriot, Rommel was no Nazi—even though at times he had been a toady to Hitler. To Rommel, the coming battle would be fought against an enemy he never hated and indeed respected. He approached that battle with professional competence rather than the zeal of a crusader.

4

WHERE AND WHEN?

IN MID-MARCH 1943, shortly after the Battle of Kasserine Pass and nearly two months before the final victory in Tunisia, the CCS appointed British Lt. Gen. Frederick Morgan to the post of chief of staff to the supreme Allied commander (designate) and charged him with "co-ordinating and driving forward the plans for cross-Channel operations this year and next year." Within a month the CCS decided that no such operation could be mounted in 1943; the final directive, issued in late April, ordered Morgan to begin planning for "a full-scale assault against the Continent in 1944, as early as possible."[1]

It would be hard to imagine a broader directive. "Where" could be anywhere between Holland and Brest; "as early as possible" could be anytime between March and September 1944. Morgan put together a staff of British and American officers, with Maj. Gen. Ray Barker of the U.S. Army as his deputy, called the group COSSAC after the initial letters of his title, and went to work.

COSSAC operated under one particularly severe constraint—the number of landing craft allotted to the operation limited the planners to a three-division assault. Coupled with the presumption that the Germans were certain to improve the Atlantic Wall, that limitation removed all temptation to plan for widely dispersed attacks. From the first, COSSAC committed the Allies to the principle of concentration of force. There would be one invasion site, the divisions landing side by side.

Where? There were many requirements. The site had to be within range of Allied fighter planes based in the United Kingdom. There had to be at least one major port close at hand that could be taken from the land side and put into operation as soon as possible. There was no thought of landing where the Atlantic Wall was complete, that is, around the French ports: the disastrous Dieppe raid by the Canadians in August 1942 convinced COSSAC that a direct frontal assault against a well-defended port could not succeed. Therefore the beaches selected had to be suitable for prolonged unloading operations directly from the LSTs and have exits for vehicles and adequate road nets behind them for rapid, massive deployment inland.

Those were tactical requirements. Most of them could be met easily on the French Mediterranean coast or in Brittany. But the strategic requirement was to land as close to the ultimate objective, the Rhine-Ruhr region, as possible, for the obvious reason that the farther away from the objective the landing took place, the greater would be the distance to be covered and the longer the supply line.

Holland and Belgium had excellent ports, but they were too close to Germany and the Luftwaffe bases, the area inland too easily flooded, too well defended. The Pas-de-Calais coast in northernmost France was ideal in every way but one—it was the obvious place to come ashore and thus it was there that the Germans had built the strongest part of the Atlantic Wall.

Le Havre, in upper Normandy on the north bank of the mouth of the Seine, was an excellent port, but it had numerous disadvantages. To take it the Allies would have to land on both sides of the river. The two forces could not be mutually supporting, which would allow the Germans to defeat them in detail. East of Le Havre the coastline is dominated by cliffs with only a few small beaches that had even fewer exits.

With Brest as its main port, and with smaller but good ports along its north coast, Brittany had advantages, but they were overshadowed by the distance from the United Kingdom and from the objective. Cherbourg was closer to both, which made the Cotentin Peninsula tempting. But the west coast of the Cotentin was open to storms coming in off the Atlantic and was guarded by the German-held Channel Islands of Guernsey and Jersey. The east coast of the

Cotentin was low-lying ground, easily flooded. Further, the narrow base of the Cotentin would make it relatively easy for the Germans to seal off the beachhead.

A process of elimination brought the choice down to the Calvados coast of Normandy. The port of Caen, although small, could be captured quickly—probably in the initial assault. There was an airfield just outside Caen, called Carpiquet, that could be captured by airborne assault on the first day. The capture of Caen would cut the railroad and highway from Paris to Cherbourg, thus simultaneously isolating the Cotentin Peninsula and putting the invaders in a position to threaten Paris.

There were other advantages. The mouth of the Orne River was the boundary between the Wehrmacht's Fifteenth Army to the northeast and Seventh Army to the southwest, and boundaries between armies are inherently areas of weakness. The attack would come against Seventh Army, which had only one panzer division (the 21st) to Fifteenth Army's five. Calvados was 150 kilometers or so from the major southern British ports of Southampton and Portsmouth.* The Cotentin Peninsula protected it from the worst effects of Atlantic storms. From the mouth of the Orne River westward there were thirty kilometers of open sand beaches, for the most part with only a gradual rise inland, and there was a good road net inland. From Arromanches westward for another ten kilometers the bluffs were almost vertical, but beginning at Colleville the bluffs receded from the coastline for a ten-kilometer stretch. Although the bluff behind was as much as forty to fifty meters high, it was not vertical and the beach was open, sandy, and 200 or so meters wide at low tide, ten meters at high tide. There were four draws with roads running down to that beach, making for suitable exits.

Already the British had collected an enormous amount of intelligence on the French coast. Shortly after Dunkirk, the BBC had broadcast an appeal for postcards gathered over the years from families who had taken prewar vacations in France; 30,000 arrived

---

* Distances are given in two ways, by meter and kilometer and by yards and miles, as is done in, respectively, France and Britain. For England, I use miles; for France, kilometers. But of course when the Allies in France talked about distances, they used yards and miles. This inevitably causes some confusion. To make comparison, a simple method is to remember that a meter is only slightly longer than a yard and may be thought of as equivalent; a kilometer is six-tenths of a mile, so just multiply by six-tenths to go from kilometers to miles (eighty kilometers are forty-eight miles; 100 kilometers are sixty miles, and so forth).

in the first post and eventually 10 million pictures were collected. Throughout 1942 and 1943 aerial reconnaissance photographs had been gathered; they were put together into panoramic photos. The French Resistance supplied information on beach obstacles, strong points, enemy units, and the like. Information on tides, currents, and topography could be dug out of old guidebooks.

So a great deal was known about the Calvados coast, but not the answer to a key question. Would the beaches west of the mouth of the Orne River support DUKWs, tanks, bulldozers, and trucks? There was reason to fear that they would not, because British geographers and geologists reported that there had been considerable erosion of the coastline over the past two centuries. The original port at Calvados, the old Roman port, had been two kilometers out from the twentieth-century shoreline. French Resistance people managed to smuggle four volumes of geological maps out of Paris, one in Latin done by the Romans, who had surveyed their entire empire for a report on fuel sources. The survey indicated that the Romans had gathered peat from the extensive reserves on the Calvados coast. If there were boggy peat fields under a thin layer of sand on the current coast, it would not hold tanks and trucks.

COSSAC had to know. The only way to find out was to obtain samples. No. 1 Combined Operations Pilotage and Beach Reconnaissance Party, consisting of Maj. Logan Scott-Bowden and Sgt. Bruce Ogden-Smith, set off on New Year's Eve 1943 in a midget submarine to take samples. They figured the Germans would be celebrating that night. Lt. Comdr. Nigel Willmott of Combined Operations was in command, with a submarine skipper and an engineer. Major Scott-Bowden and Sergeant Ogden-Smith swam ashore, carrying pistols, daggers, wrist compasses, watches, waterproof flashlights, and a dozen twelve-inch tubes.

They came in on a rising tide at the seaside village of Luc-sur-Mer on the beach later given the code name Sword. They could hear singing from the German garrison. They crawled ashore, walked inland a bit, went flat when the beam from the lighthouse swept over the beach, walked some more. They made sure to stay below the high-water mark so that their tracks would be wiped out by the tide before morning. They stuck their tubes into the sand, gathering samples and noting the location of each on underwater writing tablets they wore on their arms.

"The trouble really started," Scott-Bowden recalled, when they had filled their tubes. "The breakers were quite heavy and we were positively bogged and tattered up with all our kit, and we had a go at getting out to sea and were flung back." They took a breather, tried again, were flung back a second time. "So we went as far out in the water as we could, there were smaller waves coming over us, and watched the rhythm of these breakers until we could time it. The third attempt, having timed it right, we got out, but we got separated a bit and we swam like hell to make sure we weren't going to be pitched back in again. We didn't quite lose contact."

Suddenly Ogden-Smith started yelling. "I was thinking that he'd probably got a cramp or something," Scott-Bowden related, "but when I got close enough to him, all he was yelling was 'Happy New Year!' He's a good chap, a marvelous fellow. I swore at him, then wished him a Happy New Year too."[2]

The samples showed that the sand could bear the necessary weight. The Combined Operations Pilotage Parties (COPPs) did a series of reconnaissances all along the Calvados coast that winter, at beaches named Juno and Gold. They sometimes set the midget submarine on the sea bottom at periscope depth to take bearings and photographs. Scott-Bowden explained, "We could see things which weren't visible from air photographs as we were looking from a worm's eye view. It was quite a tricky operation, because if anybody moves inadvertently in a midget submarine and you're bottomed at periscope height on a wavy beach, you can upset the trim and put the bottom off, put the stern up, or anything, so one had to be very careful indeed."[3]

On one occasion, the submarine passed right underneath a French fishing trawler with a German spotter in the bow. Scott-Bowden was able to watch workmen on the beach using two-wheeled carts pulled by horses. He and Ogden-Smith made other swims, including one at the beach between Colleville and Vierville (by this time, late January, code-named Omaha) and did other reconnaissance missions.

At the end of January, Scott-Bowden was called to COSSAC headquarters at Norfolk House, St. James's Square (by then taken over by SHAEF), to report to Admiral Ramsay, General Bradley, General Smith, four other generals, and five more admirals. Rear Adm. George Creasy, Ramsay's chief of staff, drew the curtains and said, "Now, describe your reconnaissance."

Scott-Bowden looked at the map. It was too big, too general. "Well, I'm afraid, sir, it's going to be very difficult to give much detail from this."

"Oh," Creasy replied, "we've got another map down the

other end, it might be better." So the major followed him across the large room, looked at the map hanging there, and indicated it would do. Creasy called out, "Come on, chaps, bring your chairs down here." As the generals and admirals picked up their chairs and came over, the twenty-three-year-old Scott-Bowden thought, Oh dear, oh dear, I'm getting off to a bad start.

"I'd never been confronted with such a galaxy before," he recalled, "so I stumbled through my account. Then they started shooting questions for getting onto an hour. The Navy were not quite so interested in what I had to say, but General Bradley was. He wanted me to say whether Sherman tanks could go up this track or that track. I thought of the two wheel carts and said it must be possible. And so on."

When the brass ran out of questions, Scott-Bowden offered an opinion. "If you don't mind my saying so, sir," he told Bradley, "I think that your beach with all these tremendous emplacements with guns defilading the beaches from here and there and all over, it's going to be a very tough proposition indeed."

Bradley patted Scott-Bowden on the shoulder and said, "Yes, I know, my boy, I know."[4]

When Eisenhower and his team arrived in London to take over from COSSAC, they studied Morgan's plan and accepted his logic, except that everyone involved—Montgomery, Eisenhower, Smith, Bradley, and the others—insisted that the invasion front had to be widened to a five-division assault. They demanded, and got, an allotment of additional landing craft. Extension to the east, toward Le Havre, was not advisable because it would bring the assaulting troops directly under the Le Havre coastal guns, among the most formidable in the Atlantic Wall. Morgan had ruled out extension to the west, on the southeast corner of the Cotentin Peninsula, because the Germans were flooding the hinterland there.

Eisenhower overruled Morgan; he decided to extend to the west. He would deal with the problem of flooded areas behind the coastline by dropping the American airborne divisions inland and giving them the task of seizing the raised roads that crossed the flooded areas, so that the seaborne assault troops could use the roads to move inland.

The U.S. 4th Infantry Division would lead the way on the Cotentin, where the beach took the code name Utah. The U.S. 29th and 1st Infantry divisions would land at the beach on the

Calvados coast code-named Omaha. The British and Canadians would land on the beaches stretching westward from the mouth of the Orne, code-named (from east to west) Sword (British 3rd Division, plus British and French commandos), Juno (Canadian 3rd), and Gold (British 50th). The British 6th Airborne would land between the Orne and Dives rivers to protect the left flank.

COSSAC had been tempted to use only one army, either British or American, in the initial assault—that would make things very much simpler and eliminate what is always the weakest spot in any allied line, the boundary between the forces of the two nationalities. But it was politically impossible. As General Barker had put it in July 1943, "It can be accepted as an absolute certainty that the P[rime] M[inister] would not, for one moment, allow the assault to be made wholly by American troops. The same is true with relation to the U.S. Government. We must be practical about this and face facts."[5]

So it was settled. The invasion would come against the Calvados coast, with the British on the left and the Americans at Omaha, with an extension to the right onto the Cotentin coast at Utah.

The great disadvantage of the Calvados coast was that landing there would put the Allied armies ashore southwest of the Seine River, thus putting between them and their objective the major river barriers of the Seine and the Somme. But disadvantages could be made into advantages; in this case, COSSAC believed that the bridges over the Seine could be destroyed in preinvasion bombardments, thus making it difficult for the Wehrmacht to bring panzer divisions from the Pas-de-Calais across the river and into the battle.

The greatest advantages of Calvados were that surprise could be achieved there and that the Germans might be fooled into believing the landing was a feint, designed to draw their armor away from the Pas-de-Calais to the west of the Seine. The basic reason for surprise was that by going to Calvados the Allies would be moving south from England, away from the area the Germans absolutely had to defend, the Rhine-Ruhr, rather than east from England on the straight line toward their objective. It might be possible to persuade the Germans on an ongoing, postinvasion basis that Calvados was a feint by mounting a dummy operation aimed at the Pas-de-Calais.

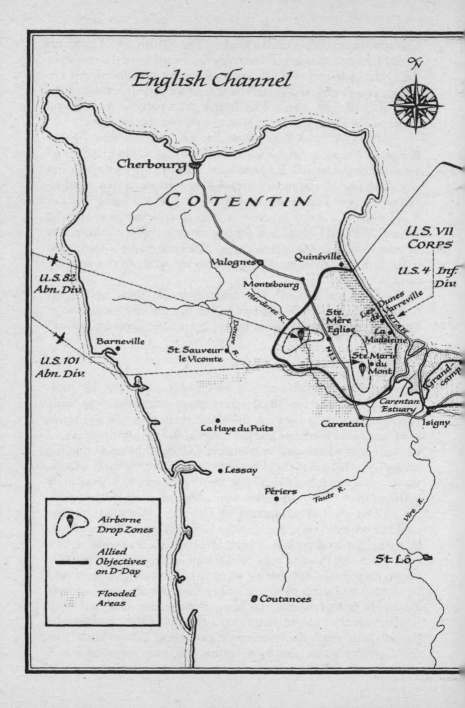

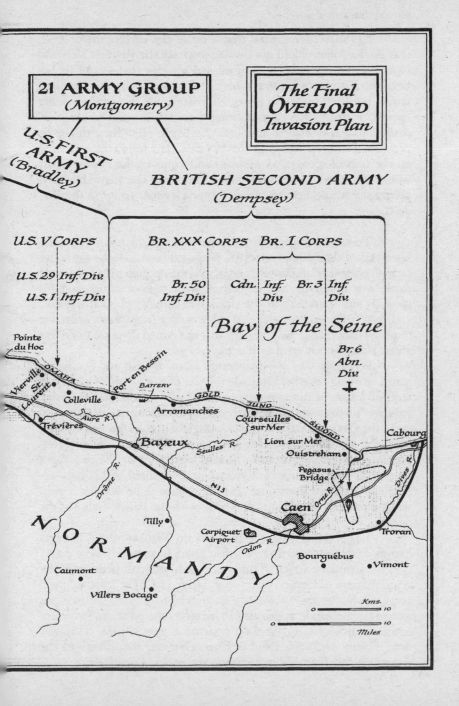

COSSAC recognized that it could not reverse the process; that is, the Allies would not be able to attack the Pas-de-Calais and mount a dummy operation aimed at Calvados that would be believable. If the attack came ashore at Pas-de-Calais, the Germans would not keep troops in lower Normandy for fear of their being cut off. Instead, they would bring their forces from lower Normandy to Pas-de-Calais and into the battle. But they might be persuaded to keep troops in the Pas-de-Calais following a landing on the Calvados coast, as the men and tanks in the Pas-de-Calais would still stand between the Allied forces and Germany. In short, geography would help to pin down the German armor in the Pas-de-Calais.

To reinforce the German need to keep their panzer armies northeast of the Seine, COSSAC proposed (and Eisenhower, after he took command, mounted) an elaborate deception plan. The code name was Fortitude; the objectives were to fool Hitler and his generals into thinking that the attack was coming where it was not, and into believing that the real thing was a feint. Each objective required convincing the Germans that the Allied invasion force was about twice as powerful as it actually was.

Fortitude was a joint venture, with British and American teams working together. It made full use of the Double Cross System; of Ultra, of dummy armies, fake radio traffic, and elaborate security precautions. Fortitude had many elements designed to make the Germans think the attack might come on the Biscay coast or in the Marseilles region or even in the Balkans. The most important parts were Fortitude North, which set up Norway as a target (the site of Hitler's U-boat bases, essential to his only remaining offensive operations and thus an area he was extremely sensitive about), and Fortitude South, with the Pas-de-Calais as the target.

To get the Germans to look toward Norway, the Allies first had to convince them that they had enough resources for a diversion or secondary attack. This was doubly difficult because of the acute shortage of landing craft—right up to D-Day it was touch and go as to whether there would be enough craft to carry six divisions ashore at Normandy as planned. Therefore, the Allies had to create fictitious divisions and landing craft on a grand scale. This was done chiefly with the Double Cross System, the talents of the American and British movie industries, and radio signals.

The British Fourth Army, for example, stationed in Scotland and scheduled to invade Norway in mid-July, existed only on the airwaves. Early in 1944 some two dozen overage British officers went to northernmost Scotland, where they spent the next months exchanging radio messages. They filled the air with an exact duplicate of the wireless traffic that accompanies the assembly of a real army, communicating in low-level and thus easily broken cipher. Together the messages created an impression of corps and division headquarters scattered all across Scotland.

Of course the messages could not read "We will invade Norway in mid-May." The Germans would never believe such an obvious subterfuge. Instead, they read "80 Div. request 1,800 pairs of crampons, 1,800 pairs of ski bindings," or "7 Corps requests the promised demonstrators in the Bilgeri method of climbing rock faces," or "2 Corps Car Company requires handbooks on engine functioning in low temperatures and high altitudes." There was no 80th Division, no VII Corps, no II Corps Car Company, but the Germans did not know that and they would come to their own conclusion as to what was going on in Scotland.[6]

Fooling the Germans was not easy; they were experts at radio deception. At the beginning of 1942 they had mounted one of the more elaborate and successful deception operations of World War II, Operation *Kreml*. Its objective had been to make the Red Army think that the main German offensive for 1942 would take place on the Moscow front, not at Stalingrad. As historian Earl Ziemke writes, *Kreml* "was a paper operation, an out-and-out deception, but it had the substance to make it a masterpiece of that highly speculative form of military art." The Germans used radio traffic to manufacture dummy armies that supposedly threatened Moscow; in most of its essentials, *Kreml* was similar to Fortitude.[7]

Thanks to the Double Cross System, however, the Allies had one advantage over *Kreml*. The turned German spies in the United Kingdom, whose reliability had been "proved" to the Abwehr over the past three years, were put to work. They sent encoded radio messages to the Abwehr in Hamburg describing heavy train traffic in Scotland, new division patches seen on the streets of Edinburgh, and rumors among the troops about going to Norway. In addition, wooden twin-engine "bombers" began to appear on Scottish airfields. British commandos made some raids on the coast of Norway, pinpointing radar sites, picking up soil samples, in general trying to look like a preinvasion force.

The payoff was spectacular. By late spring, Hitler had thirteen army divisions in Norway (along with 90,000 naval and 60,000 Luftwaffe personnel). These were hardly high-quality troops, but still they could have filled in the trenches along the Atlantic Wall in France. In late May, Rommel persuaded Hitler to move five infantry divisions from Norway to France. They had started to load up and move out when the Abwehr passed on to Hitler another set of "intercepted" messages about the threat to Norway. He canceled the movement order. To paraphrase Churchill, never in the history of warfare have so many been immobilized by so few.[8]

Fortitude South was larger and more elaborate. It was based on the First U.S. Army Group (FUSAG), stationed in and around Dover and threatening the Pas-de-Calais. It included radio traffic, inadequately camouflaged dummy landing craft in the ports of Ramsgate, Dover, and Hastings, fields full of papier-mâché and rubber tanks, and the full use of the Double Cross System. The spies reported intense activity around Dover, including construction, troop movements, increased train traffic, and the like. They said that the phony oil dock at Dover, built by stagehands from the film industries, was open and operating.

The capstone to Fortitude South was Eisenhower's selection of Lt. Gen. George S. Patton to command FUSAG. The Germans thought Patton the best commander in the Allied camp and expected him to lead the assault. Eisenhower, who was saving Patton for the exploitation phase of the coming campaign, used Patton's reputation and visibility to strengthen Fortitude South. The spies reported his arrival in England and his movements. So did the British papers (available to the Germans in a day or two via Portugal and Spain; in addition, German agents in Dublin had the London papers the day they were printed and could send on hot items by radio). FUSAG radio signals told the Germans of Patton's comings and goings and showed that he had taken a firm grip on his new command.

FUSAG contained real as well as notional divisions, corps, and armies. The FUSAG order of battle included the U.S. Third Army, which was real but still mostly in the States; the British Fourth Army, which was imaginary; and the Canadian First Army, which was real and based in England. There were, in addition, supposedly fifty follow-up divisions in the United States, organized as the U.S. Fourteenth Army—which was notional—awaiting shipment to the Pas-de-Calais after FUSAG established its beachhead.

Many of the divisions in the Fourteenth Army were real and were actually assigned to Bradley's U.S. First Army in southwest England.

Fortitude's success was measured by the German estimate of Allied strength. By the end of May, the Germans believed that the Allied force included eighty-nine divisions, when in fact the number was forty-seven. The Germans thought the Allies had sufficient landing craft to bring twenty divisions ashore in the first wave, when they would be lucky to manage six. Partly because they credited the Allies with so much strength, partly because it made good military sense, the Germans believed that the real invasion would be preceded or followed by diversionary attacks and feints.[9]

It was more important for the Germans *not* to know that Calvados was the site than it was for them to think that the Pas-de-Calais (and Norway) was. "The success or failure of coming operations depends upon whether the enemy can obtain advance information of an accurate nature," Eisenhower declared in a February 23, 1944, memorandum.[10]

To ensure security, the Allies went to great lengths. In February, Eisenhower asked Churchill to ban all visitor traffic to the coastal areas in southern England, where the base for the attack was being built and where training exercises were under way, for fear that there might be an undiscovered spy among the visitors. Churchill said no—he could not go so far in upsetting people's lives. General Morgan growled that Churchill's response was "all politics" and warned, "If we fail, there won't be any more politics."[11]

Still the British government would not act. But when Montgomery said he wanted visitors banned from his training areas, Eisenhower sent an eloquent plea to the War Cabinet. He warned that it "would go hard with our consciences if we were to feel, in later years, that by neglecting any security precaution we had compromised the success of these vital operations or needlessly squandered men's lives." Churchill gave in. Visitors were banned.[12]

Eisenhower also persuaded a reluctant War Cabinet to impose a ban on privileged diplomatic communications from the United Kingdom. Eisenhower said he regarded the diplomatic pouches as "the gravest risk to the security of our operations and to the lives of our sailors, soldiers, and airmen."[13] When the government imposed the ban, on April 17 (it did not apply to the United

States or the Soviet Union), foreign governments protested vigorously. This gave Hitler a useful clue to the timing of Overlord. He remarked in early May that "the English have taken measures that they can sustain for only six to eight weeks."[14]

With the British government cooperating so admirably, Eisenhower could not do less. In April, Maj. Gen. Henry Miller, chief supply officer of the U.S. Ninth Air Force and a West Point classmate of Eisenhower's, went to a cocktail party at Claridge's Hotel. He began talking freely, complaining about his difficulties in getting supplies but adding that his problems would end after D-Day, which he declared would be before June 15. When challenged on the date, he offered to take bets. Eisenhower learned of the indiscretion the next morning and acted immediately. He ordered Miller reduced to his permanent rank of colonel and sent him back to the States—the ultimate disgrace for a career soldier. Miller protested. Eisenhower insisted, and back he went. Miller retired shortly thereafter.[15]

There was another flap in May when a U.S. Navy officer got drunk at a party and revealed details of impending operations, including areas, lift, strength, and dates. Eisenhower wrote Marshall, "I get so angry at the occurrence of such needless and additional hazards that I could cheerfully shoot the offender myself. This following so closely upon the Miller case is almost enough to give one the shakes." That officer too was sent back to the States.[16]

To check on how well Fortitude and security were working, SHAEF relied on Ultra intercepts. Each week the British Joint Intelligence Committee issued a summary of "German Appreciation of Allied Intentions in the West," one- or two-page overviews of where, when, and in what strength the Germans expected the attack. Week after week, the summaries gave SHAEF exactly the news it hoped to receive: that the Germans were anticipating an attack on Norway, diversions in the south of France, Normandy, and the Bay of Biscay, and the main assault, with twenty or more divisions, against the Pas-de-Calais.

The Germans poured more concrete to make more fortifications in the Pas-de-Calais than anywhere else. They stationed more troops there, backed up by the panzer divisions. They concentrated their mines in the Channel off the coast of the Pas-de-Calais. They grossly exaggerated the resources available to SHAEF. They were, in short, badly fooled.

But not completely. The mobility the AEF enjoyed thanks to command of the sea and air forced the Germans to regard almost any suitable beach as a possible invasion site. At a March 19 conference at Berchtesgaden, Hitler put the problem to his senior commanders: "Obviously an Anglo-American invasion in the west is going to come. Just how and where nobody knows, and it isn't possible to speculate." But speculate he did, as the German ability to penetrate Fortitude was nonexistent and their ability to penetrate the AEF's security measures was limited. A few reconnaissance planes did get through; they did spot the buildup of shipping in the southern ports of Southampton and Portsmouth; but as Hitler pointed out, such intelligence was almost useless. "You can't take shipping concentrations at face value for some kind of clue that their choice has fallen on any particular sector of our long western front from Norway down to the Bay of Biscay," he said, because "such concentrations can always be moved or transferred at any time, under cover of bad visibility, and they will obviously be used to dupe us."

That did not stop him from guessing; indeed, he had to guess. "The most suitable landing areas, and hence those that are in most danger, are the two west coast peninsulas of Cherbourg and Brest; they offer very tempting possibilities. . . ."[17] It was a bad guess.

Adm. Theodor Krancke, commanding Navy Group West, guessed that the invasion would come between Boulogne and Cherbourg, either in the Cotentin or at the mouth of the Orne, the mouth of the Seine, or the mouth of the Somme, which was a little better—but as Boulogne to Cherbourg included most of the Kanalküste, hardly pinpoint accuracy.[18]

Rommel's guess was the Pas-de-Calais. He spent more of his time there than anywhere else on his long front, inspecting, prodding, building defenses. At the beginning of May he began to look slightly to the southwest, telling Lt. Gen. Gerhard von Schwerin, commanding the crack 116th Panzer Division of the Fifteenth Army, "We expect the invasion on either side of the Somme estuary."[19]

But all the evidence available to the Germans continued to indicate the Pas-de-Calais. The pattern of AEF air activity, for example, reinforced Fortitude. There were twice as many AEF reconnaissance flights over Fifteenth Army's sector as there were over Seventh Army's; there were almost ten times as many air raids on targets northeast of the Seine as in lower Normandy. So Rommel continued to look to the Pas-de-Calais. He was confident that if the AEF invaded there, he could defeat the assault.

On April 27, German *Schnellbootes* (abbreviated *S-Boote* and called E-boats by the Allies for "enemy boat") penetrated an Allied shipping concentration for a practice exercise—code name Tiger—and sank two LSTs. For the AEF the loss of more than 700 men was a major blow; for the Germans, the information that the Allies were practicing at Slapton Sands, on the south coast of England, was potentially useful. Hitler saw this at once. Although he had never been to England, or to the Cotentin or Calvados, he had the most amazing ability to store topographical information in his mind. In this instance, he noticed the similarity between Slapton Sands and the Cotentin beach (which was why the AEF was carrying out practice exercises at Slapton Sands) and began to insist strongly on the need to reinforce the defense in lower Normandy.[20]

Within the severe limits in which the Wehrmacht in the West was required to operate, this was done. On May 29, the weekly AEF intelligence summary included a chilling sentence: "The recent trend of movement of German land forces towards the Cherbourg area tends to support the view that the Le Havre-Cherbourg area is regarded as a likely, and perhaps even the main, point of assault."[21] Had the Germans penetrated the secret of Overlord? Only the event would tell; meanwhile, the good news was that the main panzer forces remained northeast of the Seine, with Fifteenth Army.

When? Morgan's directive declared "as soon as possible." March was out. Even if the AEF got a couple of good days to cross and land, the probability of a spring storm smashing against the Calvados coast during the establishment and buildup phase made March too risky. April 1, the target date suggested by the U.S. Joint Chiefs of Staff (JCS), was no good because of uncertain and unpredictable Channel weather and because the spring thaw in Russia would make it impossible for the Red Army to launch a coordinated offensive. Morgan therefore picked May 1. When Eisenhower took command, he moved the target date back to June 1, in order to have the use of an extra month's production of LSTs, LCVPs, and other landing craft.

The target date meant the AEF would go on the first suitable day after June 1. A number of requirements went into the

selection of D-Day, the chief of which concerned tides and moon conditions. The admirals wanted to cross the Channel in daylight to avoid confusion, to control the thousands of craft involved, and to maximize the effectiveness of the fire support. The air force generals wanted daylight before the first waves went ashore in order to maximize the effectiveness of their bombing runs. Both had to give way to the army generals' insistence on crossing at night, in order to preserve surprise up to the last minute, and landing right after first light, in order to have a full day to get established.

Rommel anticipated that the attack would come at high tide, as that would give the first waves the shortest open beach to cross, but that only showed how little he knew about amphibious operations. From the beginning, the AEF was determined to land on a rising tide so that the landing craft could run right onto the beach, then float free on the rise.

The AEF needed at least a half-moon the night of the crossing, enough to provide some illumination for the fleet and for the paratroopers, who would be dropping into France some five hours before H-Hour.

A rising tide at first light following a night with a suitable moon occurred during two periods in June, the 5th, 6th and 7th and again on the 19th and 20th. Eisenhower picked June 5 for D-Day.

The southeast coast of the Cotentin and the Calvados coast of lower Normandy would be the place. June 5 would be the date. H-Hour would be dawn.

Rommel had no inkling that the AEF suffered from a shortage of landing craft. He thought just the opposite. Further, the Double Cross spies were feeding him false information. His guess as to the date, therefore, was badly off. In April, he thought it would come in the first or third week of May. On May 6, he wrote his wife, Lucie, "I'm looking forward with the utmost confidence to the battle—it may be on May 15, it may not be until the end of the month."[22] On May 15, he wrote Lucie, "Mid-May already. And still nothing doing. . . . I think it's going to be a few more weeks yet."[23] On June 1, he consulted moon and tide tables and declared there were no good invasion tides (high tide at dawn, in his view) until after June 20. The next day he wrote Lucie, "There is still no sign that the invasion is imminent."[24]

Hitler was no better. He indulged himself in the hope that

there never would be an invasion. On April 6 he declared, "I can't help feeling that the whole thing's a shameless charade." More realistically, he went on to complain, "We've no real way of finding out what they're really up to over there."[25]

"We cannot afford to fail," Eisenhower had said. The AEF acted on that basis. There was no contingency planning. In a general ground offensive mounted in a specific area over a broad front, World War II attackers had some flexibility in their plans. If the initial assault did not force a breakthrough, follow-up units could be diverted to the flanks or held back to try again another day at another place. Overlord, however, was all or nothing. Hitler and Rommel were absolutely right in assuming that if the Wehrmacht could deny the AEF a foothold, the Allies would not be able to mount another offensive in 1944.

The size of the gamble on Overlord concentrated the minds of the men at SHAEF wonderfully, but it also increased the work load and raised tension to nearly unbearable levels. "If I could give you an exact diary account of the past week," Eisenhower wrote Mamie in late January, "you'd get some idea of what a flea on a hot griddle really does!" Toward the end of May, he wrote, "I seem to live on a network of high tension wires."[26]

5

UTILIZING ASSETS

In World War I, the side undertaking an offensive always had to worry about an enemy counteroffensive almost anywhere along the line from the Swiss border to the Channel coast. Adequate forces had to be maintained all along that line. The same was true of the Germans in Western Europe in World War II. SHAEF had an enormous advantage here. There was no possibility of a German offensive against the United Kingdom, so the AEF was free to concentrate all its resources on the point of attack.

Before 1918, when the first bombing squadrons came into being and began initial (although still very small) operations, there was no physical way a World War I attacking force could reach behind enemy lines to disrupt the movement of the enemy's men and supplies to the battle area. It could do so only through feints and deceptions. SHAEF made full use of feints and deceptions, but in addition the AEF had three means to prevent, or at least disrupt, the movement of German reserves and reinforcements to the lodgment area, isolating lower Normandy and turning it into a sort of strategic island. The three ways involved the airborne divisions, the French Resistance, and the strategic air force. Because they were new and untried, there was great controversy over how to utilize them effectively. But in the end, agreement was reached and the job was done.

• •

The initial COSSAC plan had called for using the British 6th Airborne Division in and around Caen to take the city and the airfield at Carpiquet. That was a bold plan, too bold for Montgomery, who insisted on using the division in what was essentially a defensive role, dropping it into the area between the Dives and Orne rivers to isolate Sword Beach.* Bradley, meanwhile, decided to use the U.S. 82nd and 101st Airborne divisions behind German lines in the Cotentin, to prevent the Germans from launching local counterattacks against Utah Beach and to seize the exits from that beach so that the 4th Infantry Division could move inland.

When General Marshall saw these plans, he was upset. At the beginning of the war, Marshall had held great hopes for the paratroops as a new element in warfare, but his hopes had not been realized. In September 1943, for example, a plan to drop the 82nd Airborne on airfields around Rome had been abandoned at the last minute as too risky and instead the division had been used for tactical support of the Salerno beachhead.

Early in 1944 Marshall told Eisenhower that the failure to use paratroops in a strategic role had been a severe disappointment to him. He thought the AEF could do much more to exploit its command of the air and the elite airborne divisions that had been built at such cost. Marshall felt there had been "a lack of conception" caused by a piecemeal approach, with "each commander grabbing at a piece to assist his particular phase of the operation." If he had been given command of Overlord, Marshall said, he would have insisted on a single, large airborne operation, "even to the extent that should the British be in opposition I would carry it out exclusively with American troops."

Marshall suggested to Eisenhower that the AEF use the airborne south of Evreux, some 100-plus kilometers inland from Caen. There were four good airfields near Evreux that could be quickly captured so the lightly armed airborne troops could be reinforced.

"This plan appeals to me," Marshall declared, "because I feel that it is a true vertical envelopment and would create such a strategic threat to the Germans that it would call for a major revision of their defensive plans." It would be a complete surprise,

* In addition, Montgomery hoped that his seaborne British 3rd Division at Sword Beach would be able to overrun Caen in the first hours of the invasion.

would directly threaten both the crossings of the Seine River and Paris, and would serve as a rallying point for the French Resistance. The only drawback Marshall could see was "that we have never done anything like this before, and frankly, that reaction makes me tired."[1]

Eisenhower hated to disagree with Marshall and almost never did so. Thus his reply was long and defensive. He said that for more than a year one of his favorite subjects for contemplation was getting ahead of the enemy in some important method of operation, and the strategic use of airborne troops was an obvious possibility. Nevertheless, on this one Marshall was wrong.

First, Eisenhower told his boss, he had to have the airborne on the flank at Sword and behind German lines at Utah in order to get ashore. Second, and more important, an airborne force well inland would not be self-contained, would lack mobility, and would therefore be destroyed. The Germans had shown time and again in the war that they did not fear a "strategic threat of envelopment." Using the road nets of Western Europe, they could concentrate immense firepower against an isolated garrison and defeat it in detail. Anzio was an example. An inland airborne force, cut off from all supply except what could be brought in by air, without tanks or trucks, immobile and inadequately armed, would be annihilated.

Eisenhower told Marshall that, far from being a strategic threat to the Germans, airborne troops at Evreux would just be wasted. "I instinctively dislike ever to uphold the conservative as opposed to the bold," Eisenhower concluded, but he insisted on using the 6th, 82nd, and 101st Airborne divisions as Montgomery and Bradley wanted to use them—to keep German reinforcements away from the invasion beaches.[2]

When Eisenhower took command, the Luftwaffe had been driven back into Germany to fight a defensive action, giving the Allies command of the air over France. Britain and America had put a tremendous effort into building their air fleets, including fighters but most of all medium and heavy bombers. The expense was staggering. One reason for the shortage of landing craft, for example, was the amount of steel, engines, and production capacity in general that had gone into building bombers. In addition, the air forces got first call on personnel, at the expense of the armies, where junior officer and noncom leadership suffered as a result.

Building the air armadas, in short, had been a gamble in technology and technique. The armadas gave the Allies command of the air and thousands of planes to exploit it. Those two facts gave the AEF a great asset, unique in the history of war. Was it worth the effort? That was a question no longer worth asking; the asset existed. But it left an outstanding question: How to use it.

There was no dispute about how to use it on D-Day. Everyone agreed that just before H-Hour and through D-Day, every Allied bomber that could fly would participate in the attack on the Normandy coastal defenses. But there was intense dispute over the role of the bombers in the two months preceding the invasion.

Gen. Carl Spaatz of the U.S. Eighth Air Force and Air Chief Marshal Sir Arthur Harris of RAF Bomber Command were wedded to the theory that bombers, by themselves, could win the war. Gen. J. F. M. Whiteley, a British officer who had served as Eisenhower's deputy chief of staff in the Mediterranean, had gone to the Churchill-Roosevelt-CCS conference in Quebec in September 1943. Whiteley reported that there was much discussion in Quebec about Overlord. His impression was that within the RAF and U.S. Army Air Forces (AAF, commanded by Gen. Henry "Hap" Arnold) there were powerful groups "who hoped Overlord would meet with every success, but who were sorry that they could not give direct assistance because, of course, they were more than fully occupied on the really important war against Germany."[3]

Reduced to its essentials, the dispute between the airmen and the ground soldiers was simply put. Spaatz and Harris believed that the further behind the front lines their bombers operated—that is, within Germany itself, attacking strategic targets—the more effective they could be. Eisenhower and the SHAEF staff believed that the closer to the front lines the bombers operated—that is, within France, attacking tactical targets—the more they could contribute to Overlord.

There was in addition a dispute between the bomber commanders. Although they agreed that Overlord was not really necessary, Harris and Spaatz had their own strategies. Harris felt RAF Bomber Command could bring about a German capitulation through terror bombing of German cities; Spaatz felt the Eighth Air Force could bring about a German surrender through the selective destruction of certain key industries, especially oil and synthetic-fuel production facilities.

The army commanders, most of all Eisenhower, believed

that the only way to bring about a German surrender was to overrun Germany on the ground, and that to do so required first of all
a successful Overlord. They further believed that only air superiority made Overlord feasible.

As so often happens with the military, the dispute was fought
out not over the straightforward question of targeting but rather over
the more complex question of organization and command structure.
Here things were well muddled. Although Eisenhower was the supreme commander, in fact he commanded only those forces assigned
to him by the CCS, and these did not include the Eighth Air Force
or Bomber Command. The only air power SHAEF possessed was
the British tactical air force and the American tactical air force
(Ninth Air Force), under the immediate command of Air Vice Marshal Sir Trafford Leigh-Mallory. Leigh-Mallory's experience had
been solely with fighters; he was a cautious, pessimistic sort; Harris
and Spaatz neither trusted nor liked him; they refused to serve under
him, or SHAEF.

In January, Eisenhower argued with Marshall and Arnold
about command. He insisted that Harris and Spaatz should be
under SHAEF for a period of several weeks before the invasion so
that SHAEF could pick the targets. He told Arnold he had "strong
views" on the subject. To his surprise and relief, Arnold said he
agreed that the bombers "should be placed under your direct command for the impending operations."[4]

Eisenhower intended to use the bombers to paralyze the
French railway system. He believed it could be done and that once
accomplished it would hamper German movement of reinforcements to lower Normandy. The program, called the Transportation Plan, would take time—it could not be accomplished with a
two- or three-day blitz on the eve of Overlord. The strategic air
force commanders were offering to participate in an interdiction
program that would begin shortly before D-Day and would concentrate on line-cutting, strafing, bridge-breaking, and the destruction of a few railroad focal points. The Transportation Plan called
for a prolonged attack on rail yards, sidings, stations, sheds, repair
shops, roundhouses, turntables, signal systems, switches, locomotives, and rolling stock.

Forrest Pogue, the official historian of SHAEF, writes that
"in getting the[ir] proposal adopted, Eisenhower, Tedder, and
Leigh-Mallory were vigorously opposed, on both strategic and political grounds, by most of the bomber commanders, by members

of the 21 Army Group staff, and by the Prime Minister and most of the War Cabinet."[5]

Harris and Spaatz led the protest. Harris argued that Bomber Command, built for night raids and area bombing, could not achieve the accuracy required to hit marshaling yards, repair facilities, bridges, and other pinpoint railroad targets. Tedder, the strongest advocate at SHAEF of the Transportation Plan, indeed the man who had convinced Eisenhower of its necessity, even accused Harris of juggling figures to prove that his bombers could not hit the proposed targets. Spaatz insisted that the continuing success of operations against German oil refineries would assure the greatest support for Overlord; he convinced Arnold to change his mind and support him. Spaatz argued that his Oil Plan would in the long run immobilize the Germans much more effectively than the Transportation Plan.

Eisenhower replied that the Oil Plan would have no immediate effect. The Germans had accumulated stocks of oil and gasoline in France in scattered and camouflaged depots. Only when those supplies were used up—that is, well after D-Day—would a stoppage of oil production affect German military operations in France. Spaatz shrugged off this point by saying that the Transportation Plan would be only of slight help in isolating the battlefield, while the Oil Plan would be of major help later. This was the crux of the matter: Spaatz assumed that it would be easy to get ashore and stay there; Eisenhower did not.

The Oil Plan would also allow Eighth Air Force to retain its independence from SHAEF, a point on which Spaatz insisted because of Leigh-Mallory. Eisenhower was embarrassed by Spaatz's open hostility to Leigh-Mallory and tried to reassure Spaatz that Tedder would personally supervise the air campaign. Further, as Spaatz noted in his diary, Eisenhower "tried subtly to sell Leigh-Mallory [to me], saying that . . . he felt that maybe proper credit had not been given to the man's intelligence. I told him that my views had not and would not change."[6]

Unable to persuade the air commanders, Eisenhower turned to his superiors. He convinced Churchill that Tedder could act as the "aviation lobe" of Eisenhower's brain—thus bypassing Leigh-Mallory so far as the bombers were concerned—but he could not persuade Churchill on the key point. The prime minister ruled that "there can be no question of handing over the British Bomber . . . Command as a whole to the Supreme Commander and his Deputy." Further, Churchill insisted that SHAEF air plans should be subject to CCS approval. Eisenhower objected to submitting his plans to the CCS and "demurred at anything short of complete operation control of the whole of Bomber Command and the American Strategic Forces." He felt so strongly that he told Churchill unless he was given command of the bombers he would "simply have to go home."[7]

This extreme threat—all but unique in the history of war; it evidently never occurred to Rommel to tell Hitler that unless he got control of the panzers he would "go home"—brought the British around. The War Cabinet drew up a directive that gave Eisenhower "supervision" of the bombers. Marshall suggested the word be changed to "command." The British refused, leaving Eisenhower "astonished." On March 22 he wrote in his diary, "If a satisfactory answer is not reached, I am going to take drastic action and inform the CCS that unless the matter is settled at once I will request relief from this Command." That same morning the British chiefs were meeting. When Eisenhower heard the results of their deliberations he added a postscript to his diary entry: "I was told the word 'direction' was acceptable. . . . Amen!"[8]

Tedder prepared a list of more than seventy railroad targets in France and Belgium (for the obvious reason that it would give away the invasion site, the bombing could not be concentrated around lower Normandy). On April 3 it went before the War Cabinet for approval. The British had previously forbidden air attacks on occupied countries if there was risk of high civilian casualties, and now they drew back from the Transportation Plan for that reason. "The argument for concentration on these particular targets," Churchill wrote Eisenhower, "is very nicely balanced on military grounds." He added that the Cabinet took "rather a grave and on the whole an adverse view of the proposal." Foreign Secretary Anthony Eden was especially adamant. He pointed out that after the war Britain would have to live in a Europe that was already looking to Russia "more than he would wish." He did not want the French people to regard the British and Americans with hatred.[9]

Eisenhower replied that he was convinced the Transportation Plan was necessary to the success of Overlord, "and unless this could be proved to be an erroneous conclusion, I do not see how we can fail to proceed with the program." He reminded Churchill that the French people were "slaves" and that they would benefit most from Overlord. "We must never forget," Eisenhower added in his strongest argument, "that one of the fundamental factors leading to the decision for undertaking Overlord was the conviction that our overpowering air force would make feasible an operation which might otherwise be considered extremely hazardous, if not foolhardy." He said it would be "sheer folly" to refuse approval to the Transportation Plan.[10]

Churchill put Eisenhower's views before the War Cabinet. He spoke eloquently of Eisenhower's onerous responsibilities. Care should be taken, he said, not to add unnecessarily to his burdens. Still, he complained that he had never realized that air power would assume so cruel and remorseless a form. The Transportation Plan, he feared, "will smear the good name of the Royal Air Forces across the world."[11]

Churchill wanted the French consulted. Eisenhower's chief of staff, Gen. Walter B. Smith, then talked to Gen. Pierre-Joseph Koenig, the representative of Gen. Charles de Gaulle's Algiers-based French Committee of National Liberation. "To my surprise," Smith reported, "Koenig takes a much more cold-blooded view than we do. His remark was, 'This is war, and it must be expected that people will be killed. We would take the anticipated loss to be rid of the Germans.' "[12]

Churchill was almost, but not quite, beaten down. He decided to take the issue to Roosevelt and thus force the Americans to take their share of the responsibility for approval of the plan. He told Roosevelt of the War Cabinet's anxiety about "these French slaughters" and of the British doubts "as to whether almost as good military results could not be produced by other methods." Roosevelt must decide. Roosevelt replied that the military considerations must dominate. The Transportation Plan had won.[13]

SHAEF put the bombers to work on the French railway system. By D-Day the Allies had dropped 76,000 tons of bombs (seventy-six kilotons, or about seven times the explosive power of the atomic bomb used against Hiroshima) on railway targets. The Seine River bridges west of Paris were virtually destroyed. Based on an index of 100 for January–February 1944, railway traffic dropped from 69 in mid-May to 38 by D-Day.

But by no means was this accomplished exclusively by the bombers—the French Resistance played a major role. There was some French resentment, although not so much as Eden feared. Casualties were lighter than the pessimists in the War Cabinet had predicted.

•   •

On June 3, in "Weekly Intelligence Summary No. 11," SHAEF G-2 assessed the results to date. The report began, "The enemy controlled railway system in the West has undergone and continues to undergo an attack such as no transport system has hitherto experienced either in intensity or duration." Some 1,700 locomotives and 25,000 wagons had been destroyed or put out of action, which sounded impressive, but which constituted only 13 percent and 8 percent respectively of the preraid figures. Worse, the Germans were able to replace rolling stock by taking it from French civilian needs. As the summary noted, "The prime sufferers have been the French people. French traffic has invariably been curtailed at the expense of German requirements and an already greatly strangled French economy has experienced further setbacks." Consequently, the losses "are not such that the enemy will be prevented from moving up supplies and reinforcements as required, although such movement will be less efficiently operated."

Beyond rolling stock, the Transportation Plan was directed against depots, turntables, and bridges. Some 58,000 tons of bombs had been dropped on ninety targets, inflicting great damage, but unfortunately the Germans were adept at repairs: "In many cases [the damage] has been cleared and the lines reopened within 24 hours, and in many more within 48 hours." More encouraging was the report on railway bridges across the Seine from Paris to the sea; eight of the nine had been destroyed. Of the nine highway bridges attacked, seven had been destroyed or partially damaged.

On the eve of D-Day, the SHAEF G-2 conclusion was ominous: "Evidence as to the effect on German troop movements remains unsatisfactory, but the effects till now do not appear to have been very serious."[14]

That judgment cast doubts on the wisdom of the Transportation Plan. The bomber commanders were never convinced that it was wise or effective; after the war, the official U.S. Army Air Force historians wrote, "Long after D-Day, there remained the sobering question as to whether the results of the plan were commensurate with the cost in air effort and the ruin inflicted on French and Belgian cities."[15]

But those in the best position to know, the German generals, were "strong in their belief that the various air attacks were ruinous to their counter-offensive plans."[16]

The plane that did the most damage was the B-26 Marauder, developed by the Glenn L. Martin Company. A medium bomber, it flew at low altitudes and could be extremely accurate, so it was the principal attacker of the railroad bridges and rail yards. After the war, Rommel's chief of staff, Hans Speidel, said, "Destruction of railways was making regulated railway supply impossible as early as mid-May 1944. . . . Lack of fuel paralyzed all movement. The Seine bridges below Paris and the Loire bridges below Orléans were destroyed from the air before 6 June 1944." (Speidel's statement is inscribed on the B-26 Memorial at the USAF Air Museum in Dayton, Ohio.)

In a 1946 interview, General Jodl said that "the complete construction of the coastal defenses was not yet finished and never would have been because the necessary sand and cement could no longer be brought up."[17] Gordon Harrison, the official historian of the cross-Channel attack, concluded that by D-Day the "transportation system [in France] was on the point of total collapse," and this was "to prove critical in the battle for Normandy."[18]

There was more involved in the disruption of the transportation system than just the bombers. The French Resistance played a part that was perhaps as important and that certainly was more efficient per pound of explosive.

The Resistance had grown from practically nothing in the dark days of 1940 to a considerable force by early 1944. Like all successful clandestine operations, its organization was complex and fragmented, divided regionally and politically. Its acknowledged head was Charles de Gaulle, but he was in Algiers, far from the scene and incapable of exercising anything like rigid control. Liaison was provided by the Special Operations Executive (SOE) established by the British in late 1940 (the first agents parachuted into France in the spring of 1941) and the American Office of Strategic Services (OSS), modeled on SOE. OSS began operating in 1943.

The Resistance had many significant weaknesses. It was always subject to German penetration. It was inadequately armed; in many cases totally unarmed. Lines of authority tended to be unclear. Communication within units was poor, between units almost nonexistent. It was mistrusted by the bulk of the population, as most French people wanted no trouble with the Germans and feared the consequences of stirring them up.

The Resistance had assets, including bravery, a willingness to make personal sacrifices for the goal of liberation, and fierce patriotism. Most of all, it was behind enemy lines. It could provide intelligence of the most accurate kind ("I saw it with my own eyes"), it could sabotage rail lines, bridges, and the like, and it could provide an underground army in the German rear areas that might be able to delay the movement of German forces toward the battle.

With regard to intelligence gathering, the Resistance was the best possible source on the Atlantic Wall because most of that wall was built by Frenchmen. M. Clement Marie of Port-en-Bessin in Calvados was one of many who in June 1942 was forced by the Germans to work on the construction of a major fortress at Pointe-du-Hoc (just west of what came to be called Omaha Beach). There was no heavy equipment; everything was done by shovel, by hand-cart, by horsepower, and manpower. The fortification was dug twenty-three feet deep into the ground. All the works, tunnels, trenches, and so on were covered; bunkers above soil level were also covered with topsoil and sod. Marie helped to pile earth on the sides of the bunkers, so that it gently sloped from the top to natural ground level.

Marie also worked at Pointe-de-la-Percée (the western edge of Omaha), building radar sites for the German *Kriegsmarine* (navy). He recalled the time in early 1944 when it was announced that Rommel was coming to inspect. The Germans gave the French workers an order to doff their caps when the field marshal appeared. "Very quickly," he says, "the word was spread and when Rommel came there was not a single man in Port-en-Bessin wearing a cap or hat and consequently no obligation to salute."[19]

Naturally, Rommel did not notice such a small act of defiance. Anyway, he needed more workers to make up for the absence of heavy equipment. (In many ways the Atlantic Wall was constructed in exactly the same way as the Great Wall of China, by human labor; the big difference was that the Germans had concrete and steel reinforcing rods.) "Get the French countryfolk to help erect the obstacles," Rommel told a division near Le Havre. "Pay them well and promptly for it. Point out that the enemy is least likely to invade where the most obstacles have been erected! The French farmers will be only too glad to line their purses."[20]

Naturally, the Germans never did pay enough—they established an exchange rate between the mark and the franc that was ruinous to the French—nor did they feed the workers well enough to win their loyalty. So the workers complained, and grumbled among themselves, and a few of them passed information along to active Resistance figures.

SOE had many ingenious ways of getting the information back to London, including the use of carrier pigeons dropped from airplanes. André Rougeyron was a Resistance member in Normandy; in a memoir, he described this curious wedding of an ancient method of communication with the most modern technology as follows: "I receive a visit from Ernest Guesdon. He is very happy since he found in his pasture a carrier pigeon that had been parachuted in. This is one of many pigeons discovered. This method of British information services works remarkably well. The birds are dropped at night in a cage attached to a small parachute. They are found the next morning by the user of the pasture or orchard. The equipment to accomplish this communication is meticulously put together: a packet of food for the bird, parchment envelope containing all the necessary instructions, and two moulded tubes for sending messages.

"The tubes are attached to the ring encircling the pigeon's leg. There is some very thin special paper, a pencil, and instructions on how to feed and return the bird, a questionnaire about the occupying troops, their moves, their morale, to say nothing of the defensive works."

Rougeyron was head of an escape section that rescued many young American pilots and crews shot down over France. He used the pigeons to send messages saying that the men—last names only, no rank—were safe. "We did not want to say anything else, fearing the pigeon might be shot down on its way."[21]

The Germans built a four-gun battery on the cliff just west of Port-en-Bessin. Big fortifications, big guns—155mm. Beautifully camouflaged with nets and dirt embankments, they could not be seen from the air.

The farmer on whose land they were built was furious because he could not graze his cattle or grow crops on the field. He paced off the distances between the bunkers, from the bunkers to the observation post on the very edge of the cliff, from the cliff to the bunkers, and so on. He had a blind son, eight or nine years old. Like many blind people, the boy had a fabulous memory. Because he was blind, the Germans paid little attention to him.

One day in early 1944, the boy hitched a ride to Bayeux. There he managed to get in touch with André Heintz, an eighteen-year-old in the Resistance. The boy gave Heintz his information; Heintz sent it on to England via his little homemade radio transmitter (hidden in a Campbell Soup can; today on display in the

Battle of Normandy Museum in Caen); thus the British navy, on D-Day, had the exact coordinates of the bunkers.[22]

At the little village of Benouville, on the bank of the Caen Canal where a bridge crossed the waterway, Mme Thérèse Gondrée had a café. The Germans who bought wine and snacks there did not know that she spoke German. She passed on what she picked up from their conversations to Mme Vion, the head of the local maternity hospital (and of the local Resistance), who passed it on to her superiors in the Resistance in Caen, who passed it on to SOE agents in the area, who got it back to England via radio or small airplane. Thus Maj. John Howard of the Ox and Bucks, 6th Airborne Division, who was training his company for a *coup de main* operation against the bridge on D-Day, knew a great deal about the enemy, including the location of the button that would set off the demolition charge to blow the bridge to prevent capture.[23]

The 506th Parachute Infantry Regiment (PIR) of the 101st Airborne had as one of its D-Day objectives the village of Ste.-Marie-du-Mont. Thanks to the Resistance, Lt. Richard Winters of Company E of the 506th knew, among other things, that the local German commander was seeing the local teacher and that he took his dog for a walk every day at precisely 1700 hours.[24]

M. Guillaume Mercader of Bayeux owned a bicycle shop. He had been a professional bicycle racer before the war. In an interview he related, "I could, under the occupation, renew my license and under the pretext of training I was able to travel about without difficulty." Thanks to the compulsory labor policy, he was able to gather from workers specific intelligence on defense construction, on infrastructures, on armaments, on troop locations, on beach obstacles and the like. "My responsible departmental person was M. Meslin, alias Cdt. Morvin, head of the subdivision. Every week at No. 259 Saint-Jean Street in Caen I met with him so I could hand over to him requested information we had obtained."[25]

Thanks to the information gathered and passed on from the French Resistance, supplemented and enhanced by Ultra intercepts and aerial reconnaissance, the AEF undoubtedly had better information on the enemy dispositions and strength than any attacking force in history.

•   •

Sabotage was another Resistance specialty. In the period 1941–43 it consisted of sporadic, uncoordinated pinpricks against war industries, railroads, canals, and telephone and telegraph systems. It was not of such a scale as to cause the Germans much worry. But beginning in early 1944, after SOE came under SHAEF control, railway sabotage was greatly accelerated and tied into the Transportation Plan. A resister with a stick of dynamite who knew where to place it on a bridge could be much more effective than a B-17 dropping a 500-pound bomb from 15,000 feet on the same target. The man on the spot could also time the explosion so as to take out a locomotive when the bridge went up. In the first three months of 1944 the Resistance destroyed 808 locomotives compared to 387 damaged by air attack. After the Transportation Plan went into effect, the figures were reversed: in April and May the bombers put 1,437 locomotives out of action compared to only 292 credited to the Resistance.[26]

The British hoped for more direct support from the Resistance. A committee consisting of representatives from SOE and the army considered the possibility of a national uprising. The Resistance could make a strategic contribution to Overlord if it were "backed by a general strike or by a rising on a national scale." Calmer heads prevailed. A French officer pointed out that the notion of a mass uprising "posited the existence of universal courage, whereas courage inspired only a few men—as it has always inspired the few rather than the many. And the idea of mass uprisings implied battling against modern tanks with the stone-throwing catapults of Caesar's time."[27]

SHAEF was more realistic. It wanted to use Resistance groups to prepare demolitions to blow main trunk lines leading into the lodgment area, beginning on D-Day. *Plan Vert*, it was called. By May, SOE was able to report to SHAEF that 571 railroad targets were ready for demolition. *Plan Vert* was supplemented by *Plan Tortue*, a project for blocking enemy road movements through guerrilla action—which meant in practice firing Sten and Bren guns into German columns, then running off into the woods, hoping the Germans would follow.

As the Germans were regularly picking up Resistance members and torturing them to get information, the Resistance could not be told in advance the date of D-Day. Therefore arrangements had to be made to order the execution of sabotage plans by code messages broadcast over the BBC. Leaders were told to listen to

BBC broadcasts on the 1st, 2nd, 15th, and 16th of each month. If the invasion was imminent, they would hear a preparatory code message. They would then remain on alert to listen for a confirmatory message "B," to be followed within forty-eight hours by a code launching the units into action. Each region had a different code.

In Bayeux, the action code for M. Mercader's unit was "It is hot in Suez," followed by "The dice are on the carpet." He recalled the day he heard them over the BBC: "In Bayeux, in my cellar, the radio was on. At 6:30 p.m., the first message said: 'It is hot in Suez. It is hot in Suez.' Twice. Then a definite silence. Then, 'The dice are on the carpet. The dice are on the carpet.' Twice again, as well as other messages which didn't concern us. Stunned by listening to these messages, an instant of emotion invaded me, but quickly enough, I came to myself and after having turned off the radio and climbing the steps from the cellar four at a time, I informed in the first place my wife of what I had heard. I then took my bicycle and went to contact my principal responsible people of an imminent landing. The night was going to be long."[28]

SHAEF considered limiting the sabotage activity on D-Day to lower Normandy. A strong argument for doing so was to wait in other regions until the destruction of bridges would be immediately helpful to the AEF. This applied especially to the south of France, where another landing was scheduled for mid-August. Further, if the Resistance went into action all across France, it would expose its members to identification and capture by the Germans, who meanwhile would have time to repair the damage. Those arguments gave way to the view that it was preferable to obtain the maximum amount of chaos behind enemy lines at the moment of landing, and anyway SHAEF figured that it would be impossible to keep the various Resistance groups quiet after the news of D-Day broke.

Anthony Brooks, a twenty-year-old Englishman who had grown up in French-speaking Switzerland and had been studying in France when the war began, was in 1944 an SOE agent in southern France, near Toulouse. He had been receiving airdrops of explosives, which he distributed to his Resistance people, who hid them in cesspools or even on locomotives when the drivers were Resistance. ("We would hide the explosives on an electric locomotive," he recalled, "and no German soldier is going to open up a thing that says 16,000 volts on it and it has got a key.") Some went into lavatory water tanks; they would hold up to twenty kilos of explosive. Like most SOE agents, Brooks found that his recruits were impatient, eager for action, so "we had to let them blow up trains every now and again even if it was too soon and we had no orders. Every now and again we derailed the wrong one and we had some bad press you might say and one train we derailed was a Swiss Red Cross train and there were four enormous vans full of eggs and people were trying to scoop the yolks out of the river to make omelets and cursing us all the while."[29]

In April 1944, the 2nd SS Panzer Division (the *Das Reich*) moved into a town near Toulouse named Montauban. It was refitting after hard service on the Eastern Front, receiving brand new tanks, Tigers, the biggest and best Germany could produce. The tanks were gas-guzzlers (Tigers weighed sixty-three tons and got one-half mile to the gallon). They were subject to mechanical problems. They had only steel tracks, which wore out quickly on highway travel. Therefore the Germans always moved the Tigers for any distance on railroad cars. The Tigers were concentrated in Montauban and kept under heavy guard. The railway cars they rode on were hidden in village railway sidings round Montauban, each concealed by a couple of worn-out French trucks dumped on top. These transporter cars were unguarded.

Brooks put his subagents to work. One of them was a beautiful young sixteen-year-old girl named Tetty "who was the daughter of the local boss who ran a garage and she had long ringlets and her mother was always smacking her and telling her not to play with them." All through May, Tetty and her boyfriend, her fourteen-year-old sister, and others sallied out after dark by bicycle to the cars, where they siphoned off all the axle oil, replacing it with an abrasive powder parachuted in by SOE. Brooks told Tetty and the others to throw away the oil, but "of course the French said it was ludicrous to throw away this beautiful green oil so they salvaged it as it was real high quality motor oil" that fetched a fine price on the black market.

On D-Day, the *Das Reich* got orders to move out for Normandy. The Germans loaded their Tigers onto the railway cars. Every car seized up before they reached Montauban. The damage was so extensive to the cars' axles that they could not be repaired. It was a week before the division found alternative cars, in Perigueux, a hundred kilometers away—bad luck for the tanks' tracks and fuel supply. The Resistance harassed the division from Montauban to Perigueux. As a consequence the *Das Reich,* expected by Rommel in Normandy by D plus three or four, actually arrived on D plus seventeen. Furthermore, as Brooks notes with a certain satisfaction, "No train went north of Montauban after the night of the Fifth of June until it went out flying the French flag or the Union Jack."[30]

The contributions of the paratroops on the night before D-Day, and of the bombers and the Resistance in the weeks before D-Day, cannot be appraised with precision. But it is clear that while Eisenhower never had to worry about his rear, Rommel always did.

6

PLANNING
AND PREPARING

ACCORDING TO General Eisenhower, before the battle is joined plans are everything.[1] As supreme commander, he directed a planning operation that seemed infinite in scope, was complex almost beyond description, and on which the outcome of the war depended. He insisted on and got an all-out effort from staff officers at SHAEF down through Twenty-first Army Group (Montgomery's headquarters), British Second and American First armies, the corps, divisions, battalions, and companies, and all levels of staff at the various air force, navy, and coast guard commands. As a result, Overlord was the most thoroughly planned amphibious operation in history.

When Eisenhower visited Bradley's headquarters, he told the officers, "This operation is not being planned with any alternatives. This operation is planned as a victory, and that's the way it's going to be. We're going down there, and we're throwing everything we have into it, and we're going to make it a success."

(In a 1964 interview with Walter Cronkite, Eisenhower repeated those words. He spoke with intensity, frowning a bit, giving some reminder of the power of his voice, body posture, attitude, and aura of certainty and command that he had displayed in 1944. Then he visibly relaxed, let that shy grin creep up the corner of his mouth, and added, "But there's nothing certain in war. Unless you can put a battalion against a squad, nothing is certain."[2])

The job of the planners was to make certain of as much as possible. To do that they needed to be in constant touch with troops in the field, monitoring the results of exercises and training maneuvers to decide what would work, what might work, and what wouldn't work. They had to put all that information together with the input from the other services to come up with a comprehensive plan that everyone agreed to.

The process started at the top and worked down. Eisenhower decided where and when. To deal with the objection that adding the Cotentin (Utah Beach) would be too costly because of the flooded areas behind the beach, Eisenhower's chief of staff, General Smith, suggested using airborne divisions to seize the causeways leading inland over the flooded areas. There was intense opposition from the airborne commanders, but Eisenhower ruled for Smith.[3]

By late January, Eisenhower's basic decisions were in place. On February 25 Bradley's headquarters had an outline plan drawn up; British Second Army had one completed a month later. The process moved down to corps, division, regiment, battalion levels.

Gen. Freddie de Guingand, Montgomery's chief of staff, recalled that right along the chain of command "nothing was ever proposed that didn't meet with heated opposition." If corps wanted it, division didn't. If the army proposed something and the navy agreed, the air force was sure to object.

De Guingand reported that it was Monty's Twenty-first Army Group staff that made the decision to send the DD tanks (the swimming tanks) in on the first wave, with naval guns firing over their heads. "Our reasons for using DD tanks in the van were to achieve an element of surprise which might be effective in demoralizing the enemy; also they would provide rallying points for the infantry."[4]

At the higher levels, the temptation to reach down to solve lower echelons' problems was great, but it was overcome. General de Guingand explained, "At first we all tried to discover a school solution to the composition of the assault waves—guns, engineers, tanks, infantry, in what order, where, etc., but after the first training rehearsal we decided the notion of a single formula was nonsense and we let the particular assault section solve its own problem."[5]

• •

"Its own problem" depended on the nature of the defensive works facing the particular corps, division, regiment, battalion. Each had a different problem, depending on the shape of the beach it would assault, and even more on Rommel's defensive works. But Rommel could not plan, only prepare. Planning made possible a concentration of energy and force, but it required a knowledge of where and when that Rommel did not have. Preparation for an attack anywhere required a dispersal of energy and force.

On every beach that was remotely suitable for an amphibious landing, Rommel built defenses. Offshore, the Germans' first line of defense consisted of mines anchored in the Channel, not enough to satisfy Rommel but enough to cause a major problem for the Allied navies. Onshore, the defenses differed to suit local terrain conditions, but the beach obstacles on the tidal flat between the high- and low-water marks were similar on Omaha, Utah, and the British beaches.

The tidal-flat obstacles began with so-called Belgian gates, which were gatelike structures built of iron frames ten feet high. These sat in belts running parallel to the coastline, about 150 meters out from the high-water line. Teller mines (antitank mines carrying twelve pounds of TNT) were attached to the structures, or old French artillery shells, brought in from the Maginot Line, pointed out to sea and primed to fire. Admiral Ruge had no faith in land mines and artillery shells stuck underwater, as they had no water-proofing, but the marine mines he preferred were not available in sufficient quantity.[6]

Next, at about 100 meters out from the high-water mark, a band of heavy logs were driven into the water at an angle pointed seaward, with Teller mines lashed to the tips of some of the logs. At about seventy meters from shore, the main belt of obstacles featured hedgehogs (three or four steel rails cut in two-meter lengths and welded together at their centers) that could rip out the bottom of any landing craft.

Rommel bestrode France like a colossus. He could, and did, flood the countryside by damming rivers or letting in the sea. He could and did uproot and evacuate French civilians, tear down vacation homes and buildings to give his artillery a better field of fire, cut down forests to get the trees he needed for his beach obstacles.

The obstacles forced the Allies to choose between risking

their landing craft on a full tide or coming in on a rising tide and thus giving the German soldiers an opportunity to cut down the first waves of attackers as they struggled through the tidal flat and up to the first feature of the beach, which at Omaha was a bank of shingle (small, smooth rocks),* or a line of sand dunes at Utah that could provide some cover. To make full use of the killing zone, Rommel had his static divisions (many of whose battalions were *Ost* units; in some divisions the men were 50 percent Polish or Russian) right up close.

At each of the beach exits at Omaha, for example, riflemen and machine gunners were in fire trenches on the lower part of the bluff, halfway up the bluff, and at the top. Scattered along the slopes of the draws, and on the plateau above, were hundreds of "Tobruks," circular concrete-lined holes big enough for a mortar team, a machine gun, or even the turret of a tank. The Tobruks were connected by underground tunnels. Beside and around them, the Germans had fixed fortifications of reinforced concrete looking straight down onto the beach. In them, as in the Tobruks, there were panoramic sketches of the ground features in front of them, giving range and deflection for specific targets. In other words, they were zeroed in.

Back down on Omaha Beach proper, the Germans' had twelve strong points built to provide enfilade fire the length of the beach. Big guns, 88mm and even 105mm, were put into casemates with embrasures that opened down the beach, not out to sea. The casemates had an extra wing on the seaward side to hide the muzzle blast from the Allied navies.

Up on the bluff there were eight concrete casemates and four open field positions, for 75mm to 88mm guns, all sited for both grazing and plunging fire on every yard of beach. The guns came from all over the Nazi empire, French 75s, big Russian guns, 105s from Czechoslovakia, others from Poland.

The big casemates could take any shell the Allied navies could throw against them and still protect the guns; to protect the casemates from the real threat, an infantry assault with grenades and flamethrowers, the Germans surrounded them with land mines and barbed wire.

So the GI hitting the beach in the first wave at Omaha

---

* The beach that visitors see today is considerably different from what it was in 1944. U.S. Army engineers tore down most of the seawall and entirely removed the shingle embankment during unloading operations in the summer of 1944.

would have to get through the minefields in the Channel without his LST blowing up, then get from ship to shore in a Higgins boat taking fire from inland batteries, then work his way through an obstacle-studded tidal flat of some 150 meters crisscrossed by machine-gun and rifle fire, with big shells whistling by and mortars exploding all around, to find his first protection behind the shingle. There he would be caught in a triple crossfire—machine guns and heavy artillery from the sides, small arms from the front, mortars coming down from above.

If the GI was not killed getting off his landing craft or crossing the tidal flat, if by some miracle he made it to the shingle, Rommel wanted him wounded before he got there. If not wounded, paralyzed by fear.

To keep that GI huddled there, Rommel had more mines laid. Between the shingle and the bluffs there was a shelf of beach flat (in some places marshy). Rommel loaded in the barbed wire but relied mainly on mines. They were irregularly placed throughout the shelf and of all types. Some were simple charges of TNT covered by rock and set off by trip wires. S-mines were devices of the devil; they jumped up when activated, then exploded at waist height. There were others. Altogether Rommel laid 6.5 million mines, and wanted many millions more (his goal was 11 million antipersonnel mines).[7] Behind the mines and astride the draws there were antitank ditches, two meters or so deep, and cement antitank or antitruck barriers across the exit roads.

All this was backed up by big guns at Pointe-du-Hoc, where there was to be a six-gun battery of 155s capable of firing into the mass of shipping off both Omaha and Utah beaches, another at St.-Marcouf looking right down on Utah, another at Longues-sur-Mer covering Gold, and so on.

Behind Omaha, once one got inland from the plateau, there were no fixed defenses of any kind. Mainly this reflected the impossibility of Rommel's building a genuine Atlantic Wall that had depth to it—the length was too great, the resources insufficient. Partly it reflected Rommel's all-or-nothing attitude about the battle for the beaches. But as every GI who fought in Normandy can testify, in the country of hedgerows and stone-walled villages, farmhouses, barns, and outbuildings, fixed fortifications were not needed. The hedgerow country of Normandy was ideal for fighting a defensive struggle with the weapons of the mid-twentieth century.

At Gold, Juno, and Sword, the beach obstacles were extensive, but the dunes were not so high as at Utah, and instead of bluffs behind the seawall there were French vacation homes. Some of these were torn down to give a better field of fire, some were used as strong points. There were casemates, large and small, scattered along the coast. As elsewhere, there was no depth to the defense.

At Utah, the beach obstacles were in place, but there was no bluff behind the beach, only sand dunes behind the one- to three-foot seawall, so the extensive trench system manned by infantry was absent, but the Germans had dug into the dunes a series of Tobruks with tank turrets mounted on them, connected by underground trenches, along with casemates holding heavy artillery, thousands of miles of barbed wire, and thousands of mines.

The strong point at Utah was a blockhouse at La Madeleine. It had an 88mm cannon, two 50mm antitank guns, two 75mm cannon, a 16-inch howitzer, five grenade-launching mortars, two flamethrowers, three heavy machine guns, one under an armored turret, and eight "Goliaths." These were miniature tanks hardly bigger than a child's wagon, but they were stuffed with explosives and had a radio-guidance mechanism.

Behind the dunes at Utah, a road ran parallel to the beach. Four exit roads, or "causeways" as the Americans called them, ran inland perpendicular to the beach. The causeways crossed the flooded fields created by damming up local rivers. Behind the flooded fields, Rommel had troops stationed in every village, along with field artillery presighted on the causeways. The troops came from the 709th and 716th divisions (consisting of the Georgian Battalion and 642nd *Ost* Battalion). They had almost no organic motor transport.

These inland units were used to build defenses locally, consisting of sticking logs into the ground in any open field suitable for a glider landing. The Allies had used gliders extensively if not very successfully in Sicily in July 1943, and Rommel assumed they would again. To prevent it, he devised "Rommel's asparagus," ten-foot logs driven into the ground, to be topped with shells attached by interconnecting wires. The shells didn't arrive from Paris until after D-Day, but the logs by themselves were enough to bust up a wooden glider going better than 100 kilometers per hour.

For deception purposes, Rommel built casemates that held no guns. Admiral Ruge recalled, "Dummy batteries attracted a great many Allied air attacks and helped the real guns to survive."[8]

The Americans were making extensive use of rubber, blown-up "tanks" and other heavy vehicles as part of Operation Fortitude, but the Germans did not develop such devices.

Instead, Rommel poured more concrete and planted more asparagus. Col. Gen. Georg von Sodenstern, commander of the Nineteenth Army in southern France, thought Rommel mad. He commented on Rommel's fixed defenses: "As no man in his senses would put his head on an anvil over which the smith's hammer is swung, so no general should mass his troops at the point where the enemy is certain to bring the first powerful blow of his superior material."

To which Rommel replied, "Our friends from the East cannot imagine what they're in for here. It's not a matter of fanatical hordes to be driven forward in masses against our line, with no regard for casualties and little recourse to tactical craft; here we are facing an enemy who applies all his native intelligence to the use of his many technical resources, who spares no expenditure of material and whose every operation goes its course as though it had been the subject of repeated rehearsal."[9]

He was right in his analysis of the American army but, in the view of Gen. Baron Leo Geyr von Schweppenburg, badly wrong in his conclusion about how to meet the attack. Schweppenburg commanded Panzer Group West. When Rommel began moving the 2nd Panzer Division closer to the coast, north of Amiens, Schweppenburg protested. Rommel insisted and put the leading battle group right on the coast, dug in. He growled to Admiral Ruge, "The panzer divisions are going to be moved forward, whether they like it or not!"[10]

Shortly thereafter, an angry General Schweppenburg, accompanied by Hitler's panzer expert, Gen. Heinz Guderian, confronted Rommel. The latter blandly told them he intended to dig in every tank on the coastline. Guderian was shocked. He insisted that "the very strength of panzer formations lies in their firepower and mobility." He advised Rommel to pull the tanks back out of range of Allied naval guns. He insisted that the lesson from the Sicily and Salerno landings was crystal clear—the Germans could not fight a decisive battle while they were under those naval guns. Guderian knew that an amphibious force is not at its most vulnerable when it is half ashore, half at sea. It is at its most powerful at that time, thanks to those big naval guns. He urged Rommel to think in terms of a counteroffensive launched on the Wehrmacht's terms, at some choke point inland when the enemy was overstretched. That was the way the Russians did it, with great success, as Guderian could testify.

Rommel would not budge. "If you leave the panzer divisions in the rear," he warned, "they will never get forward. Once the invasion begins, enemy air power will stop everything from moving."[11]

When Guderian reported to Hitler, he recommended pulling back and fighting inland, which specifically meant keeping command and control of the panzer divisions out of Rommel's hands. Hitler tried a weak-kneed, half-hearted compromise. On May 7, he turned over three panzer divisions to Rommel, the 2nd, 21st, and 116th. The other four panzer divisions were to be held inland. Gen. Alfred Jodl, chief of OKW, assured Rommel that, although the four divisions were under OKW's control, they "will be released for operations—without further application by yourself—the moment we can be certain about the enemy's intentions and focus of attack."[12]

That sounded reasonable, but skipped over this fact: the leadership principle had led to a situation in which a German panzer division commander would in a crisis look to not one man but three for his orders—Rommel, Rundstedt, Hitler. Jodl's sensible-sounding words also ignored the failure to choose between competing strategies. Hitler backed neither Rommel nor the Schweppenburg/Guderian team. Just as he could not trust people, neither could he trust one plan over another. He split his resources and invited defeat in detail.

Rommel got his three panzer divisions up as close as he could, especially the 21st, which went into camp around Caen. The 21st had been Rommel's favorite in Africa, where it had been decimated. It had been rebuilt around a cadre of former officers, including Col. Hans von Luck. Its commander was Gen. Edgar Feuchtinger, whose qualifications for the job were that he had organized the military displays at the annual Party rallies. He had no combat experience, knew nothing of tanks. According to Luck, Feuchtinger "was a live and let live person. He was fond of all the good things of life, for which Paris was a natural attraction." He was wise enough to leave the reality of command in the hands of his immediate subordinates.[13]

Rommel put the other two panzer divisions under his command, the 12th SS and *Panzer Lehr*, equally distant from Calais and Calvados. They were not close enough to get to the beaches in a few hours, however, a reflection of the immense front line the Germans had to cover. General Fritz Bayerlein, commanding *Panzer Lehr*, described the division as "the best equipped panzer division that Germany ever had. It was 100 percent armored; even the infantry was completely armored." When he took the command, Guderian told him, "With this division alone, you must throw the Allies into the sea. Your objective is the coast—no, not the coast, it is the sea."

Aside from the three panzer divisions, Rommel's forces had little mobility. Rundstedt, true to his analysis that fighting a mobile battle inland was preferable to fighting a pitched battle from fixed fortifications, put most of his effort in the first five months of 1944 into improving transport facilities for the coastal divisions. But Rundstedt's efforts to put wheels under his army were offset by Rommel's insistence on digging in every available soldier and gun along the coast. Anyway, as Gordon Harrison observes, "German notions of mobility in the west in 1944 hardly corresponded to American concepts of a motorized army." German "mobile" units had, at best, one or two trucks to move essential supplies, with horse-drawn artillery and general transport. The men were listed as "mobile" because they had each got a bicycle.[14]

The Wehrmacht of 1944 was a strange army. In the panzer divisions, it had highly mobile forces with superior firepower, absolutely up to date. But it did not have the fuel to sustain operations. Thanks to the Allied bombing campaign against the Romanian oil fields, Germany had desperate fuel shortages. In France, that meant the panzer divisions had to sharply curtail their training. In the infantry divisions, meanwhile, the Wehrmacht of 1944 was almost a replica of the Kaiser's army of 1918. It was dependent on rail and horse for its supplies, on foot power for movement. In organization, tactics, and doctrine, it was prepared to fight a 1918 battle, just as the Atlantic Wall was an attempt to build a replica of the World War I trench system.

Despite the handicap of inadequate equipment, the German infantry divisions could have been made more mobile through training maneuvers. But so great was Rommel's obsession with pouring concrete and sticking logs into the tidal flats that he put his fighting men to work building beach obstacles. Challenged by a subordinate who wished to emphasize training, Rommel ordered, "I hereby forbid all training, and demand that every minute be used for work on the beach obstacles. It is on the beaches that the fate of the invasion will be decided, and, what is more, during the first 24 hours."[15] Even 21st Panzer units around Caen were put to work putting in asparagus.

In March, after the spring thaw had immobilized the armies on the Eastern Front, Hitler began transferring units to the West. Rommel put them into the line where they were most needed. The Cotentin got a new division, the 91st, supposedly mobile, and the 6th Parachute Regiment, commanded by Col. Frederick von der Heydte, a legend for his exploits in Crete. His regiment was an elite, all-volunteer unit. Average age was seventeen and a half (in the 709th Infantry Division on the Cotentin, average age was thirty-six). When he arrived in Normandy, the colonel was shocked by "the mediocrity of the armament and equipment of the German divisions. There were weapons from every land that had fallen into German hands over the past thirty years." His own regiment had four kinds of grenade launchers and seven types of light machine guns.

Heydte was also shocked when he was shown a document and told to sign. It came from Hitler. He wanted each commander to give his written promise to remain in place, to hold every inch of ground, when the invasion came. Heydte refused to sign; his corps commander simply shrugged.[16]

Throughout the Cotentin, by May, Rommel had three divisions, the 243rd, the 709th, and the 91st. Along the Calvados coast he had the 352nd facing Omaha, the 716th at the British beaches, with 21st Panzer around Caen.

This was neither fish nor fowl. The whole point to pouring all that concrete and digging all those trenches along the coast was to check the enemy long enough to allow a concentrated panzer counterattack before the end of D-Day. But with only one division to cover the whole Calvados-Cotentin coastline, and only two to cover the area from Le Havre to Holland, Rommel could not possibly hope to make an early concentrated panzer attack. By denying Rommel command of the tanks, Hitler denied Rommel his strategy. At that point, a less stubborn general might have taken steps to begin implementing the strategy he didn't believe in but had been forced by circumstances to adopt. Not Rommel. He stuck to a strategy that by his own logic, given available resources, couldn't work.

On the day the battle would be joined, therefore, the mighty

Wehrmacht's armored divisions would be immobilized not so much by the Allied air forces, or by the Allied navies, or by the Resistance, as by the leadership principle of the Third Reich.

But suppose that Rommel had persuaded Hitler to put the armored divisions under his immediate command. Suppose further that he got lucky and stationed one panzer division in Bayeux, another at Carentan (as according to General Bayerlein, commander of the *Panzer Lehr* Division, he wanted to do).[17] Then suppose that on D-Day Rommel launched a panzer-led counterattack against the 4th Infantry at Utah and another at Omaha's left flank and Gold's right. That surely would have created a crisis and caused some chaos on the landing beaches, as well as many casualties.

But consider the price to the Wehrmacht. With the Allied communications network, including fire-control parties on shore and in the air in radio contact with the navy gunners, the U.S. and Royal navies, supported by Canadian, Norwegian, Polish, and French warships, would have killed every tank in the assault. In other words, Rommel's most basic idea, to stop the invaders cold on the beach, was flawed. Bringing the panzers down in range of the Allied navies was madness, as Guderian had argued. At Sicily and again at Salerno, German tanks managed to penetrate the Allied lines and get down close to the beach. There they were blasted by Allied destroyers firing point-blank. But Rommel had not been at Sicily or Salerno.

Rundstedt was right; the Germans' best hope was to fall back from the coast (as the Japanese were learning to do in the Pacific islands) and fight the battle out of range of an overwhelming naval barrage. That would have required depth to the defense, a series of strong points, as in World War I, to fall back on. Had the same amount of labor gone into building defensive positions at every choke point, river crossing, and so forth, as went into building the Atlantic Wall, then the Germans might have held on in France until winter weather closed down operations in 1944. Such a delay would not have won the war for Germany, however, because in the spring of 1945 the Allies would have been able to launch a tremendous air and land bombardment on German lines, culminating in August in an atomic bomb over Berlin.

But that would take time, and meanwhile Germany's only hope would have come into play. A long winter along the Seine or Somme would have had a terribly depressing effect on Allied morale, given a boost to the German. A long winter along the Seine would have caused Stalin to wonder whether he might not be better off reaching a compromise peace. A long winter would give the Germans time to bring in their secret weapons, most notably the ME 262.

Rommel's decision to put as much of his strength on the beaches as possible, behind the strongest fortifications possible, was based on his military judgment. Hitler's decision to approve (partly) Rommel's concept of the Atlantic Wall was based on his political megalomania. His conqueror's mentality forbade him giving up any territory without a fight.

Rommel and Hitler made fundamental errors in planning for D-Day, based on faulty judgments. The old man, Field Marshal Rundstedt, who was there for window dressing, was the one who got it right—get out from under those naval guns.

But Rommel and Hitler were land fighters. They were more afraid of airplanes than they were of ships. They looked overhead, instead of out to sea, for danger. They made a mistake.

Dr. Detlef Vogel of the *Militargeschichtliches Forschungsamt* in Freiburg comments: "It is truly amazing that the senior army commanders, who had once conducted such nimble operations, suddenly wanted to hide behind a rampart."[18]

Equally amazing was the way that Rommel, who had made his reputation as a commander who used brilliant tactics, long-range movements, and lightning strikes, had so completely adopted a defensive posture. On May 11 he visited La Madeleine on Utah Beach. The company commander at the fortification was Lt. Arthur Jahnke, a twenty-three-year-old who had been badly wounded on the Eastern Front. Rommel arrived in·his Horch, with accordions stuffed into the trunk; Rommel's habit was to give an accordion to units that were performing to his satisfaction.

Lieutenant Jahnke and his men did not get an accordion. Rommel was in a bad mood, which got worse as he strode along the dunes, followed by his staff and the hapless Jahnke. His criticism fell like hail: not enough obstacles on the beach, not enough mines around the blockhouse, not enough barbed wire.

Jahnke had enough. He protested, "Marshal sir, I string all the wire I'm sent, but I can't do more than that."

"Your hands, lieutenant! I want to see your hands!" Rommel ordered.

Bewildered, Jahnke removed his gloves. At the sight of the deep scratches that disfigured his palms, Rommel softened. "Very well, lieutenant," he said. "The blood you lost building the fortifications is as precious as what you shed in combat." As he got back into his Horch, Rommel counseled Jahnke to "keep an eye on each high tide. They surely will come at high tide."[19]

The Allies, meanwhile, went ahead with plans that they were sure would work. To them the Atlantic Wall was formidable but by no means impregnable. On April 7, Good Friday, Twenty-first Army Group had completed the overall outline plan and was ready to present it to the division, corps, and army commanders. Montgomery presided over a meeting at his headquarters, St. Paul's School (of which Montgomery was a graduate). "This exercise," he began, "is being held for the purpose of putting all general officers of the field armies in possession of the whole outline plan for Overlord, so as to insure mutual understanding and confidence." He then laid out the plan.

Working from left to right, it called for the British 6th Airborne Division to begin its assault right after midnight, with the objectives of knocking out an enemy battery at Merville, seizing intact the bridges over the Orne River and the Orne Canal, blowing the bridges over the Dives, and generally acting as flank protection. The British 3rd Division, with French and British commandos attached, was to push across Sword Beach, then pass through Ouistreham to capture Caen and Carpiquet airfield. The Canadian 3rd Division was to push across Juno Beach and continue on until it cut the Caen-Bayeux highway. The British 50th Division at Gold had a similar objective, plus taking the small port of Arromanches and the battery at Longues-sur-Mer from the rear.

At Omaha, the U.S. 1st and 29th divisions were to move up the exits, take the villages of Colleville, St.-Laurent, and Vierville, then push inland. Attached ranger battalions were to capture the battery at Pointe-du-Hoc, either by land or sea or both. At Utah, the 4th Infantry was to cross the beach, establish control of the coast road, and move west along the causeways to the high ground inland, ready to wheel to the right to drive for Cherbourg. The 101st Airborne would land southwest of Ste.-Mère-Église to secure the inland side of the causeways and to destroy the bridges in the vicinity of Carentan while seizing others to protect the southern flank at Utah. The 82d Airborne was to land west of St.-Sauveur-le-Vicomte to block the movement of enemy reinforcements into the Cotentin in the western half of the peninsula.

At the briefing, Montgomery acted on the assumption that getting ashore was not the problem. What worried him was staying ashore. He told his subordinates, "Rommel is likely to hold his mobile divisions back from the coast until he is certain where our main effort is being made. He will then concentrate them quickly and strike a hard blow. His static divisions will endeavor to hold on defensively to important ground and act as pivots to the counterattacks. By dusk on D minus 1 the enemy will be certain that the Neptune area [code name for the seaborne portion of Overlord] is to be assaulted in strength. By the evening of D-Day he will know the width of frontage and the approximate number of our assaulting divisions." Montgomery thought that Rommel would bring two panzer divisions against the lodgment on D plus one; by D plus five it would be six panzer divisions. Protecting and expanding the lodgment area would be more difficult than establishing it.[20]

With their objectives set, the generals and colonels went to work at division, regimental, and battalion levels to develop specific plans for getting ashore. As they and their staffs worked through April and into May, Rommel was building, pouring concrete, setting posts. They could not be so confident as Montgomery that getting ashore was the least of their problems. For them, it was the first of their problems, the one that had to be overcome or there would be no more problems.

The plan that emerged ran as follows:

The first regiments to hit the shore would come in on the heels of a preassault air and naval bombardment. It was designed to neutralize known gun positions and demoralize enemy troops. It would begin at midnight, with an RAF attack against coastal batteries from the mouth of the Seine to Cherbourg (1,333 heavy bombers dropping 5,316 tons of bombs). At first light, the U.S. Eighth Air Force would hit enemy beach defenses in the assault area. Strong points at Omaha were due to get hit by 480 B-24s carrying 1,285 tons of bombs. Troops scheduled to go ashore at Omaha were assured that there would be innumerable craters on the beaches, more than enough to provide protection and shelter.

Naval gunfire would commence at sunrise and continue to H minus five minutes (sunrise was at 0558, H-Hour set for 0630). At Omaha, the battleships *Texas* and *Arkansas* would fire their ten 14-inch and twelve 12-inch guns, respectively, from eighteen kilometers offshore, concentrating on Pointe-du-Hoc and enemy strong points defending the exits. They would be joined by three cruisers with 6-inch guns and eight destroyers with 5-inch guns.

If that bombardment failed to render the defenders dead, incapacitated, or immobilized by fright, smaller fire-support craft would precede the first wave to add to the Germans' misery. At Omaha, sixteen LCTs carrying four DD tanks each were fitted so that two tanks could fire up to 150 rounds per cannon over the ramp, beginning from a range of three kilometers at about H minus fifteen minutes. Ten LCTs would carry thirty-six 105mm howitzers (selfpropelled) of the 58th and 62nd Armored Field Artillery battalions; the howitzers were mounted so that they could fire 100 rounds per gun from the LCTs at a range of eight kilometers, commencing at H minus thirty minutes. Finally, fourteen LCT(R)s were outfitted as rocket launchers; each LCT(R) fired 1,000 high-explosive rockets simultaneously from three kilometers offshore. Under that cover, the first waves would land.

The plans for the assault landings varied from regiment to regiment, beach to beach. That of the 116th Infantry of the 29th Division on the western (right) flank at Omaha was representative. As the accompanying chart shows, the 116th's plan to penetrate the defenses was complex and detailed down to the seconds. At H minus five minutes, just as the naval and air bombardments lifted, and as the rockets from the LCT(R)s whistled overhead, companies B and C of the 743rd Tank Battalion (thirty-two tanks strong) would touch down on the right. These were DD tanks, which would swim ashore from 6,000 yards out. They would take up firing positions at the water's edge to cover the first wave of infantry.

At H-Hour, 0630, eight LCTs would land to the left, bringing ashore with them Company A of the 743rd Tank Battalion. With Company A there would be eight tank dozers, towing trailers of explosive to be used by combat engineers in demolishing the obstacles before the tide covered them.

At H plus one minute the first wave of infantry would touch down, Company A on the far right at Dog Green, companies E, F, and G at Easy Green, Dog Red, and Dog White. Each company was about 200 men strong; firepower included rifles, machine guns, bangalore torpedoes, bazookas, mortars and grenades. Behind these skirmishers would come engineers, followed by light artillery and antiaircraft batteries, more engineers, then at H plus fifty minutes another wave of infantry (the 116th's L, I, K, and C companies). At

LANDING DIAGRAM, OMAHA BEACH
(Sector of 116th RCT)

	EASY GREEN	DOG GREEN	DOG WHITE	DOG RED	DOG GREEN
H − 5			Co C (DD) 743 Tk Bn	Co C (DD) 743 Tk Bn	Co B (DD) 743 Tk Bn
H HOUR	Co A 743 Tk Bn			Co A 743 Tk Bn	
H + 01	Co E 116 Inf		Co G 116 Inf	Co F 116 Inf	Co A 116 Inf
H + 03	146 Engr CT		146 Engr CT	146 Engr CT	146 Engr CT — Co C 2d Ranger Bn
H + 30	Co H — HQ Co E 116 Inf — Co H AAAW Btry		Co H — HQ Co G 116 Inf — Co H AAAW Btry	Co H — Co F Co H 116 Inf — HQ Co 2d Bn AAAW Btry Demolitions Control Boat	Co B — HQ Co A 116 Inf — 1st Bn 116 149 Beach Bn 121 Engr AAAW Btry
H + 40	112 Engr Bn		121 Engr Bn	112 Engr / 149 Engr Beach Bn	Co D 116 Inf
H + 50	Co L 116 Inf		Co K 116 Inf	Co I 116 Inf	Co C 116 Inf
H + 57				Co M 116 Inf — HQ Co 3d Bn	Co B 81 Cml Wpns Bn
H + 60	112 Engr Bn		HQ & HQ Co 116 Inf	112 Engr Bn	121 Engr Bn — Co A & B 2d Ranger Bn

	EASY GREEN	DOG RED	DOG WHITE	DOG GREEN
H + 65				5th Ranger Bn
H + 70	149 Engr Beach Bn	112 Engr Bn	Alt HQ & HQ Co 116 Inf	121 Engr Bn / 5th Ranger Bn
H + 90		AT Plat 3d Bn / 29 Sig Bn	58 FA Bn Armd	
H + 100		149 Engr Beach Bn	6th Engr Sp Brig	
H + 110	111 FA Bn (3 Btrys n DUKWS)	AT Plat 2d Bn		AT Plat 1st Bn / Gn Co 116 Inf
H + 120	AT Co 116 Inf / 467 AAAW Bn	AT Co 116 Inf / 467 AAAW Bn / 149 Engr Beach Bn	467 AAAW Bn	467 AAAW Bn
H + 150		DD Tanks	HQ Co 116 Inf / 104 Med Bn	
H + 180 to H + 215		461 Amphibious Truck Co	Navy Salvage	
H + 225	461 Amph Trk Co			

NOTE: *Plan as of 11 May*

Legend:
- [ ] LCI
- M LCM
- T LCT
- A LCA
- V LCVP
- ◇ DD Tank
- D DUKW

HISTORICAL DIVISION, WAR DEPARTMENT

H plus sixty minutes two ranger battalions would come in on the right; at H plus 110 minutes DUKWs would bring in heavy artillery. At H plus three hours, Navy salvage units and truck companies would move in. By then, the beach should be clear, the fighting rifle companies moving inland.

(Brig. Gen. Norman "Dutch" Cota, second in command of the 29th Division, did not like the idea of storming ashore an hour after first light. He had little faith in the accuracy of air and naval bombardment, thought it would do little good, and wanted to land the first wave in total darkness. That way the assault troops could cross the tidal flat safely and would be able to take up firing and attacking positions at the foot of the bluff before the Germans could see them. "The beach is going to be fouled-up in any case," he declared. "Darkness will not substantially alter the percentage of accuracy in beaching—not enough to offset the handicaps of a daylight assault." He was overruled.[21])

Each movement required an exact timing schedule that would begin three and four days before H-Hour at ports in southwestern England that were up to 160 kilometers from Omaha. Men and equipment would load up on LSTs, LCIs, and LCTs. Off the mouths of the harbors the convoys would form up. After crossing the Channel, the ships would anchor off the coast of France. Men would climb down the rope nets to their LCVPs, or descend in the boats as they were lowered by the davits. They would circle, circle, circle until they got clearance to form up line abreast and go in.

There was much more to the plan of assault than outlined here, and there were variations at different sectors and beaches, but basically the 116th plan was similar to those elsewhere. The emphasis was on a crescendo of high explosives hitting the beach defenses for a half hour before the tanks arrived, to be immediately followed by the first wave of skirmishers, who should be able to take advantage of the dazed enemy and seize the trenches as well as the exits from the beach. After that it was a question of getting enough transport and firepower ashore quickly enough to take the plateau area and move inland. All this was planned out on a timetable that was exceedingly rigid and complicated—and it was done without a single computer.

When Pvt. John Barnes of Company A, 116th Infantry, attended the briefing on the assault plan, he was mighty impressed. He would be going ashore at H-Hour; one minute later E Company would come in behind him, followed by engineers at H-Hour plus three minutes. Then would come Headquarters Company and antiaircraft artillery, then more engineers, then Company L at H-Hour plus fifty minutes, and so on through the day. "It seemed so organized," Barnes recalled, "that nothing could go wrong, nothing could stop it. It was like a train schedule; we were almost just like passengers. We were aware that there were many landing boats behind us, all lined up coming in on schedule. Nothing could stop it."[22]

Others were not so sure. Capt. Robert Miller of the 175th Regiment, 29th Division, remembered his CO, Col. Paul "Pop" Good, holding up the operation plan for the regiment. "It was thicker than the biggest telephone book you've ever seen. After the briefing was completed, Colonel Good stood up, he picked it up and tried to tear it in half, but it was so thick that this strong man couldn't do it. So he simply threw it over his shoulder and said, 'Forget this goddamned thing. You get your ass on the beach. I'll be there waiting for you and I'll tell you what to do. There ain't anything in this plan that is going to go right.' "[23]

Had Eisenhower heard the remarks, he would have agreed. Whenever he said that before the battle plans are everything, he added that as soon as the battle was joined, plans were worthless.

By mid-May the plans down to regimental level were complete, but not poured in cement. Changes were made right up to D-Day in response to new information or the pace of Rommel's construction activities. At Omaha, for example, Maj. Kenneth Lord, assistant G-3 (Operations) for the 1st Division, spotted an ominous development. Up to mid-April, 1st Division staff had noted happily that the hedgehogs and Belgian gate obstacles were piled up on the beaches rather than being put in place. But when a B-17 happened to jettison some bombs onto Omaha Beach before returning to England from an aborted raid, Lord examined a photograph of the bombs exploding. He saw a series of sympathetic detonations of underwater mines just at Easy Red Beach.

Major Lord appealed to the Navy to take care of the mines, pointing out that the official landing operations manual gave the Navy responsibility up to the high-tide mark. The Navy did not disagree; it just said it did not have an ability to demolish those mines. 1st Division appealed to SHAEF and got two engineering battalions assigned to it. The division HQ put them into the first wave. When Lord informed the engineers that they would lead the way, they expressed "great shock." Lord assured them that they would have plenty of support, from the DD tanks—he pointed out that the DDs had worked "beautifully" during practice exercises.[24]

Those exploding mines caused consternation at Twenty-first Army Group. Were they electric, or pressure, or magnetic, or what? To find out, they sent Capt. George Lane, a commando working with COPPS, to bring back a sample. One night in late April he swam among the obstacles. He could find only Teller mines. He brought one back. His superiors "nearly died of fright when I presented it because it was not waterproofed, it was never meant to be an underwater mine, so they realized that the corrosion must have played havoc with its mechanism and it might go off any minute."* They told Lane "there must be something else" and sent him back, not only to look for new types of mines but to take infrared photographs of the underwater obstacles.

In May, they sent him back once again, and his luck ran out. He was captured by a German E-boat and brought to Rommel's headquarters at La Roche-Guyon. An elegant staff officer came into the room and asked, "Well, how are things in England? The weather must be beautiful. End of May is always nice in England." It turned out he had an English wife. He took Lane in to see Rommel.

"You are in a very serious situation," Rommel said, "because we think you're a saboteur."

Lane turned to the interpreter. "Please tell his excellency that I know that if he thought I was a saboteur, he wouldn't have invited me here."

Rommel laughed. "So you regard this as an invitation?"

"Yes, indeed," Lane answered, "and I consider this a great honor indeed, and I'm delighted about it."

Rommel laughed again, then asked, "So how's my friend Montgomery?"

Lane said he did not know Montgomery.

"Well what do you think he's doing?"

"I only know what I read in the *Times*. It says he is preparing the invasion."

"Do you really think there's going to be an invasion? The British will invade?"

---

* So Admiral Ruge had been right when he told Rommel that the army mines were no good for the job at hand.

"That's what I read in the *Times,* so I believe it."

"Well, if they are, this is going to be the first time that the British Army will do some fighting."

"What can you mean?" Lane demanded.

"They always get other people to do the fighting for them, the Australians, the Canadians, the New Zealanders, the South Africans. They are very clever people these English."

Rommel grew serious. "Well, where do you think the invasion is coming?"

"I certainly don't know, they don't tell junior officers. But if it was up to me, I would do it across the shortest possible way."

"Yes," Rommel nodded, "that's very interesting."

They talked politics. Rommel thought the British should be fighting side by side with the Germans against the Russians. Lane thought not.

When Lane was dismissed, he was driven to Paris and turned over to the Gestapo. But the Gestapo asked no questions, used no torture—after all, he had been interrogated by Rommel himself. So Lane was very lucky, as were the Allies—Lane's missions had all been directed against the Calvados coast of France.[25]

Other adjustments had to be made. In the Cotentin, the arrival in late May of the German 91st Division in the area where the 82nd Airborne was scheduled to come down caused a change in plan. On May 28, the drop zone was moved west, astride the Merderet, with the objective of seizing the ground between the Merderet and Douve rivers.

"Daily I viewed new aerial photographs of Utah," Col. James Van Fleet, commander of the 8th Regiment, 4th Division, recalled. "The Germans were working furiously to strengthen their defenses. It seemed a terrible assault against steel and cannon for us to make. I kept asking the Navy to land us further south, to get away from these defenses. But the Navy commander said the water was too shallow, and our boats would ground."

Van Fleet did win one fight with the Navy. The operations manual said the skippers of the LCTs would decide when to launch the DD tanks. Van Fleet had little faith in the DDs. He wanted the Navy to take them in as close as possible before launching, because the DDs moved so slowly in water and were terribly vulnerable to artillery. The Navy insisted that the skipper would decide when to launch. Van Fleet recalled, "I argued back so strongly that the

Navy backed down; the tank commander would give the launch command."[26]

Multiply Lord's and Van Fleet's experiences by hundreds to get some idea of the scope of the ever-changing planning operation. With such dedication, and with such an awesome firepower, how could the invasion not work?

Montgomery had no doubts. On May 15 he held the final great dress rehearsal for Overlord at his St. Paul's School headquarters. Churchill was there, and King George VI, and all the brass, admirals and generals from the United States, the United Kingdom, and Canada. Montgomery presided in a large lecture room; the audience looked down from a crescent-shaped auditorium; on the floor Montgomery had placed a huge colored map of lower Normandy. Churchill arrived smoking a cigar; when the king arrived Churchill "bowed in his usual jerky fashion retaining the cigar in one hand."

"As we took [our] seats," Adm. Morton Deyo of the U.S. Navy, in command of the bombardment group for Utah, later wrote, "the room was hushed and the tension palpable. It seemed to most of us that the proper meshing of so many gears would need nothing less than divine guidance. A failure at one point could throw the momentum out of balance and result in chaos. All in that room were aware of the gravity of the elements to be dealt with."

Eisenhower spoke first. He was brief. "I would emphasize but one thing," he said. "I consider it to be the duty of anyone who sees a flaw in the plan not to hesitate to say so." According to Deyo, "His smile was worth twenty divisions. Before the warmth of his quiet confidence the mists of doubt dissolved."[27]

Montgomery took over. He was wearing a well-cut battle dress with knifelike trouser creases. He looked trim and spoke in a tone of quiet emphasis. According to the note taker, Churchill occasionally interrupted him to ask questions designed to show off his military knowledge. "At one point the PM intervened, saying a trifle wryly that at Anzio we had put ashore 160,000 men and 25,000 vehicles and had advanced only twelve miles. He thought, therefore, that to take a risk occasionally would certainly do no harm." Montgomery remained "quiet and deliberate."

Montgomery's message was "We have a sufficiency of troops; we have all the necessary tackle; we have an excellent plan.

This is a perfectly normal operation which is certain of success. If anyone has any doubts in his mind, let him stay behind."

He was more realistic about Rommel's plans than he had been in April, when he had expected the enemy to hold back his tanks for the first couple of days. Now he said, "Rommel is an energetic and determined commander; he has made a world of difference since he took over. He is best at the spoiling attack; his forte is disruption; he is too impulsive for the set-piece battle. He will do his level best to 'Dunkirk' us . . . by using his own tanks well forward."

Montgomery said, "We have the initiative. We must rely on:

"(a) the violence of our assault.

"(b) our great weight of supporting fire from the sea and the air.

"(c) simplicity.

"(d) robust mentality."

He went on to say some words that later would come back to haunt him: "We must blast our way ashore and get a good lodgement before the enemy can bring sufficient reserves up to turn us out. Armoured columns must penetrate deep inland, and quickly on D-Day; this will upset the plans and tend to hold him off while we build up strength. We must gain space rapidly, and peg out claims well inland."[28]

The meeting began at 0900 hours and concluded at 1415, "thus ending," according to the minutes, "the greatest assembly of military leadership the world has ever known." Churchill was all pumped up. At the beginning of 1944 he had expressed qualms about Overlord, saying to Eisenhower on one occasion, "When I think of the beaches of Normandy choked with the flower of American and British youth, and when, in my mind's eye, I see the tides running red with their blood, I have my doubts . . . I have my doubts." Early in May Eisenhower had lunched alone with the prime minister. When they were parting, Churchill had grown emotional. With tears in his eyes he had said, "I am in this thing with you to the end, and if it fails we will go down together." But after the St. Paul's briefing Churchill grabbed Eisenhower by the arm and said, "I am hardening toward this enterprise." That was a bit late to be getting on the team, but it was good that he had finally joined up. As for Eisenhower, his confidence was high.[29]

7

TRAINING

No MATTER how brilliant the plan, no matter how effective the deception, no matter how intense the preinvasion sea and air bombardment, Overlord would fail if the assault squads did not advance. To make sure that they did, the Allies put a tremendous effort into training.

The Americans thought that they had emphasized training in 1942—indeed, that they were putting their divisions through as tough a training regimen as any in the world. In February 1943, at Kasserine Pass, they discovered that their training was woefully inadequate to the rigors of modern warfare. Men had run, commanders had panicked. Men who thought they were in top physical condition found out they weren't. "Our people from the very highest to the very lowest have learned that this is not a child's game and are ready and eager to get down to the fundamental[s]," Eisenhower wrote Marshall. "From now on I am going to make it a fixed rule that no unit from the time it reaches this theater until this war is won will ever stop training."[1] As supreme commander, he enforced that rule.

The point of the training was to get ashore. Everything was geared to the D-Day assault. The AEF later paid a price for this obsession. Nothing was done to train for hedgerow fighting; techniques suitable to offensive action in Normandy had to be learned on the spot. But of course there would be no hedgerow fighting if the AEF did not get ashore.

For some divisions the assault training had begun in the States. The airborne divisions had been formed in 1941-42 for the purpose of landing behind the Atlantic Wall, and their training reflected that goal. After jump school, the airborne troops had carried out jump, assembly, and attack maneuvers throughout the middle South.

Col. James Van Fleet took command of the 8th Infantry Regiment of the 4th Division on July 21, 1941. The 8th had been activated a year earlier for the express purpose of developing tactics to contain a blitzkrieg offensive, but when Van Fleet took over the situation had changed and he trained the 8th "as an assault unit, the American force that would make the first landings." He explained, "The initial thrust of our training was how to storm and seize enemy strong points such as pillboxes. By the time Allied forces reached Europe, the enemy would have had years to construct concrete emplacements, to shield artillery and heavy weapons. We spent long months practicing how to assault these positions, beginning with squads, and working up through the company and battalion level."

The 8th had a good mix of people, thoroughly American. As Van Fleet noted, it had historically been a Southern regiment, made up of country boys from Florida, Alabama, and Georgia. He called them his "squirrel shooters." They could find their way through the woods at night without being afraid and knew how to shoot a rifle. When the draftees began coming in, many of them were from New York and other Eastern cities. They knew nothing about weapons or woods, but they had skills the Southern boys lacked, such as motors and communications. "The marriage of North and South was a happy one," Van Fleet commented.

In training the 8th for an assault, Van Fleet emphasized coordination and firepower. If two men were attacking a pillbox, one would put continuous fire on the embrasure while the other crept up on it from the other side. When the advancing man drew fire, he went to the ground and began firing back while his partner crept closer to the objective. Eventually one crept close enough to toss a grenade into the pillbox. "This sort of attack requires bravery, confidence in your partner, and patience," Van Fleet observed. "We enacted this scenario countless hundreds of times from 1941 through 1943, often with live ammunition."[2]

Two years was a long time to be training. Men got impatient. One of Van Fleet's most aggressive lieutenants, George L. Mabry, wanted to get into the real war. He applied for a transfer to the Army Air Force. Van Fleet called him in for a chat. Knowing his commander would be upset, Mabry was shaking "like a leaf" when he reported.

"You are applying for the Air Force?" Van Fleet asked.

"Yes, sir."

"You ever been up in an airplane?"

"No, sir."

"Well, you better get over and withdraw that application. You might get sick in an airplane."

"Yes, sir."

Mabry stayed with Van Fleet. He became one of the best officers in the 4th Division.*

The 29th Division sailed for England in September 1942 aboard the *Queen Mary*, converted from luxury liner to troop transport. The *Queen Mary* sailed alone, depending on her speed to avoid submarines. At 500 miles out from the Continent, and thus within range of the Luftwaffe, an escort of British warships appeared. A cruiser, HMS *Curacao*, cut across the bow of the 83,000-ton *Queen Mary*. The *Queen* knifed into the 4,290-ton cruiser and cut her in half, killing 332 members of her crew. It was not an auspicious beginning to the great Allied invasion.

The division took over Tidworth Barracks, near Salisbury. These were the best barracks in England but woefully short of what GIs had become accustomed to in the training camps in the States. For men who had trained in the American South, the English weather was miserable. Pvt. John R. Slaughter of Company D, 116th Regiment, recalled, "Morale was not good during those first few months in the British Isles. Homesickness, dreary weather, long weeks of training without pause caused many of us to grumble."[3]

It didn't help that the 29th necessarily became an experimental outfit. It was the only large American combat unit in the United Kingdom. It had no specific mission for the first year it was there. Instead, it carried out training exercises that were, in effect,

---

* Mabry stayed in the infantry. He was awarded the Medal of Honor and retired a major general.

experiments in the development of doctrine, procedures, and techniques in amphibious assaults. In short, the men saw themselves as guinea pigs.

Making things worse, the food was awful. Britain had been at war for more than two years; there were no fresh eggs, little fresh meat, too many brussels sprouts. Lt. Robert Walker of Headquarters Company, 116th Regiment, remembered that on field problems "we were issued sack lunches. These consisted of two sandwiches made of dry brown bread; one had a glob of jelly in the middle, the other a slice of pork luncheon meat. We called them Spam and jam lunches."[4] Any American tourist who has ever purchased one of those sandwiches at a London shop knows just how bad they are.

Weekend passes to Salisbury or, even better, to London were hard to come by and highly prized. As the Yanks were paid more than double what the Tommies received, and had much better-looking uniforms, they attracted the girls. This caused considerable resentment. There was also friction between black GIs, mainly in the Services of Supply (SOS), and the white soldiers. When they mixed in a pub there was almost sure to be a fight, too often culminating in a shooting. The Army took to segregating the pubs—one night for blacks, another for whites. Overall, however, considering that by D-Day there were some 2 million Yanks on an island only slightly larger than the state of Colorado, the American "occupation" of Britain was carried out with remarkable success. It helped beyond measure that everyone had the same ultimate objective.

It helped, too, that the Americans tightened their standard of discipline. Col. Charles Canham commanded the 116th Regiment. Canham was a West Pointer, class of 1926. Pvt. Felix Branham characterized him as "a fiery old guy who spit fire and brimstone." The colonel "was so tough that we used to call ourselves 'Colonel Canham's Concentration Camp.' " If a man was a few minutes late from a pass, he was fined $30 and confined to camp for thirty days. One day Branham overheard a conversation between Canham and the CO of the 29th Division, Maj. Gen. Charles Gerhardt. Gerhardt told Canham, "You're too hard on the men."

"Goddamn it, Charles," Canham shot back, "this is my regiment and I am the one commanding it."

"You know," Gerhardt replied, "the men don't mind that

$30 but they hate that thirty days." Canham eased up, but only a bit. "I tell you, we trained," Branham declared. "We started out on various types of landing craft. We got on LSTs, LCVPs, we got on LCIs, on LCMs, we landed from British ships, we landed from American ships. You name it, our training was there. We threw various types of hand grenades. We learned to use enemy weapons."[5]

Gerhardt was a West Pointer, an old cavalryman and polo player, flamboyant in his dress, gung ho in his attitude. He did everything by the book and insisted that his men dress just right, always appear clean-shaven, even keep their jeeps spotless. He also wanted enthusiasm; one way he got it was to have the men chant their battle cry as they marched over the dunes, "Twenty-nine, let's go!" When an old-timer from the 1st Division, a combat veteran of North Africa and Sicily, heard that he yelled back, "Go ahead, twenty-nine, we'll be right behind you!"[6]

The 29th marched all over southwestern England. The men spent nights in the field, sleeping in foxholes. They learned the basic lesson infantrymen must learn, to love the ground, how to use it to their advantage, how it dictates a plan of battle, above all how to live in it for days at a time without impairment of physical efficiency. They were taught to see folds in the terrain that no civilian would notice. They attacked towns, hills, woods. They dug countless foxholes. They had fire problems, attacking with artillery, mortars, machine guns, crashing into their objectives. They concentrated single-mindedly on offensive tactics.

A member of the 29th Division recalled "loading and unloading landing craft, exiting, peeling off, quickly moving forward, crawling under barbed wire with live machine-gun fire just inches overhead and live explosions, strategically placed, detonated all around. We were schooled in the use of explosives: satchel charges and bangalore torpedoes were excellent for blowing holes in barbed wire and neutralizing fortified bunkers. Bayonets were used to probe for hidden mines. Poison-gas drills, first aid, airplane and tank identification, use and detection of booby traps and more gave us the confidence that we were ready. I believe our division was as competent to fight as any green outfit in history."[7]

They spent countless hours on the firing range. Sgt. Weldon Kratzer, Company C, 116th, remembered the day Eisenhower, accompanied by Montgomery and other big shots, came by to

watch. After a bit, Eisenhower called to Kratzer. "Sergeant, I was observing your firing," he said, "and I must compliment you." He went on, "I used to be a good shot, do you mind if I use your rifle?"
"It would be an honor, sir."

Eisenhower took the prone position, adjusted the sling, aimed, tried to pull the trigger, and nothing happened.

"Sir, your rifle is on safety," Kratzer said.

"I don't blame you for taking precautions," Eisenhower replied, blushing and taking off the safety. He blasted away at a target 600 meters off. "He wasn't bad," Kratzer reported. "Most of his shots were four or five o'clock." When Eisenhower had a total miss and Maggie's drawers went up, he called out "And the same to you, old girl."

After Eisenhower had fired a full clip, Kratzer offered to reload for him. Eisenhower said no, thanks, "You fellows need the practice more than I do." As he was leaving, Eisenhower told Kratzer, "Sergeant, I'm impressed with your marksmanship, you sure know your Kentucky windage."

"General Eisenhower," Kratzer replied, "I'm from Virginia. I use Virginia windage."

"I'll be damned," said the general. "I think we'd all be better off if we used Virginia windage."[8]

Eisenhower spent a great deal of his time in the field, inspecting, watching training exercises. He wanted to see as many men as possible and let them see him. He managed to talk to hundreds personally. In the four months from February 1 to June 1, he visited twenty-six divisions, twenty-four airfields, five ships of war, and countless depots, shops, hospitals, and other installations.

To the graduating class at Sandhurst, in the spring of 1944, Eisenhower delivered an impromptu address in which he spoke of the great issues involved. He made each graduate aware that his own chances for a happy, decent life were directly tied up in the success of Overlord. He reminded them of the great traditions of Sandhurst. He told the newly commissioned officers that they must be like fathers to their men, even when the men were twice their age, that they must keep the men out of trouble and stand up for them when they committed a transgression. Their companies must be like a big family and they must be the head of the family, ensuring that the unit was cohesive, tough, well trained, well equipped, ready to go. The response of the Sandhurst graduates, according to Thor Smith, a public-relations officer at SHAEF, was "electric. They just loved him."[9]

Beyond weapons training, physical conditioning, and getting familiar with the various landing craft, the men went through assault exercises. Everything possible was done to make them realistic, from climbing down the rope nets into the Higgins boats in a high sea to the buildings and terrain on the shore. Sgt. Tom Plumb of the Royal Winnipeg Rifles, 3rd Canadian Division, discovered when he hit the shore on D-Day near Bernières-sur-Mer (Juno Beach) that "it was identical to the beach we had been training on in Inverness, Scotland, right down to the exact locations of pillboxes."[10]

Lt. Col. Paul Thompson commanded the U.S. Assault Training Center at Woolacombe. He established training areas at suitable beaches, of which the most extensive was Slapton Sands in Devonshire on the south coast. Nearly 3,000 residents were moved out of their homes in the villages and farms in the area. At Slapton Sands the geography was a nigh replica of the Cotentin coastline. The beach of coarse gravel led inland to shallow lagoons.

Thompson, a 1929 graduate of West Point, was an outstanding engineer, an imaginative creator of realistic training exercises, and dedicated to his job, which was to develop doctrines and techniques to assault a heavily defended shore. His initial task was to train demonstration troops and put them through practice exercises for various high-ranking observers. Once his superiors approved his ideas, he became responsible for training all assault troops for the invasion.[11]

In August 1943, Thompson went to work. At Slapton Sands and eight other locations he oversaw the erection of a hedgehog area for battalion training, an assault range for company training, a beach range for firing artillery and mortars against a hostile shore from the landing craft, an artillery range, a wire-cutting range for training in the use of bangalore torpedoes and other devices for breaching wire, an infantry demolition range for training in using satchel charges against pillboxes and the breaching of underwater and land obstacles, an obstacle-course area, and a multiple-purpose range for practice in the use of flamethrowers, rockets, and grenades. Thompson also set up a training facility for engineers.

After many experiments, Thompson and his people concluded that the first waves, which would go ashore in Higgins boats with a capacity of thirty men to a boat, should be broken down into rifle-assault platoons consisting of a five-man rifle team, a four-man bangalore and wire-cutting team, a four-man rocket-launcher team, a two-man flamethrower team, a four-man BAR team, a four-man 60mm mortar team, a five-man demolition team, and two officers.

Thompson broke the training down into four phases. First, individual training on the obstacle course. Second, team training for the wire cutters and demolition men. Third, company exercises. Fourth, battalion exercises. Umpires were present to judge, criticize, and suggest. The training was hard and realistic. Live ammunition was often used and accidents happened. In mid-December a short artillery round killed four men and injured six; a couple of days later three landing craft capsized and fourteen men drowned.

The 29th Division was the first to go through the school. General Gerhardt praised the "superb training facilities," which he said made his division "capable of a successful landing on the shore of Fortress Europe."[12]

In the winter and spring of 1944, thousands of troops went through exercises every week. As they did so, observers noted what worked and what didn't and made adjustments in the plans as required. For example, the exercises indicated that the use of smoke for cover tended to confuse the assault troops as badly as it did the defenders, that smoke could not be sufficiently controlled, and that it interfered with observed fire from the warships. So smoke was out.

Experiment further convinced the planners that the best use of tanks was not as an armored force but as close-support artillery. Giving up armor's characteristics of shock and mobility, the planners decided that instead of using tanks to lead the drive through the fortifications they would instead fire from hull down in the water, giving support from behind rather than breaking through at the front.

None of these lessons, somewhat surprisingly, came from previous American experience in the Pacific. There was some correspondence between the 1st Engineer Special Brigade in Europe and the 2nd Brigade in the Pacific, and a few officers were brought from the Pacific to the United Kingdom, but for the most part there was no interchange. After North Africa, Sicily, and Italy, the commanders in Europe did not feel a need to ask their counterparts in the Pacific about their experiences.

In April and early May, assault exercises that amounted to dress rehearsals took place all over England. They included marshaling, embarkation and sailing, approach and assault, setting up the beach organization. The rehearsals brought together the units that would go to France as a team: assault forces O (for Omaha), G (Gold), U (Utah), J (Juno), and S (Sword). The Army got to know the Navy, and vice versa.

The air forces were also involved: as Leigh-Mallory's headquarters put it, "It is important that the pilots of all aircraft should see a large concentration of assault forces at sea. . . . Conversely, it is of importance that personnel in assault forces should obtain an idea of the degree of air cover and support which they might expect."[13]

Thirty-two-year-old Lt. Dean Rockwell was in charge of the training for the LCT crews. He had been a professional wrestler and high-school coach in Detroit before the war. Although he had never been on salt water, he joined the Navy after hearing a recruiting pitch from former heavyweight champion Gene Tunney. The Navy made him an instructor in physical education, but Rockwell did not approve of the Navy's PE program and said so. He voiced his criticisms so often and so loudly that he got a reputation as a "Bolshie." As a punishment he was posted to landing craft, which his senior officers regarded as a suicide squad.

Regular Navy officers thought that landing craft were ugly and unseamanlike; Rockwell loved them, and he became exceptionally clever at handling them and understanding their often strange behavior. He began with LCVPs and LCMs, got promoted to petty officer, and went to England. He was so good at his job that he got a spot promotion to lieutenant (jg), then to full lieutenant, and in March 1944 was put in command of the training program for LCTs.

Lt. Eugene Bernstein, USNR, commanding an LCT(R), remembered the training exercises as "very realistic. We would rendezvous all ships in specific convoys, load troops, tanks, ammo, and supplies of all sorts and head out. At around midnight we would open a set of orders to find that we were to go to Slapton Sands, or wherever, and go through the entire landing procedure. We would turn 180 degrees, make for Slapton Sands, fire our rockets on designated targets [if the LCT(R) was moving ahead at flank speed of ten knots when all 1,060 rockets were fired, the recoil was such that the craft was thrust backward at three knots], unload attack transports into small boats, and assault the beach. These were full scale operations with aircraft cover, major-ship bombardment, the works. Then we would go home. Soon we would be at it again. We and the British did this practice operation eleven times. So passed the spring of 1944." When it came time for the real thing, Bernstein added, "We weighed anchor and calmly got under way as though it were another practice exercise."[14]

Maj. R. Younger, who commanded an assault squadron of British tanks in the Royal Engineers, recalled that "most of the early exercises were pretty catastrophic. All sorts of things went wrong, but we were learning. . . . Vehicles broke down. Coming off a landing craft in a tank, when the sea is rough, isn't particularly easy, and sometimes we'd get a vehicle broken down on the ramp of the LCT and it had to be towed off and so on.

"We certainly needed training. Wireless, for example. You can't talk to any of your subordinate tanks without wireless and we'd never used that, and we were very verbose initially in our use of the wireless, but as we got more confident in it we got far quicker—people recognize your voice and you cut everything down, so that in the end conversations are just click click click and you know exactly what the men meant. The trouble with being verbose on the air is that somebody else has got something much more important to say and he can't get on the air because it is blocked by those long-winded statements."[15]

The joint exercises revealed flaws. In the rehearsal for the VII Corps at Utah, Operation Tiger, held on the night of April 27–28 at Slapton Sands, there were some missed schedules resulting in traffic jams and some naval craft arriving late at embarkation points. Much worse, German E-boats slipped through the British destroyer screen and sank two LSTs and damaged six others. Over 749 men were killed and 300 wounded in the explosions or drowned afterward.

Lessons were learned that saved lives on D-Day. There had been no rescue craft in the Tiger formation. Naval commanders realized that they would be needed. The men had not been taught how to use their life preservers. After Tiger, they were. It turned out that the British were operating on different radio wavelengths than the Americans, which contributed to the disaster. That was fixed.

What could not be so easily fixed was the weather. Visibility had been poor on April 27–28 and the American fighter airplanes had not shown up.

Operation Tiger was not the only training maneuver to produce casualties. The use of live ammunition led to many wounds and some deaths, as did the night jumps for the paratroopers. Maj. David Thomas was regimental surgeon of the 508th Parachute Infantry. On one training jump, a trooper's chute failed to open. "It took us three days to find him," Thomas recalled, "and when we did I took his gloves and laundered them carefully three or four times to get the sweet odor of death out of them. I'm not superstitious but I figured that those gloves couldn't be unlucky twice." He wore them on D-Day.[16]

No one had yet told the GIs and Tommies where or when they were going to attack, but the exercises made it clear to the men in such divisions as the 29th and 4th that they would be leading the way, wherever it was. Confidence was high, but there was no doubt that casualties would be taken. Rifle companies were being reinforced to the point that they were overstrength, especially in junior officers and noncoms.

Pvt. Harry Parley joined Company E, 116th, in early 1944. He never forgot the moment of his arrival: "The CO walked in, said his name was Capt. Lawrence Madill, that our company was to be first wave in the invasion, that 30-percent casualties were expected, and that we were them!" Parley commented, "It saddened me to think of what would happen to some of my fellow GIs."[17]

The U.S. 1st, 4th, and 29th Infantry divisions, the British 50th and 3rd Infantry divisions, and the Canadian 3rd Infantry Division would make the assault, supported on the flanks by the British 6th Airborne and the U.S. 82nd and 101st. The 1st and 82nd had been in combat in the Mediterranean; for the others, D-Day would be the baptism of fire (as also for the many replacements who joined the 1st Division in England). As Geoffrey Perret writes, "Overlord was the supreme task for which the wartime Army had been created: If the division-making machine really worked, it should be possible to take untried divisions such as the 4th, the 29th and 101st Airborne, put them into a battle against experienced German troops and see them emerge victorious."[18]

The infantry divisions were composed, overwhelmingly, of conscripts. The airborne divisions were all volunteer (except for the gliderborne units) and thus by definition elite. The paratroopers' motivation, in the words of Pvt. Robert Rader of the 506th Regiment, 101st Airborne, was "a desire to be better than the other guy."[19] The $50 a month extra jump pay was also an attraction. They thought of themselves as special, and they were right, but they discovered in the campaign in northwest Europe in 1944–45 that the gliderborne troops and outfits like the 1st, 4th, and 29th were almost as good as they were—a tribute to the training of the conscripts.

Still, it was true that the airborne troops underwent even tougher training than the infantry. Back in Georgia in late 1942, for example, the 506th had made a three-day forced march, carrying full equipment, of 136 miles. When the regiment got to England in September 1943, training intensified. There were numerous three-day field exercises, beginning with a jump. The regimental scrapbook described the march back to barracks: "Glancing down the line you were of the opinion that everyone had that combat expression, an unshaven face showing extreme weariness and disgust, caked mud from head to foot, and every jump suit looking as tho it had come out second best in the ordeal of the fences. You finally dragged your weary body those last few torturous kilometers, and throwing yourself across the bunk you said—'Combat can't be that rough!' "[20]

The objective of all the training, whether infantry or armored or engineers or airborne, was to make the men believe that combat could not possibly be worse than what they were undergoing, so that they would look forward to their release from training and their commitment to battle.

"But of course," Sgt. D. Zane Schlemmer of the 508th Parachute Infantry Regiment commented, "you never get enough training, I've found. Once you get into combat, you've never had enough training for combat. It is a total impossibility."[21]

Some units had highly specialized training. Major Howard of D Company of the Ox and Bucks asked the topographical people to search the map of Britain and find him some place where a river and a canal ran closely together and were crossed by bridges on the same road, as on the Orne waterways. They found such a spot outside Exeter. Howard moved his company down there and for six days, by day and by night, attacked those Exeter bridges, practicing every conceivable condition—if only one of his six gliders, each carrying a platoon, made it to the objective, that platoon knew what to do to complete the mission alone.

To make as certain as possible that the gliders did land near the bridges, the pilots (all sergeants, all members of the Glider Pilot Regiment; there were sixteen of them, two for each of the six gliders scheduled to go in on D-Day plus four reserves) went through Operation Deadstick. Col. George Chatterton, commander of the GPR, made the exercise hellishly difficult. He had the pilots land beside a small L-shaped wood, three gliders going up the L and three on the blind side. In daylight, on a straight-in run, it was relatively easy. But then Chatterton started having them release from their tug planes at 7,000 feet and fly by times and courses, using a stopwatch, making two or three full turns before coming over the wood. That was not too bad, either, because, as Jim Wallwork, pilot of no. 1 glider, explained, "In broad daylight you can always cheat a little."

Next Chatterton put colored glasses in their flying goggles to turn day into night, and warned his pilots, "It is silly of you to cheat on this because you've got to do it right when the time comes." Wallwork would nevertheless whip the goggles off if he thought he was overshooting, "but we began to play it fairly square." By early May they were flying by moonlight, casting off at 6,000 feet, eight miles from the wood. They flew regardless of weather. They twisted and turned around the sky, all by stopwatch. They did forty-three training flights in Deadstick altogether, more than half of them at night. They got ready.[22]

The U.S. 2nd and 5th Ranger battalions were composed of volunteers. Others referred to them as "suicide squads," but Lt. James Eikner of the 2nd Rangers disagreed: "We were simply spirited young people who took the view that if you are going to be a combat soldier, you may as well be one of the very best; also we were anxious to get on with the war so as to bring things to a close and get home to our loved ones as soon as possible."[23]

Naturally, such fine troops had a special mission, to capture the battery at Pointe-du-Hoc. As this would require scaling the cliff, the Rangers got into superb physical condition. In March, they went to the Highlands of Scotland, where Lord Lovat's No. 4 Commando put them through grueling speed marches (averaging twenty-five miles a day, culminating in a thirty-seven-mile march) across what was reputedly the toughest obstacle course in the world. They climbed mountains, scaled cliffs, practiced unarmed combat. They learned stealth, how to conduct quick-hitting strikes. In ten days of such training, one private's weight dropped from 205 pounds to 170 pounds.[24]

Next they practiced amphibious landing operations on the Scottish coast, hitting beaches specially prepared with barbed wire, beach obstacles, and every type of antiassault landing device that Rommel had waiting for them. In April, the rangers went to the Assault Training Center. In early May, it was off to Swanage for special training in cliff scaling with ropes, using grappling hooks trailing ropes propelled to the top of the cliff by rockets, and with extension ladders donated by the London Fire Department and carried in DUKWs.[25]

Lt. Walter Sidlowski, an engineer, marveled at the rangers. "My guys had always felt we were in good shape physically," he remembered, "but watching the rangers using most of their time double-timing, with and without arms and equipment, push-ups and various other physical exercise whenever they were not doing something else, was cause for wonder."[26]

"I can assure you," Lieutenant Eikner of the 2nd Ranger Battalion commented, "that when we went into battle after all this training there was no shaking of the knees or weeping or praying; we knew what we were getting into; we knew everyone of us had volunteered for extra hazardous duty; we went into battle confident; of course we were tense when under fire, but we were intent on getting the job done. We were actually looking forward to accomplishing our mission."[27]

The combat engineers had the most complex job. They were organized into three brigades of three battalions each; the 6th Engineer Special Brigade was attached to the 116th Regiment on the right flank at Omaha; the 5th ESB was scheduled to go in with the 16th Regiment on the left at Omaha; the 1st ESB joined the 4th Division at Utah.

Almost one-quarter of the American troops going in on the morning of D-Day would be engineers. Their tasks, more or less in this order, were to: demolish beach obstacles, blow up mines on the beach, erect signs to guide incoming landing craft through cleared channels, set up panels to bring in the troops and equipment (the color of the panel told the ships offshore which supplies to send in), clear access roads from the beach, blow gaps in the antitank wall, establish supply dumps, and act as beachmasters (traffic cops).

There were all sorts of units attached to the ESBs. Naval beach battalions had semaphores and heliographs in addition to radios in order to communicate between the beach and the fleet. A chemical battalion was ready to decontaminate anything hit by poison gas and to deal with radioactive materials (there was a fear that the Germans were far enough along in their atomic research to use such poisons). There were medical battalions, ordnance battalions, grave-registration companies, MPs to handle prisoners, DUKW battalions, signal companies to lay telephone wire—sixteen specialized units in all, organized into special companies and battalions. As Lieutenant Colonel Thompson, who took command of the 6th ESB after the work of the Assault Training Center was completed, remarked, "Was there ever a unit so meticulously put together, so precisely engineered for a specific mission as this?"[28]

The ESBs went through the Assault Training Center at Slapton Sands. Sgt. Barnett Hoffner of the 6th ESB participated in Operation Tiger, the April 27-28 exercise in which the LSTs were lost. "I was on the beach at the time with my squad. We were practicing taking up mines when we saw the bodies come floating in. I had never seen dead men before. We started down to the water's edge to get the bodies when I heard a voice yell, 'Sergeant! Get your men out of there!' I looked up and saw two stars on the shoulders and recognized that it was Major General Heubner. I got my squad out of there fast. You don't question anything a general says."[29]

The point was that everyone had a job. General Heubner wanted Sergeant Hoffner to concentrate on his. There were grave-registration crews to take care of the dead. On D-Day, the basic principle was that no one should stop to help the wounded, much less bury the dead—leave those tasks to the medics and grave-registration crews, and get on with your task.

There were many other special units, including underwater demolition teams, midget-submarine crews to guide the incoming landing craft, tiny one-man airplanes with folded wings that could be brought in on Rhino ferries (42-by-176-foot flat-bottomed pontoon barges with a capacity of forty vehicles, towed across the Channel by LSTs, powered for the run into the beach by large outboard motors), put into operation on the beach and used for naval gunfire spotting. The 743rd Tank Battalion, like the other DD tankers, spent months learning how to maneuver their tanks in the Channel. The 320th Barrage Balloon Battalion (Colored) practiced setting up their balloons on the beach. The Cherokee code talkers (forty in all, twenty for Utah, twenty for Omaha) worked on their radios—they could speak in their own language, confident the Germans would never be able to translate.

• •

All the commando units were special, but some a bit more so than others. The 1st and 8th troops of No. 10 Commandos were French; Pvt. Robert Piauge was a member of 1st Troop. Piauge was born in Ouistreham, at the mouth of the Orne River, in 1920, his father already dead as a result of a World War I wound. He joined the French army in 1939, over his mother's tearful protests, and managed to get to England in June 1940, where he rallied to De Gaulle's call to arms. He joined the French commandos, which were part of the French navy but equipped, trained, and attached to the British commandos. That the French were eager to get back was obvious, Piauge especially so after he learned he would be landing at Ouistreham, where his mother still lived.[30]

The No. 10 Commandos came from all over Europe. The various troops in No. 10 were Polish, Dutch, Norwegian, and Belgian. Like the French commandos, they were eager to get going. Like all commandos, U.S. rangers, airborne troops, and the other specialists, they trained to the absolute limit.

The men in 3 Troop, No. 10 Commando, needed no motivating. They were young European Jews who had somehow managed to make it to England. From the moment they arrived, whether from Germany or Austria or Czechoslovakia or Hungary, they pleaded for a chance to fight. Adm. Lord Louis Mountbatten, commander of Combined Operations, sent them to the commandos, where they were organized into 3 Troop, with the thought that they would go through regular commando training, then be made into specialists in patrolling and intelligence matters. The key was their language ability. If challenged on a patrol, they could answer in good German; they could also conduct instant interrogation of prisoners. They were trained in all matters pertaining to the Wehrmacht— organization, documents, weapons, and methodology.

Cpl. Peter Masters was a member of 3 Troop. Born in Vienna in 1922, he was there when the Germans marched into Austria on March 12, 1938, "so I lived under the Nazis for six months, which was quite sufficient to turn me from a kid that had been brought up as a pacifist to a volunteer eager to get into the action." In August 1938 he managed to get to London; soon he joined the commandos.

"Can you shoot?" he was asked by the recruiting officer. "Can you handle a boat? What do you know about radio?" Masters said he had once shot a BB gun, that he had rowed a boat but never sailed, and that he knew nothing about radios. He was so enthusiastic that the commandos took him anyway.

Told to take a new name so as to avoid German retribution if captured, but only given a couple of minutes to think about it, he chose "Masters." He got a dog tag with "Peter Masters" on it, plus "Church of England." He and all the others in 3 Troop had to invent stories to explain why they spoke English with an accent. Masters's story was that his parents traveled extensively and he had been raised by a German-speaking nanny who didn't have much English.[31]

Harry Nomburg was also a member of 3 Troop. "I was born in Germany," he related, "and at the age of fifteen was sent by my parents to England to escape Nazi persecution. I left Berlin on May 21, 1939. It happened to be a Sunday, Mother's Day. I never saw my parents again. At the age of eighteen, I joined the British army and in early 1943 volunteered for the commandos. Together with my green beret I was also given a brand-new name." He chose "Harry Drew," but went back to Nomburg after the war; Masters retained his English name.[32]

(There was a former member of the Hitler Youth among the American paratroopers. Fred Patheiger was born in December 1919 in Rastatt, Germany. As a teenager he joined the Hitler Youth. His aunt wanted to get married; a Nazi Party investigation revealed that his great-grandfather had been Jewish; he was kicked out of the Hitler Youth. His mother contacted relatives in Chicago; in April 1938 Patheiger immigrated to the United States. His parents, aunt, and other relatives died in the concentration camps. When he attempted to enlist in 1940, he was classified "Not Acceptable—Enemy Alien." He wrote J. Edgar Hoover of the FBI to protest, saying he wanted to fight Nazis, not Germans. Shortly thereafter he was classified "Acceptable" and joined up. He became a corporal in the 101st Airborne.[33])

The men of 3 Troop were broken up for D-Day into five-man groups, each assigned to a different commando brigade. Masters went with a bicycle troop. They had cheap collapsible bicycles with baskets on the fronts to carry their rucksacks. The bikes had no mudguards, no pedals, just stems, and Masters found them damnable. But he soldiered on, overjoyed to be of service. The Nazis, who lived by hate, had built up a lot of hatred in Europe in the past five years. From Piauge, Masters, Nomburg, Patheiger, and other young refugees, the Nazis were about to get some of their own back.

• •

Racism was at the heart of the Nazi philosophy. Racism was also present in the American army. In 1937 senior officers at the U.S. Army War College had done a study to assess the strengths and weaknesses of black soldiers. Their conclusion was that "as an individual the negro is docile, tractable, lighthearted, care free and good natured. If unjustly treated he is likely to become surly and stubborn, though this is usually a temporary phase. He is careless, shiftless, irresponsible and secretive. He resents censure and is best handled with praise and by ridicule. He is unmoral, untruthful and his sense of right doing is relatively inferior."

As to strengths, "the negro is cheerful, loyal and usually uncomplaining if reasonably well fed. He has a musical nature and a marked sense of rhythm. His art is primitive. He is religious. With proper direction in mass, negroes are industrious. They are emotional and can be stirred to a high state of enthusiasm."

In World War I, two black U.S. divisions had fought in France. One, serving with the French army, did well; it won many medals and a request from the French for more black troops. The other, serving with the American army, with white Southerners as officers and woefully inadequate training and equipment, did poorly. The War College officers in 1937 concentrated on the failure and ignored the success, which led them to conclude that blacks were not capable of combat service. Consequently, although three black infantry divisions were organized for World War II, only one, the 92nd Infantry, saw combat.

By March 1944, there were about 150,000 black American soldiers in the United Kingdom. Most of them were in Services of Supply, mainly working at the ports unloading ships or driving trucks. They were strictly segregated. In the mythology of the time, this did not mean they were objects of discrimination. Separate but equal was the law of the land back home, and in Britain.

General Eisenhower issued a circular letter to senior American commanders that ordered, "Discrimination against Negro troops must be sedulously avoided." But, he acknowledged, in London and other cities "where both Negro and White soldiers will come on pass and furlough, it will be a practical impossibility to arrange for segregation so far as welfare and recreation facilities are concerned." When the Red Cross could not provide separate clubs for blacks, Eisenhower insisted that the blacks be given equal access to all Red Cross clubs. But he went on to tell local commanders to use "their own best judgment in avoiding discrimination due to race, at the same time minimizing causes of friction through rotation of pass privileges." In other words, where there was only one Red Cross club in an area, or only a few pubs, the black soldiers would have passes one night, the whites on another.[35]

The Red Cross built twenty-seven separate clubs for black troops, but they were not enough. There was some mixing of races in white clubs, and even more in the pubs. Some ugly scenes resulted. Fist fights almost always broke out when black and white GIs were drinking in the same pub. There were some shootings, most by whites against blacks (Maj. Gen. Ira Eaker, commander of the Eighth Air Force, declared that white troops were responsible for 90 percent of the trouble), and a few killings—all covered up by the Army.

Eisenhower sent out another circular letter. He told his senior officers that in the interests of military efficiency "the spreading of derogatory statements concerning the character of any group of U.S. troops, either white or colored, must be considered as conduct prejudicial to good order and military discipline and offenders must be promptly punished. . . . *It is my desire that this be brought to the attention of every officer in this theater. To that end, I suggest that you personally talk this over with your next senior commander and instruct them to follow up the subject through command channels.*"

Lt. Gen. J. C. H. Lee, commanding Services of Supply and thus the man with the most at stake, ordered every one of his officers to read Eisenhower's letter to their immediate subordinates and warned that "General Eisenhower means exactly what he says."

The order had little effect. The racial incidents continued. Eisenhower ordered a survey done on soldiers' mail; officers censoring the enlisted men's letters reported that most white troops commented, with varying degrees of amazement, on the absence of segregation in Britain. They were indignant about the association of British women with black soldiers. They expressed fears about what effect the experience American blacks had in Britain would lead to back home after the war. Black soldiers, meanwhile, expressed pleasure with the English and delight at the absence of a color line. One officer, after analyzing censorship reports for several weeks, reported toward the end of May 1944, that "the predominant note is that if the invasion doesn't occur soon, trouble will."[36]

The best way to avoid trouble was to keep the troops, of whatever color, hard at work. Eisenhower ordered that "troops must train together, work together and live together in order to attain successful teamwork in [the coming] campaign."[37] As the white infantrymen practiced going ashore from their Higgins boats, the black soldiers loaded and unloaded LSTs and other vessels. The training was intense and seemed never to end.

The Germans in France hardly trained at all. Instead, they put more poles in the ground, more obstacles on the beach, working through April and May as construction battalions rather than going through field maneuvers. An exception was the 21st Panzer Division. Colonel Luck, commanding the 125th Regiment, put his tankers through regular night exercises. He emphasized assembly points, various routes to the coast or to the bridges over the Orne River and Canal, fire and movement, speed and dash. On May 30, Rommel inspected the division. He was enthusiastic about a demonstration with live ammunition of the so-called Stalin Organ, a rocket launcher with forty-eight barrels. That evening, Rommel told the officers of the 21st to be extremely vigilant. He closed with these words, "You shouldn't count on the enemy coming in fine weather and by day."

Staying vigilant was not easy. As Luck records, "For a *panzer* division, which in the campaigns so far had been accustomed to a war of movement, the inactivity was wearisome and dangerous. Vigilance was easily relaxed, especially after the enjoyment of Calvados and cider, both typical drinks of the region. There was, in addition, the uncertainty as to whether the landing would take place at all in our sector."[38]

In other words, even the elite of the Wehrmacht in Normandy had grown soft enjoying the cushy life of occupiers in the land of fat cattle and fine apples. For the ordinary Wehrmacht soldier, whether a teenager from Berlin or a forty-year-old Pole or Russian in an *Ost* battalion, life consisted of boring work during the day, enjoyment at night, waiting and praying that the invasion would come elsewhere—anything but getting ready for the fight of their lives.

The long occupation of France made for special problems. There was an increasing incidence of German soldiers divorcing their German wives in order to marry French women. Further, there was a danger that individuals and even units might surrender wholesale at the first opportunity. Obviously, this was so with the *Ost* battalions, but it also existed with German-born troops who, according to a December 1943 secret high command report, had "the illusion of a confrontation with an adversary who acts humanely." As Dr. Detlef Vogel of the *Militargeschichtliches Forschungsamt* put it, "As a result, hardly anyone was too much afraid of becoming a POW of the Allies. This was not exactly a favorable condition for endurability and steadfastness, as constantly demanded by the military commanders."

Dr. Goebbels put his propaganda machine to work to convince the German soldiers in the West that they faced a "life-and-death struggle, an all-out conflict." Shortly before the landing, General Jodl tried to bolster spirits by arguing, "We shall see who fights better and who dies more easily, the German soldier faced with the destruction of his homeland or the Americans and British, who don't even know what they are fighting for in Europe."

Rommel could not count on it. As Dr. Vogel writes, on the eve of the invasion "It remained quite doubtful whether the German troops in the West would resist in the same death-defying manner as they were frequently doing against the Red Army, for the often assumed motive of the German soldier defending his homeland certainly did not have the same significance to the soldiers in the West as to their brothers-in-arms on the Eastern Front."[39]

To counter such defeatism, the commanders lied to their troops. Peter Masters discovered in his interrogations of POWs on D-Day and after that the men had been told, "We will easily push them back into the sea. Stukas will dive bomb them; U-boats will surface behind their fleet and shell and torpedo them; bombers will sink their landing craft; panzers will rout them on the beaches."[40]

How many, if any, believed such fantasies is open to question. The truth is that the Wehrmacht was full of doubts, which were best expressed by Rommel's insistence that more concrete be poured, more poles stuck in the ground, rather than training for quick movement and lightning strikes. On the other side of the Channel, meanwhile, the men of the AEF were putting in nearly all their time getting ready.

8

MARSHALING
AND BRIEFING

STARTING IN the first week of May, the soldiers and sailors of the AEF began descending on southern England. They came by sea in a never-ending stream of transports and LSTs. The ships came out of the Firth of Clyde and Belfast, down the Irish Sea past the Isle of Man, from Liverpool and Swansea and Bristol. They got into formation, twenty ships, forty ships, 100 ships, to sail out into the Atlantic and then past Lands End, to turn left for their designated ports—Plymouth, Torquay, Weymouth, Bournemouth, Southampton, Portsmouth, Eastbourne, and others.

They came by land, by train, bus, truck, or on foot, men and equipment from Northern Ireland, Scotland, the Midlands and Wales. They formed up by the hundreds in companies and battalions, by the thousands in regiments, to march down narrow English roads, headed south. When they arrived in their marshaling areas, they formed up by divisions, corps, and armies in the hundreds of thousands—altogether almost 2 million men, nearly a half million vehicles. It took 54,000 men to provide necessary services for the force, including more than 4,500 newly trained army cooks. It was the greatest mass movement of armed forces in the history of the British and American armies. It culminated with a concentration of military men and weaponry in southernmost England such as the world had never seen, or would again.*

The 175th Regiment of the 29th Division marched to its assembly area, called a sausage, near Falmouth. (Sausages got their name from their shape; on the map, the long, narrow, fenced-in areas, usually beside a road, looked exactly like sausages.) There the regiment was sealed in. The men moved into tents; gravel paths had been constructed and orders were issued to stick to those paths so that German reconnaissance planes would not get photographs showing new paths beaten down by walking through the fields. Vehicles were parked close against hedges. Everything was camouflaged under wire netting. The sausages were surrounded by MPs; no one was allowed out. No fires were allowed even though the nights in mid-May in England were still cold, with frost on the ground in the mornings.

Lt. Eugene Bernstein took the LCT(R) he commanded through the Irish Sea to the Isle of Man, where he took on provisions ("mostly steaks, which we ate three times a day"), and proceeded to Falmouth, where he was told he was in the wrong place. After much confusion and many exchanges of messages, he was ordered to Dartmouth on the Dart River. On arrival, he was told to sail up the river and drop anchor across from Greenway House, Agatha Christie's home. It was a "beautiful stone mansion, with hothouses and flowers dominating the view and a winding, gravel river road running alongside." Mrs. Christie had turned it over to the U.S. Navy, which set up a headquarters there.[1]

The airborne troopers went into camps near the airfields of southern England. For the 506th PIR, that meant Uppottery; for the gliderborne troops of the Ox and Bucks, it was Tarrant Rushton. The engineers had their own marshaling areas; the 6th ECB was outside Portsmouth.

The sausages were packed with equipment. Sgt. John

---

* Had the invasion of Japan's home islands gone ahead as planned in the fall of 1945, that would have been a larger operation. On the tenth anniversary of D-Day, at a press conference, President Eisenhower predicted that the world would never again see such a concentration in so small an area because in the atomic age it would be too vulnerable. In Operation Desert Shield in 1990–91, the UN forces gathered to attack Iraq were less than one-quarter the size of the AEF. The numbers of men involved in various battles on the Eastern Front in World War II were higher than those in D-Day, but on the Eastern Front the numbers of aircraft were far below those in the United Kingdom, and of course there was no sea armada.

Robert Slaughter of the 116th Regiment, 29th Division, recalled: "Every field and vacant lot was piled high with matériel for an impending great battle. Tanks and other tracked vehicles; trucks, jeeps and weapons carriers; spotter Piper Cub airplanes; artillery pieces of all sizes; gasoline, water, food, jerry cans, boxes, drums, you name it and it was there, in abundance."[2]

The vehicles had to be waterproofed. Every moving part was protected by Cosmoline, a greasy substance that would keep out water and protect the metal from the corrosive action of salt water. Pipes emerged from the carburetors of the jeeps, tanks, and trucks for air intake. "The drivers and gunners who toiled under the camouflage nets were not careless," Lt. Ralph Eastridge of the 115th Regiment, 29th Division, observed. "Carelessness here would mean a stalled vehicle at the crucial minute that it drove down the landing ramp and headed for the beach. The gunners painstakingly covered the breeches of their weapons with rubber cloth and sealed the edges with rubber cement. The radio operators sealed the delicate radios with rubber bags."[3]

Condoms were issued, by the millions. Some were blown up into balloons or filled with water and tossed around, but most were put to more practical, if unintended, use. The infantrymen put them over the muzzles of their M-1 rifles; the rubbers would keep out sand and water and would not have to be removed before the weapons were fired. Hundreds of men put their watches in condoms and tied them off; unfortunately, the condoms were not large enough to hold wallets.

Men were given escape aids, in case of capture. "These were very Boy Scoutish things," Major Howard remarked. They included a metal file to be sewn into the uniform blouse, a brass pants button that had been magnetized so that when balanced on a pinhead it became a tiny compass, a silk scarf with the map of France on it, water-purifying tablets, and French francs (printed by the U.S. and U.K. governments, over De Gaulle's loud protest, about $10 worth to a man). "This sort of thing absolutely thrilled the troops to bits," Howard said. "I have never seen such enthusiasm about such simple things."[4]

Every soldier got a brand-new weapon. The rifles and machine guns had to be test-fired and zeroed in on the firing range. Slaughter remembered "unlimited amounts of ammo were given to each of us for practice firing. Bayonets and combat knives were honed to a keen edge."[5]

Every man was given a new set of clothing, impregnated with a chemical that would ward off poison gas. They hated those uniforms. Pvt. Edward Jeziorski of the 507th PIR spoke for all the men of D-Day when he declared, "They were the lousiest, the coldest, the clammiest, the stiffest, the stinkiest articles of clothing that were ever dreamed up to be worn by individuals. Surely the guy that was responsible for the idea on this screw-up received a Distinguished Service Medal from the devil himself."[6] (The men wore these uniforms through the Normandy campaign, in some cases longer; the chemical prevented the cloth from "breathing," so the men froze in them at night, sweated up a storm by day, and stank always.)

By contrast, the food was wonderful. "Steak and pork chops with all of the trimmings," Slaughter recalled, "topped with lemon meringue pie, were items on a typical menu, and it was all-you-can-eat." Fresh eggs—the first most of the men had enjoyed since arriving in England—plus ice cream, white bread, and other previously unavailable luxuries were devoured with relish, accompanied by the inevitable crack that "they're fattening us up for the kill."[7]

Theaters were set up inside wall tents, where first-run movies just over from Hollywood were run nonstop, with free popcorn and candy. Most soldiers can remember the names of those movies, if not the plots—favorites included Mr. Lucky with Cary Grant and Laraine Day, Going My Way with Barry Fitzgerald and Bing Crosby, and The Song of Bernadette.

Training was over. Until the briefings began, aside from firing weapons and sharpening knives, or watching movies, there was little to do. Cpl. Peter Masters remembered it as a "time without end." After the intense activity of the previous months, the superbly conditioned men quickly grew bored. According to Masters, "Total war begins in the concentration area, because when people are fully charged with ammunition, somebody will get their finger on the trigger by mistake. Occasionally there were casualties. One heard a burst and a shout—'Medics!' "[8] At Company A, 116th Regiment, a joker threw a clip of M-1 .30-caliber bullets into a burning barrel; the guys in the area laughed and cursed and ran away.[9]

As the days went by, tension mounted, tempers grew shorter. "It didn't take much of a difference of opinion to bring out the sporting instinct," Private Jeziorski recalled.[10] Fistfights were common. Lt. Richard Winters of the 506th got into a scrap with Lt. Raymond Schmitz and cracked two of Schmitz's vertebrae, which sent him to the hospital.[11] As always in an army camp, especially so in this one, rumors of every imaginable kind raced through the sausages.

Sports was one way to burn off some of the pent-up energy. At first footballs were handed out, but most company commanders put a stop to that when the games got too rough and some bones were broken. Softball was better; there were barrels full of gloves and balls and constant games of catch. A number of men recalled that these were the last games of catch they ever played because of wounds received or arms lost during the ensuing campaign.

The sausages included libraries, composed of paperback books. (The paperback revolution in publishing had begun in 1939 when Pocket Books brought out ten titles at $.25 each; Avon Books came along in 1941, quickly followed by Popular Library and Dell. There were special, reduced-size, free Armed Services Editions; 22 million copies were printed for American servicemen.) One of the most popular was *A Tree Grows in Brooklyn* but, somewhat surprisingly, the top was *The Pocket Book of Verse*. (For morale purposes, it contained none of the bitter poems from the English veterans of World War I.[12])

Gambling was the favorite boredom killer. There were virtually nonstop poker and crap games. Large amounts of money changed hands. Pvt. Arthur "Dutch" Schultz of the 505th PIR won $2,500 in a crap game. "I know because I stopped and took the time to count it," he remembered. "I had broken everyone in the game except for a staff sergeant whom I disliked intensely and who had $50 left. I was bound and determined to take all of his money. My luck changed and I lost my $2,500."[13]

There was no liquor available. A few men managed to sneak out of their sausages and go to local pubs to quench their thirst, but quick arrests by MPs brought that to an end. Maj. David Thomas, the 508th PIR's surgeon, recalled that the medics were each given a canteen of alcohol to use for sterilization purposes when they got to Normandy. He dryly remarked, "I doubt that a drop of it ever got out of England."[14]

Company commanders marched their men on the roads. This gave them some exercise and helped relieve the boredom or ease the tension; it also gave them some sense of the scope of the enterprise and a sense of confidence that a fighting force of such immensity could not be denied. Marching through the countryside and small villages, they saw unbelievable amounts of equipment, uncountable numbers of aircraft. And they saw the might of the free world gathered to destroy the Nazis; men in the uniforms of New Zealand, Norway, Poland, France, Australia, Canada, Britain, Holland, Belgium, and the United States. As Sergeant Slaughter recalled, "Soldiers from every Allied nation from all around the world seemed to be everywhere."[15]

Some of the resentment felt by the Tommies toward the Yanks came out. Corporal Masters remembered marching with 3 Troop past an American unit, also out marching. A couple of Yanks had stopped to chat with a mother and her three-year-old daughter (all communication with civilians was strictly forbidden but done anyway). Almost surely the little girl was asking the question all children in Britain had long since learned to ask of the GIs, "Got any gum, chum?"

"But as we marched past," Masters said, "a disgusted voice at the back of our lot growled at the Americans, 'At least you could let them grow up!' "[16]

Among the millions of men gathered in southern England to participate in the invasion of France, only a handful knew the secrets of Overlord—where the assault would go ashore, and when. Those few had a supersecurity designation, above Top Secret, called Bigot; they were said to be "bigoted."

Slowly the circle of those in the know widened. SHAEF and Twenty-first Army Group staff officers briefed army and corps staffs, who in turn briefed division and regimental commanders, right on down to company and platoon officers, who passed the information on to their noncoms and privates. At the lower levels the place names were not revealed until the men were actually sailing for France; otherwise the briefings were extraordinarily detailed and accurate with regard to terrain features, fairly realistic about the numbers and quality of the German defenders, and wildly optimistic about what the naval and air bombardments were going to do to those defenders.

The briefings were done on sand tables or, in the case of the 12th Regiment, 4th Division, on a huge sponge-rubber replica of the Cotentin Peninsula made to scale both horizontally and vertically, complete in minute detail with roads, bridges, buildings, power lines, hedgerows, fortifications, and obstacles. One member of the 12th recalled, "It was as though the men had been suddenly transported by plane and were looking down on the very beaches they would soon land on and the very ground over which they would have to fight."[17]

Officers were briefed at regimental level. Lt. Ralph Eastridge of the 115th Regiment, 29th Division, wrote an account of the briefing he attended. The briefing officer, the regimental S-2, began with a map of Omaha Beach. He explained that the 16th (1st Division) and 116th (29th Division) would land side by side; the 115th would follow the 116th. He described the beach obstacles and fixed fortifications at Omaha, the terrain, including the distance from the seawall to the foot of the bluff (about 200 meters), the height of the bluff (thirty meters, average), and other details.

"You can see that the defenses are heaviest at these points where the little valleys lead inland. These breaks or draws in the bluff are our beach exits, and the key to success in the initial assault will be the securing of these exits.

"The defenses include minefields, barbed wire, antitank ditches, and interlocking bands of automatic fire, concentrated at the exits. Each of these positions is manned by an estimated battalion with another battalion strung along the bluff between. They are part of the 916th Division, a static division, so-called because it is designed to fight in place from fixed positions.

"This particular static division is made up of about 40 percent Germans, many of them partially disabled. But remember, a one-armed soldier is just as capable of pulling the trigger of a fixed machine gun in a pillbox as a two-armed soldier.

"The remaining 60 percent of the division is made up of mercenaries, largely Russian, with some Poles, Jugo-Slavs, and other Balkans. . . . They are rough, simple, ignorant men and have little concern for the value of a life. They come from a part of the world where fighting has been the main occupation for generations. Their officers and noncoms are German; they will fight to the death.

"Behind this static division are mobile divisions, first-line troops. Personnel is largely German. Most have seen combat on the Russian or Italian fronts. Their weakness is a lack of transport. . . .

"Now for the plan in detail. The 16th and 116th will hit the beach in assault craft at about 0630. . . . The boats will ground out around the first of the underwater obstacles, on a rising tide. The immediate objective will be to secure the high ground above the beaches, denying the Germans direct fire and observation of the beach. Our regiment will land at H plus ninety minutes, move immediately to this village [indicating St.-Laurent-sur-Mer on the map, but unnamed], and go into position on the right. . . .

"Now this first part is a comparatively easy job. The tough job will be done by the 116th, before we land. If the 116th goes in right we should have a pushover."

"Sir," one officer asked, "what happens if the 116th doesn't clean up the beach on schedule?"

"Then we take over their mission."

"How many divisions in the first wave?" another officer asked.

"It'll be a big show," the S-2 answered with a smile, "believe me. But we need only concern ourselves with our little sector."

"When is D-Day?"

"Don't know yet. About the 3rd or 4th [of June] would be a guess."

The officers of the 115th liked that "pushover" talk, but did not believe it. Lieutenant Eastridge commented, "The prospects looked grim. The diagrams of the beach defenses indicated that the Germans had been fantastically thorough. The 116th had a rugged job ahead."[18]

Indeed, Pvt. Felix Branham of the 116th heard his briefer tell his platoon that if the men got the excess equipment they would be carrying to the beach—mortar rounds, land mines, ammo boxes, radios and batteries, and more—they would be making a contribution. The 115th coming in behind would not be as heavily laden and their men "would come in and pick up what we had carried ashore, and they would do the job, even though they had to walk over our dead bodies."[19]

Such bloodthirsty realism was uncommon. Most of the officers were upbeat and reassuring when they briefed their companies and platoons. Forty years and more later, veterans of Omaha still recalled, with some bitterness, what they were told: "The briefer explained that it would be no problem at all because the Air Force was coming over in great numbers, the Navy bombardment would be tremendous, the rocket ships would fire thousands of rockets, it was going to be a walkover, nothing to worry about. Our worries would come two or three days later when the panzer counterattacks began." (149th Combat Engineers)[20]

"We were told that many thousands of tons of bombs would

be dropped on our beach by the Ninth Air Force just prior to the invasion. My concern was that we would have trouble getting our trucks across the beach because the bomb craters would be so close and so deep." (6th ESB)[21]

"Our briefing officer gave us a pep talk. More than 1,000 bombers would do their work beforehand. The battleships would blow everything off the map—pillboxes, artillery, mortars, and the barbed-wire entanglements. Everything would be blasted to smithereens—a pushover!" (26th Regiment)[22]

"We were briefed to believe that there would be no living things on the beach, no life of any kind. It would be a piece of cake." (5th ESB)[23]

Almost every unit scheduled to invade had a similar experience. To drive home the point, junior officers, noncoms, privates were encouraged to study the sand tables or replicas whenever they wished, and thousands of them spent countless hours looking, discussing, familiarizing themselves with their objectives. They also got photographs, some only a few hours old, that revealed the most recent progress in the building of the Atlantic Wall. With that much accurate intelligence, how could the Germans stand a chance?

There was tough-guy talk. The briefer for the 91st Troop Carrier Squadron (glider-tugging pilots) gave out a warning: "Pilots will release when the C-47 leading the formation starts a gradual turn to the left to return to the coast. If any C-47 pilot cuts his glider off too soon, he'd better keep on going because if he comes back here, I'll be waiting for him."

One of the glider pilots had a question. In an entirely innocent manner, he asked, "Sir, what do we do after we land our gliders?"

The briefer was taken aback. After a silence, he confessed, "I don't know. I guess we really never thought of that really." There was nervous laughter when the glider pilot sitting next to Sgt. Charles Skidmore gave his own answer, "Run like hell!"[24]

The Army being the Army, inevitably there were some jackasses around. Sgt. Alan Anderson of the 116th Regiment remembered being called into a tent where some colonel from public relations "got up and made an impassioned and patriotic speech about what a privilege it was for us to have this opportunity to be in this great invasion which would change the history of the world, and then at the end of his speech he made the remarkable announcement that he was sorry he couldn't go with us. My buddy, Arkie

Markum, poked me and said, 'Well, he can have my place if he really wants to go!' "

The PR colonel went on to say that the Army was ready to take nearly 100 percent casualties in the first twenty-four hours. Anderson remembered, "We all turned around and looked at each other and said, 'Well, it's tough that you have to go.' "[25]

Once briefed, the troops were sealed in tight. MPs roamed the grounds and perimeter, no one allowed in without proper identification, no one allowed out without proper orders. Capt. Cyril Hendry, a British tanker, recalled that his father died on June 1 and was buried on June 3, and "I wasn't allowed to go to the funeral, I just wasn't allowed, but my brother in the army who was stationed in Damascus was allowed to fly home for the funeral."[26]

Bravado comes easy to young men who think of themselves as indestructible, but the briefings and the detailed study of the beach defenses had a sobering effect on even the most lighthearted, unreflective soldiers. For all that they told each other nothing could be worse than the training regimen, they had some sense of what bullets and shrapnel can do to a human body. For the most part they had not been in combat, but they had been reading or seeing war news ever since September 1939. In their hometown newspapers or at the newsreels at the movie theaters they had followed the sweep of the Wehrmacht across Europe, watched it defeat the best the Poles, Norwegians, Belgians, British, French, Yugoslavs, Greeks, and Russians could put against it. The men of the AEF realized that the Wehrmacht was a thoroughly combat-experienced army that had once been unstoppable and might now be impregnable.

As a consequence of these realizations, after the briefings the chaplains did a big business. After losing his $2,500, "Dutch" Shultz went to confession. The priest, a British chaplain, "really chewed me out about some of the sins I confessed to him involving the Sixth Commandment." Shultz went to Mass every chance he had "and I should mention that it was a very inspiring sight to me to see Captain Stef, Major Kellam, Major McGinty, and other battalion officers serving as altar boys."[27]

Major Thomas of the 508th didn't pay much attention at his briefing: "I had been in the airborne long enough to know that night jumps never went off as planned." Afterward, he got into a poker game. He was losing so he thought "I better go and listen to the chaplain, so as to touch all the bases. About the time I was sitting down on a cot in the last row, the only seat left in the house, Chaplain Elder says, 'Now, the Lord is not particularly interested in those who only turn to him in times of need.' I thought, 'Gee, he must have seen me come in.' So I got up and left."[28]

When John Barnes learned that his outfit, Company A of the 116th Infantry, would lead the way, he went to Mass, "thinking this might be my last time." He had been brought up by a devout mother whose heartfelt prayer had been that he would become a priest. When he graduated from high school, he had to tell her he wasn't cut out for a religious life. But as he prayed at Mass, "I decided I would make a bargain with God. If my life was spared, I'd become a priest. Then I thought that was a bad bargain, either for Him or me, so I decided I'd take my chances."[29]

There were some who decided not to take any chances. "Dutch" Schultz remembered a paratrooper who "accidently" shot himself in the foot. A 1st Division sergeant, Joseph Dragotto, watched with astonishment as a man from another company calmly put a generous portion of pipe tobacco between two pieces of bread and ate the "sandwich." That got him into the hospital—and out of the invasion. Dragotto also saw a man lift his rifle and start firing it into the pup tents. As the MPs descended on him, Dragotto wondered why he was doing such a crazy thing, "and then I realized he didn't want to go to war."[30]

Other men dealt with their fears by making their appearance even more fearsome than it already was. In the 115th Regiment, the men of one squad got a hot idea and began cutting hair, shearing it right down to the scalp. The idea quickly spread; soon the company, then nearly the whole regiment took on the appearance of a convict colony.

The paratroopers picked up on the craze, except that they left a band of hair down the middle of the scalp, so that they looked like Indians ("Mohawks," the style was called). Col. Robert Sink, commanding the 506th PIR, saw the haircutting going on and said, "I forgot to tell you, some weeks ago we were officially notified that the Germans are telling French civilians that the Allied invasion forces would be led by American paratroopers, all of them convicted felons and psychopaths, easily recognized by the fact that they shave their heads or nearly so."[31]

Junior officers and noncoms worried: were they equal to the leadership task the army had assigned to them? Sgt. Alan Anderson talked to one of his privates, George Mouser, about his fears.

Mouser responded, "Well, sarge, the only way this war is ever going to end, we're going to have to cross the Channel and we're going to have to end it. The quicker we get at it, the better. And of all the men that I have trained with, I would rather go with you into combat than anyone."[32] In the 506th PIR, Sgts. Carwood Lipton and Elmer Murray spent long hours discussing different combat situations that might occur and how they would handle them.

There were nearly 175,000 men in the sausages waiting to cross the Channel on D-Day and it is obviously impossible to generalize about their mood. Some were apprehensive, some eager, some determined, some afraid. In part, attitude depended on age. Charles Jarreau was seventeen years old; he regarded his twenty-two- and twenty-three-year-old buddies as "old men." He thought their feeling was, "Gee, let's get this thing over so we can get home." His own attitude was, "Let's get to France so we can have some fun."[33]

To venture one generalization, there was more anticipation among the Americans than the British. For the Yanks, the way home led east, into Germany. For the Tommies, they already were home. Capt. Alistair Bannerman, a platoon commander in Sussex in southeastern England, wrote a long letter, stretching over his time in his sausage, to his wife. The letter captures his mood and that of at least some of his fellow Tommies.

"We don't feel majestic at all at the moment," he wrote on May 28. "There are too many little pinpricks in this life. The eternal drill, the being pushed around, hobnailed boots and sweaty socks, and now the caged existence too. . . . I have tried explaining to my own platoon that we're about to make history and that one day their children will read of our deeds in the history books, but all I get are faint smiles.

"To soldiers . . . Churchill's radio rhetoric sounds a bit embarrassing. They have no great faith in the new world, they have no belief in any great liberating mission. They know it's going to be a charnel house. All they want is to put an end to it all, and get back to civvy street, to their homes, their private lives, their wives and loved ones."

On May 31, Bannerman wrote, "What a gigantic effort each man now has to make, to face up to something like this. Men who may have had only little of life, men with little education and little knowledge and with no philosophical supports, men with ailing, estranged or poor or needy families, men who have never been loved, men who had never had high ambitions or wanted a new world order. Yet we're all here, we're all going, as ordered, willingly into battle."[34]

In the first couple of days in June, the AEF began to load up and form up and move out for the journey across the Channel. The men left behind their duffel bags, taking with them only what they could carry—mainly weapons and ammunition, gas masks, photos of their loved ones, and a change of clothing (they were issued their cartons of cigarettes and C and K rations when they boarded). Lt. Col. Thompson spoke for all the men when he remarked, "Anyone who was there remembers with nostalgia the weeks spent in the concentration and marshaling areas."[35]

It is one of the great mysteries of World War II that although the Germans saw the buildup in southern England—they could hardly have missed it—they completely failed to draw the right conclusions from the concentration. There were nightly bombing raids over the sausages, no big deal, seldom more than a half dozen bombers, and regular flights over the harbors, with bombers dropping mines. German reconnaissance planes occasionally managed to sneak in, take some photographs, and roar away to the east. The situation cried out for a superhuman effort from the Luftwaffe to bomb the harbors and marshaling areas, but it never happened. Of course the Luftwaffe was but a shadow of its 1940 Battle of Britain self, and of course the dummy landing craft in eastern England supporting the Fortitude deception operation confused the Germans, but still to have missed the opportunity to hit the harbors and sausages with whatever they had was inexcusable and inexplicable. "It just seems a miracle," Seaman Richard Freed of the merchant marine commented.[36]

Another mystery: After the great success in late April against Tiger, when E-boats sank two LSTs and damaged six others, with no German loss, why did not the German navy make an all-out effort to use the E-boats in Caen against the Allied buildup? In fact, the E-boats made no effort at all. The German submarines, what was left of them, were meanwhile out in the North Atlantic. In the first week of June, U-boats sank two American destroyers in the mid-Atlantic, but they carried out neither reconnaissance missions nor torpedo attacks against the Overlord armada.

That the Germans failed to conclude from what they knew of the buildup that lower Normandy was the target is not so surprising. The fact that the AEF had gathered in southern England was not a giveaway as to the site of the invasion. Portsmouth is closer to the Pas-de-Calais than it is to Caen. Control of the sea meant that the fleet moving out into the Channel could head straight east, to Calais, or straight south to Calvados and the Cotentin, or southwest to Brittany. The AEF had a mobility unprecedented in the history of war. As John Keegan rightly notes, thanks to the specialized landing craft, the creation of the airborne divisions, and the utilization of command of the air to isolate the landing zone, it was precisely "where the Allies felt themselves to be at their most vulnerable in their Second Front strategy [that] their greatest strength lay; in their reliance on the sea for the movement of their forces."[37]

The Allies carried out many miniature Fortitude operations in the weeks before D-Day, sending landing craft covered by cruisers and destroyers to simulate assaults against various beaches in France. These dummy assaults kept the Germans jumpy and sometimes revealed radar sites and local Luftwaffe capacity.

Much more exact information on the Germans came from Ultra intercepts, the continuous and massive air reconnaissance, and the French Resistance. On June 3, the Joint Intelligence Sub-Committee reported on "German Appreciation of Allied Intentions Regarding Overlord." It was a most heartening document. It opened, "There has been no intelligence, during the last week, to suggest that the enemy has accurately assessed the area in which our main assault is to be made. He appears to expect several landings between the Pas de Calais and Cherbourg." It noted that the Germans continued to "overestimate the size of the Allied forces likely to be employed" and to expect landings in Norway.[38]

In "Weekly Intelligence Summary No. 11," also issued on June 3, SHAEF G-2 assessed German strength. It noted the movement of various German divisions into France and closer to the coast. Later, much was made of the shift of some formations into the Cotentin and at Omaha Beach, as if this indicated that Hitler, Rundstedt, and Rommel had finally penetrated the secret; in fact, many German units were on the move, reinforcing the Atlantic Wall from northeast to southwest (the LXVII Corps, for example, was moved on the first day of June into the Somme estuary, with headquarters at Amiens). Total German strength in France had increased almost 20 percent, from fifty to sixty divisions (ten armored); inevitably some of those reinforcements went to the invasion site, but not the panzers.[39]

Altogether, the intelligence gathered by the Allies was generally accurate, detailed, and helpful—just the opposite of the intelligence gathered by the Abwehr. The Allies knew what they were up against; the Germans could only guess.

At *Widerstandsnest* 62 (WN 62), a fortification overlooking the Colleville draw at Omaha Beach, eighteen-year-old Pvt. Franz Gockel was involved in a debate with his comrades. Half the members of his platoon argued that the Allies would come here, in the next week or two. The other half argued that the defenses at Colleville were too strong—the Allies wouldn't dare come here.

WN 62 guarded an artillery observation post that spotted for a field battery about five kilometers inland. In front of the position there were 105mm cannon zeroed in on preplanned targets. WN 62 consisted of two casemates holding 75mm guns, a 50mm antitank gun, two light and two heavy machine guns, and twenty men, all, except for the *Oberfeldwebel* and the two NCOs, under nineteen years of age. The bunkers had two-meter-thick concrete ceilings and were connected by trenches.

Private Gockel had never seen salt water before he was posted to Calvados in early 1944 with the 352nd Division. He sat behind his twin-mounted machine gun night after night, through April, May, on into June, watching, waiting, wondering. During the day, he dug. As one of his comrades put it on the afternoon of June 3, "If there will be any possibility at all of surviving an attack, it will only be with the help of this trench. Dig!"

That evening, Gockel remembered, "nothing moved on the calm surface of the water, only the slow swells made their way to the beach. The fishing boats from Grandcamp and Port-en-Bessin remained in harbor. Until May they had routinely made their excursions along the coast, but now the sea was empty."[40]

9

LOADING

EISENHOWER HAD SET D-Day for June 5. Loading for the assault began on May 31, running from west to east—from Falmouth and Fowey for the U.S. 29th Division, from Dartmouth, Torquay, and Exmouth for the U.S. 4th Division, from Weymouth and Portland for the U.S. 1st Division, from Southampton for the British 50th and Canadian 3rd divisions, from Portsmouth and Newhaven for the British 3rd Division. Those coming from a distance rode to the quays by bus or truck; those whose sausages were close to the harbors formed up into their squads, platoons, and companies and marched.

Everything was on the move, jeeps, trucks, big artillery pieces, tanks, half-tracks, motorcycles, and bicycles. Crowds gathered on the streets to watch the apparently never-ending procession. The adults were giving the V-for-Victory sign, but as one company of the 1st Division marched through a village, a boy of eleven or twelve called out to a sergeant, "You won't come back." The boy's mother gave a gasp, picked him up, and ran to the front of the column. As the sergeant passed, the boy sobbed through his tears, "You *will* come back! *You will!*"[1]

Death was on the mind of many of the men. As Pvt. Clair Galdonik remembered his bus ride to Dartmouth, "Few words were spoken among us. No joking or prankster stunts. We felt

closer to each other now than ever before."[2] Motor Machinist
Charles Jarreau of the Coast Guard was on LCI 94, watching the
gathering on the quay at Weymouth. "The troops were just flooding the docks," he recalled. "People everywhere. Priests were in
their heyday. I even saw Jews go and take communion. Everybody
scared to death."[3]

In most cases anticipation overrode fear. The men were eager
to get going. The excitement in the air was nearly overwhelming.
The Allied high command had deliberately brought the men to the
highest level of readiness, mentally and physically. Training had
been going on, in most cases, for two years or more. Although there
had been transfers and replacements, a majority of the men were in
squads and platoons that had been together since boot camp. They
had shared the drudgery and the physical and mental demands of
training, hated or loved their COs together, eaten their meals together, slept in the same foxhole on maneuvers together, gotten
drunk together. They had formed a bond, become a family. They
knew each other intimately, knew what to expect from the guy on
their left or right, what he liked to eat, what he smelled like.

Not many of them were there by choice. Only a few of them
had a patriotic passion that they would speak about. But nearly all
of them would rather have died than let down their buddies or look
the coward in front of their bunkmates. Of all the things that the
long training period accomplished, this sense of group solidarity
was the most important.

Some commanders gathered their men together for one last
talk before they boarded their transport vessels. The commander of
the 115th Regiment, Col. Eugene Slappey, looked at all the shaved
heads in his outfit, took off his helmet, scratched his own bald head,
and declared, "You men have a good idea there. Lots cleaner. But
I never realized that I had been getting ready for an invasion for a
long time."

After the laughter he grew serious, talking to his men like a
father to his sons: "There isn't much us old fellows can do now.
The success of this invasion is up to you men. We have done a lot
of planning: I wish you could know the amount of preparation that
has gone into this thing. It's the greatest military effort that the
world has seen. And all of you know the stakes, the course of
history depends on our success. It's a great satisfaction to know that
no unit was ever better prepared to go into combat; that's why we
got the job."

Slappey concluded, "I'll see you in France." As Lieutenant Eastridge walked away, he was struck by the thought, It will be a sad day for this regiment if we ever lose that old man.[4]

General Bradley gathered nearly a thousand officers in a vast aircraft hangar, the general officers on the platform, the colonels on the front-row benches, the lieutenants at the rear. Brig. Gen. Theodore Roosevelt, Jr., son of the late president, was assistant division commander of the 4th Division. Because of his age, fifty-six, and his physical condition (he had a bad heart), Roosevelt had been forced to obtain a stack of dispensations and special orders, then plea for permission to go ashore on Utah with one of the first waves. He had finally got what he wanted. He sat on the platform, grinning.

Bradley opened, "Gentlemen, this is going to be the greatest show on earth. You are honored by having grandstand seats."

Roosevelt frowned, shook his head, and in a deep bass whisper said, "Hell, goddamn! We're not in the grandstand! We're down on the gridiron!"

The acoustics of the hangar were such that everyone heard him. There was an eruption of laughter and an easing of tension. Bradley grinned and continued his pep talk.[5]

The Coast Guard and Navy crews were waiting for the men. Charles Jarreau remembered that on LCI 94 there were four officers and twenty-six men. The officers were "ninety-day wonders," graduates of officer training school, in their early twenties, but the skipper was an old man of thirty-two. He had ten years in the merchant marine and "the rules were his, not the Navy's; he did not like the Navy's." Two days before LCI 94 picked up its soldiers, he told Jarreau, "There's nobody going to leave this ship, so you go out and get the liquor you want and we are going to have a party." It started at 0700 "and boy, at the end of the day, everybody was just crapped out, but it sure relieved the tension. After a night's sleep we sobered up and started taking troops on board."[6]

Familiarity with the loading process helped immensely to ease tension. The men of the AEF had been through the drill many times. By early June 1944, the continuous stream of mounting, marshaling, embarkation, and landing had become monotonous and routine. Many of those involved commented later that they could have done it in their sleep; others said that until the definitive announcement came over the ship's loudspeaker they half believed this was just another exercise. Those were exactly the attitudes their commanders wanted them to have.

The troops indulged themselves in the age-old tendency of fighting men going into battle to carry too much stuff with them. The Assault Training Center exercises had led planners to recommend that the men in the assault waves should not carry more than forty-four pounds of equipment, but most were taking on more than double that extra weight, some even more. Partly this was the fault of the regimental commanders, who wanted the first waves to carry in land mines, satchel charges, extra ammunition, spare radios, mortars, and the like. Partly this was the men's own fault, as there was always something extra to carry—a French phrase book or a Bible, an unauthorized knife or pistol, most of all cigarettes.

The cigarettes were handed out at the quays, along with rations. Pvt. Robert Patterson of the 474th Antiaircraft Battalion told the quartermaster to never mind the cigarettes because "I don't smoke."

"You might as well take them," the quartermaster replied, "because by the time you get where you're going, you will." Forty years later Patterson commented, "He was right. On that ship I learned to smoke and did so for a lot of years thereafter."[7]

One soldier in the 4th Division was addicted to Camels. He went into a panic over the thought of running out, so he bought, borrowed, or traded for every pack he could. He went on board carrying ten cartons. Most men carried two cartons and depended on the Army to get more up to them when needed.

Vehicles were also grossly overloaded with ammunition, jerry cans, picks and shovels, canteens, field rations, weapons, and more. Nevertheless, the loading proceeded smoothly and according to the elaborate schedule. It seemed impossible that each of the thousands of ships and landing craft could find its own specific place, or that the passengers could locate the right vessels, but they did. Tanks, artillery, trucks, and jeeps backed into their LCTs— last on, first off. They used specially constructed "hards," cement aprons extending into the harbor at the right slope to accommodate the LCTs.

Men moved onto their LSTs and LCIs or other transports "in an astonishingly short time," according to Lieutenant Eastridge. Almost at once both decks of LST 459 were loaded, with vehicles and guns chained to the deck. The ship was overcrowded, with only one bunk for every three men, so they would rotate sleeping hours, eight to a man. There was insufficient space at the docks and hards for all the transports and LSTs, so many of the infantry companies were ferried out to vessels anchored in the bays on Higgins boats.

LST 459 moved away from the quay, sailed slowly to the center of the river in Plymouth harbor, and tied up to another LST. "We were side by side with so many crafts," Eastridge said, "that a man could have jumped from one deck to another for a half mile or more. Toward the sea, we could see destroyers and larger ships at anchor. The harbor was just jammed with boats."[8]

Altogether there were 2,727 ships, ranging from battleships to transports and landing craft that would cross on their own bottoms. They came from twelve nations—the United States, Great Britain, Canada, Australia, New Zealand, South Africa, France, Belgium, Norway, Poland, Greece, and Holland. They were divided into the Western Naval Task Force (931 ships, headed for Omaha and Utah) and the Eastern Naval Task Force (1,796 ships, headed for Gold, Juno, and Sword). On the decks of the LSTs were the Higgins boats and other craft too small to cross the Channel on their own. There were 2,606 of them. Thus the total armada amounted to 5,333 ships and craft of all types, more vessels—as Admiral Morison pointed out—"than there were in all the world when Elizabeth I was Queen of England."[9]

The first to move out were the minesweepers. Their job was to sweep up along the English coast in case the Luftwaffe and E-boats had dropped mines in the area, then proceed to clear five channels for the separate assault forces (O, U, G, J, and S), marking them with lighted dan buoys spaced at one-mile intervals along the 400-meter-wide channels, and finally clear the area in which the transports would anchor off the beaches. There were 245 vessels involved in this mammoth sweeping job; they began their work on the night of May 31-June 1.

On June 3, the gunfire support and bombardment ships of the Western Naval Task Force set sail from Belfast headed south through the Irish Sea. They included the battleships *Nevada*, veteran of the Pearl Harbor attack, *Texas*, the oldest in the U.S. fleet, and *Arkansas*, along with seven cruisers and twenty-one destroyers. They would lead the way. After they had rounded Lands End and passed the Isle of Wight, the LSTs, LCTs, LCMs, and the transports would follow. They were to get under way in the pre-dawn hours of June 4, rendezvous, and form up in convoys.

• •

As the troops filed onto their transports and landing craft, they were handed an order of the day from General Eisenhower. It began, "Soldiers, Sailors and Airmen of the Allied Expeditionary Force:

"You are about to embark upon the Great Crusade, toward which we have striven these many months. The eyes of the world are upon you. The hope and prayers of liberty-loving people everywhere march with you. . . .

"Your task will not be an easy one. Your enemy is well trained, well equipped and battle-hardened. He will fight savagely.

"But this is the year 1944! . . . The tide has turned! The free men of the world are marching together to Victory!

"I have full confidence in your courage, devotion to duty and skill in battle. We will accept nothing less than full victory!

"Good luck! And let us all beseech the blessing of Almighty God upon this great and noble undertaking."[10]

Sergeant Slaughter had his buddies sign his copy. He wrapped it in plastic, put it in his wallet, and carried it through Normandy all the way to the Elbe River in eastern Germany. "I still have that document framed hanging over my writing desk," Slaughter said. "It is my most treasured souvenir of the war."[11]

Thousands of those who received Eisenhower's order of the day saved it. I cannot count the number of times I've gone into the den of a veteran of D-Day to do an interview and seen it framed and hanging in a prominent place. I have one on my office wall.

Pvt. Felix Branham of the 116th Infantry got everyone on his ship to sign a 500-franc note he had won in a poker game. "One guy asked, 'Why?' and I said, 'Fellows, some of us are never getting out of this alive. We may never see each other again. We may be crippled, or whatever. So sign this.' I have that hanging on my wall in a frame. I wouldn't take *anything* for it."[12]

Officers considerably junior to Eisenhower were tempted to try their hand at inspiration. After his LST 530 took on its cargo of Churchill tanks, jeeps, trucks, six Higgins boats, and 600 British soldiers destined for Gold Beach, Lt. Tony Duke of the U.S. Navy thought he would give a speech over the ship's loudspeaker. Thoughts of Shakespeare and *Henry V* ran through his mind. But a British army colonel came up to the bridge, "put his hand on my shoulder, I'll never forget it, and said, 'Careful, young fellow. Most of my men have seen the worst of desert warfare and a good many of them were in France and evacuated through Dunkirk. So I'd advise you to go easy, go quick, and don't get dramatic or emotional.' My own emotions were thumping, straining inside of me, but I took his lead and made a very simple announcement. I realized later that I would have made a real ass out of myself if I'd let go with exactly how I did feel."[13]

The first thing most crews did was to feed the soldiers. "The Navy chow was wonderful," Eastridge recalled. "Our men were talking about transferring to the Navy for the next war."[14]

On board the transport *Samuel Chase,* Capt. Oscar Rich, an artillery observer for the 5th Field Artillery Battalion of the 1st Division (whose tiny L-5 aircraft had been disassembled, with the wings folded back and the propeller put inside the plane, which was swung on board by winch), went below to study the foam-rubber map of the Calvados coastline. "It was the most detailed thing that I had ever seen in my life. The trees were there, the trails, the roads, the houses, the beach obstacles—everything was there and I spent hours examining it. . . . I could see my first airstrip, in an apple orchard just off the draw going up from Easy Red, Omaha Beach. Everything was to scale—it was actually like being in an airplane, about 500 feet above the beach and looking at the beach and seeing the whole thing in true perspective. It was uncanny how they had built this thing." Finally he broke away from the map and joined a poker game. The players included Robert Capa, the famous *Life* magazine photographer, and correspondent Don Whitehead.[15]

Once on board, for most of the troops there was little to do except gamble, read, or spread rumors. Pvt. Clair Galdonik found a softball and two gloves. He started playing catch with a buddy but made a bad throw and the ball went over the side.[16] On his LCT, Walter Sidlowski of the 5th ESB discovered that the skipper had put the toilet off limits for Army personnel, so as to not put a strain on the facilities. Sidlowski and some buddies put their engineering skills to work and constructed hanging toilet seats, which gave some comic relief when all the seats were occupied just as an admiral's barge passed by.[17]

Men listened to the radio. They groaned when Axis Sally told them to come on over, "we are waiting for you." They cheered when the fall of Rome was announced. They read books: Lt. Frank Beetle of the 16th Regiment, 1st Division, recalled reading ("be-

lieve it or not") about Plato in a paperback edition of Will Durant's
Story of Philosophy.[18]

Some of the companies of the 2nd Ranger Battalion went on
board the *New Amsterdam,* a small passenger boat, for the journey
across the Channel. It was a British ship with a British crew—and
British food, meaning kidney stew, which caused much complaint.
The rangers being rangers, there was no sitting around waiting.
They continued their training and conditioning by stringing ropes
up to the mast to practice rope climbing. They did push-ups, sit-
ups, and even close-order drill.[19]

There were some screw ups. Capt. Robert Walker of the
116th Regiment had done practice exercises on LCVPs, LCTs,
Ducks, and LCMs. The only type of landing craft he had never
been on was an LCI. For the invasion, naturally, he was assigned
to LCI 91 and designated as billeting officer. The ship's capacity
was 180 men but he had 200 badly overloaded men on his roster. In
addition, LCI 91 was already carrying large rolls of telephone wire,
bangalore torpedoes, satchel charges, grapnels, extra flamethrowers, "and much, much more." Nevertheless, Walker managed to
crowd everyone in, then talked to the skipper, a Coast Guard lieutenant from Boston. The skipper said he had entered the Coast
Guard anticipating spending the war guarding the Atlantic Coast
near Boston, but now was about to embark on his third invasion.[20]

Lt. Charles Ryan of the 18th Regiment, 1st Division, had
been on an LCI in an exercise, so he knew what to expect when his
craft moved out into the open Channel. He described the LCI as "a
metal box designed by a sadist to move soldiers across water while
creating in them such a sense of physical discomfort, seasickness,
and physical degradation and anger as to induce them to land in
such an angry condition as to bring destruction, devastation, and
death upon any person or thing in sight or hearing. It combined the
movements of roller coaster, bucking bronco, and a camel."[21]

Around the airfields, glider troops and paratroopers checked
out their equipment for about the 1,000th time, tried to think of
some place to carry an extra pack of cigarettes or an extra grenade,
visited the models of the Cotentin or the Orne and Dives rivers one
last time—and then once more. They were tightly sealed in, ready
at a moment's notice to march out to the airfield and get into the
British-built Horsa gliders or American-built C-47s to get the invasion under way.

At another airfield, Fairford in Glouchester, a less-well-known unit prepared for the flight over the Channel. It was a Special Air Service (SAS) operation. SAS was a British army unit formed to operate behind Axis lines. It consisted of three regiments, one to work in France, plus two French battalions and a Belgian company. Capt. Michael R. D. Foot was a brigade intelligence officer in SAS. Since August 1942, he had been studying the German occupiers of France and their defenses. He had gone on a commando raid. Now he was preparing to send off some special teams to take advantage of what he knew about the Germans in Normandy (because Foot was bigoted, he was not allowed to go behind enemy lines).

Foot had experienced a difficult time in getting his teams for the operation code named Titanic (Foot had picked Titanic from a list, "trusting that would sound large to a German"). He had approached his regimental commander, who was preparing his squads for behind-the-lines bridge destruction and other acts of sabotage, to ask for four small parties of SAS troops.

"To do what?" the CO asked gruffly.

"To provide a bit of deception to assist in the landing."

"No."

"Colonel, this is an order."

"Not to me. Put it in writing if you like and I will reply in writing why I won't do it. But why should we waste paper? I will tell you why I won't do it."

He softened a bit and explained, "In the early days of the regiment we were all briefed to raid an Italian airfield. Intelligence canceled it at the last minute. We went on leave in Cairo, came back nursing our hangovers and were told, 'Right, chaps, it's on tonight, off you go.' Very few of us came back. And I swore then I was going to have no further dealings with any intelligence authority. Get out!"

Foot went to see Colonel Francks, commander of one of the other regiments in SAS, "with whom I had made my very first parachute jump, his first jump too. We were reasonable friends and he rather grudgingly agreed to Titanic, but only if it was cut down from four parties to two."

Foot agreed. He went down to Fairford, which was jammed with SAS teams preparing to go into France to fight, and there he gave his two teams—each consisting of an officer, an NCO, and two privates—the special equipment he had helped dream up and their mission.

The equipment consisted of about 500 dummy parachutists, a record player, and a mass of Very pistols and ammunition. Foot explained to the two teams that the idea was to drop the dummies, which would self-destruct on landing with a small explosion and a flash, then jump themselves carrying the equipment. On landing, they were to turn on the gramophone. The record would play snatches of soldiers' conversation, interspersed with small-arms fire. Then they should move around the area, shooting off Very pistols. One party would go in about midway between Rouen and Le Havre, the other near Isigny.

The French SAS battalion had its own special missions, including one for an advance party to seize a landing place in Brittany in order to bring the whole battalion into Brittany. The leader was a big game hunter named Bourgoin who had lost an arm but taught himself how to parachute with a single arm. The Frenchmen in the party were scheduled to be the first Allied soldiers to land in France.[22]

All across England, from four-man squads of the SAS to the overstrength divisions of the 6th, 82nd, and 101st Airborne, the men going into France by air were ready.

By the evening of June 3, the assault waves of the AEF were loaded up. Force O, carrying the 29th Division for the right flank at Omaha, coming out of Falmouth, had the longest distance to sail so it sallied forth first, during the night. To General Eisenhower, "the smell of victory was in the air."[23]

On the far shore, all was quiet. Rommel spent June 2 hunting for stags. On June 3, he drove to Paris to buy shoes for Lucie's birthday, which would come on June 6. In Paris, he conferred with Rundstedt, who agreed with him that "there is still no sign that the invasion is imminent." The tides in the Strait of Dover would not be suitable for an invasion until mid-June. Rommel checked the weather report—it indicated increasing cloudiness, high winds, and rain. He decided to go to Herrlingen for Lucie's birthday, then on to Berchtesgaden to see Hitler to beg for reinforcements. He wanted two additional panzer divisions and control of all the tanks. He wrote in his diary, "The most urgent problem is to win the Führer over by personal conversation."[24]

Although Rommel had half or less of what he calculated he required, in men, guns, mines, Rommel's asparagus, beach obstacles, and fixed emplacements, he exuded confidence. He had brought to his task outward enthusiasm and confidence. Morale was apparently high all along the Atlantic Wall, or so the German leaders told themselves. A secret Gestapo morale report claimed that the troops were actually looking forward to the invasion. "People see it as our last chance to turn the tide," it said. "There is virtually no fear of the invasion discernible."[25]

Rommel had managed to persuade some of his officers and a few of his troops that not only did they have a chance, they would prevail. Most German soldiers on the coast hoped the invasion would come far from them, but if it did hit them many were prepared to stand and fight. "*Er soll nur kommen,*" was Goebbels's sneer. ("Let them come.")

And why not? Even the *Ost* battalions had landing obstacles, barbed wire, and mines in front of their trenches and fortified pillboxes. To the rear, mortars and artillery pieces had zeroed in on every feature of the beach. At their sides were casemates holding 88mm cannon prepared to fire crisscross across their front. Behind them stood German sergeants, pistols ready. Those Allied briefers who told their men that the troops they would face on D-Day were inferior and could be expected to run away had got it wrong. Those briefers who reminded their men that the *Ost* battalions were made up of rough, simple, ignorant men with German noncoms and officers to ensure that they fought had got it right.

But for the German high command, there was the nagging problem of surrender. They feared that many of their men would take the first opportunity to turn themselves into POWs, and they too had got it right.

At Omaha Beach, Maj. Gen. Dietrich Kraiss commanded the 352nd Division, which had moved up from St.-Lô to Calvados in May. Kraiss was a veteran of the Eastern Front, where he had distinguished himself, but his disposition of his forces in Calvados left much to be desired. On the Eastern Front, the German practice was to let the Red Army attack, then counterattack with reserves held back from the front line. That was not Rommel's idea at all in Normandy, of course, but in accord with German doctrine Rommel left tactical dispositions up to his subordinates. Thus at Omaha —the only place in Kraiss's sector of the coast (stretching from the mouth of the Vire River to Arromanches) where an amphibious assault could come ashore—he had in place but one artillery battalion and two infantry battalions (from the 716th Infantry Regiment). Kraiss had his reserve, ten infantry battalions and four artillery battalions strong, as much as twelve miles back from the coast.

There was one advantage to the Germans in this arrangement: Allied intelligence had failed to see the move of part of the 352nd's strength to the coast. Briefers told the 29th Division that Omaha would be defended only by second-rate troops from the 716th Division.

Like Rommel, Colonel General Dollmann, commanding the Seventh Army in Normandy, was convinced that the deteriorating weather precluded an invasion. He ordered a map exercise to be conducted in Rennes on June 6. All divisional commanders plus two regimental commanders per division were ordered to attend. Admiral Krancke canceled E-boat sea patrols because of the foul weather.

Only the one-legged Gen. Erich Marcks, in command of the LXXXIV Corps on the western sector of the Calvados coast and in the Cotentin, was uneasy. He was especially concerned about the 716th and 352nd divisions in Calvados. Each division had a fifty-kilometer line to defend. "It's the weakest sector of my whole corps," he complained. On June 1, he went to Arromanches. Looking out to sea, he told an army captain at his side, "If I know the British, they'll go to church next Sunday for one last time, and sail Monday [June 5]. Army Group B says they're not going to come yet, and that when they do come it'll be at Calais. So I think we'll be welcoming them on Monday, right *here.*"[26]

10

DECISION TO GO

AT THE END of May, as the loading began, Air Vice Marshal Trafford Leigh-Mallory, who had doubted from the first the wisdom of dropping the two American airborne divisions into the Cotentin, came to Eisenhower at his headquarters in Southwick House (Admiral Ramsay's HQ, taken over by SHAEF for its command post for the invasion), just north of Portsmouth, to protest once again. Intelligence had discovered that the Germans had put their 91st Division into the central Cotentin, exactly where the 82nd Airborne was scheduled to drop. The 82nd had moved its drop zone to the west to avoid the Germans, but Leigh-Mallory felt not far enough.

He told Eisenhower, "We must not carry out this airborne operation." He predicted 70 percent losses in glider strength and at least 50 percent in paratroop strength even before the paratroopers hit the ground. He warned of a "futile slaughter" of two fine divisions, futile because the divisions would not be able to make any contribution to the battle. To send them into the Cotentin was "just plain sacrifice."[1]

Eisenhower went to his trailer, about a mile from Southwick House, "and thought it over again. I had no need for experts at this late time." He later described this as his most worrisome moment in the war, and wrote in his memoirs, "It would be difficult to conceive of a more soul-racking problem."

He reviewed the entire operation in his mind, then concentrated on the American airborne. He knew that if he disregarded Leigh-Mallory's warning and it proved accurate, "then I would carry to my grave the unbearable burden of a conscience justly accusing me of the stupid, blind sacrifice of thousands of the flower of our youth."[2] But he felt that if he canceled the airborne mission, he would have to cancel the landing at Utah Beach. If the paratroopers were not there to seize the causeway exits, the entire 4th Division would be endangered. But cancellation of Utah would so badly disarrange the elaborate plan as to endanger the whole Overlord operation. Further, Leigh-Mallory was only making a prediction, and the experience with airborne actions in Sicily and Italy (where Leigh-Mallory had not been present; Overlord was his first involvement with a paratroop operation), even though the airborne performance in 1943 had been flawed in many ways, by no means justified Leigh-Mallory's extreme pessimism.

"So I felt we had to put those two airborne divisions in," Eisenhower related, "and they had to take Ste.-Mère-Église and capture the causeway exits, and protect our flank." He called Leigh-Mallory to tell him of his decision and followed the call up with a letter. He wrote Leigh-Mallory, "There is nothing for it" but to go, and ordered him to see to it that his own doubts and pessimism not be spread among the troops.[3]

While Rommel was going to see Hitler to beg for more tanks and a tighter command structure, Eisenhower was visited by Churchill, who was coming to the supreme commander to beg a favor. He wanted to go along on the invasion, on HMS *Belfast*. ("Of course, no one likes to be shot at," Eisenhower later remarked, "but I must say that more people wanted in than wanted out on this one.") As Eisenhower related the story, "I told him he couldn't do it. I was in command of this operation and I wasn't going to risk losing him. He was worth too much to the Allied cause.

"He thought a moment and said, 'You have the operational command of all forces, but you are not responsible administratively for the makeup of the crews.'

"And I said, 'Yes, that's right.'

"He said, 'Well, then I can sign on as a member of the crew of one of His Majesty's ships, and there's nothing you can do about it.'

"I said, 'That's correct. But, Prime Minister, you will make my burden a lot heavier if you do it.' "

Churchill said he was going to do it anyway. Eisenhower had his chief of staff, General Smith, call King George VI to explain the problem. The king told Smith, "You boys leave Winston to me." He called Churchill to say, "Well, as long as you feel that it is desirable to go along, I think it is my duty to go along with you." Churchill gave up.[4]

With De Gaulle, it was Eisenhower asking the favor. On June 3, Churchill brought De Gaulle to Southwick House, where Eisenhower gave him a briefing on Overlord. This was the first De Gaulle knew of the plan, and he subjected Eisenhower to an hour-long lecture on what he was doing wrong; Eisenhower replied that he wished he had benefited from De Gaulle's generalship earlier but now it was too late. Then Eisenhower showed him a copy of a speech he would be making to the French people on D-Day, urging Frenchmen to "carry out my orders."

He asked De Gaulle to make a follow-up broadcast urging his countrymen to accept the SHAEF-printed francs. De Gaulle said *non*. The French people should obey him, not SHAEF; only the French government, of which he was president, had the right to issue currency. Eisenhower pleaded with him, to no avail. The whole thing was, in Eisenhower's words, "a rather sorry mess."[5]

When Churchill and De Gaulle left, Eisenhower wrote a memorandum for his diary, which he entitled "Worries of a Commander." At the top of the list was De Gaulle, and he wrote three paragraphs on the difficulties of dealing with the French. Next came weather. He was about to go to a weather conference. "My tentative thought," he wrote, "is that the desirability for getting started on the next favorable tide is so great and the uncertainty of the weather is such that we could never anticipate really perfect weather coincident with proper tidal conditions, that we must go unless there is a real and very serious deterioration in the weather."[6]

Eisenhower, his principal subordinates, and all the officers and men of the AEF had spent months training, planning, preparing for this moment. "The mighty host," in Eisenhower's words, "was tense as a coiled spring," ready for "the moment when its energy should be released and it would vault the English Channel."[7] He was determined to go if at all possible.

• •

On the morning of June 3, the LCTs in the Dart River started moving out. Hundreds of British citizens lined the shore, waving good-bye and good luck. Ens. Edwin Gale on LCT 853, a part of Flotilla 17, was twenty years old, a "ninety-day wonder." His skipper turned to Gale and said, "Edwin, you know we may not do anything as worthwhile as this again in our lives. It is a fine thing to be here."[8]

Lt. Dean Rockwell, the former high-school football coach, commanded a flotilla of sixteen LCTs. Each LCT was carrying four DD tanks, scheduled to hit the beach in front of the first wave of infantry, so he was one of the first to move out into the Channel. His LCTs began departing Weymouth late on June 3. It was soon "pitch black, no lights, no nothing. And to say pandemonium reigned is an understatement, because we not only had LCTs but picket boats and escort craft and all kinds of ships trying to sort themselves out." Radio silence prevailed, the ships could not use blinker lights, "we could not do anything but curse and swear until the whole thing got sorted out."[9]

Around the landing ships and craft, the warships circled to form up their own convoys. Storekeeper 2/C Homer Carey on LCT 505 remembered the sight of two British cruisers "in the soft twilight, racing past us headed south for the coast of France. Their shapely bows cut the water and passed us as if we were standing still. Beautiful—like two greyhounds. It was a comfort to know that they were on our side."[10]

The 2nd Battalion of the 116th Regiment was on the transport *Thomas Jefferson*. The men knew the ship well, having made two practice landings from her. Pvt. Harry Parley noted that this time, however, "humor was infrequent and forced. My thoughts were of home and family and, of course, what we were getting into. It saddened me to think of what would happen to some of my fellow GIs, whom I had grown to love." His heart went out especially to Lieutenant Ferguson, who had initiated a discussion about philosophies of death with Parley. "I did not envy him his position," Parley said. "He had come to know the men quite intimately as a result of having had to read and censor our outgoing mail. The loss of any of his men would be a twofold tragedy for him."

Private Parley carried an eighty-four-pound flamethrower, plus a pistol, shovel, life belt, raincoat, canteen, a block of dynamite, rations, and three cartons of cigarettes. He was worried about keeping up with his assault team on the dash across the beach. He scared the hell out of his buddies by using a trick he had just learned. He could set off a small flame at the mouth of his flamethrower, which would produce the same hissing sound as when the weapon was actually being fired, without triggering the propelling mechanism. Standing on the deck of the *Thomas Jefferson*, he calmly used the flamethrower to light a cigarette, sending a score or more of men scurrying in every direction.[11]

Pvt. George Roach of Company A, 116th, was saying his rosary. He was worried about casualties too, "because we were going to be in the first wave and we figured the chances of our survival were very slim." More than half the men in his company came from the same town, Bedford, Virginia. Most of the regiment came from southwestern Virginia.[12]

Sgt. Joe Pilck of the 16th Regiment, 1st Division, was on the transport *Samuel P. Chase.* "While we were riding around in the Channel," he recalled, "we were glad that this was the real thing. Not that we wanted to do it, but we knew it had to be done so we wanted to get it over with."[13]

The weather, which had been beautiful—clear skies, little wind—for the first three days of June, began to deteriorate. Clouds formed and began to lower, the wind came up, there was a smell of rain in the air. On his LCT, Cpl. Robert Miller was miserable. It started to drizzle, it was cold. He was on the open deck without shelter. The waves kicked up and started rocking his LCT. The steel deck was too slippery to lie down on, so he tried to catch some sleep on the canvas covering atop the trucks, but the wind and rain and rocking increased, so he gave it up.[14]

Pvt. Henry Gerald of the Royal Winnipeg Rifles was also on an LCT. At daylight, June 4, as the craft moved out into the Channel, he joined his mates in the crew's quarters for a briefing from his platoon leader. The LCT would "go up about twenty feet and then drop out from underneath us. Those who looked green yesterday were ghastly this morning." The deck was awash in vomit. Gerald was congratulating himself on not getting seasick when "a chap across from me began to heave up into his puke bag. He had an upper plate that came out and disappeared into the bag as he was being sick. That wasn't so bad until he reached into the bag, retrieved the plate, and popped it back into his mouth." At that sight, Gerald lost his breakfast.[15]

In the Channel, the drizzle began to turn into a cold, penetrating rain. Most of the men on the LCIs and LCTs had no shelter. The decks were slippery, the craft rocking in the choppy water. Everyone was wet and miserable. Eisenhower smelled victory in the air, but to the men of the AEF whose transports and landing craft had left harbor, the smell in the air was vomit.

During the first days of June, Eisenhower and his principal subordinates had held twice-daily meetings with the SHAEF Meteorologic Committee, at 0930 and 1600. Group Captain J. M. Stagg, twenty-eight years old and described by Eisenhower as a "dour but canny Scot,"[16] made the weather predictions, then answered questions. Eisenhower had been privately meeting with Stagg for a month to hear his predictions so he could have some sense of the basis on which Stagg made them and how good he was—knowing that, as he said, "The weather in this country is practically unpredictable."[17]

The final weather conference was scheduled for 0400, June 4, even as more ships sailed out of their harbors and those already at sea began to form up into convoys. Stagg had bad news. A high-pressure system was moving out, a low coming in. The weather on June 5 would be overcast and stormy, with a cloud base of 500 feet to 0 and Force-5 winds. Worse, the situation was deteriorating so rapidly that forecasting more than twenty-four hours in advance was highly undependable.

Eisenhower asked his subordinates for their views. Montgomery wanted to go. Tedder and Leigh-Mallory wanted a postponement. Ramsay said the navy could do its part but warned that the accuracy of the naval bombardment would be badly reduced by poor visibility and high seas and that the Higgins boats would be hard to control.

Eisenhower remarked that Overlord was being launched with ground forces that were not overwhelmingly powerful. The operation was feasible only because of Allied air superiority. Without that advantage, the invasion was too risky. He asked if anyone present disagreed. No one did. Eisenhower decided to postpone for at least one day, hoping for better conditions on June 6. At 0600 hours he gave his order to put everything on hold.

At just about that moment, Rommel began his long journey east, away from the coast, to see his wife and his führer. As he departed, in a light drizzle, he remarked, "There's not going to *be* an invasion. And if there is, then they won't even get off the beaches!"[18]

The order to postpone went out to the Allied convoys, which were under strict radio silence, in a variety of ways. Lt. Benjamin Frans, USN, was gunnery officer on the destroyer *Baldwin*. The *Baldwin* was still in Portland when the word came down. She set sail at flank speed to catch up with the leading convoys. When she did, the executive officer called over a bullhorn to the skippers of the transports and landing craft, "The operation has been postponed. Return to base." *Baldwin* caught up to the minesweeper in the van when it was within fifty kilometers of the French coast.[19]

Lieutenant Rockwell was headed toward his rendezvous point when a picket boat came alongside LCT 535 and handed him a message: "Post Mike One." That meant turn around and go back to harbor. "So we all turn around. Hundreds and hundreds of ships of various sizes." About midday, he got back to Weymouth.

For Rockwell, the postponement "was a blessing in disguise. There had been some collisions during the night. Delicate landing and launching gear was damaged, engines needed replacing or servicing."[20] Rockwell's own LCT 535 needed a new engine. He managed to get it in place before nightfall.

Ens. Sam Grundfast commanded LCT 607. He got the order to abort by flag signal. "Imagine the confusion, those hundreds of landing craft trying to get into Portsmouth harbor. We were jammed in. You could walk across that vast harbor going from boat to boat."[21] Making the sight even more vivid, every craft and ship had a barrage balloon waving in the wind overhead. The balloons were connected to the vessels by steel cables. Their purpose was to keep the Luftwaffe from making low-level passes at the fleet.

For the troops, June 4 was a terrible day. The men of the 4th Infantry Division spent it at sea—there was not time to go all the way back to Devonshire if Eisenhower decided on a June 6 landing. The transports and landing craft circled off the Isle of Wight. Waves broke over the sides, rain came down. The men were combat dressed with nowhere to go. No one wanted to play craps or poker or read a book or listen to another briefing. It was just misery.

In the harbors, or up the rivers, where the ships and craft

could drop anchor or tie up to one another, the men were not allowed off their vessels. They sat, cursed, waited. "We bitched up a storm," Private Branham of the 116th Regiment recalled, "because we wanted to go. We wanted to go. This sounds crazy, but we had come this far, we'd been sitting in England so long, we wanted to get this thing over with and get the hell home."[22]

"The waiting for history to be made was most difficult," Pvt. Clair Galdonik recalled. "I spent much time in prayer. Being cooped up made it worse. Like everyone else, I was seasick and the stench of vomit permeated our craft."[23]

The airborne troops had their feet on solid ground and were under cover from the rain, but they too were unhappy. They had got ready, made their last weapons check, packed their equipment, when word came down that the mission was off. Major Howard wrote in his diary: "The weather's broken—what cruel luck. I'm more downhearted than I dare show. Wind and rain, how long will it last? The longer it goes on, the more prepared the Huns will be, the greater the chance of obstacles on the L[anding]Z[one]. Please God it'll clear up tomorrow."[24]

Some of the enlisted men in Howard's company went to the movies. They saw *Stormy Weather* with Lena Horne and Fats Waller. The officers gathered in Lt. David Wood's room and polished off two bottles of whiskey. Twice Lt. Den Brotheridge, commanding the first platoon of D Company, fell into a depressed mood. Wood could hear him reciting a poem that began "If I should die. . . ."[25]

Pvt. Edward Jeziorski of the 507th PIR, 82nd Airborne, checked and rechecked his equipment. "Then, I remember vividly, I took my girlfriend's picture out of my wallet and taped it inside of my helmet, thinking it would be much safer there." When word of the cancellation came down, "some guys were relieved a little bit, but for most of us it was just a true misery to be held over. We were all anxious to make a move."[26]

Sgt. Jerry Eades of the 62nd Armored Field Artillery Battalion, on an LCT, got back to Weymouth late on June 4. "Of course we didn't know what was going on, but everybody was just cussing and raising Cain about another dry run. Here they had wasted another day." Sergeant Eades was Regular Army. He knew the Army had its ways, that "hurry up and wait" was the lot of the soldier, so he told one of his privates, "What the hell, we have a lot of days to waste."[27]

Lt. James Edward of the 115th Regiment got back to port in

Plymouth that afternoon. "This presented a sight not to be forgotten, just wall-to-wall ships, tied up together for lack of space. What a target, if only the Germans had known."[28]

Actually, there was one German raid that night. A squadron of four German bombers braved the storm and flew over Poole, also jammed with ships and craft. Lt. Eugene Bernstein, commanding an LCT(R), recalled that these improbable strays "were greeted by a bombardment from the ships that must have amazed them. The sky was ablaze with antiaircraft fire."[29]

Rommel spent the day on the road. He arrived in Herrlingen in time to go for a walk in the twilight with Lucie. She was trying out her new shoes, her husband's birthday present. General Salmuth of the Fifteenth Army was hunting in the Ardennes. General Dollmann of the Seventh Army was on the road to Rennes, to get ready for the map exercise scheduled for June 6. General Feuchtinger of 21st Panzer Division, accompanied by his operations officer, was on his way to Paris to visit his girlfriend. The Germans had penetrated some of the Resistance groups in France and were picking up a few of the coded phrases being broadcast to the Resistance telling the groups to prepare to go into action, but there had been so many false alarms in May, the tides in the Strait of Dover were not right, and the weather was closing in so fast that they gave the messages no great credence. As one of Rundstedt's intelligence officers put it, it would be absurd for the Allies to announce their invasion in advance over the BBC.[30] Before leaving for Rennes, General Dollmann canceled a planned alert for the night, feeling that the weather precluded an invasion. On many previous nights in May, his troops had been on full alert.

A part of the 2nd Ranger Battalion was on board an old Channel steamer, the *Prince Charles* (the ship had carried rangers into the Anzio beachhead in Italy in January). It spent the day circling off the Isle of Wight. The British skipper told Lieutenant Kerchner, "They're gonna have to run this thing shortly, or we'll have to go back. We're running out of food and fuel." According to Kerchner, "The British food wasn't all that good, so that didn't worry us too much, but the fuel did."[31]

It worried Admiral Ramsay even more. When Eisenhower had decided to postpone, the admiral had warned the supreme commander that no second postponement could be made to the 7th because the fleet would have to refuel. That meant Overlord had to go on June 6 or Eisenhower would have to accept a fortnight's postponement for the next favorable tide, on June 19.

That evening, June 4, Eisenhower met in the mess room at Southwick House with Montgomery, Tedder, Smith, Ramsay, Leigh-Mallory, Bradley, Gen. Kenneth Strong (SHAEF G-2), and various other high- ranking staff officers. The wind and rain rattled the windowpanes in the French doors in staccato sounds. The mess room was large, with a heavy table at one end and easy chairs at the other. Coffee was served and there was desultory conversation.

At 2130 Stagg came in with the latest weather report. He had good news; he said he anticipated a break in the storm. General Strong recalled that at Stagg's prediction "A cheer went up. You never heard middle-aged men cheer like that!"[32] The rain that was then pouring down, Stagg continued, would stop before daybreak. There would be thirty-six hours of more or less clear weather. Winds would moderate. The bombers and fighters ought to be able to operate on Monday night, June 5–6, although they would be hampered by scattered clouds.

When he heard that, Leigh-Mallory lost his enthusiasm. He urged postponement to June 19. Eisenhower began pacing the room, head down, chin on his chest, hands clasped behind his back.

Suddenly he shot his chin out at Smith. "What do you think?"

"It's a helluva gamble but it's the best possible gamble," Smith replied.

Eisenhower nodded, paced some more, stopped, looked at Tedder and asked his opinion. Tedder thought it "chancy" and wanted to postpone. Again Eisenhower nodded, paced, stopped, turned to Montgomery and asked, "Do you see any reason for not going Tuesday?" Montgomery looked Eisenhower in the eye and replied, "I would say—Go!"

The high command of the AEF was split. Only Eisenhower could decide. Smith was struck by the "loneliness and isolation of a commander at a time when such a momentous decision was to be taken by him, with full knowledge that failure or success rests on his individual decision." Eisenhower paced, chin tucked on his chest. He stopped and remarked, "The question is just how long can you hang this operation on the end of a limb and let it hang there?"

No one spoke up to answer that question. Eisenhower resumed pacing. The only sounds in the room were the rattling of the French doors and the rain. It hardly seemed possible that an amphibious attack could be launched in such weather. At 2145 hours, Eisenhower gave his decision: "I am quite positive that the order must be given."[33]

Ramsay rushed out to give the order to the fleet. Eisenhower drove back to his trailer to catch some sleep. By 2300 hours every vessel in the fleet had received its order to resume sailing. D-Day would be June 6, 1944. By midnight, June 4/5, the convoys began forming up. Admiral Ramsay issued an order of the day to every officer and man in his fleet: "It is our privilege to take part in the greatest amphibious operation in history. . . .

"The hopes and prayers of the free world and of the enslaved people of Europe will be with us and we cannot fail them. . . .

"I count on every man to do his utmost to ensure the success of this great enterprise. . . . Good luck to you all and Godspeed."[34]

Eisenhower woke at 0330 hours, June 5. The wind was shaking his trailer. The rain seemed to be traveling in horizontal streaks. According to Stagg, the rain should have been letting up. He dressed and gloomily drove through a mile of mud to Southwick House for the last weather meeting. It was still not too late to call off the operation, to have the fleet return to safe harbor and try again on June 19—and if the storm continued, that would have to be done.

In the mess room, steaming hot coffee helped shake the gray mood and unsteady feeling, but as Eisenhower recalled, "The weather was terrible. Southwick House was shaking. Oh, it was really storming."

Stagg came in and to Eisenhower's delight "He had a little grin on his face. He never laughed very much. He was a fine man. And he said, 'Well, I'll give you some good news.' "

He was even more certain than he had been five hours earlier that the storm would break before dawn. But the bad news was that good weather was only likely through Tuesday; Wednesday could be rough again. That raised the danger that the first waves would get ashore but the follow-up units would not.

Eisenhower asked for opinions, again pacing, shooting out his chin. Montgomery still wanted to go, as did Smith. Ramsay was concerned about proper spotting for naval gunfire but thought the risk worth taking. Tedder was reluctant. Leigh-Mallory still thought air conditions were below the acceptable minimum.

The ships were sailing into the Channel. If they were to be called back, it had to be done now. The supreme commander was the only man who could do it.

He resumed pacing. Some of those in the room thought he paced for as long as five minutes. Eisenhower thought it was about forty-five seconds: "I'm sure it wasn't five minutes," he later said. "Five minutes under such conditions would seem like a year." He reviewed in his mind the alternatives. If Stagg was wrong, at best the AEF would be landing seasick men without air cover or an accurate naval bombardment. But to postpone again would be agonizing and dangerous. The men had been briefed; they could not be held on their transports and landing craft for two weeks; the risk that the Germans would penetrate the secret of Overlord would be very high.

Typically, Eisenhower's concern was with the men. "Don't forget," he said in an interview twenty years later, "some hundreds of thousands of men were down here around Portsmouth, and many of them had already been loaded for some time, particularly those who were going to make the initial assault. Those people in the ships and ready to go were in cages, you might say. You couldn't call them anything else. They were fenced in. They were crowded up, and everybody was unhappy."

Eisenhower went on, "Goodness knows, those fellows meant a lot to me. But these are the decisions that have to be made when you're in a war. You say to yourself, I'm going to do something that will be to my country's advantage for the least cost. You can't say without any cost. You know you're going to lose some of them, and it's very, very difficult."

He stopped pacing, faced his subordinates, then said quietly but clearly, "OK, let's go."[35]

And again, cheers rang through Southwick House.[36] Then the commanders rushed from their chairs and dashed outside to get to their command posts. Within thirty seconds the mess room was empty, except for Eisenhower. His isolation was symbolic, for, having given the order, he was now powerless. As he put it, "That's the most terrible time for a senior commander. He has done all that he can do, all the planning and so on. There's nothing more that he can do."[37]

Eisenhower fortified himself with coffee and breakfast, then went down to Portsmouth to watch the ships starting out and the loading process for the follow-up units. He walked up and down the wharves. Shortly after daylight, the rain stopped, the wind began to die down. At midday he returned to his trailer, where he played a game of checkers on a cracker box with his naval aide, Capt. Harry Butcher. Butcher was winning, two kings to one, when Eisenhower jumped one of his kings and got a draw. He thought that was a good omen.[38]

After lunch, Eisenhower sat at his portable table and scrawled by hand a press release on a pad of paper, to be used if necessary. "Our landings . . . have failed," he began, "and I have withdrawn the troops. My decision to attack at this time and place was based upon the best information available. The troops, the air and the Navy did all that bravery and devotion to duty could do. If any blame or fault attaches to the attempt it is mine alone."[39]

Rommel spent a quiet June 5 with Lucie. He gathered wildflowers for a birthday bouquet. His chief of staff, Gen. Hans Speidel, prepared for a party at the chateau in La Roche-Guyon that evening. He called various friends to invite them, saying in one case, "The Old Man's gone away."[40] General Dollmann was in Rennes, ready for the map exercise to begin early on Tuesday morning. General Feuchtinger was in Paris, where he intended to spend the night with his girlfriend before driving to Rennes the next day. Other division and regiment commanders of Seventh Army had farther to travel and began setting out in the afternoon for Rennes.

On June 5, General Marcks called Col. Frederick von der Heydte to his headquarters. He said he was too worried to leave his troops that night; he would set out for Rennes at first light and wanted Heydte to join him.[41] Just outside Caen, Colonel Luck of 21st Panzer Division gave out orders for a night exercise for one of his companies, "in accordance with the plan of training every company in turn for night action."[42]

(Over in the Cotentin, other companies were also preparing for night exercises. The rifles would be loaded with wooden "bullets." GIs who later picked up clips of this "ammunition" were furious with the Germans. The GIs believed that the wooden bullets were designed to inflict horrible wounds and were a monstrous violation of the laws of warfare. Actually, the wood was soft balsa that would not penetrate a body but would indicate where the bullet hit.)

In Berchtesgaden, Hitler had a routine day. As Gen. Walter Warlimont, deputy chief of staff to General Jodl, later wrote, "On 5 June 1944 . . . German Supreme Headquarters had not the slightest idea that the decisive event of the war was upon them."[43]

On the afternoon of June 5, the Allied airborne troopers began dressing for battle. Each rifleman carried his M-1 (either broken down in a padded case called a Griswold container or already assembled), 160 rounds of ammunition, two fragmentation hand grenades, a white phosphorus and an orange-colored smoke grenade, and a Gammon grenade (two pounds of plastic explosive, powerful enough to damage a tank). Most carried a pistol—the paratroopers' greatest fear was getting shot out of the sky, next was being caught on the ground at the moment of landing, before they could put their rifles into operation—plus a knife and a bayonet. An unwelcome surprise was an order to carry a Mark IV antitank mine, weighing about ten pounds. The only place to fit it was in the musette bag, which led to considerable bitching and rearrangement of loads.

Machine gunners carried their weapons broken down, and extra belts of ammunition. Mortars, bazookas, and radios were rolled into A-5 equipment bundles with cargo chutes attached. Every man carried three days' worth of field rations and, of course, two or three cartons of cigarettes. One sergeant carried along a baseball. He wrote on it "To hell with you, Hitler," and said he intended to drop it when his plane got over France (he did).[44] There were gas masks, an ideal place to carry an extra carton of cigarettes (Capt. Sam Gibbons of the 501st PIR stuck two cans of Schlitz beer in his).[45] The men had first-aid kits with bandages, sulfa tablets, and two morphine Syrettes, "one for pain and two for eternity." They were also handed a child's toy cricket with the instructions that it could be used in lieu of the normal challenge and password. One click-click was to be answered with two click-clicks.

Pathfinders would go first to mark the drop zone with a gadget called the Eureka/Rebecca Radar Beacon System, which could send a signal up to the lead C-47 in each flight. Cpl. Frank Brumbaugh, a pathfinder with the 508th PIR, had not only the sixty-five-pound Eureka to carry, but two containers with carrier pigeons. After he set up his Eureka, he was supposed to make a note to that effect and put it in the capsule on the first pigeon's leg, then turn it loose. He was told to release the second pigeon at 0630 with information on how things were going. But when he got to the marshaling area, he discovered he had no way to feed or water the pigeons, so he let them go. Stripped, Brumbaugh weighed 137 pounds. With all his equipment, including his main and reserve chutes, he weighed 315 pounds.[46]

Around 2000 hours, Axis Sally, the "Bitch of Berlin," came on the radio. "Good evening, 82nd Airborne Division," she said. "Tomorrow morning the blood from your guts will grease the bogey wheels on our tanks." It bothered some of the men; others reassured them—she had been saying something similar for the previous ten days.[47]

Still, it made men think. Pvt. John Delury of the 508th PIR talked to his friend Frank Tremblay about their chances of coming through alive. "He thought he'd get a slight wound and survive. I thought I was going to be killed. That was the last time I saw him."[48]

Pvt. Tom Porcella, also of the 508th, was torturing himself with thoughts of killing other human beings (this was common; the chaplains worked overtime assuring soldiers that to kill for their country was not a sin). "Kill or be killed," Porcella said to himself. "Here I am, brought up as a good Christian, obey this and do that. The Ten Commandments say, 'Thou shalt not kill.' There is something wrong with the Ten Commandments, or there is something wrong with the rules of the world today. They teach us the Ten Commandments and then they send us out to war. It just doesn't make sense."[49]

When every man was ready, the regiments gathered around their commanders for a last word. Most COs stuck to basics— assemble quickly was the main point—but one or two added a pep talk. The most famous was delivered by Col. Howard "Jumpy" Johnson, in command of the 501st PIR. Every man in the regiment remembered it vividly and could quote word for word his conclusion. As Lt. Carl Cartledge described Johnson's talk, "He gave a great battle speech, saying victory and liberation and death to the enemy and some of us would die and peace cost a price and so on. Then he said, 'I want to shake the hand of each one of you tonight, so line up.' And with that, he reached down, pulled his knife from his boot and raised it high above his head, promising us in a battle cry: 'Before the dawn of another day, I'll sink this knife into the heart of the foulest bastard in Nazi land!' A resounding yell burst forth from all 2,000 of us as we raised our knives in response."[50]

After the regimental meetings, the companies grouped

around their COs and platoon leaders for a final word. The officers gave out the challenge, password, and response: "Flash," "Thunder," and "Welcome." "Welcome" was chosen because the Germans would pronounce it "Velcom." When Capt. Charles Shettle of the 506th PIR gave out the signals, Dr. Samuel Feiler, the regimental dental officer who had volunteered to accompany the assault echelon, approached him. Feiler was a German Jew who had escaped Berlin in 1938. "Captain Shettle," Feiler asked, "*Vat* do I do?"

"Doc," Shettle replied, "when you land, don't open your mouth. Take along some extra crickets and if challenged, snap twice." Later, as Shettle was inspecting each planeload prior to takeoff, he found Feiler with crickets strapped to both arms, both legs, and an extra supply in his pockets.[51]

At about 1900 hours, General Eisenhower paid a visit to the 101st Airborne Division at Greenham Common. He circulated among the men, ostensibly to boost their morale, but as Lt. Wallace Strobel of the 502nd PIR noted, "I honestly think it was his morale that was improved by being with us." Eisenhower told Capt. L. "Legs" Johnson, "I've done all I can, now it is up to you."[52] He told a group of enlisted men not to worry, that they had the best equipment and leaders in the world, with a vast force coming in behind them. A sergeant from Texas piped up, "Hell, we ain't worried, General. It's the Krauts that ought to be worrying now."[53]

With one group, Eisenhower asked, "Is there anyone here from Kansas?" Pvt. Sherman Oyler of Topeka replied, "I'm from Kansas, sir."

"What's your name, son?"

Oyler was so stricken by being addressed directly by the supreme commander that he froze up and forgot his name. After an embarrassing pause, his buddies shouted, "Tell him your name, Oyler."[54] Eisenhower gave him a thumbs up and said, "Go get 'em, Kansas."

The supreme commander turned to Lieutenant Strobel, who had a sign hanging around his neck with the number 23 on it, indicating that he was jumpmaster for plane number 23, and asked his name and where he was from.

- "Strobel, sir. Michigan."

"Oh yes, Michigan. Great fishing there. I like it." Eisenhower then asked Strobel if he was ready. Strobel replied that they had all been well prepared, well briefed, and were ready. He added that he thought it wouldn't be too much of a problem. Someone called out, "Now quit worrying, General, we'll take care of this thing for you."[55]

At approximately 2200 hours, as the daylight began to fade, the order rang out, "Chute up." Each man began the tedious task of buckling on his parachutes and trying to find an empty place to hang or tie on the small mountain of equipment he was carrying into combat. With everything strapped into place, many men found it impossible to take a last-minute pee. They marched to their planes and got their first look at the C-47s' "war paint," three bands of white painted around the fuselage and wings. (Every Allied plane involved in D-Day had been thus painted in the previous two days, using up all the white paint in England. The purpose was recognition; in Sicily, Allied ships and troops had fired on their own planes.)

Pvt. John Richards of the 508th looked at his C-47 and noted that it had a picture of a devil holding a girl in a bathing suit sitting on a tray, with an inscription saying "Heaven can wait." He thought to himself, Let's hope so.[56]

"Dutch" Schultz of the 505th, who had managed to gamble away his $2,500 in winnings, still had Jerry Columbi's watch, which he had taken in collateral for a $25 loan. It was Columbi's high-school graduation present with an inscription on the back from his parents. Columbi was in another stick. Schultz went over to him to hand back the watch, saying, "Here's your watch back, Jerry. You owe me some money and don't you forget to pay me."[57]

The 505th was at Spanhoe airfield. As Schultz was lining up to be helped into his C-47 (the men were too heavily loaded to make it into the plane on their own), he heard an explosion. A Gammon grenade carried by one of the men of Headquarters Company, 1st Battalion, had gone off. It set fire to the plane and killed three men, wounding ten others. Two unhurt survivors were assigned to another plane; they both died in combat before dawn.

A bit shaken, Schultz found his place on the plane, "and the first thing I did was reach for my rosary, having been raised a Catholic boy I had great faith in the efficacy of prayers to the Blessed Mother. And I proceeded to say one rosary after another, promising the Blessed Mother that I would never, never violate the Sixth Commandment again."[58]

As the twilight turned to darkness, the last men got on board

General Dwight David Eisenhower, Supreme Commander Allied Expeditionary Force.

Field Marshal Erwin Rommel on an inspection trip to the Atlantic Wall, early May 1944. "Our only possible chance will be at the beaches," he declared after taking command of Army Group B in France in January. He was a whirlwind of activity, full of determination.

EISENHOWER CENTER

Rommel ordered mines of all types, as well as barbed wire and wooden and metal obstacles, placed along the beaches. Here German troops run for cover as an Allied reconnaissance aircraft flies low over the beach. By mid-May a half-million obstacles were in place.

Belgian gates were underwater at high tide, topped with mines. These were piled up by American bulldozers on Utah Beach on June 8.

The Germans poured millions of tons of concrete into the Atlantic Wall. This fortified position, at St.-Marcouf behind Utah Beach, had steel-reinforced concrete walls thirteen feet thick. Despite furious air and naval attacks it was still firing on D-Day plus two.

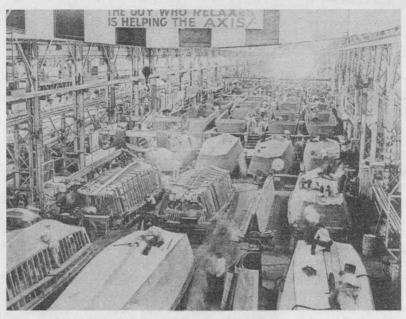

To attack the Atlantic Wall, the Allies needed assault landing craft. Andrew Higgins of New Orleans designed the LCVP "Higgins boat" and produced 20,000 of them, one of the great industrial feats of the war.

There were other production miracles. Here U.S. Army Air Force gliders arrive in England created in pars (foreground), are uncrated and have their fuselages put together (center), and have their wings attached (top) to complete the assembly.

All kinds of special craft were designed for D-Day. These are American-made "Ducks," amphibious vehicles, being checked out after arrival in England.

American troops got to England in every kind of ship imaginable. The lucky ones rode on the *Queen Mary*, shown here during a lifeboat drill. In the first half of 1944, the *Queen Mary* and the *Queen Elizabeth* brought more than a quarter-million U.S. Army troops to England.

The members of Yanks in Britain grew steadily, disrupting British life in many ways—but some things stayed the same. May 1944: Americans on maneuver, on Rockstone Road, Bassett, Southampton, while British civilians carry on.

U.S. ARMY SIGNAL CORPS

Training was intense and realistic. Here Supreme Commander Dwight Eisenhower and ground commander General Bernard Montgomery watch a tank exercise in March 1944.

While the assault forces trained, the air forces pounded the French railway system. Here B-26 Marauders of the U.S. Ninth Air Force attack railway yards in northern France, May 2, 1944, as a part of the "Transportation Plan." By June 6 over 76,000 tons of bombs had been dropped on rail targets.

IMPERIAL WAR MUSEUM

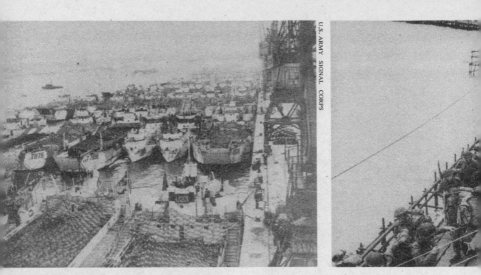

Above left, landing craft at Southampton, June 1, 1944, part of the enormous buildup in southern England for the invasion. These are LCTs (Landing Craft Tanks) and LCHs (Landing Craft headquarters).

Above right, British Royal Engineers coming aboard an LCI (Landing Craft Infantry).

Below, American LSTs (Landing Ship Tanks) at Brixham loading up for the invasion, May 27, 1944.

Above right, GIs line up for cigarettes just before loading up on the landing craft. One soldier said, "No, thanks. I don't smoke." "You might as well take them," the quartermaster replied, "because by the time you get where you're going, you will." He was right.

Below, Men from the 4th Division, U.S. First Army, loading up on an LCI, June 2. The weather was fine, although the wind was coming up.

A prayer service on an LCI. "Priests were in their heyday," a coastguardsman recalled. "I even saw Jews go and take communion." The censor has blacked out the division shoulder patches.

Ike with the 101st Airborne at Greenham Common, 1900 hours, June 5. Lt. Wallace Strobel has the card carrying his plane number, 23, around his neck. "Go get 'em," Ike is saying.

Opposite top, LCT 763 moves toward shore as USS *Arkansas* opens fire with her 12-inch guns. *Arkansas*, commissioned in 1912, was one of the "old ladies." "This was more firepower than I've ever heard in my life," said a correspondent who later covered Korea and Vietnam. "Most of us felt that this was the moment of our life, the crux of it." General Omar Bradley said of the initial salvo from the warships, "I never heard anything like it in my life."

Opposite bottom, USS *Nevada* opens fire with her ten 14-inch guns. *Nevada* had survived Pearl Harbor, the only battleship to get underway on December 7.

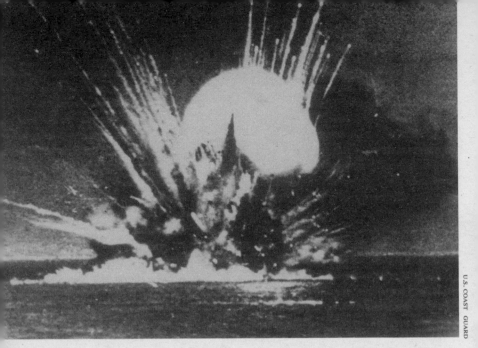

U.S. COAST GUARD

At 0537 a half-dozen German E-boats made the only *Kriegsmarine* attack of D-Day when they dashed in as close to the Allied fleet as they dared and unleashed a volley of torpedoes. The only hit was on *Svenner*, a Norwegian destroyer. "A flash of explosion occurred amidships," an observer recalled, "followed by . . . the burst of fire and smoke that shot high into the air. *Svenner* broke amidship and sank.

A weapons carrier moves through the surf to Utah Beach, its antiaircraft gun pointed skyward. No German planes appeared.

U.S. ARMY SIGNAL CORPS

Utah Beach, seen from above about midmorning, June 6. Thanks to the air and naval bombardment, and to the airborne troops behind the German lines, at Utah the assault went close to schedule.

Men from the 4th Infantry Division moving ashore at Utah, late afternoon, June 6.

Although the landing at Utah was relatively easy, there were casualties. Here medics give first aid to wounded troops at Les Dunes de Madeleine.

Gliders bringing in reinforcements and supplies to the 82nd and 101st Airborne divisions behind Utah Beach on the afternoon of June 6, over troops from the 4th Division at Les Dunes de Madeleine.

There are no photographs of the airborne night landings and action, and precious few of the paratroopers' fights on June 6. Here some Screaming Eagles of the 101st Airborne meet some local belles in Ste.-Marie-du-Mont, behind Utah Beach, the morning of June 7.

Opposite top, a Higgins boat set afire by a German machine gun. The coxswain, Coastguardsman Delba Nivens of Amarillo, Texas, managed to get the craft safely ashore, unload the men, put out the fire, and return to the transport for another load.

Opposite bottom, Unidentified troops in a Higgins boat moving into Omaha Beach, about midmorning, June 6.

U.S. COAST GUARD

THREE PHOTOS: U.S. ARMY SIGNAL CORPS

Robert Capa of *Life* magazine went in with the second wave at Easy Red sector, Omaha Beach, with Company E, 16th Regiment. He took 106 pictures, got off the beach and back to Portsmouth late on June 6, then took the train to London and turned in the film for development. The darkroom assistant was so eager to see the photos that he turned on too much heat while drying the negatives. The emulsions melted and ran down. Only eight photos survived. Here are two of them

The first waves of GIs at Omaha were hit by a tremendous barrage of machine-gun and rifle bullets, 88mm and 75mm cannon, exploding mines, mortars, and hand grenades. Company A of the 116th Regiment was the first ashore—and took more than 90 percent casualties. Here a shell-shocked soldier of the 16th Regiment collapses by the chalk cliff below Colleville.

Men from the 16th Regiment under the cliff below Colleville. At this point, about 0800, the assault plan at Omaha was dead, and the troops—who had lost their weapons in getting ashore—were leaderless and dispirited.

their planes. Eisenhower was out on the runway, calling out "Good luck!" He noticed a short private, in Eisenhower's words "more equipment than soldier," who snapped him a salute. Eisenhower returned it. Then the private turned to the east and called out, "Look out, Hitler. Here we come!"[59]

The pilots started their engines. A giant cacophony of sound engulfed the airfield as each C-47 in its turn lurched into line on the taxi strip. At the head of the runway, the pilots locked the brakes and ran up the engines until they screamed. Then, at ten-second intervals, they released the brakes and started down the runway, slowly at first, gathering speed, so overloaded that they barely made it into the sky.

When the last plane roared off, Eisenhower turned to his driver, Kay Summersby. She saw tears in his eyes. He began to walk slowly toward his car. "Well," he said quietly, "it's on."[60]

Before going to bed, Admiral Ramsay made a final entry in his handwritten diary: "Monday, June 5, 1944. Thus has been made the vital & crucial decision to stage the great enterprise which [shall?], I hope, be the immediate means of bringing about the downfall of Germany's fighting power & Nazi oppression & an early cessation of hostilities.

"I am not under [any] delusions as to the risks involved in this most difficult of all operations. . . . Success will be in the balance. We must trust in our invisible assets to tip the balance in our favor.

"We shall require all the help that God can give us & I cannot believe that this will not be forthcoming."[61]

Tired as he must have been, Ramsay caught the spirit and soul of the great undertaking perfectly, especially in his hope for what the results would be for occupied Europe and the world, his recognition that the enterprise was fraught with peril, and his confidence that God was blessing this cause.

11

CRACKING THE ATLANTIC WALL

The Airborne into Normandy

THE PATHFINDERS went in first. They preceded the main body of troops by an hour or so. Their mission was to mark the drop zones with automatic direction-finder radios, Eureka sets, and Holophane lights formed into Ts on the ground. But a cloud bank forced pilots to either climb above it or get below it, so the pathfinders jumped from too high or too low an altitude. Further, antiaircraft fire coming from the ground caused pilots to take evasive action, throwing them off course. As a consequence, of the eighteen American pathfinder teams, only one landed where it was supposed to. One team landed in the Channel.

Sgt. Elmo Jones of the 505th PIR jumped at 300 feet or so. Just before exiting the C-47 he said a brief prayer: "Lord, Thy will be done. But if I'm to die please help me die like a man." His chute popped open, he looked up to check the canopy, and just that quick his feet hit the ground. It was a "soft" landing. (One advantage of a night jump: the men could not see the ground so they did not tense up just before hitting it.) His chute settled over his head "and the first thing that I thought without even trying to get out of my parachute was, 'Damn, I just cracked the Atlantic Wall.' "

Jones assembled his team, got the seven men with the lights in place for their T, told them not to turn on until they could hear the planes coming in, set up his radio, and began sending out his ADF signal. He was one of the few pathfinders in the right place.[1]

•   •

Maj. John Howard's D Company of the Ox and Bucks was the first to go into action as a unit. Glider pilot Sgt. Jim Wallwork put his Horsa glider down exactly where Howard wanted it to land, beside the Orne Canal bridge. Lt. Brotheridge led 1st Platoon over the bridge. The Horsas carrying 2nd and 3rd platoons landed right behind Wallwork. Within minutes the men secured the area around the bridge, routing about fifty German defenders in the process. Two other platoons landed near the Orne River bridge and secured it. By 0021, June 6, five minutes after landing, D Company had taken its objectives. It was a brilliant feat of arms.[2]

As the pathfinders were setting up and Howard's men were carrying out their *coup de main* operation, the 13,400 American and nearly 7,000 British paratroopers were coming on. The Americans were following a precise route, marked at ten-mile intervals with Eureka sets and at thirty-mile intervals with aerial beacons over England. Thirty miles over the Channel a British patrol boat, "Gallup," marked the path. It was thirty additional miles to checkpoint "Hoboken," marked by a light from a British submarine. At that point the aircraft made a sharp turn to the southeast, crossed between the Channel Islands of Jersey and Guernsey (occupied by the Germans, who were sending up some flak), and headed toward their drop zones in the Cotentin. All planes were maintaining radio silence, so none of the pilots were forewarned by the pathfinder groups about the cloud bank over the Cotentin.

In the Dakotas, the men prepared themselves for "the jump in which your troubles begin *after* you hit the ground." This was the $10,000 jump (the GIs were required to buy a $10,000 life insurance policy). The flight over England and out over the Channel was a period—two hours and more—that came between the end of training, preparation, and briefing and the beginning of combat. Maj. Gen. Matthew Ridgway, commanding the 82nd Airborne, noted that "the men sat quietly, deep in their own thoughts."[3]

Lt. Eugene Brierre of Division headquarters was an aide to Maj. Gen. Maxwell Taylor, commanding the 101st Airborne. This would be Taylor's qualifying jump (five jumps were required to qualify for paratrooper wings), but he wasn't in the least excited. He had brought some pillows along and lay them on the floor of the plane. Brierre helped him get out of his chute; Taylor stretched out on the pillows and got in a solid hour's sleep. When Brierre woke him, it took five minutes to get the chute back on.[4]

Pvt. Dwayne Burns of the 508th PIR recalled, "Here we sat, each man alone in the dark. These men around me were the best friends I will ever know. I wondered how many would die before the sun came up. 'Lord, I pray, please let me do everything right. Don't let me get anybody killed and don't let me get killed either. I really think I'm too young for this.' "[5]

Pvt. Ken Russell of the 505th had just made it onto his C-47. Two weeks earlier he had been running a high fever, a result of his vaccinations, and was sent to a hospital. On June 4 he still had a high fever, but "like everyone else, I had been looking forward to D-Day since 1940—when I was still in grammar school. Now I was so afraid I would miss it." He begged his way out of the hospital and managed to rejoin his company on June 5. Flying over the Channel, he was struck by the thought that his high-school class back in Tennessee was graduating that night.[6]

Like many of the Catholic troopers, "Dutch" Schultz was "totally engrossed in my rosaries." Clayton Storeby was sitting next to George Dickson, who "was going around that rosary, giving a lot of Hail Marys. After about ten minutes, it seemed like it was helping him, so I said, 'George, when you're through with that, would you loan it to a buddy?' "[7]

"It was a time of prayer," Pvt. Harry Reisenleiter of the 508th PIR recalled, "and I guess we all made some rash promises to God." He said that so far as he could tell everyone was afraid— "fear of being injured yourself, fear of having to inflict injury on other people to survive, and the most powerful feeling of all, fear of being afraid."[8]

The pilots were afraid. For most of the pilots of Troop Carrier Command this was their first combat mission. They had not been trained for night flying, or for flak or bad weather. Their C-47s were designed to carry cargo or passengers. They were neither armed nor armored. Their gas tanks were neither protected nor self-sealing.

The possibility of a midair collision was on every pilot's mind. The pilots were part of a gigantic air armada: it took 432 C-47s to carry the 101st Airborne to Normandy, about the same number for the 82nd. They were flying in a V-of-Vs formation, stretched out across the sky, 300 miles long, nine planes wide, without radio communication. Only the lead pilot in each serial of forty-five had a Eureka set, with a show of lights from the Plexiglas astrodome for guidance for the following planes. The planes were

100 feet from wingtip to wingtip in their groups of nine, 1,000 feet from one group to another, with no lights except little blue dots on the tail of the plane ahead. That was a tight formation for night flying in planes that were sixty-five feet long and ninety-five feet from wingtip to wingtip.

They crossed the Channel at 500 feet or less to escape German radar detection, then climbed to 1,500 feet to escape antiaircraft batteries on the Channel Islands (which did fire on them, without effect, except to wake sleeping troopers—the airsickness pills the medics had handed out at the airfields had caused many men, including Ken Russell, to doze off). As they approached the Cotentin coast, they descended to 600 feet or so, the designated jump altitude (designed to reduce the time the trooper was helplessly descending).

When they crossed the coastline they hit the cloud bank and lost their visibility altogether. The pilots instinctively separated, some descending, some rising, all peeling off to the right or left to avoid a midair collision. When they emerged from the clouds, within seconds or at the most minutes, they were hopelessly separated. Lt. Harold Young of the 326th Parachute Engineers recalled that as his plane came out of the clouds, "We were all alone. I remember my amazement. Where had all those C-47s gone?"[9]

Simultaneously, to use the words of many of the pilots, "all hell broke loose." Searchlights, tracers, and explosions filled the sky. Pilot Sidney Ulan of the 99th Troop Carrier Squadron was chewing gum, "and the saliva in my mouth completely dried up from the fright. It seemed almost impossible to fly through that wall of fire without getting shot down, but I had no choice. There was no turning back."[10]

They could speed up, which most of them did. They were supposed to throttle back to ninety miles per hour or less, to reduce the opening shock for the paratroopers, but ninety miles per hour at 600 feet made them easy targets for the Germans on the ground, so they pushed the throttle forward and sped up to 150 miles per hour, meanwhile either descending to 300 feet or climbing to 2,000 feet and more. They twisted and turned, spilling their passengers and cargo. They got hit by machine-gun fire, 20mm shells, and the heavier 88mm shells. They saw planes going down to their right and left, above and below them. They saw planes explode. They had no idea where they were, except that they were over the Cotentin.

The pilots had turned on the red lights over the doors when

they crossed the Channel Islands. That was the signal to the jump-masters to order their men to "Stand up and hook up." The pilots turned on the green light when they guessed that they were some-where near the drop zone. That was the signal to go.

Many troopers saw planes below them as they jumped. At least one plane was hit by an equipment bundle; it tore off almost three feet of wing tip. Virtually every plane got hit by something. One pilot broke radio silence to call out in desperation, "I've got a paratrooper hung up on my wing." Another pilot came on the air with advice: "Slow down and he'll slide off."[11]

"In this frightful madness of gunfire and sky mixed with parachuting men and screaming planes," pilot Chuck Ratliff re-membered, "we found we had missed the drop zone and were now back out over the water. We were dumbfounded. What to do?"

Ratliff "turned that sucker around and circled back." He dropped to 600 feet. The jumpmaster pressed his way into the cockpit to help locate the drop zone. He saw what he thought was it. "We pulled back throttles to a semistall," Ratliff said, "hit the green light and the troopers jumped out into the black night. We dove that plane to 100 feet off the ground and took off for England, full bore, like a scalded dog."[12]

Sgt. Charles Bortzfield of the 100th Troop Carrier Squad-ron was standing near the jump door, wearing a headset for the intercom radio, passing on information to the jumpmaster. As the green light went on he was hit by shrapnel. As he fell from four wounds in his arm and hand he broke his leg. One trooper asked him, just before jumping, "Are you hit?"

"I think so," Bortzfield replied.

"Me too," the trooper called over his shoulder as he leaped into the night.*

In the body of the planes the troopers were terrified, not at what was ahead of them but because of the hopeless feeling of getting shot at and tumbled around and being unable to do any-

* Bortzfield's plane had to make an emergency landing in England, with the left engine gone and no hydraulic pressure left. An ambulance picked him up on the runway and rushed him to a hospital. He recalled, "I was a real celebrity because at this moment I was their only patient. All their patients had been evacuated and they were waiting for D-Day casualties. I was in the ward by 0600 when the boys were hitting the beaches. The doctors really interrogated me" (Charles Bortzfield oral history, EC).

thing about it. As the planes twisted and turned, climbed or dove, many sticks (one planeload of paratroopers) were thrown to the floor in a hopeless mess of arms, legs, and equipment. Meanwhile, bullets were ripping through the wings and fuselage. To Pvt. John Fitzgerald of the 502nd PIR, "they made a sound like corn popping as they passed through." Lt. Carl Cartledge likened the sound to "rocks in a tin can."[13]

Out the open doors, the men could see tracers sweeping by in graceful, slow-motion arcs. They were orange, red, blue, yellow. They were frightening, mesmerizing, beautiful. Most troopers who tried to describe the tracers used some variation of "the greatest Fourth of July fireworks display I ever saw." They add that when they remembered that only one in six of the bullets coming up at them were tracers, they couldn't see how they could possibly survive the jump.

For Pvt. William True of the 506th, it was "unbelievable" that there were people down there "shooting at *me!* Trying to kill Bill True!" Lt. Parker Alford, an artillery officer assigned to the 501st, was watching the tracers. "I looked around the airplane and saw some kid across the aisle who grinned. I tried to grin back but my face was frozen."[14] Private Porcella's heart was pounding. "I was so scared that my knees were shaking and just to relieve the tension, I had to say something, so I shouted, 'What time is it.' " Someone called back, "0130."[15]

The pilots turned on the red light and the jumpmaster shouted the order "Stand up and hook up." The men hooked the lines attached to the backpack covers of their main chutes to the anchor line running down the middle of the top of the fuselage.

"Sound off for equipment check." From the rear of the plane would come the call, "sixteen OK!" then "fifteen OK!" and so on. The men in the rear began pressing forward. They knew the Germans were waiting for them, but never in their lives had they been so eager to jump out of an airplane.

"Let's go! Let's go!" they shouted, but the jumpmasters held them back, waiting for the green light.

"My plane was bouncing like something gone wild," Pvt. Dwayne Burns of the 508th remembered. "I could hear the machine-gun rounds walking across the wings. It was hard to stand up and troopers were falling down and getting up; some were throwing up. Of all the training we had, there was not anything that had prepared us for this."[16]

In training, the troopers could anticipate the green light; before the pilot turned it on he would throttle back and raise the tail of the plane. Not this night. Most pilots throttled forward and began to dive. "Dutch" Schultz and every man in his stick fell to the floor. They regained their feet and resumed shouting "Let's go!" Sgt. Dan Furlong's plane got hit by three 88mm shells. The first struck the left wing, taking about three feet off the tip. The second hit alongside the door and knocked out the light panel. The third came up through the floor. It blew a hole about two feet across, hit the ceiling, and exploded, creating a hole four feet around, killing three men and wounding four others. Furlong recalled, "Basically the Krauts just about cut that plane in half.

"I was in the back, assistant jumpmaster. I was screaming 'Let's go!' " The troopers, including three of the four wounded men, dove head first out of the plane. The pilot was able to get control of the plane and head back for the nearest base in England for an emergency landing (those Dakotas could take a terrific punishment and still keep flying). The fourth wounded man had been knocked unconscious; when he came to over the Channel he was delirious. He tried to jump out. The crew chief had to sit on him until they landed.[17]

On planes still flying more or less on the level, when the green light went on the troopers set a record for exiting. Still, many of them remembered all their lives their thoughts as they got to the door and leaped out. Eager as they were to go, the sky full of tracers gave them pause. Four men in the 505th, two in the 508th, and one each in the 506th and 507th "refused." They preferred, in John Keegan's words, "to face the savage disciplinary consequences and total social ignominy of remaining with the aeroplane to stepping into the darkness of the Normandy night."[18]

Every other able-bodied man jumped. Pvt. John Fitzgerald of the 502nd had taken a cold shower every morning for two years to prepare himself for this moment. Pvt. Arthur DeFilippo of the 505th could see the tracers coming straight at him "and all I did was pray to God that he would get me down safely and then I would take care of myself."[19] Pvt. John Taylor of the 508th was appalled when he got to the door; his plane was so low that his thought was "We don't need a parachute for this; all we need is a step ladder."[20] Private Oyler, the Kansas boy who had forgotten his name when General Eisenhower spoke to him, remembered his hometown as he got to the door. His thought was "I wish the gang at Wellington High could see me now—at Wellington High."[21]

When Pvt. Len Griffing of the 501st got to the door, "I looked out into what looked like a solid wall of tracer bullets. I remember this as clearly as if it happened this morning. It's engraved in the cells of my brain. I said to myself, 'Len, you're in as much trouble now as you're ever going to be. If you get out of this, nobody can ever do anything to you that you ever have to worry about.' "

At that instant an 88mm shell hit the left wing and the plane went into a sharp roll. Griffing was thrown to the floor, then managed to pull himself up and leap into the night.[22]

Most of the sticks jumped much too low from planes going much too fast. The opening shock was intense. In hundreds if not thousands of cases the troopers swung once, then hit the ground. Others jumped from too high up; for them it seemed an eternity before they hit the ground.

Because of the way his plane rolled, Private Griffing's stick was badly separated. The man who went before him was a half mile back; the man who jumped after Griffing was a half mile forward. "My chute popped open and I was the only parachute in the sky. It took me one hundred years to get down." Below him, a German flak wagon with four 20mm guns was pumping out shells "and I was the only thing they had to shoot at. Tracers went under me and I couldn't help but pull my legs up." The flak wagon kept shooting at him even after he hit the ground. "I would have been hit through sheer Teutonic perseverance if the next flight of planes hadn't arrived and they gave up shooting at me to shoot at them."[23]

Pvt. Fitzgerald "looked up to check my canopy and watched in detached amazement as bullets ripped through my chute. I was mesmerized by the scene around me. Every color of the rainbow was flashing through the sky. Equipment bundles attached to chutes that did not fully open came hurtling past me, helmets that had been ripped off by the opening shock, troopers floated past. Below me, figures were running in all directions. I thought, Christ, I'm going to land right in the middle of a bunch of Germans! My chute floated into the branches of an apple tree and dumped me to the ground with a thud. The trees were in full bloom and added a strange sweet scent to this improbable scene." To Fitzgerald's relief, the "Germans" turned out to be cows running for cover. "I felt a strange surge of elation: I was alive!"[24]

The 506th was supposed to land ten kilometers or so southwest of Ste.-Mère-Église, but a couple of sticks from the regiment came down in the town. It was 0115. A small hay barn on the south side of the church square was on fire, evidently caused by a tracer. Mayor Alexandre Renaud had called out the residents to form a bucket brigade to get water from the town pump to the fire. The German garrison sent out a squad to oversee the infraction of the curfew.

Sgt. Ray Aebischer was the first to hit. He landed in the church square, behind the fire-brigade line and unnoticed by the German guards (the great brass bell in the church tower was ringing to rouse the citizens, drowning out the noise of his landing). He cut himself loose, then began moving slowly toward the church door, hoping to find sanctuary. The door was locked. He crawled around the church to the rear, then along a high cement wall. The Germans began firing, not at him but at his buddies coming down. He saw one man whose chute had caught in a tree get riddled by a machine pistol. Altogether, four men were killed by German fire.[25]

Pvt. Don Davis landed in the church square; he played dead, got rolled over by a suspicious German, and got away with it.* Aebischer meanwhile took advantage of the confusion to make his escape. Within a few minutes, it was quiet again over Ste.-Mère-Église; on the ground the fire-fighting effort resumed. But the German guards were now alert for any further paratroop drops.

Sgt. Carwood Lipton and Lt. Dick Winters of Company E, 506th, landed on the outskirts of the town. Lipton figured out where they were by reading the signpost in the moonlight, one letter at a time. Winters gathered together a group of squad size or less and began hiking for his company's objective, Ste.-Marie-du-Mont.

Winters did not know it, but his CO was dead. Lt. Thomas Meehan and Headquarters Company had been flying in the lead plane in stick 66. It was hit with bullets going through it and out the top, throwing sparks. The plane maintained course and speed for a moment or two, then did a slow wingover to the right. Pilot Frank DeFlita, just behind, remembered that "the plane's landing lights came on, and it appeared they were going to make it, when the plane hit a hedgerow and exploded." There were no survivors.[26]

Sgt. McCallum, one of the pathfinders for the 506th, was on the ground, about ten kilometers from Ste.-Marie-du-Mont. The

---

* Davis was killed a few days later outside Carentan. William True had been in a quonset hut with Davis in England. There were sixteen men in the hut; only three returned unscathed to England in mid-July (William True oral history, EC).

Germans had anticipated that the field he was in might be used as a drop zone, so they had machine guns and mortars around three sides of it. On the fourth side, they had soaked a barn with kerosene. When the planes carrying Capt. Charles Shettle and his company came overhead and the men started jumping out, the Germans set a torch to the barn. It lit up the whole area. As the troopers came down, the Germans commenced firing. Sgt. McCallum said, "I'll never forget the sadness in my heart as I saw my fellow troopers descend into this death trap."

Captain Shettle got down safely, despite mortar shells exploding and tracer bullets crisscrossing the field. Shettle was battalion S-3; the company he had jumped with was supposed to assemble at the barn, but that was obviously impossible; Shettle moved quickly to the alternate assembly point and began blowing his whistle. In a half hour he had fifty men around him—but only fifteen were from the 506th. The others were members of the 501st.

That kind of confusion and mixing of units was going on all over the Cotentin. A single company, E of the 506th, had men scattered from Carentan to Ravenoville, a distance of twenty kilometers. Men of the 82nd were in the 101st drop zone and vice versa. Standard drill for the paratroopers, practiced countless times, was to assemble by "rolling up the stick." The first men out would follow the line of flight of the airplane; the men in the middle would stay put; the last men out would move in the opposite direction from the airplane's route. In practice maneuvers it worked well. In combat that night it worked only for a fortunate few.

Capt. Sam Gibbons of the 501st (later long-term congressman from Florida) was alone for his first hour in France. Finally he saw a figure, clicked his cricket, got a two-click answer, and "suddenly I felt a thousand years younger. Both of us moved forward so we could touch each other. I whispered my name and he whispered his. To my surprise, he was not from my plane. In fact, he was not even from my division."[27]

Lt. Guy Remington fell into the flooded area near the Douve River. He was pulling up the bank when he heard a noise. He froze, pulled his tommy gun, then clicked his cricket. No response. He prepared to fire when he heard a voice saying "friend." He parted some bushes and there was an embarrassed Colonel Johnson, his CO, who explained, "I lost my damn cricket."[28]

Some men were alone all night. "Dutch" Schultz was one of them. When Schultz used his cricket in desperation, hoping to find someone, "I got a machine-gun burst. I brought my M-1 up and pointed it toward the Germans only to discover that I had failed to load my rifle." He crept off, thinking, I'm totally unprepared for this.[29]

Private Griffing recalled, "There were so many clicks and counterclicks that night that nobody could tell who was clicking at whom."[30] Private Storeby landed in a ditch. After cutting himself loose, he crawled to the top and heard a click. Not from a cricket; it was the distinctive sound of someone taking the safety off an M-1. Storeby pulled out his cricket "and I just clicked the living hell out of that cricket, and finally this guy told me to come on out with my hands up. I recognized his voice; it was Harold Conway from Ann Arbor, Michigan. I said, 'I don't have any idea where we are or what we're doing here or nothing.' " They set out to find friends.[31]

In contrast to almost every other battalion, the 2nd of the 505th had an excellent drop. Its pathfinders had landed in the right spot and set up their Eurekas and lights. The lead pilot, in a Dakota carrying the battalion commander, Lt. Col. Benjamin Vandervoort, saw the lighted T exactly where he expected it. At 0145 hours, twenty-seven of the thirty-six sticks of the battalion either hit the drop zone or landed within a mile of it. Vandervoort broke his ankle when he landed; he laced his boot tighter, used his rifle as a crutch, verified his location, and began sending up green flares as a signal for his battalion to assemble on him. Within half an hour he had 600 men around him; no other unit of similar size had so complete an assembly so quickly.

The 2nd Battalion's mission was to secure Neuville-au-Plain, just north of Ste.-Mère-Église. It was a long hike; Vandervoort was much too big a man to be carried; he spotted two sergeants pulling a collapsible ammunition cart. Vandervoort asked if they would mind giving him a lift. One of the sergeants replied that "they hadn't come all the way to Normandy to pull any damn colonel around." Vandervoort noted later, "I persuaded them otherwise."[32]

General Taylor was not as fortunate as Vandervoort. The commander of the 101st landed alone, outside Ste.-Marie-du-Mont. For twenty minutes he wandered around, trying to find his assembly point. He finally encountered his first trooper, a private from the 501st, established identity with his clicker, and hugged the man. A few minutes later Taylor's aide, Lieutenant Brierre, came up. The three-man group wandered around until Taylor, in the dark, physically collided with his artillery commander, Brig. Gen. Anthony McAuliffe. He didn't know where they were either.

Brierre pulled out a flashlight, the generals pulled out a map, the three men ducked into a hedgerow, studied the map, and came to three different conclusions as to where they were.

Lt. Parker Alford and his radio operator (without his radio, lost on the drop, a typical experience) joined Taylor's group. By this time it consisted of two generals, a full colonel, three lieutenant colonels, four lieutenants, several NCO radio operators, and a dozen or so privates. Taylor looked around, grinned, and said, "Never in the annals of warfare have so few been commanded by so many." He decided to set off in a direction that he hoped would take him to his primary objective, the village of Pouppeville, the foot of causeway 1.[33]

Lt. Col. Louis Mendez, commanding the 3rd Battalion of the 508th, was even worse off than Taylor. He jumped at 2,100 feet, "which was too much of a ride. I landed about 0230 and didn't see anybody for five days." In that time he may have killed more of the enemy than any other lieutenant colonel in the war: "I got three Heinies with three shots from my pistol, two Heinies with a carbine, and one Heinie with a hand grenade." He estimated that he walked ninety miles across the western Cotentin looking for another American, without success.[34]

At La Madeleine, in his blockhouse, Lt. Arthur Jahnke was confused. The airplanes overhead did not particularly worry him even though the numbers of planes flying through the night were greater than usual. But what was the meaning of the bursts of automatic and machine-gun fire he was hearing to his rear? Jahnke alerted his men, doubled the guards, and ordered a patrol to go out and reconnoiter.

Simultaneously, Pvt. Louis Merlano of the 101st, second man in his stick, landed on the dunes a few meters away from Jahnke's position. Horrified, he heard the cries of eleven of his comrades as they fell into the Channel and drowned. Half an hour later, the German patrol returned to La Madeleine with nineteen American paratroopers, including Merlano, picked up on the beach. Delighted with his catch, Jahnke tried to telephone his bat-

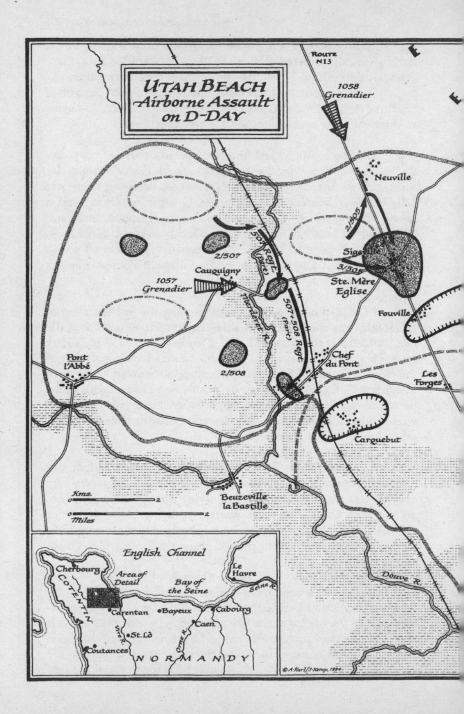

UTAH BEACH
Airborne Assault on D-DAY

ROUTE N13

1058 Grenadier

Neuville

2/505

Sige...

2/507

Cauquigny

1057 Grenadier

507 Regt. (Part)

Merderet R.

507+508 Regt. (Part)

3/505

Ste. Mère Eglise

Fouville

Pont l'Abbé

2/508

Chef du Pont

Les Forges

Carquebut

Kms.
0 — 2

0 — 2
Miles

Beuzeville la Bastille

Douve R.

English Channel

Cherbourg

Area of Detail

Bay of the Seine

Le Havre

Seine R.

COTENTIN

Carentan • Bayeux • Cabourg

Vire R.

Caen

Ome R.

• St. Lô

• Coutances

N O R M A N D Y

© A·Karl/J·Kemp. 1994.

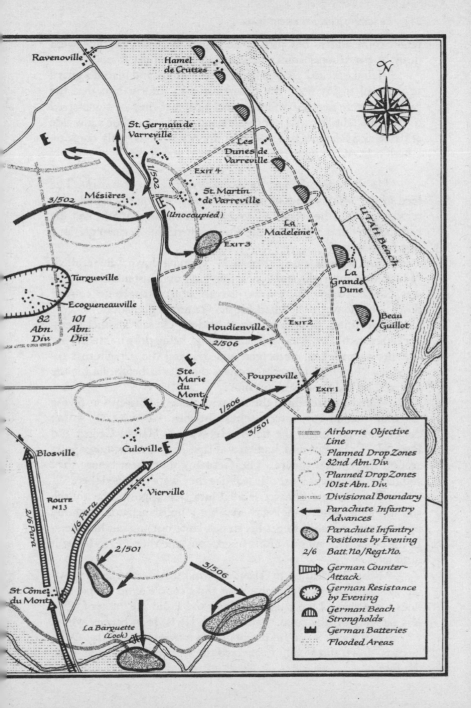

Ravenoville

Hamel
de Cruttes

St. Germain de
Varreville

Les
Dunes de
Varreville

1/502

Exit 4

3/502

Mésières

St. Martin
de Varreville

(Unoccupied)

La
Madeleine

Exit 3

UTAH Beach

Turqueville

La
Grande
Dune

Ecoqueneauville

Beau
Guillot

82
Abn.
Div.

101
Abn.
Div.

Houdienville

Exit 2

2/506

Ste.
Marie
du
Mont

Pouppeville

Exit 1

1/506

3/501

Blosville

Culoville

Vierville

Route
N13

2/6 Para

1/6 Para

2/501

St. Côme
du Mont

3/506

La Barquette
(Lock)

N

Airborne Objective
Line

Planned Drop Zones
82nd Abn. Div.

Planned Drop Zones
101st Abn. Div.

Divisional Boundary

Parachute Infantry
Advances

Parachute Infantry
Positions by Evening

2/6 Batt. No/Regt. No.

German Counter-
Attack

German Resistance
by Evening

German Beach
Strongholds

German Batteries

Flooded Areas

talion commander, but just as he began to report the line went dead. A paratrooper somewhere inland had cut the line.

Jahnke locked his prisoners into a pillbox and placed a guard in front of it. At 0400 the guard came to inform him that the prisoners were nervous and kept insisting that they be transferred to the rear. Jahnke could not understand; there would be a low tide at dawn and Rommel had told him the Allies would only come on a high tide. What were the captured men afraid of?[35]

In Ste.-Mère-Église, the fire was raging out of control. The men of the 506th who had landed in and near the town had scattered. At 0145, the second platoon of F Company, 505th, had the bad luck to jump right over the town, where the German garrison was fully alerted.

Ken Russell was in that stick. "Coming down," he recalled, "I looked to my right and I saw this guy, and instantaneously he was blown away. There was just an empty parachute coming down." Evidently a shell had hit his Gammon grenades.

Horrified, Russell looked to his left. He saw another member of his stick, Pvt. Charles Blankenship, being drawn into the fire (the fire was sucking in oxygen and drawing the parachutists toward it). "I heard him scream once, then again before he hit the fire, and he didn't scream anymore."

The Germans filled the sky with tracers. Russell was trying "to hide behind my reserve chute because we were all sitting ducks." He got hit in the hand. He saw Lt. Harold Cadish and Pvts. H. T. Bryant and Ladislaw Tlapa land on telephone poles around the church square. The Germans shot them before they could cut themselves loose. "It was like they were crucified there."[36]

Pvt. Penrose Shearer landed in a tree opposite the church and was killed while hanging there. Pvt. John Blanchard, also hung up in a tree, managed to get his trench knife out and cut his risers. In the process he cut one of his fingers off "and didn't even know it until later."[37]

Russell jerked on his risers to avoid the fire and came down on the slate roof of the church. "I hit and a couple of my suspension lines went around the church steeple and I slid off the roof." He was hanging off the edge. "And Steele, [Pvt.] John Steele, whom you've heard a lot about [in the book and movie The Longest Day], he came down and his chute covered the steeple." Steele was hit in the foot.

Sgt. John Ray landed in the church square, just past Russell and Steele. A German soldier came around the corner. "I'll never forget him," Russell related. "He was red-haired, and as he came around he shot Sergeant Ray in the stomach." Then he turned toward Russell and Steele and brought his machine pistol up to shoot them. "And Sergeant Ray, while he was dying in agony, he got his .45 out and he shot the German soldier in the back of the head and killed him."

Through all this the church bell was constantly ringing. Russell could not remember hearing the bell. Steele, who was hanging right outside the belfry, was deaf for some weeks thereafter because of it. (He was hauled in by a German observer in the belfry, made prisoner, but escaped a few days later.)

Russell, "scared to death," managed to reach his trench knife and cut himself loose. He fell to the ground and "dashed across the street and the machine gun fire was knocking up pieces of earth all around me, and I ran over into a grove of trees on the edge of town and I was the loneliest man in the world. Strange country, and just a boy, I should have been graduating from high school rather than in a strange country."

There was a flak wagon in the grove, shooting at passing Dakotas. "I got my Gammon grenade out and I threw it on the gun and the gun stopped." He moved away from town. A German soldier on a bicycle came down the road. Russell shot him. Then he found an American, from the 101st (probably a trooper from the 506th who had landed in Ste.-Mère-Église a half-hour earlier).

Russell asked, "Do you know where you are?"

"No," the trooper replied. They set out to find someone who did know.[38] *

Pvt. James Eads of the 82nd landed in an enormous manure pile, typical of Normandy. At least it was a soft landing. Three German soldiers came out of the farmhouse and ran toward him.

* M. Andre Mace, a resident of Ste.-Mère-Église, wrote that night in his diary: "ALERTE! A great number of low flying planes fly over the town—shaving the roof tops, it is like a thunderous noise, suddenly, the alarm is given, there is a fire in town. In the meantime the Germans fire all they can at the planes. We go into hiding, what is going on? Thousands [sic] of paratroopers are landing everywhere amid gun fire.

"We are huddled in M. Besselievre's garage with our friends. Our liberators are here!"

(Original in the Parachute Museum, Ste.-Mère-Église; copy in EC.)

"Oh hell," Eads said to himself, "out of the frying pan, into a latrine, now this." His rifle was still strapped to his chest. He couldn't get out of his harness (the British airborne had a quick-release device, but the Americans had to unbuckle their straps, a difficult proposition in the best of circumstances). Eads pulled his .45, thumbed back the hammer, and started firing. The first two men fell, the third kept coming. Eads had one bullet left. He dropped the last man right at his feet.

Still stuck in his harness in the manure, Eads was trying to cut himself loose when a German machine gun opened up on him. "Damn," he said aloud, "is the whole Kraut army after me, just one scared red-headed trooper?" Bullets ripped into his musette bag. He tried to bury himself in the manure. He heard an explosion and the firing stopped. He cut himself loose and began moving. He heard a noise behind him, decided to take a chance, and snapped his cricket. Two answering clicks came back at once.

"I could have kissed him," Eads recalled. "His first words were 'I got those overanxious Kraut machine gunners with a grenade, but it blew off my helmet and I can't find it.' Then he took a breath and exclaimed, 'Holy cow—you stink!' "[39]

For many of the men of the 82nd Airborne, whose drop zones were to the west of Ste.-Mère-Église, astride the Merderet River, there was a special hell. Rommel had ordered the locks near the mouth of the river, down by Carentan, opened at high tide, closed at low tide, so as to flood the valley. Because the grass had grown above the flooded area, Allied air-reconnaissance photographs failed to reveal the trap. The water generally was not more than a meter deep, but that was deep enough to drown an over-loaded paratrooper who couldn't get up or cut himself out of his harness.

Private Porcella was especially unlucky. He landed in the river itself, in water over his head. He had to jump up to take a breath. "My heart was beating so rapidly that I thought it would burst. I pleaded, 'Oh, God, please don't let me drown in this damn water.' " He bent over to remove his leg straps, but the buckle wouldn't open. He jumped up for more air, then found that if he stood on his toes he could get his nose just above the water.

Calming down a bit, he decided to cut the straps. He bent below the water and pulled his knife from his right boot. He jumped up, took a deep breath, bent down and slipped the knife between his leg and the strap, working the knife back and forth in an upward motion.

"Nothing happened. I was in panic. I came up for another breath of air and thought my heart was going to burst with fright. I wanted to scream for help but I knew that would make matters worse. I told myself, 'Think! I must think! Why won't this knife cut the strap, it's razor sharp?' "

Porcella jumped up for more air and managed to say a Hail Mary. Then he realized that he had the blade backward. He reversed it and cut himself loose.

That helped, but the weight of the musette bag and the land mine he was carrying still held him down. A few more strokes of the knife and they were gone. He moved slowly into somewhat shallower water, until it was only chest high. Then he became aware of rifle and machine-gun fire going over his head. "All the training I had received had not prepared me for this."

Suddenly there was a huge burst of orange flames in the sky. A C-47 had taken a direct hit and was a ball of flames. "Oh, my God. It's coming toward me!" Porcella cried out.

The plane was making a screaming noise that sounded like a horse about to die. Porcella tried to run away. The plane crashed beside him. "Suddenly it was dark again and it became very quiet."

Porcella resumed moving toward the high ground. He heard a voice call out "Flash." He couldn't believe it. "I thought I was the only fool in the world in this predicament." He recognized the voice. It was his buddy, Dale Cable. Porcella reached out his right hand to touch Cable, who hollered this time "Flash!" Simultaneously Cable flipped the safety off his M-1. The muzzle was within inches of Porcella's face. Porcella remembered the response and shouted back "Thunder!"

Together, they began to encounter other troopers, also sloshing around in the flooded area. After further adventures, they finally made it to high ground.[40]

Lt. Ralph De Weese of the 508th landed on his back in three feet of water. Before he had a chance to cut himself loose the wind inflated his canopy and started to drag him. The heavy equipment on his stomach (reserve chute, rifle, mine, and field bag) prevented him from turning over. His riser was across his helmet and his helmet was fastened by the chin strap so he could not get it off. His head was under water. The chute dragged him several hundred yards.

"Several times I thought it was no use and decided to open my mouth and drown, but each time the wind would slack up enough for me to put my head out of the water and catch a breath. I must have swallowed a lot of water because I didn't take a drink for two days afterward."

With his last bit of energy he pulled out his trench knife and cut the risers. "Bullets were singing over my head from machine guns and rifles, but it didn't bother me because at that point I didn't care."

De Weese finally got out, found a couple of his men, and started down a road. He saw two Frenchmen and asked if they had seen any other Americans. They couldn't understand him. He pointed to the American flag on his sleeve. One of the Frenchmen nodded happily, pulled out a pack of Lucky Strike cigarettes, and pointed down the road. "I was one happy fellow to see those Luckies."

(Two months later, back in England, De Weese wrote his mother to describe his D-Day experiences. He told her the worst part was he had no dry cigarettes himself but felt he couldn't relieve the Frenchman of those Luckies. He added that his pockets were full of little fish.)*

Pvt. David Jones of the 508th was also aquaplaned across the flooded area. He was blown to the edge; his chute wrapped around a tree and he was able to drag himself out of the water by the suspension lines. When he cut loose and climbed to the high ground, he had another fright. Back in England, during a night exercise, he had gone into a roadside pub and got into "a fairly good fistfight" with another trooper. After their buddies separated them, that trooper had vowed that once they got into combat "he was going to get my ass." Now, in Normandy, "wouldn't you know, the first person I met on the edge of that flood was that same trooper. He had me looking into the barrel of his tommy gun. Well, after we hugged and slapped each other on the back telling each other how fortunate we were to have made it through this far, we started off together."[41]

Altogether, thirty-six troopers of the 82nd drowned that night. An after-action report prepared on July 25, 1944, noted that "one complete stick from the 507th is still missing." Another 173

---

* De Weese was killed in action in Holland on September 23, 1944. A copy of his letter is in EC.

troopers had broken a leg or arm when landing; sixty-three men had been taken prisoner.[42]

Most of the POWs were taken before they could cut loose from their harness. Among them was Pvt. Paul Bouchereau, a Louisiana Cajun. He was taken to a German command post where other POWs were being harshly interrogated. The German captain, speaking English, was demanding to know how many Americans had jumped into the area.

"Millions and millions of us," one GI replied.

The angry captain asked Bouchereau the same question. With his strong Cajun accent, Bouchereau answered, "Jus' me!"

Furious, the captain had the Americans clasp their hands over their heads and marched them off, under guard. After a few minutes, for no apparent reason, the German sergeant in charge opened fire on his prisoners with his machine pistol.

"I can still recall his appearance," Bouchereau said. "He was short and stocky and mean looking. His most striking feature was a scar on the right side of his face." Bouchereau was hit near his left knee. "It felt like a severe bee sting."

The German sergeant calmed down and the march resumed. Bouchereau tried to keep up despite the squish of blood in his boot with every other step. He fell to the ground.

"A Kraut came over and rolled me on my back. He cocked his rifle and put the business end to my head. I set a speed record for saying the rosary, but instead of pulling the trigger, the German laughed, then bent over and offered me an American cigarette. I suppose I should have been grateful that my life had been spared, but instead I was furious at the physical and mental torture to which I had been subjected. My mind and heart were filled with hate. I dreamed of the day when I would repay them in full measure for my suffering."*

Lt. Briand Beaudin, a surgeon in the 508th, had a happier experience as a POW. At about 0300 he was tending to wounded men in a farmhouse set up as an aid station when it was attacked by Germans. He stuck his helmet with its red cross on a long pole and pushed it out the door. The Germans stopped firing and took the American wounded to a German aid station, "where we medics

---

* Bouchereau was liberated later that month and got his revenge in Holland (Paul Bouchereau oral history, EC).

were treated as friends by the German medical personnel." The doctors worked together through the night and the following days. Although a prisoner for some weeks, Beaudin found his stay at the 91st *Feldlazarett* to be "most interesting." He learned German techniques and taught them American methods.[43]

The Germans manning the antiaircraft batteries had done a creditable job against the Allied air armada, but the reaction on the ground against the paratroopers was confused and hesitant. Partly this was because all the division and many of the regimental commanders were in Rennes for the map exercise, but there were many additional reasons. The most important was the failure of Troop Carrier Command to drop the parachutists in tight drop zones where they were supposed to be. At 0130, headquarters of the German Seventh Army had reports of paratroop landings east and northwest of Caen, at St.-Marcove, at Montebourg, on both sides of the Vire River, on the east coast of the Cotentin, and elsewhere. There was no discernible pattern to the drops, no concentrated force—just two men here, four there, a half-dozen somewhere else.[44]

The Germans were further confused by the dummy parachutists dropped by the two SAS teams Captain Foote had organized. One party went in just before midnight between Le Havre and Rouen. An hour or so later, the commandant at Le Havre sent an agitated telegram to Seventh Army headquarters, repeated to Berlin, saying there had been a major landing upstream of him and he feared he was cut off. The second party dropped its dummies and set up its recordings of firefights southeast of Isigny. The German reserve regiment in the area, about 2,000 men strong, spent the small hours of June 6 beating the woods looking for a major airborne landing that was not there. For the Allies this was an extraordinarily profitable payoff from a small investment.[45]

The Germans could not tell whether this was the invasion or a series of scattered raids or a diversion to precede landings in the Pas-de-Calais or a supply operation to the Resistance. In general, therefore, although they fired at passing airplanes they failed completely to deal with the real threat. Here and there local company commanders sent out patrols to investigate reports of paratroopers in the area, but for the most part the Wehrmacht stayed put in its barracks. Wehrmacht doctrine was to counterattack immediately against any offensive movement, but not on this night.

Communications was a factor in the German failure. The American paratroopers had been told that if they could not do anything else, they could at least cut communication lines. The Germans in Normandy had been using secure telephone and cable lines for years and consequently had become complacent about their system. But on June 6, between 0100 and dawn, troopers acting alone or in small teams were knocking down telephone poles with their grenades, cutting lines with their knives, isolating the German units scattered in the villages.

At around 0130 the signal officer at Colonel Heydte's 6th Parachute Regiment HQ picked up a German message that indicated enemy paratroopers were landing in the vicinity of Ste.-Mère-Église. "I tried to reach General Marcks, but the whole telephone network was down," Heydte recalled.[46]

In most cases the cutting of wires was done on targets of opportunity, but in some instances it was planned. Lt. Col. Robert Wolverton, commanding the 3rd Battalion of the 506th, had been given the mission of destroying the critical communication link between Carentan and the German forces in the Cotentin. Wolverton assigned the task to Captain Shettle, CO of Company I. Shettle said he needed to know the exact location, so in late May the intelligence people had plucked a French resister out of Carentan and brought him to England. He had pinpointed for Shettle the place where the Germans had buried communication lines and a concrete casement that could be opened to gain access to it.

Within a half hour of his drop, Shettle had gathered fifteen men from Company I. He set out, found the casement, placed the charges, and destroyed it. (Years later an officer from the German 6th Parachute Regiment, deployed in the area, told Shettle that the Germans were "astounded that the American had been able to disrupt their primary source of communication so quickly."[47])

Colonel Heydte commanded the 6th Parachute Regiment. He was a professional soldier with a worldwide reputation earned in Poland, France, Russia, Crete, and North Africa. Heydte had his command post at Périers, his battalions scattered between there and Carentan. At 0030 he put his men on alert, but confusion caused by reports of landings all around the peninsula kept him from giving orders more specific than "Stay alert!" He desperately needed to get in touch with General Marcks but still could not get through.[48]

Unknown to Heydte, one platoon of his regiment, billeted

in a village near Périers, was having a party. Pvt. Wolfgang Geritzlehner recalled, "All of a sudden a courier ran toward us shouting, 'Alert, alert, enemy paratroops!' We laughed as we told him not to excite himself like that. 'Here, sit down and drink a little Calvados with us.' But then the sky was filled with planes. That sobered us up! At one stroke there were soldiers coming out of all the corners. It was like a swarm of maddened bees."

The 3,500 men of the German 6th Parachute Regiment began to form up. It did not go quickly. They were scattered in villages throughout the area, they had only seventy trucks at their disposal, many of them more museum pieces than working vehicles. Those seventy trucks were of fifty different makes, so it was impossible to provide replacement parts for broken equipment. Heydte's elite troops would have to walk into the battle. Nor would they have much in the way of heavy weapons, just hand-held material. When the colonel had requested heavy mortars and antitank guns from the General Staff, he was told with a smile, "But come now, Heydte, for paratroops a dagger is enough."

Nevertheless, the German paratroops were confident. "Frankly, we weren't afraid," Geritzlehner recalled. "We were so convinced that everything would be settled in a few hours that [when we formed up] we didn't even take our personal effects. Only our weapons, ammunition and some food. Everyone was confident."[49]

To the east, where the British and Canadian gliderborne and paratroops were landing, the Germans were also immobilized, not by what the Allies were doing but because of their own command structure. Col. Hans von Luck's 125th Regiment of the 21st Panzer Division was the one Rommel counted on to counterattack any invading forces on the east of the Orne Canal and River. At 0130 Luck got his first reports of landings. He immediately assembled his regiment and within the hour his officers and men were standing beside their tanks and vehicles, engines running, ready to go.

But although Luck had prepared for exactly this moment, knew where he wanted to go—to the Orne Canal bridge, to take it back from Major Howard—over what routes, with what alternatives, he could not give the order to go. Only Hitler could release the panzers, and Hitler was sleeping. So was Rundstedt. Rommel was with his wife. General Dollmann was in Rennes. General

Feuchtinger was in Paris. Seventh Army headquarters couldn't make out what was happening.

At 0240, the acting commander of Rundstedt's Army Group West contended, "We are not confronted by a major action." His chief of staff replied, "It can be nothing less than that in view of the depth of the penetration." The argument went on without resolution.[50]

Luck had no doubts. "My idea," he said forty years later, "was to counterattack before the British could organize their defenses, before their air force people could come, before the British navy could hit us. We were quite familiar with the ground and I think that we could have been able to get through to the bridges." Had he done so, Howard's company had only hand-held Piat antitank rockets to stop him with, and only a couple of those. But Luck could not act on his own initiative, so there he sat, a senior officer in the division Rommel most counted on to drive the Allies into the sea if they attacked near Caen, personally quite certain of what he could accomplish, rendered immobile by the intricacies of the leadership principle in the Third Reich.[51]

Beginning at 0300, the gliders began to come in to reinforce the paratroopers. On the left flank, sixty-nine gliders brought in a regiment and the commander of the 6th Airborne Division, Maj. Gen. Richard Gale. They landed near Ranville on fields that had been cleared by paratroopers who had dropped a couple of hours earlier. Forty-nine of the gliders landed safely on the correct landing zone. They brought jeeps and antitank guns.

On the right flank, fifty-two American gliders swooped down on Hiesville, six kilometers from Ste.-Mère-Église. They were carrying troops, jeeps, antitank guns, and a small bulldozer. Brig. Gen. Don Pratt, assistant division commander of the 101st, was in the lead glider. Lt. Robert Butler was the pilot in the second glider. As the gliders approached the landing zone, German antiaircraft fire caused the tug pilots in their Dakotas to climb, so that when Butler and the others cut loose from their 300-yard-long nylon tow ropes they had to "circle and circle." Planes and gliders were being shot down.

For those who survived the antiaircraft fire the problem became the Norman hedgerows. The fields they enclosed were too small for a decent landing zone. Worse, the trees were much higher than expected. (This was one of the great failures of Allied intelligence. As Sgt. Zane Schlemmer of the 82nd put it, "No one had informed us of the immense size of the French hedgerows. We were of course told that we would be in hedgerow country, but we assumed that they would be similar to the English hedgerows, which were like small fences that the fox hunters jumped over."[52]) In Normandy, the hedgerows were six feet or more high, virtually impenetrable. The roads between the hedgerows were sunken, meaning that the Germans had what amounted to a vast field of ready-made trenches. Why intelligence missed this obvious major feature of the battlefield is a mystery.

If the glider pilots came in low, they would see trees looming in front of them, try to pull up to go over, stall out, and crash. If they came in high, they couldn't get the gliders down in the small fields in time to avoid the hedgerow at the far end. The result, in the words of Sgt. James Elmo Jones of the 82nd, a pathfinder who was marking a field for the gliders, "was tragic. There's never been a greater slaughter than what took place that night. It was the most horrible thing that a person could see."[53]

In front of Lieutenant Butler, Col. Mike Murphy had the controls of the lead glider. Butler watched it take some hits from a German machine gun—General Pratt was killed, the first general officer on either side to die that day—and Murphy crashed into a hedgerow, breaking both his legs.[54]

Sgt. Leonard Lebenson of the 82nd was in a glider that hit a treetop, bounced off, hit the ground, glanced off the corner of a farmhouse, and finally crashed into another tree. "There were pieces of our glider strewn over the confines of this relatively small field, but miraculously only one guy was hurt."[55]

Lt. Charles Skidmore, a pilot, landed safely in a flooded area. He managed to get out of the water and immediately came under rifle fire. It came from a bunker holding a dozen conscripted Polish soldiers with one German sergeant in charge. The men Skidmore had brought in joined him and began firing back. There was a lull in the firefight. Then a single shot. Then shouts and laughter. Then the Poles emerged with their hands held high to surrender. They had shot the German sergeant.[56]

Private Reisenleiter of the 508th was in a field across from one where a glider came down. In the dark, with the hedgerows looming above him, he could hardly tell what was going on. He heard some crashing about on the other side and called out, "Flash."

"Flash your ass," the answer came back. "They're killing us out here and we're getting the hell out of here." Reisenleiter let them go; he figured only an American could have given such a response to the challenge.[57] *

Pvt. John Fitzgerald of the 502nd PIR watched the glider landing. "We could hear the sounds of planes in the distance, then no sounds at all. This was followed by a series of swishing noises. Adding to the swelling crescendo of sounds was the tearing of branches and trees followed by loud crashes and intermittent screams. The gliders were coming in rapidly, one after the other, from all different directions. Many overshot the field and landed in the surrounding woods, while others crashed into nearby farmhouses and stone walls.

"In a moment, the field was complete chaos. Equipment broke away and catapulted as it hit the ground, plowing up huge mounds of earth. Bodies and bundles were thrown all along the length of the field. Some of the glider troopers were impaled by the splintering wood of the fragile plywood gliders. We immediately tried to aid the injured, but knew we would first have to decide who could be helped and who could not. A makeshift aid station was set up and we began the grim process of separating the living from the dead. I saw one man with his legs and buttocks sticking out of the canvas fuselage of a glider. I tried to pull him out. He would not budge. When I looked inside the wreckage, I could see his upper torso had been crushed by a jeep."[58]

Some of the gliders carried bulldozers, to be used to make landing strips for later glider landings. Sgt. Zane Schlemmer of the 508th PIR recalled that "the sound of one glider hitting a tree was similar to smashing a thousand matchboxes all at once, and I could just visualize the poor pilot with that baby bulldozer smashing into him."[59]

The glider casualties for the 82nd were heavy. Of the 957 men who went into Normandy that night, twenty-five were killed, 118 wounded, fourteen missing (a 16 percent casualty rate). Nineteen of 111 jeeps were unserviceable, as were four of seventeen antitank guns.

Anytime a unit takes 16 percent casualties before it even gets into action, somebody had to have made a big mistake. But Leigh-

* The first thing glider troops were taught to do after a landing was to run for cover in the woods or whatever surrounded the landing zone—they were *never* to stay in the open. That may explain the response to Reisenleiter.

Mallory had feared that the gliderborne troops might take 70 percent casualties, primarily because of Rommel's asparagus. In the event, those poles in the ground were inconsequential; it was the hedgerows that caused the problems. And the jeeps and antitank guns that did survive proved to be invaluable.

By 0400, the American paratroopers and gliderborne troops were scattered to hell and gone across the Cotentin. With few exceptions, they were lost. Except for Vandervoort's 2nd Battalion of the 505th, they were alone or gathered into groups of three, five, ten, at the most thirty men. They had lost the bulk of their equipment bundles; the little blue lights attached to the bundles had mostly failed to work. Most men had lost their leg bags, containing extra ammunition, field radios, tripods for the machine guns, and the like. The few radios that they had recovered had either got soaked in the flooded areas or damaged on hitting the ground and did not work. They had taken heavy casualties, from the opening shock, from hitting the ground too hard as a result of jumping too low, from German fire, from glider crashes.

Lt. Carl Cartledge of the 501st landed in a marsh. His company was supposed to assemble on a bugle call, but the bugler drowned. He found Pvt. John Fordik and a Private Smith. Smith could not walk—he had broken his back. Others in the stick had drowned. Cartledge gathered together ten men from his platoon. They carried Smith to high ground and covered him with brush. He insisted on retaining the two homing pigeons he had with him. One had a message on its leg saying the battalion was being wiped out; the other said it was accomplishing its mission. Smith had been told to release one or the other at daylight.

As the platoon prepared to move out, Smith's last words to Cartledge were, "I'll send the right message. Don't make me out a liar."

As the platoon left, a German machine gun opened up. The men dove back into the marsh. Cartledge had no radio. He was lost, chest deep in water, taking fire without being able to return it. Private Fordik, "a tough Pennsylvania coal miner," leaned over to whisper in his ear, "You know, Lieutenant Cartledge, I think the Germans are winning this war."[60]

Ten weeks later, when the airborne troops were back in England, preparing for another jump, possibly at night, the regimental and battalion commanders of the 82nd gathered at Glebe Mount House, Leicester, for a debriefing conference. They did an analysis of what went wrong, what went right.

They started with the pilots. In the future the paratroop commanders wanted the pilots trained for combat and bad-weather missions. They wanted them forced to slow down—one suggestion was that every pilot of Troop Carrier Command be made to jump from a plane going 150 miles per hour. They wanted the pilots told that evasive action in a sky full of tracers did no good and caused much harm.

They did not say so, but it seems clear that radio silence also did more harm than good. The German antiaircraft crews were fully alerted by the pathfinder planes anyway. Had the pathfinder pilots sent back word of the cloud bank, the pilots in the main train would have been alerted. Had they been able to talk to each other on the radio, the dispersion of aircraft would not have been so great.

Only the battalion commanders of the 505th had anything good to say about the lighted-T system—Lt. Col. Edward Krause, CO of the 3rd Battalion, said that when he saw his T, "I felt that I had found the Holy Grail." None of the others had seen their Ts (which in most cases had not been set up because the pathfinders were not sure they were in the right place). No one expressed faith in the Eureka system.

There was general agreement that equipment bundles had to be tied together and a better lighting system devised. The commanders wanted every man to carry a mine (and put it to immediate use by placing it on a road; the men should be instructed to stay off the roads otherwise). Some way had to be devised to bring in a bazooka with each squad. The Gammon grenade "was very satisfactory." Each man should be issued a .45 "so as to be available immediately upon landing."

As to assembly, the commanders thought that flares would be the most effective method—but not too many. One per battalion, carried by the CO, would be sufficient. Whistles, bugles, and the like had been unsatisfactory, partly because of the noise from antiaircraft fire, partly because in hedgerow country the sound did not carry. The rolling-up-the-stick method was a failure because of the hedgerows and the scattered nature of the drops. Better radios and more of them would be a great help. The men had to be taught how to get out of their chutes faster (the simple solution to that was to get rid of those buckles and adopt the British quick-release mechanism, which was done).[61]

So the paratroop commanders found much to criticize in the operation. Still, contrary to the fear Private Fordik had expressed to Lieutenant Cartledge, the Germans were not winning the war. Scattered though they were, the paratroopers and gliderborne troops were about to go into action while the Germans, for the most part, were still holed up, badly confused.

12

"LET'S GET
THOSE BASTARDS"

The Airborne Night Attack

AT THE GLEBE MOUNT HOUSE debriefing in August 1944, the 82nd's regimental and battalion commanders concluded that the troops should be trained to assemble more quickly and to send out search parties for the equipment bundles. "It is most important, however, that the hours of darkness be used for the seizure of key points and objectives. The enemy reaction becomes increasingly violent with daylight."

Further, "prompt aggressive action by each individual is imperative immediately upon landing. An individual or small unit that 'holes up' and does nothing is ultimately isolated and destroyed. An airborne unit has the initiative upon landing; it must retain it. This is the essence of successful reorganization and accomplishment of a mission."[1]

Obviously, the commanders were unhappy with some of their troopers. Too many had hunkered down in hedgerows to await the dawn; a few had even gone to sleep. Pvt. Francis Palys of the 506th saw what was perhaps the worst dereliction of duty. He had gathered a squad near Vierville. Hearing "all kinds of noise and singing from a distance," he and his men sneaked up on a farmhouse. In it was a mixed group from both American divisions. The paratroopers had found the Calvados barrel in the cellar (there was one in virtually every Norman cellar) and "they were drunker than a bunch of hillbillies on a Saturday night wingding. Unbelievable."[2]

The 505th's historian, Allen Langdon, attempted to explain the actions of these and other men who were not acting aggressively. He wrote, "A parachute jump and in particular a combat jump (if you survived it) was so exhilarating that first-timers were apt to forget the real reason they were there—to kill Germans. The feeling was: 'We've made the jump, now the Germans should roll over and play dead.' In every regiment it seemed to take one combat jump to instill the idea that jumping was only a means of transportation. Another phenomenon noted . . . was the shock of the quick transition from a peaceful . . . situation to a war zone. Because of it, troopers were ofttimes reluctant to shoot."[3]

Pvt. Dwayne Burns was crouched beside a hedgerow. He heard a noise on the other side. "I climbed up and slowly looked over, and as I did, a German on the other side raised up and looked over. In the dark I could barely see his features. We stood there looking at each other, then slowly each of us went back down." They moved off in opposite directions.[4]

Others had similar experiences. Lt. Lynn Tomlinson of the 508th was moving down a hedgerow. He looked across at a low point in the hedge and saw four German soldiers going in the opposite direction. "They were kids. I was within five feet of them." The moon had come out, and "One of these kids saw me and smiled. I decided that if they would stay out of our way, we would stay out of theirs."[5]

Pvt. R. J. Nieblas of the 508th was crouched beside a hedgerow with a paved road on the other side. His company CO had ordered him not to fire. He heard hobnailed boots on the road, then saw a German patrol marching past. "These were young fellows, kids—well, we were too—and their sharp uniforms impressed me. We didn't fire and I thought at the time, God, I don't know if I could fire point blank at an unsuspecting man."[*]

Some of the battalion and company commanders had given their men orders not to shoot at night for fear of revealing their positions. A few went so far as to order the men not to load their rifles or machine guns. They should use grenades or, even better, their knives. The 82nd's commanders agreed at their debriefing that those orders had been a big mistake.

Sgt. Dan Furlong of the 508th would not have agreed. He

---

[*] Later that day, Nieblas saw a paratrooper hanging from a tree. Although he was obviously helpless, the Germans had shot him. That made Nieblas furious and "settled my problem about shooting an unsuspecting enemy. If he wore a German uniform, I'd shoot."

came down alone and sneaked up to a farmhouse. It was full of Germans. He could hear them talking. They must have heard him, too, because a soldier came to check out the farmyard. He came around a corner "and I was standing up against the wall. I hit him in the side of the head with my rifle butt and then gave him the bayonet and took off."⁶

Furlong was alone the remainder of the night. So were hundreds of others. "Dutch" Schultz wandered, trying to move to the sound of firefights, but before he could hook up with fellow Americans the area would become tranquil. "The peace would come, and then the noise, the violence. Then the peace, it was almost like taking a walk in the country on a Sunday afternoon, very peaceful. The peace and then again violence."⁷

Of course it was the commanders' job in a debriefing to be critical; at the time (August 1944) they were planning for the next mission, which for all they knew could be at night, so they concentrated on the shortcomings and mistakes of the D-Day operation rather than congratulating themselves on how well they and their men had done. But although the airborne assault had not been a complete success in the sense of accomplishing all assigned missions, the troopers had done enough that night to justify the operation.

The overall missions of the three airborne divisions were to disrupt and confuse the Germans so as to prevent a concentrated counterattack against the seaborne troops coming in at dawn and to protect the flanks at Sword and Utah beaches. For the 6th Airborne, that meant destroying the bridges over the Dives River and capturing intact the bridges over the Orne Canal and River, holding the dividing ridge between the Dives and the Orne, and destroying the German battery at Merville.

The Merville battery, four guns of undetermined size in four casemates, stood just east of the mouth of the Orne River, on flat, open grazing ground. The assumption by Allied planners was that those guns could cover Sword Beach to disrupt and possibly drive back the 3rd Division's landings, so they had made it a priority target. The battery would be attacked by air, land, and if necessary by naval gunfire.

The air attack, by 100 Royal Air Force Lancaster bombers, would begin at 0200. It was designed more to create foxholes around the battery and to stun the German defenders than to destroy it; even a lucky direct hit would not be sufficient to penetrate the thick, steel-reinforced concrete.

Next would come an attack by land. But just as the casemates were well defended against air bombardment, so were they prepared for a ground attack. There was a wire fence surrounding the area, with a minefield inside, then a barbed-wire entanglement, another minefield, an inner belt of barbed wire, finally a trench system for the German infantry reinforced by ten machine-gun pits. There were estimated to be 200 German soldiers defending the battery.

So formidable were these defenses, so critical were the guns, that the British assigned more than 10 percent of the total airborne strength of the 6th Division to the task. The job went to twenty-nine-year-old Lt. Col. T. B. H. Otway and his 9th Battalion. He planned to execute it by a *coup de main* operation somewhat similar to Major Howard's at the Orne Canal (Pegasus Bridge), but on a much larger scale. Howard had six gliders and 180 men; Otway had 750 men, sixty of them in gliders, the remainder paratroopers. His plan was to assemble his battalion in a wood a couple of kilometers from the battery, move into position, and attack when the gliders crash-landed inside the defenses, right against the walls of the gun emplacements. If successful, he would then fire a Very pistol as a signal of success.

The job had to be completed by 0515. If there was no success signal by then, the British warships off Sword would commence firing on Merville.

So much for plans. In the event, whereas Howard's glider pilots had put him down exactly where he wanted to be (Leigh-Mallory called lead pilot Jim Wallwork's accomplishment that night "the finest feat of flying in World War II"), Otway's pilots badly scattered his battalion. They had not hit a cloud bank, but like their American counterparts they were not accustomed to flak and thus were unable to judge how dangerous it was. They took excessive evasive action to escape what was essentially light flak; as a consequence, the 9th Battalion had a bad drop.

Otway came down just outside a German headquarters. He made his way to the assembly point in the wood, where his second in command greeted him, "Thank God you've come, sir."

"Why?" Otway asked.

"The drop's a bloody chaos. There's hardly anyone here."[8]

It was nearly 0200. Otway had fewer than 100 men with him. He needed to get into place around the battery's defenses before the gliders came, but he needed more than one-seventh of his strength to do the job. He fumed and waited.

By 0230, a total of 150 men had come in. Between them they

had but one machine gun. They had no mortars, antitank guns, radios, engineers, or mine detectors. The gliders were due in two hours. Otway decided to attack with what he had.

At 0250, the company-sized party set out, hoping to meet outside the battery a small reconnaissance party that had landed earlier with the pathfinders. On the single-file march to Merville, the main group passed a German antiaircraft battery shooting at incoming British planes and gliders. It was a tempting target of opportunity and the men wanted to attack it, but Otway's task was specific and urgent. He did not want to reveal his position and in any event his time was running out. He passed the word back down the file—no shooting.

Shortly, the commander of the reconnaissance party met Otway. His report was mixed. He had cut the outer wire fence and crossed the first minefield. The barbed wire was not as bad as had been feared. But he had no tape with him to mark the path he had followed (searching for mines with his fingers). Worse, the RAF bombardment had been a bust. Not a single bomb had hit anywhere near the battery.

At 0430, precisely on time, the gliders were overhead, flying in circles, watching for the mortar flares from Otway that were the signal to come on in. Otway watched helplessly—his men had failed to find the bundles carrying the flares. Without the flares, the pilots of the gliders assumed that something had gone wrong. Otway saw one glider skim over the battery, no more than 100 feet off the ground, then turn away to land in a field to the rear.

Otway had no choice. He gave the order to attack. It would be a frontal assault from one direction only; he did not have sufficient troops to encircle and attack from all four sides. He told the lead groups to ignore the trenches and go straight on into the casemates. Follow-up groups would take on the Germans in the trenches.

Men crept forward to blow gaps in the inner wire. When they did, German riflemen and machine gunners in the trench system began firing. Otway's men dashed forward, ignoring the mines, shouting, shooting. Many fell, but others reached the walls and put fire through the openings.

The Germans who had managed to survive the onslaught surrendered. In twenty minutes it was over. Otway sent up the Very light to signal success; a spotting aircraft saw it and passed the word on to the navy, fifteen minutes before the shelling was due to begin. Otway's signals officer pulled a pigeon from his jacket and set it free, to take word back to England that the Merville battery had been captured.

The Germans had extracted a terrible price. Fully half of Otway's 150-man force had fallen, dead or wounded. The Germans too paid a terrible price; of the 200 defenders, only twenty-two uninjured men had been taken prisoner.[9]

Otway destroyed the guns by dropping Gammon grenades down the barrels. It turned out that they were old French 75mms, taken out of the Maginot Line, set up for coastal defense against an attack east of the mouth of the Orne. They did not pose a serious threat to Sword Beach.

Nevertheless, it was a brilliant feat of arms. The British airborne had gotten off to a smashing start. Before daylight, they had taken control of the bridges over the Orne Canal and River and they had taken the Merville battery, in both cases exactly on schedule. Howard's men had hurled back a sharp local counterattack led by two old, small French tanks. They had been reinforced by paratroopers from the 7th Battalion.

Howard's plan at Pegasus Bridge had worked down to the smallest detail. Otway's plan at the Merville battery was a shambles before he hit the ground. Otway's ability to improvise and inspire and Howard's calm confidence and brilliant plan both showed the British army of World War II at its absolute best.

The 6th Airborne Division had many other adventures and successes that night. One of the more spectacular was the odyssey of Maj. A. J. C. Roseveare, an engineer with the 8th Battalion. A civil engineer before the war, Roseveare was given the task to blow the bridges over the Dives River at Bures and Troarn. For that job his squad had brought along in equipment bundles a few dozen specially shaped "General Wade" charges with thirty pounds of explosive in each.

Roseveare landed in the wrong drop zone, wandered around a bit, hooked up with Lt. David Breeze and some of his chaps, and did an inventory. The squad consisted of seven men. They had a folding trolley and a container of General Wades. They knew where they were and where they wanted to go—to Troarn, the larger of the two bridges, eight kilometers to the southeast. Roseveare had commandeered a bicycle. Even better, a medical jeep and trailer, brought in by glider, had joined up. As Roseveare remembered it, the trailer "was packed to the gunwales with bottles of blood and bandages and splints and all sorts of field dressing equipment, instruments. And I told the doctor to 'Follow me.' I thought, maybe in desperation, it would be good to have some transport. Along the way, in Herouvillette, we cut down the telephone wires, it seemed a reasonable thing to do."

Sgt. Bill Irving went to do the cutting. "I had climbed dozens of telephone poles like this in training," he said. "I got halfway and that was it, my equipment was too heavy." So in fact the wires were not cut.

The caravan, with the jeep and trailer in the rear, carried on. At a road junction five kilometers from Troarn, eight troopers from the 8th Battalion joined them. Roseveare was greatly relieved. He explained his task to them, said his sappers were ready to blow the bridge once it was secured, and concluded, "Infantry, lead the way!"

There were no officers or noncoms in the group. The eight privates looked at each other and shook their heads. The deflated Roseveare regained his composure and made a new plan. He ordered the doctor to unload the trailer.

"Did he protest?" Roseveare was asked in his interview.

"He didn't have the rights to any feelings. So we loaded all the special charges and detonating equipment into the trailer." Roseveare sent his sappers to move down to the bridge at Bures, giving them half his General Wades to blow it. Roseveare insisted on driving the jeep—"I like to be in command of things"—and the remaining seven men piled on, while an eighth, Sapper Peachey, climbed onto the trailer. He had a Bren gun and would act as tail gunner. On the front corners of the hood, Sergeant Irving and Sgt. Joe Henderson sat, Sten guns in hand. The men inside the jeep had their weapons at the ready, covering to the flank.

The jeep moved out, straining against the overload, struggling to pick up speed. Fortunately, there were no hills to climb and the route gradually descended toward the river. Roseveare nursed the jeep along, gradually gaining momentum.

He turned a corner without slowing, "and we went crash-bang into a barbed wire entanglement," Irving recalled. Irving was thrown off the jeep; there was a pile of arms and legs; the axles were entangled by barbed wire. Roseveare expected a German attack and put his men in positions of immediate defense, then held a torch for Irving as he went to work with his wire cutters. With the torch on him, Irving said, "I felt just like a pea waiting to be plucked out of the pod."

But there were no German troops in the area. The garrison in Troarn seemed to be asleep. Irving finished cutting the wire and everyone mounted up for the journey through Troarn.

They crept into Troarn. Roseveare stopped short of a crossroads and ordered Irving to go on ahead to see if all was clear.

Nothing was moving. Irving signaled the jeep to come forward, "and I turned round to check again and whistling past me was a German soldier on a bicycle, obviously returning from a night out." The men back in the jeep cut down the German with a burst of fire.

"That's done it," said Roseveare. He jammed the jeep into gear and drove straight into the main street of Troarn, running downhill to the river beyond the village. Almost immediately, the Germans had roused themselves and commenced firing.

"And the further we went," Irving said, "the more the fire coming at us, and the faster Roseveare drove the jeep, and the more we fired back and started to take evasive actions." Irving estimated that eighteen to twenty Germans were firing at them. He had started off the run perched on the left front corner of the jeep, "blazing away with my Sten gun at anything that moved." When the jeep reached the end of town, "I don't know how it happened, but I was lying flat on the bonnet of the jeep."

Irving added, "We were all so excited that there was no real feeling of being frightened."

Toward the end of the street a German rushed out of a house with an MG-34 and put it down in the middle of the road. He was a second too late; the jeep was nearly on him. But, Roseveare remembered, "he was terribly quick." He grabbed the gun and tripod and ducked into a doorway. As soon as the jeep passed, he set up and suddenly "tracers were streaming over our heads."

Once again a second too late. The jeep was now on the final long, gradual slope down to the river. It picked up speed. Roseveare began taking severe zigzags. The machine gunner could not depress his weapon enough to make it effective.

The jeep careened. Peachey fell off the trailer (he was injured and captured). "And somehow," Irving said, "Joe Henderson, who started out on the front of the jeep with me, finished up sitting back on the trailer. So in the process he climbed right over the jeep. Don't ask me how it was done, but he did it."

The squad reached the unguarded bridge. Roseveare stopped, unloaded, gave out orders. He set up guards at each end and told the sappers to place the General Wades across the center of the main arch. In a few minutes (two, Irving thought; five said Roseveare), everything was in place.

Irving asked Roseveare if he wanted to light the fuse.

"No, you light it."

"I always thought he wanted to say if the damn thing didn't go off it had nothing to do with him," Irving said in recalling the exchange.

The bridge went up in a great bang. It had a six-foot gap in the center.

Roseveare drove down river on a dirt road that soon gave out. The party abandoned the jeep to set out on foot for battalion headquarters. They got deeper into a wood. Roseveare called a halt for a rest. "After all that excitement," Irving said, "we were desperately tired. We literally flopped down and went to sleep."

The sun was appearing on the eastern horizon. They woke within the hour and got to HQ without event. There Roseveare learned that the sappers sent to do the bridge at Bures had accomplished their mission.[10]

For the Canadian airborne battalion the objective was the downstream bridge over the Dives. By 0200 Sgt. John Kemp had his squad gathered but did not know where he was. His mission was to provide protection for a team of sappers who were to blow Robehomme Bridge.

Of all things, in the dark of the night, Kemp heard a bicycle bell ringing. The rider turned out to be a French girl who had probably been out cutting telephone wires, as was being done all over Normandy, adding to the German communication woes. French-speaking Canadians talked to her; she agreed to lead them to the bridge they wanted; off they set. But she led them to a German headquarters and demanded that they assault it. Kemp refused; his job was to blow the bridge, not rouse the Germans. Reluctantly she led on. When they arrived at Robehomme Bridge, Kemp checked and found the bridge was unguarded. He posted sentries at each end and sat to wait for sappers to come up with explosives.

The girl was indignant. "Are you going to do nothing?" she asked. She had taken great risks bringing them here. "Are you going to just sit there?"

Fortunately, the sappers came up, the bridge was blown, and the girl was satisfied.[11]

• •

The British airborne as a whole had cause to be satisfied with its performance that night. It had blown the bridges it had been told to blow, captured intact the bridges it had been told to capture. It had seized some of the key villages and crossroads scattered throughout the peninsula between the Dives and Orne rivers. It had knocked out the Merville battery. It had accomplished its mission; the left flank at Sword Beach, which was the left flank for the entire invasion, was secured by the 6th Division before daybreak.

But the division was behind enemy lines. It was desperately short of heavy weapons of all kinds. Except over the narrow bridges on the Orne waterways, it had no land lines of communication with the rest of the British army—and no one could say how long it would take the Commandos to get to Pegasus Bridge.

On the right flank, the Americans were not accomplishing their specific missions as well as their British counterparts. For the 101st Airborne, the primary task was to seize the four inland exits at the western ends of the causeways in the inundated area west of Utah between St.-Martin-de-Varreville and Pouppeville. Other missions were to destroy two bridges across the Douve River, the one on the main highway northwest of Carentan and the other the railway bridge to the west. In addition, the 101st was to seize and hold the La Barquette lock and establish bridgeheads over the Douve, downstream from the lock. In sum, the 101st's mission was to open the way to the battlefield for the 4th Infantry Division landing at Utah while sealing off the battlefield from the Germans in Carentan.

The execution of the mission got off to an agonizingly slow start. It took hours, until dawn and after (in a few cases never that day), for units to come together in battalion strength, and then another week to sort out the 101st men from the 82nd.

Lt. Col. Robert Cole, commanding the 3rd Battalion, 502nd PIR, landed near Ste.-Mère-Église. His objective, the two northern exits from Utah, was ten kilometers away. It took time to figure out where he was, time to gather in the men. By 0400 he had less than fifty men gathered together. He set off. In a couple of hours of moving around Ste.-Mère-Église, the group snowballed to seventy-five men. It made contact with a small German convoy, killed several of the enemy, and took ten prisoners. As dawn came up, Cole was still an hour short of his objective.

For Lieutenant Cartledge, dawn brought a welcome respite. He had thought he was on the Douve River when he was actually on the Merderet. By 0400 he had gathered nine men. His "squad" was representative of many such units across the Cotentin. Cartledge had Lt. Werner Meyer, from intelligence, attached to division HG as an interpreter; a demolition man; three radiomen; one company clerk; two men from his own company. "With only three of us trained to fight," Cartledge said, "it was imperative we get with a larger group."

He set off toward what he thought was the coast. "When daylight came, we stopped on a hillside along a dirt road, set out our land mines in a giant circle, and pulled out our D-ration chocolate bars and canteens and ate breakfast. Meyer, Bravo, Fordik and I sat down together and talked it over, deciding which way to go."[12]

At that moment, quite a lot of 101st troopers were sitting down, talking it over. Pvt. John Fitzgerald had much to talk about but no one to talk to. Fitzgerald was from the 101st Airborne; at about 0400 he found a captain and a private from the 82nd. They set out in search of others. The gliders were coming in and a German antiaircraft battery opened fire.

"With all the noise, we were able to crawl to within twenty-five yards of the battery," Fitzgerald related. It was firing continuously. The captain whispered a brief plan of attack, then called out, "Let's get those bastards!" The private from the 82nd opened up with his BAR, hitting two Germans on the right of the platform. The captain threw a grenade that exploded directly under the gun.

"I emptied my M-1 clip at the two Germans on the left," Fitzgerald said. "In a moment it was over. Perspiration broke out on my forehead, my hands were trembling. It was the first time I had ever fired at a living thing. I noticed the torn condom hanging loosely from the end of my rifle. I had put it there before the jump to keep the barrel dry, then forgot about it."[13]

They came on another, larger battery. They attacked it and were repulsed. In the retreat they got separated. So as dawn broke, Fitzgerald was alone, wondering where he was.

Captain Gibbons of the 501st PIR put together a mixed group of a dozen men and at 0300 set off. They drove off a couple of Germans from a tiny village, roused the French residents, pointed and gestured at the map, and discovered that they had just liberated Carquebut. Gibbons knew that Carquebut was outside the 101st's sector; it was an 82nd objective. He decided to move south toward his original objective, the bridges across the Douve. It was a long way off. "When we left Carquebut," Gibbons remembered, "dawn was just beginning."

He set off with a dozen strangers toward an objective nearly fifteen kilometers away without any equipment for blowing a bridge. Later, Gibbons remarked, "This certainly wasn't the way I had thought the invasion would go, nor had we ever rehearsed it in this manner."[14]

But he was getting on with his assignment. Throughout the Cotentin, junior officers from both divisions were doing the same. This was the payoff for the extensive briefings. The platoon and company leaders knew their battalion assignments. By 0400 many of them had set off to carry out their missions, however far away the target was.

Captain Shettle found his objective before dawn, one of the few to do so. After he had blown up the communication linkup north of Carentan, he moved toward the two bridges over the Douve downstream from the lock. He was to establish a bridgehead on the far bank, not blow the bridges, which would be needed later for the hookup of the far left at Utah (which was Shettle at this moment) and the right flank coming from Omaha.

Shettle had about fifteen men with him. They came to a French farmhouse, surrounded it, called out the family, and discovered that the only German in the place was a paymaster carrying the pay for the entire 6th Parachute Regiment. Shettle made him prisoner and confiscated the money. The farmer led the group to the bridges. They were defended by machine-gun positions on the south bank, but volunteers dashed across and drove the enemy off. As dawn broke, however, German machine gunners forced Shettle's advance guard to retreat to the north bank.[15]

Just before dawn, Colonel Johnson, CO of the 501st PIR, had been able to take the La Barquette lock and establish a couple of squads on the far side.

The 82nd's mission was to seal off the Cotentin from the south by destroying the bridges over the Douve River upstream from its junction with the Merderet, at Pont-l'Abbé and Beuzeville, by occupying and holding both banks of the Merderet River, then protecting the southwest flank of VII Corps by securing the line of the Douve River. To the north, the critical objective was Ste.-Mère-Église.

At 0400 Lt. Col. Ed Krause, 3rd Battalion, 505th PIR, had gathered approximately 180 men. He put them on the road for his objective, Ste.-Mère-Église.

In the village, the fire was out, the residents had gone back to bed, and so had the German garrison. It was astonishing and inexplicable, but true. When Krause got to the edge of town without being challenged, he sent one company to move as quietly as possible through town to set up roadblocks, with mines in front. After giving the men a thirty-minute head start, Krause sent the other company into town to clear it out. A local Frenchman, half-drunk, who had guided the battalion into the town, pointed out the billets of the Germans. Thirty of them surrendered meekly; ten were shot trying to resist.

That quickly, a key objective had been taken. Krause cut the communications cable point. His men held the roads leading into Ste.-Mère-Église, most importantly the main highway from Caen to Cherbourg.*

At dawn, a disaster. A glider-landed jeep towing an antitank gun came barreling down the road from Chef-du-Pont. Before any of Krause's men could stop it, the jeep hit one of the mines, which not only "blew the hell out of it and the gun," but also killed the two men in the jeep and destroyed the roadblock.

Fortunately, Krause had already brought in two antitank guns. As the sun rose, he was holding the town the Americans had to have.[16]

Nowhere else had either American airborne division achieved its predawn objectives. Bridges had not been taken or blown, the causeway exits were not secure. Not a single American company was at full strength; only a handful were at half-strength. An hour and more after sunrise, Americans were still trying to find one another.

It led to the sobering thought that it might have been better to have come in at dawn. A daylight assembly would have been much quicker, so that by 0730 units would have been on the move— the same time or earlier than many of them got on the move in fact. (Twenty-two hours after the drop, at the end of D-Day, the 101st had assembled only about 2,500 of the 6,000 men who had dropped.[17])

But despite the time lost and relative failure at assembling,

---

* M. Andre Mace, hiding in a garage in the village, wrote in his diary: "It is real hell all over with the firing of guns, machine guns, and artillery. Around 3:00 A.M. we risk a peek to see what is going on. The Americans are the only ones in the streets of the town, there are no more Germans. It is an indescible joy. I was never as happy in all my life." (Original in the Parachute Museum, Ste.-Mère-Église; copy in EC.)

the night drop had accomplished a great deal. It had certainly confused the Germans. The junior officers, taking the initiative, had gathered together however many men they could and were setting out for their company objectives. Ste.-Mère-Église was secure.

But as dawn broke, every commander from company level on up in the American airborne felt cut off and surrounded, and was deeply worried about his unit's ability to perform its mission. Despite the mixing of personnel, the two divisions were not in contact or communication. This was not a raid. No one was coming to pluck them out. They had to fight to take ground and hold it and link up, but they had only about one-third of their men to fight with. What they most feared was being forced to circle the wagons and fight defensive actions, without radios or any idea where other Americans were, rendered passive by their weakness in numbers, perhaps even overwhelmed.

Just before dawn, Colonel Heydte finally got through to General Marcks and received his orders. He should attack with his regiment northward out of Carentan and clean out the area between that city and Ste.-Mère-Église.

Heydte set out confident he could do just that. He had under his command an overstrength regiment that was, in his opinion, worth two American or British divisions. His paratroopers were tough kids, seventeen and a half years old average age. They had been six years old when Hitler took power. They had been raised in a Nazi ideology that had been designed to get them ready for precisely this moment. They had an experienced and renowned commanding officer, a professional soldier with a record of audacity.

The 6th Parachute Regiment was a quintessential creation of Nazi Germany. The Nazis had brought together the professionalism of the German army with the new Nazi youth. They gave it new equipment. They would hurl their best against the best the Americans could put into the field. "Let them come," Goebbels had sneered.

Now they had come, and they were in scattered pockets, highly vulnerable. As the first of the sun's rays appeared, Heydte and the elite of the Nazi system marched off to take them on. The first significant counterattack of D-Day was under way. Fittingly, it would pit an American elite force against a German elite force, a trial of systems.

13

"THE GREATEST SHOW EVER STAGED"

The Air Bombardment

"As DAWN BROKE," Captain Shettle of the 506th PIR said, "we could observe one of the most impressive sights of any wartime action. Wave after wave of medium and light bombers could be seen sweeping down the invasion beaches to drop their bombs."[1]

It was the largest air armada ever gathered. It was about to enter the fray in fearsome numbers. On D-Day, the Allies flew more than 14,000 sorties to the Luftwaffe's 250 (most of those against shipping on the fringes of the invasion).*

Many pilots and bomber crews flew three missions that day, nearly every airman flew two. Spaatz, Harris, and Leigh-Mallory put everything that could fly into the attack. They held back no reserves, a sharp reminder of how far they had come in the air war since 1939–42, when the RAF was on the defensive and could not have dreamed of the day they would be leaving Great Britain uncovered.

---

* John Eisenhower graduated from West Point on D-Day. A week later, 2nd Lt. Eisenhower was driving around the beachhead with his father. Lieutenant Eisenhower was astonished to see vehicles moving bumper to bumper, in complete violation of West Point textbook doctrine. "You'd never get away with this if you didn't have air supremacy," he remarked to his father.

The supreme commander snorted. "If I didn't have air supremacy I wouldn't be here."

239

They had earned their victory in the air war and had paid a price for it, partly in equipment, mainly in human lives. It was the most hazardous service in the war. It was also the most glamorous. The foot soldiers envied and resented the airmen. To their eyes, the flyboys hung around barracks doing nothing much of anything, went out at night and got the girls, and had an excess of rank.

What the foot soldiers did not see was the Army Air Force in action. From the flyboys' point of view, they were the veterans who had been at war since 1939 (RAF) or 1942 (U.S.) while the respective armies sat around doing not much of anything.

They lived a strange existence. On bad-weather days, which were a majority, they led quiet barracks lives. On pass, they had their pick of London. On their way to action, for endless hours they were cramped, cold, tense, fearful, and bored. When they entered action they entered hell. With German flak thick enough to walk on coming up from below and German fighters coming in from behind and above, the air crews went through an hour or more of pure terror.

They were not helpless. The Allied bombers bristled with machine guns, in the nose, under the belly, on top, in the rear. Experts told them they would be better off eliminating the weight of those guns and the men who served them. (A B-17 carried thirteen .50-caliber machine guns.) With a lighter airplane, they could fly higher and faster and would be much safer. No, thanks, replied the air crews. They wanted to be able to shoot back.

They took heavy casualties. Statistically, bomber crews could not survive twenty-five missions. *Catch-22* was not fiction. Sgt. Roger Lovelace of the 386th Bomb Group had been told that he could go home after twenty-five missions. Then it was thirty, then thirty-five. On D-Day he was on his sixtieth mission (and eventually did a total of seventy-six).[2] In the two months preceding D-Day, the Allied air forces lost 12,000 men and over 2,000 planes.

They persevered and triumphed. If how much they accomplished in trying to knock out German war production is a subject of continuing controversy, what they had accomplished in driving the Luftwaffe out of France, forcing it back into Germany and a defensive role, is not. They had gone past air superiority to achieve air supremacy.

The strategic air forces had not been built to provide tactical support for the land armies. But with the climax of the Transportation Plan coming in early June, that became their task. All involved agreed that just preceding and on D-Day every bomber in Britain would participate in pounding the Atlantic Wall. There were disagreements on how specifically to do that.

The final plan was as follows: On D-Day minus two, almost half the bombing effort would be in the Pas-de-Calais as part of the Fortitude plan. The next day, half the crews rested while the others were given so-called "milk runs." The RAF Bomber Command would open D-Day with a midnight bombing of coastal batteries and Caen. At first light, the U.S. Eighth Air Force, 1,200 B-17s (Flying Fortresses) and B-24s (Liberators) strong, would bomb for one-half hour the beaches on the Calvados coast while B-26s (Marauders) from Ninth Air Force saturated Utah Beach. If the sky was clear, the bombing would cease five minutes before the troops went ashore; if cloudy, ten minutes.

Spaatz, Tedder, and Leigh-Mallory wanted a 1,500-yard safety zone; ground officers wanted 500 yards; they compromised on 1,000 yards.

After the heavies had returned to England from their dawn attack, they would refuel and go out again, this time to hit bridges and crossroads inland, or to hit Carentan, Caen, and other towns. Spaatz argued against this as inhumane and unlikely to have much impact, but Eisenhower supported Leigh-Mallory on this dispute and those were the orders.[3]

By June 4, Sgt. Roger Lovelace recalled, "the electricity of tension was so thick you could hear it, smell it, feel it." By the evening of June 5, "We felt like we were sitting on a live bomb with the fuse sizzling.

"And then it started. We heard the aircraft overhead, the Dakotas hauling the airborne. We all stood outside and looked up against the semidark sky. There were so many of them it just boggled your mind."[4]

In the briefing rooms at 0200, June 6, the men buzzed with excitement. They agreed that this had to be the invasion. The briefing officers, "grinning like a skunk eating chocolate," called them to attention, pulled back the curtain covering the map, and announced the target. As Lt. Carl Carden of the 370th Bomb Group remembered it, "Everything exploded and the cheers went up all over the room and there was a long period of joy. Now we were getting down to business and from now on the Americans were on the attack."[5]

The details of the briefing kept most spirits high; the crews

were told they would be flying high, that flak would be light and
the Luftwaffe nonexistent. Nevertheless, what about fighter cover,
someone asked. "There will be 3,500 Allied fighters over the beach
this morning," one briefer assured them.

"We were told it was our job to prepare the ground to the
best of our ability to enable the infantry to get ashore, to stay
ashore, and fight and win," Lt. John Robinson of the 344th Bomb
Group, Ninth Air Force said. "We also hoped that while they were
about it they'd kill a whole bunch of those damned antiaircraft
gunners for whom we had no love or pity."[6]

But for the Marauder crews headed for the Cotentin coast,
where they would be hitting artillery emplacements, the details of
their mission were distinctly discouraging. They would be going in
at 500 feet, if necessary.

"Did he say 500 feet?" Sergeant Lovelace asked a buddy.
"That shook us some. The last time B-26s had gone down on the
deck like that they had lost ten out of ten in a low-level mission in
Holland."[7]

The Marauder, a two-engine medium bomber built by Martin, had high tail fins, a cigar-shaped body, and short wings. The
crews called the B-26 the "flying prostitute" because she had "no
visible means of support." They had an affection for the craft that
was well expressed by Lieutenant Robinson: "The Marauders were,
without any doubt, the best bombers in the whole wide world."[8]

For Lt. J. K. Havener of the Ninth Air Force, the target was
the gun position near Barfleur at St.-Martin-de-Varreville. His
plane would carry twenty 250-pound general-purpose bombs. "Our
mission was not to knock out the gun positions but to stun the
German gunners and infantry, keeping them holed up, and to create a network of ready-made foxholes which our troops could use
when they gained a foothold on what was to become known as Utah
Beach."[9]

The B-17s were to go in at 20,000 feet, 10,000 feet lower
than normal, with bomb loads one-third heavier than usual. Targets were coastal batteries and Omaha and the British invasion
beaches. Each Fortress carried sixteen 500-pound bombs.

After the briefings, at airfields all over England, the crews
ate breakfast, then got into trucks for a ride to the revetments,
where they climbed into their bombers. They fired their engines—on the Marauders, the Pratt and Whitney 2,000-horsepower

engines sputtered and coughed and belched out smoke with fire from the exhaust—and they were ready.

Lt. James Delong was the pilot of a B-26 in the 387th Bomb Group. He was part of a thirty-six-ship formation, two boxes of eighteen in flights of six. He recalled that "the taxi out was maddening. The takeoff was just as bad. One plane took off down the right side of the runway; another would open up the throttle as the first plane reached the halfway mark to gun down the left side. It was dark and rainy. A plane in front of me went up in a ball of fire. Was my load too heavy to get off?"

He made it off the runway and began to climb. All around him, bombers were climbing, throttles wide open, using landing lights to avoid collisions. There were some anyway; airmen said that night assembly created a high pucker factor on each seat.

"Even with fifty missions under my belt, my hands were wet and I felt drained of energy," Delong admitted. His group hit a cloud bank and separated. When he emerged at 8,000 feet, the sky was clear. He could not see any of his group, so he hooked onto another group of B-26s and headed for Normandy.[10] Something similar happened to hundreds of pilots.

In his B-17, Lt. John Meyer heard the copilot on the intercom complaining about the clouds: "He was saying, 'It's a damn German secret weapon. Hitler's got another secret weapon.' "[11]

In his B-26, copilot Havener was going through "mental anguish, more so than on any of my previous twenty-four missions. I just couldn't get the thought out of my mind of those poor devils in Holland on that low-level raid. Here we were about to do the same suicidal thing with hundreds of Marauders following us at spaced and regular intervals of only a few minutes."[12]

Lt. A. H. Corry was a bombardier in a B-26. When his plane emerged from the clouds, it was alone. In a minute "I saw a plane pop out of the clouds down below. It was a B-26. So I took my blinker light and sent the code in his direction. He responded affirmatively with the code, then pulled up and stayed on our right wing. Momentarily, another popped up on the left wing. Then more and more until three flights of six planes each were formed and took course toward the invasion coast."[13]

Capt. Charles Harris was the pilot of a B-17 in the 100th Bomb Group. He was the last to take off, at 0345. "As we were absolutely Dead End Charlie in the entire Eighth Air Force, I remember glancing back a couple of times and there was not another plane in the air behind us, but as far as we could see ahead were hundreds and hundreds of planes."[14]

As the low-flying Marauders approached Utah Beach, the sky brightened and the crews saw a sight unique in world history. None of them ever forgot it; all of them found it difficult to describe. Below them, hundreds of landing craft were running into shore, leaving white wakes. Behind the landing craft were the LSTs and other transports, and the destroyers, cruisers, and battleships. "As I looked down at this magnificent operation," Lt. Allen Stephens, a copilot in a B-26 of the 397th Bomb Group said, "I had the surging feeling that I was sitting in on the greatest show ever staged."[15]

Lt. William Moriarity, a B-26 pilot, said, "As we approached the coast, we could see ships shelling the beach. One destroyer, half sunk, was still firing from the floating end. The beach was a bedlam of exploding bombs and shells."[16]

Lieutenant Corry remembered that "the water was just full of boats, like bunches of ants crawling around down there. I imagined all those young men huddled in the landing craft, doubtless scared to death. I could see what they were heading into and I prayed for all those brave young men. I thought, man, I'm up here looking down at this stuff and they're out there waiting to get on that beach."[17]

For the B-17 crews, flying mainly at 20,000 feet, up above the clouds, there was no such sight. They could see nothing but other B-17s. Those that could tucked in behind a pathfinder plane carrying radar. With radar, the lead bombardier would be able to mark a general target area. When the lead plane dropped its bombs, so would the ones following. That was not a textbook method of providing close-in ground support; such bombing was clearly inappropriate to its purpose. Eisenhower had said when he postponed the invasion that he was counting heavily on the air bombardment to get ashore; he added that the Allies would not have undertaken the operation without that asset.

Eventually, after the infamous short bombardment in late July, on the eve of Operation Cobra, Eisenhower learned the lesson that the B-17 was not a suitable weapon for tactical ground support. The testimony from the B-17 pilots and crews describing their experiences on D-Day suggests that the asset was wasted on D-Day, and that the proper use would have been to do what the

B-17 was built to do, pound away at big targets inside Germany (oil refineries, train depots, factory complexes, airfields), and leave the beach bombardment to the Marauders and A-20s (Havocs).

But not even the commanders most dedicated to the idea that strategic airpower would win the war, the ones who had opposed the Transportation Plan so strongly, ever considered for an instant not participating in D-Day. They wanted to be there, and Eisenhower wanted them there.

At 20,000 feet, with heavy clouds below and the sky just beginning to lighten, where "there" was could be a mystery. Many pilots never got themselves located. The orders were, If you can't see the target, or get behind a radar plane, bring the bombs home. In the 466th Bomb Group, sixty-eight B-17s took off, carrying 400,000 pounds of bombs. Only thirty-two were able to drop their bombs. Those that did dropped them blind through the clouds over the British beaches.

Lieutenant Carden had a brother down below. "I did not know where he was, but I wanted to be accurate. We were a little bit late because of the weather, which affected the bombing accuracy of almost every group up there with us."[18] They delayed on the split-second timing so as to avoid hitting men coming ashore; as a consequence, all the bombs from the B-17s fell harmlessly two or even three miles inland.

"It was a day of frustration," said Lieutenant Meyer. "We certainly didn't do as we had planned." The good part for the B-17s was that the flak was light and there was no Luftwaffe. "It was a milk run," Meyer concluded.[19]

At Utah Beach, it was no milk run for the Marauders. They went in low enough for the Germans "to throw rocks at us." Sergeant Lovelace recalled seeing "the first wave just a couple of hundred yards offshore, zigzagging toward the beach. We were running right down the shoreline looking for a target. We were drawing a lot of fire, not the usual 88mm but smaller rapid-fire stuff. I have this frozen image of a machine gunner set up by a barn, firing at us. For a short second I could look right down the barrel of that gun. A waist gunner or a tail gunner could return fire, but up in the top turret I felt helpless. I couldn't bring my guns below horizontal, therefore I couldn't fire on anything."[20]

Lieutenant Havener saw a plane in his box take a flak hit, do a complete snap roll, recover, and carry on. "Unbelievable!" he remarked. "Now we're on our bomb run and another of our ships takes a direct hit, blows up, and goes down. Damn that briefer and his milk run. What's with all this flak!"[21]

Sgt. Ray Sanders was in Havener's plane. "We were accustomed to heavy flak," he said, "but this was the most withering, heavy, and accurate we ever experienced."[22]

On his bomb run, bombardier Corry was well below 1,000 feet, too low to use his bombsight. He could see men jumping out of the landing craft, guys who fell and were floating in the surf, tracers coming from the bunkers, spraying that beach. He used his manual trip switch, with his foot providing the aiming point. He made no attempt to be accurate; he figured "I was making good foxholes for some of those guys coming ashore."[23]

In Havener's B-26, Sergeant Sanders "heard our ship sound like it was being blown or ripped to bits. The sound was much louder than anything I had ever heard and seemed to come from every surface of our ship. Before the terrible noise and jolting had quit, I grabbed the intercom and yelled, 'We've been hit!' And our copilot, Lieutenant Havener, came back on the intercom and said, 'No, we haven't been hit. That was our bombs going off.' We were flying that low."[24]

Lt. John Robinson recalled, "The explosions really bumped my wings at that altitude. It was like driving a car down the ties of a railroad track."[25] Many others had similar experiences, a good indication of how much of the explosive power of those bombs went up in air.

But by no means all of it, as Lt. Arthur Jahnke at La Madeleine could attest. As the Marauders came over, he huddled in his shelter and closed his eyes. A carpet of bombs hit the dunes. Sandsprouts geysered up in whirling pillars several meters high. One bomb landed only a few meters from Jahnke's shelter, burying him. Wounded in the arm, he dug himself out with great difficulty and threw himself into a bomb crater. Even in Russia, he thought, I've never seen anything like this.

Jahnke was at the site of the present-day Utah Beach museum. He had a flashback to a ceremony held on that spot just one week earlier. General Marcks had decorated him with the Iron Cross for his bravery on the Eastern Front. There had been drinking, feasting, and choir singing, followed by a performance by a troupe of visiting actors. The opening line of the play was "How long are we going to sit on this keg of dynamite?" Jahnke's men had broken up laughing.

Now the dynamite had exploded. The two 75mm cannon were destroyed, the 88 damaged, the two 50mm antitank guns gone, as were the flamethrowers. Jahnke's radio and telephone communications with the rear were *kaput*. His men had survived, huddled in their bunkers; when they emerged they were horrified. The mess corporal's assistant, an old man, came running up to Jahnke.

"Everything is wrecked, *Herr Leutnant!* The stores are on fire. Everything's wrecked!"

Shaking his head, he added, "We've got to surrender, *Herr Leutnant.*"

"Have you gone out of your mind, man?" the twenty-three-year-old Jahnke replied. "If we had always surrendered in Russia in this kind of situation the Russians would have been here long ago."

He called out a command, "All troops fall in for entrenching!" Just as they were getting into the work, here came another wave of Marauders. The men huddled in the sand. Jahnke sent a man on a bicycle to report to battalion HQ, but he was killed by a bomb.

As the bombardment ended and the sky brightened, Jahnke could see the naval armada slowly emerging out of the dark and headed straight toward La Madeleine. The sight shattered any morale the Germans had left. Jahnke's men had believed that La Madeleine, with its mighty cannon, was impregnable; now the fortress was destroyed and they were brought face to face with the reality of the naval forces rising up out of the sea. And all Jahnke had to oppose the invaders were two machine guns and two grenade launchers.[26] The American Marauders had done an outstanding job of destroying Rommel's fixed fortifications at Utah before the Germans had an opportunity to fire even one shot.

Another twin-engine bomber, the A-20 Havoc, was also effective in low-level missions, led by the 410th Bomb Group (known, at least to themselves, as "The World's Best Bomb Group," and awarded a Presidential Unit Citation). The 410th blasted Carentan, making it all but impossible for Colonel Heydte to move vehicles out of the city into the battle.

After making the bomb run, the bombers continued across the Cotentin Peninsula, then turned right, flew around the tip of the peninsula and then north to home base in England. That gave them another never-to-be-forgotten sight. As Lieutenant Delong described it, "Out over the French countryside, scattered everywhere, were parachutes, and pieces of crashed gliders. I don't believe I saw an undamaged one. I had this sick feeling that things were not going well."[27]

Lt. Charles Middleton saw parachutes "everywhere, and parts of gliders scattered all over. You could see where they had gone through the hedgerows, leaving wings behind, some burnt and some still intact although not many." Then he saw the most improbable sight: "Not far from the battle zone a farmer was plowing his field. He had a white horse and was seemingly unconcerned about all that was happening around him."[28]

By 0800, many crews were back at base, having a second breakfast. In an hour or two, they were in the air again, bombing St.-Lô and other inland targets. The RAF returned to Caen, trying to concentrate on the railroad station. The Germans in Caen, in retaliation, took eighty French Resistance prisoners out of their cells and shot them in cold blood.

In contrast to the near-total success of the B-26s at Utah, the great bombing raids by B-17s and B-24s of June 6 against Omaha and the British beaches turned out to be a bust. The Allies managed to drop more bombs on Normandy in two hours than they had on Hamburg, the most heavily bombed city of 1943, but because of the weather and the airmen not wanting to hit their own troops most of the blockbusters came down in Norman meadows (or were carried back to England), not on the Atlantic Wall. Yet the B-17 pilots and crews did their best and in some cases made important contributions, certainly far more than the Luftwaffe bomber force.[29]

At the top of the elite world of the Allied air forces stood the fighter pilots. Young, cocky, skilled, veteran warriors—in a mass war fought by millions, the fighter pilots were the only glamorous individuals left. Up there all alone in a one-on-one with a Luftwaffe fighter, one man's skill and training and machine against another's, they were the knights in shining armor of World War II.

They lived on the edge, completely in the present, but young though they were, they were intelligent enough to realize that what they were experiencing—wartime London, the Blitz, the risks—was unique and historic. It would demean them to call them star athletes, because they were much more than that, but they had some of the traits of the athlete. The most important was the lust to compete. They wanted to fly on D-Day, to engage in dogfights, to help make history.

The P-47 pilots were especially eager. In 1943 they had been on escort duty for strategic bombing raids, which gave them plenty of opportunity to get into dogfights. By the spring of 1944, however, the P-47 had given up that role to the longer-ranged P-51 (the weapon that won the war, many experts say; the P-51 made possible the deep penetrations of the B-17s and thus drove the Luftwaffe out of France).

The P-47 Thunderbolt was a single-engine fighter with classic lines. It was a joy to fly and a gem in combat. But for the past weeks, the P-47s had been limited to strafing runs inside France. The pilots were getting bored.

Lt. Jack Barensfeld flew a P-47. At 1830 June 5, he and every other fighter pilot in the base got a general briefing. First came an announcement that this was "The Big One." That brought cheers and "electric excitement I'll never forget," Lt. James Taylor said. "We went absolutely crazy. All the emotions that had been pent-up for so long, we really let it all hang out. We knew we were good pilots, we were really ready for it."[30]

The pilots, talking and laughing, filed out to go to their squadron areas, where they would learn their specific missions.

Barensfeld had a three-quarter-mile walk. He turned to Lt. Bobby Berggren and said, "Well, Bob, this is what we've been waiting for—we haven't seen any enemy aircraft for two weeks and we are going out tomorrow to be on the front row and really get a chance to make a name for ourselves."

Berggren bet him $50 that they would not see any enemy aircraft.[31]

Lieutenant Taylor learned that his squadron would be on patrol duty, 120 miles south of the invasion site, spotting for submarines and the Luftwaffe. They would fly back and forth on a grid pattern.

"We were really devastated," Taylor remembered. "I looked at Smitty and Auyer and they were both looking at the ground, all of us felt nothing but despair. It was a horrible feeling, and lots of the fellows were groaning and moaning and whatnot." Taylor was so downcast he could not eat breakfast. Instead of a knight in shining armor, he was going to be a scout.[32]

The first P-47s began taking off at about 0430. They had not previously taken off at night, but it went well. Once aloft, they became part of the air armada heading for France. Above them were B-17s. Below them were Marauders and Dakotas. The Dakotas were tugging gliders. Around them were other fighters.

Lt. (later Maj. Gen.) Edward Giller was leader for a flight of three P-47s. "I remember a rather harrowing experience in the climb out because of some low clouds. There was a group of B-26s flying through the clouds as we climbed through, and each formation passed through the other one. That produced one minute of sheer stark terror."

It was bittersweet for the P-47 pilots to pass over the Channel. Lt. Charles Mohrle recalled: "Ships and boats of every nature and size churned the rough Channel surface, seemingly in a mass so solid one could have walked from shore to shore. I specifically remember thinking that Hitler must have been mad to think that Germany could defeat a nation capable of filling the sea and sky with so much ordnance."[33]

Lt. Giller's assignment was to patrol over the beaches, to make certain no German aircraft tried to strafe the landing craft. "We were so high," he remembered, "that we were disconnected, essentially, from the activity on the ground. You could see ships smoking, you could see activities, but of a dim, remote nature, and no sense of personal involvement." Radar operators in England radioed a report of German fighters; Giller and every other fighter pilot in the area rushed to the sector, only to discover it was a false alarm.[34]

Lieutenant Mohrle also flew a P-47 on patrol that day. "Flying back and forth over the same stretch of water for four hours, watching for an enemy that never appeared, was tedious and boring."

In the afternoon, Barensfeld flew support for a group of Dakotas tugging gliders to Normandy. The P-47s, flying at 250 miles per hour, had to make long lazy S-turns to keep the C-47s in visual contact; otherwise they would overrun the glider formation. "Battle formation, 2-300 yards apart, then a turn, crossover, then we'd line up again. We were so busy we had no sense of time. Of course, we were looking for enemy aircraft, there weren't any. Mouth dry. Edge of seat. Silence. Very exciting time."

The gliders cut loose. Barensfeld descended to below 1,000 feet to shepherd them into Normandy. But for the gliders the ground was rough and the hedgerows too close together. "It was very disconcerting to see one cut loose, make the circle and hit a hedgerow. I thought, 'My God, this invasion is going to be a failure if they are depending on these gliders for any sort of part.' "[35]

The P-38 Lightning was a twin-engine, twin-boom, single-seat fighter designed by the legendary Clarence "Kelly" Johnson of Lockheed (he later designed the U-2 spy plane). The Germans called it *Gabelschwanz Teufel* (Fork-tailed Devil). Because of its distinctive shape, the Lightning was given the role of close-in support. The thought was that antiaircraft crews on the Allied warships would recognize the shape even if they failed to notice the white bands painted on the wings and booms.

But although they were closer to the action, the P-38 pilots found their high expectations quickly deflating. First, there were too many ships at sea with too many overanxious gun crews who had too much ammunition—the P-38s got shot at by their own gunships, and they found no German aircraft to shoot at themselves. "We circled and weaved in the air over our ships," Capt. Peter Moody said. "We were somewhat envious of the fighters who were allowed to break free and fly over the French coast looking for targets of opportunity. At one point I heard a British controller radio to one of his aircraft: 'Roger, Red Rover, you're free to romp and play.' "[36]

From the point of view of Lt. William Satterwhite, flying a P-38 over Omaha Beach, "German resistance appeared to be devastating. Landing craft were being capsized, some were exploding, and the contents, including men and equipment, were being spilled into the surf in great numbers and quantity."[37]

The Allies put 3,467 heavy bombers, 1,645 medium bombers, and 5,409 fighters into the air on D-Day. Not one plane was shot down by the Luftwaffe. The flak batteries managed to shoot down 113 aircraft.

Overall, except at Utah, the contributions made by the Allied air forces on D-Day could not be characterized as critical, because they had accomplished the critical mission in April and May 1944. They had isolated the battlefield from much of the French railway system, they had made it difficult to impossible for German trucks and tanks to move by day, they had driven the Luftwaffe out of the skies of France.

What they had not done was develop a workable doctrine for

the use of the heavy bombers in tactical support of ground troops, nor had they developed a working method of communication between the soldiers on the ground with those eager-to-shoot P-38 pilots over their heads. Techniques were developed, later in the war, that worked; in December 1944, in the Battle of the Bulge, the air-ground coordination was outstanding, and critical to the victory. But those techniques were not there on D-Day.

But what the air forces had accomplished before D-Day more than justified their cost. How completely the Allies controlled the skies over the battlefield was illustrated dramatically by the single Luftwaffe bombing mission against the beaches. It came at dusk on D-Day. LSTs were jammed together offshore at Omaha, Higgins boats were on the coastline, with jeeps, trucks, aid stations, tanks, men, and other equipment pressed together on the beach. A lucrative, can't-miss target.

Four twin-engined JU-88s appeared over Omaha Beach. The sky was suddenly ablaze with tracers, as every man on a machine gun or antiaircraft gun in that vast fleet opened up. "The barrage was magnificent, thunderous, and terrifying," said Lt. Donald Porter, a fighter aircraft controller on an LCI waiting its turn to go into shore. "The low trajectory of the streams of tracers, mostly .50-caliber machine guns, had us ducking. The Germans were coming in at a very low altitude so our firing was just clearing our own ships. I was huddled on the small and crowded deck with only my helmet and two blankets for protection."

Porter looked up and saw tracers converging just overhead. At that instant, "the JU-88 burst into flame from wingtip to wingtip. It seemed that the flaming plane would crash right on us and our guns were firing into him even as he burned." Some 100 yards away from the LCI, the German plane slid over and "plunged into the water with a hissing sound. Our guns were still firing into him as he hit the sea about fifty yards to the starboard."[38]

The staggering amount of hot metal the fleets poured into those JU-88s sent a signal: whatever happened on the ground, the skies above Normandy belonged to the RAF and the U.S. Army Air Force, while the Channel belonged to the Royal Navy, the U.S. Navy, and the Allied warships.

P-47 pilots were not the only ones who felt a disappointment at not being able to participate more directly in D-Day. Ground crews all over England stayed busy, refueling planes and repairing flak damage, making a direct contribution but still feeling a bit out of it. Staff officers, in London and throughout England, from the different nationalities and services, often despised by the line officers, had done their work in advance and on D-Day could only be spectators. The amount of sheer grind that the staff officers had put in denied some of them even the role of spectator.

Harry Crosby was Group Navigation Officer for the 100th Bomb Group of the Eighth Air Force. He records: "During the week before D-Day I worked twenty-four hours a day. I had to superintend the preparation of maps and flight plans. I had to set up the formations for over a hundred different missions and variations. I had to brief all our navigators as a group and each lead navigator as an individual.

"I was a minute part in the whole operation but I worked for seventy-five hours without even seeing my bed. I didn't shave. My orderly brought me a change of uniforms. I don't remember eating. I remember gallons of coffee, each cup so hot and strong it shocked me into wakefulness."

By dusk on June 5, Crosby was a zombie. His CO told him to go to bed. Crosby protested. The CO made it an order. Crosby fell onto his bed without removing his tie or shoes. He slept for twenty-four hours. So as for D-Day, "I missed it all."[39]

Shortly after Captain Shettle of the paratroops saw the sight that so impressed him, wave after wave of Marauders coming over, he spotted a German antiaircraft battery. "I had my naval radio operator send coordinates to his ship at sea. The naval gunfire came almost immediately, and after correcting their aim, they fired a barrage which silenced the antiaircraft fire."[40]

The incident illustrates the coordination and teamwork that was the hallmark of the Allied effort on June 6. A paratrooper behind enemy lines uses a naval officer who had jumped with him (probably his first jump) to contact warships at sea to silence a battery shooting at Allied aircraft. The men being protected were the men who had made it possible for the paratroopers and Navy to be there in the first place, the men of the Army Air Force.

14

A LONG, ENDLESS COLUMN OF SHIPS

The Naval Crossing and Bombardment

THE MINESWEEPERS went first. There were 255 of them. Their job was to sweep up lanes from the Isle of Wight through the Channel up to the transport anchoring area off the French coast. The mines they were after consisted of contact and antenna mines, some floating, many anchored, plus pressure mines planted on the bottom and exploded by a change in water pressure exerted by the hull of an approaching ship.[1] These mines constituted the Germans' most effective—indeed, virtually only—naval defense.

The mines could be brutally effective. One of them caused the first Allied casualties in the invasion. At about 1700 on June 5, minesweeper USS *Osprey* hit a mine that blew a large hole in the forward engine room. Fires broke out and at 1815 the ship had to be abandoned. *Osprey* sank soon after with a loss of six men.[2]

The minesweeper fleet, under the direct command of Admiral Ramsay, went on with its task. It cleared a wide channel from the Isle of Wight to Point "Z," thirteen miles southeast of the island. Around Point "Z" there was a circle of five miles' radius, nicknamed "Piccadilly Circus," through which all the following vessels would pass. From Point "Z" the minesweepers broke up into groups to sweep ten lanes to France, two for each task force (one for the slower transports, the other for the fast warships). They marked the lanes with lighted dan buoys. When that task was

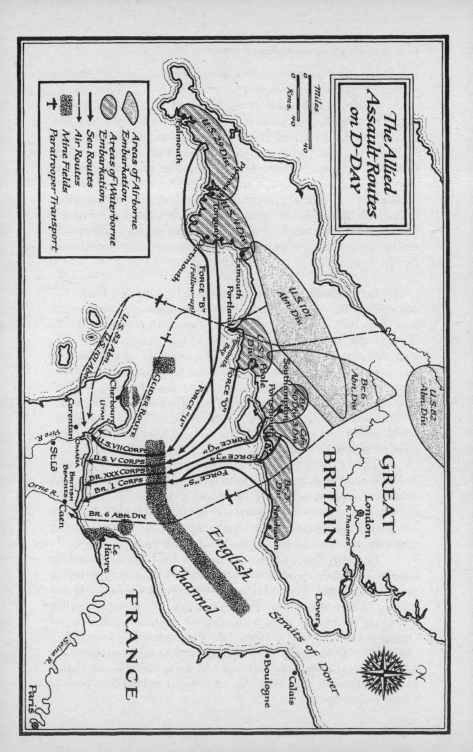

The Allied Assault Routes on D-Day

Legend:
- Areas of Airborne Embarkation
- Areas of Waterborne Embarkation
- Sea Routes
- Air Routes
- Mine Fields
- Paratrooper Transport

Kms. 40
Miles 40

GREAT BRITAIN

London
R. Thames

Dover

Straits of Dover

Calais

Boulogne

Newhaven

Portsmouth
Southampton
Poole

Portland
Portland Bill
Weymouth

Dartmouth
Plymouth

Falmouth

U.S. 29 Div.

U.S. 4 Div.
Torquay

FORCE "B" (Follow-up)

U.S. 101 Abn. Div.

U.S. 82 Abn. Div.

Br. 6 Abn. Div.

U.S. 82 Abn. Div.

U.S. 1 Div.

FORCE "O"

FORCE "U"

FORCE "G"

FORCE "J"

FORCE "S"

50 Div. & 3 Cdn. Div.

Br. 3 Div.

GLIDER ROUTE

Cherbourg

Carentan

UTAH

OMAHA

U.S. VII CORPS

U.S. V CORPS

BR. XXX CORPS

BR. I CORPS

BR. 6 ABN. DIV.

BRITISH BEACHES

St. Lô

Vire R.

Orne R.

Caen

Le Havre

Seine R.

Paris

FRANCE

English Channel

N

completed, their assignment was to move in to sweep the shallow waters off the invasion beaches.

Destroyers provided cover. The lead destroyer for the lead flotilla of minesweepers came from the first nation Hitler had overrun; it was Polish, named *Slazak*, commanded by Capt. Romuald Nalecz-Tyminski. Just behind *Slazak* was HMS *Middleton*. Next came the Norwegian destroyer *Svenner*. The minesweepers they were covering were British, Canadian, and American—a fine show of Allied unity. At 2315, June 5, the three destroyers entered channel no. 10, alongside the minesweepers that cleared the lane and marked it with dan buoys. At 0303 June 6 the job was done and the destroyers took up their patrol station opposite Ouistreham (Sword Beach).

Behind the minesweepers came the LCT flotilla. Each LCT carried four DD tanks and four jeeps with trailers full of ammunition, plus their crews. For the 29th Division's sector of Omaha (Easy Green, Dog Red, Dog White, and Dog Green), sixteen LCTs were bringing across the Channel sixty-four DD tanks. The plan was to launch the swimming tanks from five kilometers offshore. The timing had to be precise; the tanks were scheduled to climb onto the beach and commence firing at pillboxes at H-Hour minus five minutes, in order to provide cover for the first wave of infantry, which would land at H-Hour (0630, an hour after first light and an hour after dead low tide).

The LCTs were in the van because they were the slowest and most difficult to maneuver vessels in the fleet. LCTs were built from three sections bolted together to form the 110-foot craft, with the heavy machinery in the stern and the bow both high and light. They were flat-bottomed with no center board. In a strong wind or tidal current it was all but impossible to hold them on course.

Lt. Dean Rockwell commanded the LCT flotilla headed for Omaha. On June 5 he set off on his twenty-hour journey to the far shore. At Piccadilly Circus he had his first problem—LCT 713 was missing. There were ships, vessels, and boats of all types circling and trying to form up, some with a big "O" painted on the side (for Omaha), others with a "U" for Utah. Rockwell finally found LCT 713 with its "O" cruising "blithely along among ships with great big 'U's on them. I came alongside and told the captain to look around and see where he was. 'Oh,' he said, and I guided him back to where he belonged."

Rockwell headed for France. The wind was strong, holding position was difficult, even staying afloat was a problem. Those Sherman tanks weighed thirty-two tons each, plus their ammo, food, fuel, and men. "So, combined with our weight, we had very little freeboard. In fact, the seas were running in over our decks." Everyone was miserable, especially the tankers.[3]

At 0400 June 6, the LCTs reached the transport sector of Omaha. At 0415 they went from condition 1 to general quarters. At 0510 they went a kilometer closer to the beach, to their launch position five kilometers offshore. At 0522 the crews secured from general quarters to take up their beaching stations.

Although the strong westerly winds continued, they were now in the lee of the Cotentin Peninsula and the seas were relatively moderate.

Behind the LCTs came the bombardment groups, battleships, cruisers and destroyers. There were six battleships (three American, three British), twenty cruisers (three American, three French, the remainder British and Canadian), sixty-eight destroyers (thirty-one American, one Norwegian, one Polish, the others British and Canadian). The battleships were old; *Nevada*, with ten 14-inch guns, had been commissioned in 1916 and had been the only battleship to get under way at Pearl Harbor. *Texas*, mounting ten 14-inch guns, was two years older, while *Arkansas* (commissioned 1912, with twelve 12-inch guns) had been scheduled for disposal and had been saved only by the coming of the war. HMS *Warspite* was twenty-nine years old; she carried eight 15-inch guns, as did HMS *Ramillies* (commissioned 1917); HMS *Rodney*, with nine 16-inch guns, was the youngest of the battleships (commissioned 1927).

The "old ladies," navy men called the battleships. They would be dueling the heavy German batteries. In the Utah Beach sector, the Germans had 110 guns ranging from 75mm up to 170mm. Inland, they had eighteen batteries, the largest consisting of four 210mm guns in casements near St.-Marcouf. The old ladies were expendable and it was expected that one or two of them at least would be lost, but they would make their contribution by drawing the huge shells away from the beach and onto them.

The main group of destroyers came behind the cruisers and battleships, ahead of the transports, LCIs, LCCs (landing craft control, carried part of the way on LSTs before being lowered by davits to the sea), LCMs, and others. The entire fleet included 229

LSTs, 245 LCIs, 911 LCTs, 481 LCMs, all under their own power, and 1,089 LCVPs riding on LSTs to the transport area, plus various other transports, Coast Guard rescue boats, PT boats, blockships that would be sunk to create artificial harbors off Gold and Utah, and more.

The most unwieldy craft, even worse than the LCTs, were the Rhino ferries, barges hooked together carrying trucks, jeeps, bulldozers, and other heavy equipment, towed by LSTs across the Channel, with outboard motors to provide their own propulsion for the run-in to the beach.[4]

On USS *Bayfield*, an attack transport that served as headquarters for Maj. Gen. Raymond O. Barton, commander of the 4th Infantry Division, the decks were jammed with troops and sailors. Barton's deputy commander, Brig. Gen. Theodore Roosevelt, moved among the men, speaking softly and soothingly. Countless members of the 4th Division recall the words of reassurance that Roosevelt, the oldest man going ashore that day, said to them. They remember, too, that he began singing and urged them to join in. Lt. John Robert Lewis described the scene: "During the cruise across, we all assembled on the deck of the *Bayfield* and sang 'The Battle Hymn of the Republic' and 'Onward Christian Soldiers.' This was a very sobering time to sing the words, 'As God died to make men holy, let us die to make men free.' "[5]

Seaman Joseph Donlan, a radio operator on *Bayfield*, remembered thinking that at that moment his high-school class was holding graduation exercises. Had he not joined the Navy, he would have been there.[6] On LST 530, Seaman Gene Sizemore reported to Capt. Anthony Duke. Just before departing England, Sizemore had told Duke, "I'm only fifteen, Captain, and I don't want to go on this trip." (He had lied about his age when he enlisted.) Duke had replied, "Well, Sizemore, you are going anyway."

"Well, Captain, I am scared," Sizemore rejoined, "and I want to get off, NOW."

Duke said he felt sorry for him, but the best he could do was order Sizemore to report to the bridge every hour: "That way, I'll be able to see how you're doing and you'll be able to see how I'm doing." So Sizemore reported, and he was doing fine.

LST 530 was headed to Gold Beach, the second LST in a column of twelve. One of the first things Duke did was order the barrage balloon cut loose. The cables were snapping in the wind and were a danger to the crew. Other LST skippers did the same. Looking around, Duke recalled, "By God, I'll never forget the feeling of power—power about to be unleashed—that welled up in me as I viewed the long, endless columns of ships headed toward Normandy."[7]

In spite of the wind and rough sea, the crowded movement of the thousands of Allied ships and small craft ran off close to schedule, with some minor bumping but no major collisions. This remarkable feat, according to Admiral Morison, was incredible enough to "suggest divine guidance."[8]

Against this host, the Germans could put into action a handful of gunboats, a few submarines, a small fleet of E-boats, and nothing more. In World War I, Germany had challenged Britain for control of the seas; by 1944 the Germans had only three ships larger than destroyers still afloat—the cruisers *Prinz Eugen*, *Nürnberg*, and *Emden*—and they were in port on D-Day.

At 2300, *Nevada*, followed by cruisers *Quincy*, *Tuscaloosa*, and HMS *Black Prince*, Piccadilly Circus to head south-southeast for Utah. At 0230, *Nevada* reached her position, eleven miles off the coast. "As we neared our position in the Bay of the Seine," Lt. Ross Olsen recalled, "we felt like we were sneaking up on the enemy and even talked in whispers, thinking that we might be heard by the Germans on the beach, which of course was impossible. But when we cut loose the anchor, it made a tremendous noise as the anchor chain went through the hawsepipe." Olsen was sure the Germans had to have heard it.[9] Quickly the rattle of other chains running through hawsepipes filled the air, off Utah and the other four beaches.

The Germans heard nothing, saw nothing. Although there had been a steady stream of ships coming from Piccadilly Circus since well before midnight, lined up so close in their columns as to practically form a bridge from the Isle of Wight to Normandy, and although the first ships reached the transport areas around 0200, German search radar failed to pick up anything. This was partly due to German inefficiency, more to the effectiveness of preinvasion air bombardment, when the bombers had made radar sites on the coast primary targets, destroying some and damaging many more. Further, the Allied aircraft were throwing down "windows," foil strips that caused hundreds of echoes on the German radars. Admiral Krancke had canceled the usual E-boat parrols because of the foul weather, so the boats were still in port in Le Havre, Ouistreham, and Cherbourg.

At 0309, German radar finally spotted the fleet. Krancke

promptly issued orders to the shore batteries to prepare to repel an invasion. He sent the E-boat flotillas and two armed trawlers into battle; they were under way by 0348.

In the American transports, the cooks fed the soldiers Spam sandwiches and coffee. On the British LSTs, the men got a fried-egg breakfast (swimming in grease) and a tot of rum. Lt. Cmdr. B. T. Whinney (RN), the beachmaster for Gold, was astonished when at 0200 in the officers mess on *Empire Arquebus* sharply uniformed stewards wearing white gloves proffered menus.[10]

Between 0100 and 0400, depending on when the men were due to arrive at the beach, the bos'ns' whistles sounded on the LSTs: "Now hear this! All Navy hands man your battle stations." The sailors scurried to their posts. The bos'ns' whistles sounded again: "Now hear this! All assault troops report to your debarkation areas." The men climbed into their LCVPs and other craft; when the whistle sounded again, followed by the order "Away all boats!" the heavily loaded craft were swung by the davits over the side and slowly lowered into the water.

On *Empire Javelin*, a British transport carrying the 1st Battalion, 116th Infantry, 29th Division, off Omaha Beach, the davit lowering one craft got stuck for half an hour halfway down the ship's side, directly beneath the scupper. "During this half-hour, the bowels of the ship's company made the most of an opportunity that Englishmen have sought since 1776," recalled Maj. Tom Dallas, the battalion executive officer. "Yells from the boat were unavailing. Streams, colored everything from canary yellow to sienna brown and olive green, continued to flush into the command group, decorating every man aboard. We cursed, we cried, and we laughed, but it kept coming. When we started for shore, we were all covered with shit."[11]

The landing craft that had made the crossing hanging on booms over the sides of the LSTs were lowered into the water with only their coxswains aboard. As the coxswains of the LCVPs (mostly Coast Guard, almost all young, many still teenagers) brought their engines to life and began circling, the LSTs and other transports dropped their rope nets over the side.

The men descending to their Higgins boats on those scramble nets provide one of the most enduring images of D-Day. Like the paratroopers who had dropped into France during the night, the infantry and combat engineers were grossly overloaded with weapons, ammunition, and rations. Their impregnated clothing and heavy boots added to their cumbersome, awkward feeling. It was dark and the Channel swells raised and lowered the little landing craft by ten feet and more.

As the coxswains brought them alongside, officers on deck instructed their men to time their jumps off the nets into the boats—jump as the landing craft reached the top of a swell so as to shorten the distance. Many failed: there were more than two dozen broken legs in the first hour alone. A few got caught between the ship and the landing craft: at least three men were squashed to death, others badly injured.

Seaman Ronald Seaborne, a naval telegraphist going into Gold as a forward observer, was carrying his haversack, a radio, a telescopic aerial, a revolver, and an assortment of pouches. Everything was on his back, which made him top-heavy, except the aerial, which he carried in one hand, leaving only one hand free to scramble down the net. "For me, that scramble was the most difficult part of the entire Normandy operation. But for a lucky wave which almost washed the craft back onto the boat deck of the LST, and thus reduced the distance of my inevitable fall to a small one, I doubt very much whether I would have made the transit."[12] Overall, considering the difficulties, the loading went well.

On the Higgins boats, assault platoons of thirty men and two officers, carrying bangalore torpedoes, mortars, BARs, rifles, and other weapons, jammed together. They had to stand; there was insufficient room for anyone to sit. The tops of the gunwales were just about at eye level. When the boats were loaded, the coxswains pulled away from the mother ship and began to circle. The circles grew ever larger.

The boats bobbed up and down—and almost immediately most of the Spam, or eggs and rum, consumed earlier ended up on the decks, which made the decks exceedingly slippery. On Seaman Seaborne's LCM, a Royal Marine brigadier "sat majestically on the seat of a jeep, whilst the rest of us huddled miserably between the jeep and the sides of the craft trying to avoid the vast quantity of cold sea spray coming over the gunwales." Men began throwing up; the wind flung the vomit back on the jeep and the brigadier. "He shouted to all on board that anyone feeling sick was to go to the other side of the craft and within seconds the portside was full of green-faced men."

As the LCM circled, the wind came in off the port, throwing another wave of vomit on the brigadier and his jeep. "Fortunately, the brigadier then succumbed to the motion and was past caring about the dreadful state he and his jeep got into."[13]

Lt. John Ricker commanded the LCC designated as primary control vessel for Tare Green Beach, Utah. Lt. Howard Vander Beek, commanding LCC 60, set off for the coast, astern of Ricker's PC 1176. Along with the boats carrying underwater demolition teams from the Navy and the LCTs, the LCCs were in the van.

Waiting for the LCVPs and other craft to join up for the run into the beach, Vander Beek said, "We felt naked, defenseless. Although hundreds of friendly guns on U.S. battleships, cruisers, and destroyers behind us were poised and silent, ready to begin their onslaught, there were Wehrmacht batteries ahead, waiting for enough light to fire."[14]

It was a cool night and the spray hitting the men in the face was cold, but the soldiers and sailors gathered off the Normandy coast were sweating. Tension, fear, and anticipation were the dominant emotions. The drone of the engines of the landing craft began to be overwhelmed by the drone of the first waves of bombers. Behind the forward naval elements the ten swept channels were jammed bow to stern with follow-up forces. The sailors manning the 5-, 10-, 12-, and 14-inch guns on the warships were at their battle stations, ready to commence firing.

What the airborne troops had started the seaborne armada was about to continue. What Hitler had sown he was now to reap. The free peoples of the world were sending the best of their young men and the products of their industry to liberate Western Europe and crush him and his Nazi Party.

Shortly after 0520 the light began to come up in the east. Bombers began to drop their loads, German antiaircraft gunners to shoot at them. But in the transport and bombardment areas, it was ominously quiet. No German batteries opened fire; the Allied warships were not due to commence firing until 0550 (H-Hour minus forty minutes) unless they were fired upon.

On the destroyer USS McCook off Omaha, Lt. Jerry Clancy shook his head. "What I can't understand is why they don't fire on us," he told reporter Martin Sommers, standing beside him. "None of us could understand it," Sommers wrote later, "and we all wished they would start firing, so we could start firing back. That would be much better than waiting." As the air bombardment increased in intensity, "a reverent chorus of Ah's ran through the ship. . . .

Thunderous explosions rolled along the shore, followed by high bursts of multicolored flak, and then a geyser of flame here, another there. . . . The blasts were coming so fast that they merged into one roar. The shoreline became a broken necklace of flame."

Sommers and Clancy tried to make conversation but could scarcely hear each other. "I guess this is about the longest hour in history," Clancy commented.[15]

At 0535, the German batteries commenced firing on the fleet. Off Utah, Lieutenant Olsen on *Nevada* saw shells hitting all around. It seemed to him that every German gun in France was concentrated on *Nevada*. "We learned later that we were straddled twenty-seven times by shells and never hit. We had been shelled for what seemed like ages," he said, "before we saw our main battery of 14-inch guns being trained and ready to open fire."[16]

When the battleships opened fire, it was as if Zeus were hurling thunderbolts at Normandy. The noise, the concussion, the great belches of fire from the muzzles, made an unforgettable impression on every man present. Soldiers in Higgins boats could see the huge shells as they passed overhead. Seaman James O'Neal, on an LCI off Juno Beach, noted that each time the battleships let go a salvo, "they would be pushed sideways by the force of their guns, making fairly large waves, and as these waves came in toward the beach they would pass us and rock our craft."[17]

Holdbrook Bradley was a correspondent for the *Baltimore Sun* on an LST off Omaha. Six years later, he was a correspondent in Korea; twenty-five years later he covered Vietnam. As he put it in his oral history, "The sound of battle is something I'm used to. But this [the opening bombardment on D-Day] was the loudest thing I have ever heard. There was more firepower than I've ever heard in my life and most of us felt that this was the moment of our life, the crux of it, the most outstanding."

To Bradley, the initial salvo from the warships was one huge explosion, "A hell of an explosion. I never heard anything like it in my life."[18]

On the *Bayfield*, ship's stores officer Lt. Cyrus Aydlett hurried on deck to observe. "It was like the fireworks display of a thousand Fourth of Julys rolled into one," he wrote in his diary. "The heavens seemed to open, spilling a million stars on the coastline before us, each one spattering luminous, tentacle-like branches of flame in every direction. Never before has there been any more perfect coordination of firepower than that unloosed by our air and naval forces on this so-called impregnable coastline which 'Herr

Schickelgruber' had so painstakingly fortified with every obstacle man is capable of conceiving. Pillows of smoke and flame shot skyward with great force—the resounding blasts even at our distance were terrifying—concussion gremlins gave involuntary, sporadic jerks on your trouser legs—the ship shrugged and quivered as if she knew what was occurring."

One of the men watching with Aydlett shouted in his ear, "I'll bet there are a lot of dirty drawers on this ship right now."[19] There were a lot more among the Germans in the casements taking the pounding.

The Allied airborne troopers witnessed the bombardment from the receiving end, some shells falling between them and the beach, others passing overhead. John Howard at Pegasus Bridge described it this way: "The barrage coming in was quite terrific. You could feel the whole ground shaking toward the coast. Soon they lifted the barrage farther inland. They sounded so big, and being poor bloody infantry, we had never been under naval fire before and these damn great shells came sailing over, such a size that you automatically ducked, even in the pillbox, as one went over, and my radio operator was standing next to me, very perturbed about this, and finally he said, 'Blimey, sir, they're firing jeeps.' "[20]

In Vierville, the tiny village atop the bluff at the west end of Omaha, the air bombardment had awakened the populace. When the bombers passed, "a strange calm succeeded." Pierre and Jacqueline Piprel hurried to the home of M. Clement Marie because they knew he had, despite stern German orders, a pair of binoculars. "From a window in the attic the three of us in turn were able to contemplate the formidable armada, getting bigger and bigger as it closed in. We could not see the sea anymore, only ships all over."

Then came the first salvo. Naval shells descended on Vierville. Within minutes, "there was not a single glass left on the windows." One shell exploded in the upstairs bedroom "and everything fell in the dining room below." Another shell whistled through the house, coming in one window and going out another. A shell exploded in the baker's bakehouse, killing the maid and the baker's baby she was holding in her arms.[21]

Every gun in the Allied fleet was blazing away. USS *Harding*, a destroyer, Comdr. George G. Palmer commanding, opened fire at 0537 on Omaha Beach. The target was a battery east of Port-en-Bessin, range 4,800 yards. *Harding* sent forty-four rounds of 5-inch shells toward the German guns, temporarily neutralizing them. Meanwhile, near misses from the Germans sent geysers up all around *Harding;* the nearest miss was seventy-five yards over.

At 0547 *Harding* shifted her fire to three pillboxes some 3,000 yards distant, in the Colleville draw. She expended 100 rounds before smoke completely obscured the target. By then the entire shore had disappeared in clouds of smoke, dust, and debris. Commander Palmer could not see his landmarks and began to navigate by radar.

When the wind made intermittent observation possible, *Harding* opened fire on a house in the draw; twenty rounds destroyed the place. At 0610 *Harding* shifted fire to another fortified house and destroyed it after expending forty rounds. Spotting an enemy fieldpiece on Omaha Beach, with a crew preparing to fire at incoming landing craft, at 0615 *Harding* closed the shore to 1,700 yards and fired six salvos at the German gun. The shelling did not destroy the gun but it did send the German personnel scattering back into the bluffs.[22]

All the while German guns ashore blasted back. The men on *Harding* could hear the whine and scream of the shells as they passed overhead and astern. Lt. William Gentry remembered that the Germans were shooting at the battleships and cruisers seaward of *Harding,* "but their trajectories were so flat that shells were whizzing by at the level of our stacks. Some members of the crew were sure a couple of shells went between our stacks."

At 0620, as the landing craft approached Omaha Beach, the gunnery officer reported "mission completed" and Commander Palmer ordered "Cease fire."[23]

There were sixty-eight Allied destroyers off the five beaches; each of them participated in the prelanding bombardment in a manner similar to *Harding,* pounding their prearranged targets—mainly pillboxes and other fortified positions, or the spires of the church steeples—and then shifting to targets of opportunity before lifting fire to allow the landing craft to get in.

Two of the destroyers had bad luck. The Norwegian destroyer *Svenner* was on the far left flank, nearest Le Havre. At 0537 the half dozen E-boats from Le Havre, ordered into action by Admiral Krancke, dashed in as close to the fleet as they dared and unleashed a volley of torpedoes. The only hit was on *Svenner,* just off the port bow of *Slazak.* Captain Nalecz-Tyminski described the result: "A flash of explosion occurred amidships, followed by the sound of detonation and then the burst of fire and smoke that shot high into the air. *Svenner* broke amidship and sank."[24] Capt. Kenneth Wright, a commando, wrote his parents five days later: "It was rather appalling. The ship just cracked in half, and the two ends folded together as if it were a pocketknife closing."[25]

Svenner was the only Allied ship sunk by the German navy that day. Even as the E-boats fired their torpedoes, HMS *Warspite* attacked them. The battleship sank one and the remainder did a quick about-face and returned to the relative safety of Le Havre. Thus ended the sole serious attempt by the *Kriegsmarine* to interfere with the landings.

Off Utah Beach, planes laying a smoke screen between the Germans and the bombardment fleet appeared at 0610 to do their job, but the plane which should have hidden USS *Corry*, a destroyer, was shot down by flak. For a few moments, therefore, *Corry* was the only Allied ship the German gunners could see. They concentrated a heavy fire on her. *Corry* began to maneuver rapidly, firing all the while. She was taking a great risk, as only a relatively small area had been swept of mines.

Machinist Mate Grant Gullickson was down in the forward engine room. The pipes were dripping wet, the turbines hissing steam. "Our job was to give the skipper [Lieutenant Commander Hoffman] whatever he asked for, full speed ahead, emergency astern. Overhead the guns roared.

"All of a sudden, the ship literally jumped out of the water! As the floor grates came loose, the lights went out and steam filled the space." *Corry* had struck a mine amidships.

"It was total darkness with steam severely hot and choking," Gullickson said. He was in what must be one of the most terrifying situations known to man, caught in the engine room with bursting turbines, boilers, and pipes in a sinking ship. The water was rising; within minutes it was up to his waist.

"At this time, there was another rumble from underneath the ship." *Corry* had struck another mine and was all but cut in two. Hoffman headed out for sea by hand-steering his ship, but within minutes *Corry* lost all power and began to settle. At 0641 Hoffman ordered abandon ship.

Down in the forward engine room, "we grappled to open the hatch, which we did and began to evacuate," Gullickson recounted. "By the time we got up on deck, the main deck was awash and ruptured clean across. It was obvious the *Corry* was dead.

"I noticed at this time that my life belt and shirt were missing. They had been ripped from my body by the explosion. I abandoned ship on the starboard side about midship. We didn't jump off, we literally floated off because the ship was underwater." Two hours later, he and others were picked up by USS *Fitch*, given coffee laced with the ship's torpedo alcohol, and eventually transferred to a transport and taken back to a hospital in England.

"On this ship was Chief Ravinsky, the chief of the forward fire room. He had steam burns over 99 percent of his body. We tended to him and he could talk a little but the burns were too much; he passed away the next day."[26]

Seaman Joseph Dolan was stationed in the combat information center (CIC) of the *Bayfield*. "I still remember the urgent message that I copied from the *Corry*. It said *Corry* was hit and was sinking, and they had many casualties and needed help quickly. Most messages were coded, but this one was in the clear because of the urgency of the situation."[27]

Seaman A. R. Beyer of the *Fitch* was launched in a whaleboat to pick up survivors. He remembered that *Corry*'s stern stayed up to the last. He saw a man clinging to the top blade of the *Corry*'s propeller, but there were a great number of survivors clinging to debris or rafts and he picked them up first. By the time he turned back to *Corry*, the man on the propeller was gone. *Fitch* took 223 survivors on board in the course of the morning.[28]

Ens. Doug Birch was on a subchaser off Utah Beach. When the *Corry* hit the mine, "many people were blown into the water and I had the experience of finding a sailor who had B-positive blood and helping him on a direct transfusion on our deck, after he was hauled aboard. When the pharmacist mate said, 'He's dead,' I wasn't sure if it was him or me."[29]

The mines were playing hell with the Allied vessels off Utah. PC 1261 struck a mine at 0542 and sank in four minutes. At 0547, LCT 597, directly astern of PC 1176, struck a mine. Lt. Vander Beek in LCC 60 saw her lifted out of the water by the powerful force of the mine. "We were but a few yards away and felt the explosion's potent shock waves course through our craft." LCT 597 went down instantly, taking the cargo of four DD tanks with her.

At about the same time, Vander Beek learned that his sister craft, LCC 80, had fouled her screw on a dan buoy and was out of commission. That left only Vander Beek's LCC 60 as a guide for the LCTs and first wave of LCVPs at Omaha. It was an impossible task for one boat to do the work of three, made even worse by the offshore wind and strong tidal current. As Vander Beek guided the LCTs and LCVPs in to shore, he drifted to his left, so that when he signaled them to go on in, they were 500 to 1,000 meters southeast of their intended landing site. This proved to be fortuitous.[30]

By 0600, the remaining LCTs had launched their DD tanks. As the tanks swam ashore they were hampered by the head wind and tidal current. The Higgins boats comprising the first and second waves passed through them, headed for shore.

As the landing craft moved in, the battleships and cruisers continued to fire. As they belted away they raised a continuous wall of sound, so immense it could be felt as well as heard. German batteries and the drumming of the engines of the bombers overhead added to it.

Nevada was anchored off Utah. *Texas* and *Arkansas* were off Omaha. They were at anchor because the swept area was too narrow to allow maneuvering, meaning the Navy regarded the mines as more dangerous than the German batteries. The transports were behind them, the destroyers and landing craft in front, headed toward shore in columns of Higgins boats, DUKWs, LCIs, and LCTs. Supporting the battleships were the cruisers.

For *Nevada*, the initial targets for her 14-inch guns were German batteries. Her smaller guns were drenching the beach with shells. At 0620 *Nevada* turned her 14-inchers onto the beach as well; General Collins had requested this action, saying he had great confidence in the accuracy of the big guns and wanted them to knock gaps in the concrete seawall. The guns were firing point-blank, almost on the horizontal; as the great shells passed over, men on the Higgins boats swore that the vacuums created by the passing shells caused the boats to actually lift out of the water.

At Omaha, *Texas* blasted away at the battery on Pointe-du-Hoc, where the rangers were shortly scheduled to land. By 0550 it was light enough for spotter planes to direct the fire. The huge naval shells dug numerous craters in Pointe-du-Hoc, tumbled great chunks of cliff into the sea, and apparently destroyed the casemates holding the guns.

Wing Comdr. L. C. Glover was an RAF spotter for HMS *Warspite*, which was pounding away at the Villerville battery to the east of Sword Beach. He was flying midway between the ship and the shore. "I called out the order 'fire' and turned slowly broadside on to the shore to wait for the fall of shot. Suddenly, in the clear sky my aircraft experienced a most violent bump which practically shook me out of my wits. At the same moment, I saw two enormous objects moving rapidly away from me toward the shore and immediately realized that I had flown at right angles through the slipstream of *Warspite's* two ranging 15-inch 'bricks.' Awestruck, I followed the shells down quite easily with my eyes during the rest of their curved flight and saw one of them actually hit the gun emplacement we were engaging!" Less happily, Glover reported that at least two Allied planes were hit and destroyed by shells that day.[31]

At 0615, *Texas* turned her 14-inch guns on the exit road at the western end of Omaha. That road led up a ravine to the village of Vierville. As Admiral Morison put it, "The volume and accuracy of naval fire would largely determine how tough a time the 1st Battalion 116th Regiment [29th Division] would have to secure this exit after H-Hour."[32]

The Germans were firing back from their batteries at Port-en-Bessin. Nick Carbone, a sailor from Brooklyn on *Texas,* watched a great German shell skip in the water just between *Texas* and a British cruiser. Imitating a famous American voice, Carbone said, "I hate war. Eleanor hates war."[33]

On the western end of Omaha, *Arkansas* turned her guns on a battery at Les Moulins, while the cruisers and destroyers pounded away at German casemates and pillboxes situated along the bluff (where the cemetery stands today). Off the British and Canadian beaches, a bombardment just as intense was hurled at the enemy.

In short, a tremendous tonnage of shells hit the beaches and batteries. The results, for the most part, were terribly disappointing. As anyone who has visited the Normandy beaches will attest, this was not because of inaccurate fire, but rather the result of German skill in fortification building. Seaman Ian Michie, on HMS *Orion,* a cruiser, was right when he said, "Our shooting was very good and direct hits were soon being recorded. We scored thirteen direct hits on the battery before shifting target."[34] But at Longues-sur-Mer, Pointe-du-Hoc, Port-en-Bessin, St.-Marcouf, Azeville, and the other batteries, the casemates stand today, battered but unbroken. They took many direct hits, dozens in some cases, but even the 14-inch shells failed to penetrate. The shells made pock marks, they knocked away some concrete, they exposed the steel reinforcing rods, but they did not penetrate.

Many of the German gunners inside were rendered deaf or

knocked out by concussions. An official report from the Royal Navy admitted that "no serious damage either to the concrete structures or the guns in the strong points" was achieved, but pointed out that the shelling "effectively neutralized the positions by terrifying the enemy personnel in them and by preventing them from manning their weapons and firing on the troops during the landings."[35]

That was wishful thinking. Between the lifting of the naval bombardment and the landing of the first waves, many Germans managed to man their guns and commence firing. Inaccurately, it should be added: they had no spotter planes, and the forward observation posts on the edge of the cliffs were blinded by the smoke, so although they dueled with the battleships and cruisers, sitting at anchor, they scored no hits.

The smaller batteries, pillboxes, and Tobruks, the ones right on the beach or in the bluff above Omaha, also took a pounding and survived. Those on the beach had embrasures opening to the sides, not out to sea, so as to deliver enfilading fire parallel to the shoreline while being fully protected from fire from the warships. As the first wave hit, they came to life, delivering a withering fire at the tanks and infantry.

From the point of view of the soldiers going ashore, the great naval bombardment was as ineffective as the great air bombardment. According to Admiral Morison, the reason was "not enough time was allowed," and the fault was the Army's, not the Navy's, because the Army did not wish the bombardment to start before daylight. In Morison's opinion, H-Hour should have been postponed to 0730 "to give naval gunfire more time to play on beach defenses."[36]

As the warships lifted their fire and took on targets inland, LCT(R)s went into action. Lt. Eugene Bernstein was in command of the lead LCT(R) at Omaha, with thirteen other craft following him. At 3,500 meters the LCT(R)s spread out into a line abreast with 100 meters between the craft. Bernstein recalled being amazed that he was right on target and right on time.[37]

Medic W. N. Solkin was in LCT(R) 450. He remembered that each member of the crew was armed "with a fire extinguisher. Our skipper was in the conning tower with his finger on a button. We held our breath, hanging onto anything that was stationary. We fired our rockets and hell broke loose.

"The ship seemed to explode. We listed sharply and I remember being buried under arms and legs. Now the fire extinguishers came into play. Small fires broke out and smoke rose up through the bulkheads. The heat and noise were terrific. Everyone was cursing and screaming and fighting the flames that threatened to envelop the entire craft.

"I can't describe the sound of a thousand rockets being released in less than a minute. I remember a shipmate describing it as the rush of a hurricane. The craft shuddered, was thrust backward, and momentarily lost steerage."[38]

The rockets—14,000 of them—whooshed over the Higgins boats in the first wave, arching their way to the beach. As Joseph Balkoski, historian of the 29th Division, put it, "Their roar was like the final crescendo of a great symphony."[39]

To the men on the Higgins boats, it seemed that no man could possibly live through such a bombardment. Unfortunately, many of the rockets fell harmlessly into the surf. A few hit at the lower edge of the bluff and in the level areas between the bluff and the beach. The rockets set off grass fires, which provided some smoke, and caused land mines to explode—but they killed few if any German defenders.

There was one final bombardment from the sea. It came from Sherman tanks aboard LCTs approaching the shoreline. Under the circumstances—rough water, smoke and haze, extreme excitement—it was wildly inaccurate. But that those Shermans were close enough to the beach to fire was itself a near miracle, made possible by the courage and common sense of one man, Lieutenant Rockwell, who had just made what was perhaps the single most important command decision of any junior officer on D-Day.

The LCTs approaching Omaha were supposed to launch their DD tanks five kilometers offshore. They had split into two groups. The eight LCTs to the left of Rockwell's flotilla launched as planned, and all but three of the thirty-two tanks sank. The swells were too high, the tanks too low, the skirts insufficient. There was a certain gallantry involved, as tank after tank drove across the lowered ramp and into the water despite seeing the tank in front go down.

There was also a certain stubbornness and blind stupidity involved. The tank commanders could see the tank in front of them get hit by a wave, the canvas collapse, the tank disappear—but they had been given the order to launch, so launch they did. The skippers of the LCTs watched helplessly, rendered immobile by fright, unwilling to take charge. It was a pitiful sight.

Only the skipper of LCT 600, Ens. H. P. Sullivan, was

brave enough to take command. When he saw the first tank in his group of four sink he ordered the crew to pull up the ramp and then drove on into shore. Those three tanks were the only ones from his flotilla of LCTs to make it; they provided suppressing fire at Easy Green.*

Lieutenant Rockwell, off Dog White and Dog Green, made his own decision. He got on a tank radio, despite orders not to use the radio, to call Captain Elder of the 743rd Tank Battalion in a nearby LCT. Rockwell was prepared to argue, as he assumed Elder would want to follow orders. (With regard to using the radio, Rockwell later said, "At this stage of the game I was willing to take a chance, because it was necessary to get on with the invasion, is what it amounted to.")

To Rockwell's relief, Elder agreed with him. "I don't think we can make it," he said. "Can you take us right in?"

That was exactly what Rockwell wanted to hear. Using flags and Morse code, he ordered the seven other skippers of his LCT flotilla to keep their ramps up and drive into the beach. As they approached, the eager tank crews opened fire against the bluff, shooting over the bow.[40]

Rockwell's flotilla went in line abreast. On LCT 607, the skipper failed to act. Ens. Sam Grundfast, second in command (who had been a Boy Scout and could read the Morse code faster than his signalman), put it bluntly: "He froze. So the signalman looked at me, I looked at him, and I then took over the command of the boat. I gave the signal that we were obeying the order to go ashore."

As LCT 607 drove in, it hit a mine. "It literally blew us sky high. The skipper was killed. All the men were killed except two and myself. The four tanks were lost and all of the Navy personnel. I wound up in a hospital for several months, requiring extensive surgery."[41]

Seaman Martin Waarvick was on Rockwell's boat, LCT 535. "I was at my post in the forward port locker room near the bow, warming up the small Briggs & Stratton engine that we used to lower the ramp."[42] Timing was now critical. If that ramp dropped too soon, the water would be too deep; if it dropped too late, the

---

* In an after-action report dated September 22, 1944, Rear Adm. John L. Hall, commanding Assault Force "O," commented: "Because of the vulnerability of its flotation equipment and the general unseaworthiness of the entire vehicle the DD tank is not a practicable weapon for use in assault landings on open beaches." Copy in EC. Hall's conclusion was sound, but it was three months late.

tanks would not be able to do the job and the 116th Infantry would not have the help of the tanks at the moment the infantry most needed it.

The noise was deafening. The battleships and cruisers were shooting over the LCTs from behind. On each side of the lane reserved for the landing craft, the destroyers were banging away. Aircraft engines droned overhead. As Rockwell got close, the LCT(R)s let loose. On his LCT, the tank crews started up their engines.

Speaking was impossible, thinking nearly so. Further, the smoke obscured Rockwell's landmarks. But a shift of wind rolled back the smoke for a moment and Rockwell saw he was being set to the east by the tide. He changed course to starboard and increased speed; the other skippers saw this move and did the same. At the moment the naval barrage lifted, Rockwell's little group was exactly opposite Dog White and Dog Green, the tanks firing furiously.

This was the moment Rockwell had been preparing for over the past two years. This was the reason LCTs existed. But to Rockwell's amazement, what he had anticipated was not happening. He had always assumed the enemy would be firing at his LCT as it came in, but so far no German gun had done so.

At 0629 Rockwell gave the signal to Waarvick, who dropped the ramp. LCT 535 was the first ship of the first wave to launch equipment in the Omaha area. Waarvick remembered that the tanks "started out down the ramp, clanking and grinding. They sure made a racket on that steel deck." They were in about three feet of water.

The first tank lurched forward, dipped its nose to the slope, crawled ahead through the breakers to the sand fifty yards away, the water washing over its back and pouring off again. It began firing—and at that instant, so did the Germans. An 88mm gun was enfilading the beach from an emplacement to the right. Rockwell watched as 88 shells hit three of the landing craft on his right in quick succession. He expected the next shell to hit his LCT, which was lying still and broadside to the gun—a can't-miss target—when the last of his tanks went into the water. As it cleared the ramp, Waarvick raised it. The German gunners turned their fire from the LCTs onto the tanks.

And then, Rockwell recalled, "We pulled that famous naval maneuver, known through naval history as getting the hell out of there." He used his anchor to retract; he had dropped it going in, it had a separate engine to winch off, and it worked.[43]

As Rockwell backed off, the tanks he had been responsible

enough and courageous enough to put on the beach were blasting away with their 75mm cannon and .50-caliber machine guns. As LCT 535 retracted, Higgins boats carrying the 116th Regiment began moving in. It was 0630 at Omaha beach, H-Hour.

At *Widerstandsnest* 62 above the Colleville draw, Pvt. Franz Gockel had just been through the most shocking hour of his life. At 0400 he had been ordered to take his firing position behind his machine gun, but at first "nothing moved. Was it another false alarm? The minutes slowly tocked by. Was it going to be real this time? We stood at our weapons and shivered in the thin summer uniforms. The cook prepared hot red wine. An NCO appeared and checked our readiness, saying 'When they come, don't shoot too soon.' "

At first light the bombers were overhead and an incredible number of ships began to appear on the horizon. Small craft, small ships, big ships, all apparently coming right at WN 62. "An endless fleet. Heavy warships cruised along as if passing for review." Gockel tried to concentrate on his machine gun, checking it again and again, "to take my mind away from impending events."

The naval guns opened fire. "Salvo after salvo fell into our positions. Debris and clouds of smoke enveloped us. The earth shook. Eyes and ears were filled with dust. Sand ground between teeth. There was no hope for help."

The bombardment increased in its fury. "The morning dawn over the approaching landing fleet showed for us our approaching doom." Gockel was amazed that the Allies were coming at low tide. During an inspection in May, Rommel had assured the lieutenant in command of WN 62 that the Allies would come at high tide.

Gockel was even more amazed when the naval bombardment lifted and he discovered no one in his platoon had been killed, only a few wounded. "We crouched small and helpless behind our weapons. I prayed for survival."

Then, "the sea came alive. Assault boats and landing craft were rapidly approaching the beach. A comrade stumbled out of the smoke and dust into my position and screamed, 'Franz, watch out! They're coming!' "

The 75mm cannon at WN 62 fired on one of the American tanks. The tank fired back. The shell exploded inside the casemate and put the German gun out of commission.[44] It was 0630 at Omaha Beach.

15

"WE'LL START THE WAR FROM RIGHT HERE"

The 4th Division at Utah Beach

THE PLAN WAS for DD tanks to land first, at 0630, immediately after the naval warships lifted their fire and the LCT(R)s launched their 1,000 rockets. There were thirty-two of the swimming tanks at Utah, carried in eight LCTs. In their wake would come the 2nd Battalion, 8th Infantry, in twenty Higgins boats, each carrying a thirty-man assault team. Ten of the craft would touch down on Tare Green Beach opposite the strong point at Les-Dunes-de-Varreville, the others to the south at Uncle Red Beach.

The second wave of thirty-two Higgins boats carrying the 1st Battalion, 8th Infantry, plus combat engineers and naval demolition teams, was scheduled to land five minutes later. The third wave was timed for H plus fifteen minutes; it included eight LCTs with some bulldozer tanks as well as regular Shermans. Two minutes later the fourth wave, mainly consisting of detachments of the 237th and 299th Engineer Combat Battalions (ECBs), would hit the beach.

None of this worked out. Some craft landed late, others early, all of them a kilometer or so south of the intended target. But thanks to some quick thinking and decision making by the high command on the beach, and thanks to the initiative and drive of the GIs, what could have been mass confusion or even utter chaos turned into a successful, low-cost landing.

Tides, wind, waves, and too much smoke were partly responsible for upsetting the schedule and landing in the wrong place, but the main cause was the loss to mines of three of the four control craft. When the LCCs went down it threw everything into confusion. The LCTs skippers were circling, looking for direction. One of them hit a mine and blew sky high. In a matter of seconds the LCT and its four tanks sank.

At this point Lts. Howard Vander Beek and Sims Gauthier on LCC 60 took charge. They conferred and decided to make up for the time lost by leading the LCTs to within three kilometers of the beach before launching the tanks (which were supposed to launch at five kilometers), giving them a shorter and quicker run to the shore. Using his bullhorn, Vander Beek circled around the LCTs as he shouted out orders to follow him. He went straight for the beach—the wrong one, about half a kilometer south of where the tanks were supposed to land. When the LCTs dropped their ramps and the tanks swam off, they looked to Vander Beek like "odd-shaped sea monsters with their huge, doughnut-like skirts for flotation wallowing through the heavy waves and struggling to keep in formation."[1]

The Higgins boats carrying the first wave of assault teams were supposed to linger behind the swimming tanks, but the tanks were so slow that the coxswains drove their craft right past them. Thus it was that E Company of the 2nd Battalion, 8th Infantry, 4th Division, was the first Allied company to hit the beach in the invasion. The tidal current, running from north to south, had carried their craft farther left so they came in a kilometer south of where they should have been.

General Roosevelt was in the first boat to hit the shore. Maj. Gen. Barton had initially refused Roosevelt's request to go in with the 8th Infantry, but Roosevelt had argued that having a general land in the first wave would boost morale for the troops. "They'll figure that if a general is going in, it can't be that rough." Roosevelt had also made a personal appeal, saying, "I would love to do this." Barton had reluctantly agreed.

Luck was with Company E. The German fixed fortifications at the intended landing site at exit 3 were far more formidable than those where the landing actually happened, at exit 2 opposite La Madeleine, thanks to the Marauder pounding the battery there had taken. The German troops in the area were from the 919th Regiment of the 709th Division. They had been badly battered by the combined air and sea bombardment and were not firing their weapons. There was only some small-arms fire from riflemen in trenches in the sand dune just behind the four-foot concrete seawall.

In those trenches were the Germans driven from their fixed positions by the bombardment. Their leader was Lieutenant Jahnke. He looked out to sea and was amazed. "Here was a truly lunatic sight," he recalled. "I wondered if I were hallucinating as a result of the bombardment." What he saw was a DD tank. "Amphibious tanks! This must be the Allies' secret weapon." He decided to bring his own secret weapon into action, only to discover that his Goliaths would not function—the bombardment had destroyed the radio controls.

"It looks as though God and the world have forsaken us," Jahnke said to the runner by his side. "What's happened to our airmen?"[2]

At that instant, Sgt. Malvin Pike of E Company was coming in on a Higgins boat. He had a scare: "My position was in the right rear of the boat and I could hear the bullets splitting the air over our heads and I looked back and all I could see was two hands on the wheel and a hand on each .50-caliber machine gun, which the Navy guys were firing. I said to my platoon leader, Lieutenant Rebarcheck, 'These guys aren't even looking where they are going or shooting.' About that time the coxswain stood up and looked at the beach and then ducked back down. The machine gunners were doing the same and we just prayed they would get us on the beach."

The boat hit a sandbar 200 meters from the shore. (The water was shallower off exit 2 than at exit 3, which was why the Navy had insisted on going in at exit 3.) The coxswain said it was time for the infantry to go, that he was getting out of there.

Lieutenant Rebarcheck responded, "You are not going to drown these men. Give her another try." The coxswain backed off the bar, went 100 feet to the left, tried to go in, and hit the bar again. Rebarcheck said, "OK, let's go," but then the ramp got stuck.

"The hell with this," Rebarcheck called out. He jumped over the side; his men followed.

"I jumped out in waist-deep water," Sergeant Pike recalled. "We had 200 feet to go to shore and you couldn't run, you could just kind of push forward. We finally made it to the edge of the water, then we had 200 yards of open beach to cross, through the obstacles. But fortunately most of the Germans were not able to fight, they were all shook up from the bombing and the shelling and the rockets and most of them just wanted to surrender."[3]

Capt. Howard Lees, commander of E Company, led his men over the seawall to the top of the dunes. "What we saw," Sergeant Pike remembered, "was nothing like what we saw on the sand table back in England. We said, 'Hey, this doesn't look like what they showed us.' "[4] Roosevelt joined them, walking calmly up to their position, using his cane (he had had a heart attack), wearing a wool-knit hat (he hated helmets), ignoring the fire. About this time (0640) the Germans to the north in the fortifications at Les-Dunes-de-Varreville began shooting at 2nd Battalion with 88mm cannon and machine guns, but not accurately. Roosevelt and Lees conferred, studied their maps, and realized they were at the wrong place.

Roosevelt returned to the beach. By now the first Sherman tanks had landed and were returning the German fire. Commodore James Arnold, the Navy control officer for Utah, was just landing with the third wave. "German 88s were pounding the beachhead," he recalled. "Two U.S. tanks were drawn up at the high-water line pumping back. I tried to run to get into the lee of these tanks. I realize now why the infantry likes to have tanks along in a skirmish. They offer a world of security to a man in open terrain who may have a terribly empty sensation in his guts." Arnold found a shell hole and made it his temporary headquarters.

"An army officer wearing the single star of a brigadier jumped into my 'headquarters' to duck the blast of an 88.

" 'Sonsabuzzards,' he muttered, as we untangled sufficiently to look at each other. 'I'm Teddy Roosevelt. You're Arnold of the Navy. I remember you at the briefing at Plymouth.' "[5]

Roosevelt was joined by the two battalion commanders of the 8th Infantry, Lt. Cols. Conrad Simmons and Carlton Mac-Neely. As they studied the map, Colonel Van Fleet, CO of the regiment, came wading ashore. He had landed with the fourth wave, carrying the 237th and 299th ECBs.

"Van," Roosevelt exclaimed, "we're not where we were supposed to be." He pointed to a building on the beach. It was supposed to be to the left. "Now it's to our right. I figure we are more than a mile further south." Van Fleet reflected that ironically they were at the exact spot he had wanted the Navy to land his regiment, but the Navy had insisted it was impossible because the water was too shallow.

"We faced an immediate and important decision," Van Fleet wrote. "Should we try to shift our entire landing force more than a mile down the beach, and follow our original plan? Or should we proceed across the causeways immediately opposite where we had landed?" Already men were crossing the seawall and dunes in front of the officers, while Navy demolition men and engineers were blowing up obstacles behind them.

Roosevelt became a legend for reportedly saying at this point, "We'll start the war from right here." According to Van Fleet that was not the way it happened. In an unpublished memoir, Van Fleet wrote: "I made the decision. 'Go straight inland,' I ordered. 'We've caught the enemy at a weak point, so let's take advantage of it.' "[6]

The important point was not who made the decision but that it was made without opposition or time-consuming argument. It was the right decision and showed the flexibility of the high command. Simmons and MacNeely immediately set about clearing the German beach opposition, preparing to seize the eastern ends of exits 1 and 2, then cross the causeways to drive west. First, however, they needed to get their men through the seawall and over the dunes.

The engineers and naval demolition teams came in right after the first wave, also landing opposite exit 2. They were taking more fire than the first wave and could see that the spot they were headed for was not the place they had studied back in England. They could also see that they were going to be dropped in waist-deep water, so they began to lighten up their packs. The first thing that went, Sgt. Richard Cassiday of the 237th ECB remembered, were cartons of cigarettes. He had six—one man carried ten cartons. Cassiday tore open a carton, grabbed a pack out of it, and threw all the rest away. So did others. "We were wading in cigarettes up to our knees in that boat."[7]

The demolition teams consisted of five Navy Seabees (combat demolition units) and two or three Army engineers. There were ten teams. Each man carried between fifty and seventy-five pounds of explosives on his back, either TNT or composition C (a plastic explosive developed by the British that looked like a bar of laundry soap; it would burn if lit or explode when properly detonated). The

Seabee personnel tended to be older than most D-Day men; most of them were trained by miners from the western United States who where explosive experts.

The Seabees were responsible for the outermost set of obstacles, the ones that would be the first covered by the tide. The Seabees were prepared to work underwater if necessary (although without anything like the special equipment modern "frogmen" use). Orval Wakefield recalled that when the recruiter came around to ask for volunteers for the underwater demolition teams, he said that experience in the Pacific had shown how critical the teams would be to a successful invasion.

"He also explained that it was extremely hazardous duty and they needed good swimmers and we would have special training physically, mentally, and we would be expendable. We would be working with booby trapped and mined obstacles. The good thing was that we would pull no KP duty. Everything turned out to be true."

At Utah, Wakefield's team prepared the outer obstacles for demolition while incoming 4th Division troops dodged around them. The team set up their charges, got them wired together, shouted "Fire in the hole!" and blew them apart. Wakefield and his buddies then went up to the seawall, where they got into a slit trench and "just watched what was happening on the beach. When we first came in there was nothing there but men running, turning, and dodging. All of a sudden it was like a beehive. Boats were able to come through the obstacles. Bulldozers were pushing sand up against the seawall and half-tracks and tanks were able to go into the interior. It looked like an anthill."[8]

The Army engineers simultaneously went after the next set of obstacles, closer in to the beach. They attached their explosives to the obstacles, whether single poles with mines or Belgian gates, then connected the individual charges by primer cord, so that everything would go up at once. Sgt. Al Pikasiewicz was with a team from the 237th ECB. He and his buddies got their explosives in place on one set of obstacles, all connected, and ran toward the seawall to set off the primer cord. "Fire in the hole!" they shouted.

"Just before the explosions went off," Pikasiewicz remembered, "when we were up against the wall, some of the landing craft were coming in. The ramps were dropping and the men ran in and they didn't realize what they were heading into. When they heard us yelling and screaming at them they laid down behind the obstacles for protection. 'My God,' I said to Jimmy Gray, a medic. So I left the wall and ran back and grabbed men by their field packs and started screaming, 'Get the hell out of here because this is ready to blow.' I pulled about six men and yelled at the rest and headed back toward the wall. I was fifteen to twenty feet away when everything blew and a piece of shrapnel hit me in the helmet."

The team went to work closer to the seawall, hurrying to get the job done before the tide came in and covered the obstacles. "And General Roosevelt was standing there," Sergeant Cassiday said, "walking up and down the beach with his cane, and I called out, 'Go knock that bastard down, he's going to get killed!' And somebody said, 'Do you know who that is?' I said, 'Yes, it's Roosevelt, and he is going to get killed.' " Roosevelt moved on and the team blew the obstacles.[9] Within less than an hour the teams had cleared eight fifty-yard gaps in the obstacles and were going after the ones still standing.

Next, the 237th went to work blasting holes in the seawall. Tank dozers from the 70th Tank Battalion cleared the debris after the blasts. All the while 88 shells were coming in, but most of them were splashing into the water as the Germans continued to concentrate, not very effectively, on the wave after wave of landing craft.

Seaman Martin Gutekunst was a communications expert attached to the Seabees. He recalled that after the obstacles were cleared and the holes blown, "a number of the more adventurous and brave demolition men moved along the far side of the wall and got Germans to surrender." He joined them. "We could see many German gun emplacements protected by their concrete walls and roofs. Inside the bunkers they had scenery painted along the walls that represented the area as you would see it if you were outside, and narrow slits through which they could spot their fire." But no one was there to fire; the Wehrmacht soldiers had either surrendered or fled inland along the causeways.[10]

The men from the 237th ECB followed the dozers through the holes in the seawall, climbed over the dune, and saw signs saying "Achtung Meinen." The pressure from behind of men and tanks trying to get off the beach to move inland was such that the engineers were more or less forced to move forward. "Those were the first men inland," Sgt. Vincent Powell of the 237th said. "And suddenly they started stepping on mines, S- mines, Bouncing Betties. These mines bounced up and exploded. These men began screaming and running back to the beach with the blood just flowing. And that's when the tanks started in."[11]

At 0645 the swimming tanks were still chugging their way to the beach. They had been scheduled to land before the assault teams but they were not even the first tanks ashore; LCTs carrying C Company of the 70th Tank Battalion under the command of Capt. John Ahearn touched down before the DD tanks arrived. The Shermans were firing as they came in. Ahearn was in the second tank in the first LCT; Lt. Owen Gavigan commanded the tank that preceded Ahearn's. They drove through five feet of water in their waterproofed Shermans. Ahearn turned over control of the four dozer tanks to the engineers and divided the remaining fourteen Shermans into two groups, retaining control of one and giving Lieutenant Yeoman command of the other.

Ahearn turned his group left, looking for an opening through the seawall, while Yeoman turned right. Ahearn found an opening, turned toward it, and confronted a Goliath. They had been used at Anzio, but Ahearn had not been in Italy and no one had told him about the Goliaths; he could not figure out what on earth it was. Fortunately, the Goliath he faced just sat there; he later learned that the radio-control device had been blown up in the bombardment.

Ahearn got his tanks through the opening in the seawall. Looking south, he saw a German fortification. He fired some shells at the bunker. With that a couple of dozen Werhmacht troops emerged, hands above their heads, and began running toward Ahearn. He dismounted to take them in as prisoners. "They began yelling to me and gesturing at me to stay put; they were yelling 'Achtung Meinen.' With this I gestured to them to move toward the road inland, where we took them prisoner and turned them over to the infantry." They were not Germans at all, but Ost battalion troops from Georgia in the Soviet Union.

Ahearn drove south on the beach road. It turned inland, toward Pouppeville, while a dirt road continued to parallel the dunes. He detached Lieutenant Tighe with five tanks to head toward Pouppeville, which he hoped was in the hands of the 101st Airborne, and proceeded south with two tanks to see if there were any more fortifications he could assault.

His tank hit a land mine that blew the front left bogie. Ahearn radioed to Tighe to report that he was immobilized, climbed out of his tank, and proceeded on foot to scout the area. He stepped on an S-mine. The explosion threw him into the bank of a hedgerow, unconscious, his legs mangled. His crew searched for him. When he came too and yelled, they spotted him, but he cautioned them not to come up because of the mines. The crew returned to the tank, got a long rope, threw it to him, then dragged him out. Stretcher-bearers got him to a makeshift field hospital, where his foot was amputated. Engineers told him later that they removed 15,000 S-mines from that area.[12]

Lt. Elliot Richardson was CO of a medic detachment that landed with the fourth wave. "I waded ashore with my guys. There were occasional shell bursts on the beach but it didn't amount to much as most of the German guns had been put out of action. I walked up to the top of the dune and looked around. There was this barbed wire area and a wounded officer who had stepped on an antipersonnel mine calling for help."

Richardson held a brief debate with himself. It was obviously dangerous to go into the area. Nevertheless, "I decided that I should go. I walked in toward him, putting each foot down carefully and picked him up and carried him back." Richardson's men got the wounded officer on a stretcher and carried him down to an aid station on the beach.

"That was my baptism," Richardson said. "It was the sort of behavior I expected of myself."[13]

Capt. George Mabry, S-3 of 2nd Battalion, 8th Infantry, crossed the dunes and found himself with several members of G Company caught in a minefield. Three men stepped on S-mines. Colonel Van Fleet described what happened: "Mabry had a choice: to withdraw to the beach or go after the enemy. Each alternative meant crossing the minefield. Mabry chose to charge. Firing as he ran, Mabry charged twenty-five yards to an enemy foxhole. Those Germans who resisted, he killed; the others surrendered. Next he gathered a handful of G Company men, sent for two tanks, and assaulted a large pillbox guarding the causeway at exit 1."[14]

Sergeant Pike of E Company joined Mabry's group. As Mabry led the men across the causeway, headed toward Pouppeville, he caught up with Lieutenant Tighe of the 70th Tank Battalion. Tighe had lost three tanks to land mines but was moving cautiously ahead with his remaining two Shermans. Mabry put infantry in front and pushed on, urging speed because they were so exposed on the causeway and were taking mortar fire, simultaneously urging caution because of the mines. They came to a bridge over a culvert and figured it must be prepared for demolition; further, the scouts reported that they had seen some Germans duck into the culvert. Mabry sent troops out into the flooded fields to pinch in on both sides of the culvert. The Germans surrendered without putting up a fight. Mabry had them disconnect the charges, then sent the prisoners back to the beach and pushed on.[15]

After the guards put the prisoners into a landing craft, to be taken back to the *Bayfield* for interrogation, they reported to Van Fleet. It was 0940. Van Fleet radioed General Barton on *Bayfield*, "I am ashore with Colonel Simmons and General Roosevelt, advancing steadily." As new waves of landing craft came in, Van Fleet and Roosevelt sent them through the holes in the seawall with orders to move inland. Already the biggest problem they faced was congestion on the beach. There were too many troops and vehicles, not enough openings. Sporadic incoming artillery fire and the ubiquitous mines made the traffic jam horrendous. Still, at 1045 Van Fleet was able to radio Barton, "Everything is going OK." The beach area was comparatively secure, the reserve battalions were coming ashore.[16]

Mabry pushed forward on the causeway. He kept cautioning his scouts. "You know," he said to Sergeant Pike, "the paratroopers are supposed to have taken this town Pouppeville, but they may not have. Let's not shoot any of our paratroopers." Pike said OK.

The scouts got to the western edge of the flooded area. "We could see the bushes and a few trees where the causeway ended," Pike recalled, "and then I saw a helmet and then it disappeared, and I told Captain Mabry that I saw a helmet up there behind those bushes and he said, 'Could you tell if it was American or German?' and I said, 'I didn't see enough, I don't know, sir.' "

The men on the far end of the causeway shot off an orange flare. "And these two guys stood up and the first thing we saw was the American flag on their shoulder and it was two paratroopers. They said, '4th Division?' and we said, 'Yes.' "[17]

Lt. Eugene Brierre of the 101st was one of the two paratroopers. He greeted Pike and asked, "Who is in charge here?" Mabry came up and replied, "I am."

Brierre said, "Well, General Taylor is right back here in Pouppeville and wants to meet you."

It was 1110. The linkup between the 101st and 4th divisions had been achieved. Exit 1 was in American hands.[18]

Mabry talked to Taylor, who said he was moving out to accomplish further objectives, then proceeded through Pouppeville in the direction of Ste.-Marie-du-Mont. There were forty or so dead German soldiers in Pouppeville, testimony to the fight the 101st had been engaged in. Near Ste.-Marie-du-Mont, Lt. Louis Nixon of the 101st asked Mabry for a bit of help from the two tanks; Mabry detached them and they went to work (for the results, see page 304). Then it was on to Ste.-Marie-du-Mont, where the Mabry force helped the paratroopers secure the town.

The 4th Division and attached units were pouring ashore. Their main problem was with the sea, not the Germans. The waves were pitching the landing craft around, coming over the gunwales to hit the troops smack in the face, making many of the men so miserable they could not wait to get off. "The boats were going around like little bugs jockeying for position," Pvt. Ralph Della-Volpe recalled. "I had had an extra, extra big breakfast thinking it would help, but I lost it."[19]

So did many others. Marvin Perrett, an eighteen-year-old Coast Guardsman from New Orleans, was coxswain on a New Orleans-built Higgins boat. The thirty members of the 12th Regiment of the 4th Division he was carrying ashore had turned their heads toward him to avoid the spray. He could see concern and fear on their faces. Just in front of him stood a chaplain. Perrett was concentrating on keeping his place in the advancing line. The chaplain upchucked his breakfast, the wind caught it, and Perrett's face was covered with undigested eggs, coffee, and bits of bacon.

One of Perrett's crew dipped a bucket in the Channel and threw the water over his face. "How's that, skipper?", he asked.

"That was great," Perrett replied. "Do it again." The crew member did, and the infantrymen broke into laughter. "It just took the tension right away," Perrett said.[20]

Sgt. John Beck of the 87th Mortar Battalion had taken seasickness pills. They did not work; he threw up anyway. But they had an unintended effect—he fell asleep while going in.

"The explosion of shells awakened me as we approached the coast," he remembered. "My best friend, Sgt. Bob Myers from New Castle, Pa., took a number of those pills and it drove him out of his mind. He didn't become coherent until the next day. He made the invasion of Normandy and doesn't remember one thing about it!"[21]

(Who decided to hand out those pills is one of the mysteries of D-Day. They were also given to the airborne troopers, many of whom complained later that the only effect they had was to make them drowsy. They had not been used in any of the practice runs, many of which had been in water as rough as on June 6.)

As the flat-bottomed, square-bowed landing craft slammed into the waves, one anonymous green-faced GI summed up the feelings of all his buddies: "That s.o.b. Higgins—he hasn't got nothing to be proud of, inventing this boat!"[22]

Col. Russell "Red" Reeder was CO of the 12th Infantry, scheduled to land at 1030. For the first four hours of the invasion, therefore, he was watching from an LCI six kilometers out, not seeing much because of the smoke and haze. "The hands on my watch would not move," he wrote. "The time from six thirty until we landed at ten thirty was the longest four hours I ever spent." The 12th was supposed to land north of the 8th, but the coxswains followed the orders from Roosevelt to bring the follow-up waves in behind the 8th Regiment, which put the 12th two kilometers south of where it expected to be.

"It don't matter," Colonel Reeder declared when he discovered the error. "We know where to go!"

Reeder led his men through a hole in the seawall to the top of the dune, where he saw Roosevelt.

"Red, the causeways leading inland are all clogged up," Roosevelt yelled. "Look at it! A procession of jeeps and not a wheel turning." To Reeder, "Roosevelt looked tired and the cane he leaned on heightened the impression."[23]

Reeder's immediate objective was St.-Martin-de-Varreville, where he hoped to effect a linkup with the 82nd Airborne. Off to his right was exit 4, the one his regiment had been scheduled to use, but the east end of exit 2 had not been secured and was coming under fire from German artillery to the north, the battery of four 155mm cannon at St.-Marcouf. He could move his regiment right to the causeway, then use it to cross the flooded fields. But if he did that, his men would be exposed and under observation. Using causeway 2 was out of the question; it was jammed with jeeps, tanks, trucks, and troops. His option was to cross the inundated area to reach St.-Martin-de-Varreville.

Reeder made his decision. "We are going through the flooded area," he yelled. He saw Lt. Col. Charles "Chuck" Jackson, CO of his 1st Battalion, and gave him an arm signal. Jackson had just made the same judgment and set off immediately.[24]

Sgt. Clifford Sorenson was with Jackson. He recalled that "aerial reconnaissance had estimated that the flooded area was maybe ankle deep, except in the irrigation ditches, which they estimated to be about eighteen inches deep. Well, they made a big mistake. That flooded area was in some places up to your waist and the irrigation ditches were over your head. Some brave souls would swim across the irrigation ditches and throw toggle ropes back and haul the rest of us across. So much for aerial reconnaissance."

The battalion marched through the inundated fields for nearly two kilometers. "And we waded and waded and waded," Sorenson said. "An occasional sniper shot would be fired and didn't hit anybody. We were mostly interested in keeping from drowning because the bottom was slick and the footing tricky. You could slip down and maybe drown with all that equipment.

"I was so angry. The Navy had tried to drown me at the beach, and now the Army was trying to drown me in the flooded area. I was more mad at our side than I was at the Germans, because the Germans hadn't done anything to me yet."[25]

It took time, three to four hours or more, to get across, but it was accomplished without loss. When the battalion reached the high ground, Reeder signaled Jackson to turn right and proceed to St.-Martin-de-Varreville. He did. The battalion reached a crossroads, where it received some artillery fire that sent the men scattering for cover. General Roosevelt came up; he had hitched a ride on the hood of a jeep that had brought him in on causeway 2. Roosevelt spotted Colonel Jackson.

"Well, Chuck, how are things going?" he asked. Jackson explained the situation.

"Let's go up to the front," Roosevelt suggested.

"We are at the front," Jackson replied. "See those two men [about 50 meters away]. They are the leading scouts of Company A."

"Let's go talk to them," Roosevelt said. They did, got the scouts moving, and the battalion followed.[26] By late afternoon, the 8th Infantry and its supporting regiment, the 22nd, had hooked up with the 82nd Airborne at St.-Martin-de-Varreville and St.-Germain-de-Varreville. There they bivouacked for the night, somewhat short of their D-Day objective but pleased to be inland and in contact with the 82nd.

The 12th Infantry, meanwhile, had reached its D-Day objective. Captain Mabry had moved the lead elements through Ste.-Marie-du-Mont to take up an overnight position north of Les

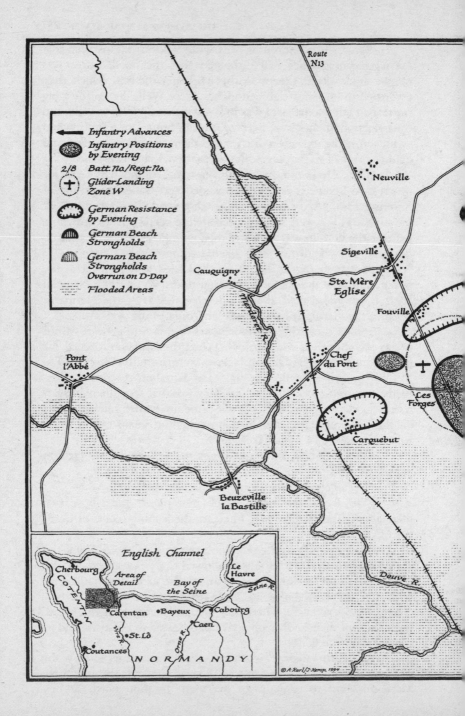

Infantry Advances

Infantry Positions
by Evening

2/8 Batt. No/Regt. No.

Glider Landing
Zone W

German Resistance
by Evening

German Beach
Strongholds

German Beach
Strongholds
Overrun on D-Day

Flooded Areas

Route
N13

Neuville

Sigeville

Cauquigny

Ste. Mère
Eglise

Fouville

Pont
l'Abbé

Chef
du Pont

Les
Forges

Carquebut

Beuzeville
la Bastille

Deuve R.

English Channel

Cherbourg

Area of
Detail

Bay of
the Seine

Le Havre

Seine R.

COTENTIN

Carentan

Bayeux

Cabourg

Caen

Orne R.

St. Lô

Vire R.

Coutances

NORMANDY

© A. Karl / J. Kemp, 1994

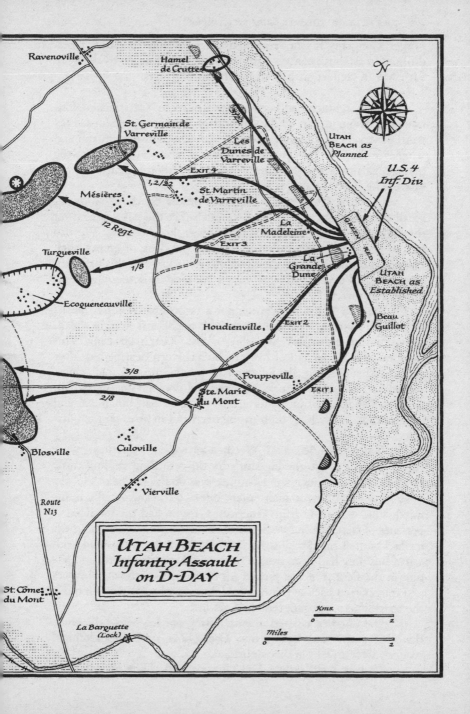

Ravenoville

Hamel
de Cruttes

St. Germain de
Varreville

Les
Dunes de
Varreville

Exit 4

UTAH
BEACH as
Planned

N

U.S. 4
Inf. Div.

1, 2, /22

Mésières

St. Martin
de Varreville

12 Regt

La
Madeleine

Exit 3

GREEN

RED

Turqueville

1/8

La
Grande
Dune

UTAH
BEACH as
Established

Ecoqueneauville

Beau
Guillot

Houdienville

Exit 2

3/8

Pouppeville

Exit 1

2/8

Ste. Marie
du Mont

Culoville

Blosville

Vierville

Route
N13

**UTAH BEACH
Infantry Assault
on D-DAY**

St. Côme
du Mont

La Barquette
(Lock)

Kms.
0   2

Miles
0   2

Forges. Company K sent a reconnaissance platoon forward to Chef-du-Pont to establish contact with the 82nd Airborne, so by dusk the 12th was in contact with both paratroop divisions.

That so much had been accomplished by the attacking battalions was due in part to the support of the Navy warships. Forward observers had accompanied the 4th Division men inland and whenever they ran into enemy artillery or tanks called back to the battleships and cruisers for suppressing fire. Spotter planes did the same. The Navy poured it on.

Lt. Ross Olsen was a gunnery officer on the *Nevada*. "I recall that our 5-inch guns fired so much that the paint peeled off the guns and all that was left showing was the blue steel. We also had to halt the guns for awhile to clear the deck of empty shell casings. Normally these were saved for reloading but this day they were dumped over the side as they were hindering the movement of the gun turrets."

On one occasion, *Nevada* got a target that required all its guns, the 14-inch as well as the 5-inch, to fire almost straight ahead. When *Nevada* unleashed the volley, it cost Olsen his hearing in his right ear and 50 percent of his left; he has worn hearing aids ever since. "The shelling also destroyed the twenty-six-foot motor whaleboat on the boat deck, knocked the door off the mess hall, peeled all the insulation material off the mess hall bulkhead, and broke almost every light bulb in the overhead fixtures on the portside."[27]

Badly wounded men, German as well as American, were being brought out to the big ships by the returning landing craft. Pharmacist Mate Vincent del Giudice was on the *Bayfield*. He was busy all day, tending to many men, but two stuck especially in his mind. One was a Mexican-American GI who had the terrible experience of stepping on two S-mines simultaneously. German medics had treated him by putting tourniquets on both legs and both arms, but they had been driven off by an American patrol and left him in the field. He was picked up by some GI stretcher-bearers and transported back to the *Bayfield*, but they had failed to remove the tourniquets and gangrene had set in.

Del Giudice assisted in amputating one leg below the knee, the other above, and both arms. The soldier also had abdominal wounds which Del Giudice debrided.

"It was a sad sight," Del Giudice said. "The man did not

complain. He had a look of resignation on him. He came out of his anesthesia, looked at his four stumps, closed his eyes and went back to sleep."

Later, Del Giudice tended a wounded German corporal, "tall, thin, a rather handsome chap with blond hair. He had been wounded on his right hand and all five fingers were dangling and his hand and fingers were blackened." Del Giudice amputated his fingers with scissors, put sulfa powder on his hand, "and for my effort I got a smile and a 'danke schön!'"[28]

Lieutenant Jahnke was in an improvised dugout on the dunes, firing with his rifle at the incoming Americans. A tank spotted him and blasted the dugout with its 75 mm cannon. Jahnke was buried alive. He felt someone dragging him out. It was a GI.

Jahnke had won an Iron Cross on the Eastern Front. His instinct was to get away—anything rather than captivity. He saw a machine pistol on the ground and dove for it. The American pushed it aside and in a calm voice said, "Take it easy, German."

The GI sent Jahnke, hands clasped over his head, to a POW enclosure on the beach. There Jahnke was wounded again by shrapnel from an in-coming German shell.[29]

Seabee Orval Wakefield was up by the seawall. He said that "by middle afternoon the beach had changed from nothing but obstacles to a small city. It was apparent that we NCD units had done our job well because as far as I could see to one side the beach was all the way opened, there was nothing holding the landing craft back. We figured our day was well spent, even though no one ever knew who we were.

"We were being questioned. 'Who are you guys? What do you do?' The coxswains didn't like us because we always had so many explosives with us. When we were inland, the Army officers wanted to know what is the Navy doing in here."

An Army medical officer spotted Wakefield's team and said he needed volunteers to carry wounded men down to the shore for evacuation to a hospital ship. "He said, 'Are you guys going to just sit here or are you going to volunteer?' We didn't think much about that idea, we had just come off the hot end of the demolition wire but finally we did volunteer to do it for him. We carried the wounded down to the shore. German shells were still coming in."

By this time, Wakefield noted, "it was no longer a rush of

men coming ashore, it was a rush of vehicles." Then he saw a
never-to-be-forgotten sight: "All of a sudden it seemed like a cloud
started from the horizon over the ocean and it came toward us and
by the time it got to us it extended clean back to the horizon.
Gliders were coming, to be turned loose inland."[30]

Reinforcements were pouring in from the sea and from the
air. Utah Beach was secure. In the morning, the Americans would
move out to cut the base of the Cotentin, to take Cherbourg, to get
on with the job of winning the war so they could go home.

At dusk, Wakefield "had my most important thought that
day." Wading into chest-deep water at first light that morning, "I
found that my legs would hardly hold me up. I thought I was a
coward." Then he had discovered that his sea bags with their explosives had filled with water and he was carrying well over 100
pounds. He had used his knife to cut the bags and dump the water,
then moved on to do his job. "When I had thought for a moment
that I wasn't going to be able to do it, that I was a coward, and then
found out that I could do it, you can't imagine how great a feeling
that was. Just finding out, yes, I could do what I had volunteered
to do."

Overall, casualties were astonishingly light. The 8th and
22nd regiments had only twelve men killed, another 106 wounded.
For the 12th Regiment, the figure was sixty-nine casualties. Nearly
all were caused by mines, either sea or land, mostly those devilish
S-mines. The 4th Division had taken heavier losses in training (in
the disaster at Slapton Sands, it lost almost twenty times as many
men as it did on June 6).

Equally astonishing was the speed with which the 4th Division and its attached units got ashore. This was thanks to the
organization, training, and skill of all those involved, whether
Army, Navy, Army Air Force, or Coast Guard. They overcame
logistical problems that seemed insurmountable. On D-Day, in
fifteen hours, the Americans put ashore at Utah more than 20,000
troops and 1,700 motorized vehicles. General Jodl had estimated
that it would take the Allies six or seven days to put three divisions
into France. At Utah alone, counting the airborne divisions, the
Americans had done it in one day.

D-Day was a smashing success for the 4th Division and its
attached units. Nearly all objectives were attained even though the
plan had to be abandoned before the first assault waves hit the

beach. By nightfall, the division was ready to move out at first light on June 7 for its next mission, taking Montebourg and then moving on to Cherbourg. It went on to fight battles far more costly than the one it won on the Cotentin beach on June 6, distinguishing itself throughout the campaign in northwest Europe, especially in taking Cherbourg, in holding the German counteroffensive at Mortain, in the liberation of Paris, in the Hürtgen Forest, and in the Battle of the Bulge.[31]

There were many reasons for the success of the 4th Division on D-Day, not least being the German reliance on mines, flooded areas, and fixed fortifications instead of high-quality troops to defend the supposedly impregnable Atlantic Wall. As important was the air and sea bombardment, and the naval shelling through the day. Credit belonged, too, to General Roosevelt and his colonels, men like Van Fleet, Reeder, and Jackson, for making quick and correct decisions. Junior officers, men like Captains Ahearn and Mabry, made indispensable contributions.

But most of all, the 4th's success was thanks to the airborne troopers behind the German lines. The paratroopers held the western exits. They confused the Germans and prevented any concentrated counterattacks aimed at the seaborne invaders. They put out of action batteries that might have brought heavy artillery fire down on Utah Beach. How the paratroopers did it, and why they were so thankful to link up with the 4th Division, whether at noon or nightfall, is its own story.

16

"NOUS RESTONS ICI"

The Airborne in the Cotentin

AT DAWN the men of the 82nd and 101st Airborne divisions were scattered in small pockets throughout an area that ran ten kilometers southwest from the mouth of the Douve River to the northern edge of Carentan, then twenty kilometers northwest from Carentan to Pont-l'Abbé, then twenty kilometers northeast to the coast near Ravenoville. Few men knew where they were. Unit cohesion was almost nonexistent. Most of the paratroopers were in groups of a half dozen to fifty men, in some cases all officers, in others all enlisted men. The groups were usually mixed, containing men from different companies, battalions, regiments, and even divisions, strangers to the leaders who were trying to get them to move on objectives to which they had not been assigned and for which they had not been briefed.

As a consequence, the airborne troops fought a score or more different engagements, unconnected to each other, many of them fights for survival rather than battles for planned objectives. For most airborne troopers D-Day was a day of confusion. But precisely because the Americans were so badly confused, the Germans were worse off—they grossly overestimated the size of the force attacking them and they could get nothing coherent or helpful from their POW interrogations.

Thanks to the initiative of individual Americans, some of

them general officers, some junior officers, some NCOs, some enlisted, the 82nd and 101st managed to overcome most of their difficulties and complete their most critical missions—seizure of Ste.-Mère-Église and the exits from Utah. The way it was done, however, was hardly textbook fashion, or in accordance with the plan.

There was virtually no overall control because it was impossible for the generals and colonels to give orders to units that had not yet formed up. The groups that had come together were unaware of where they were or where other groups were, a problem that was greatly compounded by the ubiquitous hedgerows.

Radio communication could have overcome that problem, but most radios had been damaged or lost in the drop, and those that were working were inadequate. The SCR (Signal Corps Radio)-300, which weighed thirty-two pounds, had a speaking range of five miles but only under perfect conditions. The much more common SCR-536, weighing only six pounds (and called a "walkie-talkie" because a man could talk into it and walk at the same time), had a range of less than one mile. Worse, they were easily jammed by the Germans.

Sgt. Leonard Lebenson was part of General Ridgway's headquarters group. He came in by glider and managed to find his way to Ridgway's command post, near a small farm outside Ste.-Mère-Église. He described the situation: "Ridgway's aide was there, plus a couple of staff officers and two or three other enlisted men. The command post was trying to be a directional center, but it was not really in control of anything. We were just standing there, waiting for things to develop. Ridgway, a very brave and forceful man, was continually on the move in and out, trying to exercise his control. But what we were doing was just gathering information, trying to find out what was happening. There weren't any messages, we didn't have any phones or radios, we didn't even have a map set up. We were not functioning as a CP."[1]

At the other end of the command chain, Pvt. John Delury of the 508th PIR remembered "a feeling of euphoria" as dawn came up. "The dreaded night was over, and I was still alive. But my feeling of euphoria was short-lived. Morning had arrived and with it, I found, we lost our best ally, the concealment afforded us by the night. We couldn't dig in and do a holding action because the Krauts had the communications, transportation, tanks, artillery, so once they located us they would surround us and just chew us up—so all our actions were evasive. We'd go in one direction, hit Germans, run like hell, and try again at a different route, all the time trying to find our own regiment or any other sizable friendly force."[2]

For Sgt. D. Zane Schlemmer of the 508th, "each field became a separate battleground." He had a sense of intense isolation. In this situation, he found a strange ally in the brown and white Norman cattle. Schlemmer explained: "When there were cows grazing in a field, we were pleased because we could be reasonably certain that the field was not mined. Also by watching the cows, who were by nature quite curious animals, we could tell whether there was anyone else in the field, because the cows would stand, waiting, facing anyone there in anticipation of being milked. Over all these years, I've had a place in my heart for those lovely Norman cows with their big eyes and big udders."

But the cows could only spot Germans for Schlemmer and his small group, not kill them, and the paratroopers had precious little in the way of killing weapons. "By midmorning of D-Day, more troopers had assembled, but we had no mortars, few machine guns, few bazookas, fewer radios, little medical supplies, few medics—really, not much more than a few grenades and our rifles."[3]

But despite the lack of heavy weapons they had an aggressive spirit and a can-do attitude. Sgt. Sidney McCallum of the 506th PIR got into a typical hedgerow fight, with Sgt. William Adley beside him. They were setting up when a German machine gun fired on them. McCallum and Adley dove to the ground, but not before Adley got hit in the head. The machine gun kept firing over their bodies but could not depress low enough to hit them.

"As the bullets kept hitting the hedgerow inches above our head, I asked Adley if he was hit bad, and these were his words: 'I'm dying, Mickey, but we are going to win this damn war, aren't we! You damn well f——ing A we are.' When the firing ceased, Bill was dead." McCallum concluded his story with a question: "How much farther beyond the call of duty can one go than this?"[4]

The northern exits from Utah, a kilometer or so inland from the beach across the flooded fields, were no. 4 near St.-Martin-de-Varreville and no. 3 near Audouville-la-Hubert. They were assigned to the 502nd PIR. Lt. Col. Robert Cole, commanding the 3rd Battalion of the 502nd, was the first to get there. He had landed near Ste.-Mère-Église, wandered through the night, collected a group of about seventy-five men from his own battalion, others from the 506th PIR, plus a handful of men from the 82nd Airborne, and moved out toward St.-Martin-de-Varreville. Along the way he had a skirmish with a German patrol; the Americans killed several of the enemy and took ten prisoners.

At St.-Martin, Cole sent a reconnaissance party to check out the battery there. It had been damaged by bombing and was deserted. Cole then split his force, sending one group to seize exit 3, another to take exit 4. At 0930, near Audouville-la-Hubert, the Americans saw German troops retreating across the causeway from the beach. Without loss to themselves, the Americans killed fifty to seventy-five of the enemy. By noon, the exits were securely in American hands.

Capt. L. "Legs" Johnson led a patrol down the causeway to the beach. He saw German soldiers in one of the batteries waving a white flag. "They were underground, part of the coastal defense group, and they were relatively older men, really not very good soldiers. We accepted their terms of surrender, allowing them to come up only in small groups. We enclosed them with barbed wire fencing, their own barbed wire, and they were pretty well shocked when they learned that there were a lot more of them than there were of us—there were at least fifty of those guys."

Johnson took his helmet off, set it down, lay on the ground with his helmet as a headrest, "really taking it sort of easy, waiting for the 4th Infantry Division to come up." At about 1100 the infantry were there, "and it was really sort of amusing, because we were on the beach with our faces all blackened, and these guys would come up in their boats and crash down in front of us and man, when they came off those boats, they were ready for action. We quickly hollered to them and pointed to our American flags."[5]

Inland by about a kilometer from St.-Martin-de-Varreville there was a group of buildings holding a German coastal-artillery barracks, known to the Americans from its map signification as WXYZ. Lt. Col. Patrick Cassidy, commanding the 1st Battalion of the 502nd, short of men and with a variety of missions to perform, sent Sgt. Harrison Summers of West Virginia with fifteen men to capture the barracks. That was not much of a force to take on a full-strength German company, but it was all Cassidy could spare.

Summers set out immediately, not even taking the time to learn the names of the men he was leading, who were showing considerable reluctance to follow this unknown sergeant. Summers grabbed one man, Sgt. Leland Baker, and told him, "Go up to the top of this rise and watch in that direction and don't let anything come over that hill and get on my flank. Stay there until you're told to come back." Baker did as ordered.[6]

Summers then went to work, charging the first farmhouse, hoping his hodgepodge squad would follow. It did not, but he kicked in the door and sprayed the interior with his tommy gun. Four Germans fell dead, others ran out a back door to the next house. Summers, still alone, charged that house; again the Germans fled. His example inspired Pvt. William Burt to come out of the roadside ditch where the group was hiding, set up his light machine gun, and begin laying down a suppressing fire against the third barracks building.

Once more Summers dashed forward. The Germans were ready this time; they shot at him from loopholes but, what with Burt's machine-gun fire and Summers's zigzag running, failed to hit him. Summers kicked in the door and sprayed the interior, killing six Germans and driving the remainder out of the building.

Summers dropped to the ground, exhausted and in emotional shock. He rested for half an hour. His squad came up and replenished his ammunition supply. As he rose to go on, an unknown captain from the 101st, misdropped by miles, appeared at his side. "I'll go with you," said the captain. At that instant he was shot through the heart and Summers was again alone. He charged another building, killing six more Germans. The rest threw up their hands. Summers's squad was close behind; he turned the prisoners over to his men.

One of them, Pvt. John Camien from New York City, called out to Summers: "Why are you doing it?"

"I can't tell you," Summers replied.

"What about the others?"

"They don't seem to want to fight," said Summers, "and I can't make them. So I've got to finish it."

"OK," said Camien. "I'm with you."

Together, Summers and Camien moved from building to building, taking turns charging and giving covering fire. Burt meanwhile moved up with his machine gun. Between the three of them, they killed more Germans.

There were two buildings to go. Summers charged the first and kicked the door open, to see the most improbable sight. Fifteen German artillerymen were seated at mess tables eating breakfast. Summers never paused; he shot them down at the tables.

The last building was the largest. Beside it was a shed and

a haystack. Burt used tracer bullets to set them ablaze. The shed was used by the Germans for ammunition storage; it quickly exploded, driving thirty Germans out into the open, where Summers, Camien, and Burt shot some of them down as the others fled.

Another member of Summers's makeshift squad came up. He had a bazooka, which he used to set the roof of the last building on fire. The Germans on the ground floor were firing a steady fusillade from loopholes in the walls, but as the flames began to build they dashed out. Many died in the open. Thirty-one others emerged with raised hands to offer their surrender.

Summers collapsed, exhausted by his nearly five hours of combat. He lit a cigarette. One of the men asked him, "How do you feel?"

"Not very good," Summers answered. "It was all kind of crazy. I'm sure I'll never do anything like that again."[7]

Summers got a battlefield commission and a Distinguished Service Cross. He was put in for the Medal of Honor, but the paperwork got lost. In the late 1980s, after Summers's death from cancer, Pvt. Baker and others made an effort to get the medal awarded posthumously, without success.[8] Summers is a legend with American paratroopers nonetheless, the Sergeant York of World War II. His story has too much John Wayne/Hollywood in it to be believed, except that more than ten men saw and reported his exploits.

At 0600, General Taylor made his first D-Day command decision. He had with him Brig. Gen. Anthony McAuliffe (101st artillery commander), Col. Julian Ewell (CO 3rd Battalion, 501st PIR), eighteen other officers, and forty men. With the sunrise, Taylor could see the church steeple at Ste.-Marie-du-Mont. "I know the shape of that one," he said, a payoff from the preinvasion briefing.

He was in position to move his group south, to defend the line of the Douve River, or east to exits 1 and 2. Either way he would be carrying out 101st missions. He decided to go east: "It remains for us to help the 4th Infantry Division in every way possible," he said. He set off from just south of Ste.-Marie-du-Mont for Pouppeville (called "Poopville" by the GIs) and exit 1.[9]

Lt. Eugene Brierre was in the lead, with flank guards on both sides out into the fields. As they approached Pouppeville, shots rang out. The village was held by some sixty men of the German 91st Division. They were hunkered down, occasionally firing out of second-story windows. It took Taylor's small force nearly three hours to complete the house-to-house, really window-to-window fighting. Ewell's battalion suffered eighteen casualties and inflicted twenty-five on the enemy. Nearly forty Wehrmacht troops surrendered.

In one house, Brierre found a wounded German on the floor. "His gun was near him. I almost shot him when I realized that he was seriously wounded. He signaled to me to hand him something; I saw that he was pointing toward a rosary. I grabbed his gun, unloaded it, threw it aside, picked up the rosary and handed it to him. He had a look of deep appreciation in his eyes and began to pray, passing the beads through his fingers. He died shortly thereafter."

With Pouppeville taken, Taylor had possession of exit 1. He sent Lieutenant Brierre on an eight-man patrol down the causeway with orders to make contact with the 4th Infantry Division coming in at Utah. A couple of German soldiers had fled Pouppeville headed toward the beach; four German soldiers at Utah had meanwhile fled inland along the causeway. When they met and realized they were caught in a nutcracker, they hid under a bridge. Meanwhile Captain Mabry was advancing inland along the causeway, flooded fields to both sides.

Brierre shot an orange flare up into the air to show that "we were friends. The troops came on; when they got to the bridge, six Germans came out with their hands up and surrendered. I went to the road and met Captain Mabry. I recorded the time; it was 1110." The linkup at Pouppeville was complete.[10]

Brierre took Mabry to meet Taylor. When Mabry told him how smoothly the landings at Utah were going, Taylor turned to his chief of staff, Col. Gerald Higgins, and said, "The invasion is succeeding. We don't have to worry about the causeways. Now we can think about the next move."[11]

When the German 6th Parachute Regiment moved out to attack, it was hit almost immediately by naval gun fire. "No one can imagine what it was like," Pvt. Egon Rohrs declared. "When the ships fired it was like a storm. It was hell. And it lasted, it lasted. It was unendurable. We lay on the ground, pressed against the earth." Pvt. Wolfgang Geritzlehner was in Rohrs's unit. Geritzlehner had spent two years worrying that the war would end before he could take part in it. But "at the end of one hour, I wanted only to go home. We were all terrified. There were some who cried and called for their mothers."[12]

Colonel Heydte wanted to see the situation for himself, so

he set off on his motorcycle and drove from Carentan to Ste.-Marie-du-Mont, where he climbed to the top of the church steeple, the one Taylor had spotted an hour earlier. It was fifty meters or so above the ground and gave him a magnificent view of Utah Beach.

What he saw quite took his breath away. "All along the beach," he recalled, "were these small boats, hundreds of them, each disgorging thirty or forty armed men. Behind them were the warships, blasting away with their huge guns, more warships in one fleet than anyone had ever seen before. Cannons from a single German coastal bunker were firing at the incoming American troops, who had no cover on the gently rising slope. Except for this small fortification, the German defense seemed nonexistent or, in any case, invisible."

Around the church, in the little village and beyond in the green fields crisscrossed by hedgerows, all was quiet. The Germans had a battery of four 105mm cannon at Brecourt Manor, a couple of kilometers north of Ste.-Marie-du-Mont, but the guns were not firing even though they were perfectly situated to lob shells onto the landing craft on Utah and to engage the warships out in the Channel. An identical battery at Holdy, just to the south of Ste.-Marie-du-Mont, was also not firing.[13]

No one ever found out why. As with the Germans eating breakfast at WXYZ when Summers burst in on them, it was and remains inexplicable. Of course these artillerymen were not top quality troops, nothing to match Heydte's paratroopers; many were overage, some were just kids, few had any heart for fighting American paratroopers. But the biggest problem was the absence of leadership. The junior officers and noncoms in the artillery units either would not or could not take charge and make their men do their duty. They were prepared to defend themselves from their trenches, bunkers, and stone farmhouses; they were not prepared to stand to their guns.

Heydte dashed down the circular stairs from the steeple and got on his radio. He ordered his 1st Battalion to get to Ste.-Marie-du-Mont and Holdy as quickly as possible to hold the villages and get those guns shooting.

Thus did the Wehrmacht pay the price for overextending itself. Its best troops were either dead or POWs or invalids or fighting on the Eastern Front. The garrison troops in the Cotentin were almost useless, even a detriment. Heydte's clear mission was to open the road from Carentan to Ste.-Mère-Église, concentrate his regiment to drive the small 82nd Airborne force in Ste.-Mère-

Église out of town, and by such a counterattack throw the Americans on the defensive. That was what he had intended to do, but the sad state of affairs at the batteries at Brecourt Manor and Holdy forced him to divide his force and put one of his battalions on a defensive mission.

Heydte was the only German regimental commander doing his job that morning. The others were in Rennes for the war game. That was one reason for the failure of the Wehrmacht to launch *any* coordinated counterattacks, even though it had been preparing for this day for the past six months and even though Rommel had insisted on the absolute necessity of immediate strong counterattacks while the invaders were still on the beaches.

But the war game at Rennes was only one small part of the abysmal failure of the Wehrmacht. Paralysis in the high command permeated everything. The BBC radio messages to the French Resistance were more or less ignored (for this failure at least there was an excuse; there had been so many false alarms in the preceding weeks that the German coastal units had become exhausted and exasperated by the continuous alerts; further, the messages did not indicate *where* the invasion was coming). The dummy paratroopers dropped by SAS convinced some German commanders that the whole operation was a bluff. But the major factor in the Wehrmacht's failure appears to have been a consequence of the soft life of occupation.

As early as 0615 Gen. Max Pemsel, chief of staff to General Dollmann's Seventh Army, told General Speidel at La Roche-Guyon of the massive air and naval bombardment; a half hour later Pemsel reported to Rundstedt's headquarters that the landings were beginning—but he added that Seventh Army would be able to cope with the situation from its own resources. With that news General Salmuth, commanding the Fifteenth Army, went back to bed. So did Speidel and most of Rommel's staff at La Roche-Guyon. General Blumentritt from Rundstedt's headquarters told General Jodl at Hitler's headquarters in Berchtesgaden that a major invasion appeared to be taking place and asked for the release of the armored reserve, I SS Panzer Corps outside Paris. Jodl refused to wake Hitler; permission was denied. General Bayerlein, commanding the *Panzer Lehr* division, had his tanks ready to move to the coast by 0600, but did not receive permission to do so until late afternoon.

Berlin radio reported landings in Normandy at 0700; SHAEF released its first communiqué announcing the invasion at

0930; but not until 1030 did word reach Rommel at his home in Herrlingen. He left immediately for the long drive to La Roche-Guyon but did not arrive until after dark.[14]

The cause of all this mess, beyond complacency and divided command responsibility, was the success of Operation Fortitude. As Max Hastings notes, "Every key German commander greeted the news of operations in Normandy as evidence of *an* invasion, not of *the* invasion."[15] The Calvados and Cotentin coasts were a long way from La Roche-Guyon, a longer way from Paris, an even longer way from the Pas-de-Calais, and a long, long way from the Rhine-Ruhr industrial heartland. Despite all their postwar claims to the contrary, the Germans just could not believe that the Allies would make their major, much less their sole, landing west of the Seine River. So they decided to wait for the real thing, at the Pas-de-Calais. They were still waiting three months later as the Allied armies overran France and moved into Belgium.

This from an army that claimed to be the best and most professional in the world. In fact, from the supreme commander in Berchtesgaden on down to the field officers in France to the local commanders in Normandy to the men in the barracks at WXYZ, it was an army inferior in all respects (except for weaponry, especially the 88s and the machine guns) to its Allied opponents.

The inferiority was shown again and again on D-Day. At Brecourt Manor, at 0830, just about the time Sergeant Summers started his attack at WXYZ, Lt. Richard Winters and ten men from E Company of the 506th PIR attacked the fifty-man guard at the battery of 105mms. The Germans were dug in behind hedgerows; they had extensive interconnecting trenches; they had machine guns and mortars and clear fields of fire. Winters's squad-size group had one light mortar, two light machine guns, two tommy guns, and five rifles. But although Winters was outnumbered five to one and was attacking an entrenched enemy, he and his men prevailed. They did so because they used tactics they had learned in training, plus common sense and some calculated courage.

At a cost of four dead, two wounded, Winters and his men killed fifteen Germans, wounded many more, took twelve prisoners, and destroyed four German 105mm cannon. The Americans had done the job through the quickness and audacity of a flanking attack, led by Winters, supported by suppressing fire from mortars and machine guns. One factor in their success was that this was their first combat experience. As Sgt. Carwood Lipton said, he took chances that morning he would never take again. "But we were so full of fire that day. I was sure I would not be killed. I felt that if a bullet was headed for me it would be deflected or I would move."[16]

After destroying the guns, Winters's small group disengaged. Surviving Germans still held the hedgerows around the manor house and were using their machine guns to lay down harassing fire. At about 1200, two Sherman tanks came up from the beach. Winters climbed onto the back of the first tank and told the commander, "I want fire along those hedgerows over there, and there, and there, and against the manor. Clean out anything that's left."

The tanks roared ahead. For the tankers, this was their first chance to fire their weapons at the enemy. They had a full load of ammunition for their .50-caliber and the .30-caliber machine guns and for their 75mm cannon.

"They just cut those hedgerows to pieces," Lt. Harry Welsh of Winters's company remembered. "You thought they would never stop shooting."[17]

At Holdy, members of the 1st Battalion of the 506th carried out a similar attack and destroyed that battery. Then the 506th drove Colonel Heydte's battalion out of Ste.-Marie-du-Mont. With that, the way was clear for the 4th Infantry Division to move further inland and get on with the war. The 101st had carried out its main mission—even though at no place were there more than a platoon of men from the same company gathered together. Taylor, Cassidy, Winters, Summers, and many others had seized the initiative and got the job done.

The 101st did not do so well in carrying out its second major mission, to secure the southern flank by taking the bridges over the Douve and opening the way to Carentan. This was due to the scattered drop; no sizable force of Americans was able to form up to attack. Colonel Johnson did manage to take the lock at La Barquette and establish a small bridgehead on the south bank, but he could not expand it and was pinned down by fire coming from Heydte's paratroopers in St.-Côme-du-Mont. He had no contact with any other 101st unit.

Capt. Sam Gibbons of the 501st PIR, operating independently, led a small patrol toward St.-Côme-du-Mont. He believed the village was in 501st hands, but he moved cautiously as his visibility was limited by the hedgerows. Before setting out, he shared the two cans of beer he had brought with him, then left the empty cans in the middle of the road "as a monument to the first cans of Schlitz consumed in France."

The patrol reached the bottom of the hill, with St.-Côme-du-Mont sitting at the crest. Gibbons heard a gun bolt move on the other side of a hedgerow. He looked toward the sound and saw a rifle muzzle pointed at him. "As I dove for the ditch, all hell broke loose. We had been ambushed. The German behind the hedge had his weapon set on full automatic and it sprayed bullets all over the area. Instantaneously, shots started coming from the buildings in St.-Côme-du Mont and from the hedges."

Gibbons dove to the ground. The German on the other side could not get at him without exposing himself. Gibbons lobbed a grenade over the hedge and the firing stopped. Still Gibbons could not raise his head because when he did he drew fire from the village. His patrol began returning fire, slowly at first but building up the volume as the men got into firing positions.

Gibbons made a dash for a concrete telephone pole, tried to hide behind it, found it did not give him sufficient protection, and made another dash to dive into a ditch. It was deep enough to give him protection so long as he stayed flat on his belly. He began crawling: "I had received such a shot of adrenaline I could have crawled a mile."

He did not have to go that far. After fifty meters, he found cover and was able to tell his men to slow their fire to conserve ammunition. "It was obvious that we were badly outnumbered and that the Germans were well emplaced and planned to defend St.-Côme-du-Mont stubbornly. So there we were, 200 yards north of St.-Côme-du-Mont meeting superior fire from a major force. We had no automatic weapons, no radios, only our semiautomatic rifles and a few pistols. We hardly knew each other, but we were getting well acquainted, and we were working well together."

Gibbons consulted with two lieutenants. They decided to break off the action and head north, toward Ste.-Mère-Église, in search of some friendly force. On the way, they discovered that the beer cans were gone, probably picked up by Heydte's men. At the hamlet of Blosville, although firefights small and big were going on all around the countryside, everything was quiet. "Doors all closed; windows all shuttered; cows in the field; no one stirred. The firing didn't seem to bother the cows. They just kept on eating. Occasionally one would lift its head and look at us. No one bothered us so we didn't stop." Gibbons led his patrol on toward Ste.-Mère-Église.[18]

Heydte's paratroopers had beaten off the attack and retained possession of St.-Côme-du-Mont, which blocked the road to Carentan. That was a significant victory for the Germans, as it kept them in possession of the railway and road bridges over the Douve north of Carentan, which made it possible for them to move reinforcements into the eastern Cotentin. Heydte was also able to get his 2nd Battalion to the intersection where the road from Chef-du-Pont to Ste.-Marie-du-Mont crossed the highway from Carentan to Ste.-Mère-Église.

Otherwise, as Heydte said in 1991, "The day did not work out as I expected." His 1st Battalion was forced out of Ste.-Marie-du-Mont and pushed south, where many men drowned in the floods around the mouth of the Douve. With the best regiment in the Cotentin, he was on the defensive, holding crossroads, not launching any coordinated counterattacks.[19]

One company of Heydte's men managed to get a battery of 88mms at Beaumont working. They opened fire on Colonel Johnson's position at La Barquette. Fortunately for Johnson, Lieutenant Farrell, a naval shore-fire-control officer who had jumped with the 501st, had through dogged persistence found an SCR-609 radio. With Farrell was Lt. Parker Alford, a forward observer for the 101st artillery. They tried to contact the cruiser USS *Quincy* directly, but the Germans jammed the frequency; Alford then discovered that he could reach a shore party at Utah. He asked that it relay a request to *Quincy* to lay on a barrage against Beaumont.

Quincy asked for verification of Alford's identity. He replied that he knew a naval officer who had played linebacker with the Nebraska team in the 1940 Rose Bowl game. Name him, *Quincy* called back through the shore party. Easy, Alford replied; "He is K. C. Roberts and he is a member of the shore party we are speaking through."

"Roger, Roger, where do you want the fire?" Alford gave the coordinates, *Quincy* blasted away, Beaumont was obliterated, the 88s fell silent.[20]

Captain Shettle's small group from 3rd Battalion, 506th PIR, spent the day isolated at the bridges along the lower Douve. He could not advance; the Germans made no effort to push him back. His only contact with the beach came in the late afternoon when a platoon-sized German force was seen to the rear. Shettle took about half his force and deployed to ambush the enemy. When the Americans opened fire, the "Germans" made no attempt to fight back; they threw up their hands and surrendered. "They turned out to be a Hungarian labor force fleeing from the beachhead."

As the day was ending, a German patrol came after Shettle's group. The Americans threw grenades at them. Shettle jumped up to throw one, forgetting that he had dislocated his right shoulder on a practice jump in May: "When I threw my grenade, my shoulder came out of its socket and the grenade landed in my foxhole. Fortunately, the banks of the foxhole protected me, but the next morning I found that I had blown up my prized 'Bond Street' trench coat, which was so much lighter and protective than our issue heavy rubber gear. So ended D-Day. Very little sleep, worry about our exposed position, lack of ammunition, and only hard chocolate bars for food."[21]

Those D-ration chocolate bars sustained many American paratroopers on June 6, but some found they craved real food. Pvt. Herbert James of the 508th PIR approached a Norman farmer to do some trading. James indicated he wanted eggs, but the farmer did not understand and appeared frightened.

"So I started making noises like a chicken and I hopped around and he thought I wanted a whole chicken and tried to catch one." James shook his head no and made the shape of an egg with his fingers. The farmer got some eggs; James gave him a chocolate bar in trade. Pleased with the exchange, the farmer called his small daughter from the house and gave her the bar, saying "Chocolate, chocolate" over and over. The girl took her first taste of chocolate ever and was delighted. James went back into the woods and poached his eggs on his entrenching shovel and was delighted.[22]

Lt. Carl Cartledge of the 501st PIR was even luckier. He and a few members of his platoon drove some Germans out of a farmhouse, killing six or seven of them in the process. Inside, Cartledge found the dining-room table covered with half-eaten food—Norman cheese, apples, cold meats, and cider. After bolting some food, he searched the dead Germans, looking for paybooks, unit identification, and the like. To get at one paybook, he had to open a dead German's belt buckle. "I looked at the flying-eagle belt buckle, and on it was inscribed '*Gott Mit Uns.*' And I said, 'The hell He is!' "

Cartledge was in the Vierville area, northeast of St.-Côme-du-Mont. There he found his company medic, a man named Anderson, who had been caught by the Germans as he came down. "He was hanging in a tree by his feet, his arms down, throat cut, genitals stuffed in his mouth. His medic's red-cross armband was stained with the blood that had flowed from his hair."[23]

The sight infuriated the Americans, but the Germans were

not the only ones to commit atrocities that day. Pvt. William Sawyer of the 508th remembered running into one of his buddies. "We had all been issued yellow horsehide gloves. This fellow had on red gloves, and I asked him where he got the red gloves from, and he reached down in his jumppants and pulled out a whole string of ears. He had been ear-hunting all night and had them sewed on an old bootlace."[24]

About midmorning, Lt. Jack Isaacs of the 505th PIR pulled three wounded gliderborne Americans into a farmhouse. "Shortly thereafter, we noticed a German soldier step out into the field and approach an injured man that we had left there, intending to go back for him. The German looked him over and then shot him. That Kraut didn't survive his trip back to the hedgerow."[25]

Getting help to the wounded was a major problem. Every trooper carried a first-aid kit, but it contained only bandages, sulfa tablets, and two morphine Syrettes. There were only a handful of doctors who jumped with the troops, and they had precious little equipment. Maj. David Thomas, regimental surgeon for the 508th PIR, set up his aid station in a ditch near the Merderet River.

"The thing that I remember most was a soldier who had his leg blown off right by the knee and the only thing left attached was his patellar tendon. And I had him down there in this ditch and I said, 'Son, I'm gonna have to cut the rest of your leg off and you're back to bullet-biting time because I don't have anything to use for an anesthetic.' And he said, 'Go ahead, Doc.' I cut the patellar tendon and he didn't even whimper."[26]

The confusion that characterized all airborne operations on June 6 was badly compounded for the 82nd Division because it landed astride the Merderet River. As a result of the extensive flooding, the Merderet was more a shallow lake (a kilometer or more wide and ten kilometers long) than a river. There were two crossings, one a raised road (or causeway) and bridge at La Fière, about a kilometer west of Ste.-Mère-Église, and the other a causeway and bridge at Chef-du-Pont, two kilometers south of La Fière. The 82nd had hoped to take La Fière and Chef-du-Pont during the night, then spend the day attacking westward to secure the line of the upper Douve River, but in the event the division had a terrific daylong fight for the two positions. Many of its units were isolated west of the Merderet; some of them remained surrounded and isolated for as long as four days, fighting off German tank and artillery attacks with their hand-held weapons.

Shortly after dawn, Gen. James Gavin, assistant division commander of the 82nd, had assembled nearly 300 men, mainly from the 507th PIR—about as large a group as the Americans had that morning. Gavin moved south along the railroad embankment on the edge of the flooded area to La Fière, decided that the American position on the east bank of the causeway was secure, left part of his force there, and continued on south to Chef-du-Pont with the remainder.

Meanwhile an eighty-man group under Lt. Col. Charles Timmes took possession of the hamlet of Canquigny at the west end of the La Fière causeway. When a patrol of four officers and eight enlisted men under Lt. Lewis Levy of the 507th PIR came into Canquigny, Timmes decided that the twelve-man group could hold the bridgehead. He decided to go on the offensive and moved out with his group toward his original objective, Amfreville.

Sgt. Donald Bosworth was a member of Headquarters Company, 1st Battalion, 507th. He had broken his ankle on the jump. With the aid of five other men from his company, he managed to get to a farmhouse. The farmer's wife was a schoolteacher who could speak a little English. When she answered a knock on the door, Bosworth showed her the American flag on his right shoulder. She jumped for joy, invited all the men in and hugged each one of them in turn. Then her husband offered Bosworth his small, old flatbed truck, and dug up a five-gallon can of gasoline he had buried in the yard. Bosworth and Sgt. A. J. Carlucci signed a receipt for the truck so that the couple would be able to recover its cost from Uncle Sam and set out for Amfreville. On the way they joined up with Timmes. A medic made a splint for Bosworth's ankle.

He stayed in the fight. Timmes sent him to check out a farmhouse on the other side of a hedgerow. "I started to crawl over the hedgerow to get to the other side when suddenly I was face-to-face with two Germans, not more than four feet away. They were setting up a machine gun. It seemed like an hour before any of us moved." Bosworth shot the Germans with his semiautomatic; they shot him. He was hit in the right shoulder, went flying backward off the hedgerow, and lost consciousness. Lt. Robert Law got him to the basement of a farmhouse, where he spent the rest of the day.[27] Timmes, meanwhile, was unable to penetrate the German defenses around Amfreville.

Gavin and Timmes had moved their main force out of La Fière and Canquigny on the assumption that the small groups they left behind could hold the positions and that they were mutually supporting. But the Germans held the high ground west of the causeway, which was nearly a kilometer long, and they brought the road under highly accurate sniper and mortar fire, preventing the Americans from using it.

About midmorning, the Germans launched a counterattack led by three tanks against Canquigny. Lieutenant Levy and his handful of men fought it off for over an hour. They managed to disable two enemy tanks with Gammon grenades (how the Yanks loved that British grenade; it was the best antitank weapon they had, far superior to their own bazookas—if they could get close enough*) but eventually had to withdraw northward.

Thus the bridgehead so handily won was lost. The 82nd's units were separated, each fighting its own lonely battle on either side of the swollen Merderet. Timmes's group remained isolated for two days.

To the south, at Chef-du-Pont, General Gavin and a group of about 100 men, mainly from 1st Battalion, 507th PIR, under the command of Lt. Col. Edwin Ostberg moved to seize the bridge about a half kilometer west of the village. At 1000, Ostberg led his force on a dash through the main street, headed for the bridge. The Americans were fired on from several buildings simultaneously, taking four casualties. It took nearly two hours to systematically clear the village of the enemy; retreating Germans headed for the bridge.

"We knew the bridge must be taken before the Germans could organize their defense," Capt. Roy Creek recalled, "so we made a semiorganized dash for it. We were too late. Two officers reached the bridge and both were shot, one toppling off the bridge into the water, the other falling on the eastern approach. The officer toppling into the river was Ostberg (he was rescued shortly after and lived to fight again; the other officer was dead)."

Lt. Col. Arthur Maloney and some seventy-five men arrived "and we set about dislodging the stubborn enemy." It proved to be impossible. The Germans had foxholes dug into the shoulders of the causeway and they held the high ground on the west bank. The Americans had only small arms; the Germans had tanks and artillery to supplement their machine gun and mortar fire. Two attempts to storm the bridge proved unsuccessful.[28]

The Germans counterattacked. Pvt. David Jones of the

---

* The Gammon grenade weighed about two pounds and was the size of a softball. It was a plastic explosive, point detonated.

508th PIR had just come up to the edge of the causeway. He saw tanks coming across, three French Renault tanks, "probably the smallest tanks used during the entire war, but to me they were larger than life." The lead tank had its hatch open and the black-capped tank commander was exposed from the waist up, hands resting outside the turret.

Jones turned to a buddy and said, "I think it's time to get our war started." He took careful aim and fired at the tank commander. His bullet hit the turret "and I can still remember the sound of that ricochet. The black uniform disappeared, the hatch clanged shut, the tank backed off a few feet, and our little group scattered to the four winds. Not only had I missed my first shot of World War II, but was now confronted with where and how to hide." He found a place in a vegetable garden behind a farmhouse. The tank fired a 20mm round into the side of the house and Jones and his group took off running to the nearest hedgerow.[29]

The tank moved on toward Chef-du-Pont. The other two followed. The middle tank stopped in front of the farmhouse; on the second floor, Sgts. Ray Hummle and O. B. Hill were watching. Hill handed Hummle a Gammon grenade.

"Just at that moment," he remembered, "the hatch of the tank opened and raised back and the tank commander climbed up to where his waist was out of the tank and he was looking around. Hummle dropped the Gammon grenade right into the tank. There was one awful explosion, smoke and fire all around the tank, and the commander who was standing in the hatch went straight up in the air like a champagne cork."

The other two tanks turned their guns on the farmhouse and blasted away. "The mother and the daughter who were in the building downstairs became quite excited and screamed at us to get out. And we figured that perhaps we should." Hummel and Hill fled to the nearest hedgerow. The tanks withdrew to the west.[30]

Now there was stalemate at the causeway. The Americans could not advance and would not retreat. The German infantry dug in along the causeway could fire but could not move. One of them decided to give up. He rose out of the embankment.

S. L. A. Marshall described the scene in his classic book *Night Drop*. "He called, '*Kamerad!*' Before anyone could answer, a paratrooper, not more than 20 feet away, shot him dead within clear view of the people on both sides." Marshall wrote that the shot was terribly stupid; had the man been allowed to surrender, his companions would have followed his lead.[31]

Captain Creek commented: "Having witnessed this action at close range, I would defy anyone to make a split-second judgment on what to do when an enemy soldier jumps up out of a foxhole twenty feet from you in the heat of heavy firing on both sides and in your own very first fight for your life. To this day, forty-seven years later, I don't know if the enemy soldier was trying to surrender or not. In my opinion any enemy shot during this intense action had waited too long to surrender. He was committed as the attacker was to a fight for survival."

Shortly thereafter, around midafternoon, General Gavin, who had gone back to La Fière, sent word for Colonel Maloney to bring his men and join him there. That left Creek in command of thirty-four men, with orders from Gavin to hold Chef-du-Pont at all costs. "It was pretty obvious that it couldn't cost too much. But at the same time, it was doubtful we could hold something we didn't have." Making matters worse, Creek saw a line of German infantry approaching from his left rear, while a German field piece began firing from across the Merderet.

"And then, as from heaven, C-47s began to appear, dropping bundles of weapons and ammunition. One bundle of 60mm mortar ammunition dropped right in our laps." Next came a glider-delivered 57mm antitank gun. Creek turned the mortars on the German infantry and used the AT to fire at the German fieldpiece on the west bank of the causeway. "We didn't hit it, I am certain, but we stopped it from firing."

Creek went over to the offensive. A ten-man patrol began to dash across the causeway. Five German infantrymen jumped up from their foxholes along the embankment and made a run for it. They were shot down. The others surrendered.

"That did it," Creek said. "The bridge was ours and we knew we could hold it. But as with all victors in war, we shared a let down feeling. We knew it was still a long way to Berlin."

Creek set about organizing and improving the position, tending to the wounded, gathering up the dead, German and American, and covering them with parachutes. Darkness was approaching. "When would the beach forces come? They should have already done so. Maybe the whole invasion had failed. All we knew was the situation in Chef-du-Pont, and Chef-du-Pont is a very small town.

"At 2400 hours, our fears were dispelled. Reconnaissance

elements of the 4th Infantry Division wheeled into town. They shared their rations with us.

"It was D-Day plus one in Normandy. As I sat pondering the day's events, I reflected upon the details of the fighting and the bravery of every man participating in it. We had done some things badly. But overall, with a hodgepodge of troops from several units who had never trained together, didn't even know one another, engaged in their first combat, we had done okay. We captured our bridge and we held it."[32]

Ste.-Mère-Église was a quiet little village with a couple of hundred gray stone houses. The town square, built around a gray Norman church, contained the usual Norman shops selling eggs, cheese, meat, dresses and suits, cider and wine, newspapers, bread, and a pharmacy. It had a *hotel de ville* and a hospital. It was a village in which nothing much of consequence had happened for ten centuries. The most exciting times were the festivals and weddings.

The N-13 ran through the village, heading north to Cherbourg, south to Carentan, then east to Caen and on to Paris. Without the use of the N-13 the Germans to the north of Ste.-Mère-Église would be cut off; without control of Ste.-Mère-Église, the American paratroopers along and beyond the Merderet would be cut off and the 4th Infantry Division unable to move west and north.

Thus the battle for Ste.-Mère-Église took on an importance out of all proportion to the intrinsic value of the village. The staff of the 82nd Airborne had agreed during the planning stage of the invasion that the place would be the division's defensive base. If the 4th Infantry failed to gain a foothold or the linkup was delayed, all the division's units would fall back on Ste.-Mère-Église until relieved. The village had to be held for an additional reason; the second flight of gliders was scheduled to land around the village just before dusk.

The 3rd Battalion, 505th PIR, commanded by Lt. Col. Edward Krause, had taken possession of the town just before daylight. Lt. James Coyle of Headquarters Company was with Krause. Coyle recalled a Frenchman who came out of his house to talk. "He spoke little or no English and I spoke but a little French, but I understood him well enough to sense his concern: He wanted to know if this was a raid or if it was the invasion." Coyle reassured him.

"Nous restons ici," Coyle said ("We are staying here"). "We were not leaving Ste.-Mère-Église."[33]

Pvt. John Fitzgerald of the 502nd PIR, who had been misdropped, came into town at dawn. He saw troopers hanging in trees. "They looked like rag dolls shot full of holes. Their blood was dripping on this place they came to free."

On the edge of town, Fitzgerald saw a sight "that has never left my memory. It was a picture story of the death of one 82nd Airborne trooper. He had occupied a German foxhole and made it his personal Alamo. In a half circle around the hole lay the bodies of nine German soldiers. The body closest to the hole was only three feet away, a potato masher [grenade] in its fist.* The other distorted forms lay where they had fallen, testimony to the ferocity of the fight. His ammunition bandoliers were still on his shoulders, empty of M-1 clips. Cartridge cases littered the ground. His rifle stock was broken in two. He had fought alone and, like many others that night, he had died alone.

"I looked at his dog tags. The name read Martin V. Hersh. I wrote the name down in a small prayer book I carried, hoping someday I would meet someone who knew him. I never did."[34]

Colonel Vandervoort, despite his broken ankle, was moving his battalion, the 2nd of the 505th, toward Ste.-Mère-Église. His mission was to guard the northern approaches to the village. He therefore detached 3rd Platoon of D Company (Lt. Turner Turnbull commanding) and sent it to Neuville-au-Plain with orders to set up a defense there.

Vandervoort entered Ste.-Mère-Église, where he got lucky. There was a glider-delivered jeep in good working order, which allowed Vandervoort to get out of his wheelbarrow and become more mobile. He conferred with Krause (who had shrapnel wounds in his leg); they agreed that Vandervoort would be responsible for the eastern and northern sides of the village, Krause for the southern and western ends. They did not have enough men to set up an all-around perimeter defense but they could block the roads.

Vandervoort had another piece of luck. Capt. Alfred Ireland of the 80th Airborne Antiaircraft Battalion, who had come in by glider shortly after dawn, reported that he had two working 57mm AT guns. (Commenting later on his ride into Normandy and the crash landing of his glider, paratrooper Ireland said of the glider-borne troops, "Those guys don't get paid enough."[35] That was

---

* The German grenade, with its long handle, could be thrown much more easily and farther than the American oval-shaped fragmentation grenade. But the amount of metal on the potato masher was not nearly as much as on the fragmentation grenade. Thus, as William Tucker of the 505th PIR put it, the Germans could use the potato masher "as an assault weapon. They could throw it and run right after it. We threw that damn frag grenade, we would run for cover ourselves."

literally true; the glider troops did not get the extra $50 per month jump pay the paratroopers received.)

Vandervoort set up one of the AT guns at the northern end of Ste.-Mère-Église and sent the other north to Neuville-au-Plain to support Turnbull.

Turnbull was half Cherokee. His men called him "Chief," but not in his presence. "He was a good guy," Pvt. Charles Miller remembered. "I used to box with him."[36] Turnbull had put two of his squads along a hedgerow to the east of Neuville-au-Plain, the third to the west. Vandervoort set up the AT gun in town, pointing north, then talked to Turnbull, who told him nothing much had happened since he set up some four hours earlier. It was now about 1300.

While they were talking, a Frenchman rode his bicycle up to them and announced in English that some American paratroopers were bringing in a large contingent of German prisoners from the north. Sure enough, when Vandervoort and Turnbull looked in that direction there was a column of troops marching in good order right down the middle of the N-13, with what appeared to be paratroopers on either side of them waving orange flags (the American recognition signal on June 6).

But Vandervoort grew suspicious when he noticed two tracked vehicles at the rear of the column. He told Turnbull to have his machine gunner fire a short burst just to the right of the approaching column, which by now was less than a kilometer away.

The burst scattered the column. "Prisoners" and "paratroopers" alike dove into the ditches and returned fire, the perfidious Frenchman pedaled madly away, and the two self-propelled (SP) guns that had aroused Vandervoort's suspicion began to move forward behind smoke canisters.

At a half kilometer, the SPs opened fire. One of the first shots knocked out Turnbull's bazooka team, another was a near miss on the American AT gun. Its crew scattered, but with some "encouragement" from Vandervoort the gunners remanned the AT and with some fast and accurate shooting put the German SPs out of action. But the German infantry, a full-strength company from the 91st *Luftlande* Division, outnumbering Turnbull's force more than five to one, began moving around his flanks, using hedgerows for cover.

Vandervoort saw that Turnbull would be overrun quickly without reinforcements, so he had his jeep driver take him back to Ste.-Mère-Église, where he dispatched Lt. Theodore Peterson and Lieutenant Coyle with 1st Platoon of E Company to go to Neuville to cover Turnbull's withdrawal.

Turnbull, meanwhile, was extending his lines to the east and west in order to force the Germans to make a wider flanking move, but by 1600 he had about run out of men and room. He was taking heavy casualties, primarily from accurate German mortar fire. Of the forty-three men he had led into Neuville-au-Plain, only sixteen were in condition to fight, and some of them were wounded. Nine of Turnbull's men were dead.[37]

Turnbull was prepared to make a last stand, a sort of Custer at the Little Big Horn in reverse, when the platoon medic, Corp. James Kelly, volunteered to stay behind and look after the wounded. Pvt. Julius Sebastain, Cpl. Ray Smithson, and Sgt. Robert Niland offered to form a rearguard to cover the retreat of the remainder of the platoon, those who could still walk.

Just as Turnbull began the retreat, E Company moved into Neuville-au-Plain. "We hit fast and hard," Sgt. Otis Sampson recalled. He was handling the mortar and he was good at it. He began placing shells smack in the middle of the German force that was coming in on the flank.

"The Jerries were trying to move some men from the left of a lane to the right. One man at a time would cross at timed intervals. I judged when another would cross and had another round put in the tube. The timing was perfect."

Sampson kept moving his mortar around "so as not to give Jerry a target." The rifle squads kept up a steady fire. The momentum of the German advance was halted. Meanwhile Lieutenants Peterson and Coyle took a patrol to meet Turnbull and the few men he had left with him.

"And we started our journey back to Ste.-Mère-Église," Sampson said. "I could hear the Jerries yelling as we were leaving. It reminded me of an unfinished ball game, and they were yelling for us to come back and finish it. We withdrew in a casual way as one would after a day's work. I walked alongside Lieutenant Turnbull. He was a good man."[38]

The twenty-eight badly wounded men left behind and two of the three volunteers who provided a rearguard were captured. (The third volunteer, Sgt. Bob Niland, was killed at his machine gun. One of his brothers, a platoon leader in the 4th Division, was killed the same morning at Utah Beach. Another brother was killed that week in Burma. Mrs. Niland received all three telegrams from the War Department announcing the deaths of her sons on the same day. Her fourth son, Fritz, was in the 101st Airborne; he was snatched out of the front line by the Army.) The most critical of the wounded were evacuated to a hospital in Cherbourg by the Germans and were eventually freed when that city was taken on June 27. The others were freed on the night of June 7-8 when American tanks overran Neuville-au-Plain. Turnbull was killed in Ste.-Mère-Église on June 7 by an artillery round.[39]

Turnbull's heroic stand allowed Krause and Vandervoort to concentrate on an even stronger counterattack from the 795th Regiment south of Ste.-Mère-Église. It was as big a counterattack as the Germans mounted on D-Day, and it was supported by 88mm guns firing from high ground south of the village.

"The impact of the shells threw up mounds of dirt and mud," Private Fitzgerald recalled. "The ground trembled and my eardrums felt as if they would burst. Dirt was filling my shirt and was getting into my eyes and mouth. Those 88s became a legend. It was said that there were more soldiers converted to Christianity by the 88 than by Peter and Paul combined.

"When the firing finally stopped, it was midafternoon. We still held the town and there was talk of tanks coming up from the beaches to help us. I could not hold a razor steady enough to shave for the next few days.

"Up until now, I had been mentally on the defensive. My introduction to combat had been a shocker but it was beginning to wear off. I found myself pissed off at the Germans, the dirt, the noise, and the idea of being pushed back."[40]

Others felt the same. When Colonel Krause sent I Company to strike at the enemy flank, it moved out aggressively. It caught a German convoy in the open and with bazookas and Gammon bombs destroyed some tanks. The accompanying German infantry withdrew under a hail of fire. "With the last light of day," Fitzgerald said, "the last German attack came to a halt."[41]

Reinforcements came in by glider. They tried to land all around Ste.-Mère-Église, but the pilots were taking small-arms fire from the surrounding Germans and in any case the fields were too short and the hedgerows too high. Every glider seemed to end up crashing into a hedgerow.

"I was standing in a ditch when a glider suddenly came crashing through some trees," Lieutenant Coyle remembered. "I had not seen it coming and of course could not hear it as it made no sound. I just had time to drop face down in the ditch when the glider hit, crashed across the road, and came to rest with its wing over me. I had to crawl on my stomach the length of the wing to get out from under."[42]

Sergeant Sampson dove to the ground as a glider crashed into a hedgerow. "The tail end of the glider was sticking up at a forty-five-degree angle. I went to see if I couldn't help. As I came up, a hole started to appear on the right side of the glider. The men were kicking out an exit. Like bees out of a hive, they came out of that hole, jumped on the ground, ran for the trees and disappeared. I tried to tell them they were in friendly country, but they passed me as if I wasn't even there."

During the night, the Germans were firing flares, shooting rifles, mortars, and occasionally 88s at Ste.-Mère-Église, yelling out orders and threats at the Americans. "They seemed to be so sure of themselves," Sampson said. "A barrage would hit us, and then they would open up with their machine pistols, yelling as if to attack. Then it would quiet down and then burst out anew. I snuggled up close to my mortar and caressed the barrel. How I wanted to fire it. But we were too intermingled; I might have hit some of our own men.

"The enemy never came on. Maybe they thought with all their yelling and firing we would give our positions away by running. I wondered what had happened at the beaches. The infantry should have been with us by now.

"Many things ran through my mind. I was afraid the invasion had been a failure. I was thinking of my country and the people we were trying to help. I was almost certain I would never see daylight again. I can't say I was afraid. I just wanted a chance to take as many Jerries with me as possible. I wanted them to come where I could see them. I wanted to see a pile of them in front of me before they got me. It would have been so much easier dying that way."[43]

Ste.-Mère-Église was secure, if barely. The official history records this as "the most significant operation of the 82d Airborne Division on D-Day."[44] Another victory for the 82nd had been won by Captain Creek at Chef-du-Pont. On the west side of the Merderet, however, the bulk of the 82nd was scattered in small, isolated pockets, surrounded, fighting for survival rather than seizing objectives. Communication between units was almost nonexistent. General Ridgway feared that his division might be destroyed before it could consolidate and before the 4th Infantry reached it.

To the east, toward the beaches, the 101st had opened the causeways and linked up with the seaborne American troops. Many of its men were unaccounted for; of the 6,600 troopers of the 101st who had dropped into Normandy during the night, only 2,500 were fighting together in some kind of organized unit at the end of the day. Some of its units, like Colonel Johnson's at La Barquette and Captain Shettle's at the lower Douve bridges, were isolated and vulnerable, but the 101st had accomplished its main mission, opening the way inland for the 4th Infantry.

The casualty rate cannot be stated with accuracy; the airborne records for Normandy do not distinguish between D-Day losses and those suffered in the ensuing weeks. It was perhaps 10 percent, which was much lower than Air Vice Marshal Leigh-Mallory had feared and predicted, but incredibly high for one day of combat.

It would almost seem to have been too high a price, except that, thanks to the airborne, the 4th Division got ashore and inland with an absolute minimum of casualties. That was the payoff for the largest night drop of paratroopers ever made.

Leigh-Mallory had urged Eisenhower to cancel the air drop and bring the airborne divisions into the beaches as follow-up troops. Eisenhower had refused and he was surely right. Without the airborne fighting behind the German lines, the 4th Infantry would, probably, have gotten ashore and over the sand dunes without too much difficulty, as the German defenders on the shoreline were too few and of poor quality and so were badly battered by the Marauders. But getting across the causeways over the flooded area back from the dunes would have been costly, perhaps impossible, without the airborne.

The 101st had accomplished two critical missions; its men had taken the exits from the rear, and they had knocked out German cannon at Brecourt Manor, Holdy, and other places, cannon that could have been used with deadly effectiveness against the infantry and landing craft.

General Marshall had urged Eisenhower to drop the airborne much further inland, as much as sixty kilometers from the beach. Eisenhower had refused to do so. He had reasoned that lightly armed paratroopers far behind German lines would have been more a liability than a help, isolated and vulnerable, unable to act aggressively. The experience of the 82nd Airborne west of the Merderet would seem to show that Eisenhower was right.

17

VISITORS TO HELL

The 116th Regiment
at Omaha

IF THE GERMANS were going to stop the invasion anywhere, it would be at Omaha Beach. It was an obvious landing site, the only sand beach between the mouth of the Douve to the west and Arromanches to the east, a distance of almost forty kilometers. On both ends of Omaha the cliffs were more or less perpendicular.

The sand at Omaha Beach is golden in color, firm and fine, perfect for sunbathing and picnicking and digging, but in extent the beach is constricted. It is slightly crescent-shaped, about ten kilometers long overall. At low tide, there is a stretch of firm sand of 300 to 400 meters in distance. At high tide, the distance from the waterline to the one- to three-meter bank of shingle (small round stones) is but a few meters.

In 1944 the shingle, now mostly gone, was impassable to vehicles. On the western third of the beach, beyond the shingle, there was a part-wood, part-masonry seawall from one to four meters in height (now gone). Inland of the seawall there was a paved, promenade beach road, then a V-shaped antitank ditch as much as two meters deep, then a flat swampy area, then a steep bluff that ascended thirty meters or more. A man could climb the bluff, but a vehicle could not. The grass-covered slopes appeared to be featureless when viewed from any distance, but in fact they contained many small folds or irregularities that proved to be a critical physical feature of the battlefield.

There were five small "draws" or ravines that sloped gently up to the tableland above the beach. A paved road led off the beach at exit D-1 to Vierville; at Les Moulins (exit D-3) a dirt road led up to St.-Laurent; the third draw, exit E-1, had only a path leading up to the tableland; the fourth draw, E-3, had a dirt road leading to Colleville; the last draw had a dirt path at exit F-1.

No tactician could have devised a better defensive situation. A narrow, enclosed battlefield, with no possibility of outflanking it; many natural obstacles for the attacker to overcome; an ideal place to build fixed fortifications and a trench system on the slope of the bluff and on the high ground looking down on a wide, open killing field for any infantry trying to cross no-man's-land.

The Allied planners hated the idea of assaulting Omaha Beach, but it had to be done. This was as obvious to Rommel as to Eisenhower. Both commanders recognized that if the Allies invaded in Normandy, they would have to include Omaha Beach in the landing sites; otherwise the gap between Utah and the British beaches would be too great.

The waters offshore were heavily mined, so too the beaches, the promenade (which also had concertina wire along its length), and the bluff. Rommel had placed more beach obstacles here than at Utah. He had twelve strong points holding 88s, 75s, and mortars. He had dozens of Tobruks and machine-gun pillboxes, supported by an extensive trench system.

Everything the Germans had learned in World War I about how to stop a frontal assault by infantry Rommel put to work at Omaha. He laid out the firing positions at angles to the beach to cover the tidal flat and beach shelf with crossing fire, plunging fire, and grazing fire, from all types of weapons. He prepared artillery positions along the cliffs at either end of the beach, capable of delivering enfilade fire from 88s all across Omaha. The trench system included underground quarters and magazines connected by tunnels. The strong points were concentrated near the entrances to the draws, which were further protected by large cement roadblocks. The larger artillery pieces were protected to the seaward by concrete wing walls. There was not one inch of the beach that had not been presighted for both grazing and plunging fire.

Watching the American landing craft approach, the German defenders could hardly believe their eyes. "Holy smoke—here they are!" Lieutenant Frerking declared. "But that's not possible, that's not possible." He put down his binoculars and rushed to his command post in a bunker near Vierville.

"Landing craft on our left, off Vierville, making for the beach," Cpl. Hein Severloh in *Widerstandsnesten* 62 called out. "They must be crazy," Sergeant Krone declared. "Are they going to swim ashore? Right under our muzzles?"

The colonel of the artillery regiment passed down a strict order: "Hold your fire until the enemy is coming up to the waterline."

All along the bluff, German soldiers watched the landing craft approach, their fingers on the triggers of machine guns, rifles, artillery fuses, or holding mortar rounds. In bunker 62, Frerking was at the telephone, giving the range to gunners a couple of kilometers inland: "Target Dora, all guns, range four-eight-five-zero, basic direction 20 plus, impact fuse."[1]

Capt. Robert Walker of HQ Company, 116th Regiment, 29th Division, later described the defenses in front of Vierville: "The cliff-like ridge was covered with well-concealed foxholes and many semipermanent bunkers. The bunkers were practically unnoticeable from the front. Their firing openings were toward the flank so that they could bring flanking crossfire to the beach as well as all the way up the slope of the bluff. The bunkers had diagrams of fields of fire, and these were framed under glass and mounted on the walls beside the firing platforms."[2]

A. J. Liebling, who covered the invasion for the *New Yorker*, climbed the bluff a few days after D-Day. "The trenches were deep, narrow, and so convoluted that an attacking force at any point could be fired on from several directions," he wrote. "Important knots in the system, like the command post and mortar emplacements, were of concrete. The command post was sunk at least twenty-five feet into the ground and was faced with brick on the inside. The garrison had slept in underground bombproofs, with timbered ceilings and wooden floors." To Liebling, it looked like "a regular Maginot Line."[3]

Four things gave the Allies the notion that they could successfully assault this all-but-impregnable position. First, Allied intelligence said that the fortifications and trenches were manned by the 716th Infantry Division, a low-quality unit made up of Poles and Russians with poor morale. At Omaha, intelligence reckoned that there was only one battalion of about 800 troops to man the defenses.

Second, the B-17s assigned to the air bombardment would hit the beach with everything they had, destroying or at least neutralizing the bunkers and creating craters on the beach and bluff that would be usable as foxholes for the infantry. Third, the naval bombardment, culminating with the LCT(R)s' rockets, would finish off anything left alive and moving after the B-17s finished. The infantry from the 29th and 1st divisions going into Omaha were told that their problems would begin when they got to the top of the bluff and started to move inland toward their D-Day objectives.

The fourth cause for confidence that the job would be done was that 40,000 men with 3,500 motorized vehicles were scheduled to land at Omaha on D-Day.

In the event, none of the above worked. The intelligence was wrong; instead of the contemptible 716th Division, the quite-capable 352nd Division was in place. Instead of one German battalion to cover the beach, there were three. The cloud cover and late arrival caused the B-17s to delay their release until they were as much as five kilometers inland; not a single bomb fell on the beach or bluff. The naval bombardment was too brief and generally inaccurate, and in any case it concentrated on the big fortifications above the bluff. Finally, most of the rockets fell short, most of them landing in the surf, killing thousands of fish but no Germans.

Captain Walker, on an LCI, recalled that just before H-Hour, "I took a look toward the shore and my heart took a dive. I couldn't believe how peaceful, how untouched, and how tranquil the scene was. The terrain was green. All buildings and houses were intact. The church steeples were proudly and defiantly standing in place.* 'Where,' I yelled to no one in particular, 'is the damned Air Corps?' "[4]

The Overlord plan for Omaha was elaborate and precise. It had the 116th Regiment of the 29th Division (attached to the 1st Division for this day only) going in on the right (west), supported

---

* At the pre-assault briefing, Walker had been told, "This mock-up shows the land behind the beach as green, but it won't look that way on D-Day. The pulverizing from the bombing, naval shells, and rockets will turn it brown. And don't depend on those village church steeples as landmarks, because all buildings will be flattened."

by C Company of the 2nd Ranger Battalion. The 16th Regiment of
the 1st Division would go in on the left. It would be a linear attack,
with the two regiments going in by companies abreast. There were
eight sectors, from right to left named Charlie, Dog Green, Dog
White, Dog Red, Easy Green, Easy Red, Fox Green, and Fox Red.
The 116th's sectors ran from Charlie to Easy Green.

The first waves would consist of two battalions from each of
the regiments, landing in a column of companies, with the third
battalion coming in behind. Assault teams would cover every inch
of beach, firing M-1s, .30-caliber machine guns, BARs, bazookas,
60mm mortars, and flamethrowers. Ahead of the assault teams
would be DD tanks, Navy underwater demolition teams, and
Army engineers. Each assault team and the supporting units had
specific tasks to perform, all geared to opening the exits. As the
infantry suppressed whatever fire the Germans could bring to bear,
the demolition teams would blow the obstacles and mark the paths
through them with flags, so that as the tide came in the coxswains
would know where it was safe to go.

Next would come the following waves of landing craft,
bringing in reinforcements on a tight, strict schedule designed to
put firepower ranging from M-1s to 105mm howitzers into the
battle exactly when needed, plus more tanks, trucks, jeeps, medical
units, traffic-control people, headquarters, communication units—
all the physical support and administrative control required by two
overstrength divisions of infantry conducting an all-out offensive.

By H plus 120 minutes the vehicles would be driving up the
opened draws to the top of the bluff and starting to move inland
toward their D-Day objectives, first of all the villages of Vierville,
St.-Laurent, and Colleville, then heading west toward Pointe-du-
Hoc or south to take Trevières, eight kilometers from Omaha.[5]

Eisenhower's little aphorism that plans are everything before the battle, useless once it is joined, was certainly the case at
Omaha. Nothing worked according to the plan, which was indeed
useless the moment the Germans opened fire on the assault forces,
and even before.

With the exception of Company A, 116th, no unit landed
where it was supposed to. Half of E Company was more than a
kilometer off target, the other half more than two kilometers to the
east of its assigned sector. This was a consequence of winds and
tide. A northwest wind of ten to eighteen knots created waves of

three to four feet, sometimes as much as six feet, which pushed the landing craft from right to left. So did the tidal current, which with the rising tide (dead low tide at Omaha was 0525) ran at a velocity of 2.7 knots.

By H-Hour, not only were the boats out of position, but the men in them were cramped, seasick, miserable. Most had climbed down their rope nets into the craft four hours or more earlier. The waves came crashing over the gunwales. Every LCVP and LCA (landing craft assault, the British version of the Higgins boat) shipped water. In most of them, the pumps could not carry the load, so the troops had to bail with their helmets.

At least ten of the 200 boats in the first wave swamped; most of the troops were picked up later by Coast Guard rescue craft, often after hours in the water; many drowned. Another disheartening sight to the men in the surviving boats was the glimpse of GIs struggling in life preservers and on rafts, personnel from the foundered DD tanks.[6]

In general, the men of the first wave were exhausted and confused even before the battle was joined. Still, the misery caused by the spray hitting them in the face with each wave and by their seasickness was such that they were eager to hit the beach, feeling that nothing could be worse than riding on those damned Higgins boats. The only comforting thing was those tremendous naval shells zooming over their heads—but even they were hitting the top of the bluff or further inland, not the beach or the slope. At H minus five minutes the fire lifted.

Chief Electrician's Mate Alfred Sears was in the last LCVP of sixteen in the first wave. Going in, the ensign had told him "all the German strong points will be knocked out by the time we hit the beach." Sears went on, "We were so confident of this, that on the way in most of my men and I were sitting on top of the engine room decking of the landing craft, enjoying the show, fascinated by the barrage from the rocket ships. About one thousand rockets shattered the beach directly where we were to land. It looked pretty good."

Lt. Joe Smith was a Navy beachmaster. His job was to put up flags to guide the landing craft from A Company, 116th Regiment. His Higgins boat may have been the first to hit the beach. "The Germans let us alone on the beach. We didn't know why, we could see the Germans up there looking down on us; it was a weird feeling. We were right in front of a German 88 gun emplacement, but fortunately for us they were set to cover down the beach and not toward the sea, so they could not see us."

A Higgins boat carrying an assault team from A Company came in behind Smith. The men in it figured that what they had been told to expect had come true: the air and naval bombardments had wiped out the opposition. The ramp went down.

"Target Dora—fire!" Lieutenant Frerking shouted into the telephone. When the battery opened fire, eager German gunners throughout the area pulled their triggers. To Frerking's left there were three MG-42 positions; to his front a fortified mortar position; on the forward slopes of the bluff infantrymen in trenches. They exploded into action.[7]

"We hit the sandbar," Electrician's Mate Sears recalled, "dropped the ramp, and then all hell poured loose on us. The soldiers in the boat received a hail of machine-gun bullets. The Army lieutenant was immediately killed, shot through the head."[8]

In the lead Company A boat, LCA 1015, Capt. Taylor Fellers and every one of his men were killed before the ramp went down. It just vaporized. No one ever learned whether it was the result of hitting a mine or getting hit by an 88.[9]

"They put their ramp down," Navy beachmaster Lt. Joe Smith said of what he saw, "and a German machine gun or two opened up and you could see the sand kick up right in front of the boat. No one moved. The coxswain stood up and yelled and for some reason everything was quiet for an instant and you could hear him as clear as a bell, he said, 'For Christ's sake, fellas, get out! I've got to go get another load.'"[10]

All across the beach, the German machine guns were hurling fire of monstrous proportions on the hapless Americans. (One gunner with Lieutenant Frerking at strong point 62 fired 12,000 rounds that morning.) Because of the misplaced landings, the GIs were bunched together, with large gaps between groups, up to a kilometer in length, which allowed the Germans to concentrate their fire. As the Higgins boats and larger LCIs approached the beach, the German artillery fired at will, from the Tobruks and fortifications up the draws and on top of the bluff and from the emplacements on the beach.

Motor Machinist Charles Jarreau, Coast Guard, was on LCI

94. His skipper was an "old man" of thirty-two years, a merchant mariner who did things his own way. His nickname was "Popeye." He had stashed a supply of J&B scotch aboard and told the cook that his duty that day was to go around to the crew "and keep giving them a drink until they didn't want anymore or until we ran out; essentially we drank most of the day. Didn't have any food, but I drank all day and didn't get the least bit intoxicated. It had absolutely no effect."

LCI 94 was in the first wave, right behind the Navy demolition teams and the beach-marking crew. "By this time, it was getting pretty hot. Popeye looked at our sign and said, 'Hell, I'm not going in there, we'll never get off that beach.' So he aborted the run. The rest of the LCIs in our flotilla went in where they were supposed to go and none of them got off the beach. They were all shot up. Which made our skipper go up in our esteem by one hell of a lot."

Popeye cruised down the beach about 100 meters, turned toward shore, dropped his stern anchor, and went in at one-third speed until he ran aground twenty meters or so offshore. The ramps went down and the men from the 116th moved down them. As they disembarked, the ship lightened. Popeye had his engines put into reverse, used the small Briggs & Stratton motor to pull on the anchor chain, and backed off. Five men from his twenty-six-man crew were dead, killed by machine-gun fire. Twenty of the 200 infantrymen were killed before they reached the beach.[11]

Pvt. John Barnes, Company A, 116th, was in an LCA. As it approached the shore, line abreast with eleven other craft, someone shouted, "Take a look! This is something that you will tell your grandchildren!"

If we live, Barnes thought.

Ahead, he could see the single spire of the church at Vierville. A Company was right on target. The LCA roared ahead, breasting the waves. "Suddenly, a swirl of water wrapped around my ankles, and the front of the craft dipped down. The water quickly reached our waist and we shouted to the other boats on each side. They waved in return. Our boat just fell away below me. I squeezed the CO2 tube in my life belt. The buckle broke and it popped away. I turned to grab the back of the man behind me. I was going down under. I climbed on his back and pulled myself up in a panic. Heads bobbed up above the water. We could see the other boats moving off toward shore."

Some men had wrapped Mae Wests around their weapons and inflated them. Barnes saw a rifle floating by, then a flamethrower with two Mae Wests around it. "I hugged it tight but still seemed to be going down. I couldn't keep my head above the surface. I tried to pull the release straps on my jacket but I couldn't move. Lieutenant Gearing grabbed my jacket and used his bayonet to cut the straps and release me from the weight. I was all right now, I could swim."

The assault team was about a kilometer offshore. Sergeant Laird wanted to swim in, but Lieutenant Gearing said, "No, we'll wait and get picked up by some passing boat." But none would stop; the coxswains' orders were to go on in and leave the rescue work to others.

After a bit, "we heard a friendly shout of some Limey voice in one of the LCAs. He stopped, his boat was empty. He helped us to climb on board. We recognized the coxswain. He was from the *Empire Javelin*. He wouldn't return to the beach. We asked how the others made out. He said he had dropped them off OK. We went back to the *Empire Javelin*, which we had left at 0400 that morning. How long had it been? It seemed like just minutes. When I thought to ask, it was 1300."[12]

Barnes and his assault team were extraordinarily lucky. About 60 percent of the men of Company A came from one town, Bedford, Virginia; for Bedford, the first fifteen minutes at Omaha was an unmitigated disaster. Companies G and F were supposed to come in to the immediate left of Company A, but they drifted a kilometer further east before landing, so all the Germans around the heavily defended Vierville draw concentrated their fire on Company A. When the ramps on the Higgins boats dropped, the Germans just poured the machine-gun, artillery, and mortar fire on them. It was a slaughter. Of the 200-plus men of the company, only a couple of dozen survived, and virtually all of them were wounded.

Sgt. Thomas Valance survived, barely. "As we came down the ramp, we were in water about knee-high and started to do what we were trained to do, that is, move forward and then crouch and fire. One problem was we didn't quite know what to fire at. I saw some tracers coming from a concrete emplacement which, to me, looked mammoth. I never anticipated any gun emplacements being that big. I shot at it but there was no way I was going to knock out a German concrete emplacement with a .30-caliber rifle."

The tide was coming in, rapidly, and the men around Valance were getting hit. He found it difficult to stay on his feet—like most infantrymen, he was badly overloaded, soaking wet, exhausted, trying to struggle through wet sand and avoid the obstacles with mines attached to them. "I abandoned my equipment, which was dragging me down into the water.

"It became evident rather quickly that we weren't going to accomplish very much. I remember floundering in the water with my hand up in the air, trying to get my balance, when I was first shot through the palm of my hand, then through the knuckle.

"Pvt. Henry Witt was rolling over toward me. I remember him saying, 'Sergeant, they're leaving us here to die like rats. Just to die like rats.' "

Valance was hit again, in the left thigh by a bullet that broke his hip bone. He took two additional flesh wounds. His pack was hit twice, and the chin strap on his helmet was severed by a bullet. He crawled up the beach "and staggered up against the seawall and sort of collapsed there and, as a matter of fact, spent the whole day in that same position. Essentially my part in the invasion had ended by having been wiped out as most of my company was. The bodies of my buddies were washing ashore and I was the one live body in amongst so many of my friends, all of whom were dead, in many cases very severely blown to pieces."[13]

On his boat, Lt. Edward Tidrick was first off. As he jumped from the ramp into the water he took a bullet through his throat. He staggered to the sand, flopped down near Pvt. Leo Nash, and raised himself up to gasp, "Advance with the wire cutters!" At that instant, machine-gun bullets ripped Tidrick from crown to pelvis.

By 0640 only one officer from A Company was alive, Lt. E. Ray Nance, and he had been hit in the heel and the belly. Every sergeant was either dead or wounded. On one boat, when the ramp was dropped every man in the thirty-man assault team was killed before any of them could get out.[14]

Pvt. George Roach was an assistant flamethrower. He weighed 125 pounds. He carried over 100 pounds of gear ashore, including his M-1 rifle, ammunition, hand grenades, a five-gallon drum of flamethrower fluid, and assorted wrenches and a cylinder of nitrogen.

"We went down the ramp and the casualty rate was very bad. We couldn't determine where the fire was coming from, whether from the top of the bluff or from the summer beach-type homes on the shore. I just dropped myself into the sand and took my rifle and fired it at this house and Sergeant Wilkes asked, 'What are you firing at?' and I said, 'I don't know.' "

The only other live member of his assault team Roach could see was Pvt. Gil Murdoch. The two men were lying together behind an obstacle. Murdoch had lost his glasses and could not see. "Can you swim?" Roach asked.

"No."

"Well, look, we can't stay here, there's nobody around here that seems to have any idea of what to do. Let's go back in the water and come in with the tide." They fell back and got behind a knocked-out tank. Both men were slightly wounded. The tide covered them and they hung onto the tank. Roach started to swim to shore; a coxswain from a Higgins boat picked him up about halfway in. "He pulled me on board, it was around 1030. And I promptly fell asleep."

Roach eventually got up to the seawall, where he helped the medics. The following day, he caught up with what remained of his company. "I met General Cota and I had a brief conversation with him. He asked me what company I was with and I told him and he just shook his head. Company A was just out of action. When we got together, there were eight of us left from Company A ready for duty."

(Cota asked Roach what he was going to do when the war was over. "Someday I'd like to go to college and graduate," Roach replied. "I'd like to go to Fordham." Five years to the day later, Roach did graduate from Fordham. "Over the years," he said in 1990, "I don't think there has been a day that has gone by that I haven't thought of those men who didn't make it."[15])

Sgt. Lee Polek's landing craft was about to swamp as it approached the shore. Everyone was bailing with helmets. "We yelled to the crew to take us in, we would rather fight than drown. As the ramp dropped we were hit by machine-gun and rifle fire. I yelled to get ready to swim and fight. We were getting direct fire right into our craft. My three squad leaders in front and others were hit. Some men climbed over the side. Two sailors got hit. I got off in water only ankle deep, tried to run but the water was suddenly up to my hips. I crawled to hide behind a steel beach obstacle. Bullets hit off it, others hit more of my men. Got up to the beach to crawl behind the shingle and a few of my men joined me. I took a head count and there was only eleven of us left, from the thirty on the craft. As the tide came in we took turns running out to the water's edge to drag wounded men to cover. Some of the wounded were hit again while on the beach. More men crowding up and crowding up. More people being hit by shellfire. People trying to help each other.

"While we were huddled there, I told Jim Hickey that I would like to live to be forty years old and work forty hours a week and make a dollar an hour (when I joined up I was making thirty-seven-and-a-half cents an hour). I felt, boy, I would really have it made at $40 a week.

"Jim Hickey still calls me from New York on June 6 to ask, 'Hey, Sarge, are you making forty bucks per yet?' "[16]

Company A had hardly fired a weapon. Almost certainly it had not killed any Germans. It had expected to move up the Vierville draw and be on top of the bluff by 0730, but at 0730 its handful of survivors were huddled up against the seawall, virtually without weapons. It had lost 96 percent of its effective strength.

But its sacrifice was not in vain. The men had brought in rifles, BARs, grenades, TNT charges, machine guns, mortars and mortar rounds, flamethrowers, rations, and other equipment. This was now strewn across the sand at Dog Green. The weapons and equipment would make a life-or-death difference to the following waves of infantry, coming in at higher tide and having to abandon everything to make their way to shore.

F Company, 116th, supposed to come in at Dog Red, landed near its target, astride the boundary between Dog Red and Easy Green. But G Company, supposed to be to the right of F at Dog White, drifted far left, so the two companies came in together, directly opposite the heavy fortifications at Les Moulins. There was a kilometer or so gap to each side of the intermixed companies, which allowed the German defenders to concentrate their fire.

For the men of F and G companies, the 200 meters or more journey from the Higgins boats to the shingle was the longest and most hazardous trip they had ever experienced, or ever would. The lieutenant commanding the assault team on Sgt. Harry Bare's boat was killed as the ramp went down. "As ranking noncom," Bare related, "I tried to get my men off the boat and make it somehow to get under the seawall. We waded to the sand and threw ourselves down and the men were frozen, unable to move. My radioman had his head blown off three yards from me. The beach was covered with bodies, men with no legs, no arms—God it was awful."

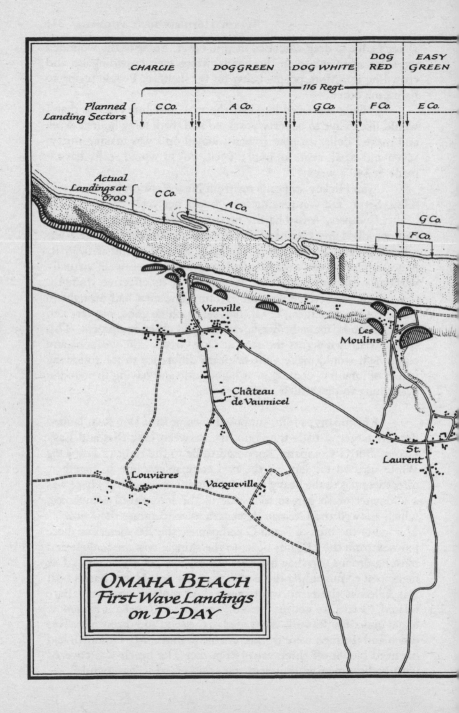

OMAHA BEACH
First Wave Landings
on D-DAY

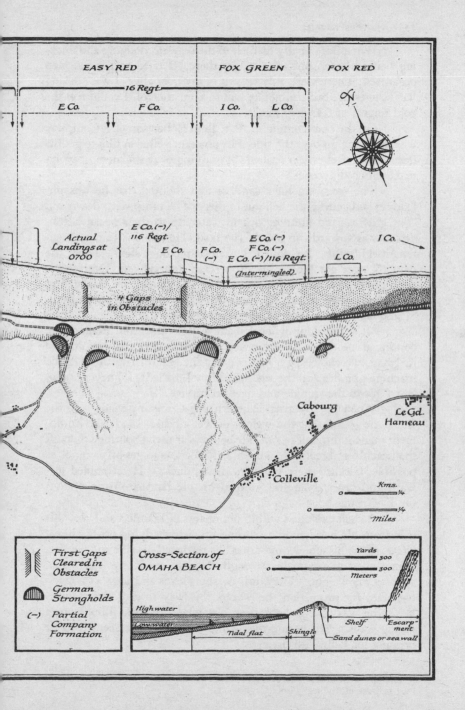

EASY RED   FOX GREEN   FOX RED

16 Regt.

E Co.   F Co.   I Co.   L Co.

N

Actual Landings at 0700

E Co.(–)/ 116 Regt.

E Co.

F Co. (–)

E Co. (–) F Co. (–) E Co. (–)/116 Regt. (Intermingled)

L Co.

I Co.

4 Gaps in Obstacles

Cabourg

Le Gd. Hameau

Colleville

Kms.
0   ¼

0   ¼
Miles

First Gaps Cleared in Obstacles

German Strongholds

(–) Partial Company Formation

Cross-Section of OMAHA BEACH

Yards
0   300

0   300
Meters

High water

Low water

Tidal flat   Shingle

Shelf   Escarpment

Sand dunes or sea wall

When Bare finally made it to the seawall, dodging and ducking behind beach obstacles to get there, "I tried to get the men organized. There were only six out of my boat alive. I was soaking wet, shivering, but trying like hell to keep control. I could feel the cold fingers of fear grip me."[17]

On the boat coming in, Pvt. John Robertson of F Company was throwing up over the side. His sergeant yelled at him to get his head down. Robertson replied, "I'm dying of seasickness, it won't make much difference."

The coxswain hit a sandbar and shouted that he was unloading and getting the hell out of there. The ramp went down and "our guys started jumping out in water up to their necks." Robertson was toward the rear of the boat. He saw his leader, Lieutenant Hilscher, get killed by an exploding shell. Then the flamethrower got blown up. Robertson jumped out. Despite his sixty pounds of ammunition and other equipment, he managed to struggle his way inland, to where the water was about a foot deep. "I just lay there wondering what I was going to do.

"It wasn't long when I made a quick decision. Behind me, coming at me, was a Sherman tank with pontoons wrapped around it. I had two choices; get run over by the tank or run through the machine-gun fire and the shelling. How I made it, I'll never know. But I got to the shingle and tried to survive."[18]

When Sgt. Warner Hamlett of F Company made it to the shore, he found that the weight of wet clothes, sand, and equipment made it difficult to run. He could hear men shouting, "Get off the beach!" and realized "our only chance was to get off as quick as possible, because there we were sitting ducks." He stumbled forward and saw a hole and jumped in. He landed on top of Pvt. O. T. Grimes.*

A shell exploded within ten meters of Hamlett and blew his rifle from his hands while sending his helmet flying off his head. Crawling on his elbows and knees, he retrieved his rifle and helmet, then waited to regain his strength "and to see if my legs would support my weight." They did. By short leaps and advances, using obstacles for protection, he worked his way toward the shingle. While he was resting behind an obstacle, "Private Gillingham, a young soldier, fell beside me, white with fear. He seemed to be begging for help with his eyes.

* "On our recent 1987 annual reunion," Hamlett said, "O. T. told me his back still hurt because of my heavy boot."

"I said, 'Gillingham, let's stay separated, 'cause the Germans will fire at two quicker than they will at one.' He remained silent as I jumped and ran forward again."

A shell burst between them. "It took Gillingham's chin off, including the bone, except for a small piece of flesh. He tried to hold his chin in place as he ran toward the shingle. He made it and Bill Hawkes and I gave him his morphine shot. We stayed with him for approximately thirty minutes until he died. The entire time he remained conscious and aware that he was dying."

From the beach, to the GIs, that shingle looked like the most desirable place in the world to be at that moment. But when they reached it, they found concertina wire covering it, no way to get across without blowing the wire, nothing on the other side but more death and misery. And although they were now protected from machine-gun and rifle fire coming down from the German trenches on the bluff, they were exposed to mortar fire. The few who made it had no organization, little or no leadership (Lieutenant Wise of F Company, one of the few officers to make it to the wall, was trying to force a gap in the concertina when he was hit by a bullet in the forehead and killed), only a handful of weapons. They could but huddle and hope for follow-up waves to bring in bangalore torpedoes to blow the wire.

E Company, 116th, landed farthest from its target. Scheduled to come in at Easy Green, it actually landed on the boundary between Easy Red and Fox Green, a kilometer off and intermixed with men from the 16th Regiment, 1st Division. Pvt. Harry Parley was a flamethrower, so far as he is aware "the only flamethrower to come off the beach unscathed."[*] He landed with a pistol, a holster, a shovel, a Mae West, a raincoat, a canteen, a block of dynamite, and his eighty-pound flamethrower.

"As our boat touched sand and the ramp went down," Parley recalled, "I became a visitor to hell." Boats on either side were getting hit by artillery. Some were burning, others sinking. "I shut everything out and concentrated on following the men in front of me down the ramp and into the water."

He immediately sank. "I was unable to come up. I knew I was drowning and made a futile attempt to unbuckle the flamethrower harness." A buddy grabbed his flamethrower and

---

[*] Pvt. Charles Neighbor, of E Company, was an assistant flamethrower who made it ashore and took over when his No. 1 became a casualty.

pulled Parley forward, to where he could stand. "Then slowly, half-drowned, coughing water, and dragging my feet, I began walking toward the chaos ahead."

He had 200 meters to go to the beach. He made it, exhausted. Machine-gun fire was hitting the beach. As it hit the sand "it made a 'sip sip' sound like someone sucking on their teeth. To this day I don't know why I didn't dump the flamethrower and run like hell for shelter. But I didn't." He was behind the other members of the team. "Months later, trying to analyze why I was able to safely walk across the beach while others running ahead were hit, I found a simple answer. The Germans were directing their fire down onto the beach so that the line of advancing attackers would run into it and, since I was behind, I was ignored. In short, the burden on my back may well have saved my life."

When Parley reached the shingle, he found chaos. "Men were trying to dig or scrape trenches or foxholes for protection from the mortars. Others were carrying or helping the wounded to shelter. We had to crouch or crawl on all fours when moving about. To communicate, we had to shout above the din of the shelling from both sides as well as the explosions on the beach. Most of us were in no condition to carry on. We were just trying to stay alive.

"The enormity of our situation came as I realized that we had landed in the wrong sector and that many of the people around me were from other units and strangers to me. What's more, the terrain before us was not what I had been trained to encounter. I remember removing my flamethrower and trying to dig a trench while lying on my stomach. Failing that, I searched and found a discarded BAR. But we could see nothing above us to return the fire. We were the targets."

Parley lay behind the shingle, "scared, worried, and often praying. Once or twice I was able to control my fear enough to race across the sand to drag a helpless GI from drowning in the incoming tide. That was the extent of my bravery that morning."[19] Not true, as will be seen.

Capt. Lawrence Madill of E Company was urging his men forward. "One of the episodes I remember the most was debarking from the landing craft and trying to take shelter from the enemy fire behind one of their obstacles," recalled Walter A. Smith. "Captain Madill came up behind me and others, ordering all that could move to get off the beach. I looked up at him and his left arm appeared to be almost blown off."

Madill made it to the seawall, where he discovered that one

of his company mortars had also made it but had no ammunition. He ran back to the beach to pick up some rounds. As he was returning, he was hit by machine-gun fire. Before he died, Madill gasped, "Senior noncom, take the men off the beach."[20]

As what was left of A, F, G, and E companies of the 116th huddled behind obstacles or the shingle, the following waves began to come in: B and H companies at 0700, D at 0710, C, K, I, and M at 0720. Not one came in on target. The coxswains were trying to dodge obstacles and incoming shells, while the smoke drifted in and out and obscured the landmarks and what few marker flags there were on the beach.

On the command boat for B Company, the CO, Capt. Ettore Zappacosta, heard the British coxswain cry out, "We can't go in there. We can't see the landmarks. We must pull off."

Zappacosta pulled his Colt .45 and ordered, "By God, you'll take this boat straight in."

The coxswain did. When the ramp dropped, Zappacosta was first off. He was immediately hit. Medic Thomas Kenser saw him bleeding from hip and shoulder. Kenser, still on the ramp, shouted, "Try to make it in! I'm coming." But the captain was already dead. Before Kenser could jump off the ramp he was shot dead. Every man in the boat save one (Pvt. Robert Sales) was either killed or wounded before reaching the beach.[21]

Nineteen-year-old Pvt. Harold Baumgarten of B Company got a bullet through the top of his helmet while jumping from the ramp, then another hit the receiver of his M-1 as he carried it at port arms. He waded through the waist-deep water as his buddies fell alongside him.

"I saw Pvt. Robert Ditmar of Fairfield, Connecticut, hold his chest and heard him yell, 'I'm hit, I'm hit!' I hit the ground and watched him as he continued to go forward about ten more yards. He tripped over an obstacle and, as he fell, his body made a complete turn and he lay sprawled on the damp sand with his head facing the Germans, his face looking skyward. He was yelling, 'Mother, Mom.'

"Sgt. Clarence 'Pilgrim' Robertson had a gaping wound in the upper right corner of his forehead. He was walking crazily in the water. Then I saw him get down on his knees and start praying with his rosary beads. At this moment, the Germans cut him in half with their deadly crossfire."

Baumgarten had drawn a Star of David on the back of his

field jacket, with "The Bronx, New York" written on it—that would let Hitler know who he was. He was behind an obstacle. He saw the reflection from the helmet of one of the German riflemen on the bluff "and took aim and later on I found out I got a bull's eye on him." That was the only shot he fired because his damaged rifle broke in two when he pulled the trigger.

Shells were bursting about him. "I raised my head to curse the Germans when an 88 shell exploded about twenty yards in front of me, hitting me in my left cheek. It felt like being hit with a baseball bat only the results were much worse. My upper jaw was shattered, the left cheek blown open. My upper lip was cut in half. The roof of my mouth was cut up and teeth and gums were laying all over my mouth. Blood poured freely from the gaping wound."

The tide was coming in. Baumgarten washed his face with the cold, dirty Channel water and managed not to pass out. The water was rising about an inch a minute (between 0630 and 0800 the tide rose eight feet) so he had to get moving or drown. He took another hit, from a bullet, in the leg. He moved forward in a dead man's float with each wave of the incoming tide. He finally reached the seawall where a medic dressed his wounds. Mortars were coming in, "and I grabbed the medic by the shirt to pull him down. He hit my hand away and said, 'You're injured now. When I get hurt you can take care of me.' "*

Sgt. Benjamin McKinney was a combat engineer attached to C Company. When his ramp dropped, "I was so seasick I didn't care if a bullet hit me between the eyes and got me out of my misery." As he jumped off the ramp, "rifle and machine-gun fire hit it like rain falling." Ahead, "it looked as if all the first wave were dead on the beach." He got to the shingle. He and Sergeant Storms saw a pillbox holding a machine gun and a rifleman about thirty meters to the right, spraying the beach with their weapons. Storms and McKinney crawled toward the position. McKinney threw hand grenades as Storms put rifle fire into it. Two Germans jumped out; Storms killed them. The 116th was starting to fight back.[22]

---

* Baumgarten was wounded five times that day, the last time by a bullet in his right knee as he was being carried on a stretcher to the beach for evacuation. He went on to medical school and became a practicing physician. He concluded his oral history, "Happily, in recent years when I've been back to Normandy, especially on Sept. 17, 1988, when we dedicated a monument to the 29th Division in Vierville, I noted that the French people really appreciated us freeing them from the Germans, so it made it all worthwhile."

• •

At 0730 the main command group of the 116th began to come in, including the regimental commander, Col. Charles Canham, and the assistant commander of the 29th Division, Brig. Gen. Norman Cota. They were in an LCVP with an assault team from Company K. The boat got hung up on a beach obstacle to which a Teller mine was attached. Although the boat rose and fell in the swells, by some miracle the mine did not go off, but the LCVP was under heavy machine-gun, mortar, and light-cannon fire. Three men, including Maj. John Sours, the regimental S-4, were instantly killed as the ramp went down.

Pvt. Felix Branham was in that boat. "Colonel Canham had a BAR and a .45 and he was leading us in," Branham said. "There he was firing and he got his BAR shot out of his hand and he reached and he used his .45. He was the bravest guy."[23]

The scene the commanders saw as they struggled their way to the beach was described by Cota's aide-de-camp, Lt. J. T. Shea, in a letter he wrote ten days later: "Although the leading elements of the assault had been on the beach for approximately an hour, none had progressed farther than the seawall at the inland border of the beach. [They] were clustered under the wall, pinned down by machine-gun fire, and the enemy was beginning to bring effective mortar fire to bear on those hidden behind the wall." The beach was jammed with the dead, the dying, the wounded, and the disorganized.

When Cota got to the wall, he made an immediate and critical command decision. He saw at once that the plan to go up the draws was obsolete. It simply could not be done. Nor could the men stay where they were. They had to get over the shingle, get through the heavily mined swamp, and climb the bluff to drive the Germans from their trenches and take the draws from the inland side.

Lieutenant Shea described Cota's actions: "Exposing himself to enemy fire, General Cota went over the seawall giving encouragement, directions, and orders to those about him, personally supervised the placing of a BAR, and brought fire to bear on some of the enemy positions on the bluff that faced them. Finding a belt of barbed wire inside the seawall, General Cota personally supervised placing a bangalore torpedo for blowing the wire and was one of the first three men to go through the wire."

Six mortar shells fell into the immediate area. They killed

three men and wounded two others, but Cota was unharmed. "At the head of a mixed column of troops he threaded his way to the foot of the high ground beyond the beach and started the troops up the high ground where they could bring effective fire to bear on the enemy positions." Behind him, engineers with mine detectors began marking a path through the minefield, using white tape.[24]

Some of the boats in the follow-up waves got in relatively unscathed. It was a question of luck and numbers. The luck was avoiding mined obstacles, now well underwater. The numbers of boats coming in meant that the Germans could no longer concentrate their fire; they had too many targets. By 0730 what was supposed to have happened with the first wave was beginning to take place—the assault teams were coming forward on every sector of the beach (not always or even usually the right one).

Others had bad luck. LCI 92, approaching Dog White about 0740, was hit in the stern by an 88 as it made its first attempt to get through the obstacles. Sgt. Debs Peters of the 121st ECB was on the craft. He recalled, "We lost headway and turned sideways in the waves and were parallel to the beach for a few seconds. We were hit directly midship and blew up. Those of us on deck were caught on fire with flaming fuel oil and we just rolled overboard. I fell into the water and went down like a rock." He inflated his Mae West and popped to the surface.

"The Germans were raking the whole area with machine-gun fire. I held onto one of those poles until I could get my breath, then moved to another one. I finally got within about fifty yards of the shore. Now the tide was in full, it almost reached the road."

When Peters reached the beach "I was loaded so heavy with water and sand that I could just stagger about." He got behind a tank; it got hit by an 88. Shrapnel wounded the man beside him and hit Peters in the cheek. He was lucky; he was one of the few survivors from LCI 92.[25]

Capt. Robert Walker of HQ Company was on LCI 91, just behind LCI 92. (LCI 94, the one "Popeye" the skipper decided not to take in on that sector, was just to the left of LCIs 91 and 92.) As it approached the beach, LCI 91 began taking rifle and machine-gun fire. Maneuvering through the obstacles, the LCI got caught on one of the pilings and set off the Teller mine. The explosion tore off the starboard landing ramp.

The skipper tried to back off. Walker moved to the port-side ramp, only to find it engulfed in flames. A man carrying a flamethrower had been hit by a bullet; another bullet had set the jellied contents of his fuel tank on fire. Screaming in agony, he dove into the sea. "I could see that even the soles of his boots were on fire." Men around him also burned; Walker saw a couple of riflemen "with horrendous drooping face blisters."

The skipper came running to the front deck, waving his arms and yelling "Everybody over the side." Walker jumped into water about eight feet deep. He was carrying so much equipment that despite two Mae Wests he could not stay afloat. He dropped his rifle, then his helmet, then his musette bag, which enabled him to swim to where he could touch bottom.

"Here I was on Omaha Beach. Instead of being a fierce, well-trained, fighting infantry warrior, I was an exhausted, almost helpless, unarmed survivor of a shipwreck." When he got to waist-deep water he got on his knees and crawled the rest of the way. Working his way forward to the seawall, he saw the body of Captain Zappacosta. At the seawall, "I saw dozens of soldiers, mostly wounded. The wounds were ghastly to see."

(Forty-nine years later, Walker recorded that the scene brought to his mind Tennyson's lines in "The Charge of the Light Brigade," especially "Cannon to right of them/Cannon to left of them/Cannon in front of them/Volley'd and thunder'd." He added that so far as he could tell every GI knew the lines, "Theirs not to reason why/Theirs but to do and die," even if the soldiers did not know the source. Those on Omaha Beach who had committed the poem to memory surely muttered to themselves, "Some one had blunder'd.")

Walker came to Cota's conclusion. Any place was better than this; the plan was *kaput*; he couldn't go back; he set out on his own to climb the bluff. He picked up an M-1 and a helmet from a dead soldier and moved out. "I was alone and completely on my own."[26]

Maj. Sidney Bingham (USMA 1940) was CO of 2nd Battalion, 116th. When he reached the shingle he was without radio, aide, or runner. His S-3 was dead, his HQ Company commander wounded, his E Company commander dead, his F Company commander wounded, his H Company commander killed, "and in E Company there were some fifty-five killed out of a total of something just over 200 who landed."

Bingham was overwhelmed by a feeling of "complete futility. Here I was, the battalion commander, unable for the most part to influence action or do what I knew had to be done." He set out to organize a leaderless group from F Company and get it moving up the bluff.

By this time, around 0745, unknown others were doing the same, whether NCOs or junior officers or, in some cases, privates. Staying on the beach meant certain death; retreat was not possible; someone had to lead; men took the burden on themselves and did. Bingham put it this way: "The individual and small-unit initiative carried the day. Very little, if any, credit can be accorded company, battalion, or regimental commanders for their tactical prowess and/or their coordination of the action."

Bingham did an analysis of what went wrong for the first and second waves. Among other factors, he said, the men were in the Higgins boats far too long. "Seasickness occasioned by the three or four hours in LCVPs played havoc with any idealism that may have been present. It markedly decreased the combat effectiveness of the command."

In addition, "The individual loads carried were in my view greatly excessive, hindered mobility, and in some cases caused death by drowning." In his view, "If the enemy had shown any sort of enthusiasm and moved toward us, they could have run us right back into the Channel without any trouble."

From June 6, 1944, on to 1990, Bingham carried with him an unjustified self-criticism: "I've often felt very ashamed of the fact that I was so completely inadequate as a leader on the beach on that frightful day." That is the way a good battalion commander feels when he is leading not much more than a squad—but Bingham got that squad over the shingle and into an attack against the enemy, which was exactly the right thing to do, and the only thing he could do under the circumstances.[27]

The Germans did not counterattack for a number of reasons, some of them good ones. First, they were not present in sufficient strength. General Kraiss had but two of his infantry battalions and one artillery battalion on the scene, about 2,000 men, or less than 250 per kilometer. Second, he was slow to react. Not until 0735 did he call up his division reserve, *Kampfgruppe Meyer* (named for the CO of the 915th Regiment of Kraiss's 352nd Division), and then he decided to commit only a single battalion, which did not arrive until midday. He was acting on a false assumption:

that his men had stopped the invasion at Omaha. Third, the German infantrymen were not trained for assaults, only to hold their positions and keep firing.

One German private who was manning an MG 42 on top of the bluff put it this way, in a 1964 radio interview: "It was the first time I shoot at living men. I don't remember exactly how it was: the only thing I know is that I went to my machine gun and I shoot, I shoot, I shoot."[28]

The sacrifice of good men that morning was just appalling. Capt. Walter Schilling of D Company, who had given a magnificent briefing to his magnificently trained men, was in the lead boat in the third wave. He was as good a company CO as there was in the U.S. Army. The company was coming into a section of the beach that had no one on it; there was no fire; Schilling remarked to Pvt. George Kobe, "See, I told you it was going to be easy." Moments later, before the ramp went down, Schilling was killed by a shell.[29]

Lt. William Gardner was the company executive officer, a West Point graduate described by Sgt. John Robert Slaughter as "young, articulate, handsome, tough, and aggressive. He possessed all the qualities to become a high-ranking officer in the Army."[30] The ramp went down on his boat some 150 meters from shore. The men got off without loss. Gardner ordered them to spread out and keep low. He was killed by machine-gun fire before he made the shore.

Sgt. Slaughter's boat was bracketed by German artillery fire. At 100 meters from shore, the British coxswain said he had to lower the ramp and everyone should get out quickly. Sgt. Willard Norfleet told him to keep going: "These men have heavy equipment and you *will* take them all the way in."

The coxswain begged, "But we'll *all* be killed!"

Norfleet unholstered his .45 Colt pistol, put it to the sailor's head and ordered, "All the way in!" The coxswain proceeded.

Sergeant Slaughter, up at the front of the boat, was thinking, If this boat don't hurry up and get us in, I'm going to die from seasickness. The boat hit a sandbar and stopped.

"I watched the movie *The Longest Day*," Slaughter recalled, "and they came charging off those boats and across the beach like banshees but that isn't the way it happened. You came off the craft, you hit the water, and if you didn't get down in it you were going to get shot."

The incoming fire was horrendous. "This turned the boys into men," Slaughter commented. "Some would be very brave men, others would soon be dead men, but all of those who survived would be frightened men. Some wet their britches, others cried unashamedly, and many just had to find it within themselves to get the job done." In a fine tribute to Captain Shilling, Slaughter concluded, "This is where the discipline and training took over."

Slaughter made his way toward shore. "There were dead men floating in the water and there were live men acting dead, letting the tide take them in." Most of Company D was in the water a full hour, working forward. Once he reached shore, for Slaughter "getting across the beach to the shingle became an obsession." He made it. "The first thing I did was to take off my assault jacket and spread my raincoat so I could clean my rifle. It was then I saw bullet holes in my raincoat. I lit my first cigarette [they were wrapped in plastic]. I had to rest and compose myself because I became weak in my knees.

"Colonel Canham came by with his right arm in a sling and a .45 Colt in his left hand. He was yelling and screaming for the officers to get the men off the beach. 'Get the hell off this damn beach and go kill some Germans.' There was an officer taking refuge from an enemy mortar barrage in a pillbox. Right in front of me Colonel Canham screamed, 'Get your ass out of there and show some leadership.' " To another lieutenant he roared, "Get these men off their dead asses and over that wall."[31]

This was the critical moment in the battle. It was an ultimate test: could a democracy produce young men tough enough to take charge, to lead? As Pvt. Carl Weast put it, "It was simple fear that stopped us at that shingle and we lay there and we got butchered by rocket fire and by mortars for no damn reason other than the fact that there was nobody there to lead us off that goddamn beach. Like I say, hey man, I did my job; but somebody had to lead me."[32]

Sgt. William Lewis remembered cowering behind the shingle. Pvt. Larry Rote piled in on top of Lewis. He asked, "Is that you shaking, Sarge?"

"Yeah, damn right!"

"My God," Rote said. "I thought it was me!" Lewis commented, "Rote was shaking all right."

They huddled together with some other men, "just trying to

stay alive. There was nothing we could do except keep our butts down. Others took cover behind the wall."

All across Omaha, the men who had made it to the shingle hid behind it. Then Cota, or Canham, or a captain here, a lieutenant there, a sergeant someplace else, began to lead. They would cry out, "Follow me!" and start moving up the bluff.

In Sergeant Lewis's case, "Lt. Leo Van de Voort said, 'Let's go, goddamn, there ain't no use staying here, we're all going to get killed!' The first thing he did was to run up to a gun emplacement and throw a grenade in the embrasure. He returned with five or six prisoners. So then we thought, hell, if he can do that, why can't we. That's how we got off the beach."[33]

That was how most men got off the beach. Pvt. Raymond Howell, an engineer attached to D Company, described his thought process. He took some shrapnel in helmet and hand. "That's when I said, bullshit, if I'm going to die, to hell with it I'm not going to die here. The next bunch of guys that go over that goddamn wall, I'm going with them. If I'm gonna be infantry, I'm gonna be infantry. So I don't know who else, I guess all of us decided well, it is time to start."[34]

18

UTTER CHAOS REIGNED

The 16th Regiment at Omaha

THE 16TH INFANTRY REGIMENT of the 1st Division (the Big Red One) was the only first-wave assault unit on D-Day with combat experience. It didn't help much. Nothing the 16th had seen in the North Africa (1942) and Sicily (1943) landings compared to what it encountered at Easy Red, Fox Green, and Fox Red on June 6, 1944.

Like the 116th, the 16th landed in a state of confusion, off-target, badly intermingled (except L Company, the only one of the eight assault companies that could be considered a unit as it hit the beach), under intense machine-gun, rifle, mortar, and artillery fire from both flanks and the front. Schedules were screwed up, paths through the obstacles were not cleared, most officers—the first men off the boats—were wounded or killed before they could take even one step on the beach.

The naval gunfire support lifted as the Higgins boats moved in and would not resume until the smoke and haze revealed definite targets or until Navy fire-control officers ashore radioed back specific coordinates (few of those officers made it and those that did had no working radios). Most of the DD tanks had gone down in the Channel; the few that made it were disabled.

As a consequence, the German defenders were able to fire at presited targets from behind their fortifications unimpeded by incoming fire. The American infantry struggled ashore with no support whatsoever. Casualties were extremely heavy, especially in the water and in the 200 meters or so of open beach. As with the 116th to the right, for the 16th Regiment first and second waves D-Day was more reminiscent of an infantry charge across no-man's-land at the Somme in World War I than a typical World War II action.

"Our life expectancy was about zero," Pvt. John MacPhee declared. "We were burdened down with too much weight. We were just pack mules. I was very young, in excellent shape. I could walk for miles, endure a great deal of physical hardship, but I was so seasick I thought I would die. In fact, I wished I had. I was totally exhausted."

Jumping off the ramp into chest-deep water, MacPhee barely made it to the beach. There, "I fell and for what seemed an eternity I lay there." He was hit three times, once in the lower back, twice in the left leg. His arm was paralyzed. "That did it. I lost all my fear and knew I was about to die. I made peace with my Maker and was just waiting."

MacPhee was lucky. Two of his buddies dragged him to the shelter of the seawall; eventually he was evacuated. He was told he had a million-dollar wound. For him the war was over.[1]

As the ramp on his Higgins boat went down, Sgt. Clayton Hanks had a flashback. When he was five years old he had seen a World War I photograph in a Boston newspaper. He had said to his mother, "I wish I could be a war soldier someday."

"Don't ever say that again," his mother had replied.

He didn't, but at age seventeen he joined the Regular Army. He had been in ten years when the ramp went down and he recalled his mother's words. "I volunteered," he said to himself. "I asked for this or whatever was to come." He leaped into the water and struggled forward.[2]

Pvt. Warren Rulien came in with the second wave. Dead soldiers floated around in the water, which had risen past the first obstacles. He ducked behind a steel rail in waist-deep water. His platoon leader, a nineteen-year-old lieutenant, was behind another rail.

The lieutenant yelled, "Hey, Rulien, here I go!" and began attempting to run to the shore. A machine gun cut him down. Rulien grabbed one of the bodies floating in the water and pushed it in front of him as he made his way to the shore.

"I had only gone a short distance when three or four soldiers began lining up behind me. I shouted, 'Don't bunch up!' and moved out, leaving them with the body. I got as low as I could in the water until I reached a sandbar and crossed it on my belly." On the inland side of the sandbar the water was up to his chest. He moved forward. "On the shore, there were officers sitting there, stunned. Nobody was taking command." He joined other survivors at the seawall.[3]

The coxswain on Pvt. Charles Thomas's boat was killed by machine-gun fire as he was taking his craft in. A crew member took over. The platoon leader had his arm shot off trying to open the ramp. Finally the ramp dropped and the assault team leaped into the surf. Thomas had a bangalore torpedo to carry so he was last man in the team.

"As I was getting off I stopped to pick up a smoke grenade, as if I didn't have enough to carry. The guy running the boat yelled for me to get off. He was in a hurry, but I turned around and told him that I wasn't in any hurry."

Thomas jumped into chest-deep water. "My helmet fell back on my neck and the strap was choking me. My rifle sling was dragging under the water and I couldn't stand." He inflated his Mae West and finally made it to shore. "There I crawled in over wounded and dead but I couldn't tell who was who and we had orders not to stop for anyone on the edge of the beach, to keep going or we would be hit ourselves."

When he reached the seawall, "it was crowded with GIs all being wounded or killed. It was overcrowded with GIs. I laid on my side and opened my fly, I had to urinate. I don't know why I did that because I was soaking wet anyway and I was under fire, and I guess I was just being neat."

Thomas worked his way over to the left, where "I ran into a bunch of my buddies from the company. Most of them didn't even have a rifle. Some bummed cigarettes off of me because I had three cartons wrapped in waxed paper." Thomas was at the base of the bluff (just below the site of the American cemetery today). In his opinion, "The Germans could have swept us away with brooms if they knew how few we were and what condition we were in."[4]

Capt. Fred Hall was in the LCVP carrying the 2nd Battalion headquarters group (Lt. Col. Herb Hicks, CO). Hall was battalion S-3. His heart sank when he saw yellow life rafts holding men in life jackets and he realized they were the crews from the DD tanks. He realized "that meant that we would not have tank support on the beach." The boat was in the E Company sector of Easy Red. E Company was supposed to be on the far right of the 16th, linking up with the 116th at the boundary between Easy Green and Easy Red, but it came in near the boundary between Easy Red and Fox Green, a full kilometer from the nearest 116th unit on its right (and with sections of the badly mislanded E Company of the 116th on its left).

There was nothing to be done about the mistake. The officers and men jumped into the water and "it was every man for himself crossing the open beach where we were under fire." Fourteen of the thirty failed to make it. Hall got up to the seawall with Hicks and "we opened our map case wrapped in canvas, containing our assault maps showing unit boundaries, phase lines, and objectives. I remember it seemed a bit incongruous under the circumstances."

The incoming fire was murderous. "And the noise—always the noise, naval gunfire, small arms, artillery, and mortar fire, aircraft overhead, engine noises, the shouting and the cries of the wounded, no wonder some people couldn't handle it." The assistant regimental commander and the forward artillery observer were killed by rifle fire. Lieutenant Colonel Hicks shouted to Hall to find the company commanders. To Hall, "It was a matter of survival. I was so busy trying to round up the COs to organize their men to move off the beach that there wasn't much time to think except to do what had to be done."

Hicks wanted to move his men to the right, where the battalion was supposed to be, opposite the draw that led up the bluff between St.-Laurent and Colleville, but movement was almost impossible. The tide was coming in rapidly, follow-up waves were landing, the beach was narrowing from the incoming tide, "it became very crowded and the confusion increased." So far as Hall could make out, "there was no movement off the beach."[5]

In fact, one platoon from E Company, 16th Regiment, was making its way up to the top of the bluff. It was led by Lt. John Spaulding of E Company. He was one of the first junior officers to make it across the seawall, through the swamp and beach flat, and up the bluff.

At 0630, Spaulding's boat hit a sandbar. He and Sgt. Fred Bisco kicked the ramp down in the face of machine-gun, mortar, and artillery fire. Spaulding jumped into the water. To his left he could see other E Company boats, but to his right there was nothing. His platoon was the far-right flank of the 16th Regiment.

He spread his men and moved toward shore. The water depth at the sandbar was about a meter, but moving inland the platoon ran into a runnel where the water was over the men's heads. A strong undercurrent was carrying them to the left (Spaulding said he had learned to swim in the Ohio River; he found the current at Omaha was much stronger). Sergeant Streczyk and medic George Bowen were carrying an eighteen-foot ladder to be used for crossing the antitank ditch. Spaulding grabbed it. "Streczyk yelled at me, 'Lieutenant, we don't need any help,' but hell I was trying to get help, not to give it."

In these desperate circumstances, Spaulding ordered his men to abandon their heavy equipment and get ashore. There went the ladder, the flamethrower, the mortars, one of the two bazookas, and some of the ammunition. Most men were able to hold onto their rifles; to Spaulding's surprise, they were able to fire as soon as they came ashore: "It shows that the M-1 is an excellent weapon," he commented.

The platoon took only a couple of casualties getting ashore. Luck was with Spaulding; he had come in at a spot where the German defenses were not particularly heavy, and besides the Germans had bigger targets than an isolated platoon. Once the men reached the beach, they stood up and started moving across the sand.

"They were too waterlogged to run," Spaulding said, "but they went as fast as they could. It looked as if they were walking in the face of a real strong wind." At the seawall, Sgt. Curtis Colwell blew a hole in the wire with a bangalore. Spaulding and his men picked their way through.

Spaulding took his 536 radio off his shoulder, pulled the antenna out and tried to contact his CO. The radio didn't work. The mouthpiece had been shot away. "I should have thrown it away, but training habits were so strong that I carefully took the antenna down as I had always been taught to do and put the 536 back on my shoulder. Your training stays with you even when you are scared."

Once across the seawall, the platoon began to take heavier small-arms fire. One man was killed. The swamp and beach flat to the front were mined. Sergeant Streczyk and Pvt. Richard Gallagher went forward to investigate. "We can't cross here," they shouted and went to the left where they found a little defilade through the mined area. The platoon crossed to the base of the bluff, then began to climb it, following a faint trail.

"We could still see no one to the right and there was no one up to us on the left," Spaulding said. "We didn't know what had become of the rest of E Company. Back in the water boats were in flames. I saw a tank ashore, knocked out. After a couple of looks back, we decided we wouldn't look back anymore."

There was a pillbox to Spaulding's left, its machine gun firing down on the beach. "We fired but couldn't hit them. We were getting terrific small-arms fire ourselves but few were hit." By this time the platoon was about halfway up the bluff, smack in the middle of the extensive German trench system. Pvt. Gallagher, in the lead, sent word that he had found a path toward the right that was in defilade, behind some trenches in a mined area. Spaulding moved forward.

Sergeant Bisco called out, "Lieutenant, watch out for the damn mines." The place was infested with them, Spaulding recalled, "but we lost no men coming through them, although H Company coming along the same trail a few hours later lost several men. The Lord was with us and we had an angel on each shoulder on that trip."

A machine gun was firing from above. Sergeant Blades fired the platoon's only bazooka at it and missed. He was shot in the left arm; a private was shot down; Sergeant Phelps moved up with his BAR and was hit in both legs. Spaulding decided to rush the machine gun.

"As we rushed it the lone German operating the gun threw up his hands and yelled, 'Kamerad.' We needed prisoners for interrogating so I ordered the men not to shoot."

The "German" turned out to be Polish. He told Spaulding (Sergeant Streczyk interpreting) there were sixteen other Poles in the nearby trenches and said they had taken a vote on whether to fight and had voted not to, but the German noncoms forced them to fire. "He also said that he had not shot at us, although I had seen him hit three. I turned the PW over to Sergeant Blades, who was wounded. Blades gave his bazooka to another man and guarded the prisoner with a trench knife."

Spaulding moved his wounded men into a defile where Pvt. George Bowen, the medic, gave them first aid. Spaulding paid Bowen a tribute: "He covered his whole section of the beach that day; no man waited more than five minutes for first aid. His action did a lot to help morale. He got the DSC for his work."

Spaulding moved his platoon up the bluff, taking advantage of every irregularity in the ground. "Coming up along the crest of the hill Sgt. Clarence Colson began to give assault fire from his BAR as he walked along, firing the weapon from his hip. He opened up on the machine gun to our right, firing so rapidly that his ammunition carrier had difficulty getting ammo to him fast enough." It was about 0800. Americans were clearing out the trenches and advancing toward the high ground.[6]

Spaulding and his men, and other small units in the 116th and 16th led by such men as Capt. Joe Dawson and Capt. Robert Walker, were doing a great thing. The exemplary manner in which they had seized their opportunity, their dash, boldness, initiative, teamwork, and tactical skills were outstanding beyond praise. These were exactly the qualities the Army had hoped for—and spent two years training its civilians-turned-soldiers to achieve—in its junior officers, NCOs, and enlisted men.

The industrial miracle of production in the United States in World War II was one of the great accomplishments in the history of the Republic. The job the Army did in creating and shaping the leadership qualities in its junior officers—just college-age boys, most of them—was also one of the great accomplishments in the history of the Republic.

At 0800 the small groups making their way up the bluff were unaware of each other. Spaulding and his men were about midway between Colleville and St.-Laurent. The latter village was their target. There they expected to link up with E Company, 116th, coming in from their right. Actually, E Company, 116th, had been on their *left* on the beach, and was still stuck behind the seawall.

L Company of the 16th was on the far left. It came in at 0700, a half hour late, almost a kilometer from its target. Scheduled to land at the foot of the draw that led directly to Colleville, instead it was at Fox Green, the eastern edge of Omaha Beach, at the place where the tidal flat almost reached the bluff and where the first rise of the bluff was clifflike in steepness.

Because the boats were late, the tide had covered the outermost line of beach obstacles. No company had been scheduled to land on Fox Red, so no engineers had been there to blow the obstacles. Pvt. Kenneth Romanski saw the boat to his right blow up. He looked left and that boat also hit a mine. He saw a GI go up about ten feet in the air, arms and legs outstretched and his whole body in flame.

"About that time, our platoon leader, Lieutenant Godwin, said, 'Back it up! Back it up! Put the damn thing in reverse.' " The British coxswain did. He pulled back about 100 meters and went over to the left.

"Drop the ramp," Lieutenant Godwin ordered. "Drop the ramp!" The water was eight feet deep. Romanski moved out and immediately hit bottom. He threw away his rifle and bangalore, inflated his Mae West, and swam toward shore, or rather paddled as best he could until his feet touched bottom. Then he crawled to the beach, jumped up, and ran the few meters to the base of the cliff.

"There were already men there, some dead, some wounded. There was wreckage. There was complete confusion. I didn't know what to do. I picked a rifle from a dead man. As luck would have it, it had a grenade launcher on it. So I fired my six grenades over the cliff. I don't know where they went but I do know that they went up on enemy territory."

Romanski looked back to the beach and saw a sight "I'll never forget. There was a body rolling with the waves. And his leg was holding on by a chunk of meat about the size of your wrist. The body would roll, then the leg would roll. Then the leg would roll back and then the body would roll back."

To L Company's right there was a tiny draw leading up the far eastern edge of the bluff. An unknown officer was attempting to get the men to move to the right and up the draw.

"I need help!" Romanski heard him shout. "I need help! Come on over here. I need some men!"

Romanski moved in that direction. The company was down to 125 men, but it was intact and better organized than any other on the whole of Omaha Beach. Romanski joined the unknown officer, who had gathered twenty men. They started up the draw, other platoons following.[7]

Between Spaulding's platoon on the right and L Company on the left, companies E, F, and I were badly intermixed, off schedule and off target, hung up on the obstacles or the beach or huddled up against the seawall, taking casualties but not firing back.

Pvt. H. W. Shroeder was among them. He came in with the third wave. As his boat approached the sandbar "we were hearing noises on the side of the landing craft like someone throwing gravel against it. The German machine gunners had picked us up. Everybody yelled, 'Stay down!' The coxswain backed it out, relocated, and came in again, and I noticed the lieutenant's face was a very gray color and the rest of the men had a look of fear on their faces. All of a sudden the lieutenant yelled to the coxswain, 'Let her down!'

"The ramp dropped and we could get a look at the beach and it was sickening. We were supposed to have tanks. There were two tanks there. One was knocked out and the other was out of ammo, and the only good they were doing was the GIs were piling up behind them to get out of the fire that was coming down and looked like a red snowstorm, there were so many tracers coming from so many different directions."

Shroeder moved out with his assault team, got through the obstacles and across the beach, and threw himself down at the seawall. "There were GIs piled two deep. I started checking my .30-cal machine gun and it was full of sand and water." He cleaned it and "stayed there for an hour or so."[8]

The coxswain on the boat carrying the CO of I Company, Capt. Kimball Richmond, got swept to the east almost to Port-en-Bessin. He was going to land there but Richmond could see it was the wrong place. He redirected the coxswain, who backtracked to the west until he was off Fox Green, the designated target. An hour had been lost. When the coxswain finally got to the right place and dropped the ramp, he was immediately hit by machine-gun fire. He was still able to maneuver the boat. He ordered the ramp pulled up, then backed off out of the range of the machine gun. He circled until Captain Richmond picked a spot and told him to go in. It was about 0800 and the tide had covered the outer obstacles. Going in, the coxswain hardly knew which to fear more, mines or machine guns.

About 100 meters from shore, as Pvt. Albert Mominee remembered it, "the craft gave a sudden lurch as it hit an obstacle and in an instant an explosion erupted followed by a blinding flash of fire. Flames raced around and over us. The first reaction was survival; the immediate instinct was the will to live. Before I knew it I was in the water."

Mominee was five feet one inch tall and in water well over his head. He dropped his rifle and equipment, inflated his Mae West, and swam toward shore, machine-gun bullets hitting around him, killing some GIs, wounding others.

"About fifty yards from shore the water was shallow enough for me to wade. Thirty yards to go and then twenty. I was exhausted and in shock. I heard a voice shouting, 'Come on, Little One! Come on! You can make it!' It was Lieutenant Anderson, the exec, urging me on. It seemed like someone had awakened me from a dream. I lunged toward him and as I reached him, he grabbed my hand and pulled me out of the water, then practically dragged me to the cover of the seawall. Only six out of thirty in my craft escaped unharmed.

"Looking around, all I could see was a scene of havoc and destruction. Abandoned vehicles and tanks, equipment strung all over the beach, medics attending the wounded, chaplains seeking the dead. Suddenly I had a craving for a cigarette. 'Has anybody got a smoke?' I asked."[9]

I Company had taken more than one-third casualties. F Company, landing earlier at Fox Green, was simply gone as a fighting unit; some individuals had made it to the shingle but they were mostly without weapons.

G Company came in at 0700. The CO, Capt. Joe Dawson, was first off his boat, followed by his communications sergeant and his company clerk. As they jumped, a shell hit the boat and destroyed it, killing thirty men, including the naval officer who was to control fire support from the warships.

Dawson expected to find a path up the bluff cleared out by F Company, but "as I landed I found nothing but men and bodies lying on the shore." He got to the shingle where survivors from other boats of G Company joined him.[10] Among them was Sgt. Joe Pilck. He recalled, "We couldn't move forward because they had a double apron of barbed wire in front of us, and to our right it was a swampy area we couldn't cross and to the left they had minefields laid out so we couldn't go there."[11]

"Utter chaos reigned," Dawson recalled, "because the Germans controlled the field of fire completely." He realized that "there was nothing I could do on the beach except die." To get through the barbed wire he had Pvts. Ed Tatara and Henry Peszek put two bangalore torpedoes together, shoved them under the wire, and blew a gap. They started through the minefield and up the bluff, engaging the enemy.

The fortified area above the beach in the Easy and Fox sectors was far too extensive to be thoroughly cleaned out by Spaulding's and Dawson's small units, but they—and other units—were making a significant contribution to reducing the volume of fire pouring down on the 16th Regiment.

Spaulding's and Dawson's and the other small groups that were working their way to the top were like magnets to the men along the shingle embankment. If they can make it so can I, was the thought.

Simultaneously, the men were being urged forward by other junior officers and NCOs, and by the regimental commander, forty-seven-year-old Col. George Taylor. He landed about 0800. Pvt. Warren Rulien watched him come in. "He stepped across the sandbar and bullets began hitting the water around him. He laid down on his stomach and started crawling toward shore, his staff officers doing the same."

"He had a couple of tattered-ass second louies following him," according to Pvt. Paul Radzom, who was also watching. "They looked like they were scared to death."

When Taylor made it to the seawall, Rulien heard him say to the officers, "If we're going to die, let's die up there."[12] To other groups of men, Taylor said, "There are only two kinds of people on this beach: the dead and those about to die. So let's get the hell out of here!"[13]

Men got to work with the bangalores, blowing gaps in the barbed wire. Engineers with mine detectors moved through, then started laying out tape to show where they had cleared paths through the minefields. Others hit the pillboxes at the base of the bluff. "I went up with my flamethrower to button up the aperture of a pillbox," Pvt. Buddy Mazzara of C Company remembered, "and Fred Erben came in with his dynamite charge. Soon some soldiers came out of the pillbox with their hands up saying, 'No shoot. No shoot. Me Pole.' "[14]

Private Shroeder, his machine gun cleaned and ready to fire, watched as a rifleman moved out. "So the first man, he started out across, and running zigzag he made it to the bluff. So we all felt a little better to see that we had a chance, we were going to get off.

And the minefield was already full of dead and wounded. And finally it came my turn and I grabbed my heavy .30-cal and started up over the shingle and across the minefield, trying to keep low. Finally I got to the base of the bluff." There he ducked behind the old foundation of a house. Two others joined him. "It was just the three of us there, we couldn't find our platoon leaders or our platoon sergeants or anybody."

But they could see two heartening sights. One was Americans on the crest of the bluff. The other was a line of POWs, sent down by Captain Dawson under guard. The enemy prisoners "were really roughed up. Their hair was all full of cement, dirt, everything. They didn't look so tough. So we started up the bluff carrying our stuff with us, and others started following us."[15]

Lt. William Dillon gathered the survivors from his platoon, joined three bangalores together, shoved them under the barbed wire, blew a gap, dashed through, crossed the swamp, swam across an antitank ditch filled with water, and made it to the base of the bluff.

"I knew that the Germans had to have a path up the hill that was clear of mines. I looked around. When I was younger I'd been a good hunter and could trail a rabbit easily. I studied the ground and saw a faint path zigzagging to the left up the hill, so I walked the path very carefully. Something blew up behind me. I looked back and a young soldier had stepped on a mine and it had blown off his foot up to his knee. I brought the others up the path. At the top we saw the first and only Russian soldiers I have ever seen."[16]

In his column for June 12, 1944, Ernie Pyle wrote, "Now that it is over it seems to me a pure miracle that we ever took the beach at all. . . . As one officer said, the only way to take a beach is to face it and keep going. It is costly at first, but it's the only way. If the men are pinned down on the beach, dug in and out of action, they might as well not be there at all. They hold up the waves behind them, and nothing is being gained.

"Our men were pinned down for a while, but finally they stood up and went through, and so we took that beach and accomplished our landing. We did it with every advantage on the enemy's side and every disadvantage on ours. In the light of a couple of days of retrospection, we sit and talk and call it a miracle that our men ever got on at all or were able to stay on."[17]

• •

It was not a miracle. It was infantry. The plan had called for the air and naval bombardments, followed by tanks and dozers, to blast a path through the exits so that the infantry could march up the draws and engage the enemy, but the plan had failed, utterly and completely failed. As is almost always the case in war, it was up to the infantry. It became the infantry's job to open the exits so that the vehicles could drive up the draws and engage the enemy.

Exhortation and example, backed by two years of training, got the GIs from the 16th Regiment to overcome their exhaustion, confusion, and fear and get out from behind the shingle and start up the bluff. Colonel Taylor and many others pointed out the obvious, that to stay behind the "shelter" was to die. Retreat was not possible.

Captain Dawson, Lieutenants Spaulding and Dillon, and many others provided the example; their actions proved that it was possible to cross the swamp, the antitank ditch, the minefields, and find paths to the top of the bluff.

As they came onto the beach, the junior officers and NCOs saw at once that the intricate plan, the one they had studied so hard and committed to memory, bore no relationship whatsoever to the tactical problem they faced. They had expected to find ready-made craters on the beach, blasted by the bombs from the B-17s, to provide shelter in the unlikely event that they encountered any small-arms fire when they made the shoreline. They had expected to go up the draws, which they anticipated would have been cleared by the DD tanks and dozers, to begin fighting up on the high ground. They had expected fire support from tanks, half-tracks, artillery. Nothing they had expected had happened.

Yet their training had prepared them for this challenge. They sized up the situation, saw what had to be done, and did it. This was leadership of the highest order. It came from men who had been civilians three or even two years earlier.

Sgt. John Ellery of the 16th Regiment was one of those leaders. When he reached the shingle, "I had to peer through a haze of sweat, smoke, dust, and mist." There was a dead man beside him, another behind him. Survivors gathered around him; "I told them that we had to get off the beach and that I'd lead the way." He did. When he got to the base of the bluff, he started up, four or five men following. About halfway up, a machine gun opened up on them from the right.

"I scurried and scratched along until I got within ten meters of the gun position. Then I unloaded all four of my fragmentation grenades. When the last one went off, I made a dash for the top. The other kids were right behind me and we all made it. I don't know if I knocked out that gun crew but they stopped shooting. Those grenades were all the return fire I provided coming off that beach. I didn't fire a round from either my rifle or my pistol."

In giving his account, Ellery spoke about leadership. "After the war," he said, "I read about a number of generals and colonels who are said to have wandered about exhorting the troops to advance. That must have been very inspirational! I suspect, however, that the men were more interested and more impressed by junior officers and NCOs who were willing to lead them rather than having some general pointing out the direction in which they should go."

Warming to the subject, Ellery went on: "I didn't see any generals in my area of the beach, but I did see a captain and two lieutenants who demonstrated courage beyond belief as they struggled to bring order to the chaos around them." Those officers managed to get some men organized and moving up the bluff. One of the lieutenants had a broken arm that hung limply at his side, but he led a group of seven to the top, even though he got hit again on the way. Another lieutenant carried one of his wounded men thirty meters before getting hit himself.

"When you talk about combat leadership under fire on the beach at Normandy," Ellery concluded, "I don't see how the credit can go to anyone other than the company-grade officers and senior NCOs who led the way. It is good to be reminded that there are such men, that there always have been and always will be. We sometimes forget, I think, that you can manufacture weapons, and you can purchase ammunition, but you can't buy valor and you can't pull heroes off an assembly line."[18]

The truth of Ellery's strongly felt opinion is obvious, but it is not the whole truth nor is it fair to Colonel Taylor (forty-seven-year-old men do not lead twenty-year-old men up steep bluffs) or to General Cota. Nor is it fair to the assembly line. It was the assembly line that had gotten the 16th Regiment and all the others across the Atlantic ocean, across the English Channel, and to the Normandy beach with weapons in their hands. Courage and bold leadership had taken over at that point and put small groups of infantry on top of the bluff, but without support they were not going to do much damage to the Germans or even stay there long. They had to have reinforcements, and not just infantry reinforcements.

In a way, the men on the top were in a position similar to World War I infantry who led the way through no-man's-land in frontal assaults. They had penetrated the enemy trench system, but as with their fathers in World War I, the follow-up waves were taking machine-gun fire from the flanks while enemy artillery pounded them from the rear. The men in front were isolated.

This was where the incredible production feats of American industry came into play. The larger landing craft, the LCMs and LCTs and LSTs and Rhino barges, were, by 0830 or so, bringing in a staggering quantity of armed and armored vehicles. The 16th Regiment at Omaha already had lost more vehicles in the water and on the beach, all of them brought from across the Atlantic, than the entire German 352nd Division ever dreamed existed. And there were almost uncountable numbers of other vehicles waiting an opportunity to land.

But at 0830 all those tanks, DUKWs, half-tracks, self-propelled artillery, trucks, and jeeps were more of a problem than a solution, and it was getting worse, because as the tide moved toward its high-water mark the beach area kept shrinking. At this point General Bradley contemplated sending follow-up waves over to the British beaches, because until someone could open the draws so the vehicles could exit the beach and get up to the road net on the high ground, the vehicles caught in the traffic jam on the beach were just targets, not weapons.

That someone was spelled i-n-f-a-n-t-r-y.

19

TRAFFIC JAM

Tanks, Artillery, and Engineers at Omaha

IN NORTH AFRICA in 1943 General Eisenhower had reprimanded a general officer who had built an elaborate, bombproof underground HQ for himself, where he stayed during the Kasserine Pass battle. Eisenhower told him to go on a front-line inspection tour and explained to the reluctant warrior the simplest truth of war: "Generals are expendable just as is any other item in an army."[1]

War is waste. Men and equipment—and generals—are expendable so long as their destruction or death contributes to the ultimate goal of victory. At Omaha Beach, they were expended in fearful numbers. Hundreds of young men and boys, trained at enormous expense, were killed, many—perhaps most—of them before they could fire one shot. Equipment losses were staggering. Hundreds of tanks, trucks, self-propelled artillery, jeeps, and landing craft of all types went to the bottom or were destroyed on the beach by German artillery. Thousands of radios, rifles, machine guns, ammunition boxes, K and D rations, BARs, bazookas, flamethrowers, gas masks, hand grenades, and other matériel were destroyed, abandoned, or sunk.

The equipment had made a long journey, from factories in California, Illinois, Michigan, and the Deep South to East Coast ports, then across the Atlantic to England, by truck or rail to Portsmouth, finally across the Channel, only to go to the Channel bottom off Omaha Beach. Some of those vehicles still rest there today. Aside from the German gunners, the major culprits were the runnels, deep trenches just inside the shallow sandbars, and the mined obstacles, which at high water took a ghastly toll.

The first vehicles on Omaha Beach were Sherman tanks. They arrived at H-Hour minus thirty seconds, in Lt. Dean Rockwell's flotilla. The LCTs hit a sandbar fifteen meters or so off the shoreline, where they dropped their ramps and the tanks drove off. Those coming off Rockwell's LCT dipped into the runnel, gunned their waterproofed engines, and climbed toward the beach.

As the tanks went clanking and grinding down the ramp, a German 88mm gun that was enfilading the beach took them under fire. As Rockwell retracted, he noticed two of the tanks get hit by 88 shells. One of them was burning. The following two, and others from the battalion, stayed offshore, about half under water, and commenced firing their machine guns and 75mm cannons.[2]

Not all the tanks got that far. Ens. F. S. White, skipper of LCT 713, later reported to Rockwell: "The ramp was again lowered, and the first tank was launched. The water was much deeper than expected, and as the tank went off the ramp it went to the bottom and settled. The tank commander gave the order to abandon tank and the entire crew was brought back to the ship by means of a heaving line thrown from the ship." Ensign White retracted, moved 100 meters east, and beached a second time. The other three tanks made it to the water's edge even as LCT 713 took a direct hit.[3]

Pvt. J. C. Friedman was a tank driver in the 747th Tank Battalion. His LCT came in on the third wave. Through his periscope he could see "tanks, half-tracks, jeeps, and trucks being blown up by land mines. The noise of gunfire and gun powder as well as the smell of death seemed to be all around us. Everyone in my tank was praying. I kept thinking, Is this the end of me? Constant shelling and shrapnel flying off the tank seemed to indicate an unleashing of the powers of hell. I wondered if all this was worth the lives taken and if we would see the next day."[4]

Col. John Upham commanded the 743rd Tank Battalion. It went in on the heels of the first wave. He stayed a few hundred meters offshore, directing his tanks by radio. When his LCT went in at 0800, he jumped over the side and waded ashore to join his tanks. Still on foot, he began to direct their fire. A rifle bullet tore through his right shoulder but he refused medical attention. He came upon Pvt. Charles Leveque and Cpl. William Beckett, who had abandoned their tank after a track had been knocked off. Upham, his right arm dangling uselessly, directed them to the seawall. Beckett commented, "You couldn't get the colonel excited—not even *then*."[5]

Sgt. Paul Radzom was excited. He was in command of a half-track equipped with multibarreled .50-caliber machine guns. As his LCT approached the shore, machine-gun rounds started bouncing off the side. The ramp went down and "out we go. We were not supposed to be in more than eight feet of water. They dumped us off in fifteen feet. Our track didn't go anywhere but down. I had the boys elevate that barrel straight up in the air, as high as it would go. There was about six inches of that barrel up above the water, when the swells weren't hitting it. I lost everything including my helmet.

"I swam back and got back on that ramp and the rest of the crew did, too, except old 'Mo' [Carl] Dingledine, who couldn't swim. Last time I saw Mo he was clinging to that barrel. Never found out what happened to old Mo." (Ens. Edward Kelly, commanding LCT 200, spotted Dingledine as he was retracting and picked him up.)

Radzom's LCT backed off and came in again. He jumped on Sergeant Evanger's half-track as it drove off the ramp. His crew followed him. The track made it to shore. "There was supposed to be a road cleared out for us. Then we were supposed to go in about five miles and secure a position. We couldn't have gotten five yards." The track got hit and Radzom jumped off. He picked up a helmet, then a rifle.

"I saw a first louie laying there dead. There was the neck of a bottle sticking out of his musette bag. I snitched it. It was a bottle of Black & White scotch." He rejoined Evanger's crew and passed the bottle around. "That was the first time and the only time in my life that I drank scotch. I never felt a thing." He got hit with shrapnel in the face, side, and back, and eventually was evacuated.[6]

Cpl. George Ryan was a gunner on a 105mm howitzer. The vehicle was called an M-7. The cannon was mounted on a Sherman tank chassis. There were four M-7s on the LCT. The skipper saw that his designated landing site on Easy Red was too hot so he said he was going down a little way to find a softer spot.

"Nobody was arguing with him," Ryan remembered.

The skipper turned toward shore and just that quick the

craft was stuck on a sandbar. Ryan's CO shouted, "Every man for himself," and over the side the CO jumped.

"Holy smokes," Ryan remarked. "He was just gone. We lowered the ramp. Everybody in the first M-7 took a deep breath and they gave it the gun, down the ramp they went and into the water. The thing almost disappeared from sight, but the driver gave it the gun and broom, right out of the water it came. He did it so fast."

The second M-7 drove off "and it went glonck. It just disappeared from sight. The guys started popping up like corks. They swam in."

Shells were bursting around the LCT. "We gotta get off this thing," someone in Ryan's crew shouted, and they all jumped into the water. Ryan held back. "I wasn't so much afraid of them bullets or the shells as I was of the cold Channel water. I cannot swim."

Ryan threw off all his equipment, inflated his Mae West, and began to tiptoe in off the ramp when "some German opened up on the side of the LCT with his machine gun, blblblblang. That convinced me. Into the water I dove. I pushed with all my might and then I started going. I'm swimming and I'm swimming. Somebody taps me on the shoulder and I look up. I was in a foot of water, swimming. You talk about the will to live. If they hadn't stopped me I would have swam two miles inland."

Ryan made it to the seawall. He threw himself down beside a 16th Regiment infantryman. "You got a cigarette?" Ryan asked.

A bit later, a piece of shrapnel made a scratch on Ryan's hand. Nothing much, "almost like a cat would give you." Soon a medical officer came along. He said, "Every man on this beach deserves the Purple Heart, just for being here. Give me your names, fellows. If you are wounded I can take care of you. If you are dead, I can't. If there's nothing wrong with you, I can see that you get a Purple Heart anyway."

"How about this, Major?" Ryan asked, showing his scratch. The doctor said he would get him the medal. But Ryan thought, "No, I can't do this. It would cheapen it so much. A guy loses a leg and gets the Purple Heart; I get it for a scratch; that just ain't fair. I turned it down."[7]

Another crew chief on an M-7 was Sgt. Jerry Eades. There were two M-7s on his LCT. They were hooked by cable to two half-tracks behind; directly behind one of the half-tracks, also connected by cable, was a truck, while a jeep was behind the other.

The M-7s were supposed to drag a half-track and a truck or jeep to shore.

As the landing craft approached the beach, the 105mm howitzers fired at the bluff. At first "it was just like a picnic," because no one was firing back. "All of a sudden, shells hit the water around us and we knew we were back in the war [Eades had been in North Africa and Sicily]. We came alive. It was a feeling of, well, I don't know how to explain fear, a feeling that went over you that you knew that the next breath could be your last. Of course, we were continuing to do our job." They would fire, lower the elevation, fire again, one shell every thirty seconds.

There were some GIs, infantry, on the LCT. There was nothing they could do but "wait for the slaughter. Us guys on the guns, at least we felt like we were doing something, shooting back. As long as you were shooting, you felt like you were in the war. But as for me, I would think, Let me hold my control, not let the guys see how scared I am, not lose control. That was my biggest fear, being caught afraid."

At 2,000 meters, the howitzers could not depress sufficiently to hit the bluff, so they stopped firing. German machine-gun bullets began to zing off the LCT. "I got down as low as possible, wishing I could push right on through the bottom of the boat, with the helpless feeling of 'I can't do anything now.' " The LCT was "going awfully slow. We were all having that urge like at a horse race, kind of shaking your shoulders to get the horse to run faster; we were trying to get this boat to go faster."

Eades looked at his watch. It was 0800. "All of a sudden I was real hungry. My thoughts drifted back to a bar and grill in El Paso, when I was in the old horse cavalry down there. The California Bar & Grill. They served a tremendous big taco for $.10 and an ice cold Falstaff beer for $.10. I could imagine myself sitting there at the bar with a beer and a taco for $.20 and here I was with maybe $200 in my pocket and I couldn't even buy a beer and taco."

When the LCT grounded on a sandbar (after three unsuccessful tries) and dropped the ramp, the skipper was "running madly around the boat shouting, 'Get them damn things off my boat! Get those damn things off my boat!' My lieutenant had his arm up; when he dropped his arm forward, I kicked the driver in the back of the head and off we went. I heard a kind of 'glub glub blub blub' sound. The water was deeper than our air intake and we were immediately flooded."

Eades thought about "all the stuff we had just lost. The Navy boys had given us fifty pounds of sugar, thirty pounds of coffee, fifty cartons of cigarettes, and we had lost all this stuff—and our gun."

Eades made it to shore and up to the shingle, where he asked himself, "Just what in the hell am I doing here when I could be back in Ft. Bliss, Texas." He was old Army, with an arm full of hash marks, an experienced goldbrick who knew how to avoid the tough assignments and garner the soft ones. To his consternation, he ended up spending D-Day as a rifleman on Omaha Beach, about the worst predicament an old soldier could find himself in. He organized "a kind of a provisional platoon" of infantry, engineers, and artillerymen, and up the bluff he led them.[8]

Because so many vehicles went glub glub, many specialists found themselves ending up as ordinary infantry. Capt. R. J. Lindo was a liaison officer for the Navy. He landed at 0730, with two men to carry his radio. His job was to direct naval gunfire in support of the 18th Regiment. But "my worst fears and my best training were for naught as we lost our radios coming in from the LCT to the beach. So there I was, helpless to assist in any way. I became instead a part of the infantry attack."[9]

Sgt. William Otlowski, a veteran of North Africa and Sicily, came in on a DUKW. He was in command of an M-7, which was far too heavy for the DUKWs to carry in anything but calm water. His DUKW was slammed up and down by a wave as it backed off its LST ramp. The rudder hit the ramp and got bent.

"So we're going around in little tight circles and we can't straighten out, so the coxswain, a Navy boy, he decided to shut off the motor, which was a mistake, because that shut off the pumps and the DUKW started to fill with water and of course we sank."

Otlowski yelled at his crew to keep together, hold hands, stay in a circle. A passing LCVP, returning to its mother ship for another load, picked them up. They transferred to a Rhino ferry.

The Rhino hit a sandbar. A lieutenant tied a rope to a jeep and told the driver to take off to test the water depth. The jeep promptly sank.

"Hey, men," the lieutenant called out, "grab the rope and pull up the jeep." Just then an 88 burst on one side of the Rhino, then another on the far side.

Otlowski yelled to the lieutenant, "Those are 88s, and the third one's going to hit right in the middle, get your men off this f—ing boat!'

"He said, 'Sergeant, stay where you are!'

"I said, 'To hell with you, Lieutenant, if you want to die, go ahead. Okay, men let's go!' " Otlowski and his crew jumped ship and swam to shore.

"I looked back, the third 88 had hit smack in the middle of that damn barge and every consecutive shot was right on target."

Otlowski picked up a rifle, ammunition belt, and helmet "and scooted up across the beach to the seawall." He saw a young soldier walking behind it, with a big roll of communication wire on his back. A lieutenant spotted the soldier and called out, "Oh, boy, do we need that. Sit down right here. Give me that wire."

The soldier replied, "I can't, Lieutenant. What will I do with this?" In his right hand he was carrying his left arm. Otlowski helped get the wire off his back, gave him some morphine, and yelled for a medic.[10]

Charles Sullivan was a Seabee on a Rhino. He helped bring in three loads on D-Day. Most of the vehicles were destroyed before they could fire a shot, but he concluded, "In twenty-eight years of service, three wars, fourteen overseas tours of duty, thousands of faces, only Normandy and D-Day remain vivid, as if it happened only yesterday. What we did was important and worthwhile, and how many ever get to say that about a day in their lives."[11]

Sullivan's comment brings to mind Eisenhower's remark to Walter Cronkite that no one likes to get shot at, but on D-Day more people wanted to get in on it than wanted to get out.

A tremendous tonnage of tanks, half-tracks, M-7s, jeeps, trucks, and other vehicles had attempted to come into Omaha between 0630 and 0830. Many had sunk, others were destroyed, and the few survivors were caught on an ever-shrinking beach with no place to go. The vehicles were more of a problem than they were an offensive weapon.

Beside and between the tanks, half-tracks, M-7s, and the rest, the Higgins boats were coming in, carrying the 116th and 16th regiments. With them were demolition teams composed of Seabees and Army engineers (five of each in a team). There were sixteen teams, each assigned to a distinct sector of the beach with the job of blowing a gap some fifty meters wide. Not one landed on target.

A Seabee described his experience: "As we dropped our ramp, an 88mm came tearing in, killing almost half our men right there, the officer being the first one. We all thought him the best officer the Navy ever had. . . . From then on things got hazy to me. I remember the chief starting to take over, but then another shell hit and that did it. I thought my body torn apart."

Bleeding heavily from shrapnel in his left leg and arm, the Seabee looked around and saw no one alive. Fire on the Higgins boat was about to set off the demolition charges. "So I went overboard and headed for the beach." He reached the obstacles, looked back, and saw the craft blow up.

"That got me. Not caring whether I lived or not, I started to run through the fire up the beach." He made the seawall, later picked up a rifle, and spent the day with the 116th as an infantryman.[12]

Other demolition teams had better luck. They got off their craft more or less intact and went to work, ignoring the fire around them. They were better off than the infantry; the GIs who landed at the wrong place and whose officers were wounded or killed before they made the seawall did not know what to do next. Not even heavy gunfire puts such a strain on a soldier's morale as not knowing what to do and having no one around to tell him. The demolition teams, however, could see immediately what to do. Even if they were at the wrong place, there were obstacles in front of them. They started blowing them.

Comdr. Joseph Gibbons was the CO of the demolition teams at Omaha. He strode up and down the beach, giving help where it was required, supervising the operation. The first two of his men he met told him the whole of the rest of their team had been killed. They had no explosives with them. Gibbons told them to get behind the seawall until he found a job for them. Then he found a team that had landed successfully and was already fastening its charges to the obstacles. The men moved methodically from one obstacle to another, fixing the charges to them.[13]

Pvt. Devon Larson of the engineers made it ashore. He was alone but he had his explosives with him so he went to work anyway. "Lying on the beach, I saw only two steel obstacles in front of me. Both with Teller mines atop of them. I wrapped a composition C pack around the base, piled about a foot of sand on my side so that the explosion would be away from me, pulled a fuse lighter from my helmet, yelled 'Fire in the hole!' and pulled the fuse. I heard several more shouts of 'Fire in the hole!' to my left. I rolled to the right. The explosion rolled me a little farther, but my two steel posts were gone. No more obstacles were in front of me or on either side, so I headed for the seawall."[14]

• •

Altogether, the demolition teams were able to blow five or six partial gaps instead of the sixteen that had been planned, and the gaps that did exist were not properly marked by flags. As the tide rose, this situation caused immense problems for the coxswains bringing in the follow-up waves of infantry and vehicles.

Seaman Exum Pike was on patrol craft 565. The job was to guide LCIs and other craft into the beach. But with landmarks obscured by smoke and haze and with no clear path through the obstacles, PC 565 could not accomplish its mission. It became, in effect, a gunboat, firing its machine guns at the bluff, from which Pike could see "a rain of fire that appeared to be falling from the clouds." Pike remembered seeing a DUKW hit an obstacle and set off the mine. "I saw the bodies of two crewmen blown several hundred feet into the air and they were twisting around like tops up there, it was like watching a slow-motion Ferris wheel."

Then PC 565 took a hit. Six men were wounded. "Blood was gushing down the gunwales of that boat like a river." Recalling the scene forty-five years later, Pike commented, "I have often told my two sons I have no fear of hell because I have already been there."[15]

Ens. Don Irwin was the skipper of LCT 614. His crew consisted of another ensign, the executive officer, and twelve Navy enlisted men. His cargo consisted of sixty-five GIs, two bulldozers, and four jeeps with ammunition-carrying trailers. He was scheduled to go in at 0730.

"As we headed toward the beach," Irwin recalled, "the most ear-splitting, deafening, horrendous sound I have ever heard or ever will took place." The *Texas* was firing over the top of LCT 614. Irwin looked back "and it seemed as if the *Texas*'s giant 14-inch guns were pointed right at us." Of course they were not; they were aiming at the bluff. "You'll never know how tremendously huge a battleship is," Irwin commented, "until you look up at one from fairly close by from an LCT."

Irwin was headed toward Easy Red. So far no Americans had landed on that section of the beach. To Irwin, it seemed "tranquil." He allowed himself to think that the briefing officer had been right when he said, "There won't be anything left to bother you guys when you hit the beach. We're throwing everything at the Germans but the kitchen sink, and we'll throw that in, too."

But as Irwin ran LCT 614 onto a sandbar and dropped the ramp, "all hell tore loose. We came under intense fire, mainly rifle and machine gun." When the first two men from the craft went down in water over their heads, Irwin realized the water was still too deep, so he used his rear anchor and winch to retract. He spent the next hour trying to find a gap in the obstacles where he could put his cargo ashore. Finally he dropped the ramp again; the bulldozers made it to the shore "only to be blasted by German gunners with phosphorus shells which started them burning."

The GIs were trying to get off, but when the first two got shot as they jumped off the ramp, the others refused to leave. Irwin had orders to disembark them. The orders stressed that to fail to do so could result in a court martial. He had been told that, if necessary, he should see to the execution of the order to disembark at gunpoint.

"But I could in no way force human beings to step off that ramp to almost certain wounding or death. The shellfire had grown even more intense. Pandemonium everywhere, with lots of smoke and explosions. Bodies in the water.

"The men in my crew, who were still at their battle stations and who had been standing erect on our way to the beach, were now flattened out against the craft as if they were a part of it. A couple of them were yelling, 'Skipper, let's get out of here!'

"After an hour of trying to get my load of troops and vehicles off, believe me I was ready."[16]

It was now 0830. Men and vehicles, almost none of them operating, were jammed up on the beach. Not a single vehicle and not more than a few platoons of men had made it up the bluff. At this point, the commander of the 7th Naval Beach Battalion made a decision: suspend all landing of vehicles and withdraw those craft on the beach.

Ensign Irwin got the order to retract over his radio. He was told that the beach was too hot and that he should go out into the Channel, anchor, and await further orders. It was the most welcome order he ever received, but the one that he had the most difficulty in executing. As he began to retract, his LCT suddenly stopped. It was hung up on an obstacle. It could have been panic time, but Irwin kept his head. He eased forward, then back again and floated free. His crew began taking in the anchor cable. But just when the anchor should have been in sight, it stuck.

"Try as we might we couldn't free that anchor. I gave the

command 'All engines ahead, full!' This did cause the anchor to move, and soon coming to the surface was a Higgins boat that had been sunk with our anchor hooked into it."

Irwin turned his LCT, gave it a couple of shakes, and freed the anchor. He got out to deep water and dropped the anchor.*

The 0830 general order to retract craft on the beach and postpone the landing of others until gaps in the obstacles had been blown added to the confusion. With nowhere to go, over fifty incoming LCTs and LCIs began to turn in circles.

For most of the skippers and crews, this was the first invasion. They were amateurs at war, even the old merchant mariners commanding the LSTs. The crews were as young as they were inexperienced.

Seaman James Fudge was on one of the two LSTs that had made it to the beach. When the order came to get off, "this is where our ship got in trouble, where our captain panicked. We had dropped our stern anchor. We had not unloaded a thing. The LST to our right got hit with an 88. And what our skipper needed to do was give the order 'Haul in the stern anchor! All back full!' But he said, 'All back full!' and forgot about the anchor. So he backed over his stern anchor cable and fouled the screws."

The LST was helpless in the water, about 500 meters offshore. Eventually, it was off-loaded by a Rhino. Fudge said, "It was quite difficult to unload tanks from the LST to the Rhino. You had to have a crane, it was a terrible time in a somewhat choppy sea to have a barge to unload trucks and tanks without dropping them in the water. But we didn't lose any."

Fudge recalled that "an admiral came by on an LCVP and in front of the whole crew he scolded our skipper for being so thoughtless as to back over his own cable. He had some very insulting things to say to our skipper. Directly. He was a very angry man."[17]

While the LST was being unloaded, Fudge saw a sight that almost every man on Omaha Beach that morning mentioned in his oral history. The incident was later made famous by Cornelius Ryan in *The Longest Day*. At about 0900, zooming in from the British beaches, came two FW-190s. The pilots were Wing Comdr. Josef Priller and Sgt. Heinz Wodarczyk. Ryan recorded that when they

---

* Six hours later Irwin went back in and got most of his cargo ashore. One sergeant refused to drive his jeep off the ramp; not until D-Day plus one did he go ashore, and then at a British beach.

saw the invasion fleet, Priller's words were "What a show! What a show!" They flew at 150 feet, dodging between the barrage balloons.

Fudge commented, "I can remember standing sort of in awe of them and everyone was trying to fire at them. People were shouting, 'Look, look, a couple of Jerries!' " Every 40mm and 20mm in the fleet blasted away.

So far as Fudge could make out, many of the gunners were hitting the ship next to them, so low were Priller and Wodarczyk flying. No one hit the planes. As Priller and Wodarczyk streaked off into the clouds, one seaman commented, "Jerry or not, the best of luck to you. You've got guts."[18]

There was one battalion of black soldiers in the initial assault on Omaha, the 320th Barrage Balloon Battalion (Colored). It was a unique outfit attached to the First Army. The troopers brought in barrage balloons on LSTs and LCIs in the third wave and set them up on the beach, to prevent Luftwaffe straffing. (About 1,200 black soldiers landed on Utah on D-Day, all of them truck drivers or port personnel from segregated quartermaster companies.) Black Coast Guard personnel drove Higgins boats and black sailors manned their battle stations on the warships. Overall, however, it was remarkable that so few black servicemen were allowed to participate in the initial attack against the Nazi regime, and a terrible waste considering the contributions of black combat troops in Korea and Vietnam.*

It was the Navy's job to get the men to shore, the tankers and artillerymen's jobs to provide suppressing fire, the infantry-

---

* In December 1944, during the crisis of the Battle of the Bulge, Eisenhower allowed black truck drivers to volunteer for combat infantry posts. Nearly 5,000 did, many of them giving up their stripes for the privilege of fighting for their country. Initially they were segregated into all-black platoons, with white officers. They compiled an outstanding record. A staff officer from the 104th Division remarked on the performance of the black platoons: "Morale: Excellent. Manner of performance: Superior. Men are very eager to close with the enemy and to destroy him. Strict attention to duty, aggressiveness, common sense and judgment under fire has won the admiration of all the men in the company. The colored platoon has a calibre of men equal to any veteran platoon." A few white officers declared that the black troops were too aggressive and occasionally overextended themselves, but when the black units suffered losses and could no longer function as platoons, the survivors were formed into squads and served in white platoons. This was the beginning of integration in the U.S. Army. Mr. James Cook of Sharon Hills, Pennsylvania, provided information on the 320th.

men's job to move out and up, the demolition teams' job to blow gaps in the obstacles, and the engineers' job to blow remaining obstacles, provide traffic control on the beach, blast the exits open, and clear and mark paths through the minefields. For the engineers, as for the others, the first couple of hours on Omaha were full of frustration.

Sgt. Robert Schober was with the 3466 Ordnance Maintenance Company. His unit's job was to dewaterproof vehicles. His tools were crescent wrench, screwdriver, and pliers. The task was simple: tighten fan belts, open battery vents, remove packing from various parts of the engine. When Howell got to the beach, "I felt a ding on the helmet. When I realized it was a bullet, I was no longer scared. I made up my mind that when the next wave of infantry took off for the seawall, I was going too. I did, and dug in when I arrived." He and his buddies stayed there through the morning, because they could not locate any vehicles that needed dewaterproofing.[19]

At least they made it to the wall. Cpl. Robert Miller, a combat engineer with the 6th ESB, did not. He was in an LCT that landed around 0700 on Easy Red. He glanced to his right "and saw another LCT, with the skipper standing at the tower, receive a blow from the dreaded German 88. After the smoke cleared both the skipper and tower had disappeared."

Miller worried about the trucks packed full of dynamite on his LCT taking a hit from an 88, but that turned out to be the wrong worry: the craft was rocked by a blast from an underwater mine. The ramp was jammed, a half-track up front badly damaged, many of the men on board wounded.

"The skipper decided to pull back to dump off the half-track, transfer the wounded, and repair the ramp. As this was being done a Navy officer in a control craft pulled alongside and raised hell with the skipper, saying we should not be sitting there and to get our a— into the beach where we belonged."

The skipper took the LCT back in and managed to drop the ramp in eight feet of water about 100 meters offshore. He told the engineers, "Go!" Miller's platoon commander objected "in no uncertain terms, reminding the skipper his orders were to run us onto the beach, but the skipper refused to budge."

A jeep drove off. It went underwater but the waterproofing worked and it managed to drive to the shore. The trucks also made it, only to get shot up. The men came next. Miller went in over his head. He dropped his rifle and demolition charges, jumped up from the Channel floor, got his head above water, and started swimming to the beach.

"It was a very tough swim. The weight of the soaked clothes, boots, gas mask, and steel helmet made it near impossible but I did reach hip-deep water finally and attempted to stand up. I was near exhaustion.

"At last I reached shore and was about fifteen feet up the beach when a big white flash enveloped me. The next thing I knew I was flat on my back looking up at the sky. I tried to get up but could not and reasoned, my God, my legs had been blown off since I had no sensation of movement in them and could not see them for the gas mask on my chest blocked the view. I wrestled around and finally got the gas mask off to one side. I saw my feet sticking up and reached my upper legs with my hands, and felt relieved that they were still there, but could not understand my immobility or lack of sensation."

Miller had been hit in the spinal cord. It was damaged beyond repair. Those first steps he took on Omaha Beach were the last steps he ever took.

A medic dragged him behind a half-track and gave him a shot of morphine. He passed out. When he came too he was at a first-aid station on the beach. He passed out again. When he regained consciousness, he was on an LST. He eventually made it to a hospital in England. Four months later, he was in a stateside hospital. A nurse was washing his hair. "To her and my own astonishment, sand was in the rinse water, sand from Omaha Beach."[20]

Sgt. Debbs Peters of the engineers was on an LCI. When the craft was about 300 meters offshore, a shell hit it in the stern, then another midships. "Those of us on deck were caught on fire with flaming fuel oil and we all just rolled overboard." Peters inflated his Mae West and managed to swim to an obstacle to take cover and catch his breath. Then he managed to stand and tried to run to the seawall, "but I was so loaded with water and sand that I could just stagger about." He crouched down behind a burning Sherman tank; almost immediately a shell hit the tank. (That was an experience many men had at Omaha; the urge for shelter sent them to knocked-out tanks, half-tracks, and other vehicles, but it was a mistake, because the tanks were targets for German artillery.)

Peters managed to reach the seawall. There he found Capt.

John McAllister and Maj. Robert Steward. "We agreed that we should get out of there if we expected to live and Major Steward told me to go ahead and find the mines." Peters had no equipment for such a search other than his trench knife, but he went ahead anyway.

"I jumped up on the road and went across, fell down into a ditch, up again, through a brier patch, then up against the bluff." He climbed carefully, probing for mines with his knife, leaving a white tape behind to mark the route. Near the top of the bluff he started taking machine-gun fire. Bullets ripped open his musette bag and one put a hole in his helmet. He tossed a grenade in the direction of the pillbox and the firing ceased. He had done his job, and more.[21]

Pvt. John Zmudzinski of the 5th ESB came in at 0730 on an LCI. "Our job was supposed to be to bring in our heavy equipment and cut the roads through the beach and bring the cranes and bulldozers in." Zmudzinski got ashore without getting hit. On the beach he saw some men freeze and just lie there. Beside them, he saw "a GI just lying there calmly taking his M-1 apart and cleaning the sand out of it, he didn't seem to be excited at all."

At the seawall, Zmudzinski threw himself down beside his CO, Capt. Louis Drnovich, an All-American football player at the University of Southern California in 1939. "He was trying to get things moving. He sent me down the beach to see if one of our bulldozers got in. I came back and told him nothing that heavy was getting in at that time. There was a half-track part way up to the exit road and Captain Drnovich sent me there to see what was holding him up. I went and hid behind it; it was all shot up and under heavy fire. When I got back to report, Captain Drnovich was gone."

Drnovich had gone back to the beach and climbed into a knocked-out tank to see if he could get the cannon firing. As he was making the attempt, he was hit and killed.

At the seawall, Zmudzinski found that he was protected from machine-gun fire but taking mortar rounds. "It was a matter of Russian roulette. I didn't know whether to stay where I was or go down the beach. It was just a matter of chance, whoever got hit." He saw half-tracks on the beach getting hit "and then one whole LCT loaded with half-tracks catch fire and burn up."[22]

Pvt. Allen McMath was a combat engineer who came in on the third wave. He found swimming difficult but managed to reach a pole sticking up in the water. "I held on to it for awhile to get my wind. I happened to look up. There on top of that pole was a Teller mine and that scared me so darned bad I took off and headed on in for shore."

A wave hit McMath and tumbled him. He was drifting parallel with the shore when a Higgins boat came straight at him. He tried to grab the front of the boat but there was nothing to hold onto, so he slid under and came up behind. "I still don't know how I missed that prop.* After that ordeal was over I was glad I hadn't caught onto the boat as it was hit soon after it passed over me."

McMath finally made shore. He picked up a rifle and cleaned the blood and sand off it. Then he took some dry socks off a dead soldier and changed his socks.

"I found some cigarettes that were dry and wouldn't have taken any amount of money for them." He moved up to the seawall. He could find no members of his company. Looking around, "there in a foxhole was a kid I had practically lived with most of my civilian life. What a surprise. I crawled into his hole and we had a little chat about how glad we were that we had both made it."[23]

Pvt. Al Littke was a combat engineer who came in with the first wave on an LCM. His initial task was to act as a pack horse; he was to carry demolition charges to the obstacles and drop them there. Then he was to continue to the beach and clear minefields. He draped his demolition charges over one shoulder, his M-1 over another, and carried a suitcase with his mine detector in his hand. He jumped off the ramp into knee-deep water, took a few steps, and fell into a runnel.

"I let go of my suitcase and I hit bottom. I pushed myself off; it was a good thing I had my life preserver on. I did a little dog paddle-breast stroke until my knees hit solid ground, then I got up and started to walk in."

When he reached the beach, Littke dropped his demolition charges beside an obstacle, then went on to the seawall. "It was pretty crowded there." Nevertheless, he kept his mind on his job. He fired a clip from his M-1 toward the bluff, reloaded, crossed the seawall, and got to the base of the bluff. When he started to move up, "about a foot in front of me little puffs of dirt flew up, about a dozen." He dug a foxhole and waited "for how long I do not know."

Unlike the leaderless infantry behind him, Littke knew what

---

* One of the features of the Higgins boat was a protected, enclosed propeller.

he was supposed to do and he was determined to do it. "I thought I'd better go up and look for mines. I had a roll of tape that brought it to my attention. I tied a stick around the tape and I took off again." As he moved up the bluff, leaving a trail marked by his tape behind, he went cautiously, watching for prongs sticking above the surface indicating Bouncing Betties or for any indentation in the sand indicating possible Teller mines or box mines. When he found some, he probed with his bayonet to dislodge and disarm them. After his tape ran out, he ran back to his foxhole.

Littke looked back at the beach. He saw an LCI unloading, soldiers coming down the two sides. "All of a sudden there was a flash on the portside, it hit right where the GIs were coming down the ladder. GIs fell into the water screaming and hollering for medics. I thought that if I ever got out of this alive, I would never miss going to church on Sundays again."

Just then an infantryman from the 116th Regiment appeared. He looked down at Littke in the foxhole and asked, "Kid, are you all right?" Littke said he was. The soldier started up the trail Littke had just marked; a half-dozen other GIs followed. Littke said to himself, "Hell, I might as well go with them."

He jumped up to do so when he heard someone call out, "Fatty!" It was a corporal from his platoon. Littke joined him to help a wounded man into a foxhole, then asked the corporal if he knew where their sergeant was. Back on the beach. Littke started down. He saw a sickening sight; a wounded soldier had crouched behind a tank for shelter. Shells were hitting near the tank. Littke could hear the tank commander yelling, "Let's get the hell out of here, they're zeroing in on us!" The tank backed up and crushed the soldier.

Later that morning, on the beach, Littke had what must have been a moment of intense satisfaction. He ran into a brigadier general and a colonel. The general asked him, "Son, how do we get to the top?"

"I just pointed toward my white tape."[24]

Pvt. John Mather of the engineers followed Littke's path. His team was more or less intact, led by a Lieutenant Allen. The men were carrying picks, shovels, bangalore torpedoes, bazookas and rockets, mine detectors, and satchel charges. They had landed at the wrong place, but Allen decided to go through the same gap Littke had used and stick to the marked path. When they reached the top Allen realized they were nowhere near their initial objective. A platoon from the 116th Regiment was exchanging fire with Germans in the next hedgerow. The engineers were not equipped for a firefight. Allen returned to the beach and tried to locate the exit he was supposed to be using. He led the men up another trail, found he was still in the wrong place, and again returned to the beach.

"At this point," Mather commented, "I started to get angry and frustrated at the lack of action on our part." He joined Lieutenant Allen, who was in consultation with the company commander. The CO was in a state of shock; he had lost half his men. "He looked like hell and very dispirited. I asked the lieutenant if there wasn't something we could do but got a negative answer. I'm sure he would have been willing but he couldn't get the CO to take action. So we sat in our holes and listened to the sound of the mortars swishing overhead and watched the tide go out."[25]

Lt. Barnett Hoffner of the 6th ESB came in on the rising tide. "The sight of the waves breaking onshore choked us up. It seemed like thousands of homeless were floating in a long line all around us. When our ramp dropped and we charged out into the water wading toward the beach, we went through what looked like hell itself. On the fifty or so yards of sand between the seawall and the water line lay blasted tanks, trucks, tractors, dozers, tangles, anything, blazing trucks filled with gas, everything was blown up. Of the sixteen teams we had trained for the demolition, only five came in for their assignments and three of them had nothing with them. All their equipment was gone. And only three bulldozers out of sixteen were left and they couldn't maneuver because the infantrymen were taking cover behind them."[26]

Lt. Col. Frank Walk was an assistant beachmaster for the ESB. His responsibility was to serve as traffic patrol officer, to direct incoming vehicles to open exits so they could climb to the top. But there were no open exits, and in any case Walk—who landed at about 0800—could not get off the beach. He and his radioman and his runner were under intense small-arms fire, "and one thing they spent a lot of time teaching us in the Army was how to dig foxholes. That is wasted training time. It is a natural instinct when you're under fire to dig a hole as fast as you can even if you have to do it with your fingernails. No one has to teach you how to dig a hole."

When the fire let up a bit, Walk moved to the seawall and located his CO, who had landed with an earlier wave. The CO was shell-shocked. "He was really just not at all in control of himself. He had gone completely berserk." He had to be evacuated; Walk took command.

By this time, around 0830, more brass was coming ashore. Lieutenant Colonel Walk was awfully junior to be giving assistant division commanders orders, but he did it anyway.

"They were accustomed to having their way," Walk commented. "So I would say, 'General, I'm sorry to tell you, you can't take those units through that exit. You've got to go over there.' "

"Who says so?"

"Well, General, I say so. I'm the traffic control officer here."[27]

Col. Paul Thompson, who had run the assault training center back in England, commanded the 6th ESB. He came in on an LCI at about 0830. Very little was going the way it was supposed to go, the way he had trained the assault units to take a fortified beach.

Thompson wanted to get things moving. He noticed a group of combat engineers held up by barbed wire on the beach road. "Some of the engineer personnel were trying to blow it with bangalore torpedoes, and of course I had conducted that exercise hundreds of times in training and it seemed to me they were going about it kind of clumsy." Thompson went forward to show them how to shove the bangalore under the wire. He got hit twice by rifle fire, one bullet through the right shoulder, the other through the jaw. The wound was unique because it was from the inside of the mouth out: Thompson had been shouting orders when he got hit.[28]

Thompson had longed to see the divisions he had trained take the beach and move inland. He had longed to see his engineers do the job they had been trained and equipped to do. He had longed to participate in the fight for the first 1,000 yards. It was not to be.

Thompson's frustration that morning was shared by every survivor of the first two hours of the battle, whether tankers or infantrymen or artillerymen or engineers or demolition teams. Many thought they had failed. When the 0830 order to cease landing came through, men were close to despair. At Omaha at least, Rommel's fixed defenses seemed to have stopped them cold.

At *Widerstandsnest* 62, Pvt. Franz Gockel thought so. At 0630 he had opened fire with his machine gun. The sand shaken loose by the naval bombardment caused it to jam. "I tore the belt from the feed tray, shook it clean, and slapped it back into the tray. At that instant the machine gun was torn from my hands by an explosion. I have no idea how I survived."

Gockel grabbed his rifle and began firing as "the first closely packed landing troops sprang from their boats, some in knee-deep water, others up to their chests. Within seconds the first wave of assault troops collapsed after making only a few meters headway. Assault craft careened leaderless back and forth on the water.

"On came the second waves of assault craft. Again we opened fire. The beach became strewn with dead, wounded and shelter-seeking soldiers. They reached the low stone wall, but the safety offered there was temporary. Our mortar crews had waited for this moment and began to lay deadly fire on preset coordinates along the sea wall. Mortar rounds with impact fuses exploded on target. The shell splinters, wall fragments, and stones inflicted severe casualties. The waves of attackers broke against our defenses."

Gockel and his comrades had plenty of ammunition for their rifles and machine guns, plenty of hand grenades stored nearby, plenty of mortar rounds. They had taken only light casualties. When at 0830 transports began turning out to sea without unloading their troops, "we believed the Americans were initiating a withdrawal."[29]

20

"I AM A DESTROYER MAN"

The Navy at Omaha Beach

THE SEABEES on the demolition teams, naval beachmasters, and spotters for the warships were the first Navy men on the beach. The beachmasters' job was to put up flags to guide the landing craft assigned to a particular sector, but twelve of the sixteen beachmaster teams never made it to shore, and the four who did were at the wrong place.[1]

Seaman Robert Giguere was on an LCI that hit a floating mine as she was going in, wounding or killing about half the men on board. The skipper dropped the ramp on the left side; the one on the right wouldn't work. A Coast Guardsman swam to shore with a rope; Giguere and infantry from the 16th Regiment used the rope to help themselves get ashore. On the way in, Giguere was hit in the left arm, but it was only a flesh wound. Ashore, he could not find any members of his beach party, so he picked up a rifle as he made his way to the seawall. There he switched from being a sailor assisting a beachmaster to a soldier.

At the seawall, Giguere heard Colonel Taylor say, "We might as well get killed inland as here on the beach." Giguere pointed to the markings on his helmet indicating that he was a Navy man; Taylor told him to join the infantry. Someone put a bangalore under the barbed wire; Giguere joined a small group from the 16th and crossed the road, only to be pinned down by a pillbox.

"I threw a couple of grenades in the pillbox openings," Giguere recorded. "I guess that helped to finish it off." He worked his way up the bluff. Late that morning he participated in a rush on a house that proved to have no Germans in it, but there were five Frenchmen in the cellar. A lieutenant told him to escort them down to the beach for interrogation.

On the beach, Giguere found that "artillery was landing everywhere. I was wounded again. When I came to, I was in the 40th General Hospital in Cirencester, England. It was my eighteenth birthday."[2]

The few beachmasters who made it ashore could hardly do their jobs in the chaotic conditions. Still, they tried to help out as best they could. Seaman William O'Neill was on an LCT. He recalled spotting a beach-party member "half crouching, waving his semaphore flags furiously at us. Without much thought, I grabbed a pair of flags and scrambled to the top of the wheelhouse and gave him a king, which means go ahead. His message was stay low, keep your head down. I really had some evil thoughts about getting that gratuitous advice."

Looking around, O'Neill could see that "our chances of reaching the beach at that place were very poor, but the chances of being slaughtered by machine gun and mortar fire were very high." He decided to pass his insights on to his skipper.

The skipper, an Ensign Phillips, was a "ninety-day wonder," but O'Neill thought he was "just great. Unassuming, never unjustly critical, a courageous and resourceful leader. It was a privilege to have served with him."

O'Neill did not think so much of Phillips's executive officer, another ensign, "who was a kind man but in battle he became literally paralyzed, unable to give orders or even to move." The third officer, an Ensign Fox, "was an absolute joy, bright, brave, and cool; we would do anything for him. His father was a Methodist bishop and his mother president of the Women's Christian Temperance Union in Maryland. He would dutifully pass around the temperance literature his mother would send, then lead the march to the nearest pub. He would point to himself as living proof that the ministers' kids were the worst in town."

Up on the wheelhouse, O'Neill was "really excited. I said to the skipper, 'What the hell are you doing here? You'll get us all killed! There's more of a chance to get in to our right.' "

Ensign Phillips agreed and off to the right the LCT moved,

sailing parallel to the beach for a kilometer or two, where other LCTs were moving in. Phillips closed the beach. He could see tanks sinking in runnels, so he asked for a volunteer who would test the water depth by wading into shore before the bulldozer in the front of his LCT unloaded.

"That was a nutty idea," O'Neill commented, but someone did volunteer "to be a human depth finder." Phillips ran onto the sandbar. At that moment, an LCT to the right, carrying seven half-tracks, dropped her ramp and the lead vehicle was hit just as it left the ramp. O'Neill saw "an immediate explosion and the entire LCT erupted in flames and then the ammunition began to explode so it was really quite a mess."

Ensign Phillips gave the order to drop the ramp. The volunteer jumped into the water, but the bulldozer driver did not wait to see the result; he just drove off, almost overrunning the volunteer. The driver had his blade raised to its maximum position, which provided an excellent shield for him. Down into the runnel he went. The waterproofing worked and he chugged his way forward, dragging a line of jeeps attached by cable behind him.

O'Neill remembered "my last vision of my friend Bill Lynn was of him sitting in his jeep being pulled along into deep water and then disappearing beneath the surface and then appearing soaking wet, water sloshing out of the jeep, some fifty yards further."

On the LCT, the gun crews were firing their 20mm guns into the bluff. So far as O'Neill could tell, "We were the only U.S. offensive activity in that area. Even the tanks were sheltered behind the sand dunes, unable to fire over them. Our orders had been to land, retract, and return for another load, but instead we stayed and continued to fire."

The executive officer cowered in the hold, but Ensign Fox led O'Neill and others ashore to bring wounded men to the LCT. "We filled our bunks, our inside decks, and every available space on the main deck. The wounds were gross. There was one medic and our cook to tend to all of them, and we did our best using our inexpert hands as well as we could."[3]

It was about 0830. So far the Navy had not done any better than the Army in carrying out the plan for Omaha. The 12-inch and 14- inch shells from the prelanding bombardment had mostly gone over the top of the bluff. The skippers on the landing craft had mostly put their men and cargoes ashore in the wrong places. The cutting edge of the invasion force, the infantry from the 116th and 16th regiments, had taken horrendous casualties; the survivors were mostly huddled at the seawall. They were receiving precious little fire support.

The Allies controlled the air over Normandy, which with the rarest of exceptions on D-Day kept the Luftwaffe from strafing the lucrative targets on the beach or bombing the beach or ships offshore, but the Air Force could contribute little in the way of direct support to the troops on the beach. The heavy bombers did not have the pinpoint accuracy required to hit the bluff but miss the beach; after the preassault bombardment, the big bombers returned to England, refueled and reloaded, and then hit targets such as railroads and crossroads well inland. That helped considerably in the following days by making German movement difficult, but it contributed nothing to the battle of June 6.

Later in the war, the Allied fighter pilots and the Army developed an efficient, indeed deadly, ground-to-air radio communication system, but even had the system been in place on D-Day it wouldn't have helped much, as 80 percent of the radios with the infantry at Omaha were lost in the surf or destroyed on the beach.

LCTs had managed to land some tanks, but most of them had been disabled. The Navy had been unable to get many field artillery pieces ashore. About all the help the infantry was receiving was coming from those little 20mm guns on the LCTs. That wasn't much.

The warships at sea had big guns, but they had lifted their fire as the first waves went in and were under orders not to resume firing until they had a definite target radioed to them from fire-control parties ashore. But the fire-control parties had not made it ashore, and there was no shore-to-ship liaison. The gunships closest to the shore, the destroyers, did not dare fire into the bluff, even when they could see fortified positions, for fear of hitting advancing American infantry.

"It was most galling and depressing," Commander W. J. Marshall of the destroyer *Satterlee* wrote in his action report, "to lie idly a few hundred yards off the beaches and watch our troops, tanks, landing boats, and motor vehicles being heavily shelled and not be able to fire a shot to help them just because we had no information as to what to shoot at and were unable to detect the source of the enemy fire."[4]

Lt. Owen Keeler was the gunnery officer on the destroyer

Frankford. He too was frustrated because he had no targets. Aside from all the other problems, "German camouflage was excellent, so we could not see who was where or pinpoint anything to shoot." His skipper, Lt. Comdr. James Semmes, decided to go in closer for a better look. Navigating by fathometer and seaman's eye, he got to within 400 yards, as close as he could possibly go without running aground, but "the camouflage on the beach was still good. We could not spot a target—and we did not know how far our troops had advanced."[5]

Destroyer *Harding's* executive officer and navigator, Lt. William Gentry, shared the feeling of helplessness. He watched DUKWs sink: "All we could do was stay clear of the assault craft and hold ourselves ready for counterfire."[6] (Chief Engineer Lt. Ken Shiffer on *Harding* was able to make a small contribution. He went up on deck to see the assault. "All of a sudden I saw a heavily loaded DUKW. The coxswain yelled, 'Which way is the beach?' I realized that the DUKW was so low in the water he couldn't make out the low-lying shoreline. I pointed to the east and he steamed away."[7])

The skipper of *Harding,* Capt. George Palmer, wrote in his action report, "This ship ceased firing while troops landed on beach and we commenced patrolling area about 2000 yards offshore searching for targets of opportunity. The smoke on the beach was so heavy that no targets could be seen and unobserved fire was deemed unsafe."[8]

After two hours of such frustration, skippers began to act on their own responsibility. Evidently the first to do so was Lt. Comdr. Ralph "Rebel" Ramey on *McCook.* He sailed into the western sector of Omaha, close enough to see that the troops were not getting up the bluff. He began blasting away with his 5-inch guns at the Vierville exit, hitting gun positions, pillboxes, buildings, and dug-in cliff positions. Two guns set into the cliff, enfilading the beaches, were particular targets. After almost an hour of shooting, one of the German guns fell off the cliff onto the beach and the other blew up.[9]

Pvt. Ernest Hillberg of the 1st Division was on a Higgins boat. The coxswain had received orders not to land yet, so "with those shells flying past," Hillberg remembered, "he decided we had to find a place to hide. *McCook* was a great place to hide. So we hid behind her. I'm sure there were a hundred small craft hiding behind *McCook,* which was slowly but methodically cruising along the coast, spotting the gun emplacements and taking them under fire. It was beautiful to see. We were scared to death *McCook* was going to run aground."[10]

Other destroyers were joining *McCook*. Lt. W. L. Wade commanded an LCI group that was circling offshore, waiting for orders to go in. He described the scene in front of him at 0930: "Enemy fire on the beaches was terrific—105mm, 88mm, 40mm, mortars, machine guns, mines, everything. Destroyers were almost on the beach themselves, firing away at pillboxes and strong points."[11]

The scene looked different to different men, in at least one case to men standing next to each other on the same bridge. At 0856 *Harding* went to the command vessel for Omaha, *Ancon*, to pick up Adm. Charles Cooke and Maj. Gen. Thomas Handy, who wanted to go close in to observe. *Harding* then cruised the beach, firing away as she did so.

Admiral Cooke declared that "the landing was a complete disaster" and commented that "the troops were pinned to the beach." But to Lieutenant Gentry, *Harding*'s executive officer, "it looked to us Navy destroyer types as if everything was proceeding according to the book. Troops were moving off the beach inland, enemy fire appeared to have died down, and it seemed to me the U.S. Army was getting its act together." But Cooke "kept muttering disaster."[12]

At 0950 Adm. C. F. Bryant, commanding the gunfire support group off Omaha, called all destroyers over TBS (Talk Between Ships) radio: "Get on them, men! Get on them! They are raising hell with the men on the beach, and we can't have anymore of that! We must stop it!" Every destroyer off Omaha responded, the skippers taking the risk of running aground (several did scrape bottom but got off), firing point-blank at targets of opportunity on the bluff.[13]

Comdr. Robert Beer on *Carmick* went in to within 900 meters of the beach, where he could keep up a visual communication of a sort with the troops ashore. When he saw a tank fire a single shot at a certain point on the bluff, Beer blasted the same spot. When he could see riflemen firing at a target, he laid into it with his 5-inch shells.[14]

Seaman Edward Duffy was in the radio room of *Shubrick*. His skipper was engaging shore batteries in what Duffy called

"Dodge City shootouts." He had two packs of cigarettes and a pound box of lemon drops with him; he went through both, plus a dozen cups of "Godawful coffee" in three hours. (It was years before he ate another lemon drop; "When I eat one now it brings back a lot of memories.")

Down in the radio room, "We could hear the projectiles exploding in the water around us. We were below the main deck at just about the water level, so the sounds of the explosions reverberated within the steel hull.

"I was scared. I had my life jacket very securely tied tightly about my (then) skinny frame. I expected at any moment to hear a shell come crashing through the bulkhead. I kept repeating to myself a prayer to the Blessed Virgin Mary. Then I became so tired of being scared I began paying attention to what the ship was doing."

Shubrick moved close in and pounded away point-blank. Duffy could "see" the battle over his earphones. "The spotters would report to all stations what was happening." At one point, the range finder reported a German officer walking on the crest. "Our officers suspected that he was scouting and spotting for the guns in this area. We trained our main battery and director in his direction, took a range on his location, and sent him a four-gun salute. A direct hit and the tension was relieved because we had gotten one of the bastards ourselves."[15]

That a destroyer could fire a salvo at a single individual indicates what a superb job American industry had done in supplying the men of D-Day. *Shubrick* fired 440 rounds that day; *McCook* 975; *Carmick* 1,127; *Satterlee* 638; the other destroyers between 500 and 1,000 rounds of 5-inch shells. They were supposed to save half their ammunition for possible German surface attack, or for antisubmarine work, but in many cases the destroyers returned to England with few or no rounds remaining in the locker.

Frankford fired away from shoal water 800 meters off the beach. Gunnery Officer Keeler recalled: "A tank sitting at the water's edge with a broken track fired at something on the hill. We immediately followed up with a 5-inch salvo. The tank gunner flipped open his hatch, looked around at us, waved, dropped back in the tank, and fired at another target. For the next few minutes he was our fire-control party. Our range-finder optics could examine the spots where his shells hit."[16]

A bit later *McCook* had the perhaps unique experience of forcing German troops to surrender. As "Rebel" Ramey was firing at a cliff position, German soldiers appeared waving a white flag and attempting to signal the ship by semaphore and flashing light. For nearly an hour Ramey's semaphore man tried to establish communications, he using broken German, they using poor English.

When Ramey tired of the game and signaled that he was resuming fire, a prompt answer came back—"Ceize fire!" Ramey had his man signal to the Germans that they should come down the bluff and surrender themselves. They understood and did, coming down single file with hands up to turn themselves over to GIs on the beach.[17]

Admiral Morison got it right when he wrote, "This destroyer action against shore batteries . . . afforded the troops the only artillery support they had during most of D-Day."[18] The cruisers and battleships, unable to go in close, were banging away at major emplacements on the cliffs east and west of Omaha whose position was known before the invasion and with good effect, but the troops ashore could neither see nor sense the results. But the effect on the troops on Omaha of the destroyers' heroic and risky action was electric.

Before he got hit in his spinal column, while he was still on his LCT, Cpl. Robert Miller could see "a destroyer ahead of us with heavy smoke pouring from its stack. It seemed to be out of control and heading right for the beach. I thought, my God, they're going to run aground and be disabled right in front of the German emplacement, when the ship made a hard left pulling parallel to the beach, blazing away with every gun it had point-blank at the position. Puffs of smoke and mounds of dirt flew everywhere on the hillside as the destroyer passed swiftly by."[19]

Seaman Giguere was on the beach when a destroyer "came in as close to shore as could be. She was firing at a pillbox just over my head. It was a funny feeling hearing the shells go over my head."[20] Seaman O'Neill, also on the beach, recalled, "The destroyers were firing their 5-inch shells point-blank at the pillboxes, you could see the shells as they went screaming overhead and smacked against the thick concrete walls. They bounced skyward off the sloping sides of those pillboxes, but they managed to get a few of them into the gun ports. The enemy fire soon stopped."[21]

Lt. Joe Smith, a Navy beachmaster, remembered seeing "the destroyers come right into the beach firing into the cliff. You could see the trenches, guns, and men blowing up where they would hit. They aimed right below the edge of the cliffs where the trenches were dug in. There is no question in my mind that the few Navy destroyers that we had there saved the invasion." In his conclusion, Smith spoke for every man who witnessed the scene: "Believe me, I am a destroyer man from that day on."[22]

Forty-five years later, James Knight, an Army engineer on a demolition team who landed at 0630 at Fox Red, wrote a letter to the crew of the *Frankford*, published in the *U.S. Naval Institute Proceedings*. Knight said that he had been pinned down until, "at about 1000 or 1030, a destroyer loomed out of the sea . . . headed straight toward me. Even though she wasn't listing or smoking, my first thought was that she had either struck a mine or taken a torpedo and was damaged badly enough that she was being beached."

But the destroyer began to turn right. Before she was parallel to the beach she was blazing away with all her guns. Shells landed just a few feet over Knight's head. He watched her proceed westward along the beach, firing constantly. He expected to see her pull out to sea at any moment "when suddenly I realized she was backing up and her guns had yet to pause. She backed up almost to where she had started, went dead in the water for the second time . . . and again headed toward the other end of the beach, with all guns still blazing."

Over the years since D-Day, Knight tried to find out the name of the destroyer, but neither Ryan nor Morison nor any other author mentioned the incident (although Morison did say that *Frankford* went in closest that morning). Then Knight saw a notice of a reunion for the *Frankford* in the *VFW Magazine*. He attended the reunion, in 1989. There he confirmed that the destroyer that had so impressed and helped him was the *Frankford*.

In his letter to the crew, Knight wrote, "Regardless of the time of arrival, nearly every living person on Omaha was pinned down from the time he reached the dune line until after you made your 'cruise.' Not long after you swung out to sea, there was movement on the beach, which eventually enabled the infantry to advance up the slope onto the flat land and beyond."[23]

The chief of staff of the 1st Division, Col. S. B. Mason, wrote Rear Adm. J. L. Hall on July 8, 1944, after an inspection of the German defenses at Omaha. Those defenses should have been impregnable, Mason wrote, and indeed the Germans had hurled back everything the Army had thrown at them. "But there was one element of the attack they could not parry. . . . I am now firmly convinced that our supporting naval fire got us in; that without that gunfire we positively could not have crossed the beaches."[24]

When Maj. Gen. Leonard Gerow went ashore at 1900 hours on D-Day, to establish his V Corps headquarters on the beach, his first message back to General Bradley on *Augusta* was: "Thank God for the United States Navy!"[25]

The Navy was part of a team. Indispensable, obviously, especially the destroyers, but still just a part. Much hard fighting remained before the bluff and high ground could be secured even after *Frankford* and the others had expended virtually all their ammunition and withdrawn. What the Navy had done was to give the men on Omaha a fighting chance. It was up to the infantry to exploit it. The first task was to open those exits and relieve the traffic jam on the beach. To do that, the infantry had to get to the top and come down on the German defenders from the rear.

The outstanding job the Navy did of destroying German pillboxes on the bluff was matched by the outstanding job the Navy did of caring for the wounded. Medical care began on the beach, with men dragging the wounded out of the water to keep them from drowning in the rising tide. Chief Yeoman Garwood Bacon of the 7th Naval Beach Battalion was on an LCI that hit a mine at 0810 on Dog Green. Many were wounded; the craft was burning. With the other members of his team, Bacon got a rubber raft into the water; he got aboard while they pitched onto it a radio set and medical packs plus their weapons and ammunition. As machine-gun and rifle fire whined past their ears, they pushed the raft through the obstacles to shallow water, then unloaded the contents on the sand.

"Hey, Bacon," Seaman Johnakin called out, "do you think that we can make it out to the ship again? Some of those wounded guys will never make it ashore."

"I'll give it a try if you will," Bacon replied.

They tossed their packs, tommy guns, and helmets onto the beach, grabbed the raft, and began crawling backward out into deeper water, again dodging obstacles and trying to avoid bullets as they picked up wounded men from the water. "In a matter of a few minutes some fifteen wounded or nonswimmers were crammed into-it or hanging on the outside of the raft, and with the help of free hands and feet flailing the water we all managed to reach shore once more where several able-bodied men helped to take the wounded to the protection of the seawall and administer first aid wherever possible."[26] An Army Signal Corps photographer took a snapshot of the scene; it became one of the best-known photos of Omaha Beach.

Bacon grabbed a carbine (someone had already picked up his tommy gun) and made his way to the shingle seawall. He saw a group of fifty or so men, "all prostrate on the sand or rocks. Thinking they were lying there held down by gunfire, I threw myself down between two soldiers and buried my face in the sand. Suddenly I realized there was no rat-a-tat-tat of a machine gun whining overhead so I lifted my head cautiously and looked around. The sickening sight that met my eyes froze me on the spot. One of the men I had dropped between was headless, the other was blown half apart. Every last one of them was dead." He could render no first aid to dead men, so he set off in search of his party.[27]

German snipers would shoot at the Army medics (universally praised by the veterans of D-Day as the bravest of the brave) as they tried to tend wounded men on the beach who could not be moved. Wounded men who could be dragged to the seawall were treated by the medics as best they could, which wasn't much more than applying tourniquets, giving wounds a quick cleaning, applying sulfa and/or the new wonder drug penicillin (the U.S. pharmaceutical industry had produced a record-breaking 100 million units of penicillin the previous month[28]), giving a shot of morphine, and waiting for an opportunity to take the man by litter down to a landing craft that was going back to the mother ship for another load.

Seaman O'Neill and a beach engineer carried a stretcher to O'Neill's LCT. When they set the litter down, O'Neill saw that one side of the wounded man's face was gone. "His eyeball and teeth and jawbone were plainly visible. It looked like one of those medical drawings or a model. I asked him how he was doing. He said he felt OK."

O'Neill continued to bear the stretcher until his LCT was jammed with wounded. An Army medic and the cook on the LCT took over. The medic had some blood plasma, but his supply was soon exhausted. As the LCT moved out toward the transport area, where the wounded could be transferred to a hospital ship, O'Neill heard the medic say, "This man's going to need some plasma or else he isn't going to make it."

"There isn't any more," the cook said, tears in his eyes.

They were still an hour and a half away from the hospital ship. When they finally got there, the ship was ready for them, with booms rigged to load litters. The LCT tied up alongside; hospital corpsmen came off the ship and aboard the LCT with medical supplies of all types. One by one, the wounded were lifted by litter to the ship.[29]

Time was the great danger to the wounded. Pain could be endured or handled—a combination of shock and morphine helped (when a medic or a GI administered a shot of morphine he would tag the man so that another soldier coming along later would not give a second shot)—but loss of blood could not. But if the flow could be stopped and the man put into a doctor's hands on a hospital ship, the chances of survival were good.

The crews on the landing craft did their best to get the wounded to treatment. Sgt. Stanley Borkowski of the 5th ESB was running a DUKW back and forth from a Liberty ship to the beach, carrying cargo. On the return trips he brought wounded to the hospital ship, which was anchored about two miles out. "I do not wish to comment about the wounded soldiers," Borkowski said in his oral history, his voice choking with the thought of what he had seen. "I was glad to get them to the hospital. My prayers are always with them."[30]

The LCI on which correspondent A. J. Liebling of the New Yorker was riding picked up some wounded men from Omaha Beach to take out to a hospital ship. Three of them had to be sent up in wire baskets, "vertically, like Indian papooses. A couple of Negroes on the upper deck dropped a line which our men made fast to the top of one basket after another. Then the man would be jerked up in the air by the Negroes as if he were going to heaven.

"A Coast Guardsman reached up for the bottom of one basket so that he could steady it on its way up. At least a quart of blood ran down on him, covering his tin hat, his upturned face, and his blue overalls. . . . A couple of minutes after the last litter had been hoisted aboard, an officer leaned over the rail and shouted down, 'Medical officer in charge says two of these men are dead. He says you should take them back to the beach and bury them.' A sailor on deck said, 'The son of a bitch ought to see that beach.' " The skipper of the LCI refused the absurd order.[31]

Seaman Ferris Burke was a sixteen-year-old on LST 285, which served as a hospital ship. "The doctors were outstanding," he recalled. "Just unbelievable. They worked for hours, amputating arms and legs, removing shrapnel, patching bullet wounds, and trying to calm down some men who were completely out of their minds."

Burke had an awful experience for a sixteen-year-old (or anyone else for that matter). He remembered Dr. Slattery asking him to go down to the shipfitter's shop and get half a dozen pieces of angle iron, two feet long. Burke did. When he returned with the metal Dr. Slattery told him to tape the arms and legs he had amputated to the metal and throw them overboard. Later, when Burke told the shipfitter what he had used the angle iron for, the shipfitter was "a bit upset because he had given me very good metal. He said if he had known what the doctor wanted the metal for he would have given me some scrap from around the shop instead of the good stuff."[32]

There were many heartbreaking scenes. Pharmacist Mate Frank Feduik recalled administering morphine to a GI on the deck of an LST. He was lying on a stretcher. "He suddenly raised his body and let out an awful yell. He had realized that his right leg was missing. I pushed him back down and I remember him saying, 'What am I gonna do? My leg, I'm a farmer.'"[33]

War creates many strange juxtapositions, perhaps none stranger than this: men who are doing their utmost to kill other men can transform in a split second into lifesavers. Soldiers who encounter a wounded man (often an enemy) become tender, caring angels of mercy. The urge to kill and the urge to save sometimes run together simultaneously.

Captain Palmer on *Harding* was prowling just off the beach, blazing away with every gun on his ship. Palmer was described by Lieutenant Gentry as a man full of "autistic energy and nervous tension." The medical officer on *Harding* was a Dr. McKenzie. At 1024 McKenzie had persuaded Palmer to cease firing long enough to launch the ship's boat so that he could go ashore to render medical aid to wounded men on a Higgins boat that had been hit. Upon completion of that duty, although under intense rifle and machine-gun fire, McKenzie had the ship's boat take him to a DUKW holding some wounded so that he could tend to them. Then he returned to *Harding*.

On board, McKenzie faced an emergency. Ens. Robert Reetz had acute appendicitis. Only an immediate operation could save his life. McKenzie asked Palmer to cease fire so that he could operate. Palmer reluctantly agreed. After a half hour or so, Palmer sent Lieutenant Gentry down to the wardroom that had been converted to an operating room to see what was holding things up.

McKenzie told Gentry he had given Reetz "enough anesthesia for two people but still couldn't get him quieted down enough to operate." Ens. William Carter was there, along with three others trying to hold Reetz down. (Carter remembered that "Dr. McKenzie had promised for months to let me assist in an operation; this was the first major one and he called for me to assist.") The overhead light was out; Carter held a lantern with one hand and Reetz with the other. It took another forty-five minutes for the anesthesia to do its work, "with the captain calling down every five minutes for a progress report," as Gentry put it. Finally, after one and a half hours, the operation was successfully completed. Captain Palmer let go a "Thank God" and ordered all guns to commence firing.[34]

The medics were not the only men on the beach whose job was not to destroy but to preserve. The Army Signal Corps and the Coast Guard sent photographers ashore to record the battle. These were the men on the beach who carried only cameras and black-and-white film. They went in with the first waves.*

Perhaps the bravest and certainly the best known that day was Robert Capa of *Life* magazine, who went into Omaha with Company E in the second wave. His craft mislanded at Easy Red. Capa was last off. He paused on the ramp to take a photograph. The coxswain "mistook my picture-taking attitude for explicable hesitation and helped me make up my mind with a well-aimed kick in the rear." Capa got behind an obstacle and shot a roll of film. He dashed forward to gain the protection of a burned-out tank in waist-deep water. He wanted to get to the seawall "but I could not find any hole between the shells and bullets that blocked the last twenty-five yards." He stayed behind the tank, repeating a sentence he had learned in the Spanish Civil War (where he had taken one of the best-known photographs of combat in the Twentieth Century, of a soldier just as he got hit in the chest): "*Es una cosa muy seria. Es una cosa muy seria.*" ("This is a very serious business.")

---

* In 1991, one of my students remarked, "World War II? Isn't that the one they fought in black and white?"

Capa finally made it to the seawall, where he threw himself to the ground. "I found myself nose to nose with a lieutenant from our last night's poker game. He asked me if I knew what he saw. I told him no and that I didn't think he could see much beyond my head. 'I'll tell you what I see. I see my ma on the front porch, waving my insurance policy.' "

Mortars were landing all around. Capa kept shooting, inserting new rolls of film and shooting some more. He ran low on film. Turning to the beach, he saw an LCI.

"I did not think and I didn't decide it. I just stood up and ran toward the boat." Holding his cameras high above his head, he waded out to the LCI. "I knew that I was running away. I tried to turn but couldn't face the beach and told myself, 'I am just going to dry my hands on that boat.' "

Coast Guardsman Charles Jarreau was on the LCI, picking up wounded men to take back to a hospital ship. He spotted Capa: "Poor fellow, he was there in the water, holding his cameras up to try to keep them dry, trying to catch his breath." Capa called out for help; the skipper told him to come aboard. "He was really grateful to get out. He came aboard. He took pictures on our ship, which appeared in *Life* magazine."[35]

Capa got back to Portsmouth later that day, then went by train to the developing studios in London. He turned in his film for development. The darkroom assistant was so eager to see the photos that he turned on too much heat while drying the negatives. The emulsions melted and ran down. Of the 106 pictures Capa had taken, only eight were salvaged and they were blurry.

Capa was understandably upset until he realized that the gray, murky photos of men hiding behind beach obstacles or coming ashore from Higgins boats caught the chaos and fear on Omaha Beach exactly. Thanks in part to the overeager developer, Capa had taken some of the most famous photographs of D-Day.[36]

Hollywood director and producer John Ford was head of a photographic unit for the Office of Strategic Services. On D-Day, he had a team of Coast Guard cameramen working for him. They crossed the Channel on destroyer USS *Plunket*, carrying $1 million worth of camera gear. Twenty years later, Ford talked about his experiences to writer Pete Martin for the *American Legion Magazine*. Ford had brought with him to Omaha Beach his wonderful director's eye; his oral history needs to be quoted at some length.

"When we started," Ford told Martin, "we were the last ship out in our huge convoy. . . . Suddenly our flotilla was switched about . . . which put out *Plunket* in the lead. I am told I expressed some surprise at leading the invasion with my cameras."

Plunket dropped anchor at 0600 off Omaha Beach. "Things began to happen fast."

Ford saw the first wave go in. "They didn't have a chance.

"Neither did the LCMs bringing in bulldozers and more tanks. They really caught hell. Later I heard that only three bulldozers out of 30 or 40 made it. I also remember seeing landing craft swing out of control and smash against obstacles where they touched off a mine and blew sky high. On a later day, much later, I discovered that it was this very week that the first U.S. shipyards were getting ready to lay off hundreds of men as war-time orders slackened."

The objective of Ford's team was "simple, just take movies of everything on Omaha Beach. Simple, but not easy." Ford off-loaded onto a DUKW. Going in, "I remember watching one colored man in a DUKW loaded with supplies. He dropped them on the beach, unloaded, went back for more. I watched, fascinated. Shells landed around him. The Germans were really after him. He avoided every obstacle and just kept going back and forth, back and forth, completely calm. I thought, *By God, if anybody deserves a medal that man does.* I wanted to photograph him, but I was in a relatively safe place at the time so I figured, *The hell with it.* I was willing to admit he was braver than I was."

The infantry also made a vivid impression on Ford: "The discipline and training of those boys who came ashore in the later waves of landing craft, throwing up and groaning with nausea all the way into the beach, was amazing. It showed. They made no mad rush. They quietly took their places and kept moving steadily forward."

When Ford hit the beach, he ran forward and began directing his photographers to selected spots (mainly behind beach obstacles). They began setting up and shooting. "I wouldn't let them stand up. I made them lie behind cover to do their photographing. [Nevertheless] I lost some men. To my mind, those seasick kids were heroes. . . . I take my hat off to my Coast Guard kids. They were impressive. They went in first, not to fight, but to photograph.

"My memories of D-Day come in disconnected takes like unassembled shots to be spliced together afterward in a film.

"I was reminded of that line in 'The Red Badge of Courage' about how the soldiers were always busy, always deeply absorbed in their individual combats.

"My staff and I had the job of 'seeing' the whole invasion for the world, but all any one of us saw was his own little area. . . . In action, I didn't tell my boys where to aim their cameras. They took whatever they could. . . . There was no panic or running around."

The film went back to London, where it was processed. Most of it was in Kodachrome, which was transferred to black-and-white for release in the newsreels in movie theaters. "My cutting unit . . . worked 24-hour watches, picking out the best part of the film that had been shot. I'm sure it was the biggest cutting job of all time. They worked four-hour shifts—on four, off four. . . . Very little was released to the public then [because] apparently the Government was afraid to show so many American casualties on the screen."[37]*

---

* Not until 1945 did the government release movie or still photos of dead American soldiers. In his 1964 interview with the *American Legion Magazine*, Ford said, "All of it [the D-Day film] still exists today in color in storage in Anacostia near Washington, D.C." Where it was thirty years later the Eisenhower Center has been unable to discover.

21

"WILL YOU TELL ME
HOW WE DID THIS?"

The 2nd Ranger Battalion
on D-Day Morning

ON THE AFTERNOON of June 5, Lt. Col. James Earl Rudder, CO of the Ranger Force (2nd and 5th Ranger battalions), paid a visit to companies A, B, and C of the 2nd Battalion on their transport, the *Prince Charles.* He was going to lead companies D, E, and F on an assault at Pointe-du-Hoc, a sheer cliff some forty meters high about seven kilometers west of the right flank of Omaha Beach. A, B, and C were going in at the Charlie sector of Omaha, to the immediate right of Company A of the 116th Regiment.*

Rudder, a 1932 graduate of Texas A&M, where he received a commission in the reserves, had been a college football coach and teacher before going on active duty in 1941. He knew how to give inspirational talks before going into action. On this occasion, he told companies A, B, and C, "Boys, you are going on the beach as the first rangers in this battalion to set foot on French soil. But don't worry about being alone. When D, E, and F take care of Pointe-du-Hoc, we will come down and give you a hand with your objectives. Good luck and may God be with you."[1]

In the event, almost none of this worked out, not for A, B, and C or for D, E, and F. Most of the game plan had to be aban-

---

* The ranger companies' strength was seventy men each, less than half the size of regular infantry assault companies.

doned even before the action began. C Company was alone when it landed, and virtually alone through the day. D, E, and F companies came in at the wrong time from the wrong direction at Pointe-du-Hoc. Most of the special equipment for scaling the cliff never made it to the shore; much of what did failed to work. When the companies nevertheless made it to the top, they found that their objective, five 155mm cannon capable of dominating both Utah and Omaha beaches, were not in the casemates. Apparently what the rangers had accomplished in one of the most famous and heroic actions of D-Day had gone for naught and the skills and sacrifices of one of the most elite and highly trained forces in the Allied army had been wasted. But in fact what the rangers accomplished at Omaha and at Pointe-du-Hoc was critical to the ultimate success at both American beaches.

Ten years after the event, Colonel Rudder visited the site with his fourteen-year-old son and *Collier's* reporter W. C. Heinz. Looking up at the cliff at Pointe-du-Hoc, he asked, "Will you tell me how we did this? Anybody would be a fool to try this. It was crazy then, and it's crazy now."[2]

The plan was for Company C to land on the far right flank of Omaha Beach and follow Company A of the 116th Regiment up the Vierville draw, pass through the village, turn right, and clear out the area between the beach and the coastal road (about a kilometer inland) running from Vierville to Pointe-du-Hoc. In that area the Germans had some twenty pillboxes, bunkers, Tobrucks, and open gun emplacements, plus a radar station. The schedule called for Company C to accomplish its mission in two hours, that is, by 0830. Companies A and B would land at 0730 at Pointe-du-Hoc, if given a signal that Rudder needed them there for reinforcement: if no signal was received (presumably meaning that Rudder's force had failed), they would land at the mouth of the Vierville draw, from which spot they would move to the high ground, turn right, and proceed west on the coastal road to attack Pointe-du-Hoc from the land side.

For ranger companies A, B, and C, in short, everything depended on Company A of the 116th Regiment securing the Vierville draw and the village itself in the initial moments of the assault. But Company A of the 116th was wiped out at the beach. Company C of the rangers came in a few minutes later, at 0645, in an isolated position, at the far western edge of Omaha, just beyond the Vierville draw; the closest American troops were more than two kilometers to the east at Dog Red.

Going in on the heels of the naval bombardment, before the Germans opened fire, the rangers were in a cocky mood. "It's going to be a cinch," one of them said. "I don't think they know we're coming." Sgt. Donald Scribner recalled the men in his boat singing "Happy Anniversary" to Sgt. Walter Geldon—June 6, 1944, was Geldon's third wedding anniversary.[3] They cheered when the LCT(R)s launched their rockets, only to groan when they saw the rockets fall short and harmlessly in the water. Their dismay increased as they realized, in the words of Lt. Gerald Heaney, "there was no one on the beach in front of us and we were going to touch down in a sector that had not been invaded by other American soldiers."

When Heaney's LCA hit a sandbar, the British coxswain called out a cheery "This is as far as I go, Yanks" and lowered the ramp. German machine-gun fire ripped across the boat. The first man out was immediately hit. Heaney saw he had no chance if he went down the ramp, so he jumped over the side.

"All around me men were being killed and wounded. I ran as hard as I could toward shore, and I remember being so exhausted when I reached the shore that it was all I could do to make it to the cliff."[4]

The CO of C Company, Capt. Ralph Goranson, recalled, "Going across the beach was just like a dream with all the movement of the body and mind just automatic motion." He made it to the shelter at the base of the cliff. To Sgt. Marvin Lutz, crossing the beach was "like a horrible nightmare." Nevertheless, like his CO, he moved automatically—the payoff from the training maneuvers.[5]

The cliff was sheer, about thirty meters high, just to the west of the Vierville draw. At its base men were out of sight of German machine gunners but still vulnerable to mortar fire and to grenades dropped over the edge by Germans on top. They were concussion grenades, universally called "potato mashers" by the GIs because of their shape. As they came down, Pvt. Michael Gargas called out, "Watch out fellows! Here comes another mashed potato!"[6]

Sergeant Scribner's boat was hit three times by artillery fire. The first shell tore the ramp completely off the boat, killing the men in front and covering the others with blood. The second hit the port side. Scribner started to climb over the rear starboard side when he noticed a 60mm mortar lying on the bottom of the craft. He stopped to pick it up when the third shell tore out the starboard side. Somehow he made it into the water.

"I was carrying a radio, my rifle, my grenades, my extra ammunition, my bedroll, all my gear, and I started sinking in the Channel. I didn't think I was ever going to stop going down."

Scribner made it to the shore—he cannot recall how—and tried to run across the beach. "I remember dropping three different times. Each time I did, machine guns burst in front of my face in the sand. I didn't stop because I knew what was coming; I dropped because I was so tired." When he made it to the base of the cliff, "I looked back, and I saw Walter Geldon lying out on the beach with his hand raised up asking for help. Walter never made it. He died on his third wedding anniversary."[7]

Lt. Sidney Salomon, leading 2nd Platoon of C Company, was first off his boat. He went to the right into chest-deep water as automatic weapons and rifle fire sprayed the debarking rangers. The second man off, Sgt. Oliver Reed, was hit. Salomon reached over and pulled him from under the ramp just as the craft surged forward on a wave. He told Reed to make it the best he could and started wading toward the shore. "By this time, the Germans had zeroed in on the ramp. Ranger after ranger was hit by small-arms fire as they jumped into the water, and in addition mortar shells landed around the craft, making geysers of water."

Salomon made the base of the cliff. He looked back. "Bodies lay still, where they had fallen, trickles of blood reddening the sand. Some of the wounded were crawling as best they could, some with a look of despair and bewilderment on their tortured and painracked faces. Others tried to get back on their feet, only to be hit again by enemy fire. Bodies rolled back and forth at the water's edge, the English Channel almost laughing as it showed its might over man and played with the bodies as a cat would with a mouse."[8]

Of the sixty-eight rangers in Company C, nineteen were dead, eighteen wounded. Only thirty-one men made it to the base of the cliff. The company had yet to fire a shot.[9] Its experience in the first few minutes on French soil had been nearly as disastrous as that of A Company, 116th.

But the rangers had some advantages. Despite the grenades and mortar fire, they were more secure at the base of the cliff than the survivors of A Company were at the seawall on the other side of the Vierville draw. Their company commander, Capt. Ralph

Goranson, along with two platoon leaders, Lts. William Moody and Sidney Salomon, were with them to provide leadership. And they were elite troops, brought to a fever pitch for this moment. For example, Sergeant Scribner recalled Sgt. "Duke" Golas: "He had about half his head blown away by a grenade and he was still standing at the bottom of the cliff firing his weapon, hollering at the Krauts up above to come out and fight."[10]

The officers, meanwhile, realized the company was alone, that the Vierville draw was not only not opened but was bristling with German defenders, and that their only alternative—other than cowering at the base of the cliff and getting killed—was to climb the cliff. Fortunately, they had been through cliff-climbing training and had some special equipment for the task.

Lieutenants Moody and Salomon and Sgts. Julius Belcher and Richard Garrett moved to their right until they found a crevice in the cliff. Using their bayonets for successive handholds, pulling each other along, they made it to the top of the crest. There Moody attached some toggle ropes to stakes in a minefield and dropped them to the base of the cliff, enabling the remainder of the company to monkey-walk them to the top. By 0730 Company C of the 2nd Ranger Battalion, or what was left of it, was on the crest. According to the official Army history, it "was probably the first assault unit to reach the high ground."[11]

On the cliff, the rangers saw what they always called thereafter a fortified house. Actually, it was not fortified, although it might as well have been, as it was a typical Norman stone farmhouse. It overlooked the draw and was surrounded by a maze of communications trenches. Behind the house the Germans had numerous Tobruks and other types of pillboxes, plus an extensive trench system. From the house, the Germans were firing on the rangers.

C Company's mission was to move west along the high ground, but Captain Goranson decided to first of all attack the house and clean out the trenches behind it. Lieutenant Moody led a patrol against the house. He kicked in the door and killed the officer in charge, then began a search through the trenches. Moody was killed by a bullet through his forehead. Lieutenant Salomon took command of the patrol. It moved down the trenches using white phosphorus grenades to clear out pillboxes.

Sgts. George Morrow and Julius Belcher spotted a machine gun that was enfilading the western end of Omaha Beach, one of those guns that had killed so many rangers an hour earlier. It was firing continuously down at the beach again, as the follow-up waves attempted to get across the sand. In a pitiless rage, Belcher ran toward the position, oblivious of his own safety. He kicked in the door of the pillbox and threw in a white phosphorus grenade. As the phosphorus began to burn on their skins, the Germans abandoned their gun and ran out the door, screaming in agony. Belcher shot them down as they emerged.[12]

Not everyone was brave. Lieutenant Heaney recalled "an officer whose name I will not use. He had been one of the most physically active officers all during training. We all felt that he would be an outstanding combat soldier. But I found this officer in the bottom of a slit trench crying like a baby and totally unable to continue. Sergeant White assigned one of his men to bring him back to the beach for evacuation and this was the last I ever heard of him."[13]

Captain Goranson meanwhile had seen a section of men from the 116th Regiment landing just below the cliff (it was a kilometer off course). He sent a ranger down to guide them to the top, providing C Company with its first reinforcements. The Germans were constantly reinforcing, bringing men in from the draw and the village via their communications trenches. There were far more German than American reinforcements. At Utah, the paratroopers prevented the Germans from sending reinforcements forward to the beach; at Omaha there were no paratroopers, and the Germans had freedom of movement behind the beach.

An all-day firefight ensued on the cliff to the west of the Vierville draw. Goranson was not strong enough to dislodge the Germans; his men would clear out a trench, move on, only to have fresh German troops reoccupy the position. Lieutenant Salomon was leading a "platoon" of three men. He described a typical action: "We proceeded further down the trench, around a curve. We came upon a German mortar crew in a fixed gun position. Some more grenades, more rifle and tommy-gun fire, as we continued through the trenches."[14] To Sergeant Scribner, it seemed that the day would never end.

Lieutenant Salomon despaired. Looking down on the beach below, he saw chaos. "Up until noon D-Day," he later commented, "I thought the invasion was a failure and I wondered if we could make a successful withdrawal and try the invasion some time again in the near future."[15]

For most of the rangers this was the first combat experience. It was a mark of how well they had been trained, and a textbook example of what training can accomplish, that they completely outfought the Germans in their fortified positions. They did so not by fighting regardless of loss but by using basic tactics carried out with enthusiasm balanced by proper caution. The next day a U.S. Army Quartermaster burial party reported the result: there were sixty-nine German dead in and around the fortified house and trench system, two American.

For C Company of the rangers and the section from the 116th, this was an isolated action. They were the only Americans on the west side of the Vierville draw. They were completely out of touch because all of the radios had been lost. They did get some help from the Navy, not always welcome. Unaware that the rangers were on the cliff, destroyers fired some 20mm and 5-inch guns on the position. Sergeant Scribner saw a 5-inch shell score a direct hit on a pillbox; he was amazed that it only "put in a dent about six inches deep. Those Germans really knew how to build their emplacements."

Sgt. William Lindsay was in a concrete pillbox when it received two direct hits from 5-inch shells. He lost a tooth and was knocked silly by the concussion. Three times during the day he had to be stopped by fellow rangers from walking off the cliff. That evening, he confronted Colonel Taylor of the 116th. Red-faced, cursing, he accused Taylor of stealing his rifle. All the while he had the rifle slung over his shoulder.[16] The incident gave the rangers who saw it a laugh (after Lindsay recovered his senses, as he did in a few hours) and a certain sympathy for the Germans caught inside their casemates when 14-inch shells from the battleships exploded against them.

"I was worried as all hell on top of the cliff," Sgt. Charles Semchuck later said about the day, "just waiting for the Jerries to push us back into the Channel. They had the chance to do it. D-Day night, when we made contact with our A and B companies, my spirits and morale rose a hundred percent. . . . I felt like doing handsprings for I was so happy. I knew then that the Jerries had muffed their one chance for victory. I never again want to be in another D-Day." Sergeant Lutz echoed that last sentiment: "Brother, I say this, no more D-Days for me if I can help it!"[17]

C Company had not completed its mission. Indeed, it could be said it never even got started on its mission. Its action was minor in scale, a small-unit engagement of inconsequential size when measured by the number of men involved. Yet it was critical. By occupying the Germans on the west side of the Vierville draw and on the cliff, the rangers diverted some of the machine-gun fire that otherwise would have added to the carnage on the beach. By no means did the rangers do it alone, but without them the passage up the Vierville draw would have been, at best, even more costly; at worst, no Americans would have gotten up that draw on D-Day.

Companies A and B of the 2nd Rangers came in at 0740 on Dog Green; the 5th Ranger Battalion came in at 0750 on Dog White, to the east of the mouth of the Vierville draw. There they became, in effect, a part of the 116th Infantry, to the point that many of the ad hoc fighting units formed on the beach were composed of a mix of rangers and infantry from the 116th. Thus the experience of the rangers on the east side of the draw is best understood when told together with that of the 116th drive to the top of the bluff, as related in the following chapter.

The Allied bombardment of Pointe-du-Hoc had begun weeks before D-Day. Heavy bombers from the U.S. Eighth Air Force and British Bomber Command had repeatedly plastered the area, with a climax coming before dawn on June 6. Then the battleship *Texas* took up the action, sending dozens of 14-inch shells into the position. Altogether, Pointe-du-Hoc got hit by more than ten kilotons of high explosives, the equivalent of the explosive power of the atomic bomb used at Hiroshima. *Texas* lifted her fire at 0630, the moment the rangers were scheduled to touch down.

Colonel Rudder was in the lead boat. He was not supposed to be there. Lt. Gen. Clarence Huebner, CO of the 1st Division and in overall command at Omaha Beach, had forbidden Rudder to lead companies D, E, and F of the 2nd Rangers into Pointe-du-Hoc, saying, "We're not going to risk getting you knocked out in the first round."

"I'm sorry to have to disobey you, sir," Rudder had replied, "but if I don't take it, it may not go."[18]*

The rangers were in landing craft assault (LCA) boats manned by British seamen (the rangers had trained with British commandos and were therefore accustomed to working with British sailors). The LCA was built in England on the basic design of

---

* James W. Eikner, a lieutenant with Rudder on D-Day, comments in a letter of March 29, 1993, to the author: "The assault on the Pointe was supposed to be led by a recently promoted executive officer who unfortunately managed to get himself thoroughly drunk and unruly while still aboard his transport in Weymouth harbor. This was the situation that decided Col. Rudder to personally lead the Pointe-du-Hoc assault. The ex. ofc. was sent ashore and hospitalized—we never saw him again."

Andrew Higgins's boat, but the British added some light armor to the sides and gunwales. That made the LCA slower and heavier—the British were sacrificing mobility to increase security—which meant that the LCA rode lower in the water than the LCVP.

On D-Day morning, all the LCAs carrying the rangers took on water as spray washed over the sides. One of the ten boats swamped shortly after leaving the transport area, taking the CO of D Company and twenty men with it (they were picked up by an LCT a few hours later. "Give us some dry clothes, weapons and ammunition, and get us back in to the Pointe. We gotta get back!" Capt. "Duke" Slater said as he came out of the water. But his men were so numb from the cold water that the ship's physician ordered them back to England.[19]) One of the two supply boats bringing in ammunition and other gear also swamped; the other supply boat had to jettison more than half its load to stay afloat.

That was but the beginning of the foul-ups. At 0630, as Rudder's lead LCA approached the beach, he saw with dismay that the coxswain was headed toward Pointe-de-la-Percée, about half-way between the Vierville draw and Pointe-du-Hoc. After some argument, Rudder persuaded the coxswain to turn right to the objective. The flotilla had to fight the tidal current (the cause of the drift to the left) and proceeded only slowly parallel to the coast.

The error was costly. It caused the rangers to be thirty-five minutes late in touching down, which gave the German defenders time to recover from the bombardment, climb out of their dugouts, and man their positions. It also caused the flotilla to run a gauntlet of fire from German guns along four kilometers of coastline. One of the four DUKWs was sunk by a 20mm shell. Sgt. Frank South, a nineteen-year-old medic, recalled, "We were getting a lot of machine-gun fire from our left flank, alongside the cliff, and we could not, for the life of us, locate the fire."[20] Lt. James Eikner, Rudder's communications officer, remembered "bailing water with our helmets, dodging bullets, and vomiting all at the same time."[21]

USS *Satterlee* and HMS *Talybont*, destroyers, saw what was happening and came in close to fire with all guns at the Germans. That helped to drive some of the Germans back from the edge of the cliff. D Company had been scheduled to land on the west side of the point, but because of the error in navigation Rudder signaled by hand that the two LCAs carrying the remaining D Company troops join the other seven and land side by side along the east side.

Lt. George Kerchner, a platoon leader in D Company, recalled that when his LCA made its turn to head into the beach, "My thought was that this whole thing is a big mistake, that none of us were ever going to get up that cliff." But then the destroyers started firing and drove some of the Germans back from the edge of the cliff. Forty-eight years later, then retired Colonel Kerchner commented, "Some day I would love to meet up with somebody from *Satterlee* so I can shake his hand and thank him."[22]

The beach at Pointe-du-Hoc was only ten meters in width as the flotilla approached, and shrinking rapidly as the tide was coming in (at high tide there would be virtually no beach). There was no sand, only shingle. The bombardment from air and sea had brought huge chunks of the clay soil from the point tumbling down, making the rocks slippery but also providing an eight-meter buildup at the base of the cliff that gave the rangers something of a head start in climbing the forty-meter cliff.

The rangers had a number of ingenious devices to help them get to the top. One was twenty-five-meter extension ladders mounted in the DUKWs, provided by the London Fire Department. But one DUKW was already sunk, and the other three could not get a footing on the shingle, which was covered with wet clay and thus rather like greased ball bearings. Only one ladder was extended.

Sgt. William Stivison climbed to the top to fire his machine gun. He was swaying back and forth like a metronome, German tracers whipping about him. Lt. Elmer "Dutch" Vermeer described the scene: "The ladder was swaying at about a forty-five-degree angle—both ways. Stivison would fire short bursts as he passed over the cliff at the top of the arch, but the DUWK floundered so badly that they had to bring the fire ladder back down."[23]

The basic method of climbing was by rope. Each LCA carried three pairs of rocket guns, firing steel grapnels which pulled up either plain three-quarter-inch ropes, toggle ropes, or rope ladders. The rockets were fired just before touchdown. Grapnels with attached ropes were an ancient technique for scaling a wall or cliff, tried and proven. But in this case, the ropes had been soaked by the spray and in many cases were too heavy. Rangers watched with sinking hearts as the grapnels arched in toward the cliff, only to fall short from the weight of the ropes. Still, at least one grapnel and rope from each LCA made it; the grapnels grabbed the earth, and the dangling ropes provided a way to climb the cliff.

To get to the ropes, the rangers had to disembark and cross the narrow strip of beach to the base of the cliff. To get there, the rangers had two problems to overcome. The first was a German machine gun on the rangers' left flank, firing across the beach. It killed or wounded fifteen men as it swept bullets back and forth across the beach.

Colonel Rudder was one of the first to make it to the beach. With him was Col. Travis Trevor, a British commando who had assisted in the training of the rangers. He began walking the beach, giving encouragement. Rudder described him as "a great big [six feet four inches], black-haired son of a gun—one of those staunch Britishers." Lieutenant Vermeer yelled at him, "How in the world can you do that when you are being fired at?"

"I take two short steps and three long ones," Trevor replied, "and they always miss me." Just then a bullet hit him in the helmet and drove him to the ground. He got up and shook his fist at the machine gunner, hollering, "You dirty son of a bitch." After that, Vermeer noted, "He crawled around like the rest of us."[24]

The second problem for the disembarking rangers was craters, caused by bombs or shells that had fallen short of the cliff. They were underwater and could not be seen. "Getting off the ramp," Sergeant South recalled, "my pack and I went into a bomb crater and the world turned completely to water." He inflated his Mae West and made it to shore.

Lieutenant Kerchner was determined to be first off his boat. He thought he was going into a meter or so of water as he hollered "OK, let's go" and jumped. He went in over his head, losing his rifle. He started to swim in, furious with the British coxswain. The men behind him saw what had happened and jumped to the sides. They hardly got their feet wet. "So instead of being the first one ashore, I was one of the last ashore from my boat. I wanted to find somebody to help me cuss out the British navy, but everybody was busily engrossed in their own duties so I couldn't get any sympathy."

Two of his men were hit by the machine gun enfilading the beach. "This made me very angry because I figured he was shooting at me and I had nothing but a pistol." Kerchner picked up a dead ranger's rifle. "My first impulse was to go after this machine gun up there, but I immediately realized that this was rather stupid as our mission was to get to the top of the cliff and get on with destroying those guns.

"It wasn't necessary to tell this man to do this or that man to do that," Kerchner said. "They had been trained, they had the order in which they were supposed to climb the ropes and the men were all moving right in and starting to climb up the cliff." Kerchner went down the beach to report to Colonel Rudder that the D Company commander's LCA had sunk. He found Rudder starting to climb one of the rope ladders.

"He didn't seem particularly interested in me informing him that I was assuming command of the company. He told me to get the hell out of there and get up and climb my rope." Kerchner did as ordered. He found climbing the cliff "very easy," much easier than some of the practice climbs back in England.[25]

The machine gun and the incoming tide gave Sgt. Gene Elder "a certain urgency" to get off the beach and up the cliff. He and his squad freeclimbed as they were unable to touch the cliff. When they reached the top "I told them, 'Boys, keep your heads down, because headquarters has fouled up again and has issued the enemy live ammunition.' "[26]

Other rangers had trouble getting up the cliff. "I went up about, I don't know, forty, fifty feet," Pvt. Sigurd Sundby remembered. "The rope was wet and kind of muddy. My hands just couldn't hold, they were like grease, and I came sliding back down. As I was going down, I wrapped my foot around the rope and slowed myself up as much as I could, but still I burned my hands. If the rope hadn't been so wet, I wouldn't have been able to hang on for the burning.

"I landed right beside Sweeney there, and he says, 'What's the matter, Sundby, chicken? Let me—I'll show you how to climb.' So he went up first and I was right up after him, and when I got to the top, Sweeney says, 'Hey, Sundby, don't forget to zigzag.' "[27]

Sgt. William "L-Rod" Petty, who had the reputation of being one of the toughest of the rangers, a man short on temper and long on aggressiveness, also had trouble with a wet and muddy rope. As he slipped to the bottom, Capt. Walter Block, the medical officer, said to Petty, "Soldier, get up that rope to the top of the cliff." Petty turned to Block, stared him square in the face, and said, "I've been trying to get up this goddamned rope for five minutes and if you think you can do any better you can f—ing well do it yourself." Block turned away, trying to control his own temper.[28]

Germans on the top managed to cut two or three of the

ropes, while others tossed grenades over the cliff, but BAR men at the base and machine-gun fire from *Satterlee* kept most of them back from the edge. They had not anticipated an attack from the sea, so their defensive positions were inland. In addition, the rangers had tied pieces of fuse to the grapnels and lit them just before firing the rockets; the burning fuses made the Germans think that the grapnels were some kind of weapon about to explode, which kept them away.

Within five minutes, rangers were at the top; within fifteen minutes, most of the fighting men were up. One of the first to make it was a country preacher from Tennessee, Pvt. Ralph Davis, a dead shot with a rifle and cool under pressure. When he got up, he dropped his pants and took a crap. "The war had to stop for awhile until 'Preacher' could get organized," one of his buddies commented.[29]

As the tide was reducing the beach to almost nothing, and because the attack from the sea—although less than 200 rangers strong—was proceeding, Colonel Rudder told Lieutenant Eikner to send the code message "Tilt." That told the floating reserve of A and B companies, 2nd Rangers, and the 5th Ranger Battalion, to land at Omaha Beach instead of Pointe-du-Hoc. Rudder expected them to pass through Vierville and attack Pointe-du-Hoc from the eastern, landward side.

On the beach, there were wounded who needed attention. Sergeant South had barely got ashore when "the first cry of 'Medic!' went out and I shrugged off my pack, grabbed my aid kit, and took off for the wounded man. He had been shot in the chest. I was able to drag him in closer to the cliff. I'd no sooner taken care of him than I had to go to another and another and another." Captain Block set up an aid station.[30]

"As I got over the top of the cliff," Lieutenant Kerchner recalled, "it didn't look anything at all like what I thought it was going to look like." The rangers had studied aerial photos and maps and sketches and sand table mock-ups of the area, but the bombardment from air and sea had created a moonscape: "It was just one large shell crater after the other."[31]

Fifty years later, Pointe-du-Hoc remains an incredible, overwhelming sight. It is hardly possible to say which is more impressive, the amount of reinforced concrete the Germans poured to build their casemates or the damage done to them and the craters created by the bombs and shells. Huge chunks of concrete, as big as houses, are scattered over the kilometer-square area, as if the gods were playing dice. The tunnels and trenches were mostly obliterated, but enough of them still exist to give an idea of how much work went into building the fortifications. Some railroad tracks remain in the underground portions; they were for handcarts used to move ammunition. There is an enormous steel fixture that was a railroad turntable.

Surprisingly, the massive concrete observation post at the edge of the cliff remains intact. It was the key to the whole battery; from it one has a perfect view of both Utah and Omaha beaches; German artillery observers in the post had radio and underground telephone communication with the casemates.

The craters are as big as ten meters across, a meter or two deep, some even deeper. They number in the hundreds. They were a godsend to the rangers, for they provided plenty of immediate cover. Once on top, rangers could get to a crater in seconds, then begin firing at the German defenders.

What most impresses tourists at Pointe-du-Hoc—who come today in the thousands, from all over the world—is the sheer cliff and the idea of climbing up it by rope. What most impresses military professionals is the way the rangers went to work once they got on top. Despite the initial disorientation, they quickly recovered and went about their assigned tasks. Each platoon had a specific mission, to knock out a specific gun emplacement. The men got on it without being told.

Germans were firing sporadically from the trenches and regularly from the machine-gun position on the eastern edge of the fortified area and from a 20mm antiaircraft gun on the western edge, but the rangers ignored them to get to the casemates.

When they got to the casemates, to their amazement they found that the "guns" were telephone poles. Tracks leading inland indicated that the 155mm cannon had been removed recently, almost certainly as a result of the preceding air bombardment. The rangers never paused. In small groups, they began moving inland toward their next objective, the paved road that connected Grandcamp and Vierville, to set up roadblocks to prevent German reinforcements from moving to Omaha.

Lieutenant Kerchner moved forward and got separated from his men. "I remember landing in this zigzag trench. It was the deepest trench I'd ever seen. It was a narrow communications trench, two feet wide but eight feet deep. About every twenty-five yards it would go off on another angle. I was by myself and I never felt so lonesome before or since, because every time I came to an angle I didn't know whether I was going to come face to face with a German or not." He was filled with a sense of anxiety and hurried to get to the road to join his men "because I felt a whole lot better when there were other men around."

Kerchner followed the trench for 150 meters before it finally ran out near the ruins of a house on the edge of the fortified area. Here he discovered that Pointe-du-Hoc was a self-contained fort in itself, surrounded on the land side with minefields, barbed-wire entanglements, and machine-gun emplacements. "This is where we began running into most of the German defenders, on the perimeter."[32]

Other rangers had made it to the road, fighting all the way, killing Germans, taking casualties. The losses were heavy. In Kerchner's D Company, only twenty men were on their feet, out of the seventy who had started out in the LCAs. Two company commanders were casualties; lieutenants were now leading D and E. Capt. Otto Masny led F Company. Kerchner checked with the three COs and learned that all the guns were missing. "So at this stage we felt rather disappointed, not only disappointed but I felt awfully lonesome as I realized how few men we had there."

The lieutenants decided that there was no reason to go back to the fortified area and agreed to establish a perimeter around the road "and try to defend ourselves and wait for the invading force that had landed on Omaha Beach to come up."[33]

At the base of the cliff at around 0730, Lieutenant Eikner sent out a message by radio: "Praise the Lord." It signified that the rangers were on top of the cliff.[34]

At 0745, Colonel Rudder moved his command post up to the top, establishing it in a crater on the edge of the cliff. Captain Block also climbed a rope to the top and set up his aid station in a two-room concrete emplacement. It was pitch black and cold inside; Block worked by flashlight in one room, using the other to hold the dead.

Sergeant South remembered "the wounded coming in at a rapid rate, we could only keep them on litters stacked up pretty closely. It was just an endless, endless process. Periodically I would go out and bring in a wounded man from the field, leading one back, and ducking through the various shell craters. At one time, I went out to get someone and was carrying him back on my shoulders when he was hit by several other bullets and killed."[35]

The fighting within the fortified area was confused and confusing. Germans would pop up here, there, everywhere, fire a few rounds, then disappear back underground. Rangers could not keep contact with each other. Movement meant crawling.* There was nothing resembling a front line. Germans were taken prisoner; so were some rangers. In the observation post, a few Germans held out despite repeated attempts to overrun the position.

The worst problem was the machine gun on the eastern edge of the fortified area, the same gun that had caused so many casualties on the beach. Now it was sweeping back and forth over the battlefield whenever a ranger tried to move. Rudder told Lieutenant Vermeer to eliminate it.

Vermeer set out with a couple of men. "We moved through the shell craters and had just reached the open ground where the machine gun could cover us also when we ran into a patrol from F Company on the same mission. Once we ran out of shell holes and could see nothing but a flat 200-300 yards of open ground in front of us, I was overwhelmed with the sense that it would be impossible to reach our objective without heavy losses." The heaviest weapon the rangers had was a BAR, hardly effective over that distance.[36]

Fortunately, orders came from Rudder to hold up a moment. An attempt was going to be made to shoot the machine gun off the edge of that cliff with guns from a destroyer. That had not been tried earlier because the shore-fire-control party, headed by Capt. Johnathan Harwood from the artillery and Navy Lt. Kenneth Norton, had been put out of action by a short shell. But by now Lieutenant Eikner was on top and he had brought with him an old World War I signal lamp with shutters on it. He thought he could contact the *Satterlee* with it. Rudder told him to try.

Eikner had trained his men in the international Morse code on the signal lamp "with the idea that we might just have a need for them. I can recall some of the boys fussing about having to lug this old outmoded equipment on D-Day. It was tripod-mounted, a dandy piece of equipment with a telescopic sight and a tracking

* Pvt. Robert Fruling said he spent two and a half days at Pointe-du-Hoc, all of it crawling on his stomach. He returned on the twenty-fifth anniversary of D-Day "to see what the place looked like standing up" (Louis Lisko interview, EC).

device to stay lined up with a ship. We set it up in the middle of the shell-hole command post and found enough dry-cell batteries to get it going. We established communications and used the signal lamp to adjust the naval gunfire. It was really a lifesaver for us at a very critical moment."

Satterlee banged away at the machine-gun position. After a couple of adjustments, Satterlee's 5-inch guns blew it off the cliffside. Eikner then used the lamp to ask for help in evacuating wounded; a whaleboat came in but could not make it due to intense German fire.[37]

The rangers were cut off from the sea. With the Vierville draw still firmly in German hands, they were getting no help from the land side. With the radios out of commission, they had no idea how the invasion elsewhere was going. The rangers on Pointe-du-Hoc were isolated. They had taken about 50 percent casualties.

A short shell from British cruiser Glasgow had hit next to Rudder's command post. It killed Captain Harwood, wounded Lieutenant Norton, and knocked Colonel Rudder off his feet. Lieutenant Vermeer was returning to the CP when the shell burst. What he saw he never forgot: "The hit turned the men completely yellow. It was as though they had been stricken with jaundice. It wasn't only their faces and hands, but the skin beneath their clothes and the clothes which were yellow from the smoke of that shell—it was probably a colored marker shell."

Rudder recovered quickly. Angry, he went out hunting for snipers, only to get shot in the leg. Captain Block treated the wound; thereafter Rudder stayed in his CP, more or less, doing what he could to direct the battle. Vermeer remarked that "the biggest thing that saved our day was seeing Colonel Rudder controlling the operation. It still makes me cringe to recall the pain he must have endured trying to operate with a wound through the leg and the concussive force he must have felt from the close hit by the yellow-colored shell. He was the strength of the whole operation."[38]

On his return trip in 1954, Rudder pointed to a buried blockhouse next to his CP. "We got our first German prisoner right here," he told his son. "He was a little freckle-faced kid who looked like an American. . . . I had a feeling there were more of them around, and I told the rangers to lead this kid ahead of them. They just started him around this corner when the Germans opened up out of the entrance and he fell dead, right here, face down with his hands still clasped on the top of his head."[39]

• •

Out by the paved road, the fighting went on. It was close quarters, so close that when two Germans who had been hiding in a deep shelter hole jumped to their feet, rifles ready to fire, Sergeant Petty was right between them. Petty threw himself to the ground, firing his BAR as he did so—but the bullets went between the Germans, who were literally at his side. The experience so unnerved them they threw their rifles down, put their hands in the air, and called out "Kamerad, Kamerad." A buddy of Petty's who was behind him commented dryly, "Hell, L-Rod, that's a good way to save ammunition—just scare 'em to death."[40]

In another of the countless incidents of that battle, Lt. Jacob Hill spotted a German machine gun behind a hedgerow just beyond the road. It was firing in the general direction of some hidden rangers. Hill studied the position for a few moments, then stood up and shouted, "You bastard sons of bitches, you couldn't hit a bull in the ass with a bass fiddle!" As the startled Germans spun their gun around, Hill lobbed a grenade into the position and put the gun out of action.[41]

The primary purpose of the rangers was not to kill Germans or take prisoners, but to get those 155mm cannon. The tracks leading out of the casemates and the effort the Germans were making to dislodge the rangers indicated that they had to be around somewhere.

By 0815 there were about thirty-five rangers from companies D and E at the perimeter roadblock. Within fifteen minutes another group of twelve from Company F joined up. Excellent soldiers, those rangers—they immediately began patrolling.

There was a dirt road leading south (inland). It had heavy tracks. Sgts. Leonard Lomell and Jack Kuhn thought the missing guns might have made the tracks. They set out to investigate. At about 250 meters (one kilometer inland), Lomell abruptly stopped. He held his hand out to stop Kuhn, turned and half whispered, "Jack, here they are. We've found 'em. Here are the goddamned guns."

Unbelievably, the well-camouflaged guns were set up in battery, ready to fire in the direction of Utah Beach, with piles of ammunition around them, but no Germans. Lomell spotted about a hundred Germans a hundred meters or so across an open field, apparently forming up. Evidently they had pulled back during the bombardment, for fear of a stray shell setting off the ammunition dump, and were now preparing to man their guns, but they were in no hurry, for until their infantry drove off the rangers and reoccupied the observation post they could not fire with any accuracy.

Lomell never hesitated. "Give me your grenades, Jack," he said to Kuhn. "Cover me. I'm gonna fix 'em." He ran to the guns and set off thermite grenades in the recoil and traversing mechanisms of two of the guns, disabling them. He bashed in the sights of the third gun.

"Jack, we gotta get some more thermite grenades." He and Kuhn ran back to the highway, collected all of the thermite grenades from the rangers in the immediate area, returned to the battery, and disabled the other three guns.

Meanwhile Sgt. Frank Rupinski, leading a patrol of his own, had discovered a huge ammunition dump some distance south of the battery. It too was unguarded. Using high-explosive charges, the rangers detonated it. A tremendous explosion occurred as the shells and powder charges blew up, showering rocks, sand, leaves, and debris on Lomell and Kuhn. Unaware of Rupinski's patrol, Lomell and Kuhn assumed that a stray shell had hit the ammo dump. They withdrew as quickly as they could and sent word back to Rudder by runner that the guns had been found and destroyed.[42]

And with that, the rangers had completed their offensive mission. It was 0900. Just that quickly, they were now on the defensive, isolated, with nothing heavier than 60mm mortars and BARs to defend themselves.

In the afternoon, Rudder had Eikner send a message—via his signal lamp and homing pigeon—via the *Satterlee*: "Located Pointe-du-Hoc—mission accomplished—need ammunition and reinforcement—many casualties."[43]

An hour later, *Satterlee* relayed a brief message from General Huebner: "No reinforcements available—all rangers have landed [at Omaha]."[44] The only reinforcements Rudder's men received in the next forty-eight hours were three paratroopers from the 101st who had been misdropped and who somehow made it through German lines to join the rangers, and two platoons of rangers from Omaha. The first arrived at 2100. It was a force of twenty-three men led by Lt. Charles Parker. On the afternoon of June 7 Maj. Jack Street brought in a landing craft and took off wounded and prisoners. After putting them aboard an LST he took the craft to Omaha Beach and rounded up about twenty men from the 5th Ranger Battalion and brought them to Pointe-du-Hoc.

The Germans were as furious as disturbed hornets; they counterattacked the fortified area throughout the day, again that night, and through the next day. The rangers were, in fact, under siege, their situation desperate. But as Sgt. Gene Elder recalled, they stayed calm and beat off every attack. "This was due to our rigorous training. We were ready. For example, Sgt. Bill Stivinson [who had started D-Day morning swaying back and forth on the London Fire Department ladder] was sitting with Sgt. Guy Shoff behind some rock or rubble when Guy started to swear and Bill asked him why. Guy replied, 'They are shooting at me.' Stivinson asked how he knew. Guy's answer was, 'Because they are hitting me.' "[45]

Pvt. Salva Maimone recalled that on D-Day night "one of the boys spotted some cows. He went up and milked one. The milk was bitter, like quinine. The cows had been eating onions."[46]

Lieutenant Vermeer said he could "still distinctly remember when it got to be twelve o'clock that night, because the 7th of June was my birthday. I felt that if I made it until midnight, I would survive the rest of the ordeal. It seemed like some of the fear left at that time."[47]

The rangers took heavy casualties. A number of them were taken prisoner. By the end of the battle only fifty of the more than 200 rangers who had landed were still capable of fighting. But they never lost Pointe-du-Hoc.

Later, writers commented that it had all been a waste, since the guns had been withdrawn from the fortified area around Pointe-du-Hoc. That is wrong. Those guns were in working condition before Sergeant Lomell got to them. They had an abundance of ammunition. They were in range (they could lob their huge shells 25,000 meters) of the biggest targets in the world, the 5,000-plus ships in the Channel and the thousands of troops and equipment on Utah and Omaha beaches.

Lieutenant Eikner was absolutely correct when he concluded his oral history, "Had we not been there we felt quite sure that those guns would have been put into operation and they would have brought much death and destruction down on our men on the beaches and our ships at sea. But by 0900 on D-Day morning the big guns had been put out of commission and the paved highway had been cut and we had roadblocks denying its use to the enemy. So by 0900 our mission was accomplished. The rangers at Pointe-du-Hoc were the first American forces on D-Day to accomplish their mission and we are proud of that."[48]

22

UP THE BLUFF AT VIERVILLE

The 116th Regiment and 5th Ranger Battalion

At 0830 all landing ceased at Omaha Beach. The men already ashore were going to have to move out, attack German positions, reduce the murderous fire coming in on the beach, secure the high ground, move inland, come down from behind to drive the Germans from their entrenchments around draws, then blow the cement roadblock and clear paths before vehicle traffic could move off the beach and up the draw.

The men already ashore would have to do these jobs without land-based artillery support and without reinforcements of men or supplies. This was the moment Eisenhower had feared above all others. The Americans had a sizable force ashore, about 5,000 fighting men, but because they were now cut off from the sea they were as much potential hostages as potential offensive threat.

This was the moment Rommel had anticipated above all others. His enemy was caught half on, half off, unable to reinforce or withdraw. And unable to advance, apparently, so strong were the defenses at the exits from the beach. The Overlord plan had called for the exits to be open by 0730. At 0830, they remained sealed shut and unapproachable.

The Americans on the beach had just been through a baptism of fire that was heart-stopping. They were at 50 percent strength or less, without unit cohesion. They were exhausted, frightened, confused, wounded.

To a watching German, they looked like beaten troops. When the landings stopped at 0830 the commander of *Widerstandsnest* 76, a fortified position near Vierville, reported by phone to 352nd Division HQ: "At the water's edge at low tide near St.-Laurent and Vierville the enemy is in search of cover behind the coastal obstacles. A great many vehicles—among these ten tanks—stand burning at the beach. The obstacle demolition squads have given up their activity. Debarkation from the landing boats has ceased, the boats keep farther seaward. The fire of our strong points and artillery was well placed and has inflicted considerable casualties among the enemy. A great many wounded and dead lie on the beach."[1]

That was the view from above. The view from offshore was similar. The half-tracks, jeeps, and trucks that had survived the difficulties of getting close enough and unloading under artillery fire found themselves on a narrowing strip of sand without any open exits through the impassable shingle embankment. Sailors could see the vehicles immobilized by engine trouble or artillery hits. Those capable of movement were immobilized by the hopeless traffic jam. The vehicles were sitting targets for German artillery and mortar fire.

But even as the landings ceased, individuals and groups were moving off the beach and up the bluff between the Vierville and Les Moulins exits. Others began to follow. They had the support of the destroyers and of the surviving tanks on the beach, but mainly they were on their own.

As always in war, the infantry (in this case including engineers, Coast Guard, artillery observers, Seabees, and other specialists acting as ad hoc infantry) got stuck with war at its cutting edge, where it is at its most shocking, dangerous, and decisive. The most extreme experience a human being can go through is being a combat infantryman, and nowhere in World War II was the combat more extreme than at Omaha in the early morning hours of June 6.

The 116th Regiment and the 5th Ranger Battalion (plus two companies from the 2nd Rangers) experienced war at its most horrible, demanding, and challenging. They were on the right (western) half of the beach. The 116th was a Virginia National Guard outfit, part of an ordinary infantry division. The 5th Ranger Battalion was an elite, all-volunteer force. How they responded to this crisis, with the fate of Omaha Beach and perhaps the invasion as a whole at stake, was testimony to the marvelous job General Marshall and all those old Regular Army officers and noncoms had done in turning these children of the Depression into first-class fighting men. Pvt. Felix Branham remarked at the end of his oral history, "I've heard people say we were lucky. It wasn't luck. When we landed on Omaha Beach, we were well trained, we had good leaders, and the Lord God Almighty was with us, and that's all I can say."

Branham also observed, "Each one of us had our own little battlefield. It was maybe forty–fifty yards wide. You might talk to a guy that pulled up right beside of me, within fifty feet of me, and he got an entirely different picture of D-Day."[2]

That was certainly the case on the right flank (and the left flank as well, as will be seen) at Omaha. Going up the bluff was often a lonely experience. Capt. Robert Walker went a third of the way up before he found a dead soldier from the 116th and was able to arm himself with an M-1 and protect himself with a helmet.

"At this point I could not see anyone from the 116th and I realized that I was alone and completely on my own." Walker decided to go to the top and proceed to the right, to the regimental assembly point at Vierville. "I passed many dead bodies, all facing forward." Near the top, he heard groans nearby. He investigated; it was a German soldier with a bad wound in his groin.

The German cried out for *wasser*. Walker replied, in German, that his canteen was empty. The German told Walker there was *ein born* (a spring), just over there. Sure enough, Walker found a delightful spring-fed pool with clear water. He filled his canteen and brought water to his enemy. Before continuing his own odyssey, looking for Germans to kill, Walker returned to the spring, refilled his canteen, went back to the wounded enemy soldier, and filled his canteen cup.

The wounded German was the only soldier from either side Walker saw on his climb up the bluff.[3] His isolation was unusual, possibly unique. Although few men saw any Germans until they got to the top of the bluff, most came up with buddies, in small groups. As soon as they got over the seawall and the flat and began to climb, they discovered they were in the safest place on Omaha Beach. The defilade and smoke from grass fires provided some coverage. Because they were between exits, they were in an area not so heavily defended as the draws. The German trenches were dug at angles to shoot flanking fire at the beach, not directly downward. There were folds and irregularities in the bluff to use to advantage.

Fire support for the advancing Americans, other than their own hand-held weapons, came from tanks and destroyers. The tanks were leading a hard life. They were caught on the sand between high water and the embankment, unable to get over the shingle to the beach flat, open targets for enemy guns. Still, they kept firing. One tank maintained its fire until the rising tide drowned out its cannon.

The 741st Tank Battalion report on D-Day noted: "The tanks continued to fire on targets of opportunity during the infiltration of the infantry, which was moving directly forward, making an assault on the bluff behind the beach. Due to the fact that exit Easy 3, which was to have been used as an exit from the beach by both infantry and tanks, was still in enemy hands and commanded by several artillery pieces, consisting mostly of 88mm guns, the infantry was forced to make their direct approach under the protecting fire of tank weapons."[4]

Maj. Sidney Bingham, CO of the 2nd Battalion, 116th, said that the tanks "saved the day. They shot the hell out of the Germans, and got the hell shot out of them."[5]

The same was true of the destroyers. Between them, the tankers and the sailors knocked out pillboxes as targets of opportunity and thus made it possible for the infantry to get up the bluff. But it was the infantry who had to do it.

Someone had to set an example to get the men started. That someone could be a general officer, a colonel, a major, a company commander, a platoon leader, or a squad leader. Medic Cecil Breeden remembered, "When I got to about where the 29th Memorial now stands, Colonel Canham, Colonel [John] Metcalfe, and some other officers had set up a command post. Canham was shot through the hand. I fixed it. A man came along looking for a noncom, saying there was a sniper up there. Metcalfe said that he wasn't a noncom but would he do? They both left going up the hill, bearing to the left."[6]*

General Cota was an inspiration. After leading a group to the base of the bluff and almost getting blown away by a barrage of mortar shells, he led a column of men up the bluff. They moved

---

* Metcalfe commanded the 1st Battalion, 116th Infantry. "I first saw him in Vierville, late on D-Day," Capt. John Raaen commented. "I was extremely impressed with his manner, his attitude, his knowledge. He was KIA shortly after D-Day." (Maj. Gen. John Raaen to author, March 12, 1993.)

slowly, following in Cota's footsteps, for fear of mines. Those mines imposed considerable delay in every sector. No one charged up the bluff; the Americans moved up cautiously, in single file.

Cota's group finally reached the top of the bluff above Hamel-au-Prêtre (a small group of beach villas blasted away by now), about midway between Vierville and St.-Laurent. Germans in trenches and behind hedgerows immediately brought Cota's force under crossed interlocking bands of machine-gun fire. Cota arranged the men into ad hoc fire and maneuver teams. He had one team lay down a steady stream of covering fire against the German positions and led others in a series of short rushes across the open fields. Dumbfounded by such aggressiveness, the Germans fled. This may have been the first effective American infantry attack in the campaign in northwest Europe.[7]

Cota came upon the dirt road that ran parallel to the beach. He turned right, toward Vierville. There was very little fire. In Vierville, the Americans met their first French civilians. There was no celebration, hardly an exchange of greetings; mostly, the Frenchmen and Americans stared at each other as the Americans moved through the village. On the west side of Vierville, Cota sent some rangers who had joined him in the direction of Pointe-du-Hoc. They encountered stiff resistance. When their attack bogged down, Cota hastened to the front of the column and assisted the platoon leader in the disposition of his forces.

C Company of the 116th, one of the few to fight intact on D-Day, came into Vierville. The men of the company remembered Cota walking down the narrow main street, twirling a pistol on his index finger like an Old West gunfighter. "Where the hell have you been, boys?" he asked.[8]

Colonel Canham came up. Cota sent him east, toward St.-Laurent, with orders to help clear the bluff so that others could climb up it. Then Cota, accompanied by his aide, Lieutenant Shea, and four riflemen, prepared to start down the Vierville draw, still held by the Germans. *Texas* was pounding away with her 14-inch guns at the cement roadblock at the mouth of the draw. Shea recalled that "the concussion from the bursts of these guns seemed to make the pavement of the street in Vierville actually rise beneath our feet in a bucking sensation." As Cota set off, Shea remarked that he hoped the firing would lift. Cota said he hoped not, as it would force the Germans to keep their heads down.

But the firing lifted, and Germans in a fortification on the east side of the draw began firing at Cota's little group. The riflemen responded. Five Germans, dazed from the bombardment, gave up. Cota ordered them to lead the way through the minefields down the draw. The group made it to the beach.

Ten days later, Lieutenant Shea wrote a report of Cota's actions after returning to the beach: "General Cota, though under constant sniper and machine-gun fire from the high ground beyond the beach, progressed eastward along the beach, herding and reorganizing tank units, engineer demolition units, supplies of demolitions, bulldozers, and in general directing units suffering from the initial confusion of landing under fire so that their efforts could be effectively bent toward the establishment of the beachhead."[9]

Despite the shelling from *Texas*, the concrete wall in front of the draw still blocked the movement of vehicles inland. "Can you blow up that antitank wall at the exit?" Cota asked an engineer colonel. It was fourteen feet thick at the base, twelve feet high, and six feet thick at the top.

"We can, sir, just as soon as the infantry clean out those pillboxes around there," the colonel replied.

"We just came down through there," declared Cota. "There's nothing to speak of there. Get to it!"

But the engineers did not have any TNT. Cota saw a bulldozer down the beach, piled high with explosives. He turned to a group of soldiers huddled at the seawall. "Who drives this thing?" he demanded. No answer. "Well, can anyone drive the damn thing?" Still no answer.

"They need TNT down at the exit," Cota said. "I just came through there from the rear. Nothing but a few riflemen on the cliff, and they're being cleaned up. Hasn't anyone got guts enough to drive it down?" A soldier stepped forward. "That's the stuff!" Cota called out.[10] The engineers blew the wall, but by no means did that open the draw. Engineers needed more bulldozers to clear an approach from the beach, to clear the rubble from the wall, to clear the mines, and to fill in the antitank ditch. They got to work.

Cota was accosted by a sailor whose LCT had been destroyed. Brandishing a rifle, he asked, "How in hell do you work one of these? This is just the goddamn thing that I wanted to avoid by joining the Navy—fighting like a goddamn foot soldier." And he started working his way up the bluff.[11]

Many men moved out on their own. Lt. Henry Seitzler was one of them. Seitzler was a forward observer for the Ninth Air

Force. With no radio, he had no specific assignment. He picked up a rifle and some grenades and became an infantryman. "I remember," he said in his oral history, and then paused. He apologized: "Pardon me if I stop every once in awhile. These things are so very real.

"Even after all these years I can see it again in my mind, just like it was happening right now. I went to the seawall and stuck my head up between machine-gun bursts to see what was going on. I looked right in the eyes of a young American. He was dead. His eyes were wide open. He was blond, crew-cut. I thought about his mother."

Looking back down the beach, Seitzler noticed that "Jerry would deliberately shoot the medics. I think that the hottest place in hell is reserved for the man that would do that." Turning back to face the bluff, Seitzler crossed the seawall and began to make his way to high ground.[12]

After dragging some wounded GIs off the beach, Pvt. Harry Parley found an opening in the barbed wire. "A few men had already gone through. I could see them picking their way up the slope. As I started up, I saw the white tape marking a safe path through the mines, and I also saw the price paid to mark that path. A couple of GIs had been blown to death and another was being attended to by a medic. As I passed, I could see that both his legs were gone and tourniquets were being applied. In the weeks that followed, I was to see much worse, but that particular memory remains with me still."

As Parley neared the top, a destroyer commenced firing at a pillbox on the crest. "I remember foolishly standing about forty feet below and watching in amazement the power and accuracy of the Navy fire landing just above me. It was like sitting in the very first row of a movie looking up at the screen."

Parley traded his BAR for an M-1 with another GI. "He wanted more firepower and I wanted less weight to carry. Finally reaching the top, I found an area entirely devoid of vegetation, marked by shell craters and covered by a maze of trenches, dugouts, and firing positions used by the Germans earlier in the morning."

Parley also saw his first enemy soldiers, two prisoners, hands on head, being passed back down the slope. They were Asians. (In general, the *Ost* soldiers in Wehrmacht uniforms tended to surrender as soon as GIs got near them. They were mainly in the trenches.

Ethnic Germans inside concrete fortifications tended to fight on.)[13]

Captain Sink, CO of HQ Company, 116th, landed at 0800 just east of Les Moulins draw. The beach "had its share of the dead, the dying, the wounded, and disorganized." HQ Company was supposed to be at the Vierville draw; Sink's orders were to proceed up that draw to the village to set up a regimental CP and assembly area. But Sink took one look and decided that lateral movement on the beach through the masses of men and equipment and heavy fire was out. He made an instant decision to breach the wire obstacles in his front, wade the swamp, climb the bluff, and proceed to Vierville along the dirt road. The regimental adjutant declined to accompany Sink; he took out his entrenching tool and started to dig in on the beach. Sink went ahead.

After wading through the swamp, Sink and Lieutenant Kelly found a path up the bluff. They passed an unoccupied gun emplacement located on a natural shelf about halfway up. Looking back, they could see the men of the company carefully working their way through the breach in the barbed wire and following up the path in single file.

Sink and Kelly came out in an open field at the top of the bluff, where they immediately came under small-arms fire. Advancing by creeping and crawling for several hundred feet, they reached a spot where it was safe to stand. Looking down the bluff, they were dismayed to discover that only six men were still climbing; the others had dropped back to the beach. Sink sent a runner to return to the beach, round up the men, and get them started again.

Sink and Kelly drew machine-gun fire from St.-Laurent. They fell back and encountered a group from 3rd Battalion, 116th, including the battalion CO, Lt. Col. Lawrence Meeks. It was 1000. Meeks ordered 3rd Battalion to move against St.-Laurent. Sink's mission was to establish the CP at Vierville, so he decided to return to the beach to get his missing men moving.[14]

Sgt. Warner Hamlett and some of his buddies from F Company, 116th, got over the seawall only to be held up at the base of the bluff by machine-gun fire from pillboxes. They tried to put them out of action by attaching TNT to long poles, but barbed wire surrounding the pillboxes kept the Americans from getting close enough to the positions to insert the explosive.

"We decided to run between the pillboxes and enter the trenches that connected the boxes. We entered those trenches, slipped behind the pillboxes, and threw grenades into them. After the explosion, we ran into the boxes to kill any survivors. Rows of pillboxes stood between us and the top of the bluff. Slowly, one by one, we advanced. The bravery and gallantry of the soldiers was beyond belief."

Hamlett was wounded in the leg and back. When he got to the top of the bluff, "Sergeant England told me to go back to the beach and get a medic to tag me so that I could be transported back to a hospital ship. As I painfully walked back to the beach, thousands of parts of bodies lined it. They were floating, heads, arms, legs. I realized what being in the first wave was all about."

Hamlett concluded his oral history, "I was in the hospital in England for two months. I was then sent back to the front lines. In all, I saw seven months of combat and was wounded twice more. I would do it all over again to stop someone like Hitler. I am Warner H. Hamlett."[15]

Companies A and B of the 2nd Rangers, along with the 5th Ranger Battalion, had alternate missions. If they got word by 0700 from Colonel Rudder ("Praise the Lord" was the signal) indicating that the 2nd Rangers had possession of Pointe-du-Hoc, they were to go in there and provide reinforcements. If they did not get the message, they were to go in at Dog Green and Dog White, proceed up the Vierville draw, turn right, and go overland to the aid of their comrades at Pointe-du-Hoc.

Lt. Col. Max Schneider of the rangers was in command. He delayed making his landing decision as long as possible. By 0715 he could delay no longer. His craft were midway between Pointe-du-Hoc and Vierville.

"Schneider had to choose," Capt. John Raaen, CO of HQ Company, 5th Rangers, wrote in a memoir. "Emotion ran high to go in and assist the 2nd at the Pointe, but our orders under the plan were to shift to Vierville [if the message was not received] and shift we did."

It was a critical and wise decision. The rangers provided badly needed support for the 116th at Vierville, and Rudder's men would soon accomplish the mission at the Pointe on their own.

Shortly after the craft made their turn toward the beach, Schneider got the message sent from Rudder's CP, "Praise the Lord." It came too late; Schneider was already committed.[16]

Companies A and B of the 2nd Rangers hit the beach first. Pvt. Jack Keating was in A Company. He recalled that as his LCA approached the beach, *Texas* was firing "right over our little old boat, and every time she fired it almost lifted our boat out of the water." The LCA came in at the boundary between Dog Green and Dog White, just east of the Vierville draw. No one had landed at that spot yet and it was still free of fire. The CO of A Company, Capt. Dick Merrill, called out, "Fellows, it's an unopposed landing."

The coxswain dropped the ramp and the Germans began firing. "The first few minutes in the water," Keating said, "I will never forget as long as I live. There were machine guns, rifle fire, mortar fire, 88s, and God knows what else. And it felt as though every German was aiming at me."

It took Keating a half hour to make his way to the beach. "It's not like in Hollywood," he commented. "The actors jump into the water and in three seconds they're charging up the beach. Well, it isn't like that."

When he finally struggled ashore, Keating got behind a tank with two buddies. "We got behind the engine to get some heat back into our bones and had our first cigarette on French soil."

After catching his breath, "I got my wits, as most everybody did, and realized now there's only one way to go, baby, and that's you gotta go in." As he moved across the beach, his musette bag was ripped open by a burst of machine-gun fire. "It ruined my cans of plums and peaches, my bars of candy, my K rations, cigarettes, everything was ruined."

On the beach, Keating encountered a captain from the 116th who had been shot in the head and twice through the chest "and he was still alive. He asked me if I would take him to the aid station down the beach. I said, 'There's only one way I can do it: I'll crawl. You get on my back and I'll crawl.' It was about 100 yards down the beach. I finally got him there."[17]

Colonel Schneider observed the landing efforts of the two companies. He saw that "it was a disaster." Captain Raaen commented, "Schneider was battlewise. He wasn't about to waste his battalion in a fruitless assault, so he made his second decision: he ordered the British crews to move east, parallel to the beach, until he found the relatively quiet Omaha Dog Red beach. There our two columns did by the right flank and our assault was on."[18]

Sgt. Victor Fast was Schneider's interpreter. In his view,

"Colonel Schneider's presence of mind and shrewd calculations—a Ranger mind working, not afraid to make a decision—saved a multitude of lives, maybe hundreds."[19]

The two companies from the 2nd Rangers had taken casualties almost as bad as the companies from the 116th, but the 5th Rangers got to the seawall with only six casualties out of some 450 men. Lt. Francis Dawson* of D Company described his experience: "The skipper made an abrupt turn to the left and a tremendous wave hit the craft and we were lifted over several obstacles. Then the ramp opened and I was out. Five days on ship had taken its toll on my legs. After standing for several hours with the sea pounding, my legs just would not move fast enough." But he made the seawall—which at that spot was constructed of wooden timbers—and sent a runner to inform Lt. George Miller, D Company CO, where his platoon was located.[20]

When Captain Raaen landed, "I saw a dismaying sight. Obstacles everywhere. Wounded and dead, lying in the sand. The crack of machine-gun fire passing us by. The puffs in the sand where bullets hit. Those awful 20mm antiaircraft cannon shells bursting overhead. And of course the artillery shells bursting around us."

Despite the fire, Raaen was able to trot ashore. Later, to his amazement, he found he had lost only one man from his company. He looked around "and at that point I realized that *no one* had left that part of the beach." The rangers had landed on a sector containing assault teams of the 116th whose men were shell-shocked, leaderless, unorganized. Fear had gripped them, and some of the rangers too. Raaen pointed to the seawall and called out, "Ranger headquarters, there!" Simultaneously, he tried to get his life belt off but could not. His radioman was beside him, "cringing with fear. I called him over and told him to cut it off."

"Oh, sure, Captain," the man replied. He stood up beside Raaen and cut it off. "From there on he was never afraid again, nor was I. I had seen in my first minute of combat what showing complete lack of fear could do for your men." There was another factor in the recovery. In general, the men cringing at the seawall were as confused as they were exhausted and shell-shocked. In the wrong sectors with none of their leaders present, they just did not

---

* Dawson stayed in the Army. He headed a Special Forces unit in Vietnam, where he made 125 night combat jumps. He retired as a colonel.

know what to do. On being given a specific assignment and carrying it out, most men got a grip on themselves and went on to do their duty.

Although the 5th Rangers had a much easier time coming in at around 0745 than the 116th had experienced at 0630, things were bad enough. As LCIs followed the rangers' LCAs to Dog White, German artillery began to pound the beach. Raaen saw an LCI ramp get hit by an 88 just as the flamethrower man stepped onto it. "In an instant the boat was a mass of flames. It was horrible to see. I looked away. There were other things to do."[21]

Father Joe Lacy was on the beach, tending to the wounded. Lacy was described by one ranger as a "small, old, fat Irishman." The rangers had insisted that he could never keep up with them in combat, but he had insisted on coming along. On the transport on the night of June 5-6, he told the rangers, "When you land on the beach and you get in there, I don't want to see anybody kneeling down and praying. If I do I'm gonna come up and boot you in the tail. You leave the praying to me and you do the fighting."

On the beach, men saw Father Lacy "go down to the water's edge and pull the dead, dying, and wounded from the water and put them in relatively protected positions. He didn't stop at that, but prayed for them and with them, gave comfort to the wounded and dying. A real man of God."[22]

When Lt. Jay Mehaffey reached the seawall he could hear only German fire, "and I had the impression that the invasion had failed and that all other Americans had been killed or captured. At that moment on Omaha Beach the invasion of France had ceased to exist and it was in effect a military disaster. The grand design of battalions achieving D-Day objectives had collapsed completely."[23]

But in fact the rangers were getting organized and to work. Captain Raaen saw an old sergeant set up a .30-cal water-cooled machine gun on a tripod. An engineer lieutenant in a green sweater was helping him, carrying water and ammunition. They set up, "the sergeant got behind it and began to traverse and search the bluff to our right front, and I could see troops from the 116th trying to fight their way up the bluffs. The sergeant was firing in support of their advance."

The engineer lieutenant was "absolutely oblivious to the German fire around him. He yelled down at the troops that were huddled up against the seawall, cowering, frightened, doing nothing and accomplishing nothing, 'You guys think you're soldiers?!' To no avail."

General Cota came down the beach. In the Hollywood version, he calls out "Rangers lead the way!" and off they charged. In the real thing, the battlefield noise was such that he couldn't be heard ten feet away. What he did was move from group to group. The first he encountered included Raaen, who recognized him (Cota's son was a West Point classmate of Raaen's). Raaen reported the location of Colonel Schneider's CP.

Cota started encouraging individuals and small groups to move out on their own, saying, "Don't die on the beaches, die up on the bluff if you have to die, but get off the beaches or you're sure to die." To Raaen, he said, "You men are rangers and I know you won't let me down."[24]

Cota found Schneider at his CP. Cota remained standing; Schneider stood upright to converse. According to one witness, Cota said, "We're counting on you rangers to lead the way." Sergeant Fast, Schneider's interpreter, remembered Cota saying, "I'm expecting the rangers to lead the way."[25]

Whatever Cota's exact words, the motto of the Rangers became "Rangers lead the way." It is a valid motto, well earned, but insofar as it implies that it was necessary for the rangers to be inspired to lead, it needs some correcting.

The rangers did not feel that they needed a kick in the butt from Cota. "There was little or no apprehension about going through the wire and up the hill," Cpl. Gale Beccue of B Company, 5th Rangers, remembered. "We had done that in training so many times that it was just a matter of course." He and a private went about their business; they shoved a bangalore torpedo under the barbed wire and blew gaps, then started up. They encountered little opposition: "The German forward positions had been pulling back to prepare rear positions." Meanwhile, German artillery was concentrating on the follow-up landing craft, making it "a lot worse on the beach than when we had landed."[26]

As for the implication in the Ranger motto that it took rangers to lead the 116th off the beach, the fact is that the first organized company to the top at Vierville was Company C, 116th. By the time the rangers landed, many other individuals from the 116th had gone up. They preceded the rangers. The members of the 116th still at the seawall came from those companies that had been decimated in the first wave. Although they seemed helpless, they were just waiting for someone to tell them what to do, and give them some equipment—they had no bangalore torpedoes, no BARs, no machine guns, no radios, no officers—and some support. When the platoon leaders from the rangers started moving, they joined in. It is a small point, and the Rangers certainly had no intention of casting aspersions on the 116th when they adopted their motto, but it rankles with some of the survivors of the 116th.

As Captain Raaen crossed through the gap in the barbed wire, leading his men, he recalled, "There was little Tony Vullo, the smallest man in the battalion, lying across a ruined pillbox with his trousers down, having his gluteus maximus treated for a bullet wound." He had been shot by a single bullet at such an angle that he had four separate bullet holes in his butt. "Of course, the men enjoyed ribbing him as we went by."[27]

For some, going up the bluff was relatively safe. Lieutenant Dawson and his platoon from D Company of the 5th Rangers were among those. He reached the top, then turned parallel to the beach and began moving along the crest in a bent-over position, shooting or throwing grenades down on the Germans in the trenches below him.*

Captain Raaen's headquarters company was held up by machine-gun fire. Lieutenant Dawson could see the German firing position. It was seventy-five meters away, on the military crest of the bluff, and held two men. Dawson motioned for his BAR man to come forward, but the German machine gunners spotted his movement, turned on him, and killed him.

Dawson retrieved the BAR and attacked the German position, firing from the hip as he did so. The two terrified Germans jumped out of the pillbox and began to flee up the bluff. Dawson cut them down.

That freed Raaen. He moved on up and encountered heavy smoke from a brushfire. "Captain, can we put on our gas masks?" one of the men called out.

Raaen doubted that it was necessary but reluctantly gave permission. As the smoke thickened, he decided to put on his own. He took his helmet off, put it between his knees, with his left hand

---

* Most of the men who got to the top that morning tended to move straight inland to their assembly point at Vierville. Had more of them done as Dawson did, the 1st and 29th divisions and supporting units would have gotten off the beach much sooner.

ripped open the cover of the gas-mask bag, and pulled out the mask. He had forgotten about the apple and orange he had stuffed in the bag; they went bouncing down the bluff.

He put on his mask, took a deep breath, "and nearly died. I had forgotten to pull the plug on the front that allowed the air to come through. I had to rip off my mask, take a couple more gasps of smoke, put the mask back on, rip off the tab, and I could breathe easily. I reorganized myself, took two steps, and I was out of the smoke. I was so furious that I kept my mask on for about ten or twenty more feet just to punish myself for having weakened and put on the mask."[28]

Pvt. Carl Weast was in the area. He heard someone holler "Gas!" Weast put on his mask, but he had cracked the edge of his facepiece and could tell by smell that it was only grass smoke, "so I took my damn gas mask off and threw it away. That's the last time during the entire war that I ever carried a damn gas mask."[29]

As Colonel Schneider's HQ group went up the bluff it ran into German prisoners coming down. Schneider told his interpreter, Sergeant Fast, to find out what he could from them. Fast had no training in this sort of thing, but he proved to be a natural at it.

"I picked the youngest, most timid-looking, lowest-ranking Kraut I could find." He moved him away from the others and informed the prisoner, "You are going to tell me what I want to know." Then Fast told the prisoner to relax, "For you the war is over." Then he made threats: "You have three choices. Tell me nothing at all and I'll send you over to the Russians. Give me information and if you leave any doubt in my mind that you're telling the truth I'll turn you over to my Jewish buddy standing here next to me and he'll take you behind that bush over there." (Fast said in his oral history that the Jewish buddy was Herb Epstein, "and he had not shaved for a couple of days, he was big and burly, I remember he had a .45 on his hip and a ranger knife in his boot, and an automatic tommy gun.")

"Third, if you tell me what you know and convince me you are telling the truth I'll send you to America and you will have a good life until the war is won and then you'll get to go home."

Then the first question: "Did you see all the American and British bombers overhead earlier this morning?"

"*Ja,*" the prisoner replied. Good, Fast thought, now he is in a yes mood. The prisoner went on to indicate the position of minefields and pointed out hidden fortifications along the bluff. He said there were no German troops in Vierville (which was true) but there were "many" stationed inland, and gave other useful information.[30]

Schneider's HQ group got to the top, as did other rangers to the left and right. What they could see was an open field and a maze of hedgerows. Germans with machine guns were firing from behind the bushes.

Private Weast was furious. He wanted to know, "Where the hell was this Air Force bombardment that was supposed to blow all this stuff out of there. Hell, I didn't see a bomb crater nowhere! Nowhere did I see a bomb crater."[31]

The Army's official history states, "The penetrations of the beach defenses made between 0800-0900 represented a definite success achieved by determined action in the face of great difficulties."[32]

The penetrations had been made by about 600 men, mainly from C Company, 116th, and the rangers. They had penetrated and made it to the top—but they had no radios, no heavy weapons, no tanks, no supporting artillery, no way to communicate with the Navy. All the exits were still blocked, the beach was still jammed with vehicles that could not move, taking heavy artillery fire. The reserve regiments were not coming ashore.

The 116th and the rangers were still on their own. They were mixed together. Moving toward the Germans in the hedgerows, encountering fire, moving to outflank the positions, the ad hoc assault groups tended to split up, resulting in progressive loss of control as movement proceeded inland. When Colonel Canham reached the top, shortly after 0900, and set up his CP, he found rangers and 116th elements scattered all through the field ahead, some headed for the coastal road to Vierville, some engaged in firefights with Germans in the bushes.

The situation was by no means under control. A victory had not yet been won. But there was now a sizable American force on top of the bluff. The battle for Omaha Beach had not gone according to plan, but thanks to men like General Cota, Colonels Schneider and Canham, Captains Raaen and Dawson, and innumerable lieutenants and noncoms, disaster had been averted.

23

CATASTROPHE CONTAINED

Easy Red Sector, Omaha Beach

"OMAHA BEACH," General Bradley wrote three decades after D-Day, "was a nightmare. Even now it brings pain to recall what happened there on June 6, 1944. I have returned many times to honor the valiant men who died on that beach. They should never be forgotten. Nor should those who lived to carry the day by the slimmest of margins. Every man who set foot on Omaha Beach that day was a hero."[1]

Bradley's command post was a twenty-by-ten-foot steel cabin built for him on the deck of the cruiser USS *Augusta*. The walls were dominated by Michelin motoring maps of Normandy. There was a plotting table in the center of the room, with clerks at typewriters along one side. Bradley was seldom there; he spent most of the morning on the bridge, standing beside Adm. Alan G. Kirk, the Western Naval Task Force commander. Bradley had cotton in his ears to muffle the blast of *Augusta*'s guns, binoculars to his eyes to observe the shore.[2]

For Bradley, it was "a time of grave personal anxiety and frustration." He couldn't see much except smoke and explosions. He was getting no reports from his immediate subordinate, Maj. Gen. Leonard Gerow, commander of V Corps (1st and 29th divisions), no news from the beach, only scattered bits of information from landing-craft skippers returning to the transport area for another load, and they were muttering words like "disaster," "terrible casualties," and "chaos."

"I gained the impression," Bradley later wrote, "that our forces had suffered an irreversible catastrophe, that there was little hope we could force the beach. Privately, I considered evacuating the beachhead. . . . I agonized over the withdrawal decision, praying that our men could hang on."[3]

Those were the thoughts of a desperate man faced with two apparently hopeless options. At 0930, with the tide rushing in to fully cover all the obstacles, and with hundreds of landing craft circling offshore, while the congestion on the beach was still so bad that all landings were still suspended, sending in the follow-up waves as reinforcements according to the planning schedule would only add to the problem—but not sending them in would leave the forces already ashore isolated and vulnerable to a counterattack.

Bradley's private thoughts notwithstanding, as for retreat, "It would have been impossible to have brought these people back," as General Eisenhower flatly and rightly declared.[4] With almost no radios functioning, there was no way to recall the men from the 116th and 16th regiments and the rangers who were already—although unknown to Bradley or any other senior officer—making their way up the bluff. The men at the shingle could have been ordered to fall back to the beach for withdrawal, but if they had obeyed they would have been slaughtered—Omaha Beach was one of the few battlegrounds in history in which the greater danger lay to the rear. In any case, the landing craft ashore were *kaput*. Those offshore were jammed with men and vehicles.

Withdrawal was not an option. Nor was the alternative that Bradley played with in his mind, sending follow-up waves to Utah or the British beaches, not just because that might well have meant sacrificing the men ashore at Omaha Beach but even more because it would have left a gap of some sixty kilometers between Utah and Gold beaches, which would have jeopardized the invasion as a whole.

As head of the U.S. First Army, Bradley had more than a quarter of a million men under his immediate command. But standing on the bridge of *Augusta*, he was a helpless observer, desperate for information. On the beaches the plans could be modified or abandoned as circumstances demanded; on the *Augusta*, Bradley was stuck with the overall strategic plan.

On the amphibious command ship USS *Ancon*, General

Gerow had his command post. For the first three hours of the assault he was as blind as Bradley. He sent the assistant chief of staff of V Corps, Col. Benjamin Talley, in a DUKW to cruise offshore and report on the battle. Talley found that even from 500 meters he couldn't see much. It was obvious that the beaches were jammed, that enemy artillery and machine-gun fire was effective, and that the exits had not been opened. He could not see up the bluff because of the smoke, so he was unaware of the progress of individuals and small units who had managed to reach high ground. Talley was also unaware of the 0830 order from the 7th Naval Beach Battalion commander to suspend landings, so he was disturbed by the failure of landing craft to go ashore. At 0930 he informed Gerow that the LCTs were milling around offshore like "a stampeded herd of cattle."[5]

At 0945 Gerow made his initial report to First Army. It was sketchy and alarming: "Obstacles mined, progress slow. 1st Battalion, 116th, reported 0748 being held up by machine-gun fire—two LCTs knocked out by artillery fire. DD tanks for Fox Green swamped."[6]

Five minutes later, Maj. Gen. Clarence Huebner, commanding the 1st Division, received a radio report from the beach: "There are too many vehicles on the beach; send combat troops. 30 LCTs waiting offshore; cannot come in because of shelling. Troops dug in on beaches, still under heavy fire."[7] Huebner responded by ordering the 18th Regiment to land at once on Easy Red—but only one battalion was loaded in LCVPs; the other two had to be transshipped from their LCIs to LCVPs, and in any case the prohibition on further landings was still in effect.

Bradley sent his aide, Maj. Chester Hansen, and Admiral Kirk's gunnery officer, Capt. Joseph Wellings, in a torpedo boat to the beach to report, but all he got back was a message from Hansen: "It is difficult to make sense from what is going on."[8]

From the generals' point of view, disaster loomed, a disaster they could do nothing about. The generals were irrelevant to the battle.

On Omaha, the situation was so bad that the evacuation of the wounded was toward the enemy. This may have been unique in military history. The few aid posts that had been set up were at the shingle seawall. Medics took great risks to drag wounded from the beach to the aid posts. There was little that could be done for them beyond bandaging, splinting, giving morphine and plasma (if the medics had any supplies). The medical units landed off schedule and on the wrong beach sectors, often without their equipment. The 116th lost its entire regimental supply of plasma in two LCIs sunk off the beach.

Nevertheless, as a staff officer of the 116th recalled, "First-aid men of all units were the most active members of the group that huddled against the seawall. With the limited facilities available to them, they did not hesitate to treat the most severe casualties. Gaping head and belly wounds were bandaged with rapid efficiency."[9]

The situation looked worse to the medical teams than it did even to the generals offshore. Maj. Charles Tegtmeyer, regimental surgeon of the 16th, who landed at 0815, described what he saw: "Face downward, as far as eyes could see in either direction were the huddled bodies of men living, wounded and dead, as tightly packed together as a layer of cigars in a box. . . . Everywhere, the frantic cry, 'Medics, hey, Medics,' could be heard above the horrible din."

Tegtmeyer's medics, now wading, now stumbling over prone men, bandaged and splinted wounded as they came upon them, then dragged them to the shelter of the shingle. "I examined scores as I went," Tegtmeyer declared, "telling the men who to dress and who not to bother with." In many cases it was simply hopeless. Tegtmeyer reported a soldier with one leg traumatically amputated and multiple compound fractures of the other. "He was conscious and cheerful," Tegtmeyer noted, "but his only hope was rapid evacuation, and at this time evacuation did not exist. An hour later he was dead."[10]

Confusion in the planned landing sequence compounded the chaos. The first men of the 61st Medical Battalion to wade ashore on Easy Red were members of the headquarters detachment. They landed with typewriters, files, and office supplies on a beach strewn with dead and wounded. They abandoned their typewriters, scavenged for medical equipment among the debris, and went to work on the casualties around them. Forward emergency surgery never got started on Omaha that day; of the twelve surgical teams attached to the 60th and 61st Medical battalions, only eight reached shore and none of them had proper operating equipment. Like the clerks from the HQ detachment, the surgeons pitched in to give first aid.[11]

•   •

At 0950, General Huebner gave the order for the 18th Regiment of the 1st Division to go ashore at Easy Red, the largest of the eight designated sectors. It lay just to the east of the middle of Omaha Beach. The right flank of Easy Red was the dividing line between the 29th and 1st divisions. Two first-wave companies of the 16th Regiment were supposed to have landed on Easy Red, with three additional companies coming in on the second wave.

But the mislandings were such that what was to have been the most heavily attacked sector was actually the loneliest—only parts of one company came ashore there in the first hour, parts of two others in the next three hours. But at 1000, with the 1st Battalion of the 18th coming in and the 115th Regiment of 29th Division mislanding right on top of the 18th, it became the most crowded and bloodiest of all the beach sectors.

At 1000, the tide was nearly at its highest mark. All the obstacles were covered. The skippers on the larger landing craft were afraid to try to go ashore, and they had orders from the Navy Beach Battalion to stay away. But the 18th's 1st Battalion officers had orders from their CO to go in. There were some fierce arguments between the skippers and the soldiers.

The stalemate was broken at about 1010 when LCT 30 drove at full speed through the obstacles, all weapons firing. LCT 30 continued the fire after touchdown. At about the same time, LCI 544 rammed through the obstacles, firing on machine-gun nests in a fortified house. These exploits demonstrated that the obstacles could be breached and gave courage to other skippers, who began to give in to the demands of the Army officers and move in.[12]

The destroyers helped immeasurably in this attack. As noted, they sailed in close and pounded the enemy—when they could spot him. *Harding*'s action report noted, "At 1050 observed enemy pillbox which was firing on our troops down draw north of Colleville, thereby delaying operations on the beach. Opened fire on pillbox and demolished it, expending 30 rounds."[13]

Adm. Charles Cooke, along with Maj. Gen. Thomas Handy of General Marshall's staff at the War Department, were on *Harding*. Cooke recorded that as *Harding* closed the beach, "We saw an LCT dash in opposite a draw firing her guns at some German position at Colleville. The German batteries were hidden in the shrubbery, had the advantage, and the LCT was badly shot up."[14]

So were many others. The Navy report for the transport

group carrying the 18th ashore listed twenty-two LCVPs, two LCIs, and four LCTs as lost at the beach, either to mined obstacles or to enemy artillery fire.

Sgt. Hyman Haas was lucky. LCTs to the right and left of his were burning. "The machine-gun fire was right into them. Mortars were blowing around them. Artillery pieces were blowing beside them. But we had landed in a spot that seemed to be immune."

Haas commanded a half-track (M-15). When he drove off the LCT, "the water reached up to my neck. My driver, Bill Hendrix, had his head just above water. We kept going. Some screwball gave a rebel yell. Sgt. Chester Gutowsky looked at him and growled, 'You schmuck!! Why don't you shut up?' "

When Haas reached shore, "I was breathing very heavily with excitement, eyes darting in all directions, looking, waiting, seeing. It was quite bewildering." He started thinking straight immediately. Haas ordered Hendrix to drive back into the water, then to turn the M-15 into firing position. He began to blaze away with his 37mm gun, aiming at a pillbox on the west side of the E-1 exit. The first three rounds were short. He adjusted his range setter, and "the next ten shots went directly into the porthole of the pillbox."

(Later that day, Haas drove up to the pillbox. "There, lying on the parapet, was a German officer, bleeding from the mouth, obviously in his last moments of life, being held by another wounded German. McNeil came running over. He says, 'Haas, that's your pillbox.' It took my breath away. It's one thing to fire impersonal, but I was responsible for that dying German officer and the wounded men in there. I felt awful and shocked at the sight."[15])

With that kind of support, the 18th got ashore, but not without loss and not without confusion, a confusion compounded by the mislanding of the 115th Regiment of the 29th Division, which was supposed to land on Dog Red but instead came in starting at 1030 on Easy Red, right on top of the 18th. This caused a horrendous mix-up of men and units, and imposed delays, but it put a lot of firepower on Easy Red, where it was badly needed.

As the 18th came ashore, it appeared to the officers that no progress at all had been made. The regimental action report declared, "The beach shingle was full of tractors, tanks, vehicles, bulldozers, and troops—the high ground was still held by Germans who had all troops on the beach pinned down—the beach was still

under heavy fire from enemy small arms, mortars, and artillery."[16]
Capt. (later Maj. Gen.) Al Smith was executive officer, 1st Battalion, 16th Regiment. He had landed on Easy Red at 0745. "About 500 yards offshore I began to realize we were in trouble," he recalled. "The nearer we got to the beachline, the more certain I was that the landing was a disaster. Dead and wounded from the first waves were everywhere. There was little or no firing from our troops. On the other hand, German machine guns, mortars, and 88s were laying down some of the heaviest fire I'd ever experienced."

About half of Smith's battalion made it to the defilade afforded by the shingle embankment. Smith made contact with Brig. Gen. Willard Wyman, the assistant division commander. Wyman asked if the men were advancing by fire and movement, as taught at the Infantry School.

"Yes, sir!" Smith snapped back. "They're firing, we're moving."

He followed the path made earlier that morning by Captain Dawson of G Company up the bluff. "Near the top, I can recall the most pleasant five-minute break of my military career. With our column at one of its temporary standstills, [Capt.] Hank [Hangsterfer, CO of HQ Company] and I moved to the side to sit down and eat apples provided by the ship's mess. We also had time for a wee nip of Scotch whisky—my farewell gift from a little old English lady."

Smith set up the battalion CP beside a dirt road.* "About this time a telephone line reached me from regimental HQ at the base of the bluffs. Colonel [George] Taylor [CO of the 16th] asked about our situation and what he could do to help. I told him we could use tanks—the sooner, the better. He promised to do everything possible."[17]

It was 1100. Taylor ordered all tanks available to go into action up the E-3 draw. Capt. W. M. King got the order. He ran along the beach, notifying each tank as he came to it to proceed to E-3 and move up. When he reached the last tank, King found the commander wounded. He took over. Backing away from the shingle, King drove

---

* General Smith, in a 1993 letter to the author, recalls, "Today, the site would be very near the Rotunda of our Normandy memorial." Captain Dawson, also in a 1993 letter, remarks: "I am proud and indeed honored that the esplanade dividing the monument from the reflecting pool and graves is centered at the exact spot where we made the opening from the beach."

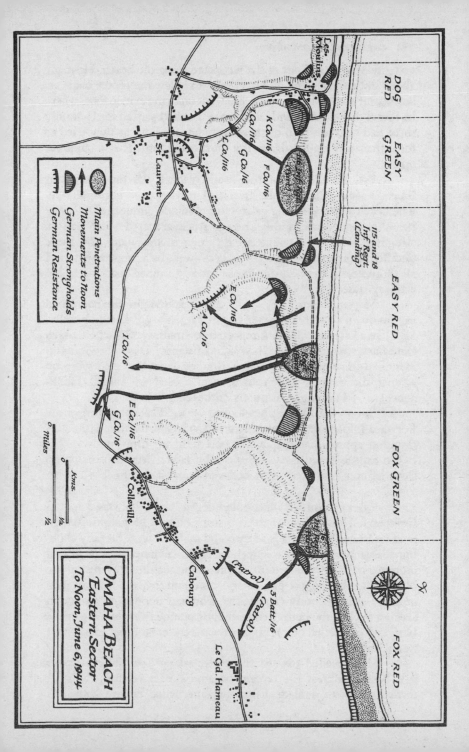

OMAHA BEACH
Eastern Sector
To Noon, June 6, 1944.

Main Penetrations
Movements to Noon
German Strongholds
German Resistance

Les Moulins

DOG RED

EASY GREEN

St Laurent

K Co./116
G Co./116
F Co./116
G Co./116

115 and 18
Inf Regt
(Landing)

EASY RED

E Co./116
A Co./116

I Co./116

E Co./116
G Co./116

Colleville

Cabourg

(Patrol)
(Patrol)
3 Batt./16

Le Gd. Hameau

FOX GREEN

FOX RED

N

0 miles ½
0 kms. ½

east, weaving in and out of the wreckage along the beach. He made about 200 meters when he hit a mine that blew the center bogie assembly off and broke the track. He went on to the exit on foot, where he found that, of the handful of tanks that had started for E-3, only three had arrived. Two of these were knocked out as they tried to force their way up the draw; the third backed off. E-3 was not yet open.

Pvt. Ray Moon of the 116th reached the top about this time. "I looked back at the beach. The view was unforgettable. The beach was a shooting gallery for machine gunners. The scene below reminded me of the Chicago stockyard cattle pens and its slaughter house. We could see the men in the water and those huddled along the sea wall. There was little movement and all those below were sitting ducks for any trained marksmen and artillery observers."[18]

Mortar fire, artillery shells, and machine-gun fire continued to rain down on the beach. At higher HQ, Easy Red continued to look like a calamity. Gerow reported to Bradley, "Situation beach exits Easy still critical at 1100. 352nd Infantry Division (German) identified [this was the first that Bradley knew his men were up against the 352nd, which had been missed by Allied intelligence]. . . . Fighting continuous on beaches."[19]

But on the spot, things looked better. Colonel Talley of the Forward Information Detachment reported shortly after 1100, "Infiltration approximately platoon [strength] up draw midway between exits E-1 and Easy 3," and a bit later, "Men advancing up slope behind Easy Red, men believed ours on skyline."[20]

One of those GIs on the skyline was Capt. Joe Dawson of G Company. How he got there is a story he tells best himself: "On landing I found total chaos as men and material were literally choking the sandbar just at the water's edge. A minefield lay in and around a path extending to my right and upward to the crest of the bluff. After blowing a gap in the concertina wire I led my men gingerly over the body of a soldier who had stepped on a mine in seeking to clear the path. I collected my company at the base of the bluff and proceeded on. Midway toward the crest I met Lieutenant Spaulding.

"I proceeded toward the crest, asking Spaulding to cover me. Near the crest the terrain became almost vertical. This afforded complete defilade from the entrenched enemy above. A machine-gun nest was busily firing at the beach, and one could hear rifle and mortar fire coming from the crest.

"I tossed two grenades aloft, and when they exploded the machine gun fell silent. I waved my men and Spaulding to proceed as rapidly as possible and I then proceeded to the crest where I saw the enemy moving out toward the E-3 exit and the dead Germans in the trenches.

"To my knowledge no one had penetrated the enemy defenses until that moment.

"As soon as my men reached me we debouched from that point, firing on the retreating enemy and moving toward a . . . wooded area, and this became a battleground extending all the way into town."

In an analysis of how he became the first American to reach the top of the bluff in this area, written in 1993, Dawson pointed out: "The Battle of Omaha Beach was 1st, Deadly enemy fire on an exposed beach where total fire control favored the defender and we were not given *any* direct fire support from the Navy or tanks. 2nd, the poor German marksmanship is the *only* way I could have made it across the exposed area because I could not engage the enemy nor even see him until I reached the machine gun. 3rd, the fortunate ability to control my command both in landing together and debouching up the bluff together as a fighting unit. 4th, our direct engagement of the enemy caused him to cease concerted small-arms, machine-gun and mortar fire with which he was sweeping the beach below."*

While Dawson moved on Colleville, Spaulding went to the right (west), toward St.-Laurent. Spaulding spread his men over an area of some 300 meters and advanced. They spotted a German machine gunner with a rifleman on each side of him, firing down on the beach from their dugout. Sergeant Streczyk shot the gunner in the back; the riflemen surrendered. Spaulding interrogated the prisoners but they were ethnic Germans and refused to give any information. With the prisoners in tow, Spaulding moved west.

"We were now in hedgerows and orchard country," he told Sgt. Forrest Pogue of the Army's Historical Division in a February

---

* Dawson's route to the top was approximately the same as the paved path that today leads from the beach to the lookout with the bronze panorama of Omaha Beach on the edge of the American cemetery. His oral history and a written memoir are in EC.

1945 interview. "We crossed through two minefields. No one was lost; we still had an angel on each shoulder."

The E Company platoon came upon a fortified position overlooking the E-1 draw. Sgt. Kenneth Peterson fired his bazooka into it but no one came out. Spaulding was about to move on when he spied a Tobruk.

"Sergeant Streczyk and I went forward to investigate. We discovered an underground dugout. There was an 81mm mortar with beautiful range cards and lots of ammunition, and a position for a 75mm cannon, overlooking E-1 draw. The dugout was of cement, had radios, excellent sleeping facilities; dogs. We started to drop a grenade in the ventilator, but Streczyk said, 'Hold on a minute,' and fired three shots down the steps into the dugout. He then yelled in Polish and German for them to come out. Four men did. They brought out two or three wounded."

Germans from the other side of the draw began to fire on Spaulding's platoon. The GIs fired back. American destroyers commenced firing into the draw (it was about 1000). Spaulding started down the line of communication trenches, which led to the cliff overlooking the beach. "We were now behind the Germans so we routed four out of a hole and got thirteen in the trenches. The trenches had Teller mines, hundreds of grenades, numerous machine guns."

Spaulding inspected the trenches. There, he admitted, "I did a fool thing." He had lost his carbine when he landed, had picked up a German rifle only to discover he did not know how to use it, and had traded it to a soldier for another carbine. But he failed to check the carbine. In the trenches, "I ran into a Kraut and pulled the trigger, but the safety was on. I reached for the safety catch and hit the clip release, so my clip hit the ground. I ran about fifty yards in nothing flat. Fortunately, Sergeant Peterson had me covered and the German put up his hands. That business of not checking guns is certainly not habit-forming."

Spaulding tried to use the 81mm mortar but no one in his platoon could operate the German weapon. Meanwhile, he sent nineteen German prisoners back to the beach, guarded by two of his men. He told the men to turn the prisoners over to anyone who would take them and to ask where the rest of E Company was located. He set off his last yellow smoke grenade to let the American destroyers know that he had possession of the fortification, because "their fire was getting very close."

At this point, about 1030, Lieutenant Hutch and nine enlisted men caught up with Spaulding. "I was very glad to see them," Spaulding told Pogue. Hutch brought word that Spaulding should change his objective from St.-Laurent to Colleville, that is, head east instead of trying to cross the E-1 draw.[21]

The terrain was flat, an area of apple orchards and hedgerows. Germans from the 352nd Division were present in company strength. The fighting now took on a new form. Instead of firing on the beach from the extensive trench system on the bluff, the Germans were hidden in hedgerows. Their main weapon was the fearfully effective MG-42. They had clear fields of fire over the open fields. The inexperienced GIs found it difficult to locate enemy fire positions in terrain affording so much cover, a difficulty exacerbated by sniper fire coming from no one could tell where. With no mortars, tanks, or supporting artillery, and with inadequate communications with the destroyers, the American infantrymen could advance hardly at all. Again and again, the E Company platoon ran into pockets of resistance in prepared positions built around machine guns dug in along the hedgerows. When Spaulding and Hutch bypassed such positions, the platoon got split up, so there was progressive loss of control. Still, they managed to move forward and catch up with and join Captain Dawson and G Company.

Dawson was experiencing similar difficulties in moving on Colleville. Dawson led by example and gave orders that were simple, direct, impossible not to understand: "I said, 'Men, there is the enemy. Let's go get them.' "

Company G worked its way to within a kilometer of Colleville. Dawson paused under a large oak tree. "There, a very friendly French woman welcomed us with open arms and said, 'Welcome to France.' "

Dawson advanced to the edge of Colleville. The dominant building, as always in the Normandy villages, was a Norman church, built of stone, its steeple stretching into the sky. "Sure enough," Dawson noted, "in the steeple of the church there was an artillery observer." He dashed inside the church with a sergeant and a private.

"Immediately, three Germans inside the church opened fire. Fortunately, we were not hit by this burst. But as we made our way through the church the private was killed, shot by the observer in the tower. I turned and we secured the tower by eliminating him. My sergeant shot the other two Germans and thus we took care of the opposition at that point."

As Dawson ran out of the church, a German rifleman shot at him. Dawson fired back with his carbine, but not before the German got off a second shot. The bullet went through Dawson's carbine and shattered the stock. Fragments from the bullet went through his kneecap and leg, which "caused my knee to swell and caused me to be evacuated the next day."

Beyond the church, G Company ran into heavy fire from a full German company occupying the houses in Colleville. Built of stone, the positions were all but impregnable to small-arms fire. G Company got into what Dawson called "a very severe firefight," but could not advance.[22]

It was shortly after noon. Maj. William Washington, executive officer of the 2nd Battalion, 16th Regiment, came up, arriving at about the same time as Spaulding's platoon. Washington set up a CP in a drainage ditch just west of Colleville. He sent the E Company platoon to the right (south) of the village. Spaulding moved out and got separated from Dawson. Germans moved into the gap; in forty minutes Spaulding's platoon was surrounded. Just that quickly, Spaulding realized that instead of attacking, he was being counterattacked. He set up a defensive position in the drainage ditches. Several squads of Germans came toward the platoon. Spaulding's men were able to beat them off.

Spaulding saw a runner coming from the battalion CP with a message from Major Washington. "The Germans opened fire on him. After he fell they fired at least a hundred rounds of machine-gun ammunition into him. It was terrible but we do the same thing when we want to stop a runner bearing information."

Spaulding's platoon spent the remainder of the day in the ditches, fighting a defensive action. By nightfall, Spaulding was down to six rounds of carbine ammunition; most of his men were down to their last clip. The platoon was still surrounded.

It had been the first platoon to take prisoners. It had eliminated several machine-gun posts on the bluff, and the Tobruk looking down the E-1 draw. It had landed with thirty men; by nightfall, two had been killed, seven wounded. Five men in the platoon were awarded DSCs, personally presented by General Eisenhower: they were Lt. John Spaulding, Kentucky; Sgt. Philip Streczyk, New Jersey; Pvt. Richard Gallagher, New York; Pvt. George Bowen, Kentucky; Sgt. Kenneth Peterson, New Jersey.[23]

Major Washington dug in, expecting a major German tank counterattack, as he had experienced in Sicily. "We spent all night of the first day wrestling 57mm antitank weapons up the cliff with ropes with jeeps and winches and everything else."

By daylight, June 7, there had been no counterattack. What Washington did see at first light was astonishing enough: two GIs leading fifty German POWs into the American line. The Americans turned out to be privates who had been mislanded and captured by the Germans. Both American privates were of Polish extraction; the "German" soldiers were Polish conscripts; when darkness fell the GIs persuaded their captors to hide out in the bushes and surrender at first light.

(Washington had a personal piece of good luck. War correspondent Dan Whitehead asked him how he got across the beach safely. Washington relates: "I don't know what I told him, but it sounded good in print. He wrote that I said it was my wife's prayers that carried me across the beach. So that went over good back home."[24])

Casualties in the Easy Red sector were awful. In F Company, 16th Regiment, every officer and more than half the NCOs were down by the end of the day. The losses in the other platoons of E Company were almost as heavy. The carnage made an indelible impression on the S3, Capt. Fred Hall. He concluded his oral history with these words: "My wife and I walked Easy Red Beach in May 1982. It was soon enough to return."[25]

Spaulding fought on through the campaign in northwest Europe. He continued to provide inspired leadership and, as he told Pogue in the 1945 interview, he learned a lot about combat in the process that he wished he had known on D-Day. He was lucky, he said.[26]

Most survivors from Easy Red have a "Lord was I lucky" story to tell. Sgt. John Ellery recalled that in the fighting outside Colleville, "I was about to climb through a break in the hedgerow when my ID bracelet on my right wrist got hung up on a rather sturdy piece of brush. I slid back down and broke off the branch to get loose. Meanwhile, a fellow from another company decided to pass by me and go on over. As his head cleared the top of the hedgerow, he took a round right in the face, and fell back on top of me, dead."

Ellery went looking for the sniper. "I evened the score. It was a clean shot and the only one that I fired on D-Day."

Ellery decided that he was hungry. He thought one of his

apples would taste good. He dug around in his musette bag "and discovered that my apples had become applesauce. So I settled for a K ration, and enjoyed it. I enjoyed it so much that I decided to have another. It seemed to me that I wasn't likely to outlast my supply of rations, so there was no point in going hungry."[27]

The sight of Americans on the bluff and the procession of prisoners coming down with their hands over their heads gave heart to the men on the beach and to the generals on *Ancon* and *Augusta*. But at 1200, Easy Red was by no means a safe place to be. The machine-gun fire had let up in the area between E-3 and E-1, thanks to the platoons that had gone up the bluff, eliminating pillboxes as they climbed, but the mortar and artillery fire continued to pour down—not as accurate as it had been earlier, because forward observation posts had been overrun or destroyed, but in greater volume.

Reinforcements were coming ashore, primarily from the 115th Regiment. Its 1st Battalion, combat-loaded in LCVPs, went in at 1100 side by side with, or immediately behind, the craft carrying the 18th Regiment ashore. But at 1200 the other two battalions of the 18th, loaded in LCIs, were still milling about the line of departure. It was an hour after high water and the ebb was running so fast it was difficult for the LCIs to avoid stranding, so they discharged their troops into LCVPs, which shuttled between them and the shore. The Germans caught on to this and started hitting the transfer points with shells. LCI 490 was unable to hook up with any LCVPs, but the skipper did spot an LCM. He traded his load of troops for the LCMs unwanted load of high explosives, to which he promptly gave the "deep six."[28]

Pvt. Eldon Wiehe was a truck driver for HQ Battery, 1st Division Artillery. His LCT, carrying seven deuce-and-a-half trucks loaded with ammunition, was scheduled to go in at 0830, but at 1130 it was still circling offshore, out of range of the German guns. When it did turn toward shore, an LCT to the right got hit by an 88mm shell, so the skipper on Wiehe's LCT turned around and headed back into the Channel. After a bit he headed toward shore again, came under heavy gunfire, and backed off once more. At 1200 a patrol craft came by and a control officer with a bullhorn yelled, "The skipper of that craft, take that craft in, you've been in twice and backed off twice, now take it in this time and do not come back until it is unloaded."

The tide was receding but still high enough to cover the obstacles. Shells were exploding around the LCT. The skipper got in as far as he was going to go that day and, still well offshore, lowered the ramp. Wiehe's lieutenant protested: "Take us in closer."

"Get off," the skipper replied.

The first truck drove off and immediately sank, the water far above the exhaust pipe.

"Take us in closer!" the lieutenant screamed at the skipper.

"Get off," the skipper replied. "I've got to unload and get back to sea."

One after the other, the remaining six trucks drove off and sank. The drivers climbed out, inflated their Mae Wests, and swam in to shore. As he got out of the water, Wiehe heard a shell coming in. He jumped into a shell hole. "When that shell burst," he related, "I panicked. I started crying. My buddies got me behind a burned-out craft, where I cried for what seemed like hours. I cried until tears would no longer come. [Finally] I stopped crying and came to my senses."

There were pillboxes off to Wiehe's left, at the opening of E-3 draw, firing down the beach. He saw two bulldozers head for the positions, blades down. The dozers piled sand on the pillboxes and put them out of action. "On the return trip to the beach, one of the dozers took a direct hit. The man on it seemed like he flew all to pieces." Wiehe and the other drivers in his group picked up rifles and carbines and became infantry. "We loaded up and moved forward," Wiehe said.

In concluding his oral history, Wiehe recalled his crying episode and declared, "To this day I've never shed another tear. I would give anything to have one good cry or one good laugh. I hurt inside but I cannot get my emotions out since that day. I've never been able to."[29]

By 1200, Americans from the 16th, 18th, 115th, and 116th regiments had been coming ashore at Easy Red for five and a half hours. They had made no gains at E-3 draw (directly north of Colleville). The traffic jam was still horrendous. Dead and wounded were strewn about the beach and behind the seawall.

But what looked like catastrophe, wasn't. Although the situation was far from being well in hand, it was improving, especially at E-1. Thanks to Spaulding and Dawson, the fortification on the east side of the draw had been neutralized; the fortification on the west side was still in action but was being contained by Company M, 116th Regiment. Dozers had made a gap through the dune line just east of the draw and were making it ready for vehicles to pass through.

Best of all, a penetration had been made almost exactly between E-1 and E-3 by companies E, I, and G of the 16th Regiment and Colleville was under attack. To the right, five companies from the 116th had gone up the bluff between D-3 and E-1, while to the left of E-3 patrols from three companies of the 16th had done the same.

At 1309, Gerow was able to make his first favorable report to Bradley: "Troops formerly pinned down on beaches Easy Red, Easy Green, Fox Red advancing up heights behind beaches."[30]

"The situation everywhere on the beach was still grave," Bradley later wrote, "but our troops . . . were inching inland. . . . I gave up any thought of abandoning Omaha Beach."[31]

Maj. Gen. Charles Gerhardt, CO of the 29th Division, later wrote a report entitled "Battle Lessons and Conclusions" on D-Day. He summarized the lessons learned in two sentences: "No reports of disaster should be allowed. THEY ARE NEVER TRUE."[32]

24

STRUGGLE FOR THE HIGH GROUND

Vierville, St.-Laurent, and Colleville

JOHN RAAEN, the twenty-two-year-old captain with the 5th Rangers, commanding HQ Company, was the son of an Army officer. Born at Fort Benning, a January 1943 graduate of West Point, Raaen loved the Army. He stayed in for forty years and fought in three wars. He retired as a permanent major general. "I wouldn't change a single day of my military life," he concluded his oral history. "There were bad days, all right, but they made the good days better."

On June 6, 1944, within minutes of going into combat for the first time, Raaen had learned an important lesson—that to give a frightened man something specific to do would work wonders for his nerves. When he got up the bluff at Vierville later that morning, he learned some more lessons: don't trust intelligence and don't make assumptions about terrain until you have seen it with your own eyes.

"As we had looked at the maps and the models of the Normandy area," Raaen related, "we had recognized hedgerows surrounding all of the fields. Of course we were all familiar with hedgerows from England." Like virtually every other officer in the invasion, Raaen assumed that the French hedgerows would be similar to those in England—low, compact, built as much for fox hunters to jump over as to maintain a barrier. Reconnaissance photos from the air did not show the height of French hedgerows. "As soon as we got to the top of the crest off the beach," Raaen said, "we immediately found out that French hedgerows were different. In France, the hedgerow was a mound of dirt from six to ten or twelve feet high with heavy hedges on top and roots that worked down into the mounds, and the mounds themselves were very effective barriers. You simply could not pass through a hedgerow. You had to climb up something and then at the top you were practically blocked by the jungle of the plant roots and trunks, vines, branches, everything." Usually, there was a single gap in the hedgerow, to allow the farmer to get his cows or equipment in and out, but the gaps were covered by machine-gun fire.*

"The Germans would dig into the back of a hedgerow," Raaen remembered, "put a machine-gun nest in there, and then cut a very small slit looking forward, providing them with a field of fire with what was for practical purposes absolute protection. You couldn't see them as they fired." Typically, the Germans would place their MG-42s at the corners opposite the gap, so that they could bring crossing fire to bear on anyone who ventured into the gap or out into the field. Further, they had presighted mortar and artillery fire on the field. In the initial hedgerow fighting, the Germans would allow a squad of GIs to get into the field, then cut them down.

Eventually, the Yanks learned to fight hedgerow-style. They would use TNT to blast a hole in the hedge away from the gap, then send a Sherman tank into the hole so that it could fire white phosphorus shells—terrifying to the Germans, loved by the Yanks—into the far corners. Or they would weld steel rails (picked up from the beach obstacles, thus turning Rommel's defenses into their own assets) to the front of a Sherman, so that when it drove into the hedge the rails would dig into the earth and prevent the tank from going belly-up against the skyline with its unarmored bottom an easy target for German gunners. But those methods were developed only after a couple of weeks of hedgerow fighting, and in any case there were no tanks on top until late in D-Day.

When Raaen set up his company CP in a field outside Vier-

* Fifty years later, many of those centuries-old hedgerows are gone. As Norman farmers began to acquire tractors after World War II, they needed bigger gaps to get in and out, and bigger fields to work in, so they began knocking down the hedgerows. One of the best places to see hedgerows as the GIs saw them is along the Merderet River west of Ste.-Marie-du-Mont and Ste.-Mère-Église.

ville, it came under artillery fire. He quickly learned another lesson. "After five minutes under artillery fire, you learned when you
had to duck and when you didn't. You could tell from the sound of
the incoming rounds where they were going to hit. If they were
going to hit fifty yards away, it was too much trouble to hit the dirt.
You just stayed up and kept moving. Of course, if they were going
to come in a little closer than that, you hit the dirt and prayed."

The objective of the 5th Ranger Battalion was Pointe-du-
Hoc. That meant moving through Vierville and west along the
coastal road. But Colonel Schneider, always quick to make a decision on the basis of what he was seeing even when it meant abandoning the plan, sent a patrol from Raaen's company to the left
(east) to link up with patrols coming up the Les Moulins draw.
Raaen did, moving in the ditches and sunken roads between the
hedgerows, and "we ran into a patrol of 1st Division troops [actu-
ally, Company K of the 116th Regiment, 29th Division, attached to
the 1st Division for June 6]. It included one paratrooper from the
101st who had landed in water off Omaha Beach, and the 1st
Division boys had fished him out and he was now fighting with
them."

The linkup, probably the first for the Americans coming up
at Vierville and those coming at St.-Laurent, cut off the Germans
on the bluff between Dog Green and Easy Green beaches, as well
as those between the crest and the coastal road. Raaen observed that
"any reasonable commander should have attempted to move his
troops off the beach defenses and inland so that they could continue
to fight instead of being captured in the mop-up operations." But
the Germans—and the *Ost* troops on whom German NCOs held
pistols—remained loyal to their führer's and Rommel's doctrine of
standing and fighting in place. Raaen felt that they had to have
known "they were being caught in a trap," but they stayed in their
trenches and pillboxes. Something similar was going on over to the
west, near Colleville.[1]

Lieutenant Frerking of the Wehrmacht, who had been directing fire on the beach through the morning, finally was blasted
out of his bunker. A Sherman tank got it. His last message before
fleeing was: "Gunfire barrage on the beach. Every shell a certain
hit. We are getting out." He had waited too long. His battery was
out of ammunition, and he and most of his men were killed trying
to escape.

Other German batteries were running low on ammunition. Colonel Ocker, commander of the artillery of the 352nd Division, telephoned to tell 1st Battery that a truck with more shells was coming. "It's on its way already," he promised. It was, but it took a direct hit from a 14-inch naval shell. The explosion left nothing describable.[2]

Most Germans did not know it yet, but they had lost the battle. They had expended most of their immediately available ammunition and failed to stop the assault. Things were in reverse. With land lines of communication, the Germans should have been able to move unlimited quantities of ammunition to their guns—as they had done in World War I. But Allied naval and air power had turned the Calvados coast into something like an island, which meant the Germans in the front lines would have to fight with what they had at hand. Meanwhile, the Americans should have found it difficult to supply their men ashore as they had no ports and everything from bullets to shells had to be brought in over water to an open beach. Yet it was the Americans who had a steady stream of reinforcements and fresh supplies coming into the battle and the Germans could do nothing to stop them.

The general German failure to fall back and regroup once American patrols had infiltrated the German line was a major mistake. Still it had some benefits: Germans in observation posts on the bluff and crest could call in artillery fire on the beaches and keep the exits under fire, so long as ammunition held out, while those in the trenches and pillboxes could continue to direct aimed fire on the beaches. But the price was far too high. Staying in place meant the Germans could not form up for concentrated counterattacks against the squads, platoons, and companies that had made it to the top at a time when the GIs had no artillery support and no weapons heavier than BARs, .30-caliber machine guns, and mortars.

"They could have swept us off with a broom," one ranger declared,[3] but instead the Wehrmacht soldiers stayed in their fixed defenses, from which they could still kill Americans but not win the battle. They paid the price for Hitler's obsession with defending every square inch of his conquered empire, and for Rommel's obsession with stopping the invasion cold on the beach.

On the high ground, too, the Germans fought a strictly defensive action. Partly this was because the hedgerows were such marvelous defensive positions, mainly it was because they were receiving few reinforcements even as the Americans sent wave after wave of combat infantry onto the beach and into the battle. The Germans were supposed to counterattack immediately, in battalion strength, but because they were confused with their senior commanders absent, because they had their troops scattered in platoon strength in the small villages of Normandy and it took time to assemble them, because they were still a horse-drawn army for the most part, and mainly because the Allied air forces, which had done so little to help the infantry on the beach, did an outstanding job of strafing and bombing bridges, crossroads, and assembly points inland all through D-Day, thus hampering German movement to the sound of the guns, the Germans were unable to launch even one company-strength counterattack at Omaha Beach on D-Day.

They fought effectively, inflicting casualties and for the most part holding their hedgerows, thus preventing the Americans from getting inland more than a couple of kilometers—far short of their intended D-Day objectives—but they fought isolated, confused, small-unit actions designed to delay and harass and hold rather than to drive the Americans off the high ground.

As Raaen was establishing contact with K Company, 116th, Colonel Schneider pushed the remainder of the 5th Rangers across the coastal road, intending to go around Vierville to the south and head out for Pointe-du-Hoc. But the leading companies were held up by machine guns firing from hedgerows south of the road. Three times Schneider tried to outflank the German positions, only to run into new ones.

"We ran into the doggonest bunch of Germans you ever did see," Pvt. Donald Nelson recalled. "We got pinned down and we really couldn't move." Colonel Schneider came up and wanted to know what the trouble was.

"Snipers," Nelson replied.

"Can't you get them?" Schneider asked.

"No, sir, we can't even see them," Nelson answered.

Schneider took his helmet off, got a stick, put the helmet on the stick, and eased it up.

"The moment that helmet got up above the hedgerow," Nelson said, "the snipers started shooting at it. That's the way we got a few of the snipers."

Nelson was on "the very tip of the front line." He wanted to see more so he and a buddy "crawled up on this hedgerow and took our helmets off and a five-man German machine-gun crew set their gun right in front of us. We laid real quiet and watched them. They were about twenty feet from us. They got the machine gun all set up and pulled the slide back and put a shell in the chamber. My buddy tapped me on the side of my foot with his foot, and I tapped him back. We let them have it. I covered him while he went and rolled them over to see if they were all dead. They were."[4]

As the rangers continued to extend their line to the south in the attempt to outflank Vierville, Company C of the 116th Regiment moved through the village, without opposition. Company B of the rangers joined up; the combined forces then moved west, along the coastal road, toward Pointe-du-Hoc. At about 500 meters out of Vierville they were stopped by machine-gun fire from hedgerows. For the next few hours the Americans tried to outflank the positions, only to run into new ones. Every attempt to move across an open field was checked by German rifle and automatic-weapon fire at ranges of 200–300 meters.

A major problem for the Americans was keeping up the momentum of the advance. This is always a problem for an attacking force, made much worse at Omaha by the natural and inevitable tendency of the men who had made it up from the hell on the beach to the comparative quiet of the high ground to feel that they had triumphed—and thus done their job for that day. In addition, they were exhausted. Furthermore, as with the paratroopers at Utah, when the men got into a village they had immediate, easy access to wine. Sgt. William Lewis of the 116th recalled spending the afternoon of D-Day "trying to get organized outside Vierville. I had liberated a big jug of wine and we all had a drink."[5]

(The residents of Vierville were, of course, terrified. Pierre and Fernand Piprel decided to flee to the south. On the way, they saw some soldiers crouching behind a hedgerow. Pierre Piprel said it was "hard to tell who they were since we did not know the Allied uniforms. Arriving close, I asked them, English? and they answered, No, Americans. Seeing their packs of Lucky Strikes, we knew we were safe. They let us go on."[6])

The absence of radios, the lack of unit cohesion, and the nature of the terrain also contributed to the inability to maintain momentum west of Vierville. Where individuals could set an example and lead the way up the bluff, in the hedgerows the brave got cut down when they exposed themselves by dashing forward.

"We were under observation all afternoon long," Cpl. Gale Beccue of the rangers recalled. "One man moving alone would draw sniper fire, but any concentration of men would bring in the artillery and mortar rounds. We had the village secure but outside Vierville we had only fleeting glimpses of the Germans."[7]

Those who led the way off the beach and up the bluff had a much better chance than those who tried to lead on top. The men behind the seawall could see for themselves that to stay where they were was to die, that they could not fall back, that only by following advancing columns did they have any chance at all. On top, a man crouched behind a hedgerow was safe right where he was.

Isolation contributed to the loss of momentum, as it led many men to the conclusion that their groups were on their own—as was indeed often the case. "From noon through the balance of June 6," Pvt. Harry Parley of the 116th said, "I am unable to recall chronologically what happened to me. The rest of the day is a jumbled memory of running, fighting, and hiding. We moved like a small band of outlaws, much of the time not knowing where we were, often meeting other groups like ours, joining and separating as situations arose, always asking for news of one's company or battalion."

Parley related one incident from the early afternoon. He was moving along a road when he heard the characteristic clank of a tracked vehicle, then the roar of a German cannon. "Terrified, I turned, ran like hell, and dove into a roadside ditch. Already there was a tough old sergeant from the 1st Division lying on his side as one would relax on a sofa. I screamed at him, 'It's a tank—what the hell do we do now?' "

The sergeant, a veteran of North Africa and Sicily, stared calmly at Parley for a few seconds, poker-faced, and said, "Relax, kid, maybe it will go away." Sure enough, it did.[8]

Colonel Canham, CO of the 116th, moved out of Vierville at around 1200 to set up his HQ at the prearranged CP location, the Chateau de Vaumicel, a half kilometer south of the village. In the process, his HQ group (three or four officers and a couple of enlisted men) got isolated behind a hedgerow just short of the chateau. Pvt. Carl Weast with a platoon of rangers came on the scene; Canham spotted the men and ordered them to act as his CP guard.

The chateau was full of Germans. A German riding a bicycle came up the road. The rangers shot him, then took up outpost positions around the chateau. Weast watched as a platoon of German soldiers came out of the chateau and formed up in a column around an old two-wheeled horse buggy with wounded in it. The Germans were unaware of the presence of Americans; they had their rifles slung over their shoulders.

"They were pulling the cart along, two guys shoving and two guys pulling. We waited until they got real close, maybe ten yards, and we stepped out in the road with our weapons pointed at them and they surrendered immediately.

"Now, with this kind of a situation, what in the hell do you do with twenty-five prisoners? We put them in an orchard and we put one man guarding them and we tried to interrogate them. Hell, there were no Germans! They were all Hungarians, Romanians, Russians, anything but Germans. There was one German noncom, middle-aged, and this guy looked like he wanted to do anything but fight a war. He was just happy as hell to be a prisoner, although he was concerned about a German counterattack, but not nearly as concerned as we were.

"The situation was becoming very, very tenuous. Here was Colonel Canham with 1500 yards of front to cover, and he had a total of about thirty-five men to do it with, expecting a German armored attack. Oh, man, you talk about bad spirits."

As the afternoon wore on, there was talk among the rangers about shooting the prisoners, but Weast pointed out that "not only is that illegal and immoral, it's stupid." When the light began to fade, "we had them lay real close to each other and we put a man with a BAR at the end and we made it plain to them that when it got dark we wouldn't be able to observe them but we could hear them and if anybody made any move we were going to get the whole bunch of them with the BAR. They lay there through the night and believe me, those were some damn quiet enemy."[9]

At 1400 Lt. Jay Mehaffey of the rangers was on the outskirts of Vierville. He lost a man who had been crossing a gap in a hedgerow to a German sniper. Just then a ranger came down the road with eight German POWs. Mehaffey lined the prisoners up in the gap, hands clasped over their helmets, then had his men get past the gap behind the prisoners.

"We didn't have time to fool with prisoners," he said, so onee' safely beyond the gap he just waved to the Germans to continue on down the bluff and find someone to whom they could surrender.[10]

•   •

Colonel Canham's isolation was complete. His only working radio belonged to the liaison officer from the 743rd Tank Battalion and even he could not contact any of the tanks still down on the beach. Canham did get some help—that may not have been needed—from the Navy. At 1350, a signalman on LCI 538 at Dog Green beach sent a visual message to destroyer *Harding*: "Believe church steeple to be enemy artillery observation post, can you blast it?"

Harding replied, "Which church do you mean?"

"Vierville."

"Don't you mean the church at Colleville?"

"No, Vierville."

Harding called the commander of Force O Forward Observers to report the request. CFOFO replied five minutes later, granting permission to fire on the church for one minute. *Harding's* action report noted, "At 1413 opened fire at a range of 3200 yards and completely demolished church, expending 40 rounds, every shell of which landed on the target."[11]

The incident was typical in a number of ways of not only D-Day but of the later fighting in France. Whenever the Americans took artillery fire they were convinced that the Germans were using the spires of nearby churches for observation posts and used their own artillery to knock those spires down. Sometimes they were right about the OP, often they were wrong; in any case there were few standing spires left in Normandy after the battle.

In the case of Vierville, the town was in American hands (unknown to LCI 538 and *Harding*) and none of those on the spot thought the spire was being used as an OP. *Harding* claimed a ranger officer later confirmed that the church contained four enemy machine guns "which were completely demolished."

Harding's claim to have hit the church with every shell was contradicted by Mayor Michel Hardelay of Vierville, who said that the first shell exploded in his house, causing the wall of the second floor to collapse. The second hit the bakery, killing the maid and the baker's baby. The following shells hit the surrounding buildings as well as the church. The GIs in the town took some casualties from the naval fire.[12]

Such contradictions in the testimony of eyewitnesses, well known among witnesses to traffic accidents, are commonplace in war; in the case of the D-Day fights at Vierville, St.-Laurent, and Colleville, they are exacerbated by the nature of the action—small groups without knowledge of what was going on around them, no radio or other contact, each group engaged in its own battle.

When the American destroyers had a spotter, they could be deadly accurate. Private Slaughter of the 116th saw *Satterlee* do some fine work. Slaughter was on the edge of the Vierville draw. He spotted Sgt. William Presley leading a small band of men. Presley was six feet four inches, weighed 230 pounds, and was, according to Slaughter, "the epitome of a first sergeant: rugged-looking, immaculate, and gifted with a booming voice."

In front of Presley there was a naval forward observer, lying face down, dead, with a radio strapped to his back. Presley had been observing a battery of *Nebelwerfer*, 105mm mottars, firing from a fixed position a couple of hundred meters to his front. The shells were playing hell with the reinforcements arriving on the beach. Presley retrieved the radio and made contact with *Satterlee*. He said he had a target and gave the coordinates. *Satterlee* fired; Presley gave a correction; another shell, another correction; then Presley called, "Fire for effect."

Slaughter, watching all this, recalled, "We heard the salvo, 'Boom-ba-ba-boom-ba-ba-boom-ba-be-boom!' Soon the shells came screaming over on the way to the German tormentors. 'Ker-whoom-ker-whoom-ker-whoom! Ker-whoom-oom-oom-ker-whoom-oom-oom!' The ground trembled under us. The exploding shells saturated the area, some of them landing too close for comfort to our position. That action put the *Nebelwerfer* out of action and earned Presley the Distinguished Service Cross."

Shortly thereafter, Slaughter saw his first German prisoner. He was being interrogated by a German-speaking American officer armed with a carbine. The captive was on his knees, hands behind his head. The American demanded to know where the minefields were located. The prisoner replied with his name, rank, and serial number.

"Where are the damn minefields?" the officer shouted. With an arrogant look on his face, the prisoner gave his name, rank, and serial number. The American fired his carbine between the German's knees. With a smirk on his face, the German pointed to his crotch and said, "*Nicht hier.*" Then he pointed to his head and said, "*Hier!*"

The American interrogator gave up and waved the prisoner away. Slaughter commented, "This convinced me that we were fighting first-rate soldiers."[13]

"At nightfall the Vierville area was the weakest part of the beachhead," the Army official history states.[14] The 5th Rangers and elements of the 1st Battalion, 116th, with some combat engineers, were holding defensive positions west and southwest of the village. Many were surrounded. (One ranger platoon had, amazingly, managed to make it to Pointe-du-Hoc, almost without incident.) Communication ranged from poor to completely absent. The Vierville draw remained closed almost until dark. Dog Green, White, and Red sectors on the beach were still under heavy artillery fire and few landings had been attempted after 1200, which meant that few reinforcements were coming up to help.

Lt. Francis Dawson of the rangers had already earned a DSC for his actions in getting men off the beach. When he got to Vierville his unit was stopped on the west side by machine-gun fire. "We failed to eliminate this gun, so we withdrew and came back to the Vierville road and tried to outflank it. But as night fell, we were not too far from Vierville. We dug in."[15]

Others had similar experiences. Lieutenant Mehaffey got through Vierville in the midafternoon, then stopped. "Our right flank was the English Channel, our left flank our own outposts. We held this position the rest of D-Day. We were less than a mile from where we had landed."[16]

Pvt. Paul Calvert of the 116th, after describing the route his company followed to Vierville, declared, "The end of the day saw this group completely fatigued, demoralized, disorganized, and utterly incapable of concerted military action. The men were scattered from captured German positions overlooking the Vierville draw to the designated CP with Colonel Canham."[17]

But the Germans at Vierville were also fatigued, demoralized, disorganized, and incapable of concerted action. From behind their hedgerows, German snipers and machine gunners could delay and harass and stop the American advance—but they could not push the men from the rangers and the 116th back down the bluff.

The village of Vierville had not been defended by the Germans, but St.-Laurent held a company of infantry from the 352nd Division. The Germans were dug in on the high ground commanding the upper end of the Les Moulins draw. They were on both sides of the road coming up the draw and controlled the approaches to the main crossroad on the western outskirts of the village. Maj. Sidney Bingham, CO of 2nd Battalion, 116th, organized a series of attacks against the German position, only to be stopped by machine-gun fire from positions which his men were unable to locate.

In the afternoon, the GIs at St.-Laurent got help from the 115th Regiment, 29th Division. The 115th landed at E-1 draw just before noon, but it took many hours for the regiment to clear the beach and launch an assault on St.-Laurent from the northeast. It was slowed by mines—and by a rumor sweeping through the troops that American mine detectors could not locate German mines, so that the paths marked out by white tape were not safe. German snipers on the bluff caused some casualties and many delays.

"We moved cautiously and hesitantly, partly because of fear and partly because of the strangeness of the situation," Sgt. Charles Zarfass recalled. St.-Laurent was only about a kilometer up from the beach, but the 2nd Battalion, 115th, did not start its attack against the village until late afternoon, while the 1st Battalion did not reach its objective south of St.-Laurent until 1800.[18]

Pvt. John Hooper got near St.-Laurent in midafternoon. "Creeping forward, ever so cautiously, I tripped a Bouncing Betty mine. It popped into the air and I hit the ground expecting to be blown to bits. It fell back to earth with a thump—a dud. Greatly fatigued, I just lay there wondering if the war would last much longer."

Hooper got up and advanced, only to be held up by machine-gun fire coming from a wood. A prolonged firefight ensued. Rifle ammunition for the GIs was running critically low. A lieutenant with an M-1 and binoculars told Hooper to cover him—he intended to climb a tree and "get those bastards."

"That's not a good idea, Lieutenant," Hooper said. The lieutenant glared at him, turned, climbed the tree, found a good firing position, and shot three times. Then he came crashing down, screaming, "My God, I'm hit."

Hooper and a buddy dragged him to a hedgerow. He had been shot in the chest. They called for a medic who gave him some morphine.

"What a thorough waste," Hooper commented to his buddy. "All the money spent on commissioning this guy and he's trying to act like a Sergeant York. Didn't last a day. What a terrible waste." The lieutenant died that evening.[19]

By late afternoon, E-1 was open for tracked vehicles. At 2000 hours, Major Bingham sent a runner to ask for tank support in the assault on St.-Laurent. Three tanks from the 741st Tank Battalion came up. They destroyed sniper and machine-gun nests in the vicinity of the village. But just as the infantry began to move in,

5-inch shells from American destroyers came pouring down. As at Vierville, the troops at St.-Laurent had no way of contacting the Navy, and they took some casualties as a result of the bombardment.

After the naval fire lifted, the fighting in St.-Laurent reached a crescendo. GIs ducked around corners, threw grenades into windows, kicked in doors, and sprayed interiors with their BARs and carbines. The Germans, taking advantage of the stone houses that might as well have been fortresses, fought back furiously.

In the midst of this street fighting, several men from the 115th were startled to see Lt. Col. William Warfield, CO of the 2nd Battalion, calmly sitting on a curb with his feet extended into the street, tossing pebbles at a scruffy dog.

Another strange sight: General Gerhardt had come ashore in the late afternoon and set up 29th Division HQ in a quarry in the Vierville draw. He could not get much information on how things were going up on top for his regiments, but he could see a long file of men trudging up the draw. He spotted a passing soldier eating an orange. When the man tossed the orange peel away, Gerhardt sprang up from the maps he was studying and gave the GI a furious tongue-lashing for littering.[20]

By nightfall, 29th Division troops held positions north, east, and south of St.-Laurent and parts of the town. Elements from five battalions had spent the afternoon fighting through an area of about a square mile without securing it—and it was defended by only a single German company. That spoke well for the German defenders—and showed what excellent defensive positions hedgerows and stone houses on narrow streets provided, as well as how difficult it was in World War II for infantry lacking on-site artillery, tank, or mortar support to carry out a successful assault.

But although the Germans had done well and the Americans had failed to reach their objectives, the prospects for the next day were decidedly dismal for the Germans. The GIs had fresh supplies coming up from the beach, plus reinforcements, plus all those vehicles waiting for a chance to drive up the draws and get into the action. The Germans were all but surrounded, they had no hope of fresh supplies or reinforcements, and they were badly outnumbered.

At Colleville, as in the other two villages, small separate battles developed throughout the afternoon. Advancing American

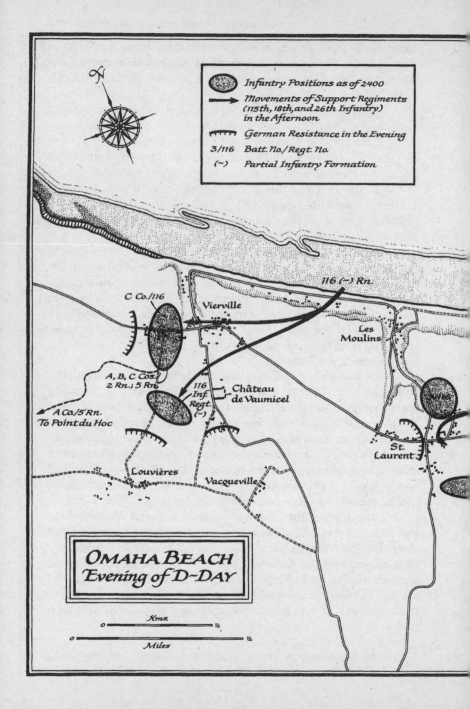

Infantry Positions as of 2400

Movements of Support Regiments
(115th, 18th, and 26th Infantry)
in the Afternoon

German Resistance in the Evening

3/116   Batt. No./Regt. No.

(~)   Partial Infantry Formation

116 (~) Rn.

C Co./116

Vierville

Les
Moulins

A, B, C Cos.
2 Rn.; 5 Rn.

116
Inf.
Regt.
(~)

Château
de Vaumicel

3/116

A Co./5 Rn.
To Point du Hoc

St.
Laurent

Louvières

Vacqueville

OMAHA BEACH
Evening of D-DAY

Kms.
0 ———————— ½

0 ———————— ½
Miles

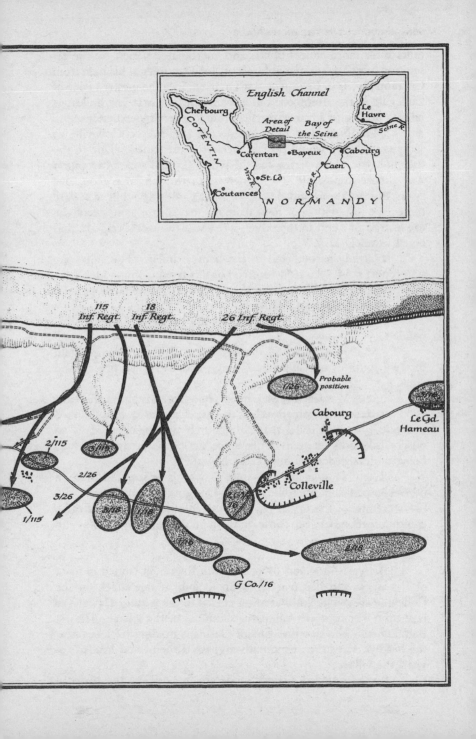

English Channel

Cherbourg

COTENTIN

Area of
Detail

Bay of
the Seine

Le
Havre

Seine R.

Carentan

Bayeux

Cabourg

Caen

Vire R.

St. Lô

Orne R.

Coutances

N O R M A N D Y

115
Inf. Regt.

18
Inf. Regt.

26 Inf. Regt.

1/26

Probable
position

Cabourg

Le Gd.
Hameau

2/115

3/11

2/26

1/115

3/26

3/18

1/18

2/3/18

Colleville

3/16

2/18

G Co./16

units were more or less blind, and coordinated action by the assaulting forces was impossible. Capt. Joe Dawson got his men from G Company, 16th Regiment, 1st Division, into the western edge of Colleville in the afternoon, but after seizing the first few buildings he was unable to advance further, due to a terrible experience.

"The Navy had been given orders to fire on Colleville as soon as visibility would permit," Dawson explained. "Due to the haze of battle which permeated the whole sky and area, observation was almost impossible. Nevertheless, in the late afternoon, our Navy did go ahead and decide to level Colleville while we were there. We lost sixty-four men from our naval fire, as it swept the town from one end to the other. That was the worst tragedy that befell us on D-Day."[21]

Harding participated in the bombardment. The ship's action report read, "At 1854 received orders from Commander Task Force to open fire for two minutes on Colleville Church, range 3500 yards, which was complied with.

"At 1857 ceased fire, church badly battered, 73 rounds expended.

"At 1935 again received orders from CTF to open fire again for two minutes on Colleville Church and to spread fire around area.

"At 1937 opened fire again on same target, range at this time 3800 yards, scoring numerous hits on church and area. Sixty rounds expended. It is believed that this church was being used as an observation post for mortar fire since the beach at this time was being bombarded apparently from inland."[22]

The CTF was just guessing; Dawson's losses, and those of other companies in Vierville and St.-Laurent, to so-called friendly fire were one of the prices paid for the complete absence of radio communication between those on the high ground and the Navy in the Channel.

Between 1100 and 1400, the 18th Regiment landed in front of E-1 draw and began moving up to join in the attack on the Colleville area. The 2nd Battalion passed to the west of Dawson to take up positions a half kilometer southeast of the village. The 1st Battalion ran into two platoons of Germans holding trenches near the head of E-1 draw, eventually bypassed them, and headed toward the village.

"As we moved against moderate fire toward the town of

Wounded men from the 1st Division at Omaha Beach.

Survivors from a destroyed Higgins boat are helped onshore. This may have been the only battle in history in which the wounded were brought forward, toward the front line, for first aid from the medics.

Below, by midday, junior officers and noncoms had taken charge and led small groups of men up the bluff at Omaha. By 1400, men from the 29th and 1st divisions were working their way inland. Here troops disembark from a Higgins boat. On the beach are half-tracks and a Duck.

Opposite top, once the beachhead was won, the Allies had a seemingly inexhaustible flow of reinforcements to bring into the battle. Here a Sherman tank unloads from an LST at Omaha Beach, June 8.

Opposite bottom, a part of the price of victory. Coastguardsmen haul a sailor up over the side of their landing craft; he had survived the sinking of his Higgins boat after it hit a mine off Omaha Beach.

U.S. COAST GUARD

The coxswain of this Higgins boat was hit by machine-gun fire off Omaha Beach. He is being moved from his craft to a Coast Guard transport for treatment and eventual transfer to England.

An LCT brings out wounded assault troops from Omaha Beach. They were taken to LSTs serving as hospital ships, then to England. Total Allied casualties were about 4,900 killed, wounded, and missing. Of these, more than 2,000 were hit on Omaha.

The cliff at Pointe-du-Huc. The rangers climbed it in the face of fierce resistance. Returning to the scene ten years later, the CO, Col. James Earl Rudder, asked a reporter, "Will you tell me how we did this?"

A portion of the battleground at Pointe-du-Hoc. Rudder's men took fearful casualties driving the Germans out of their fortifications—but by 0900, June 6, they had accomplished their objective, the destruction of the big guns.

TWO PHOTOS:
COURTESY OF MRS. JAMES EARL RUDDER

The face of the enemy. Old men and boys made up much of the Wehrmacht manning the Atlantic Wall. Great care had to be taken in offering and accepting a surrender on D-Day. U.S. Ranger Alban Meccia wrote, "I saw a German officer shoot one of his men in the back when he started to walk over to us with his hands up. One of our guys saw a flag of surrender, and stood up to wave to the Germans to come on over, and was shot between the eyes."

Poles and Czechs—*Ost* battalion troops—on Utah Beach, gathered for transfer to the LST in the background for shipment to England. there are lots of smiles—but these prisoners later expressed their disappointment at being sent to POW camps in England rather than the United States.

"For you the war is over," and these German POWs—officers and enlisted men—couldn't be happier.

A badly damaged German fortification at Omaha Beach, showing the extent of the steel reinforcing rods and the thickness of the concrete. This fortification looked down on Easy Red sector and had a 75mm cannon that fired through the morning. It was finally put out of action by infantry tossing grenades into it.

A German soldier lies dead outside a machine-gun emplacement he so vainly defended on Utah Beach near Les dunes de Madeleine.

A young American, two even younger Germans at Utah Beach. Hitler had bet that his youth, deliberately raised for this moment in his totalitarian society, would outfight the soft, spoiled children of democracy. Hitler lost the bet.

Left, Maj. Gen. Percy Hobart attached all types of gadgets to the British tanks, this one a flail tank. The steel chains thrashing ahead of the rotating drum would set off mines harmlessly.

Opposite, another of "Hobart's funnies," this one a thirty-foot metal bridge that folded in half. The Americans were scornful of such devices, but the British used them to good effect on their beaches.

British troops from the 50th Division debarking from LCIs at Gold Beach, midday of June 6.

Troops from the 9th Canadian Brigade, 3rd Canadian Division, going ashore at mid-morning on Juno Beach. The Canadians on D-Day paid the Germans back for Dieppe. They made the deepest penetrations of any Allied force.

Arromanches and its artificial harbor, code name Mulberry, on the right flank of Gold Beach, in a photograph taken in September 1944. There was a similar artificial harbor off Omaha Beach, but it was destroyed by a gale between June 19 and 22. Between June 6 and 16, the Americans landed 278,000 men and 35,000 vehicles at Omaha, while the British had put ashore 279,000 men and 46,000 vehicles at Gold.

Commandos from Lord Lovat's Special Service Brigade landing at La Brèche on Sword Beach. Sherman DD (Duplex Drive) amphibious tanks are leading.

Men of No. 4 Commando advancing in Ouistreham, supported by Sherman DD tanks still wearing their skirts. After taking Ouistreham in house-to-house fighting, the commandos moved inland to link up with the 6th Airborne Division.

British casualties from the South Lancashire and Middlesex regiments being helped ashore on Queen White sector of Sword Beach, about 0750, June 6.

Gliders of the British 6th Airborne Division near Ranville, about a kilometer from Pegasus Bridge. Of the 355 gliders that took part in British airborne operations on D-Day, 100 pilots were killed or wounded.

Above and right, the end of the day at Omaha Beach. American men and equipment coming ashore in staggering numbers. One pilot thought, as he looked down on this scene, that Hitler must have been mad to think he could beat the United States.

Opposite bottom, there was lots more to come. On D-Day plus one, troops of the 2nd Division move inland from Easy Red sector, near St. Laurent, Omaha Beach. The column curves around a German strongpoint that did great damage on D-Day.

TWO PHOTOS U.S. COAST GUARD

A part of the continuous stream of men and equipment sailing from England to France, June 7. In the background, a Rhino ferry loaded with ambulances eases toward the beach.

Only a handful of German planes dared to fly anywhere near the invasion beaches; those who did after dark on D-Day were greeted by a tremendous barrage (and only one in six of the shells being fired were tracers). In the foreground, an American transport vessel that hit a mine is slowly sinking.

Colleville," Lt. Charles Ryan of Company A related, "I became aware of a small group of men moving steadily toward Colleville. As I reached my position, I saw that it was my battalion commander, Lt. Col. Robert York, who was one of the greatest combat leaders of WWII or any other war.

"He had his command group with him. He paused to say, 'Keep moving, boys, through town to the other side. We're getting a handle on this thing but we still have a long way to go.' Then he moved ahead."

At 1730, Ryan's platoon reached the coastal road, where it assumed defensive positions for the anticipated counterattack. "That night," Ryan remembered, "we were subjected to continuous machine-gun and rifle fire." He paused, then went on: "But there was a beachhead. The 1st Division was ashore.

"The Sixth of June, 1944, was an exhausting day, a frightening day, an exhilarating day, a sorrowful day, and a joyous day. It was a day when the men in the 1st Division lived up to the division motto, 'NO MISSION TOO DIFFICULT, NO SACRIFICE TOO GREAT. DUTY FIRST.'

"Now, forty-five years later, it's hard for me to believe that I was a part of this. I still correspond with some of the men in my D-Day platoon and we're all still proud of what was done and happy that we were a part of it and completely bewildered as to why we survived. But we're bewildered by lots of things these days."[23]

At 1900, the 1st Division CO, General Huebner, landed on Easy Red and set up his CP. At 2030 General Gerow and the advance HQ of V Corps left the *Ancon* for shore. On the high ground inland, the men of the 29th and 1st divisions were scattered and isolated in eighteen different pockets around the three villages. There was no continuous line. They had no artillery or heavy mortars, only a few tanks, no communications with the naval or air forces. For the night, they were on the defensive, dug in.

But they were there. The presence of so much brass on the beach was proof that they had secured the beachhead and won the battle.

The German defenders had inflicted very heavy casualties on the assaulting force at Omaha Beach. V Corps suffered 2,400 dead, wounded, and missing in putting 34,000 troops of the 55,000-

man assault force ashore. Losses of 7.2 percent in one day are horrendous, but that was five percentage points less than anticipated.[24]

The 352nd Division suffered 1,200 killed, wounded, and missing, or about 20 percent of its total strength. The 29th and 1st divisions had accomplished their basic objective, establishing a foothold, even if they had not driven anywhere near as far inland as they had planned or hoped. The 352nd Division had not accomplished its objective, stopping the assault on the beach.

The experiences of Pvt. Franz Gockel of the 352nd provide some vivid images of what the day was like for a German infantryman. At 0830 he had thought the battle won, but the Americans had continued to land. To his left and right, American squads and platoons had bypassed WN 62, then attacked it from the rear, "making it necessary for us to defend ourselves from attack from behind." At noon, he got a half ration of bread and a mess tin of milk, but no supplies or reinforcements came in. A runner sent to get help was never seen again. The Americans pressed on and "our resistance became weaker."

Gockel was shot through the left hand. The medic who put a bandage on smiled and said it looked like a good *Heimatschuss* (million-dollar wound). American troops got into the network of trenches and suddenly they were only twenty meters away.

Gockel grabbed his rifle and ran toward Colleville. On the outskirts he linked up with his company CO and the few survivors from WN 62. The Americans were already in the village.

The CO ordered Gockel and fifteen other wounded men into a truck for transport to a hospital in Bayeux. The route was blocked. Ruins and rubble covered the crossroads—here was the payoff from the B-17s and battleship bombardment. "Dead cattle lay in the pastures. The supply units had also suffered their share of casualties. Many of them were immobilized."

Gockel's truck came under fire from a strafing RAF fighter plane. He and his comrades jumped out. Those with light wounds proceeded on foot toward Bayeux. En route they commandeered a French farmer's horse and wagon. In Bayeux they found that the hospital had been evacuated. They were told to proceed to Vire. They found that city badly damaged and still burning from air bombardment. They spent the night in a farmhouse, drinking Calvados.

Of the twenty men from WN 62, only three escaped unwounded, and they were taken prisoner. Gockel concluded, "None of my comrades who had survived the invasion continued to believe in victory."[25]

The German failure at Omaha Beach had many causes. The attempt to defend everywhere had scattered the division in driblets here, droplets there. Furthermore, the CO of the 352nd, General Kraiss, completely misinterpreted Allied intentions. At 0200, when he received reports about paratroopers landing on his left flank between Isigny and Carentan, he thought that the Americans were trying to separate the 352nd from the 709th. At 0310 he ordered his division reserve, called *Kampfgruppe Meyer* after the CO of the 915th Regiment, to move from its positions south of Bayeux all the way to the Vire estuary. But it was a wild-goose chase; the paratroopers were a handful of 101st men who had been misdropped.

At 0550 Kraiss realized his error. He told Meyer to halt the *Kampfgruppe* and await further orders. Within a half hour the Americans began landing at Omaha, but not until 0735 did Kraiss commit reserves to the area, and then he sent only one battalion from the *Kampfgruppe*. At 0835 he sent the other two battalions against the British 50th Division at Gold Beach. Splitting the 915th in this fashion meant it was nowhere able to strike a telling blow. The battalions were also hours late in arriving at the battle areas, because as they moved they were shot up by Allied fighters and hit by Allied bombers.

Inadequate intelligence in many cases, and none at all in others, badly hampered Kraiss, but he was as guilty of passing on bad information as he was a victim of receiving it. At 1000 he reported penetrations in the forward positions of the 352nd at Omaha but indicated that they were not dangerous. At 1335 he advised Seventh Army HQ that the American assault had been hurled back into the sea, except at Colleville, which he said was being counterattacked by the 915th. Not until 1800 did he admit that the Americans had infiltrated through the 352nd's strong points, but even then he claimed that only Colleville was in danger.

At 1700, Field Marshal Rundstedt demanded that the Allied bridgehead be wiped out that evening. A few minutes later, General Jodl sent out an order from OKW—all available forces should be thrown into the battle. At 1825, Kraiss ordered his last uncommitted unit, the engineer battalion, to move to St.-Laurent and fight as infantry. By the time the engineers got there, it was dark, too late to do anything but dig in and wait for daylight.

Shortly before midnight, June 6, Kraiss admitted to his corps commander, General Marcks, that the 352nd desperately needed help. "Tomorrow the division will be able to offer the enemy the same determined resistance it did today [but] because of heavy casualties . . . reinforcements must be brought up by the day after tomorrow. Losses of men and material in the resistance nests are total."

Marcks replied, "All reserves available to me have already been moved up. Every inch of the ground must be defended to the utmost capacity until new reinforcements can be brought up."[26]

In sum, the fighting power of the 352nd had been frittered away in stubborn defensive action by small groups who were able to delay but not to stop the American advance. Rommel's insistence on close-up defense of the beach had made the initial assault phase harder for the Americans but at excessive cost for the Germans— and it had not worked. "In that respect," the Army's official history states, "V Corps had surmounted a severe crisis, and the success of its hard fight should be measured in other terms than the size of the beachhead."[27]

The 352nd was used up. No reinforcements were immediately available. Those coming to the sound of the guns from the interior of France, whether infantry or panzer, were going to have to run a gauntlet of air and naval gunfire to get there.

The Atlantic Wall had been cracked at Omaha Beach, and there was nothing behind it in the way of fixed fortifications— except those awful hedgerows.

How did V Corps do it? The sheer weight of the assault was one of the deciding factors, but by itself not enough to ensure victory. Pvt. Carl Weast of the rangers has an answer to the question. In his oral history, he was relating a story about his company commander, Capt. George Whittington.

"He was a hell of a man," Weast said. "He led people. I recall the time a week or so after D-Day when we shot a cow and cut off some beef and were cooking it over a fire on sticks. Captain Whittington came up and threw a German boot next to the fire and said, 'I'll bet some son of a bitch misses that.' We looked at the boot. The German's leg was still inside of it. I'll bet by God he did miss it."

That same day, Weast heard the executive officer of the 5th

Ranger Battalion, Maj. Richard Sullivan, criticizing Captain Whittington for unnecessarily exposing himself.

"Whittington said to Sully, 'You saw it happen back on that goddamn beach. Now you tell me how the hell you lead men from behind.' "

Weast's introduction to combat came on D-Day. He fought with the rangers through the next eleven months. He concluded that the Allied high command had been right to insist that "there be practically no experienced troops in the initial waves that hit that beach, because an experienced infantryman is a terrified infantryman, and they wanted guys like me who were more amazed than they were frozen with fear, because the longer you fight a war the more you figure your number's coming up tomorrow, and it really gets to be God-awful."

Weast made a final point: "In war, the best rank is either private or colonel or better, but those ranks in between, hey, those people have got to be leaders."[28]

At Omaha Beach, they were.

25

"IT WAS JUST FANTASTIC"

Afternoon on Omaha Beach

BY EARLY AFTERNOON a majority of the German pillboxes on the beach and bluff had been put out of action by destroyers, tanks, and infantry, suppressing if not entirely eliminating machine-gun fire on the beach. Sniper fire, however, continued. The Germans made use of the maze of communication trenches and tunnels to reoccupy positions earlier abandoned and resumed firing.

Worse, artillery from inland and flank positions kept up harassing fire on the beach flat, some of it haphazard, some of it called in by OPs on the bluff. Even the haphazard fire was effective, because the traffic jam remained—it was hardly possible for a shell or mortar fired on the beach flat to miss.

Capt. Oscar Rich was a spotter for the 5th Field Artillery Battalion. He was on an LCT with his disassembled L-5 plane. He came to Easy Red at 1300. "I'd like to give you first my impression of the beach, say from a hundred yards out till the time we got on the beach," he said.

"Looking in both directions you could see trucks burning, tanks burning, piles of I don't know what burning. Ammunition had been unloaded on the beach. I saw one pile of five-gallon gasoline cans, maybe 500 cans in all. A round hit them. The whole thing just exploded and burned.

"I've never seen so much just pure chaos in my life. But what I expected, yet didn't see, was anybody in hysterics. People on the beach were very calm. The Seabees were directing traffic and bringing people in and assigning them to areas and showing them which way to go. They were very matter-of-fact about the whole thing. They were directing traffic just like it was the 4th of July parade back home rather than where we were."

While the LCT circled offshore, looking for a place to go in, a mortar round hit it in the bow. The skipper, an ensign, nevertheless saw a likely spot and moved in. The beachmaster waved him off. He had forgotten to drop his sea anchor so "we had one heck of a time trying to get off the sandbar, but finally we made it," Rich said.

"I felt sorry for this ensign, who was really shook up after taking this round in the bow and forgetting to drop his sea anchor. And he asked me, 'Lieutenant, do you know anything about running ships?' and I said, 'Hell, man, I've been running boats all my life.' Actually, the biggest I'd ever run was a skiff fishing in the river, but he said, 'You want to run this?' and I said, 'I sure as hell do.'

"I got one of the sailors and told him, 'Son, you've got one job and one job only.' He said, 'What's that?' I said, 'When we get within 100 yards of the shore, you drop this sea anchor whether I tell you to or not.' "

The LCT went in again. Somehow the sailors managed to drop the bow, even as the craft took another hit in the engine room. Two jeeps ran off. To Rich's dismay, "They forgot to hook my airplane on and I didn't have a jeep." A Seabee came over with a bulldozer, hooked a rope onto the tow bar for the L-5, pulled it onto the beach, unhooked the plane, told Rich he had other work to do, wished him luck, and drove off. "So there I was with an airplane, no mechanic, no help, and no transportation."

Rich saw the beachmaster. "He couldn't have been over twenty-five years old. He had a nice handlebar mustache and he was sitting in a captain's chair there on the beach, and he had a radio and a half dozen telephones and a bunch of men serving him as runners and he was just keeping everything going. People came up to him and wanted to know this, that, or the other. He never lost his temper. He never got excited. He would just tell them and they'd go away. He was only a lieutenant, but these Army colonels and generals would come up and demand this and demand that and he'd say, 'I'm sorry, I haven't got it. You'll just have to take what you've got and go on with it.' They would shake their heads and go off and leave him.

"When he'd spot an open space, why, he'd say, 'Let's get a

craft in there. Let's get a boat in there. Let's get that one out of the way. Get a bulldozer over and shove that tank out of the way. Make room for somebody to come in here.' He kept that beach moving. I have no idea who he was, but the Navy certainly should have been proud of him, because he did a tremendous job."

Rich told the beachmaster he needed a jeep to pull his L-5 off the beach. "He said, 'There's one over there. There's nobody in it. Go take it.' "

Rich did, and wove his way through the congestion to the E-1 draw, his plane in tow. Then he drove up the draw. Rich was possibly the first to do so—it had just opened.

On top, Rich found the apple orchard outside St.-Laurent where he was supposed to be and began to assemble his plane. With no mechanic to help, he was not making much progress. From time to time he would get some help from a GI who could not resist the temptation to tinker with a machine. Sooner or later a noncom or officer would yell at the soldier to get the hell back to the battle and Rich would be on his own again. Not until dark did he get his plane ready to fly.[1]

Rich was lucky. German artillery and mortar fire concentrated on the exits; without spotter planes, the Navy could not locate the sources of the fire. As the afternoon wore on, the shelling got heavier. Adm. Charles Cooke and Maj. Gen. Tom Handy of the War Department, observing the action from the deck of *Harding,* decided they needed a closer look. They off-loaded onto an LCI, closed the beach, transferred to an LCM, and went in through a gap in the obstacles.

"The beach was strewed with wrecked landing craft, wrecked tanks, and various other vehicles," Cooke recalled. "It was also strewed with dead and wounded."

Handy went to the right, Cooke to the left. Shells burst all around them, throwing sand in their faces, forcing them to hit the beach, in Cooke's case inflicting some slight shrapnel wounds. After a couple of hours, they rejoined and decided to get out, because, as Cooke said, "the shelling was getting very much heavier, increasing the casualty toll and it appeared highly desirable to leave."[2]

Lt. Vince Schlotterbeck of the 5th ESB spent seven hours on an LCT cruising just out of range of the German guns, waiting for an opportunity to go in. Like most others, the skipper had cut loose the barrage balloon—there were no German planes strafing the fleet, and the balloons gave the Germans a target to spot and zero in on. Schlotterbeck spent the time perched atop the landing ramp, watching whatever caught his eye.

"The underwater obstacles could be seen plainly, since the tide was not all the way in. The wreckage on the beach and in the water was greater than anything I had ever imagined. Tanks were strewn along the beach, some half submerged. We could see that there were only two or three tanks on which we could depend."

At 1830, the LCT tried to run in. "We headed for a likely spot but ran onto a sandbar and had to back off because the water was too deep. Just as we cleared, a shell threw up a spray in the exact spot where we had been grounded." The skipper tried again. He found a gap in the obstacles "but a big ship loaded with ammunition was grounded and burning fiercely. The almost continuous explosions made it too dangerous to land there, so we sought again." Finally the skipper saw a good spot at Fox Red and turned toward it, but an LCI raced him to the gap, cutting in front of the LCT and causing it to land on another sandbar. This time it was stuck, period.

"Our engines throbbed at top speed, and our craft seemed ready to disintegrate from vibration. The stern anchor had been dropped and was being pulled in, but instead of pulling us off the anchor just dragged along in the sand. The engines screamed with power, never ceasing."

Meanwhile, the LCI that had beat the LCT to the gap had lowered its ramps and men were wading into shore. "Suddenly, a shell burst in their midst and we never saw any of them again. Then the Germans sent a shell into the front of the craft, one in the middle, and one in the rear."

Schlotterbeck's LCT finally floated free on the rising tide. The officers on the craft held a conference to decide whether to wait until after midnight, when the tide would be full, or to continue to attempt to get ashore.

"Everyone was in favor of going in as soon as possible because we did not like the idea of hitting the beach after dark, so we kept on trying. And at about 2000 we found the right spot." Schlotterbeck waded ashore.

"My mind had already been made up to the fact that a horrible sight would greet me, and it is a good thing that I had prepared myself because the number of casualties was appalling.

The number of dead was very great, but what struck us hardest was the boys who had been wounded and were trying to hitch rides back to the transports. Wounded were walking along the beach trying to pick up a ride. Those who were more severely wounded came in pairs, supporting each other, when they rightfully should have been stretcher cases."

Schlotterbeck had to walk on dead bodies to proceed up the bluff. "At one point I was ready to walk on a body face up when the soldier slowly opened his eyes and I almost twisted myself out of shape to avoid him. Luckily, I missed him."[3]

Pvt. M. C. Marquis of the 115th Regiment had his own unnerving experience. On his LCVP going in that afternoon, he had of all things exchanged shoes with Corporal Terry: "We thought we got a better fit." Going up the bluff, Terry was in front of Marquis. He stepped on a mine. It split open his foot and shoe. "As I walked by," Marquis reported, "I said, 'So long, Terry.' I still wonder if he made it to the hospital."

As Marquis climbed, a dozen German prisoners guarded by a GI descended. "These were the first Germans we saw. They didn't look so tough."

An American went down, hit by a sniper. A medic hurried over to treat the wounded man. The sniper shot the medic in the arm. "Hey," the medic shouted angrily, "you're not supposed to shoot medics!"

Marquis got to the top and moved forward with his squad to join the fight in St.-Laurent. Just as he arrived, naval gunfire came in. He got showered with bricks and mortar, but a helmet he had picked up on the beach protected him. The squad retreated and dug in beside a hedgerow.[4]

Down on the beach men went about their work despite the shelling. The demolition teams were making progress in their vital task of clearing paths through the obstacles. As the tide dropped in the afternoon, they methodically blew up Rommel's Belgian gates and tetrahedra, ignoring sniper fire. They completed three gaps partially opened in the morning, made four new ones, and widened others. By evening they had thirteen gaps fully opened and marked and had cleared about one-third of the obstacles on the beach.[5]

The engineers, meanwhile, were opening the exits for vehicles. This involved blowing the concrete antitank barriers, filling in the antitank ditch, removing mines, and laying wire mesh on the sand so the jeeps and trucks could get across. By 1300, they had E-1 open to traffic.

Movement began at once, but within a couple of hours new trouble loomed; the vehicles coming up on the plateau were unable to get inland because the crossroad at St.-Laurent was still in enemy hands. For an hour or so vehicles were jammed bumper to bumper all the way from the beach to the plateau. At 1600 the engineers pushed a branch road south that bypassed the defended crossroad and movement resumed. At 1700, the Vierville exit (D-1) was opened, further relieving the congestion on the beach.[6]

Tanks, trucks, and jeeps made it to the top, but almost no artillery did. By dusk, elements of five artillery battalions had landed, but they had lost twenty-six guns to enemy fire and most of their equipment. Except for one mission fired by the 7th Field Artillery Battalion, American cannon, the queen of the battlefield, played no part in the battle on D-Day. The two antiaircraft battalions scheduled to land never even got ashore; they had to wait for D plus one. Over fifty tanks were lost, either at sea or on the beach.[7]

Planners had scheduled 2,400 tons of supplies to reach Omaha Beach during D-Day, but only 100 tons got ashore. A large proportion of what did arrive was destroyed on the beach; precious little of it got up to the plateau. Troops on top had to fight with what they carried up the bluff on their backs. They ran dangerously low on the three items that were critical to them—ammunition, rations, and cigarettes. Some did not get resupplied until D plus two; the rangers at Pointe-du-Hoc had to wait until June 9 for fresh supplies.

Despite the shelling, the congestion, and the obstacles, all through D-Day afternoon landing craft kept coming in, bringing more tanks and infantry. Lt. Dean Rockwell of the Navy, who had brought his LCT flotilla to Omaha Beach at H-Hour and landed the first tanks, made a return trip at 1400. His experience was typical of the skippers trying to get ashore in the follow-up waves.

"We cruised along the beach parallel for hundreds of yards," he recalled, "looking for an opening through the obstacles. One time we tried to nose our way through but made contact with one of the obstacles, which had a mine that detonated and blew a hole in our landing gear, which meant that we could not let our ramp down."

Rockwell finally made it to shore, but the damage to his

LCT prevented him from discharging his tanks and trailers. "We were able, however, to put the poor soldiers ashore." They were from a medical detachment. "Let me say," Rockwell went on, "I have never seen anybody who liked less to follow through on an assignment than they. The beach was literally covered with military personnel backed up, held down by the fire from the enemy. The enemy was bombarding the beach from mortars back over the bluff. The Germans had predetermined targets, and bodies and sand and material would fly when these mortars went off. Anyway, we put the poor soldiers ashore and we felt very, very sorry for them, but we thanked God that we had decided to join the Navy instead of the Army."[8]

Ernest Hemingway, a correspondent for *Collier's,* came in on the seventh wave, in an LCVP commanded by Lt. (jg) Robert Anderson of Roanoke, Virginia. To Hemingway, the LCVP looked like an iron bathtub. He compared the LCT to a floating freight gondola. The LCIs, according to Hemingway, "were the only amphibious operations craft that look as though they were made to go to sea. They very nearly have the lines of a ship." The Channel was covered with bathtubs, gondolas, and ships of all kinds, "but very few of them were headed toward shore. They would start toward the beach, then sheer off and circle back."

As Anderson's LCVP made its way toward shore, *Texas* was firing over it at the antitank barrier at one of the exits. "Those of our troops who were not wax-gray with seasickness," Hemingway wrote, "were watching the *Texas* with looks of surprise and happiness. Under the steel helmets they looked like pikemen of the Middle Ages to whose aid in battle had suddenly come some strange and unbelievable monster." To Hemingway, the big guns "sounded as though they were throwing whole railway trains across the sky."

Anderson had a hard time finding his designated landing area, Fox Red. Hemingway tried to help him navigate. They argued about landmarks. Once Anderson tried to go in, only to receive intense fire. "Get her the hell around and out of here, coxswain!" Anderson shouted. *"Get her out of here!"* The LCVP pulled back and circled.

Hemingway could see infantry working up the bluff. "Slowly, laboriously, as though they were Atlas carrying the world on their shoulders, men were [climbing]. They were not firing. They were just moving slowly . . . like a tired pack train at the end of the day, going the other way from home.

"Meantime, the destroyers had run in almost to the beach and were blowing every pillbox out of the ground with their five-inch guns. I saw a piece of German about three feet long with an arm on it sail high up into the air in the fountaining of one shell-burst. It reminded me of a scene in *Petroushka*."

Anderson finally got to the beach. So did the other twenty-three LCVPs from *Dorothy Dix*. Six were lost to mined obstacles or enemy fire. Hemingway concluded, "It had been a frontal assault in broad daylight, against a mined beach defended by all the obstacles military ingenuity could devise. The beach had been defended as stubbornly and as intelligently as any troops could defend it. But every boat from the *Dix* had landed her troops and cargo. No boat was lost through bad seamanship. All that were lost were lost by enemy action. And we had taken the beach."[9]

Capt. James Roberts, aide to General Gerow, went ashore at 1700 on Easy Red. "As we approached, we were hit with artillery fire, fragments were knocking us around," he remembered. "Several people were hit, including the skipper of our LCI. He was killed. Simultaneously we hit a sandbar and we were still a hundred or so yards from shore. There was mass confusion and fear and frankly I was in a panic. It is very difficult to dig a hole in a steel deck, and there isn't much cover on an LCI."

Roberts got off in chest-deep water and made his way to shore. "The beach was just a complete shambles. It was like an inferno. There were bodies everywhere and some wounded being attended to. As I went by a tank I heard people screaming for morphine. The tank was on fire and they were burning to death. There wasn't a thing that I could do about that and it was pretty nerve-shaking."

Shells were bursting all around. Roberts got off the beach as fast as he could. His job was to move up to St.-Laurent to set up a CP. As he climbed the bluff, a sniper opened fire. The bullet went over Roberts's head. Roberts tried to fire back, but his carbine was filled with sand and sea water and would not work, so he dove into a foxhole and cleaned it. When it was working, the sniper had gone.

Roberts got to the top of the bluff but could find no one from his HQ Company, nor any working radio, so "I didn't have much to do." He returned to the crest of the bluff and looked back at the Channel. "It was just fantastic. Vessels of all kinds as far as you could see."

Soon others from his HQ Company joined him, and Roberts set up V Corps CP north of St.-Laurent. Someone brought along tentage. Roberts set up a pup tent for General Gerow's first night ashore. When Gerow arrived, around 2100, his concerns were establishing communications and the possibility of an armored counterattack. V Corps had no contact with the British 50th Division on the left nor with the U.S. VII Corps on the right (nor, come to that, with the rangers at Pointe-du-Hoc). If the Germans did counterattack, V Corps was on its own.

Roberts's concern was his general's safety. The front line was only a half kilometer forward of corps HQ, "which is not the way the military planners like it to be."

As darkness fell, Roberts broke out one of his K rations and ate his first food of the day. Then he found a GI blanket and curled up in a ditch for the night. "Around midnight when things seemed to be fairly quiet I remember thinking, Man, what a day this has been. If every day is going to be as bad as this I'll never survive the war."[10]

There was no German counterattack. Rommel's plans for fighting the D-Day battle were never put into motion. There were many reasons.

First, German surprise was complete. The Fortitude operation had fixed German attention on the Pas-de-Calais. They were certain it would be the site of the battle, and they had placed the bulk of their panzer divisions north and east of the Seine River, where they were unavailable for counterattack in Normandy.

Second, German confusion was extensive. Without air reconnaissance, with Allied airborne troops dropping here, there, everywhere, with their telephone lines cut by the Resistance, with their army, corps, division, and some regimental commanders at the war game in Rennes, the Germans were all but blind and leaderless. The commander who was most missed was Rommel, who spent the day on the road driving to La Roche-Guyon— another price the Germans paid for having lost control of the air; Rommel dared not fly.

Third, the German command structure was a disaster. Hitler's mistrust of his generals and the generals' mistrust of Hitler were worth a king's ransom to the Allies. So were Hitler's sleeping habits, as well as his *Wolkenkuckucksheim* ideas.

The only high-command officer who responded correctly to the crisis at hand was Field Marshal Rundstedt, the old man who was there for window dressing and who was so scorned by Hitler and

OKW. Two hours before the seaborne landings began, he ordered the two reserve panzer divisions available for counterattack in Normandy, the 12th SS Panzer and *Panzer Lehr*, to move immediately toward Caen. He did so on the basis of an intuitive judgment that the airborne landings were on such a large scale that they could not be a mere deception maneuver (as some of his staff argued) and would have to be reinforced from the sea. The only place such landings could come in lower Normandy were on the Calvados and Cotentin coasts. He wanted armor there to meet the attack.

Rundstedt's reasoning was sound, his action decisive, his orders clear. But the panzer divisions were not under his command. They were in OKW reserve. To save precious time, Rundstedt had first ordered them to move out, then requested OKW approval. OKW did not approve. At 0730 Jodl informed Rundstedt that the two divisions could not be committed until Hitler gave the order, and Hitler was still sleeping. Rundstedt had to countermand the move-out order. Hitler slept until noon.

The two panzer divisions spent the morning waiting. There was a heavy overcast; they could have moved out free from serious interference from Allied aircraft. It was 1600 when Hitler at last gave his approval. By then the clouds had broken up and Allied fighters and bombers ranged the skies over Normandy, smashing anything that moved. The panzers had to crawl into roadside woods and wait under cover for darkness before continuing their march to the sound of the guns.[11]

"The news couldn't be better," Hitler said when he was first informed that D-Day was here. "As long as they were in Britain we couldn't get at them. Now we have them where we can destroy them."[12] He had an appointment for a reception near Salzburg for the new Hungarian prime minister; other guests included diplomats from Bulgaria, Romania, and Hungary. They were there to be browbeaten by Hitler into doing even more for the German war economy. When he entered the reception room, his face was radiant. He exclaimed, "It's begun at last." After the meeting he spread a map of France and told Goering, "They are landing here—and here: just where we expected them!" Goering did not correct this palpable lie.[13]

Nazi propaganda minister Goebbels had been told of the Allied airborne landings at 0400. "Thank God, at last," he said. "This is the final round."

Goebbels's and Hitler's thinking was explained by one of Goebbels's aides, who had pointed out in an April 10, 1944, diary entry: "The question whether the Allied invasion in the West is coming or not dominates all political and military discussion here.

"Goebbels is afraid that the Allies dare not make the attempt yet. If so, that would mean for us many months of endless, weary waiting which would test our strength beyond endurance. Our war potential cannot now be increased, it can only decline. Every new air raid makes the petrol position worse."[14] It had been galling to the Nazis that the Allies had been able to build their strength in England, untouchable by the Luftwaffe or the Wehrmacht. Now they had come within range of German guns.

But Hitler was more eager to hit London than to fight a defensive war. He had a weapon to do it with, the V-1. It had first been flown successfully on Christmas Eve, 1943; by June 1944, it was almost ready to go to work. The V-1 was a jet-powered plane carrying a one-ton warhead. It was wildly inaccurate (of the 8,000 launched against London, only 20 percent even hit that huge target), but it had a range of 250 kilometers and flew at 700 kilometers per hour, too fast for Allied aircraft or antiaircraft to shoot down.

On the afternoon of June 6, Hitler ordered the V-1 attacks on London to begin. As was so often the case, he was giving an order that could not be carried out. It took six days to bring the heavy steel catapult rigs from their camouflaged dumps to the Channel coast. The attack did not begin until June 12, and when it did it was a fiasco: of ten V-1s launched, four crashed at once, two vanished without a trace, one demolished a railway bridge in London, and three hit open fields.[15]

Still, the potential was there. Fortunately for the Allies, Hitler had picked the wrong target. Haphazard bombing of London could cause sleepless nights and induce terror, but it could not have a direct military effect. Had Hitler sent the V-1s against the beaches and artifical harbors of Normandy, by June 12 jammed with men, machines, and ships, the vengeance weapons (Goebbels picked the name, which was on the mark—they could sate Hitler's lust for revenge but they could not effect the war so long as they were directed against London) might have made a difference.

On D-Day, Hitler misused his sole potential strategic weapon, just as he misused his tactical counterattack force. His interference with his commanders on the scene stands in sharp contrast to Churchill and Roosevelt, who made no attempt at all to tell their generals and admirals what to do on D-Day, and to Eisenhower, who also left the decision-making up to his subordinates.

Eisenhower was up at 0700 on June 6. His naval aide, Harry Butcher, came by his trailer to report that the airborne landings had gone in and the seaborne landings were beginning. Butcher found Eisenhower sitting up in bed, smoking a cigarette, reading a Western novel. When Butcher arrived, Eisenhower washed, shaved, and strolled over to the tent holding the SHAEF operations section. He listened to an argument about when to release a communiqué saying that the Allies had a beachhead (Montgomery insisted on waiting until he was absolutely sure the Allies were going to stay ashore) but did not interfere.

Eisenhower wrote a brief message to Marshall, informing the chief of staff that everything seemed to be going well and adding that the British and American troops he had seen the previous day were enthusiastic, tough, and fit. "The light of battle was in their eyes."[16]

Eisenhower soon grew impatient with the incessant chatter in the tent and walked over to visit Montgomery. He found the British general wearing a sweater and a grin. Montgomery was too busy to spend much time with the supreme commander, as he was preparing to cross the Channel the next day to set up his advance HQ, but the two leaders did have a brief talk.

Then Eisenhower paid a visit to Southwick House to see Admiral Ramsay. "All was well with the Navy," Butcher recorded in his diary, "and its smiles were as wide as or wider than any."[17]

At noon Eisenhower returned to the tent, where he anxiously watched the maps and listened to the disturbing news coming from Omaha. He called some selected members of the press into his canvas-roofed, pine-walled quarters and answered questions. At one point he got up from his small table and began pacing. He looked out the door, flashed his famous grin, and announced, "The sun is shining."[18]

For the remainder of the day he paced, his mood alternating as he received news of the situation on the British and Canadian beaches and on Omaha and Utah. After eating, he retired early to get a good night's sleep.

The supreme commander did not give a single command on D-Day. Hitler gave two bad ones.

As dusk descended on Omaha Beach, intermittent shellfire continued to come down. Men dug in for the night wherever they could, some in the sand, some at the seawall, some on the bluff slopes, some behind hedgerows on the plateau. There were alarms caused by overeager troops, occasional outbursts of firing. There were no rear areas on D-Day.

Still, things had quieted down considerably. Lt. Henry Seitzler was a forward observer for the U.S. Ninth Air Force. He was taking "a lot of heckling and ribbing from the guys" because of the failure of the air forces to bomb and strafe the beaches as promised. "Of course, I had nothing to do with it; they just wanted to needle somebody.

"My biggest problem was to try to stay alive. My work didn't really start till D plus three, and here I'd gone in at H plus two hours on D-Day and I had been in the thickest and hottest part of it, and I had no real work to do, no assignment, except as far as I could see to stay alive, because I had no replacement."

Late in the afternoon, Seitzler and some members of a beach brigade decided they were hungry. "So we went out and climbed on a burned-out LCI. We broke into the pantry. Boy, that was really something. It hadn't been damaged. We brought a lot of stuff out and ate it on the beach under the seawall. The Navy really lived fine. We had a boned chicken, boned turkey, boned ham. We had everything you could think of, and we made pigs out of ourselves because we were half starved by that time."

When they finished, they decided they needed to top off their picnic on the beach with some coffee. They built a small fire behind the shingle seawall, using wood they had scavenged from one of the blasted-out vacation homes, and made Nescafé.

For Seitzler, that turned out to be a mistake. When it was full dark, the rule was that every man should stay in his foxhole. Anything that moved would be shot. But the Nescafé had a diuretic effect on Seitzler.

"So it was quite a problem, I'll tell you. If I made any noise or anything, I could very well get shot. All I could do was get up, ease up on the edge of my foxhole, roll over a couple of times, use an old tin can to do my business, throw it away, and roll back, very slowly and quietly. I called it 'suffering for sanitation.' I have never been able to drink Nescafé since."[19]

The next morning, Pvt. Robert Healey of the 149th Combat Engineers and a friend decided to go down the bluff to retrieve their packs. Healey had run out of cigarettes, but he had a carton in a waterproof bag in his pack.

"When we walked down to the beach, it was just an unbelievable sight. There was debris everywhere, and all kinds of equipment washing back and forth in the tide. Anything you could think of seemed to be there. We came across a tennis raquet, a guitar, assault jackets, packs, gas masks, everything. We found half a jar of olives which we ate with great relish. We found my pack but unfortunately the cigarettes were no longer there.

"On the way back I came across what was probably the most poignant memory I have of this whole episode. Lying on the beach was a young soldier, his arms outstretched. Near one of his hands, as if he had been reading it, was a pocketbook (what today would be called a paperback).

"It was *Our Hearts Were Young and Gay* by Cornelia Otis Skinner. This expressed the spirit of our ordeal. Our hearts were young and gay because we thought we were immortal, we believed we were doing a great thing, and we really believed in the crusade which we hoped would liberate the world from the heel of Nazism."[20]

26

THE WORLD HOLDS ITS BREATH

D-Day on the Home Fronts

AT 0700 MOUNTAIN WAR TIME (1300 French time), three teenage cowboys from western Montana strode into the Mecca Café in Helena, the state capital. The previous afternoon, the cowboys had joined the Navy at the Helena recruiting station. They were full of bluff and bluster and themselves.

"Food! Service! Attention!" they shouted at the waitress. She and the customers realized that the boys would be shipping out in a few hours, almost certainly their first trip out of Montana. The boisterous bad behavior of the "sailors" was forgiven. The waitress gave them "super de luxe" treatment, while around the tables the customers resumed their conversations over the coffee cups.

Someone switched on the radio. "Supreme Headquarters, Allied Expeditionary Force has just announced that the invasion has begun. Repeat, D-Day has come."

A reporter for the *Helena Independent-Record* was in the café. He wrote, "The news was first met with unbelief, and then rapt silence. Food was forgotten. Not a single voice was raised in request for service; no one wanted anything. They only sat and listened, and wondered."[1]

Not until the invention of the telegraph did people on the varied home fronts of wars know that a great battle was under way even as it was being fought. For Americans in 1861–65, the first

486

news came from the bulletins in the newspapers, bulletins that said little more than that a great battle was being fought in Pennsylvania or Mississippi. Over the next few days the papers would report on the battle. Then would come the seemingly never-ending lists of the dead. Gettysburg and Vicksburg were fought simultaneously, which meant that in the first days of July 1863 virtually every American knew someone who was in one of the battles. Son, husband, father, mother, brother, sister, grandson, girlfriend, uncle, friend—they all had to hold their breath. Wait, pray, worry, pray some more, and wait some more.

In World War I, Americans again had such agonizing experiences. By World War II, wire transmission had improved; Americans whose loved ones were in the Pacific or North Africa or Italy heard radio reports of battles as they happened, and within a week or so could see carefully censored moving-picture film from the battle (*never* showing dead or badly wounded Americans). What they could not know was how their loved one had fared. For that they could only wait and pray that the man from Western Union did not knock at their door.

On D-Day, a vast majority of the American people was involved. Most of them had made a direct contribution, as farmers providing the food, as workers in defense plants making planes or tanks or shells or rifles or boots or any of the myriad items the troops needed to win the war, or as volunteers doing the work at hundreds of agencies. The bandages they had rolled, the rifles they had made, were being put to use even as they heard the news. They prayed that they had done it right.

Andrew Jackson Higgins caught the spirit well. He was in Chicago on D-Day; he sent a message to his employees in New Orleans: "This is the day for which we have been waiting. Now, the work of our hands, our hearts and our heads is being put to the test. The war bonds you have bought, the blood you donated are also in there fighting. We may all be inspired by the news that the first landings on the continent were made by the Allies in our boats."[2]

The workers at Higgins Industries and the workers in defense plants around the nation had sacrificed their daily routines to make the invasion possible. They had jobs, which was a blessing to a generation that had just gone through the Depression, and they were well paid (although nobody got rich on an hourly wage). But they sacrificed to do it.

Polly Crow worked the night shift at the Jefferson Boat Company outside Louisville, Kentucky. She helped make LSTs.

She wrote her husband, who was in the Army, about their savings—something young couples in the Depression could only dream about: "We now have $780 in the bank and 5 bonds which sho looks good to me and as soon as I get the buggie in good shape I can really pile it in."

To make that money, Mrs. Crow worked a ten-hour night shift. She cared for her two-year-old son during the day; her mother looked after the child at night. She did volunteer work at the Red Cross. She shared her apartment with another woman and her mother.[3]

There were tens of thousands of young women like Mrs. Crow. Quickie marriages had become the norm, a million more during the war than would have been expected at prewar rates. Teenagers got married because the boy was going off to war, and in many cases, in the moral atmosphere of the day, if they wanted to have a sexual experience before he left they had to stand in front of a preacher first.

When the boy husbands left for war to become men, the girl wives became women. They traveled alone—or with their infants—to distant places on hot and stuffy or cold and overcrowded trains, became proficient cooks and housekeepers, managed the finances, learned to fix the car, worked in a defense plant, and wrote letters to their soldier husbands that were consistently upbeat.

"I write his dad everything our baby does," one young mother explained, "only in the letters I make it sound cute."[4]

Women in uniform were a new phenomenon for the Americans of the 1940s. They were in every branch of service, but more strictly segregated by their sex than blacks were by their race. The names of those segregated organizations were condescending: Women's Army Auxiliary Corps (WAAC), Women's Auxiliary Air Force (WAAF), Women's Auxiliary Ferry Squadron (WAFS), and WAVES, an acronym for Women Accepted for Volunteer Emergency Services (in late 1944 the Navy dropped the acronym and the women were called Women Reserves).

The women in uniform did everything the men did, except engage in combat. They were clerks, mechanics, administrators, radio operators, photo interpreters, cooks, meteorologists, supply sergeants, test pilots, transport pilots, and much more. Eisenhower felt he could not have won the war without them.[5]

They did not have an easy time. Cruel and vicious jokes were told about them—although not by the wounded about the nurses.

These pioneering women persevered and triumphed. The contribution of the women of America, whether on the farm or in the factory or in uniform, to D-Day was a *sine qua non* of the invasion effort.*

D-Day for the young women who had husbands they hardly knew stationed in the ETO was an especially trying experience, but then few Americans were without personal worries. Nearly every American knew someone in the Army, Army Air Force, Navy, or Coast Guard stationed in the European theater. Only a handful knew if the soldier or sailor or airman was in action on D-Day or if he was going in later, but they all knew that before the war was won their loved one would be in a combat zone.

Now it had started. The buildup phase was over. The United States was committed to throwing into the battle all the vast forces she had brought into existence over the past three years. That meant their boy, brother, husband, boyfriend, employee, fellow student, cousin, nephew was either already in combat or soon would be.

In Helena and New York, throughout the nation, they sat and wondered and listened to the radio and dashed out on the streets for the latest edition of the newspaper with a front-page map of the French coast. The home front heard and read about World War II. What Americans heard and read on D-Day was dismayingly lacking in details.

The official Nazi news agency, Transocean, was first to announce the invasion. The Associated Press picked it up and put it on the wire. The *New York Times* had it on the streets at 0130, but it was a headline only—no story. At 0200 Eastern War Time, the networks interrupted their musical programs with a flash announcement: "German radio says the invasion has begun." The Germans reported a naval battle off Le Havre and airborne landings north of the Seine (these were the dummy parachutists). Commentators quickly pointed out that there was no confirmation from Allied sources, and warned that it might well be a trick designed to get the Resistance in France to rise up prematurely and thus expose the organization to destruction.

At 0932 in London (0332 Eastern War Time) SHAEF re-

---

* Britain and America utilized their womanpower to the fullest in World War II. In Japan, women were urged by the government to stick to their traditional role and have more babies. In Germany, Hitler's romantic notions led him to give cash awards to German women who had more babies, and in Germany womanpower was not utilized until the very last months of the war.

leased a brief communiqué from General Eisenhower, read by his press aide, Col. Ernest Dupuy: "Under the command of General Eisenhower, Allied naval forces, supported by strong air forces, began landing Allied armies this morning on the northern coast of France."

SHAEF also sent by radio to New York a recording of Eisenhower reading his order of the day. It was a marvelous reading, rich in tone, resonant, and it provided a unifying experience, since it had been broadcast over the loudspeakers on the LSTs and transports in the southern England harbors before D-Day, so the American people heard what the invading force had heard.

By 0415 Eastern War Time NBC had an eyewitness report from London by a reporter who had flown with the 101st Airborne. Through the morning, more eyewitness reports came from reporters who had been at sea and returned to London. They had seen a lot of smoke, ships, and planes, little else. There was nothing from the beaches.

People listened to each new announcement breathlessly, only to be disappointed. To Eustace Tilley, pseudonymous "Talk of the Town" correspondent for the New Yorker, it was maddening: "The idiot babble of the radio followed us wherever we went."[6] The incoming news was so slow there were long periods, hours and more, when nothing new came over the wire. But the tension was so great that people wanted to hear something, so the broadcasters kept repeating themselves and quoting each other.

The commentators had a terrible time with French placenames. They needed some geography lessons. Their attempts at military analysis ranged from misleading to silly. They chattered away, with little to say except that it was on. They talked about everything except the one thing that was uppermost in the minds of many in the audience, casualties. That was forbidden by the Office of War Information (OWI).

Radio's shortcomings were caused primarily by OWI, but the SHAEF censorship policies contributed. SHAEF refused to give out the information the American people most longed to hear—what divisions, regiments, squadrons, ships were involved. It would not be more specific in its identification of the site of the landings than to say they had taken place on "the French coast." The reason for this strict censorship was to keep the Fortitude operation alive; the price in the United States was heightened anxiety.

Radio could not provide information, but it could provide inspiration. After the recording of Eisenhower's reading of his order of the day, the king of Norway spoke to his people, followed by the premiers of the Netherlands and Belgium, then the king of England. All these were repeated throughout the day.

Thin as the news was on the radio, it was a comfort. A California woman wrote Paul White, a CBS announcer: "It is 0321 here on the Pacific Coast. I was fortunate enough to hear the first radio news of D-Day break from CBS this morning, as I have spent all my evenings waiting at the radio these past two months. . . . Your London report from Mr. Murrow gave me a feeling that though I'm at least one world's distance from my husband and alone, I will not feel that way as long as you and your staff keep on the job."[7]

On D-Day, Franklin Roosevelt used the power of radio to link the nation in a prayer. Throughout the day the networks broadcast the text, which was printed in the afternoon editions of the newspapers; at 2200 Eastern War Time the president prayed while Americans across the country joined him:

"Almighty God: Our sons, pride of our nation, this day have set upon a mighty endeavor . . .

"Lead them straight and true; give strength to their arms, stoutness to their hearts, steadfastness in their faith. . . .

"These men are lately drawn from the ways of peace. They fight not for the lust of conquest. They fight to end conquest. They fight to liberate. . . . They yearn but for the end of battle, for their return to the haven of home.

"Some will never return. Embrace these, Father, and receive them, Thy heroic servants, into Thy kingdom. . . .

"And, O Lord, give us faith. Give us faith in Thee; faith in our sons; faith in each other. . . . Thy will be done, Almighty God. Amen."[8]

"What does the 'D' stand for?" a passerby asked Eustace Tilley.

"Why, it just stands for 'Day,' " the *New Yorker* correspondent rightly answered.* Writing about the incident, he went on: "D-Day was a unique experience, a colossal moment in history."

His stroll about town took him to Times Square, where a crowd watched the electric news bulletin. "AND ONE GERMAN

---

* *Time* magazine reported on June 12 that "so far as the U.S. Army can determine, the first use of D for Day, H for Hour was in Field Order No. 8, of the First Army, A.E.F., issued on Sept. 20, 1918, which read, 'The First Army will attack at H-Hour on D-Day with the object of forcing the evacuation of the St. Mihiel salient.' "

GUN IS STILL FIRING," it read. "Nobody seemed to think that the one German gun was trivial; it was solemnly weighed along with the other bits of news from the beachheads." A reporter for the New York Times noted that "people stood on the sidewalk near the curb or against the plate glass windows of shops and restaurants on all sides of the little triangle looking up, always looking up to catch even a glimpse of the invasion news."

Tilley joined a hundred or so citizens outside the Rialto Theatre. Men were "clustered together and were talking about the course of history during the past twenty-five years. . . . Everybody waited his turn and made his points without raising his voice more than was necessary. . . . The sober talk was still going on when we left."

He went to one of the network broadcasting studios "and found the corridors full of radio actors, all somewhat upset by the cancellation of the soap-opera programs."

Over the radio, he heard once again the Eisenhower recording. "General Eisenhower's words are tied up with the image of D-Day that will, we think, remain in our mind the longest. Up in the Modern Museum, an old lady, seated on an angular plywood chair, was reading the General's message aloud to several other old ladies who stood clustered around her. 'I call upon all who love freedom to stand with us,' she read, in a thin voice, and a shiver ran through the group."[9]

New York City on June 6, 1944, was a bustling, prosperous place. Everyone had jobs and more cash than there were products to buy. Apartments were hard to impossible to find; people doubled and tripled up. Bars and movie theaters were jammed. The spring season on Broadway was a big success, topped by Oklahoma! by Richard Rodgers and Oscar Hammerstein, Paul Robeson in Othello, Milton Berle in Ziegfeld Follies, and Mary Martin in One Touch of Venus (with music by Kurt Weill, book by S. J. Perelman and Ogden Nash, staged by Elia Kazan, with dances by Agnes de Mille)—those were the days.

Broadway shut down on D-Day. The actors went to the Stage Door Canteen to perform a scene or two from their plays for servicemen. Only one table, "The Angel's Table," was available to nonservicemen; it was reserved "for those civilians whose mildly royal donations win them the privilege of admission to the Canteen." The donations went to the servicemen's organizations.[10]

The New York Daily News threw out its lead articles and

printed in their place the Lord's Prayer. The *New York Daily Mirror* eliminated all advertising from its columns so as to have room for invasion news.

Stores shut down. Macy's closed at noon. Still there was a large crowd around it, because the store set up a loudspeaker that carried radio programs. When one announcer read a dispatch that warned Americans against rejoicing, according to a reporter for the *New York Times*, "the faces of those who stood listening were grim and subdued."

Lord & Taylor never opened at all. President Walter Hoving said he was sending his 3,000 employees home to pray. "The store is closed," he announced. "The invasion has begun. Our only thought can be of the men who are fighting in it. We have closed our doors because we know our employees and customers who have loved ones in battle will want to give this day to hopes and prayers for their safety."[11]

Baseball games and racing programs were canceled. In his column "Sports of the Times," Arthur Daley raised the question of whether all sports events should be canceled until the war was won and decided not. "Once the stunning impact of the invasion news has worn off," he wrote, "there will not be the same irresistible urge to glue ear to radio for last-minute bulletins and human nature again will demand entertainment as a distraction from the war— movies, the theater and all other diversions, including sports." Daley said no one resented the "youths playing games" while others died, because everyone knew that the baseball players were either 4-F or too old. The entire Yankee starting lineup of 1941, he reminded readers, was in uniform—military, not baseball. But bad as the replacements were, Daley wanted the season to "struggle along as best it can. After all, it still is part of our American way of life and that is one of the things we are fighting for."[12]

Wall Street went about its business. The New York Stock Exchange called for two minutes of silent prayer at the opening, then went to work. The headline in the June 7 edition of the *Wall Street Journal* read: "INVASION'S IMPACT; MARKS BEGINNING OF END OF WAR ECONOMY; NEW PROBLEMS FOR INDUSTRY." That might be characterized as putting first things first.

The market had suffered a case of "invasion jitters" for two months. According to *Time* magazine, "The New York Stock Exchange has quivered on every D-Day rumor. But on D-Day, taking its courage firmly in hand, the Exchange: 1) had its busiest day of the year, turning over 1,193,080 shares; 2) saw the Dow-Jones industrial average rise to 142.24, a new peak for 1944." AT&T, Chrysler, Westinghouse, General Motors, Du Pont, and retail-store stocks all hit new highs for 1944.[13]

As always, Wall Street was concerned with the future. As the *Journal* put it, "Invasion has raised the curtain on reconversion." As soon as it was clear that the invasion had succeeded, "a limited reconversion to civilian production will be possible. Contract cancellations will increase, freeing manpower, materials and facilities for a small-scale start on production of new consumer goods. Assuming all goes as planned, that time is thought to be two to four months off."[14]

(In December 1944, the GIs paid for this unrealistic optimism. Orders for artillery shells were cut back during the summer; when the great German counteroffensive in Belgium began, American batteries were always short of and some ran out of ammunition.)

The *New York Times* financial section gave a patriotic cast to its report on Wall Street's day: "The stock market gave a salute of confidence to the Allied invasion forces in a buying splurge. . . . The motor issues continued to attract the greatest speculative demand, while other industrials with high post-war ratings shared in the advance, which found support from all sections of the nation."[15]

New Yorkers more concerned with the present than the future came in large numbers to the Civilian Defense Volunteer Office on Fifth Avenue, to sign up for bandage rolling, administering vision tests, checking prices for the Office of Price Administration, nurses' aides, day-care, aides at Red Cross and other servicemen's centers, the USO, and the dozens of other jobs volunteers were doing all across the city. Record numbers gave blood.[16]

The mayor, Fiorello La Guardia, talked to reporters at Gracie Mansion at 0340. He said: "We can only wait for bulletins and pray for success. It is the most exciting moment in our lives."[17]

The editors of the *New York Times* tried to put some perspective on D-Day in their lead editorial for the June 7 edition. "We have come to the hour for which we were born," they wrote. "We go forth to meet the supreme test of our arms and of our souls, the test of the maturity of our faith in ourselves and in mankind. . . .

"We pray for the boys we know and for millions of unknown boys who are equally a part of us. . . .

"We pray for our country. . . .

"The cause prays for itself, for it is the cause of the God who created man free and equal."[18]

North of New York City, it was graduation day at West Point. Among the graduates was Cadet John Eisenhower; among the families gathered was Mrs. Dwight D. Eisenhower. On June 3, from Portsmouth, General Eisenhower had written to Mamie, "This note will probably reach you soon after you return to Washington [from West Point]. There's nothing I would not have given to have been with you and John on June 6, but *c'est la guerre!*

"Anyway I'm so deep in work that I'll actually be lucky to remember on the exact date—that it does mark his graduation."[19]

Mamie found out about D-Day from a *New York Post* reporter, who woke her with a telephone call to her room at the Hotel Thayer at West Point.

"The invasion?" Mamie exclaimed. "What about the invasion?"

On June 9 General Eisenhower sent a telegram to Mamie. Never one to overstate things, he wrote: "DUE TO PREVIOUS PLANS IT WAS IMPOSSIBLE FOR ME TO BE WITH YOU AND JOHN MONDAY BUT I THOUGHT OF YOU AND HOPE YOU AND HE HAD A NICE TIME WITH THE FAMILY. I SEND YOU MUCH LOVE WITH THIS NOTE AS TIME HAS NOT PERMITTED LETTER WRITING RECENTLY AND PROBABLY WILL NOT FOR A WHILE BUT I KNOW YOU UNDERSTAND."

(Monday was June 5. Evidently Eisenhower remembered that John had graduated on D-Day, which had been scheduled for June 5, and mixed the dates.)[20]*

In New York and throughout the land, bells tolled. The greatest of these was the Liberty Bell. It had last been tolled on July 8, 1835, for the funeral of Chief Justice John Marshall. At 0700 on D-Day, Philadelphia mayor Bernard Samuel tapped the bell with a wooden mallet, sending its voice throughout the country over a radio network. Then he offered a prayer.

The impulse to pray was overwhelming. Many people got

---

* A week later, 2nd Lt. John Eisenhower joined Supreme Commander Dwight Eisenhower in London (Marshall arranged it). He stayed three weeks before going to Infantry School at Fort Benning. John's West Point obsessions came to play immediately on his arrival in London; walking with his father at SHAEF HQ, he asked in great earnestness, "If we should meet an officer who ranks above me but below you, how do we handle this? Should I salute first and when they return my salute, do you return theirs?" The supreme commander snorted, then said: "John, there isn't an officer in this theater who doesn't rank above you and below me" (John Eisenhower, *Strictly Personal* [Garden City, N.Y.: Doubleday, 1974], p. 63).

their first word of the invasion as they began their daily routines; after they recovered their breath, they said a silent prayer. Others heard the news broadcast on loudspeakers during their night shifts on assembly lines around the country. Men and women paused over their machines, prayed, and returned to work with renewed dedication.

Across the United States and Canada, from the Atlantic to the Pacific, from the Arctic to the Gulf Coast, the church bells rang. Not in triumph or celebration but as a solemn reminder of national unity and a call to formal prayer. Special services were held in every church and synagogue in the land. Pews were jammed with worshipers.

In Washington, General Pershing issued a statement. The commander of the World War I AEF said, "Twenty-six years ago American soldiers, in co-operation with their Allies, were locked in mortal combat with the German enemy. . . . Today, the sons of American soldiers of 1917-18 are engaged in a like war of liberation. It is their task to bring freedom to peoples who have been enslaved. I have every confidence that they, together with their gallant brothers-in-arms, will win through to victory."[21]

At the Capitol building, the politicians were going about their business. On D-Day, the House voted 305 to 35 to proceed with the courts-martial of Maj. Gen. Walter Short and Rear Adm. Husband Kimmel in order to fix responsibility for the Pearl Harbor disaster. "It's all politics," one congressman confessed. The Democrats (who opposed but felt they could not vote against the resolution, which they had been delaying for two years) charged that the Republicans were seeking to make a campaign issue in an effort to embarrass President Roosevelt. The Republicans (who sponsored the resolution and were unanimous for it) charged that the Democrats were trying to delay any possible disclosures until after the presidential election.[22] Both charges were true.

In midafternoon, Roosevelt held a press conference. Over 180 reporters filled the executive office almost to capacity. According to the *New York Times* reporter, "They found Mr. Roosevelt looking tired around the eyes but smiling. He sat at his desk in shirtsleeves, wearing a dark bow tie. He smoked a cigarette stuck into a yellow amber holder."

"How do you feel about the progress of the invasion?" a reporter asked.

"It's up to schedule," the president replied, then smiled.

He went on to say he had reports from General Eisenhower that indicated only two destroyers and one LST had been sunk and that losses among the fliers were less than 1 percent.

Other points: General Eisenhower alone decided the actual date and place. Stalin had known of the plan since the Teheran meeting and was pleased with it. A second front a year ago would have been impossible due to lack of men and equipment. The war was not over by any means; this operation is not even over, and this is no time for overconfidence.[23]

After the conference, Roosevelt conferred with Admiral King and General Marshall. At their rarefied level, and so far removed from the battle, they couldn't tell the president much more than what was coming over the radio.

Marshall was stopped as he left the Oval Office by a reporter who asked if he had spent the night at his desk.

No, Marshall replied. Then he smiled a little bit and said simply, "I had done my work before."[24]

In Bedford, Virginia, the local newspaper, the *Bulletin*, printed a prayer written by Mrs. H. M. Lane of nearby Altavista: "Dear Father and Great Maker of all things: Beauty that dies the soonest, lives the longest. Who can fail to see the beauty and sacrifice our brave lads are making? Because they cannot keep themselves for a day, we'll keep them forever in memory and give them immortality."

A reporter for the *Bulletin* wrote, "News of the invasion brought a feeling of uneasiness to hundreds of Bedford county homes for many of them have sons, husbands and brothers in the army in England. Old Company A [of the 116th Regiment] has been in training there for nearly two years and probably was among the first landing forces, and hundreds of other Bedford county men will ultimately be thrown into the fight, and among them some casualties can be expected." He noted that every church in town was filled to capacity for special services.

A month later, on July 6, the *Bulletin* reported that "Old Company A" had received "high praise" for its role in D-Day, and went on, "So far there have been no reports of fatalities, but as yet the government has given out no complete list of casualties. There has been considerable uneasiness about the fate of the men, as it seemed too much to hope that all of them could have come safely through the landing ordeal and subsequent fighting."

In the July 20 issue, the *Bulletin* reported that the 116th had been awarded a presidential citation, and it recorded the awful news that on July 19 fourteen families in Bedford were informed that their sons had been killed on June 6. There would be more to come. The editor wrote, "They died as all free men should die— gallantly and unafraid. They knew what was before them. But there was no shirking or hesitation, no holding back, no attempt to escape the issue."[25]

(At the Normandy American Cemetery and memorial, over-looking Omaha Beach, there are eleven sons of Bedford buried along with 9,386 other American war dead from the Normandy campaign. The cemetery is beautifully and perfectly maintained by the American Battle Monuments Commission. No American can visit the site without feeling a surge of pride, nor can any American suppress a flow of tears. In the circular chapel, there are inscribed these words: "Think not only upon their passing. Remember the glory of their spirit.")

The historic St. Louis Cathedral in New Orleans, from the first early Mass until Benediction Tuesday night, was full. A mother of a paratrooper, "my only child," prayed by the side of a policeman with "two boys over there." A pretty young bride knelt before a statue of Our Lady of Prompt Succor while in a nearby pew a sailor, home on leave, prayed.

Canal Street store owners had planned for D-Day for three months; when it came, they turned their employees to selling war bonds rather than goods. The idea was picked up in a number of other cities. On Canal Street, patriotic music and appeals to buy bonds filled the air. Bonds went at a record pace. One woman counted out $18.75 in dimes for a bond. She explained, "I've been saving this money to buy a bond on the day of invasion. I hope it will be a day I can remember happily. My husband is with the airborne troops and he's been in England for a long time waiting for this."[26]

Record crowds at the Red Cross blood donor center on Carondelet, record numbers of volunteers at the various civilian agencies, but in a city that will seize on any excuse for a parade, there was no parade. The Times Picayune explained, "New Or-leans was hoarding its parades for V-Day."

Andrew Higgins reminded his employees that there was a long-way to go, and not just in Europe: "There should not be letup on our part until our boats have carried our troops onto the shores of Japan."[27]

• •

In Ottawa, Prime Minister Mackenzie King reported to the House of Commons that the landings were making good progress. He warned that there was still much to do. Opposition leader Gordon Graydon said there were no divisions of opinion on this day. From the ranks of the French-speaking members, Maurice Lalonde rose to acclaim, in French, "the historic fact that from the belfry of time has rung out the hour of the deliverance of France."

On D-Day Canada, like the United States, was united as never before. French-Canadians and English-speaking Canadians had equal stakes in the invasion and were single-minded about the goal. M. Lalonde asked special permission of the House: could "The Marseillaise" be sung? For the first time in Canadian parliamentary history, all the members joined in singing "The Marseillaise," followed by "God Save the King."[28]

In Columbus, Ohio, Mayor James Rhodes ordered the air-raid sirens and factory whistles sounded as a call to prayer at 7:30 P.M. The entire city came to a complete stop for five minutes—cars, buses, trucks, and pedestrians halted and people prayed.[29] In Columbus, as elsewhere, the Red Cross got a record blood donation, factory production was up, absenteeism down, churches were full. The Red Cross put out a call: "Every woman in Franklin County is asked to go immediately to the surgical dressing unit in her community," and was overwhelmed with volunteers. The Truck-Tractor & Equipment Company took out a full-page advertisement in the Columbus Star with the banner headline reading "Next Stop: Berlin," and with a brief text: "Today is a fitting day to ask ourselves, am I doing enough? If I met a man who was there, could I look him squarely in the face and say, I did my share?"[30]

In Milwaukee, the Red Cross blood donor center was overwhelmed by people wanting to give blood. In Reno, Nevada, the gambling dens closed and only sixteen couples filed for divorce, less than 10 percent of the usual weekday number. Elsewhere, an uglier side of American life was at work; in Cincinnati, 450 workers at the Wright Aeronautical Corporation went on strike, which tied up the plant. Their grievance was that seven Negro workers had been transferred into a shop theretofore manned entirely by white personnel. William Green, president of the American Federation of Labor, called on American workers to consider themselves part of the invasion force and to stay at their jobs "under any and all circumstances."[31]

In Birmingham, Alabama, the News reported that 1,500 miners at Republic Steel had gone out on a wildcat strike. The editors at the News were outraged. So were union officials. "Damn the strikers," the president of the state American Federation of Labor said. "To think that this great day should find AFL people away from their jobs is inconceivable."

In Marietta, Georgia, police sirens and church bells began sounding at 3:00 A.M. "Many citizens were hysterical," the Atlanta Constitution reported, "as wave after wave of sirens blasted their ears. Police cars, their sirens wide open, sped through the residential districts."

Columnist Ralph Jones quoted his wife, whose remarks, he felt, were typical. Their son was in England, possibly already in Normandy. "Even if it meant I had to die," Mrs. Jones said, "I should like to be a part of that invasion. It is the biggest and greatest and most spectacular thing in all history."

After a pause, she went on, "I just can't worry all the time about young Ralph. If I did I'd go crazy. He's in no greater danger than hundreds of thousands of sons of other mothers."[32]

In Missoula, Montana, "There was discussion everywhere, but the tremendous import of the news threw a hush over the spirit of the city, which was definitely noticeable."[33]

At the veterans hospital in Helena, one soldier on crutches exclaimed, "This is it, brother. We've got 'em on the run now." Another called out from his bed, "Boy, do I wish I could be there!"

There was a silence in the ward. "Yeah," the boy on crutches finally said, without enthusiasm. Then he thoughtfully added: "I'll bet that beach is like hell on the Fourth of July."[34]

At Lawson General Hospital, near Atlanta, wounded German POWs took the news with derisive laughter and a "just you wait" attitude. One of them told a reporter, "The high command will simply let the Allies penetrate a few miles and then pinch them off with the thousands of SS elite guards who are stationed near Paris."[35]

In Dallas, Texas, patriotism ran high. At 0235 a hospital intern and a city ambulance driver helped Mrs. Lester Renfrow give birth to a daughter. She heard sirens going and asked what was the cause. Told that the invasion had begun, she named her little girl Invasia Mae Renfrow.[36] In Norfolk, Virginia, Mrs. Randolph Edwards named her June 6 daughter Dee Day Edwards.[37]

• •

On June 4, Mollie Panter-Downes reported in her "Letter from London" for the *New Yorker*, "Everyone is existing merely from one ordinary day to the next, waiting for the great, extraordinary one."

Panter-Downes noted an unexplainable rise in the rental of punts on the Thames and a record crowd at a cricket match at Lord's. Then she turned to a phenomenon of the war in Britain that was always an irritant and sometimes costly, the prohibition on any weather news either in the newspapers or over radio. In May, frosts wiped out the famous Vale of Evesham berry and plum crops. "The fruit growers regret that the official secrecy on weather conditions was not relaxed for once to give them a warning which might have helped save some of the fruit."

The loss was a serious one for the British diet, made worse by a drought that had damaged the hay crop, meaning less milk. The weather was the natural topic of conversation in a rural pub Panter-Downes dropped in on, the one she expected to hear, but instead "the one topic, as much there as in London clubs and bars, is the invasion."[38]

On June 6, Panter-Downes sensed something that other commentators missed: "For the English," she wrote, "D-Day might well have stood for Dunkirk Day.

"The tremendous news that British soldiers were back on French soil suddenly revealed exactly how much it had rankled when they were seen off it four years ago."

There was no celebrating, however; far from it. "The principal impression one got on the streets was that nobody was talking. . . . Everybody seemed to be existing wholly in a preoccupied silence of his own. . . . Everywhere, individual silences."

Business was extremely bad. Taxi drivers said it was their worst day in months. Theaters and movie houses were half empty, all but unheard of in 1944. The pubs didn't fill, either. Londoners stayed home. "Everybody seemed to feel that this was one night you wanted your own thoughts in your own chair."

In the countryside, "Everything is different now . . . every truck on the road, every piece of gear on the railways, every jeep and half-track which is heading toward the front has become a thing of passionate concern.

"Farmers who wanted gray skies for their hay's sake now want blue ones for the sake of their sons, fighting in the skies and on the earth across the Channel." Women who gathered at train crossings where troops headed for the battle went by "didn't know whether to wave or cheer or cry. Sometimes they do all three."[39]

King George VI made a D-Day broadcast to the nation. "Four years ago," he began, "our Nation and Empire stood alone against an overwhelming enemy, with our backs to the wall. . . . Now once more a supreme test has to be faced. This time the challenge is not to fight to survive but to fight to win the final victory for the good cause."

The king knew that nearly all his subjects were listening and realized that the mothers and wives among them deserved special concern. "The Queen joins with me in sending you this message," he said. "She well understands the anxieties and care of our womenfolk at this time and she knows that many of them will find, as she does herself, fresh strength and comfort in such waiting upon God."

The king called on his subjects to pray: "At this historic moment surely not one of us is too busy, too young, or too old to play a part in a nation-wide, perchance a world-wide, vigil of prayer as the great crusade sets forth."[40]

The House of Commons went about its business. The first question came from Mr. Hogg, Oxford. He asked the secretary of state for war "whether he could give an assurance that all ranks of the Army had been informed that unless A.F.B. 2626 was completed they would not have a vote at the next General Election whether or not they were on the old register; and on what scale A.F.B. 2626 had been issued to units."

The secretary of state for war, Mr. John Grigg, replied at ten-minutes length that it was being done.

Another member wanted to know if the prime minister would consider the complete restoration of the abbey of Monte Cassino as a memorial to the heroes who had captured it, to be done at the expense of Germany as a part of reparations. Labor leader Clement Attlee, member of the coalition War Cabinet, replied that is was "premature to consider such proposals."

The secretary of state for the colonies, Col. Oliver Stanley, rose-tò remind the House that in many of the colonies "there are large numbers of people who are condemned to live at an abysmal level of existence. The standard of living of the peoples in the Colonial areas should be built up." Mr. Attlee, in replying to another question, switched the area for postwar concern from the colonies to the home front. He urged "the composition and terms of reference of the proposed Royal Commission on the subject of equal pay between men and women."

John Grigg made an unhappy announcement about men who had been overseas for five years or more: "I much regret that owing to the shortage of men it may be necessary, at any rate for the time being, to send such men overseas again after a period of three months in this country instead of six months as hitherto."

A member pressed the secretary of the treasury to see to it that members of the Association of Office Cleaners were referred to as such instead of as charwomen or charladies, which was resented by the 2,400 members of the association. The secretary replied that the word "cleaners" would henceforth be used.

As the mundane gave way to the silly in Commons, the tension built. Rumors buzzed around about when the great man would appear on this, his greatest day.

Churchill sent word to expect him at noon.

When Churchill entered Commons, every seat was taken, every member was leaning forward expectantly. They were not so much expecting (or even wanting) to be swept away by Churchillian eloquence as they were eager for whatever news the prime minister could tell them.

The master toyed with his audience. Churchill began with Rome. He was obviously enjoying his old role of war reporter ("still this country's best reporter," Raymond Daniell wrote in the *New York Times*). Churchill went into fifteen minutes of detail about how Rome was taken, then an analysis of the meaning of the event. It was all welcome news, the kind that prime ministers love to be in a position to tell the members, but the members squirmed on their benches. They wanted to hear about how it was going on the other side of the Channel.

Finally Churchill got to it. "I have also to announce to the House that during the night and early hours of the morning the first of a series of landings in force upon the European continent has taken place. So far, the commanders . . . report that everything is proceeding according to plan. And what a plan!

"Landings on the beaches are proceeding at various points at the present time," he said. "The fire of shore batteries has been largely quelled. Obstacles which were encountered in the sea have not proved as difficult as was apprehended."

He left to great cheers. He returned four hours later to add more detail. "There is very much less loss than we expected. The many dangers and difficulties which at this time yesterday appeared extremely formidable are behind us.

"A very great risk had to be taken in respect to the weather, but General Eisenhower's courage is equal to all necessary decisions that have to be taken in these extremely difficult and uncontrollable matters."

He referred to Maj. John Howard's operation at Pegasus Bridge and claimed that British troops had "fought their way into the town of Caen, nine miles inland."

Churchill was fond of saying that the first casualty of war is truth. His rosy report fell, at times, into that category. But he was telling the truth when he described the airborne landings as having taken place "on a scale far larger than anything that has been seen so far in the world."[41]

For Edward R. Murrow in London, it was a day of frustration. CBS put him in charge of coordinating the work of its many correspondents and reading the various announcements coming from SHAEF and others. He would much rather have been in France. Adding to his woes, radio correspondents had precious little to pass on to the States. Mobile transmitters were not set up on the beach or even on ships. Reporters who went into the beach in landing craft, including Bill Downs, Larry LeSueur, and Charles Collingwood, could not broadcast.

Finally, in the small hours of June 7 (2300, June 6 in New York), Murrow got what he wanted. It was a recording that had been made at daybreak just off the French coast, sent back to London by small boat. "I think you'll like this," Murrow told New York as he put it on. It was George Hicks of ABC, reporting from the *Ancon*. He described the array of ships, while in the background could be heard the exchanges between the German batteries and the Allied warships. That broadcast, cutting through the static and punctuated by the sounds of battle, became the most widely listened-to account of the D-Day landings.[42]

In Paris, the military governor, General Stulpnagel, issued a proclamation that was broadcast by French Radio: "German troops have been given orders to shoot any person who is seen to be cooperating with the Allied invasion forces, or who gives shelter to Allied soldiers, sailors, or airmen. Such Frenchmen will be treated as bandits."

Prime Minister Pierre Laval of the Vichy government broadcast a national appeal to his countrymen to ignore Eisenhower's call over BBC for resistance: "With sadness I read today of the orders given to Frenchmen by an American general. . . . The French government stands by the armistice of 1940 and appeals to Frenchmen to honor their country's signature. If you took part in the present fighting, France would be plunged into civil war."

Marshal Pétain called on Frenchmen to stand with the Germans: "The Anglo-Saxons have set foot on our soil. France is becoming a battlefield. Frenchmen, do not attempt to commit any action which might bring terrible reprisals. Obey the orders of the government."[43]

Parisians listened and kept their own counsel. The country as a whole was quiet. Resisters went into action, of course, but most French people were not in the Resistance. In Normandy, and everywhere between Normandy and the German border, people were apprehensive about their village or farm or city becoming a battlefield. They could hardly be sure who was going to win; the Germans were there, among them, occupying their country, while the Allies were only a hope. They did the sensible thing, kept quiet and kept their thoughts to themselves.

In the smaller cities in the south of France, people were more open with their feelings. Anthony Brooks of SOE walked into Toulouse at dawn. He knew from the BBC broadcasts the hour had come and he was putting his operation into action. But only he and other Resisters knew that this was D-Day.

"So I walked into Toulouse through the market garden area and there were all these little one-story houses and these enormous great stretches with lettuces and onions and they were thinning them out, like a painting.

"Suddenly as I was walking past a house, just after sunrise, shutters were flung open and a little girl, I suppose eight years old, stark naked, shouted in the local jargon, 'They've landed!' and the liberation of Europe had begun."

Brooks went to a meeting in Toulouse, where "we lifted our glass for a very early morning drink, white wine, because we never really believed that we would see it. I mean liberation. I couldn't believe when I was parachuted into France in 1942 that I'd ever see D-Day."[44]

One famous American expatriate who was a French resident wrote down her feelings and her perception of the effect on the Germans. In 1940, Gertrude Stein had fled Paris when the Germans entered. "They all said, 'Leave,' " Stein wrote in 1945, "and I said to Alice Toklas, 'Well, I don't know—it would be awfully uncomfortable and I am fussy about my food.' "

But they went. Stein and Alice Toklas lived in the village of Belley at the corner made by Italy and Switzerland. Stein's attitude was, "Alice Toklas could listen to the wireless, but as for me I was going to cut box hedges and forget the war."

Of course she could not. On June 5, 1944, she wrote, "To-night Rome is taken it is a pleasure and such a pleasure . . . and it has taken everybody's mind a little off their feelings about the [Allied] bombardments in France about the civilians killed. . . . But to-night Rome is taken and everybody has forgotten the bombardments, and for the French to forgive and forget and forget and forgive is very easy just as easy as that. Rome is taken and it is not the end but the beginning of the end."

Stein went walking on the morning of June 6 to celebrate. She passed "some German soldiers they said most pitifully how do you do, I naturally said nothing, later on I was sitting with the wife of the mayor in front of her house a German soldier passed along the road and he politely bowed to us and said how do you do, they have never done this before.

"Well to-day is the landing and we heard Eisenhower tell us he was here they were here and just yesterday a man sold us ten packages of Camel cigarettes, glory be, and we are singing glory hallelujah, and feeling very nicely, and everybody has been telephoning to us congratulatory messages upon my birthday which it isn't but we know what they mean. And I said in return I hoped their hair was curling nicely, and we all hope it is, and to-day is the day."[45]*

In Rome, a celebration was already under way when the news came. The celebration just got bigger. Daniel Lang in his "Letter from Rome" reported to the *New Yorker* that the Italians were ecstatic. "They love a winner just a little more than the rest of the world does," and they were "out by the thousands, jamming the square on which Mussolini used to stage his pep rallies. They

* Stein published her memoir of the war in the fall of 1945. She was liberated in the fall of 1944 by two soldiers from the 45th Infantry Division. "Were we excited," she wrote. "How we talked that night, they just brought all America to us every bit of it, they came from Colorado, lovely Colorado, I do not know Colorado but that is the way I felt about it lovely Colorado. . . . They have asked me to go with them to Voiron to broadcast with them to America and I am going and the war is over and this certainly this is the last war to remember."

cheered and applauded as though they were watching the best opera of their lives. They shouted whatever scraps of English they knew. One wild old man yelled 'Weekend! Weekend!' over and over again. Many had huge bouquets of flowers, from which they kept plucking small bunches to toss at soldiers in jeeps and lorries, or at tank drivers. Dozens of people were waving British, French and American flags. Where they had been hidden, only the Italians knew."[46]

In Amsterdam, Anne Frank heard the news over the wireless in her attic hideaway. " 'This is D-Day,' came the announcement over the English news," she wrote in her diary. Then, in English, she wrote, "This is *the* day." She went on, "The invasion has begun! The English gave the news. . . . We discussed it over breakfast at nine o'clock: Is this just a trial landing like Dieppe two years ago?" But through the day, confirmations that this was really it kept coming on the wireless.

"Great commotion in the 'Secret Annexe'!" Frank wrote. "It still seems too wonderful too much like a fairy tale. Could we be granted victory this year, 1944? We don't know yet, but hope is revived within us; it gives us fresh courage and makes us strong again. . . . Now more than ever we must clench our teeth and not cry out. France, Russia, Italy, and Germany, too, can all cry out and give vent to their misery, but we haven't the right to do that yet!

"The best part of the invasion is that I have the feeling that friends are approaching. We have been oppressed by those terrible Germans for so long, they have had their knives so at our throats, that the thought of friends and delivery fills us with confidence!

"Now it doesn't concern the Jews any more; no, it concerns Holland and all occupied Europe. Perhaps, Margot says, I may yet be able to go back to school in September or October."[47]

In Moscow, the crowds were joyous. People literally danced in the streets, *Time* reported, and its correspondent claimed that "This was the happiest capital." In the lobby of the Metropole Hotel, an ecstatic Muscovite threw her arms around the correspondent and exclaimed, "We love you, Americans. We love you, we love you. You are our real friends."[48]

Restaurants were packed in Moscow on the evening of June 6, packed with people celebrating—Russians dancing with British and American diplomats and reporters. Alexander Werth was at one such gathering when "a party of Jap diplomats and journalists came in and behaved and danced provocatively and ostentatiously and were nearly beaten-up by some Americans."

Pravda gave the invasion news four columns with a large photograph of Eisenhower, but no comment was made on the significance—the editors had to wait for Stalin to give his line. Not for a week did the dictator speak about the realization of that second front for which he had for so long been pleading. When he did, he was generous and forthright: "This is unquestionably a brilliant success for our Allies. One must admit that the history of wars does not know of an undertaking comparable to it for breadth of conception, grandeur of scale, and mastery of execution." He pointed out that "Invincible Napoleon" had not managed to cross the Channel, nor "Hitler the Hysteric."

"Only the British and Americans troops succeeded in forcing the Channel. History will record this action as an achievement of the highest order." After that statement, *Pravda* was enthusiastic for the achievement.[49]

In Berlin, people went quietly about their duties. Few talked of the invasion, although the radio was full of announcements. The Nazi propaganda line was "Thank God, the intense strain of the nerve war is over." But the *Times* correspondent in Stockholm reported that "the scale of General Eisenhower's first blow made a deep impression on the general public in Berlin, especially as the German spokesmen emphasize its magnitude and disconcertingly add that it is not yet certain whether this is the main invasion force."

Mainly, though, the Nazi broadcasters went to work to convince people that it was necessary for them to fight against the British and Americans in France in order to save Germany from the horror of a Red Army occupation. In a totalitarian state it was impossible to tell how many, if any other than Hitler and his henchmen, believed such logic.[50]

27

"FAIRLY STUFFED WITH GADGETS"

The British Opening Moves

Lt. George Honour, Royal Navy Reserves, was the skipper of X23, a midget submarine seven meters in length with a crew of four. Along with the skipper of X20, Honour had a unique view of the invasion. At first light, he was anchored a couple of kilometers off Ouistreham (Sword Beach); X20 was off Juno. The submarines were between the invaders and defenders in no-man's water.

X23 and X20 were there because of the requirements of the DD tanks. There were only narrow strips where the swimming tanks that would lead the invasion could climb up the beaches; the submarines would serve as their guides so that they could land bang on target.

The British tanks, Churchills and Shermans, were equipped for a variety of tasks. There were flail tanks with drums out front that carried chains that lashed the ground as the drums turned (powered by their own small engines) and set off mines safely in front of the tank. There were tanks carrying fascines for getting over antitank ditches and drainage ditches, others that carried heavy bridging equipment for crossing larger gaps. To accommodate some of the special equipment, the 75mm cannon on the tanks had been replaced by little snub-nosed heavy mortars. Those mortars could hurl twenty-five-pound high-explosive charges over a short distance, less than fifty meters, to blast holes in cement walls and blockhouses. Other tanks dragged 400-gallon trailers of fuel, which could shoot a high-pressure jet of flame over a range of 100 meters.

Captain Hammerton of the 79th Armored Division had been introduced to "Hobart's Funnies" by their inventor, Maj. Gen. Percy Hobart, at the Oxford training area in East Anglia. "General Hobart gathered everybody around and said, 'I have some news for you. You have heard of the Lord Mares Show,' and everybody's heart stopped beating, 'and you know about the people who come afterwards to clear up the mess. Well, your job is going to be the very opposite. You're going in front to clear up the mess. You are going to be line clearers, flails.' "

Hammerton went on, "They were experimenting with flails, snakes, scorpions, and all the other strange menagerie of things. They had bull's-horn plows which fitted to the front of the Churchills and carved an enormous plow furrow and the idea was they would turn any mines over the side. The snake was a flexible and the serpent a rigid tube. The snake was fired from a harpoon gun, then pumped full of nitroglycerin; the serpent was pushed in front of a tank, stuffed with high explosive. The idea was when detonated they would set off the mines."[1]

The snub-nosed tanks had a multiplicity of extra lugs welded on the body, with heavy tow ropes fixed on beside them; the purpose was to drag obstacles out of the way or to move disabled vehicles. The tanks, called Mk. VIII AVREs, provided a loading platform for extra gear.

Maj. Kenneth Ferguson of the British 3rd Division commanded an assault squadron of Hobart's Funnies at Sword Beach. He recalled loading onto an LCT. His unit contained two flail tanks, a tank carrying a thirty-foot metal bridge folded in half and sticking straight up in the air in front of the tank, and a tank carrying log carpets—two drums (nearly as large as the tank itself) attached to the front, one over the other, that could lay down matting over the sand. The flails would go first, then the bridge to provide a way to get over the seawall, then the carpet layer making a road surface for the fighting tanks. DD tanks would precede them in, set up at the water line, and blast fortified positions.

As Ferguson finished overseeing the loading of his Funnies, one of the seamen called out, "Oh, sir, I say, you've forgotten the piano!"

Ferguson wanted personal mobility once he got ashore, so he loaded a motorcycle and a bicycle on top of his AVRE.[2] Thousands of British troops took bicycles with them; there is no record of any American doing so (although one 101st commander tried, but his men threw it out over the Channel).

Capt. Cyril James Hendry commanded a troop of Funnies. During the crossing, the skipper of the LCT said to him, "Your bridge is acting as a sail, can you lower it a bit?" Hendry unfolded the bridge so that the far end rested on the tank in front, which helped. [3]

The British counted heavily on these specialized tanks to help them get ashore and break through the first line of defenses. They were a bit put off by the American refusal to use their inventions (except for the DD tank concept, which the British insisted the Americans butchered by launching from too far out). Some British officers wondered if there was a touch of hurt pride involved. In their view it would be rather a nice thing if the Yanks would utilize British brains to guide American brawn, but the Americans had insisted they would do the job with their own equipment.

At Utah, the Americans had been right. Although they could have used flail tanks, overall the armored units performed well at Utah. Not so cumbersome or slow as the overloaded British specialized tanks, they sped inland and participated in important actions, in the process achieving most D-Day objectives at Utah.

At Omaha, British specialized tanks would have had no function to serve in overcoming the first problem, getting through the shingle. Of all the beaches, only Omaha had a shingle so high and so slippery, impossible for a tank to cross. Once some gaps were blown, the American tankers could have put some of the British gadgets to good use, especially the fascines and bridging equipment. But the Yanks had bulldozers for that work, which was completed in time for a few tanks to make it to the plateau before dark.

It would be too large a generalization to say that the British wanted to fight World War II with gadgets, techniques, and espionage, rather than men, to outthink more than outfight the Germans; and that the Americans wanted to fight it out in a head-to-head encounter with the Wehrmacht. Still, many people, from both countries, felt such generalizations had merit. Connected to that feeling was the British sense that the Americans took needless casualties because of their aggressive head-on mentality, and the American sense that the British were going to take needless casualties because their caution and refusal to press an attack home regardless of loss was going to prolong the war.

Whatever measure of truth there was in those widely held

perceptions, certain it is that on D-Day the British used far more gadgets than the Americans, beginning with X23 and X20.

"We were fairly stuffed with gadgets," Lieutenant Honour recalled of X23. The submarine had a diesel engine and an electric motor, two bunks, a toilet (the escape hatch), a cooker, electronic equipment to send out signals, oxygen bottles (taken from Luftwaffe planes shot down over England, as they were the lightest bottles available in Britain), and more.

"So we had all these wretched gadgets," Honour said, "and the worst was the wretched mast." It was eighteen feet in length and had to be lashed to special stanchions on the shell of the submarine. "It folded miserably," Honour complained.

Code name for this operation was Gambit. Honour was not a chess player; he looked the word up in the dictionary and was a bit set back to read "throwing away the opening pawns."

Gambit required a special kind of man. Everyone on the submarine had to be able to do every job: handle all machinery and electronic gear, navigate, dive, and much more. They also had to be able to handle, without loss of effectiveness, being cooped in an enclosed boat hardly bigger than a canoe for forty hours and more. Some volunteers found in their trials that they couldn't take one hour of it. "Let me out!" one man cried after forty-five minutes.

With five men on board (the extra was a seaman who was going to take a rubber raft toward the shore, anchor, and provide a final marker for the DD tanks), X23 and X20 set off at 1800 on Friday night, June 2. Two trawlers escorted them past the Isle of Wight. At that point they dove and set off for their destinations, X23 at Sword, X20 at Juno.

Sunday morning, June 4, just before dawn, X23 came up for air. "And we had hit it right on the nose. We were right where we should have been. We had a quick look to see what was around." To Honour's surprise, the Germans had a light turned on to mark the entrance to the Orne River. As dawn began to break, he submerged to periscope depth and checked out the church steeples and other landmarks to make doubly sure he was on target. "There was a cow grazing on the shore there," Honour remembered. He took the submarine down to the bottom of the Channel, dropped anchor, and waited.

At midday on Sunday, Honour came back to periscope depth to see what was going on. "There were lorry loads of Germans coming down to the beach and playing beach ball and swimming. They were having their Sunday make and mends, coming down, lorry loads, having a lovely time. We were saying, 'Little do they know.' "

Back to the bottom for more waiting. Up again at midnight, with the radio turned on for coded messages. One came, in the clear, by voice message from the Isle of Wight, for X23 and X20: "Your aunt is riding a bicycle today." That meant the invasion had been postponed for one day. Back to the bottom for an additional twenty-four hours of waiting.

It was cold, wet, stuffy, and cramped inside the submarine. Honour and his crew fiddled around with the gyroscope to give them something to do. They worried about the oxygen; no one knew how long the air in the bottles would last. They played poker. They tried to sleep, in shifts on the two bunks. They could not smoke cigarettes, a real deprivation. The gyroscope was fixed; there was nothing to do.

"We didn't like this twenty-four-hour bit," Honour declared. "We didn't know about the oxygen, how these damned bottles were getting on. Whether they were half empty or nearly empty."

When the submarines came to the surface at midnight, June 5-6, there was no postponement message. After recharging the batteries, back to the bottom. At 0500 on D-Day, back to the top, swinging on the anchor. The weather was miserable. The wind in the Channel was making one- to three-meter swells. There was no possibility of launching the rubber boat. There was some question whether they could get the mast properly mounted. Waves were breaking over the submarine. It was slippery and pitching in the waves. Those below were handing up tools and equipment: "What the hell's this?" those on top would inquire.

X23 completed the job at about 0520 and immediately began sending out radio signals and flashing the green light from the top of the mast. Green meant they were on station; red would have meant they were off station. They turned on the radio underneath the boat; Honour described it as "a dreadful thing that sent out an underwater ping." The ping could be picked up by sonar, thus marking the spot.

The light was coming up. Lieutenant Honour looked out to sea "and gradually in the distance you could make out the bigger ships and then the smaller ones, the destroyers, and then all hell broke loose." Over X23 sailed the 14-inch shells from the battleships, the 5-inchers from the destroyers. On shore, bombers and fighters were hitting the beach. "I was standing quietly, watching all this," Honour said, "when suddenly my cap was whisked off by one of those LCT(R)s firing about 1,000 rockets."

Then came the DD tanks, "these poor wretched tanks," Honour called them. "They just poured off those LCTs. And they had twin screws and they set off and made a line abreast and they all set off in line with the shore."

One tank started going round and round. Apparently it had bent a screw. It started taking water and down it went. "The chaps came up," Honour said. "They got out just like in a submarine, one hatch."

The remainder of the tanks headed toward shore. "As they passed us," Honour noted, "we cheered them and they cheered us. That was our job done, then."

Honour's orders were to rendezvous with his trawler and return to England. Fearful that his little boat might get smashed by an LCT or LCM, he tied a large white sheet to the mast, and went out on the surface toward the transport area.

"As far as the eye could see, you had these landing craft, either the small ones or the tank landing craft. All along, people going ashore from them. And the bigger landing ships, you could see the little landing craft being lowered and leaving the sides and everybody going on to the shore. It was a hive of activity every way you looked."

Honour made it back to England and went on to other adventures in the war. Asked forty-seven years later if he had ever discovered how much oxygen he had left, he replied, "No, we never knew at all. Didn't much care."[4]

Thanks to X20 and X23, the DD tanks were on target. But they were too slow, too cumbersome to fight the combined effects of wind, swells, and tidal current. They were scheduled to hit the beach first to bring suppressing fire to bear immediately, but as they slowly made their way toward shore, the LCTs bearing the specialized tanks began to pass them. "They were rather run down," Maj. Kenneth Ferguson remembered. As his LCT passed the DD tanks, "I realized they weren't going to be there."[5]

"There" was a thirty-kilometer stretch of sandy beach stretching from Ouistreham at the mouth of the Orne River to Arromanches, where there was a small fishing harbor. Here and there a cliff jutted out to sea; between Luc-sur-Mer and Lion-sur-Mer there was a stretch of a kilometer or so where the cliff was sheer and ten meters high, clearly unsuitable for an invasion. But most of the remainder was suitable until just east of Arromanches, where the tableland rose and the cliffs ran straight down to the sea, and at a height of thirty meters. The Germans had put a *Wurzburg* radar installation on top of the cliff, but Allied bombers had knocked it out in May.

To the west of the opening at the tiny port of Arromanches the cliffs rose sheer again and ran on for another twelve kilometers to Fox Red, the eastern edge of Omaha Beach.

Gold, Juno, and Sword beaches were similar to Utah in that they all had a gradual, almost imperceptible rise inland. In all four cases there was no high ground at the foot of the beach to overcome, no one shooting down on them.

But the British beaches differed from Utah in a number of ways. They were far more built up with seaside resorts and homes. The British infantry would have to rout out the enemy in street-to-street fighting. The British beaches were not so extensively flooded as Utah, and the British had a more extensive road system available. And they had a major objective, according to General Montgomery the most important of all the D-Day tasks—to capture Caen.

Caen was a city of critical importance to the Germans, far more than Carentan or Bayeux. Caen opened the direct route to Paris. The Germans would be certain to rush armored reinforcements to Caen as soon as possible; Montgomery wanted to seize the city as part of the opening shock and surprise. He wanted to get Caen before the Germans could get their armor there. The airmen were pushing for Caen, too; they wanted to set up a forward base at the well-developed Carpiquet airfield just west of Caen, and they wanted to get started on D-Day.

It was six weeks before these objectives were realized, and it only happened then because the Americans had broken out on the western flank and were threatening to envelop Caen. Montgomery later claimed that it had always been his intention to hold on his left (at Caen) and break out on his right (at St.-Lô). There is an overlong historical controversy about the claim. It generally breaks down along nationalistic lines: most British historians back Monty; all American historians say Monty's claim was false, a cover-up. It is not necessary to go into the details, already far too much written about. It is not possible to go into Montgomery's heart to see what he really intended. It is possible to observe his actions. We know what he said to others.

What Montgomery said was that Caen was critical and that he would have it by the end of D-Day.

To get Caen, the British had made their major commitment. The 6th Airborne landed east of the River Orne so as to prevent German tanks from getting to Caen. John Howard's Ox and Bucks had landed at Pegasus Bridge to open that crossroads to the inland push on Caen. The commandos were put into the operation.

The British official historian later concluded that the D-Day objectives were "perhaps over-ambitious—namely, the capture of Bayeux and the road to Caen, the seizure of Caen itself and the safeguarding of the Allies' left flank with a bridgehead east of the Orne. . . . Caen is eight miles from the coast . . . and Bayeux six or seven. There was no possibility of taking them that day unless the advance was made as rapidly as possible."[6]

Montgomery promised that the British would advance rapidly. At the final briefing, at St. Paul's on May 15, he had said he would get "well inland" on D-Day and "crack about and force the battle to swing our way." He said it was possible he would get to Falaise, fifty kilometers inland, the first day. He intended to send armored columns quickly toward Caen, for "this will upset the enemy's plans and tend to hold him off while we build up strength. We must gain space rapidly and peg claims well inland." He said he intended to take Caen the first day, break through the German lines and drive along the coast toward the Seine River.[7]

Those were heavy commitments. To take them on required confidence and optimism. The optimism especially ran high. In late May intelligence reported the presence of the 21st Panzer Division around Caen, with a regiment on each side of the Orne. Montgomery's headquarters decided to keep the information from the troops (John Howard and his men were not informed, nor were they given adequate antitank weapons).

Not only did British headquarters suppress information that could have been invaluable to men going into battle for fear of dampening their morale—shades of World War I—headquarters made no positive use of the quite accurate intelligence about the position of 21st Panzer. The official historian of British intelligence in World War II wrote, "There is no indication in the surviving evidence that it [the information] prompted any consideration of the need to revise and strengthen the British plans for the capture of Caen. . . . despite strong warnings from the intelligence authorities, they proceeded without bargaining for the possibility that 21st Panzer might be widely deployed around Caen."[8]

The reason given was that it was too late to change the plans. But during those same final days, the U.S. 82nd Airborne changed its drop zones on the basis of the latest intelligence on German positions in the Cotentin.

British intelligence had a similar break in September 1944, just before the airborne landings at Arnhem in Operation Market Garden, and again was frustrated when Montgomery refused to use the intelligence. The British were outstanding in gathering intelligence, lousy in using it.

The obstacles on the British beaches were similar to those at Utah. The inland defenses varied considerably because the battlefield was so different. At Gold, Juno, and Sword, once men and vehicles were over the seawall and across the antitank ditch, they were in paved village streets. Once through two or three blocks, they were out in the wheat fields. Large fields—the terrain between Ouistreham and Caen is flat and mainly free of hedgerows.

To prevent a British breakout into the open ground, the Germans had built some formidable defenses. At Riva Bella, a village just west of Ouistreham, there was an emplacement that had twenty-two pieces of all types, including twelve 155mm cannon. At Houlgate, about ten kilometers from Sword's left flank, there was a battery with six 155mm guns. Even closer, at Merville, there were four 75mm guns. At Longues, halfway between Omaha and Gold beaches, the German battery consisted of four 155mm Czech guns, set back about a kilometer from the coast, with a steel-reinforced concrete observation post right on the edge of the cliff (and able to communicate with the batteries by underground telephone line).

Scattered along the beach were extensive emplacements, holding 75s, 88s, mortars, and machine guns. As always, the embrasures opened along the beach, not out to sea, and the concrete was much too thick and too well reinforced to be vulnerable to even the largest naval shell. Such positions would have to be taken by infantry. In the dunes, the Germans had some Tobruks, but not nearly so many as at Omaha; nor were the infantry trenches so extensive.

The commander of the German 716th Infantry Division was *Generalleutnant* Wilhelm Richter. He was responsible for the defense of the British beaches, and he was pessimistic about his chances to hold against a serious invasion. More than a third of his men were from *Ost* battalions, primarily from Soviet Georgia and Russia. One general staff officer remarked in a May report, "We are asking rather a lot if we expect Russians to fight in France for Germany against the Americans."[9]

Richter's strong points and resistance nests were spaced about 800 meters apart, in some places more than a kilometer apart. Richter commented that they were beaded along the coast like a string of pearls. There was no depth to the position whatsoever. For reinforcement, Richter had to rely on 21st Panzer; twelve kilometers away and paralyzed by Hitler's orders, or the 12th Panzer Division, which had one regiment north of Caen, some twenty kilometers away.

The British attack on General Richter's 716th Division began shortly after midnight with a bombing raid along the coast. In this part of the Calvados coast, the population was considerably denser than at Omaha or Utah, and French civilians suffered badly. Mlle Genget, who lived in the seaside village of St.-Côme-de-Fresne, at the western tip of the British invasion, kept a diary: "Awakened this morning at 1 a.m. by a distant bombardment, we got dressed . . . We heard the big bombers coming in and constantly passing over our heads." She and her parents stayed in the corner where the walls were thickest.

At dawn, "Suddenly a big gun is fired from the sea and the smaller cannon of the Boches were answering. . . . Everything in the house—doors, windows, and everything in the loft seem to be dancing. We had the impression that all sorts of things were falling in the court-yard. We were not feeling very brave!"[10]

Mme d'Anselm lived in Asnelles, a village off Gold Beach. The Germans had a gun emplacement at the bottom of her garden. Mme d'Anselm had seven children. She had dug a trench in her garden, "just big enough to shelter the eight of us and a couple of others," she said.

When the bombing began, Mme d'Anselm hurried her little troop into the trench. They stayed until dawn. One of the boys seized the opportunity of a lull when the bombing lifted to climb the garden wall to see what was happening.

"Mummy, Mummy!" he called out. "Look—the sea—it's black with boats!"[11]

28

"EVERYTHING WAS WELL ORDERED"

The 50th Division at Gold Beach

THE UDT (UNDERWATER DEMOLITION TEAM) MEN and the Royal Engineers began to touch down on Gold Beach at 0735, followed immediately by the first wave of LCTs carrying tanks and LCAs bringing in infantry assault teams. It was an hour later than the American landings because the tide moved from west to east and low tide came later on the British beaches. But the wind at Gold was coming almost straight in from the northwest, piling up the water to such a depth that the outer line of obstacles was underwater before the UDT men could get to them.

The later time of the attack was fortunate in that it gave the bombers and battleships longer to work over the beach defenses. Many of the Germans were in the resort houses that dotted the coast, concentrated at Le Hamel (right-center of Gold Beach) and La Rivière (left flank boundary with Juno Beach). Unlike the concrete emplacements, the houses could be set on fire by naval shells and air-dropped bombs.

The official British observer described the initial action: "Just as it was getting light, a tremendous bombing attack was delivered inland and fires which appeared to come from Ver-sur-Mer and La Rivière could be clearly seen. Apart from some flak, there was no enemy opposition of any sort, although it was broad daylight and the ships must have been clearly visible from the beaches. It was not until the first flight of assaulting troops were away and the cruiser H.M.S. *Belfast* opened fire that the enemy appeared to realize that something out of the ordinary was afoot. For some time after this the anchorage was ineffectually shelled by the enemy coastal battery situated about three-quarters of a mile inland. Shooting was very desultory, and inaccurate, and the guns of only 6- to 8-inch calibre."[1]

As Lt. Pat Blamey's LCT moved toward shore, shells from naval guns ranging from 5-inch to 14-inch whistled overhead. Blamey commanded a Sherman tank with a twenty-five-pounder cannon mounted on it; behind him in the LCT were four twenty-five-pounder field-artillery pieces that he would be towing ashore. The battery commenced firing when it was twelve kilometers from shore, and continued to fire a steady three rounds per minute until down to three kilometers.

"This was a period of furious activity," Blamey remembered. "Ammo boxes and shell cases jettisoned overboard as I called out the ranges received from the control craft. The noise was terrific, but nothing compared with the blast from the rocket ships when they opened up as our assault craft closed the beach."[2]

The beach obstacles proved to be more dangerous than German infantry or artillery. German snipers concentrated their fire on UDT teams, so that almost no clearing of lanes had been completed. LCTs landed first, near Asnelles, where they disgorged two companies of Hobart's Funnies. Twenty of the LCTs hit mined obstacles, suffering moderate to severe damage, losing some tanks and some men.

This "damn the torpedoes, full speed ahead" approach by the LCTs was in accord with the rules for guidance handed out to the coxswains by the Royal Navy. "*Hedgehogs, stakes or tetraheda will not prevent your beaching provided you go flat out,*" those instructions read. "Your craft will crunch over them, bend them and squash them into the sand and the damage to your outer bottom can be accepted. So drive on.

"Element C, however, is an obstacle to LCTs [but] at full speed you can bend them and pass partially over them.

"Therefore, avoid Element C if you can. If you cannot, try and hit it a glancing blow, preferably near the end of a 'bay.' This will probably turn it, or drive its supports into the sand. A second blow may enable you to squeeze through or past it.

"Do not worry too much about how you are to get out again.

The first and primary object is to get in and land without drowning the vehicles."[3]

Once the ramp went down, the men and vehicles rushed off the craft. A commando explained why: "The reason we stormed Normandy like we did was because the soldiers would rather have fought the whole German Army than go back on the ships and be as seasick as they were going over. My God! Those soldiers couldn't wait to get on dry land. Nothing would have got in their way . . . they would have torn tanks to pieces with their bare hands."[4]

They didn't have to, because there were no German tanks on the beach. Even the infantry resistance was ineffective. When Blamey drove off his LCT, towing the artillery pieces, he found that "local strong points had been neutralized by the bombardment. Shelling and mortaring from inland was slight and inaccurate. Except for some dozen Jerries, the beach was deserted of enemy. The ones I saw were completely shattered by the bombardment. They appeared to be Mongolians."

To Blamey, it seemed like "an ordinary exercise. The only difference that there was were the LCTs blowing up on the beach obstacles and swinging about." He went to work, laying out the line for his guns, putting up flags where he wanted the twenty-five-pounders to position themselves (the British landed some 200 of these excellent antitank guns on D-Day, a much better record than the American artillery achieved).

"One wasn't conscious of being in the middle of a hurly-burly," Blamey said. "Everything was very well ordered. Things were arriving, being unloaded. All those nice little French villas just inland had been set on fire and almost all were destroyed. I was more frightened of making a cock-off of my job and letting the side down than anything else."

Asked if the organization was better than he had expected, Blamey replied, "It was absolutely like clockwork. We knew it would be. We had every confidence. We had rehearsed it so often, we knew our equipment, we knew it worked, we knew given reasonable conditions we would get off the craft." He gave the credit to the Navy and the RAF; in his opinion, "they made our landing a pushover."

As the second wave began to arrive and the tide reduced the width of the beach, Blamey had his gunners cease fire and prepare to move inland. He hooked the pieces up to his tank and drove to the outskirts of Asnelles, where he stopped to brew up some tea before proceeding on to just west of Meuvaines, where he began to take fire from German 88s on a ridge ahead. Blamey lined up his cannon and replied; soon enough the German fire was silenced.[5]

The sectors at Gold were, from west to east, Item, Jig, King, and Love. The attackers from the Northumbrian (50th) Division were the Devonshire, Hampshire, Dorsetshire, and East Yorkshire regiments, accompanied by the Green Howards and Durham Light Infantry, plus engineer, communication, and artillery units, followed by the 7th Armoured Division, the famous "Desert Rats."

Blamey had landed at Jig; Seaman Ronald Seaborne, a forward observer for the *Belfast*, landed to his left at Love. Everyone on Seaborne's LCM was seasick: "We had had a fried egg breakfast, washed down by a tot of rum (not my choice but mandatory for all those going ashore.)"

The LCM ran aground 200 meters or more from the waterline, but Seaborne—carrying his radio—was as eager as everyone else to "run down the ramp and into the water—anything to abandon that instrument of torture."

LCAs passed Seaborne as he struggled through the chest-deep water. "By the time I was on the beach there were 200 or so troops already there effectively dealing with the straggling rifle fire coming from the defenses of La Rivière." After the bombardment the Germans had taken, Seaborne was surprised that any of them were still alive, much less firing back.

Seaborne's party consisted of a Royal Artillery captain, a bombardier, and a leading telegraphist. They crossed the seawall and the coastal road. The captain told Seaborne to report to *Belfast* that the beachhead was secure and that the party was going inland, then begin hiking toward Crepon.

Seaborne was unable to raise *Belfast*. After a quarter of an hour of frustration, he decided to follow the captain. "As I walked along a lane in the direction of Crepon, I could not see another person.

"Suddenly, from a field ahead, three men in German uniforms emerged. I thought this was the end of the war for me, but they raised their hands about their heads and by a mixture of French, German and English, I learned that they were Russians. I pointed the way to the beach and proceeded on. Before long I came to a small church. After halfway through the graveyard a shot whistled by me. I dropped to the ground amid a mass of poppies, then moved slowly toward a stone tombstone for safer shelter. Another shot rang out. I hid behind the tombstone, peered round it, and spotted a German helmet. I fired back and for the next few minutes it was real cowboys and Indians stuff. With the last of my ammunition, I got a lucky ricochet on my enemy, who slumped from his hiding place into my full view. I went over and looked at him and found I was gazing at a young boy, presumably one of the Hitler *Jugend*. I felt sick—sicker even than I had done on the LCM an hour or so previously."[6]

Lt. Comdr. Brian T. Whinney, RN, was beachmaster for Item and Jig sectors. He landed at 0745, some 150 meters from the waterline. On the way in, "considerable fire developed on the beaches and offshore from enemy batteries inland and mortars. Many near misses were observed among the LCAs of the assault wave."

Whinney made his way to the seawall, where "I became aware of a group of about a dozen men sitting quite quietly, apparently gazing out to sea. It took a few seconds for me to realize that they were the Germans who had been manning the beach defenses." They were waiting to surrender.

Further east, at Le Hamel, the German troops were sticking to their guns. One machine gun in a pillbox was firing with great effect, supported by mortar rounds dropping onto the shrinking beach. All tanks on the beach had been put out of action, either by mined obstacles or mortar shells. Without tanks, the engineers had been unable to clear any exits in the sector.

The Germans in Le Hamel (from the 1st Battalion, 916th Regiment, part of the 352nd Division) were somewhat protected in brick houses and hotels and they maintained a steady fire onto the beach. Whinney decided to suspend landings opposite Le Hamel and diverted follow-up waves to his right and left, where the opposition was less and exits had been opened. "I also stopped the clearance of beach obstacles in front of Le Hamel as no landing craft were beaching and with the heavy surf and enemy fire it was too great a risk for the personnel concerned."

Whinney went to the top of the seawall, where he was driven to take cover behind a disabled tank. Other men joined him. "The disabled tank was a great boon to us," Whinney remembered, "as it gave a narrow cone of shelter from the fire from the pillbox.

Without it we would have been in much worse trouble. The only tank to get off our beach successfully was a flail tank which succeeded in deafening the lot of us by blowing off his waterproofing before proceeding inland to support the marine commandos."

Whinney and his little party were soon joined by an improbable comrade. A Fleet Air Arm small plane, piloted by a Royal Navy lieutenant commander, was shot down by his own ship while reporting to it. The pilot managed to eject and come down safely by parachute, landing in the surf.

"We met him as he staggered ashore. He was almost speechless with rage, demanding a boat forthwith. The crossest man I've ever seen and I didn't envy the gun crew responsible for his ditching."[7]

(The next day there was a somewhat similar incident at Omaha. Pvt. Joseph Barrett was in the 474th AAA. A P-51 came out of the clouds, down low; the 474th shot it down. The pilot, a lieutenant, dropped by parachute onto the beach. He was wearing his class-A uniform and carrying a bottle of whiskey. He said he had a date in London that night and was only supposed to make a single pass over the beach. "He was mad as hell," Barrett recalled, "but in our defense we had been told to shoot at anything lower than 1,000 feet."[8])

Except at La Rivière, which held out until 1000, and Le Hamel, which held out until midafternoon, the German defenses on Gold were incapable of stopping the onrush of men and vehicles from the 50th Division. Nor were there hedgerows inland to check their momentum. What the Germans counted on was their counterattack capability. *Kampfgruppe Meyer* was stationed near Bayeux and it had often practiced maneuvers for getting to the beach in a hurry.

But at 0400, June 6, the regiment had gone off on a wild-goose chase to attack reported large-scale enemy airborne landings near Isigny. At 0800 General Kraiss realized his mistake and ordered a countermarch back to the Bayeux area, for a counterattack toward Crepon. But it took an hour for the order to reach the regiment, which then had to march some thirty kilometers to reach its start point. The march was made partly on foot, partly by bicycle, partly by French trucks that kept breaking down. It consumed another five hours before the lead elements were approaching the assembly position. Thus did Kraiss's main reserve spend the critical hours of D-Day marching across the countryside, first this way, then that.

While the 915th was marching east, it lost one of its three battalions, as Kraiss split the 2nd Battalion off and sent it to Colleville to meet the threat there from the U.S. 1st Infantry Division. When the body of *Kampfgruppe Meyer*, passing to the south of Bayeux, reached the Brazenville assembly area it was 1730 hours and the British were already in possession of Brazenville. Instead of attacking, *Kampfgruppe Meyer* was thrown on the defensive. Colonel Meyer was killed. There was no counterattack at Gold Beach.

But *Kampfgruppe Meyer* served a purpose for the Germans; the opposition it put up at Brazenville checked the advance of the 50th Division. Due to the unusually high tide, and the delay in clearing the beach obstacles, the follow-up waves from the division had been two hours or more late in getting ashore. The road to Bayeux was open until 1730, but the British were too late to take advantage of the opportunity. Still, they managed to get to Brazenville in time to check Meyer, and were in a position to move out to Bayeux the following day.[9]

The pattern was repeated all across the British and Canadian beaches. The assault teams got across the beach and through the crust of the German defense system with relatively little difficulty, but the follow-up waves were delayed by the unusually high tide and the abundance of beach obstacles. Inland, the assault teams failed to advance as quickly or as far as Montgomery had wanted them to go. The tendency was to stop to brew up a tea and congratulate themselves on having accomplished their objective—getting ashore.

When they moved out in the afternoon, they did so cautiously, relying on their artillery or Hobart's Funnies to subdue the opposition. There were some tanks and artillery opposing the advance, and the Germans were rushing reinforcements to the area, which was far more critical to them than anything on the American front. Bayeux sat astride the N-13, the highway that ran from Caen to Cherbourg, while Caen was the gateway to Paris to the east.

The adventures of Seaman Seaborne during the day illustrate in microcosm the British problems after clearing the beach. After his firefight with the German sniper in the graveyard, Seaborne hurried to catch up with the captain of his forward observation team. When he did, he found that the captain had joined up with the leading infantry units. They were unable to advance because of a single German tank concealed in a field beside the road.

The captain had Seaborne contact *Belfast* on his radio and prepare to give coordinates to the cruiser so it could blast the tank, but the infantry commander asked him to not call in naval shells because his men were too close to the tank. Seaborne's captain suggested falling back 100 meters or so, but the infantry leader would not do that either.

"It is no use just keeping up with the troops," the captain commented to Seaborne. "If we are to do anything useful we must be ahead—then we can bring *Belfast* into play without risk to our side."

The team set off for Creully—the infantry staying in place, neither attacking the tank nor backing off from it—and reached the village, some seven kilometers inland, about midday. There was no opposition, although eight soldiers in German uniforms surrendered to the team. Five of them were Russians; three hotly denied being Russian—they were Lithuanians who hated the Russians just as much as they did the Germans. The British sent them packing toward the beach.

Seaborne's team pushed on. At 1500 it reached the N-13 at the village of St.-Leger, midway between Bayeux and Caen. "Here we cautiously crossed the road and entered the cluster of houses beyond. We found a truly rustic setting—a village green, a café, a tall tree in the middle of the green, and two or three benches on the grass. Everything was very quiet and very still. Who said that there was a war on?

"It was very pleasant, but not what we had come for." The captain decided to climb the tree to spy out the land. "So up we went. Suddenly, below us, we heard a rumble. Looking down we saw a German half-track enter the square and park below our tree." Six German soldiers climbed out, relieved themselves against the tree, then climbed back in. "We hoped that this was the only reason for the stop, but to our dismay the half-track did not move." Ten minutes later another half-track lumbered into the square, quickly followed by a third.

The captain whispered to Seaborne, "Send a signal to *Belfast*—send 'Cut off in Daedalus' " (code name for St.-Leger).

The telegraphist went white. "Don't be daft," he whispered furiously. "What bloody good will that do? Jerry will hear the Morse key for sure."

The captain hissed back, "This is mutiny in the face of the enemy. I'll have you shot."

"Belt up," the telegraphist fired back, "or you'll get us all shot."

Seaborne made his own decision—he sent no message.

The Germans got themselves sorted out. Half of them took off on one half-track headed east, the other half jumped in a second half-track to head west, leaving the third vehicle unattended in the square. The telegraphist scurried down the tree trunk, Seaborne right beside him. They crossed wires and got the half- track started, jumped in and took off, the captain scrambling aboard as the vehicle moved out, shouting curses at the telegraphist and at Seaborne.

"We charged back over the N-13," Seaborne remembered, "and down the lane toward Creully. Near this village we stopped and got out. I reported back to *Belfast* and soon after we made contact once more with our own troops."[10]

Seaborne's little party was the only British unit from Gold to cross the N-13 that day. It had made the deepest penetration of any Allied unit. But it had not accomplished anything positive and ended up settling down for the night in Creully.

The 47th Royal Marine Commandos landed at Item sector, on the far right, near St.-Côme-de-Fresne. The beach obstacles played havoc with their landing craft; fifteen out of sixteen were damaged. Initially machine gun fire was heavy; one marine called out to his mates, "Perhaps we're intruding. This seems to be a private beach." But the Germans from the 352nd Division soon packed it in and, once ashore, the Royal Marines found it tame, "like another exercise back home." The medical teams had so little to do that they began unloading ammunition.

The marines' task was to push on inland, turn right (west), pass to the south of Arromanches and Longues, and take Port-en-Bessin from the rear. Port-en-Bessin was midway between Omaha and Gold; the marines were supposed to link up with the Americans at the tiny port. But neither the marines nor the Americans got to Port-en-Bessin before nightfall, although the marines did get to within a kilometer of it and took the port the next day.[11]

In their trek to the west, the marines passed Longues-sur-Mer. On the steep cliff on the outskirts of the village, the Germans had a superbly built large observation post, linked by underground telephone lines to a battery of four 155mm cannon about a kilometer back from the cliff. The observation post consisted of two floors. The bottom floor, mainly below the ground, had a direction-finder room, a long, narrow aperture, a chart room, a telephone exchange, and other equipment. The upper floor was protected by a concrete slab more than a meter thick, reinforced by steel rods and supported by steel bars. It housed a range finder. The guns were in four separate fortifications, also with meter-thick reinforced concrete and underground magazines.

This was the battery whose exact coordinates the British had obtained thanks to the blind son of the farmer who owned the land and thanks to André Heintz's radio reports over his homemade wireless set.

Shortly after dawn, the battery—which had been pounded by tons of bombs from the air and shells from the sea in the pre-invasion bombardment, but was hardly scratched—opened fire on the battleship *Arkansas*, anchored five kilometers off Omaha Beach. *Arkansas* returned fire, supported by two French cruisers. The battery then turned its cannon to fire toward HMS *Bulolo*, the headquarters ship for Gold Beach, which was some twelve kilometers out in the Channel. The firing was accurate enough to force *Bulolo* to change its position.

At this point HMS *Ajax*, famous for its participation against the German pocket battleship *Admiral Graf Spee* off Montevideo on the River Plate on December 13, 1939, got into a ship-vs.-fortification duel with the Longues-sur-Mer battery. *Ajax* was some eleven kilometers offshore, but its firing was so accurate that within twenty minutes two of the German cannon fell silent. They had not been destroyed, but the shock and concussion from direct hits on the concrete emplacement so shattered the German artillerymen that they abandoned the position.

On a third emplacement, *Ajax* scored what was either the most accurate or the luckiest hit of the invasion—perhaps both. There were no survivors so there is no way to know exactly what happened, but the on-site evidence five decades later indicates what must have happened. The entire breech mechanism of the 155mm cannon is simply gone. The barrel, three-inches-thick steel, lies in pieces: The emplacement looks as if a tactical nuclear weapon had gone off inside.

Evidently *Ajax* sent one of its 6-inch shells through the

embrasure of the emplacement at a moment when the breech was open and the gunners were loading a shell into it. The shell must have gone off in the breech. At that same instant, the steel door leading to the magazine below must have been open; the fire from the explosion ran down into the magazine and set off the piles of 155mm ammunition stored there.

What a bang that must have been. It tore off the concrete roof, scattering automobile-size chunks of it all around. One has to doubt that even one piece of any of the gunners survived.

Twenty-five years later, the skipper of *Ajax* was entertaining a young American student studying in England. She was the daughter of an American woman he had been dating during the war, and had just returned from a visit to Normandy. She got him to talking about his duel with the battery at Longues-sur-Mer. He described it, then said he had often wondered but never found out how he had the exact coordinates of those well-camouflaged emplacements.

"Why," the girl replied, "I know. I've just talked to André Heintz [then professor of history at the University of Caen] and he told me." She then related the story of the blind boy and his father pacing off the distances and getting the information to Heintz in Bayeux.[12]

Mlle Genget was a resident of St.-Côme-de-Fresne, where the Royal Marines landed. On the evening of June 6, she wrote in her diary, "What seemed impossible has really happened! The English have landed on the French coast and our little village has become famous in a few hours! Not one civilian killed or wounded. How can we express our surprise after such long years of waiting in wonderment and fear?"

In the morning she and a friend went to the edge of the cliff to see what was happening. "From there what a sight met our eyes! As far as we could see there were ships of all kinds and sizes and above floated big balloons silvery in the sun. Big bombers were passing and repassing in the sky. As far as Courseulles one could see nothing but ships."

Mlle Genget returned to St.-Côme, where she encountered British soldiers. "The English had thought that all civilians had been evacuated from the coast and were very surprised to find the inhabitants had stayed in their homes. Our little church had received a direct hit on the roof and fire broke out, but with the help of the villagers it was soon overcome. Guns were firing. What a noise everywhere and smell of burning!"

She wondered if she were dreaming. "Is it all really true?" she wrote. "We are at last liberated. The enormous strength that all this war material represents is fantastic, and the way it has been handled with such precision is marvelous. . . . A group of Tommies pass and ask us for water. We fill their bottles, say a few words, and, having given chocolate and sweets to the children, they continue on their way."[13]

On the beach, Lieutenant Commander Whinney noted that as night came on "all was quiet. An eerie feeling remained. There was not a soul in sight." He went to a farmhouse, which backed onto the pillbox that had given so much trouble at Le Hamel in the forenoon, and was surprised to hear a noise inside. He knocked on the door "and to my astonishment an old lady appeared. She seemed quite unconcerned. She had apparently been there all day, carrying out her household chores as usual."[14]

By nightfall on June 6, the British at Gold Beach had penetrated some ten kilometers inland and hooked up with the Canadians at Creully on their left. They were on the cliff looking down on Arromanches. They had not taken Bayeux or crossed the N-13, but they were in position to do so the next day. They had put 25,000 men ashore at a cost of 400 casualties. It was a good start.

29

PAYBACK

The Canadians at Juno

ON AUGUST 19, 1942, the 2nd Canadian Division, supported by British commandos and a small unit of American rangers, made an amphibious assault on the port of Dieppe, on the upper Norman coast about 100 kilometers from Le Havre. It was a raid, not an invasion. It was poorly planned and badly executed. The Canadians suffered terrible losses; three-quarters of them were killed, wounded, or taken prisoner within six hours; all seven battalion commanders were casualties.

At Dieppe, the Germans had fortified positions holding 88mm cannon on the cliffs on each side of the beach, plus machine-gun pillboxes and entrenched troops. The beach consisted entirely of shingle, impossible for tanks to cross and difficult for men. There had been no preassault bombardment from ships or planes. The attacking infantry outnumbered the defenders by only a two-to-one ratio, and the defenders were top-quality troops.

Allied propaganda tried to play Dieppe as a rehearsal from which critical lessons were learned, lessons that were applied on June 6, 1944. But in fact the only lesson learned was Do Not Attack Fortified Ports Head-On. Dieppe was a national disaster. The Canadians owed the Germans a bit of payback. They got it on Juno Beach.

• •

Courseulles-sur-Mer, in the center of Juno Beach, was the most heavily defended point in the long stretch from Arromanches on the far right of the British beaches to Ouistreham on the far left. St.-Aubin and Langrune, to the left (east) of Courseulles, were well defended also. General Richter's 716th Division had eleven heavy batteries of 155mm guns and nine medium batteries, mainly 75s. All were supposed to be in fortified bunkers, but only two bunkers were complete. Elsewhere the crews were protected by unroofed bunkers or earthen gun pits in open fields.

There were *Widerstandnester* at Vaux, Courseulles, Bernières, and St.-Aubin, each heavily fortified with reinforced concrete. The *Widerstandnester* were supported by trenches and gun pits, surrounded by barbed wire and minefields. All weapons were sighted to fire along the beach in enfilade, not out to sea; the zones of fire were calculated to interlock on the formidable array of beach obstacles situated just below the high-water mark. To the Germans, as John Keegan noted, "The combination of fixed obstacles and enfilading fire from the resistance nests was deemed to guarantee the destruction of any landing force."[1]

But General Richter had some serious problems. His *Widerstandnester* were a kilometer apart. His mobility was practically nonexistent—the 716th used horses to move its artillery and supplies, while its men moved by foot. Their weapons were a hodgepodge of captured rifles and cannon. The men were under eighteen or over thirty-five years of age, or veterans of the Eastern Front in their midtwenties who had suffered more or less disabling wounds, or *Ost* battalion troops from Russia and Poland. Their orders were to stand fast. Giving an inch of ground was forbidden, and German NCOs were there to enforce those orders (in any case, the encircling minefields and barbed wire would keep them in just as much as it would keep the Canadians out). Man for man, they were hardly a match for the young, tough, magnificently trained Canadians, and they were outnumbered by the Canadians in the first wave at a ratio of six to one (2,400 Canadians, 400 Germans).

The Canadian 3rd Division contained lumberjacks, fishermen, miners, farmers, all tough outdoorsmen and all volunteers (Canada had conscription in World War II, but only volunteers were sent into combat zones). Sapper Josh Honan "volunteered" in a way familiar to all veterans. He was a surveyor in an engineer company in Canada in late 1943 when a colonel called him to headquarters.

"You're Irish," the colonel declared.

"Yes, sir."

"An Irishman always likes a good scrap, doesn't he? We got a job we'd like you to do."

Honan replied that he would just as soon stay with his company. "We're all together, sir, we're going overseas and I don't want to get separated from my mates."

"Never mind about all that, you may meet them again in England."

Honan asked what the job was; the colonel replied that he could not say. "The only thing I can tell you about it is that there are many men in England today who would gladly change places with you."

"Just one will do," Honan responded.

"Well, you Irish will have your little joke. I can promise you that you will be totally pleased that you took this job."

"Will I?"

"Oh, yes, I know you Irish, you enjoy a good scrap, don't you?"

In his interview, Honan commented, "I wasn't too keen on this jolly-good-scrap business talk," but there it was. A few days later he was on his way to England, where he discovered that the job was just about the worst imaginable—he was to precede the first wave and blow up beach obstacles.

On the night crossing on his LST, Honan noted that the men he was with (the Regina Rifle Regiment, headed toward Mike sector of Juno) spent their time alternating between using their whetstones to sharpen knives, daggers, and bayonets and playing poker. He saw one man who had a knife with a wooden haft covered with leatherwork with a big diamond-like gem inserted into it "sharpening it like mad." Others were "playing poker like nothing I'd ever seen before. There was no use in holding back, nothing made any difference, bet the lot. When officers came around they would sort of cover the money with the blankets they were playing on."

Asked if the officers didn't try to stop the men from gambling, Honan said matter-of-factly, "You couldn't stop anybody from doing anything at that stage."

Honan saw a single ship steaming through his convoy, between the rows of ships, "and as it passed we could see on the prow the solitary piper silhouetted against the evening sky and the thin lament coming across, 'We No' Come Back Again.' It was very touching and everybody was hushed and everybody just stood there watching, not a sound from anyone, and then gradually it passed by and faded away in the distance. And we often thought that we no' come back again."[2]

The Canadians were scheduled to land at 0745, but rough seas made them ten minutes and more late, and extremely seasick ("Death would be better than this," Pvt. Henry Gerald of the Royal Winnipeg Rifles moaned to one of his mates[3]). They had been told in the final briefings that all the pillboxes, machine guns, and artillery pieces would be *kaput* as a result of the air and naval bombardments, but things did not work out that way.

The midnight June 5/6 air bombardment by RAF Bomber Command was heavy enough—the 5,268 tons of bombs dropped was the heaviest raid the British had yet mounted in the war—but it was woefully inaccurate. American B-17s came over at first light, but as at Omaha they delayed dropping their bombs up to thirty seconds after crossing the aiming point. As a result, the bombs fell well inland. Very few of the fortifications were hit, none on Juno.

Royal Navy cruisers and battleships began firing at 0600. The destroyers went into action at 0619. At 0710 the tanks and twenty-five-pounders on LCTs joined in, followed by the rockets from the LCT(R)s. It was the heaviest bombardment ever fired from ship to shore. But the smoke and haze was such that very few of the shells actually hit their targets (a target-analysis team later calculated that only about 14 percent of the bunkers were destroyed).

The smoke was so thick that for the most part the German defenders could not see out to sea. At 0645 Seventh Army's routine morning report to OB West read: "Purpose of naval bombardment not yet apparent. It appears to be a covering action in conjunction with attacks to be made at other points later." Occasionally the wind would sweep away the smoke; when it did, the Germans could see "countless ships, ships big and small, beyond comprehension."[4]

The bombardment lifted at 0730, when the first wave was supposed to be landing. This gave the Germans time to recover and man their guns. "All the softening up did was alert the enemy of the landing," Private Henry remarked, "and give them the chance to be settled in for our guys to run into."[5] Another soldier in the Royal Winnipeg Rifles commented, "The bombardment had failed to kill a single German or silence one weapon."[6]

Yet as the Canadian landing craft approached the beach

obstacles, mostly underwater due to the strong northwest wind, there was an eerie silence. The Germans were not firing, which the Canadians found encouraging; they did not yet realize the reason was all the German guns were sighted to fire down the beach.

Josh Honan was on an LST, waiting to be off-loaded onto an LCA for the final run of five kilometers or so to the beach. One of his mates asked, "Do you think this might just be a rehearsal?"

"It looks a bit elaborate for that," Honan replied.

Honan had his own fantasy, that his demolition team would be forgotten by the officer in charge. "It was like being called for the dentist," Honan said. "I was hoping that I wouldn't be next, that maybe somebody else would go before me. But then this fellow with the bullhorn called out, 'Sapper assault team, report to your boat stations on number six deck, NOW!' "

Safely loaded, Honan's LCA joined five others and began to circle. He went to the ramp to watch the action. He noted that all the Canadian soldiers had deeply suntanned faces, while the British coxswains and crews were moon white. He looked for landmarks but could not see any through the smoke. The LCA was pitching and bucking in the waves. "The rougher it got," Honan said, "the less I looked around me to see what was happening to anybody else."

The craft started closing up on each other, but not in an organized fashion. The LCAs began losing way and losing steerage, bumping into each other and into beach obstacles.

When the leading craft—mostly carrying engineers and UDT teams—reached the outer line of obstacles, a quarter or more of them set off Teller mines. The mines were not big enough to blow the craft out of the water or otherwise destroy them (the open tops allowed most of the explosive power to escape into the air), but they made holes in the bottoms or damaged the ramps.

Honan's LCA came in opposite Bernières-sur-Mer. Honan tried to give the coxswain directions to avoid obstacles, "but he hadn't enough steerage for the boat to answer. So we finished up by running on top of one of the obstacles with the ramp up against it. We could see the mine just beside us; one bump and bang.

"So Major Stone [Honan's CO] said, 'I'm going over.' I said, 'Bloody good luck to you,' but my orders were to try to keep Stonie alive so I had to go over after him."

Honan dumped all his equipment overboard—rifle, explosives, walkie-talkie, the works—and dove into the water after his major.

"And Stonie was starting to swim for the front of the boat,

and I said, 'Bugger it, I've got to do that too,' so I swam to the front and the obstacle was wired onto two adjacent tetrahedrons and the major had cutting pliers and he said, 'I'll cut the wires,' and I said, 'OK, I'll take out the detonators.'

"So I got astride the tetrahedron, wrapped my legs around it, and started to unscrew the detonators. Stonie shouted to get a dozen men off the craft and for the others to go to the stern to help lift the prow off the obstacle. So a dozen soldiers dove in and we all got our shoulders to the prow and pushed."

It was about 0800. The leading LCAs carrying assault teams were dropping their ramps. Canadians were making their way on foot through the obstacles up onto the beach.

The Germans commenced firing. Snipers and mortar crews were aiming at the landing craft as machine guns concentrated on the first wave of infantry. Bullets were creating miniature geysers around Honan. He, Major Stone, and the men managed to free the LCA. Its ramp went down and the infantry made toward shore as Honan moved to the next obstacle to remove the detonator on its mine.

"My mates were attacking the pillboxes; that was their business and I was doing my business. I was a sitting duck, I didn't have anything to work with except my bare hands." The rising tide covered the obstacles faster than Honan could unscrew the detonators. Honan remarked, "I could do my job only by wrapping my legs around the obstacles to keep from being floated away, and I could only use one hand."

At about 0815 he decided, "Bugger this lark, I'm going ashore." He swam for the shore. There he saw a headless corpse. The man had apparently been wounded in the water and then run over by an LCA. The propeller had cut his head off. He was clutching in his hand the knife with a diamond-like gem inserted into the leather wrapped around the handle that Honan had noticed during the night.

When Honan reached the seawall, a couple of the chaps hauled him up and over. One of them pulled out a flask of whiskey and offered Honan a drink.

"No thanks," Honan said.

The soldier took a slug himself and asked, "Why not? You're not an 'effin teetotaler are you?"

"I'm not," Honan replied, "but I'm afraid that stuff will make me feel brave or some bloody thing like that."

Honan moved into the village, where he took shelter until

the German machine-gun fire was suppressed. "I had done my bit," he explained. "I was watching the others get on with it." Until the tide receded, he could do no more demolition of obstacles.

Soon the guns fell silent and the people began coming out into the street, waving for the liberators, throwing bouquets of roses. The village priest appeared.

"Monsieur le curé," Honan said in his best high-school French, "I hope that you are pleased that we have arrived."

"Yes," the priest replied, "but I will be better pleased when you are gone again," as he pointed sadly to the hole in the top of his seventeenth-century church.

The barber came out and asked Honan if he would like a cognac. No, Honan replied, "but I could do with a shave." The barber was happy to comply, "so I went in and sat in the chair in my wringing-wet battle dress, the water squelching in my shoes, and he gave me a shave."

Refreshed and rested, Honan returned to the beach to go back to work. "I was in time to see the DD tanks coming ashore. Two of them came out of the water, I had never seen nor heard of them before. So this was like sea monsters for me coming out of the deep. Those two tanks pulled up their skirts and ducked around the village with the other girls."[7]

Sgt. Ronald Johnston was a tank driver. At 0500, out in the Channel, in the anchorage area, he off-loaded from an LST onto a Rhino ferry, an experience he found disconcerting as he had not done the maneuver previously and the steel tracks slipped on the steel deck of the Rhino and his tank almost plunged into the sea. Finally he got to his designated position. There was a jeep in front of him.

Johnston walked up to the jeep driver and asked, "That jeep is waterproofed, isn't it?"

"Yeah, why?"

"I sure as hell hope so, because if it stalls I'm going right over the top of it." When the ferry made the shoreline, Johnston recalled, the jeep driver all but broke his neck looking back to make sure the Sherman tank wasn't coming on.

The jeep made it OK, Johnston right behind. He was horrified when he made the shore and discovered he had to run over dead and wounded infantry. "We just had to put it out of our minds," he commented, "just forget it. There was only one way forward."

Johnston's tank carried two motorcycles strapped onto the exhaust pipes and was towing an ammunition trailer. Cordite was wrapped around the waterproofing and exhaust pipes, all connected by wire. When the motorcycles were removed, Johnston got the word from the tank commander to hit the button that ignited the cordite and blew the waterproofing off. "It made a hell of an explosion."

On the beach, "It was unreal. Machine-gun fire, mostly wild. A lot of the infantry were still in the water and they couldn't get in. They took cover behind the tanks."

A commando officer told Johnston to turn left. "I looked and I said, 'Oh, my God, no.' "

The commando asked why not. Johnston replied, "I'm not going to run over any more of my own buddies today."[8]

Sgt. Tom Plumb was with a mortar platoon of the Royal Winnipeg Rifles. He went in on an LCT. When the ramp dropped and the tanks drove off, the LCT was pushed back into deeper water. The skipper nevertheless ordered the sergeant in charge of the first section to drive off in his mortar carrier. The sergeant protested that the water was too deep but the skipper was adamant.

The first carrier drove off and immediately sank in four meters of water. The men came floating up, choking and cursing.

The skipper ordered the next carrier off, but the sergeant rebelled and demanded a dry landing. The skipper threatened him with a court martial, but the sergeant held fast. Finally the skipper conceded, raised the ramp, circled, came in again, and Plumb and the others made a dry landing. "That landing craft commanding officer was later given a dishonorable discharge," Plumb commented with some satisfaction.[9]

The skipper had reason to be hesitant, reason to want to pull that famous naval maneuver known as getting the hell out of there. All around him, all across Juno Beach, landing craft were setting off Teller mines. Many did so coming in; more did so when their troops and vehicles disembarked, because they then floated higher in the water and wave action pushed them against mined obstacles. Half or more of the craft at Juno were damaged, a quarter sunk.

Sgt. Sigie Johnson of the Regina Rifles was first out of his LCA. It had stuck on a sandbar; when Johnson took a couple of steps forward he was in over his head. "Then a swell came along and it lifted the boat and it went right over the top of me." He paused in his interview, shook his head, and said with wonder in his voice, "And I'm still here telling about it." One of his mates was hit in the stomach and the legs. Despite his wounds, he went straight for a pillbox.

"He shot one of the gunners, and the other one, he got his hands around his throat. He strangled the German, then he died himself, and when we found him he still had his hands around the German's throat."

A DD tank swam ashore, dropped the skirts, and began blasting with its 75mm cannon. Unfortunately, the tank had blasted at some Canadian infantry. Johnson got over to the tank and was able to get the captain to cease fire. Asked how the friendly fire could have happened, Johnson replied, "That tank was one of the first ones in and they saw troops and I guess everybody's uniform was black from being wet anyway, and they just started firing." Johnson pointed to a 37mm gun in front of a building and got the tanker to blast it.[10]

For the infantry assault teams it was a matter of chance whether they landed on their sector before any tanks got ashore, or landed side by side with tanks, or followed tanks ashore. In general, the DD tanks were late—if they arrived at all—while skippers of LCTs who decided to hell with the orders, we are going all the way in, put their tanks in even as the UDT men started working on the obstacles.

It was also a matter of chance whether the infantry landed dry or in deep water. Sergeant McQuaid, an Irishman, jumped off his ramp into neck-deep water. Amid many other curses, he shouted, "Oh, the evil of it. They're trying to drown me before I even get up on the beach."[11]

The Germans opened fire as the infantry made their way through the obstacles up to the seawall. The Canadians in the first wave took dreadful casualties, in some companies every bit as bad as the first wave at Omaha. B Company of the Winnipegs was cut down to one officer and twenty-five men before it reached the seawall. D Company of the Regina Rifles lost half its strength even before it reached the beach.

The regimental historian described the scene: "A Company found the bombardment had not cracked the huge casemate on their sector. This fortress had reinforced concrete walls four feet thick and housed an 88mm gun as well as machine guns. In addition there were concrete trenches outside the fort liberally sprinkled with small arms posts." Men survived by getting behind tanks until they could reach the seawall.[12]

The Queen's Own Rifles landed at Bernières, accompanied by DD tanks from the Fort Garry Horse (10th Armored Regiment). Sergeant Gariepy drove one of the tanks.

"More by accident than by design," he recalled, "I found myself the leading tank. On my way in I was surprised to see a friend—a midget submarine who had been waiting for us for forty-eight hours. He waved me right on to my target. . . . I remember him very very distinctly standing up through his conning hatch joining his hands together in a sign of good luck. I answered the old familiar army sign—To you too, bud!

"I was the first tank coming ashore and the Germans started opening up with machine guns. But when we came to a halt on the beach, it was only then that they realized we were a tank when we pulled down our canvas skirt, the flotation gear. Then they saw that we were Shermans.

"It was quite amazing. I still remember very vividly some of the machine gunners standing up in their posts looking at us with their mouths wide open. To see tanks coming out of the water shook them rigid."

Gariepy's target was a 75mm gun firing enfilade across the beach. Infantry got behind him as he drove his tank forward. "The houses along the beach were all full of machine gunners and so were the sand dunes. But the angle of the blockhouse stopped them [the crew of the 75mm] from firing on me. So I took the tank up to the emplacement, very very close, and destroyed the gun by firing at almost point-blank range." The infantry following Gariepy gained the relative safety of the seawall.[13]

In the midst of this uproar, the pipers with the Canadian Scottish Regiment piped away. The pipers had played the regiment out of the harbor when they left England, played again as they clambered into their assault boats, and yet again as they hit the beach. Cpl. Robert Rogge was an American who had joined the Canadian army in 1940. He went in with the Black Watch (Royal Highland Regiment).

"It was something," he recalled. "While I was wading onshore I could hear one of our pipers playing 'Bonnie Dundee' on the ship behind us and we were really getting piped into action."[14]

Pvt. G. W. Levers of the Canadian Scottish Regiment kept a diary. He jotted notes in it as best he could as his LCA moved toward shore. "Craft is bobbing around like a cork. We are not due to touch down until 0745. As we gradually near the shore we can see the different ships firing, also batteries of rockets firing. When they go off there is a terrific flash of flame. We are within half a mile of shore by now and several of the chaps are quite seasick.

"The engines are speeded up and we are making our run for the shore. We can see the beach although the seas are running high. We can see a big pillbox with the shells bursting around it and apparently doing no damage at all.

"The machine-gun bullets are starting to whine around our craft and the boys are keeping their heads down. Here we go, the ramp is down."

Levers tucked his diary away and went down the ramp. Later, catching his breath at the seawall, he pulled it out and wrote, "We were in water up to our waists and sometimes up to our chests. We waded ashore and it was pretty slow work. We hit the beach and machine guns were making us play hopscotch as we crossed it at the walk."[15]

As Levers's experience indicates, the initial assault at Juno was like the initial assault at Omaha, but once the Canadians reached the seawall there were significant differences. There were more tanks on Juno, especially more specialized tanks designed to help the infantry over the seawall (which was considerably higher at Juno than at Omaha), through the barbed wire, and across the minefields. The flanking fire was as intense at Juno as at Omaha, and the fortified pillboxes and gun emplacements just as numerous and formidable.

At Omaha, one in nineteen of the men landed on D-Day became casualties (nearly 40,000 went ashore; there were 2,200 casualties). At Juno, one in eighteen were killed or wounded (21,400 landed; 1,200 were casualties). The figures are misleading in the sense that most men landed in the late morning or afternoon at both beaches, but a majority of the casualties were taken in the first hour. In the assault teams at both beaches the chances of being killed or wounded were close to one in two.

The biggest difference between the beaches was that at Juno there was no bluff behind the seawall. Once across and through the villages, the Canadians were in relatively flat, open country with few hedgerows, few fortifications, and almost no opposition.

The trick was to get over the seawall and through the villages. That was where Hobart's Funnies came into play. Tanks carrying bridges put them up against the seawall. Flail tanks beat their way through minefields. Tanks with bulldozers pushed barbed wire out of the way. Churchill crocodile tanks, towing 400 gallons of fuel in armored trailers, with a pipeline under the belly to the flame guns in front, shot out streams of flame at pillboxes. Tanks carrying fascines dropped them into the antitank ditches, then led the way over.

Sgt. Ronald Johnston drove his tank up to the seawall. His captain fired forty rounds of armor-piercing ammunition against it, cutting it down. A bulldozer cleared away the rubble. Johnston drove through and reached the street running parallel to the beach. The tank was buttoned-up; Johnston was looking through a periscope. He did not see a slit trench "and I went left and the damn track went in the slit trench and there we sat. But the Lord was with us."

The tank came to a halt in a position that had its .50-caliber machine gun looking right down the throat of some German infantry in the trench. The gunner gave a blast, killing or wounding a few Germans. Twenty-one other Germans put their hands up. Another British tank came through the gap, hooked onto Johnston's tank, and pulled it out of the trench.[16]

Capt. Cyril Hendry, the troop commander who had unfolded his bridge on the LCT so that it would not act as a sail, was "terrifically busy" on the run into shore. "Getting all our tanks started up, warmed up, lifting that damn bridge, getting everybody into position, making sure all the guns were loaded and this sort of thing, everybody so flaming seasick, it was rough."

When he drove off the ramp, he was pleased to see an armored bulldozer already on the beach, using its winch to pull barbed wire off the seawall. "I had to drop my bridge on the sand dunes so that the other tanks could climb and drop down on the far side." The first of the Funnies to cross began flailing a path for the follow-up vehicles and infantry.

When the flail tank reached "this bloody great hole of a tank trap," it turned aside to allow a Sherman carrying a fascine to move forward and drop the fascine into the hole. Then the Sherman started to cross, only to slide down into an even deeper hole, evidently created by a naval shell. Hendry drove forward with his bridge, which had a thirty-foot reach. The combination tank trap and crater was sixty feet wide. Hendry used the turret of the sunken tank as a pier. After he got his bridge in place, the far end resting on the sunken Sherman, another bridge-carrying tank crossed and, also using the sunken tank for support, dropped its bridge to reach the dry ground on the far side.

By 0915 the two bridges resting on the sunken tank were secure enough for flail tanks to cross. Infantry came after them and rushed the houses from which machine-gun fire was coming.[17]*

The Canadian infantry moved across the seawall and into the street fighting in the villages, or against pillboxes, with a fury that had to be seen to be believed. One who saw it happen was Pvt. Gerald Henry. His company of the Royal Winnipegs was scheduled to land at 0800, but it was late, so he was an observer for the initial action. His comment was to the point: "It took a great deal of heroics and casualties to silence the concrete emplacements and the various machine gun nests."[18]

Sergeant Sigie Johnson saw one of the bravest acts possible in war. A pioneer platoon was held up by barbed wire. It was supposed to use a bangalore torpedo to blow a gap, but the torpedo failed to explode. A soldier, unknown to Johnson, threw himself over the wire so that others could cross on his back. Johnson saw others crawl through barbed wire and minefields to get close enough to the embrasures of pillboxes to toss in grenades. He concluded his interview with these words: "Very few publications ever get the truth of what our Winnipeg infantry faced and did."[19]

Every platoon in the Canadian assault companies had an assigned sector in the villages to attack. In some cases they met almost no resistance once over the seawall. Company B of the Regina Rifles, for example, cleared the east side of Courseulles in a matter of minutes. But A Company, at the western side, was held up and badly hurt by machine guns, an 88mm gun beside the harbor entrance, and a 75mm out to the right flank. Fortunately, fourteen of the nineteen DD tanks launched by B Squadron of the 1st Hussars provided support for the infantry, who worked their way through the trenches and dugouts connecting the concrete positions.

* The sunken tank was a Churchill with the 26th Assault Engineer Squadron, Royal Engineers, under the command of the 7th Canadian Infantry Brigade. Later on D-Day the 85th Field Company, Royal Engineers, improved the bridge. It remained in use until 1976. When a new bridge was built, the tank that had served as a pier was lifted out of the crater and placed at a gap in the sand dunes just west of Courseulles, where it sits today, a memorial to all those from Britain and Canada who came to liberate France.

Sergeant Gariepy nearly got stuck in Courseulles. His tank ended up in a narrow street "and there was one of those funny-looking trucks with a charcoal burner on the running board. I couldn't get my tank by, and I saw two Frenchmen and a French woman standing in a doorway looking at us. So I took my earphones off and told them in good Quebec French, 'Now will you please move that truck out of the way so I can get by?'

"They must have been frightened because they wouldn't budge. So I then called them everything I could think of in the military vocabulary. They were amazed to hear a Tommy—they thought we were Tommies—speak French with the old Norman dialect!' " But they finally moved the truck and Gariepy was able to push inland.[20]

B Company of the Queen's Own Regiment, attacking Bernières, also ran into undamaged fortifications. Before it was able to get around and behind the guns and put them out of action it took sixty-five casualties. But within an hour, Courseulles and Bernières were in Canadian hands.[21]

The North Shore (New Brunswick) Regiment assault teams hit St.-Aubin. Within an hour A Company, on the right, cleared its immediate front with a loss of twenty-four men. B Company, attacking the village itself, ran into a reinforced-concrete casemate with steel doors and shutters, with well-prepared entrenchments around it and 100 German soldiers inside. Not until tanks lobbed several twenty-five-pound petards against the bunker and cracked the concrete to stun the defenders did the Germans surrender. Half the garrison was by then dead or wounded.[22]

As at Omaha, strong points that the attackers thought they had cleared came alive after the Canadians passed through. Germans infiltrated via their trench system back into the positions and resumed the fight. Within the villages, the Germans would pop up at one window, then another, fire a round or two, then disappear. Street fighting, sometimes heavy, sometimes sporadic, went on through the day. The North Shore assault teams did not have St.-Aubin fully secured until 1800.

Follow-up waves came in steadily. Many of the men in them carried bicycles, which in some cases actually worked (although by the end of the day most of the bikes had suffered the fate of most of the gas masks carried ashore, that is, they were discarded). Using the bikes and their feet, the reinforcements passed over the seawall and through the villages to dash forward and seize crossroads and bridges inland.

C Company of the Canadian Scottish reached the area between Ste.-Croix and Banville, where follow-up elements of the Royal Winnipegs were involved in a firefight with German defenders. A platoon commander from the company described what happened: "An LMG [light machine gun] which sounded like a Bren opened up from a position about 150 yards away. We 'hit the dirt' and I shouted, 'This must be the Winnipegs! When I say "UP"—all up together and shout "WINNIPEGS." '

"We did, and to our surprise two enemy infantry sections stood up. . . . They too were a picture of amazement. . . . Their camouflage was perfect and it was no wonder we did not see them earlier. But the stunned silence did not last long. There was only one course of action, and to a man the platoon rushed the enemy position. It was a bitter encounter with much hand-to-hand fighting."[23]

At 0930 the 12th Field Regiment, Royal Canadian Artillery, began landing. The gunners drove their self-propelled 105mm guns onto the beach, lined them up only a few meters inland, and began firing, sometimes over open sights. The assault sappers from the Royal Canadian Engineers meanwhile were clearing the beach and opening exits, allowing tanks and other vehicles to move inland.

By 1200 the entire Canadian 3rd Division was ashore. The Winnipegs and Reginas, supported by tanks, had penetrated several kilometers inland and captured the bridges over the River Seulles. No German tanks had been seen. Early in the afternoon the Canadian Scottish had passed its leading battalion through the Winnipegs and captured Colombiers-sur-Seulles.

Sgt. Stanley Dudka of the North Nova Scotia Highlanders landed at 1100. "Our instructions were to break through immediately hitting the beachhead, to stop at nothing, not to fight unless we had to, but to get to Carpiquet airport [just west of Caen, fifteen kilometers inland] and to capture and consolidate the airport."

For a variety of reasons, the Highlanders did not get that far, or even close to Carpiquet. Dudka explained that, first of all, his platoon was held up on the beach by German fire and congestion and did not get started inland until 1400. When the Highlanders did move, they had only got a couple of kilometers inland when it was time for tea. ("The British and Canadian armies can't fight three and a half minutes without tea," according to Robert Rogge, the American volunteer in the Black Watch.)

Dudka brewed up his tea and met his brother Bill, also a Highlander. "We had our tea together and cautioned each other to be careful, like brothers do. Then we started on our way." The march was slow, as each man was carrying approximately ninety pounds of gear, land mines, ammunition, and weapons.

"The tanks got too far ahead of us at times," Dudka went on. "This was caused by the anxiety of Canadians to get into the action." When the Highlanders were about halfway to Carpiquet, it was 2000. Orders came down to dig in for the night, put out patrols, and prepare for a counterattack.[24]

Another cause of delay was the tendency to stop to loot— always the bane of infantry commanders trying to hurry their men forward. Corporal Rogge noted that as the Black Watch moved through the farmhouses that the Germans had been using for billets, men would break away from the column to do a bit of looting. Luger pistols, binoculars, and cloth swastikas were the most sought-after items.[25]

Sergeant Dudka described a further problem. "The grass and wheat in France was ready to be cut, and the visibility was nil. When we dug in or laid down, we had no visibility whatsoever, just a bunch of grass in front of you. You couldn't see where the others were at. We had not been prepared for that."[26]

Private Henry of the Winnipegs called it "a very slow day. We were sort of on the move all day, but didn't travel very far without stopping to take cover in ditches or whatever cover was available. My first day in France was one of amazement. I seemed to always be far enough away from danger, yet was always a part of it. When we dug in for the night it was a welcome stop."[27]

At the end of the day Private Levers brought his diary up to the minute. After making it to the seawall and resting for a few minutes, his platoon cut the wire and started inland. "We keep moving along—have to cross six or seven tank obstacles. They are ditches four to five feet deep and six to eight feet across and filled to the brim with water. There is a heavy machine gun firing up ahead and we go off on the left flank to try and round him up." On completing that task, "we start out immediately for our second objective. We bypass two big straw stacks which are in reality pillboxes. We leave them for the troops coming up behind."

Two Germans appeared in a barley field and came in with

their hands in the air. "There are two more hiding in the field, so we start looking for them with the bayonet. I happened to come across him first and am just going to sink the bayonet home when he shouts, 'Russky.' I pulled up my rifle when the bayonet was about two inches from his chest and turned him over to our officer."

Levers's platoon kept moving. It spotted a machine gun and closed the distance. "As we get close we come under a crossfire of machine guns. By this time I am pretty cocky and have all the confidence in the world. I was ahead of my section, which was in the lead and was on the right flank. We were in grass which gave us cover from the machine-gun fire. I crawled up to a barbed-wire fence which was about a hundred yards from an enemy slit trench. I saw a Boche well exposed and like a sucker raised myself to take aim. I drew a nice bead and was just squeezing the trigger when a machine-gun bullet smacked me down. It hit me in the right leg and went through the thigh from left to right. Two inches higher and I would have stopped being a man."

Levers crawled back to his platoon. A medic dressed his wound. Soldiers in German uniforms came across the field, hands in the air. They were Poles and Russians. Levers was put to guarding them. Eventually he was carried back to the beach and transported by landing craft to a hospital ship. By evening, June 7, he was back in England, where he had started out on the afternoon of June 5.[28]

Shortly after 1800, the North Nova Scotia Highlanders reached Beny-sur-Mer, five kilometers inland. There the Canadians were greeted by the sight of excited French civilians looting German barracks. Men were carrying off bags of flour, wheelbarrows full of army boots, bread, clothes, furniture. Women were taking chickens, butter, sheets, and pillows. The parish priest was helping to liberate a set of dishes. The French took time off from their looting to offer the Canadians glasses of milk and wine.

The Canadians pushed on to the south, against light resistance. One troop of 1st Hussar tanks crossed the Caen-Bayeux railway, fifteen kilometers inland. It was the only unit of the Allied invasion force to reach its final objective on D-Day. But it had to pull back because the infantry had not kept up. The tanks refueled and stocked up on ammunition to prepare for the expected counterattack.

To the west, the Canadian Scottish had made a ten-kilometer penetration and linked up with the British 50th Division at Creully. Between them, the British 50th Division and the Canadian 3rd had landed 900 tanks and armored vehicles, 240 field guns, 280 antitank guns, and over 4,000 tons of stores.

The Canadians had failed to reach their D-Day objective to the south, the N-13, while to the east there was a four- to seven-kilometer gap between the Canadians and the British 3rd Division at Sword Beach.

The reasons the Canadians did not achieve all their objectives were many. For a start, the objectives had been wildly optimistic, especially for men going into combat for the first time. They were late in hitting the beaches. The high tide and strong wind hampered the landings. The obstacles were more formidable than expected (Canadian engineers complained that the obstacles off Juno Beach were much heavier, stronger, and more numerous than those they had practiced against in England). The air and sea bombardments had been disappointing. The schedule for landing was too tight, too many vehicles were brought ashore too soon, creating congestion that took hours to straighten out. As a consequence, the attack lost its initial momentum.

Finally, once ashore and through the villages, there was a tendency for men to feel that they had done their bit.[29]

The German soldiers encountered by the Canadians gave cause for optimism. They were young or old, Pole or Russian, not the tough fanatical Nazis the Canadians had anticipated. Wehrmacht POWs were a dispirited, sorry-looking lot. But the Canadians knew the Germans had better troops in the area, especially the 21st Panzer Division, and they anticipated strong, determined counterattacks. So they dug in short of their objectives.

But as John Keegan writes of the Canadian 3rd Division, "At the end of the day its forward elements stood deeper into France than those of any other division."[30] Insofar as the opposition the Canadians faced was stronger than that at any other beach save Omaha, that was an accomplishment in which the whole nation could take considerable pride.

After two years, the Canadians had given the Wehrmacht a payback for Dieppe.

30

"AN UNFORGETTABLE SIGHT"

The British at Sword Beach

SWORD BEACH ran from Lion-sur-Mer to Ouistreham at the mouth of the Oran Canal.* In most areas there were vacation homes and tourist establishments just inland from the paved promenade that ran behind the seawall. There were the usual beach obstacles and emplacements in the sand dunes, with mortar crews and medium and heavy artillery pieces inland. Primarily, however, the Germans intended to defend Sword Beach with the 75mm guns of the Merville battery and the 155mm guns at Le Havre.

But Lieutenant Colonel Otway's 6th Airborne Division men had taken and destroyed the Merville battery, and the big guns at Le Havre proved to be ineffective against the beach, for two reasons. First, the British laid down smoke screens to prevent the Germans' ranging. Second, the Le Havre battery spent the morning in a duel with HMS *Warspite* (which it never hit), a big mistake on the Germans' part as the targets on the beach were much more lucrative.

Nevertheless, the 88mms on the first rise, a couple of kilometers inland, were able to put a steady fire on the beach to supplement the mortars and the machine-gun fire coming from the

* The eight-kilometer stretch from the left flank at Juno (St.-Aubin) and the right flank of Sword (Lion-sur-Mer) was too shallow and rocky to permit an assault. Ironically, at Ouistreham there was a monument to the successful repulse of a British landing attempted on July 12, 1792.

windows of the seaside villas and from pillboxes scattered among the dunes. In addition, there were antitank ditches and mines to impede progress inland, as well as massive concrete walls blocking the streets. These defenses would cause considerable casualties and delay the assault.

The infantry assault teams consisted of companies from the South Lancashire Regiment (Peter sector, on the right), the Suffolk Regiment (Queen sector, in the middle), and the East Yorkshire Regiment (Roger sector, on the left), supported by DD tanks. Their job was to open exits through which the immediate follow-up wave, consisting of troops of commandos and more tanks, could pass inland to their objectives. Meanwhile, UDT units and engineers would deal with the obstacles. Other regiments from the British 3rd Division scheduled to land later in the morning included the Lincolnshire, the King's Own Scottish Borderers, the Royal Ulster Rifles, the Royal Warwickshire, the Royal Norfolk, and the King's Shropshire Light Infantry. H-Hour was fixed for 0725.

On the run-in to the beach, Brigadier Lord Lovat, CO of the commando brigade, had his piper, Bill Millin, playing Highland reels on the fo'c'sle on his LCI. Maj. C. K. King of the 2nd Battalion, the East Yorkshire Regiment, riding in an LCA, read to his men the lines from Shakespeare's *Henry V*: "On, on, you noble English! whose blood is fet from fathers of war-proof. . . . Be copy now to men of grosser blood and teach them how to war! The game's afoot: Follow your spirit."[1]

DD tanks were supposed to land first, but they could not swim fast enough because of the tide. LCTs and LCAs passed them. At 0726 the first LCTs began touching down, accompanied by the LCAs carrying the infantry assault teams. Sporadic machine-gun and mortar fire, accompanied by 88mm shells fired from inland, greeted them—not so heavy as at Juno or Omaha, much heavier than at Utah and Gold.

Royal Marine frogmen jumped over the sides of their craft and went to work on the obstacles as infantry descended into the surf over the ramps and worked their way ashore. Casualties were heavy, but a majority of the assault teams managed to make it to the dunes. Although some of the men were shocked into a temporary helplessness, most began to put out suppressing fire against the emplacements. Shermans and Churchills, firing their .50-caliber machine guns and 75mm cannon, were a great help—and they provided some protection for the men crossing the beach.

Maj. Kenneth Ferguson was in the first wave of LCTs. He was on the far right, opposite Lion-sur-Mer. His craft was hit by a mortar bomb. Ferguson had tied a motorcycle beside the turret of his Sherman; the bomb set off the petrol in the tank of the cycle and put the craft in great danger, as it contained ammunition carriers, bangalores, and petrol drums. Ferguson told the coxswain to back off and drop the ramp, so as to put the deck cargo awash. Then he drove his tank down the ramp.

Immediately behind Ferguson came a bridge-carrying Sherman. A German antitank gun took them under fire. The Sherman drove right up to it and dropped its bridge directly onto the emplacement, putting the gun out of action. Flail tanks went to work clearing paths through the mines.

"They drove off the beach flailing," Ferguson said. "They flailed straight up to the dunes, then turned right flailing and then flailed back to below the high-water mark." Other tanks used bangalores or snakes or serpents to blow gaps in the barbed wire and the dunes. Still others of Hobart's Funnies dropped their bridges over the seawall, followed by bulldozers and then fascine-carrying tanks that dropped their bundles of logs into the antitank ditches.

When that task was complete, the flail tanks could cross to the main lateral road, about 100 meters inland, and begin flailing right and left to clear the way for the infantry. "We were saved by our flail tanks," Ferguson said. "No question about it."

Still, the infantry assault teams were stopped by sniper and machine-gun fire coming from Lion-sur-Mer. The commandos coming in the second wave were supposed to pass right through Lion and move west, to link up with the Canadians at Langrune-sur-Mer, but they too were held up by the German fire. Ferguson's orders were to proceed south toward Caen, but instead he had to turn west to help out at Lion.

"I was cross about going to help those commandos, I was angry about that. I was angry at people not getting off the beaches as fast as they could and getting away. People tended to hang around too much."

Reflecting on those words, Ferguson went on to say, "It seems entirely natural though. I suppose it could have been done better on D-Day, I don't know. We'd done our bit, though." Taking it all in all, he concluded, "We got off the beach bloody quickly."[2] But not through Lion, where German resistance continued.

The Germans had a battery in a wood near Lion, protected by infantry in trenches and behind sandbags. The commandos could not dislodge the Germans; the battery maintained its fire against the beach. At 1441, the naval forward observer with the commandos got through on his radio to Captain Nalecz-Tyminski, skipper of the Polish destroyer *Slazak*. "With excitement in his voice," Nalecz-Tyminski wrote in his action report, the observer said that "the commandos were pinned down by heavy enemy fire, that neither they nor himself could raise heads from their foxholes, that the situation was very serious and that their task was vital for the whole operation. He insistently requested twenty minutes bombardment of each target, commencing with the woods."

Nalecz-Tyminski's orders were not to fire any bombardments unless the fall of shell could be observed and reported by a forward observer, but "In view of the seriousness of the situation I could not waste the time for requesting permission to carry out bombardment without it being corrected by the forward observer. I ordered my gunnery officer to commence firing at the generally described targets."

Slazak blasted away with her 4-inch guns for forty minutes. Nalecz-Tyminski then informed the observer that the bombardment was completed. The observer responded that the Germans were still holding out and requested a further twenty minutes of fire. *Slazak* did as asked. "When that bombardment was completed, we heard on the radio his enthusiastic voice saying: 'I think you saved our bacon. Thank you. Stand by to do it again.' "

After a bit, another request for support. *Slazak* complied. After that action, the gunnery officer reported to Nalecz-Tyminski that out of 1,045 rounds of ammunition held in the magazines at the start of the day, only fifty-nine rounds remained. Nalecz-Tyminski had to break off. He so informed the forward observer, wishing him the best of luck. The observer acknowledged the message and concluded with the words "Thank you from the Royal Marines."[3]

Despite the pounding, the Germans in Lion held on, not only through D-Day but for two days thereafter. The long gap between Langrune on the Canadian left at Juno and Lion on the British right at Sword remained in German hands.

Etienne Robert Webb was the bowman on an LCA carrying an assault team to the extreme left of Roger sector. Going in, "We caught one of those obstacles and it ripped the bottom of the craft like a tin-can opener." The LCA sank. Webb swam to shore, "where I thought what in the bloody hell am I going to do now?" He joined his mates.

"There was all this activity, bugles sounding, bagpipes playing, men dashing around, the commandos coming in off a landing craft and just moving off the beach as if it was a Sunday afternoon, chatting and mumbling away at whatever they were going to go through to do their little bit of stuff." The beachmaster spotted Webb and his mates and told them to "keep out of the way, keep out of trouble and we will get you off."

Webb got ashore at 0730. By 0800 "there was no fighting on the beach. None at all. It was all inland." Mortars were dropping on the beach, coming from inland, along with shells and occasional sniper fire, all of which the commandos and East Yorks ignored as they went about their business. At 1100 Webb was evacuated by an LCI.[4]

Those commandos seen by Webb were French, led by Commandant Philip Kieffer. On June 4, as they loaded up, the French commandos—men who had been evacuated at Dunkirk four years earlier, or who had escaped from Vichy France to join De Gaulle's Free French—were in a gay mood. "No return ticket, pliz," they had told the military embarkation control officers when they boarded their LST.

On the morning of June 6, they were part of the initial contingent of commandos making the run-in to the beach in LCAs. At the last minute the commander of the group, Lt. Col. Robert Dawson, Royal Marine Commandos, waved the Frenchmen forward so that they would be the first to set foot on shore.[5]

One of those Frenchmen was Pvt. Robert Piauge, twenty-four years old, whose mother lived in Ouistreham. He was on LCI 523, commanded by Sub-Lt. John Berry, which had got hung up on a beach obstacle. Piauge and the other commando jumped into the sea, so impatient were they to get back to France. Piauge landed in chest-deep water. He waded ashore, the third Frenchman to arrive.

Mortars were exploding around him, some heavy shells coming down, a bit of small-arms fire, a lot of noise. Piauge made it to shore and got about ten meters across the beach when a mortar exploded beside him, riddling him with shrapnel (he still carries twenty-two pieces of steel in his body today). His best friend, next to him, was killed by the same mortar. A British medic examined Piauge's wounds, pronounced him "fini," gave him a shot of morphine, and moved on to treat men who could be saved.

Piauge thought of his mother, who had protested tearfully against his joining the French army in 1939, as her husband had died as a result of World War I wounds. Then he thought of France, and "I began to cry. Not out of sorrow for myself, nor because of my wounds, but at the great joy that I felt at being back on French soil." He passed out.

Piauge was picked up by a medic, carried out to a hospital ship by an LCI, treated for his wounds, and eventually recovered in a hospital in England. He lives today in a seaside apartment in Ouistreham. From his living-room window he can look out at the spot where he landed.[6]

The commandos carried on. Moving with dash and determination, they crossed the seawall and attacked the German defenders at Riva-Bella and Ouistreham, driving them from their pillboxes and fortified houses. They took the heavily fortified Casino strong point from the rear after bitter fighting.

Maj. R. "Pat" Porteous, who had won the Victoria Cross at the Dieppe raid (after being wounded in one hand, he led a one-handed bayonet charge) commanded a British troop in No. 4 Commando. His task was to go left, to the edge of Ouistreham, to destroy a German fire-control tower in a medieval fortress and a nearby coastal battery, then go to help relieve Major Howard's *coup de main* party at Pegasus Bridge.

Porteous lost nearly a quarter of his men getting over the seawall, either to mined obstacles, mortar fire, or machine-gun fire coming from a pillbox to his left. "We got off that beach as fast as we could. We put down smoke grenades which gave us quite a bit of cover to get across the beach. The pillbox was protected by concrete and they were safe as could be, but the smoke let us get over the beach."

Porteous turned left on the coastal road, fought his way through the streets, got to the battery, and discovered that the "guns" were telephone poles. "We learned afterward from a Frenchman that the battery had been withdrawn about three or four days before D-Day and had been resighted some three kilometers inland," Porteous recalled. "As we got into the position they started bringing down fire on the old battery position. We lost a lot of chaps there."

Porteous realized that the German observers in the medieval tower were communicating with the gunners at the inland battery. He moved to the bottom of the tower. "There was a single staircase up the middle of the tower and these Germans were up on top.

They were safe as could be; the walls were ten feet thick." One of his men tried to climb the staircase but the Germans dropped a grenade on him. Another of Porteous's men fired his PIAT hollow-charge missile projectile at the tower, but it failed to penetrate.

"So the PIAT was useless. We tried to give the German observers a squirt with a flamethrower, but they were too high; we couldn't get enough pressure from those little backpack flamethrowers that we had." There was no way to dislodge the observers; Porteous was taking casualties from rifle fire coming from the tower; he decided to leave it to someone else and set off for Pegasus Bridge.

His men did not move very fast. "We were still soaking wet, carrying our rucksacks, we really looked like a lot of snails going on. But we met no Germans, except a few dead ones lying about." They did meet a few Frenchmen. At one farmhouse, "It was very sad, a man rushed out and cried, 'My wife has been wounded. Is there a doctor?'

"At that moment I heard a mortar bomb approaching. I went flat and as I got up I saw his head rolling down the road. It was kind of awful. Luckily I had gone down faster."

Porteous's troop moved overland toward Pegasus Bridge. "There was a big field of strawberries. Most of the chaps waded into the field and began eating strawberries. The poor little French farmer came to me and said, 'For four years the Germans were here and they never ate one.' "

The troop took time to brew up a bit of tea. "One of my subalterns was brewing himself a cup and he had a little tommy cooker thing; he had his mess kit in one hand and a tin of tea in the other and a mortar bomb went off that blew him head over heels backwards, filled his coffee cup with holes, filled his mess kit with holes, all he had was he was just winded."[7]

Capt. Kenneth Wright was the intelligence officer with No. 4 Commando. On June 11, he wrote his parents ("Dearest Old Things" was the salutation) about his experiences. He described the loading, the journey across the Channel, the sinking of the Norwegian destroyer *Svenner*, the run-in to the beach in his LCA.

Wright went on, "Just as we were getting ready to disembark, there was a terrific jar [from an exploding mortar bomb] and all the party fell over on top of each other. I felt quite numb in my right side [from numerous shrapnel wounds]—no pain, just a sudden absence of feeling, a feeling of being knocked out of breath. At the same moment, the ramp was lowered and the naval bloke said, 'This is where you get off.'

"So I got off, but only after a bit of preliminary gasping for breath and struggling. It seemed ages before I got myself up and off the boat. There were quite a few who could not follow me off, including our Padre. I got off into about 3 ft. of water. It was nearly 7.45 and I remember wondering for a second if Nellie would have called you yet!"

Wright had fifty meters to wade "and what with the weight of the rucksack and the water to push through, I was nearly exhausted by the time I got clear. When I got on the beach I just sat down and dumped the rucksack with all my belongings in it.

"The beach by now was covered with men. They were lying down in batches in some places to avoid overcrowding round the exits: some were sitting up: most of them were trotting or walking across the sand to the dunes. There were a good many casualties, the worst of all being the poor chaps who had been hit in the water and were trying to drag themselves in faster than the tide was rising.

"The behaviour of the men on these beaches was terrific. Our Frenchmen came pouring across the beach chattering madly and grinning all over their faces. We all went through the same gap in the wire at the back of the beach, everyone queuing up and taking their turn as if it were a Pay Parade. I sat down under a wall and watched the Commandos file through on to the main road inland. Everyone happy and full of beans." A soldier brought Wright some liberated Calvados.

That helped ease his pain. He joined Dr. Joe Paterson, the Commando medical officer, who had been wounded in the head and leg but was still carrying on. Paterson attended to Wright's wound and told him to stay put and await evacuation. Two Frenchmen brought Wright some more Calvados "and a host of good wishes. I got into a house and lay down on a large feather bed: and that was the end of my participation in the Invasion."

Wright was carried back to the beach, where he spent nearly twenty-four hours on a stretcher out in the open. Eventually he got back to a hospital in England.[8]

Lord Lovat came in to the left of No. 4 Commando. He was, and is, a legend. At Dieppe, his commandos had done a fine piece of work in destroying a German fortification, but had some men killed in the process. Orders came to withdraw. Scots *never* leave their dead behind. Bringing them down the cliff in a hurried retreat was impossible. Lovat had gasoline poured over them and burned the bodies.

Lovat was with Comdr. Rupert Curtis, commander of the 200th Flotilla (LCIs). As the LCIs were coming in, Curtis recalled, "a lumbering LCT passed close, having discharged her tanks. Lord Lovat asked me to hail her and through my megaphone I spoke to a sailor on her quarterdeck. 'How did it go?' He grinned cheerfully, raised his fingers in the familiar V-for-Victory sign, and said with relish, 'It was a piece of cake.' This was encouraging but I had reason to doubt his optimistic report because the enemy was obviously recovering from the shock of the initial bombardment and hitting back."

Going in, Curtis raised the flag that meant "Assume arrowhead formation," and each craft fanned out to port or starboard, forming a V that presented less of a target for the Germans. To his left, on the beach, Curtis could see an LCT on fire and stranded. "Judging from the wounded at the edge of the waves the German mortar fire was laid accurately on the water's edge.

"Now was the moment. I increased engine revolutions to full ahead and thrust in hard between the stakes. As we grounded I kept the engines moving at half ahead to hold the craft in position on the beach and ordered 'Out ramps.' The commandos proceeded to land quite calmly. Every minute detail of that scene seemed to take on a microscopic intensity, and stamped in my memory is the sight of Shimi Lovat's tall, immaculate figure striding through the water, rifle in hand and his men moving with him up the beach to the skirl of Bill Millin's bagpipes."9

Amid all the carnage, exploding shells, smoke, and noise on Sword Beach, some of the chaps with Pvt. Harold Pickersgill claimed that they saw a most remarkable sight, an absolutely stunningly beautiful eighteen-year-old French girl who was wearing a Red Cross armband and who had ridden her bicycle down to the beaches to help with the wounded.

Pickersgill himself met a French girl inland later that day; she had high-school English, he had high-school French; they took one look at each other and fell in love; they were married at the end of the war and are still together today, living in the little village of Mathieu, midway between the Channel and Caen. But he never believed the story of the Red Cross girl on the beach.

"Oh, you're just hallucinating," he protested to his buddies. "That just can't be, the Germans wouldn't have allowed civilians to come through their lines and we didn't want any civilians messing about. It just didn't happen."

But in 1964, when he was working as a shipping agent in Ouistreham for a British steamship line, Pickersgill met John Thornton, who introduced him to his wife, Jacqueline. Her maiden name was Noel; she had met Thornton on D plus four; they fell in love and married after the war; he too worked as a shipping agent in Ouistreham. It was Jacqueline who had been on the beach, and the story was true.[10]

Pickersgill arranged an interview for me with Jacqueline for this book. "Well," she said, "I was on the beach for a silly reason. My twin sister had been killed in an air raid a fortnight before in Caen, and she had given me a bathing costume for my birthday, and I had left it on the beach, because we were allowed about once a week to remove the fences so we could pass to go swimming, and I had left the costume in a small hut on the beach, and I just wanted to go and pick it up. I didn't want anybody to take it.

"So I got on my bicycle and rode to the beach."

I asked, "Didn't the Germans try to stop you?"

"No, my Red Cross armband evidently made them think it was OK."

"There was quite a bit of activity," she went on in a grand understatement, "and I saw a few dead bodies. And of course once I got to the beach I couldn't go back, the English wouldn't let me. They were whistling at me, you know. But mostly they were surprised to see me. I mean, it was a ridiculous thing to do. So I stayed on the beach to help with the wounded. I didn't go back to the house until two days after. There was a lot to do." She changed bandages, helped haul wounded and dead out of the water, and otherwise made herself useful.

"I remember one thing horrible which made me realize how stupid I was, I was on top of the dune and there was a trunk, completely bare, no head on it. I never knew if it was a German or an Englishman. Just burned completely."

When asked what her most vivid lingering memory of D-Day was, she replied, "The sea with all the boats on it. All the boats and planes. It was something which you just can't imagine if you have not seen it. It was boats, boats, boats and more boats, boats everywhere. If I had been a German, I would have looked at this, put my weapon down, and said, 'That's it. Finished.' "[11]

Jacqueline and John Thornton (he came in on the second wave on D-Day) live today near the village of Hermanville-sur-Mer, in a lovely home with a lovely garden. She is still an extraordinarily handsome woman, as beautiful as she is brave. British veterans whose wounds she bandaged still visit her to say thanks, especially on the anniversaries of D-Day.

Pvt. Harry Nomburg (using the name "Harry Drew") was one of those Central European Jews who had joined the commandos and been put into 3 Troop, No. 10 Commando, where he and his fellow Jews were given special training in intelligence and made ready for battlefield interrogation of German POWs. He wore the green beret of the commandos with pride and went ashore full of anticipation about the contribution he was going to make to bringing Hitler down.

He waded ashore carrying his Thompson submachine gun high above his head. He had been issued a thirty-round magazine for the tommy gun, something new to him—he had always before carried a twenty-round magazine. "Alas, nobody had informed me that when filled with the thirty rounds of .45-caliber bullets, the magazine would get too heavy and therefore easily come loose and drop off. It therefore should never be loaded with more than twenty-eight rounds.

"Not knowing, I filled it all the way with the result that the magazine got lost in the water and I hit the beaches of France and stormed the fortress of Europe without a single shöt in my gun."

Looking around, Nomburg saw the armada stretching along the entire length of the horizon. He noticed three bodies in the surf, "yet the opposition turned out to be far lighter than I had expected."

As he moved across the beach, to the sound of the bagpipes, "I noticed a tall figure stalking just ahead of me. At once I recognized the brigadier and, getting close to him, I shyly touched his belt from behind while thinking to myself, 'Should anything happen to me now, let it at least be said that Private Drew fell by Lord Lovat's side!' "

Nomburg crossed the seawall and ran into two Wehrmacht soldiers, who surrendered to him. Nomburg was sure that they had been fed nothing but propaganda and lies, so he wanted to enlighten them about the true situation on Germany's many fronts. The latest news he had heard before boarding his LCI in England was that the Allied forces stood within fifteen kilometers of Rome. With great satisfaction, he reported that fact to his prisoners.

"They looked at me in amazement and replied that they had just heard over their own radio that Rome had fallen! So as it turned out they were telling me rather than I telling them." He sent them back to a POW cage on the beach and proceeded toward his destination, Pegasus Bridge.[12]

Cpl. Peter Masters, a Jew from Vienna who was also a member of 3 Troop, No. 10 Commando, had his own odyssey on D-Day. He was the second man out of his LCI. He was carrying his rucksack and a tommy gun with a thirty-round magazine ("which was no good at all because it tended to drop off from the tommy gun because of the extra weight"), with 200 spare rounds, four hand grenades (two fragmentation and two smoke), a change of clothing, a blanket, two days' rations, a full-sized spade ("the entrenching tools the army issued us were not good enough to dig deep holes in a hurry"), and a 200-foot rope to haul inflatable dinghies (carried by others) across the Orne waterways in the event the bridges had been blown. That would have been more than enough for a horse to lug ashore, but in addition Masters had a bicycle, as did all the others in his troop.

"Nobody dashed ashore," he remarked. "We staggered. With one hand I carried my gun, finger on the trigger; with the other I held onto the rope-rail down the ramp, and with the third hand I carried my bicycle."

The order on which the greatest stress had been laid was "Get off the beach." Masters did so as best he could, noticing on the way in two soldiers digging a foxhole in the water. "I could never figure out why they were doing that. Being a beginner, I did not know enough to be really frightened." When he got to the dune he saw his 3 Troop skipper, Maj. Hilton-Jones. "I couldn't think of anything better to do, so I saluted him. It must have been the only salute on the beach on D-Day."

Crossing the dune with his bicycle and rope, "we passed a few fellows sweeping mines with a mine detector. But we could not wait. Our leader, Captain Robinson, went right past them. They shouted, 'Hey, what are you doing?' Robinson said, 'Sorry about that, fellows, but we've got to go.' "

The infantrymen who had preceded the commandos "seemed to be sitting around here and there, not doing anything in particular." Masters was critical of their passivity until he heard a signaler next to him, crouching in a ditch, decoding a message for an officer: "No. 2 Platoon, six men left, sir."

"So I thought they must have been doing something, and we were going where whatever happened to them had happened." The troop passed under a mortar barrage to get to its assembly point, a couple of kilometers inland on the edge of a wood. It had to cross a plowed field to get there.

Snipers were firing from the wood. Mortars were falling. "To make matters worse, we had to cross and recross a muddy creek full of water. The bicycles proved very difficult to hold onto while slipping in the water, which was considerably deeper than what we had waded through at the beach."

There was a furrow running toward the wood. The troop used it for cover, "crawling stealthily toward the assembly point. I joined the queue. At first, I tried to crawl, reach back, and drag the bicycle toward me, but that proved so exhausting that I soon changed my method. The only way was to push it upright, visible for miles, while I was well down in the furrow, with only my arm holding it up, but at least it rolled better upright."

The furrow got shallower at a couple of hundred meters from the wood. German fire became more accurate. A couple of British tanks came up and blasted the wood. Masters got up "and pushing my bicycle and running over everybody who happened to be in my way, I made it to the wood."

Lord Lovat was walking about in the assembly area, urging people on. "He seemed to be a man perfectly at ease, and shots and the noise in general didn't seem to bother him at all. 'Good show, the Piper,' he said as Piper Millin came dashing up. Millin was panting and catching his breath, dragging the bagpipes as well as all his other equipment."

"Come on, get a move on, this is no different than an exercise," Lovat called out.

"He was very calm," Masters observed. "He carried no weapon other than his Colt .45 in his holster [Lovat had handed his rifle to a soldier who had dropped his in the water]. He had a walking stick, a slim long stick forked at the top. It's called a wading stick in Scotland."

There were a couple of prisoners in the assembly area. Lovat noticed Masters and said, "Oh, you are the chap with the languages. Ask them where their howitzers are."

Masters did, but got no reaction. One of the prisoners was

a big burly balding fellow. Commandos gathered around and began saying, "Look at that arrogant German bastard. He won't even talk to our man when he's asking questions."

The blank faces on the Wehrmacht prisoners made it clear to Masters that they were not understanding one word of his German. He looked at their paybooks and realized that one of the prisoners was a Pole, the other a Russian. He recalled that Poles learned French in school, so he tried his high-school French.

"That Pole's face lit up and he started to talk immediately. But Lovat spoke a lot better French than I did and he took over the interrogation and I pushed on with my bicycle troops, feeling a bit put out as I had been preempted by a better linguist."

On the far side of the wood there was a paved road, "so we started riding our bicycles, a pleasant change from what we had been through so far." The troop rode into Colleville-sur-Mer (subsequently renamed Colleville-Montgomery). The place was a shambles; it had been badly damaged by the air and sea bombardment. There were dead cows and maddened cows in the fields surrounding the village. The people stood in their doorways.

"They gazed and gazed and waved at us, heedless or beyond caring about the danger of shells and shrapnel. One young man in a light blue smock and dark blue beret, as the farmers in Normandy are wont to dress, pasted up posters on a doorway. On the posters it said 'Invasion,' and carried instructions on what to do. They had obviously been waiting for this day, and as we went by they said, 'Vive les Tommies!' and 'Vive la France!' " It was 1030.

The troop carried on south, toward Pegasus Bridge. Masters had been told to make sure he was properly used by the officer commanding the troop he was attached to. Masters's skipper had told him, "The troop commander will be very busy and preoccupied with his own thing, but don't you come back and tell me he was too busy to use you. Pester him. Ask whether you may go on reconnaissance patrols. Make sure that all your training isn't going to waste."

"I conscientiously did precisely that," Masters said. "Captain Robinson, however, was indeed preoccupied and considered me a nuisance. Whenever I asked whether I might go along with a patrol or do this or that, he simply said 'No.' He sent one of his men with whom he had been in North Africa, or with whom he had been training for the past several years and in whom he had greater confidence than this funny 'Johnny come lately' with the accent who had joined his troop at the very last minute."

Approaching the villages of Le Port and Benouville, in the valley of the Orne waterways, the troop was pinned down by machine-gun fire. A commando riding his bicycle was killed.

"Now there's something you can do, Corporal Masters," Robinson said. "Go on down to the village and see what's going on."

"Well, it wasn't very difficult to tell what was going on," Masters commented. "I envisioned a reconnaissance patrol and asked how many people I should take. And the Captain said, 'No, no, I just want you to go by yourself.' That didn't bother me. I said, 'I will go around the left here and please look for me to come back in a sweep around the right-hand side.'

"You don't seem to understand what I want you to do," said Robinson. "I want you to go straight down the road and see what is going on."

Masters got the point: Robinson wanted to know where the fire was coming from and he intended to use Masters as a target to draw fire. Rather than send one of his own men, he had decided to send this recently attached stranger.

"It felt rather like mounting the scaffold of the guillotine, though I could hardly blame him for using me rather than one of his own men for this suicidal task. But I had been trained to figure out angles, so I frantically looked for some angle to improve the odds, but there really didn't seem to be one. There were no ditches or cover. It was broad daylight."

Masters remembered a film he had seen, with Cary Grant, called *Gunga Din*. He recalled Grant, facing a completely hopeless situation, surrounded by Indian rebels from the Khyber Pass. Grant had faced the Indians just before they overwhelmed him and said quite calmly, "You're all under arrest."

Masters started walking down the road, yelling at the top of his voice, in German, "Everybody out! Come out! You are totally surrounded! Give yourselves up! The war is over for you! You don't have a chance unless you surrender now!"

No Germans surrendered, but neither did they fire. "They probably figured that nobody would come out like a lunatic like that unless he had an armored division right behind him, and in any case they could shoot me any time they felt like it, so they awaited developments."

Finally, from behind a low stone parapet, a German popped up. Masters went down on one knee. Both men fired. The German had a *Schmeisser*. His burst missed. Masters's tommy gun fired one shot and jammed. Just as he thought it was all up for him, Captain

Robinson—evidently feeling he had seen enough—gave an order to fix bayonets and charge. The troop charged right past the prone Masters. A corporal got to the parapet first, firing his Bren. He drove the Germans from the position, wounding two of them.

Masters ran up to do an interrogation. One man was not fit to talk, he just moaned. The other was a fifteen-year-old boy from Graz in Styria, Austria. He claimed he had never fired. Masters pointed to his half-empty machine gun belt. The boy said it was the others who had fired.

The British corporal with the Bren gun stood next to Masters. The Austrian boy was in great pain from his wound. "How do you say 'I'm sorry' in German?" the corporal asked. *"Es tut mir leid,"* I said, "or *Verzeihung."*

" '*Verzeihung*,' the corporal tried to say to the boy. He was a good soldier and a good man, and he told me he had never shot anybody before. The next day he was killed leading a charge firing his Bren gun from the shoulder."

Masters continued his interrogation, but the Austrian boy didn't know much. He demanded to be evacuated. Impossible, Masters replied. Arrangements would be made in due course.

Two British tanks appeared. The commandos were taking fire from a nearby house. With gestures, the commandos pointed to it. "The tank turret swung around with that weird motion of almost animate machinery. The gun cracked twice. It breached the wall of the house from about three yards distance." That silenced the fire and the commandos proceeded on toward Pegasus Bridge.

To their delight, the commandos found the bridges intact and held by Howard's Ox and Bucks. "The maroon bereted gliderborne chaps from the airborne division on either side of the road leading to the bridge beamed their welcome for our green berets. 'The commandos have come,' said the glider people."[13]

It was 1300. The seaborne commandos had achieved their most critical objective. They had linked up with the airborne troops on the east side of the Orne waterways.

On the right flank of Sword Beach, there was no linkup with the Canadians. And into the gap, at 1600, the Germans launched their only serious counterattack of D-Day.

Colonel Oppeln, commanding the 22nd Regiment of the 21st Panzer Division, had received orders at 0900 to attack the British airborne troopers east of the Orne. He had set out to comply, but progress was slow due to Allied fighter planes shooting up his column. Then at 1200 Oppeln got new orders: about turn, pass through Caen, attack into the gap between the Canadians and British. It took an additional four hours to carry out the maneuver. At 1400 the regiment had at last reached the jumping-off line north of Caen. There it joined the 192nd Panzer Grenadier Regiment.

Major Vierzig commanded one of the battalions of the 22nd Panzer Regiment. He set out on foot to join the commander of the Panzer Grenadiers, Major Gottberg. He found Gottberg, and the two majors climbed a nearby hill, where they found General Marcks, who had arrived from St.-Lô, along with Colonel Oppeln. "A real old-time generals' hill," Vierzig commented.

Marcks walked over to Oppeln and commented, "Oppeln, if you don't succeed in throwing the British into the sea we shall have lost the war."

The colonel thought, Is victory or defeat to depend on my ninety-eight tanks? But he suppressed the thought, saluted, and said, "I shall attack now."

Marcks drove over to the 192nd Panzer Grenadier regiment and gave his order: "Press on to the coast."

The Grenadiers were an elite unit, well equipped. They had trucks and armored personnel carriers for transportation, plus a variety of small arms. Their thrust went well; almost without opposition, they reached the beach at 2000. "We've made it!" they called on their radios. "We've made it!"

To themselves, the Grenadiers were saying, "If our tanks join up with us now, we shan't get dislodged from here."

But by the time the tanks started rolling, the Canadians to the west and the British to the east had been alerted. They had antitank guns plus tanks of their own. The 22nd Panzer Regiment had a gauntlet of fire to run.

The lead tank took a direct hit and blew up. One by one, others suffered the same fate. Within a few minutes five tanks had blown up.

Allied fighter aircraft joined in. Lt. John Brown of the Royal Canadian Air Force was flying a Hawker Typhoon. His squadron dropped bombs on the German tanks, "and we then individually attacked the tanks, firing our cannon at them from all angles."

Oppeln had to call off the advance. He put his regiment on the defensive with these orders: "Tanks to be dug in. Position must be held." The counterattack had fizzled out. The Panzer Grenadiers at the beach waited in vain for tank support. The gap remained, but the Germans were incapable of exploiting it.[14]

Late in the afternoon, Colonel Oppeln came upon a desperate General Richter lamenting that his whole division was finished. As the broken remnants of the 716th Division streamed past him, Oppeln asked for orders or information about the enemy positions. Richter looked at him blankly and did not, could not, respond.[15]

The British had put 29,000 men ashore at Sword. They had taken 630 casualties, inflicted far more, and had many prisoners in cages. At no point had they reached their far-too-optimistic D-Day objectives—they were still five kilometers short of the outskirts of Caen—but they had an enormous follow-up force waiting in the transport area in the Channel to come in as reinforcements on D plus one. The 21st Panzer Division had lost its best opportunity to hurl them into the sea, and the bulk of the German armor in France was still in place in the Pas-de-Calais area, waiting for the real invasion.

Toward dusk, Commander Curtis had his LCI make a run along the coast. "We set off on a westerly course parallel to the shore," he later reported, "and we now had a grandstand view of the invasion beaches for which many would have paid thousands. Past Luc-sur-Mer, St.-Aubin, Bernières, and Courseulles in the Canadian sector, past La Rivière lighthouse and Le Hamel and so to Arromanches. It was all an unforgettable sight. Through the smoke and haze I could see craft after craft which had been driven onto the beach with relentless determination in order to give the troops as dry a landing as possible. Many of these craft were now helplessly stranded on obstacles and I could not help feeling a sense of pride at the spirit which their officers and crews had shown.

"We anchored off Arromanches and stood by for air attack that night. Already parts of the prefabricated Mulberry harbors were under tow from England to be placed in position off Arromanches and St.-Laurent. It was clear that the battle for the foothold in the British and Canadian sectors had gone well enough."[16]

31

"MY GOD, WE'VE DONE IT"

The British Airborne on D-Day

THE EXTREME LEFT FLANK of the Overlord invasion was critical to the success of the whole, because it was there, between the Dives River and the Orne waterways, that the Allied force was most vulnerable to German armored counterattacks. Col. Hans von Luck's 125th Regiment of 21st Panzer was in the immediate area, east of Caen; the 12th SS Panzer Division and Panzer Group *Lehr* were between Normandy and Paris, within a few hours march of the invasion site; east of the Seine River there were nine additional panzer divisions that could be brought into the battle within a day or two. If they reacted actively and energetically, the Germans could counterattack the British at Sword within twenty-four hours with more than 1,000 tanks, many of them brand-new Tigers with 88mm cannon. Not only were the Tigers mounting better guns, they were heavier and better armored than the Shermans and Churchills.

But thanks to the brilliant execution of Fortitude, the Tigers east of the Seine were immobilized. Fortunately for the Allies, the panzer divisions west of the Seine were immobilized by Hitler's insistence that only he could order them into action. Best of all for the Allies, the one man who might have ignored those orders and launched an immediate counterattack, Gen. Edgar Feuchtinger, CO of 21st Panzer, was in Paris with his girlfriend.*

* Feuchtinger later claimed that he was in his headquarters, issuing orders, but according to Colonel Luck and others who were in a position to know, that claim was a cover-up.

Still, the German garrisons between the Orne and Dives had some old French tanks, self-propelled guns, armored personnel carriers, and an abundance of Moaning Minnies (rockets) mounted on a variety of vehicles. This gave the Germans a firepower in the battle area that was superior to anything the 6th British Airborne Division possessed.

The British had come into the battlefield, by glider and by parachute, shortly after midnight June 6. They had achieved their principal nighttime objectives, blowing the bridges over the Dives to isolate the area, destroying the battery at Merville that threatened Sword Beach, and capturing intact the bridges over the Orne waterways. Those offensive tasks completed, their daytime objectives were to set up a strong defensive position along the ridge that was the divide between the valleys of the Orne and the Dives (where the key point was the crossroads in the village of Varaville) and to hold the bridges over the Orne waterway, so that the seaborne commandos and British armor could cross and reinforce along the ridge.

At dawn at Pegasus Bridge, over the Orne Canal, Major Howard's gliderborne D Company of the Ox and Bucks was holding on, barely. The German garrison in Benouville had come to life. Although it mounted no serious counterattacks, it was putting the Ox and Bucks under heavy rifle, mortar, and rocket fire. British movement over the bridge, which was under observation from a nearby chateau, was difficult to impossible.

As the firefight went on, Corp. Jack Bailey saw an unexpected sight. A woman, "dressed in black, as women of a certain age do in France, with a basket over her arm, walked between us and the Germans." Everyone on both sides stopped firing and stared. "And she was gathering her eggs! She stooped over not three feet from my firing position and gathered one in. When she had completed her task and strolled off, we resumed firing."[1]

At 0900, Howard "had the wonderful sight of three tall figures walking down the road." They were Maj. Gen. Richard Gale, the 6th Division CO, who had landed by glider during the night and established his CP at Ranville, Brig. Hugh Kindersley, the Air Landing Brigade CO, and Brig. Nigel Poett, CO of the 5th Parachute Brigade. All three were over six feet tall.

"They came marching in very smartly and it really was a wonderful sight because they were wearing red berets and in battle dress and marching in step," Howard said. "It was a pure inspiration to all my chaps seeing them coming down."[2]

Lt. Richard Todd of the 5th Parachute Brigade, who had parachuted in during the night and joined the Ox and Bucks just before dawn (and who later became a famous British actor; he played John Howard in the movie *The Longest Day*) said that "for sheer bravado and bravery" the march-past of Gale, Kindersley, and Poett "was one of the most memorable sights I've ever seen."[3]

As he marched along, Gale called out "Good show, chaps" to the Ox and Bucks. After Howard assured him that the bridges were in British hands but warned him that a determined counterattack could well change that situation, Gale crossed Pegasus Bridge to go into Benouville. There he conferred with Col. Geoffrey Pine Coffin,* who commanded a battalion of the 5th Brigade and who had joined up with Howard during the night, then established his CP in Benouville.

Fighting continued in the village. Pine Coffin said he needed help; Gale ordered Howard to send one of his three platoons into Benouville. When Lt. Tod Sweeney got the order to cross the bridge and put his platoon into fighting positions in Benouville, he "thought this was a little bit unfair. We'd had our battle throughout the night. We rather felt that we should be left alone for a little bit and that the 7th Battalion should not be calling on our platoon to come help it out."[4]

But help it must, as less than half of the 7th Battalion had yet made it to Benouville from the drop zones. Not until 1200 had a majority of the battalion arrived. The British were being hard-pressed by Germans in French tanks and other armored vehicles. "The day went on very, very, very wearing," Pvt. Wally Parr recalled. "All the time you could feel enemy movement out there and closer contact coming."[5]

Maj. Nigel Taylor, commanding a company of the 7th Battalion in Benouville, remembered that it "was a very long wait" for the commandos to link up. "I know the longest day and all that stuff, but this really was a hell of a long day. Where were the commandos?"[6]

At 1300, the first commandos (Peter Masters's outfit) arrived, followed shortly thereafter by Lord Lovat and bagpiper Bill

---

* "Is that a code name, sir?" Pvt. Wally Parr asked Howard when told that Pine Coffin's battalion would be the first to reinforce the Ox and Bucks at Pegasus Bridge.

Millin, who was playing away. It was quite a sight. "Lovet strode along," Howard said, "as if he were on exercise back in Scotland." There was a Churchill tank with the commandos. "Everybody threw their rifles down," Sgt. Wagger Thornton of the Ox and Bucks recalled, "and kissed and hugged each other, and I saw men with tears rolling down their cheeks. I did honestly. Oh, dear, celebrations I shall never forget."[7]

Lovat met Howard at the east end of the bridge. "John," Lovat said as they shook hands, "today history is being made." Howard briefed him on the situation. Lovat's objective was Varaville; Howard told him to be careful crossing Pegasus Bridge, as it was still under heavy sniper fire. Lovat nevertheless marched his men across rather than have them dash over as individuals, an act of bravado that cost the commandos a dozen casualties. The doctor who treated them noted that most were shot through their berets and killed instantly; commandos coming later started putting on their helmets to dash across the bridge. More British tanks came in from the coast, some crossing the bridge, others moving into Benouville to help in the defense. The linkup was now solid.[8]

At 1400, Luck finally received permission to attack the bridge. But as he set out with his tanks and self-propelled vehicles, Allied aircraft spotted the movement and called in naval fire. "All hell broke lose," Luck remembered. "The heavy naval guns plastered us without pause. We lost radio contact and the men of the reconnaissance battalion were forced to take cover." Luck ordered the commander of the lead battalion to break off the attack and dig in near Escoville.[9]

Lt. Werner Kortenhaus was in the battalion. "We failed," he said, "because of heavy resistance from the British navy. We lost thirteen tanks out of seventeen."[10] Like the other regiment of 21st Panzer west of the Orne, the 125th abandoned its counterattack and went on the defensive. Howard's Ox and Bucks, with help from the paratroopers and then from the commandos, had held Pegasus Bridge.

East of the bridge, in the area between the ridge and the Orne waterways, British airborne troops were engaged in scattered firefights. Peter Masters recalled riding his bicycle to Ranville and beyond and seeing "people welcoming us, gliders and parachutists, but we never knew exactly how far we were in possession of the road, how far it was reasonably safe to cycle on. At times there was fire from the woods and instinctively one cycled faster to regain cover and dip into a less exposed stretch."

Masters was headed toward Varaville. By this time, around 1400, "a number of the commandos were riding German bicycles, army issue, heavy black things, much better than ours; their rightful owners had abandoned them galore by the side of the road. Some of our chaps were mounted on colorful civilian bikes, ladies' bikes, anything would do to get to Varaville.

"At last we approached the village. Canadian parachutists [from the 1st Canadian Parachute Battalion of the 6th Airborne Division] told us they were still fighting for the place."[11]

The Canadians had started their attack on Varaville during the night, at about 0330. An anonymous British captain (who had landed at 0200 in the River Dives) reported that when he joined the fight just before dawn "Complete chaos seemed to reign in the village. Against a background of Brens, Spandaus and grenades could be heard the shouts of British and Canadians, Germans and Russians. There was obviously a battle in progress."[12] The Russians in Wehrmacht uniforms had been told that if they retreated their German NCOs would shoot them and that if they surrendered the Allies would shoot them as traitors, so they put up a stiff resistance until late afternoon.

By 1900 the Canadians had taken the village. They thought that with the job accomplished, they would be evacuated back to England. "They gave us all their cigarettes," Masters remembered, "Sweet Caporal cigarettes from Canada, which we appreciated greatly, on the premise they didn't need them as they would be going home soon."

"Give 'em hell, boys," the Canadians called out to the commandos. "Give 'em hell."

A sergeant with Masters informed the Canadians that they were indulging themselves in a fantasy. He pointed out, "If a general has you under his command, do you suppose he's going to let you go in the middle of a battle?" The Canadian paratroopers spent three months in Normandy before being withdrawn.

On D-Day afternoon, having reached Varaville, the commandos dug in and awaited counterattacks.[13]

Brig. John Durnford-Slater was the planning officer for the commandos. In the late afternoon he joined Shimi Lovat on the ridge south of Varaville. Lovat's men were beating off occasional counterattacks. "Shimi was magnificent," Durnford-Slater reported. "Every time a mortar bomb burst I jumped a couple of feet while he stood rock still. I felt thoroughly ashamed.

"A runner came rushing up from No. 4 Commando. 'We're being heavily counterattacked, sir,' he said to Lord Lovat.

" 'Tell 4 Commando to look after their own counterattacks, and don't worry me until things get serious,' Shimi said. We then resumed our conversation."

Durnford-Slater and Maj. Charlie Head picked up a Bren gun and offered to man a post for the night. "We were anxious to prove ourselves."

"No, thank you," Lovat replied.

A bit downcast, Durnford-Slater and Head went down the road, back toward the Orne. On the way, Durnford-Slater saw a huge German soldier standing by a ditch.

"Shoot him if he moves an inch!" Durnford-Slater shouted to Head. The German's hands flew up.

"*Kaput*," the German said with a grin on his face. He was supposed to be acting as a sniper but he was delighted to be taken prisoner.

Durnford-Slater had his batman hold a pistol on the prisoner while conducting an interrogation. The prisoner was wearing a fine lumber jacket.

"You ought to have that," Head said to Durnford-Slater. Head told the batman to strip the jacket from the German. The batman unthinkingly handed his pistol to the prisoner. Durnford-Slater recalled, "The situation was ludicrous: a German prisoner with a loaded revolver, faced by an unarmed British brigadier, a major, and a private soldier. Fortunately this particular prisoner had no guts at all. He surrendered his jacket. Then he handed back the gun."[14]

As the sun began to go down over the Channel, Maj. Nigel Taylor settled himself into a chair outside the Gondrée café at Pegasus Bridge. He had been wounded in the leg. After a medic dressed the wound, "Georges Gondrée brought me a glass of champagne, which was very welcome indeed after that sort of day, I can tell you. And then, just as it was getting dark, there was a tremendous flight of aircraft, British aircraft, that came in and they did a glider drop and a supply drop on our side of the canal. It was a marvelous sight, it really was. Hundreds of gliders, hundreds of the damned things, and of course they were also dropping supplies on chutes out of their bomb doors. All this stuff coming down, and then it seemed only a very few minutes afterward, there were all these chaps in jeeps, towing antitank guns and God knows what, coming down the road and over this bridge."[15]

As the reinforcements marched over the bridge to join the paratroopers and glider troops east of the Orne, Wally Parr and other enlisted men in Howard's company called out, "Where the hell you been?" and "War's over" and "A bit late for parade, chaps" and other such nonsense.[16]

There were 308 Horsa gliders in the flight, bringing in two glider battalions of 1,000 men each, accompanied by thirty-four of the larger Hamlicar gliders bringing in jeeps, artillery, and supplies. The landing zones had been cleared by paratroopers, on both sides of the Orne waterways.

Capt. Huw Wheldon, later a famous BBC broadcaster and producer, was in a Horsa. When his platoon landed, "all our weapons were at the ready. There were gliders all around, some up-ended and grotesque, some in the act of landing. They seemed huge."

Where Wheldon came down, there was no firing. "The next thing I noticed, and shall never forget, was the sight of the troops, ever sensitive to unexpected opportunity, standing on the quiet grass in the twilight and relieving themselves with the absent-minded look that men assume on these occasions. First things first.

"That done, off we went. The entire company had landed, 120 strong, in five gliders; not a single man was hurt or missing." Engineers and signalers, artillerymen and weapons, supply and transport and repair services, medical units and even chaplains came down all around. "All in all," Wheldon commented, "it seemed, even at the time, an extraordinary and even breathtaking piece of organisation."[17]

Not everything worked. After sunset, forty DC-3s from 233 Squadron of the RAF crossed the Channel carrying 116 tons of food, ammunition, explosives, spare radios, medical stores, and petrol to drop by parachute to the 6th Airborne Division. The crossing was uneventful, but when the Dakotas passed over the naval vessels off the mouth of the Orne River, the ships opened fire on the low- and slow-flying aircraft. Two were forced to turn back with severe damage and one ditched in the Channel; five more were missing and the rest scattered. Only twenty-five tons of supplies were recovered.

The Royal Navy's trigger-happy gunners had failed to recognize the Dakotas; they blamed the aircraft for failing to identify themselves soon enough, adding the excuse that a lone enemy night fighter had attacked them not long before.[18]

Capt. John Tillett of the Air Landing Brigade had spent the bulk of D-Day at the airfield at Tarrant Rushton in England, waiting for word that the landing zones in Normandy had been cleared. Tillett had charge of some homing pigeons that were to be used to bring back news should the radios fail. A squadron leader in the RAF had trained the pigeons "and he was so proud of them. They were all in baskets. Unfortunately, during the waiting period, some of the chaps fell for this temptation and killed, roasted, and ate the pigeons."

Finally at 1830 the bombers towing the gliders began to take off, with some 900 Spitfires providing cover. As the fleet approached the French coast, Tillett recalled, "The sky was full of aircraft for miles in all directions and they were all ours. There was the mass of shipping off the beaches, thousands of ships of every shape and size." At 2130 his glider pilot cast off and the Horsa began to spiral down to land.

"We hit the ground with a splintering crash and our glider came to a shuddering halt. Other gliders were landing around us, some hitting one another, they were landing from all different directions.

"We leapt out of the glider and took our position all around for defense. To my astonishment, there in front of me was a German in a trench, a real live German. We had been training for three years to fight Germans but I wasn't prepared for this. We got ready to shoot him but then looking at him I could see that he was absolutely terrified and there was no question of him shooting us. He couldn't move. We made him prisoner."

Tillett and his platoon set off at a trot for the ridge. "Just as we got to it we could hear tank noises and two tanks came up and to my horror I saw the leading tank had a swastika painted on its side so we turned tail and disappeared over this cornfield in 'Jesse Owens' speed, looking for some sort of hole to get into as this tank swung its turret toward us.

"So within two minutes of landing we had a.) taken a prisoner, b.) advanced boldly, and c.) pulled full flight."

The tanks turned out to be British. The lead tank had knocked out a German tank earlier in the day and chalked a swastika on its side. Tillett got his men back on the ridge and dug in for the night.[19]

One major in the Air Landing Brigade had noticed a paperboy selling the afternoon London *Evening Standard* outside his airfield before taking off. The headline was "SKYMEN LAND IN EUROPE." The major bought the entire stock, loaded them into his glider, and distributed them in Normandy that night, so that at least some of the paratroopers were able to read about themselves in a London paper the same day they had been dropped.[20]

As darkness fell the 6th Airborne Division was in place. The airborne chaps were, in Huw Wheldon's words, "safely on dry land, and what is more, many of us, probably most of us, were where we were supposed to be." But the British army as a whole had not achieved its goal of taking Caen and Carpiquet.

Something like a paralysis had crept over the men. The British airborne troops going into battle shortly after midnight, and those who had arrived in the morning and afternoon, had been engaged in bold and aggressive offensive operations. Less than twenty-four hours later they were on the defensive, digging in, waiting for counterattacks.

They would soon regret not pushing on into Caen while the Germans were still in a state of shock and disorganization. They have been strongly criticized by the Americans for losing their momentum. But the fact is that with the exception of some paratroopers and units of the U.S. 4th Division at Utah, none of the Americans reached their D-Day objectives either. The Americans too tended to feel after they had cleared the beaches that they had done enough for one day.

Major Taylor put it best. Sitting outside the Gondrée cafe as it grew full dark, he sipped his champagne and felt good. "And at that moment I can remember thinking to myself, My God, we've done it!"[21]

32

"WHEN CAN
THEIR GLORY FADE?"

The End of the Day

As FULL DARKNESS came to Normandy, about 2200, unloading at
the beaches ceased. Nearly 175,000 American, Canadian, and British troops had entered Normandy, either by air or sea, at a cost of
some 4,900 casualties.* From the American airborne on the far
right to the British airborne on the far left, the invasion front
stretched over ninety kilometers. There was an eighteen-kilometer
gap between the left flank at Utah and the right flank at Omaha
(with Rudder's rangers holding a small piece of territory in between
at Pointe-du-Hoc), an eleven-kilometer gap between Omaha and
Gold, and a five-kilometer gap between Juno and Sword. These
gaps were inconsequential because the Germans had no troops in
them capable of exploiting the opportunity.

For the Germans, the battlefield was isolated. Rommel had
been right about that at least; Allied command of the air had made
it difficult to impossible for the Germans to rush men, tanks, and
guns to the scene of the action. For the Allies, virtually unlimited
men, tanks, guns, and supplies were waiting offshore for first light
on June 7 to begin unloading, and behind them were even more men,
tanks, guns, and supplies in England waiting to cross the Channel.

---

* No exact figures are possible, either for the number of men landed or for casualties, for D-Day alone.

There was little depth to the penetration, nowhere more than ten kilometers (Juno) and at Omaha less than two kilometers. But everywhere the Allies had gone through the Atlantic Wall. The Germans still had the advantage of fighting on the defensive, and the hedgerows, especially in the Cotentin, gave them excellent ready-made positions. But their fixed fortifications on the invasion front, their pillboxes and bunkers, their trench system, their communications system, their emplacements for the heavy artillery, were with only a few exceptions *kaput*.

The Germans had taken four years to build the Atlantic Wall. They had poured thousands of tons of concrete, reinforced by hundreds of thousands of steel rods. They had dug hundreds of kilometers of trenches. They had placed millions of mines and laid down thousands of kilometers of barbed wire. They had erected tens of thousands of beach obstacles. It was a colossal construction feat that had absorbed a large percentage of Germany's material, manpower, and building capacity in Western Europe.

At Utah, the Atlantic Wall had held up the U.S. 4th Division for less than one hour. At Omaha, it had held up the U.S. 29th and 1st divisions for less than one day. At Gold, Juno, and Sword, it had held up the British 50th, the Canadian 3rd, and the British 3rd divisions for about an hour. As there was absolutely no depth to the Atlantic Wall, once it had been penetrated, even if only by a kilometer, it was useless. Worse than useless, because the Wehrmacht troops manning the Atlantic Wall east and west of the invasion area were immobile, incapable of rushing to the sound of the guns.

The Atlantic Wall must therefore be regarded as one of the greatest blunders in military history.*

The Allies had made mistakes. Dropping the U.S. 82nd and 101st Airborne in the middle of the night was one. Almost surely it would have been better to send them in at first light. The great assets of the Allied bomber and warship fleets were not used to full effect in the too-short and too-inaccurate preinvasion bombardment. The single-minded concentration on getting ashore and cracking the Atlantic Wall was, probably, inevitable, so formidable did those fixed fortifications appear, but it was costly once the assault teams had penetrated. It led to a tendency on the part of the

* The parallel with the Maginot Line is obvious but should not be overstressed. As the Wehrmacht went around, not through, the Maginot Line in 1940, we cannot know if it could have been penetrated.

men to feel that, once through the Wall, the job had been done. Just when they should have been exerting every human effort possible to get inland while the Germans were still stunned, they stopped to congratulate themselves, to brew up a bit of tea, to dig in.

The failure to prepare men and equipment for the challenge of offensive action in the hedgerow country was an egregious error. Allied intelligence had done a superb job of locating the German fixed defenses and a solid if not perfect job of locating the German units in Normandy, but intelligence had failed completely to recognize the difficulties of fighting in the hedgerows.

Allied errors pale beside those of the Germans. In trying to defend everywhere they were incapable of defending anywhere. Their command structure was a hindrance rather than a help. Rommel's idea of stopping the invasion on the beach vs. Rundstedt's idea of counterattacking inland vs. Hitler's compromise between the two prevented an effective use of their assets. Using Polish, Russian, and other POWs for construction work made sense; putting them in Wehrmacht uniforms and placing them in trenches, hoping that they would put up a stiff resistance, did not.

The Wehrmacht's many mistakes were exceeded by those of the Luftwaffe, which was quite simply just not there. Goering called for an all-out effort by the Luftwaffe on D-Day, but he got virtually none at all. The Allies' greatest fear was a massive air bombardment against the mass of shipping and the congestion on the beaches, with Goering putting every German plane that could fly into the attack. But Goering was in Berchtesgaden, agreeing with Hitler's self-serving, ridiculous assertion that the Allies had launched the invasion exactly where he had expected them, while the Luftwaffe was either in Germany or redeploying or grounded due to administrative and fuel problems. Once the terror of the world, the Luftwaffe on June 6, 1944, was a joke.*

The *Kriegsmarine* was no better. Its submarines and cruisers were either in their pens or out in the North Atlantic, hunting merchant shipping. Except for one minor action by three E-boats, the *Kriegsmarine* made not a single attack on the greatest armada ever gathered.

The V-1s, on which Hitler had placed such high hopes and to which he had devoted so much of Germany's technological and

* A Wehrmacht joke had it that if the plane in the sky was silver it was American, if it was blue it was British, if it was invisible it was ours.

construction capacity, were not ready. When they were, a week after D-Day, he launched them against the wrong target.

The German's tactical and strategic mistakes were serious, but their political blunders were the greatest of all. Their occupation policies in Poland and Russia precluded any enthusiasm whatsoever by their *Ost* battalions for their cause—even though nearly every one of the conscripted *Ost* troops hated the communists. Although German behavior in France was immeasurably better than in Poland and Russia, even in France the Germans failed to generate enthusiasm for their cause, and thus the Germans were unable to profit from the great potential of conquered France. What should have been an asset for Germany, the young men of France, became an asset for the Allies, either as saboteurs in the factories or as members of the Resistance.

What Hitler regarded as the greatest German assets—the leadership principle in the Third Reich, the unquestioning obedience expected of Wehrmacht personnel from field marshal down to private—all worked against the Germans on D-Day.

The truth is that despite individual acts of great bravery and the fanaticism of some Wehrmacht troops, the performance of the Wehrmacht's high command, middle-ranking officers, and junior officers was just pathetic. The cause is simply put: they were afraid to take the initiative. They allowed themselves to be paralyzed by stupid orders coming from far away that bore no relation to the situation on the battlefield. Tank commanders who knew where the enemy was and how and when he should be attacked sat in their headquarters through the day, waiting for the high command in Berchtesgaden to tell them what to do.

The contrast between men like Generals Roosevelt and Cota, Colonels Canham and Otway, Major Howard, Captain Dawson, Lieutenants Spaulding and Winters, in adjusting and reacting to unexpected situations, and their German counterparts could not have been greater. The men fighting for democracy were able to make quick, on-site decisions and act on them; the men fighting for the totalitarian regime were not. Except for Colonel Heydte and a captain here, a lieutenant there, not one German officer reacted appropriately to the challenge of D-Day.

As darkness came on, the Allied troops ashore dug in, while the Allied air forces returned to England and the Allied armada prepared for the possibility of a Luftwaffe night attack. It came at 2300 and it typified the Luftwaffe's total ineffectiveness.

Josh Honan remembered and described it: "Suddenly everything started banging and we all went to see what it was, and it was a German reconnaissance plane. He wasn't all that high and he wasn't going all that fast. And he did a complete circle over the bay and every ship had every gun going and you never saw such a wall of tracer and flak and colored lights going up in your life and the German quite calmly flew all around over the bay, made another circle, and went home."[1]*

Pvt. John Slaughter of the 116th Regiment, U.S. 29th Division, also described the scene: "After dark an enemy ME-109 fighter plane flew over the entire Allied fleet, from right to left and just above the barrage balloons. Every ship in the English Channel opened fire on that single airplane, illuminating the sky with millions of tracer bullets. The heroic Luftwaffe pilot defied all of them—not even taking evasive action. I wondered how he ever got through that curtain of fire."[2]

All along the invasion front, men dug in. Capt. John Raaen of the 5th Ranger Battalion was outside Vierville, off Omaha Beach. "By now it was getting dark and it was necessary to organize ourselves for nighttime counterattacks and infiltration from the Germans," he said in his oral history. "Headquarters Company was in a small farmyard, located to the south of the road. At this point I learned my next mistake—I had not brought an entrenching tool.

"A French farmyard is more like brick than it is like dirt. For centuries animals have been pounding it down. The sun has been baking it. There was just no way that I could dig a hole to protect myself. The enlisted men had their entrenching tools and a couple of them offered to dig me a hole but I said, 'No. You go take care of yourselves. Dig your own holes and after you are safe and secure then you can give me your shovel and I will dig me a hole.'

"It was cold as the darkness came on us. I mean really cold. There was a haystack in the farmyard." Raaen decided to lie down in it. "I'm just a city boy. I learned a little bit about haystacks in French barnyards that night because it wasn't a haystack, it was a manure pile. I hardly had lain down in the warmth of that manure pile when I was covered with every kind of bug you could think of.

---

* Honan went on: "Now that convinced me of the absolute futility of antiaircraft fire. There was one plane and he flew quite a regular course at a medium altitude with about 20,000 guns firing at him and he did a second circle and went away home."

I came out of that thing slapping and swinging and pinching, doing all I could to rid me of all those vermin and biting bugs.

"I went to the farmhouse. Inside an old French woman was putting fagots on a fire. It was a very tiny fire." Lieutenant Van Riper, a platoon leader in Raaen's company, was there. "Van Riper and I spent the rest of the night warming our hands over that little tiny fire of fagots alongside that little old French woman. It was sort of an ignominious ending to a rather exciting day."[3]

Pvt. Harry Parley, 116th Regiment, 29th Division, said in his oral history that "the last hours of June 6 are quite vivid in my memory. As darkness came, we found ourselves in a hedgerow-enclosed field. Dirty, hungry, and dog tired, with no idea as to where we were, we decided to dig in for the night. We could hear the far off sound of artillery and see the path of tracer fire arcing in the distance.

"As we spread out around the field, I found myself paired off with my sergeant. We started to dig a foxhole, but the ground was rock hard and we were both totally exhausted by the time the hole was about three inches deep. Finally, standing there in the dark, aware that it was useless to continue, my sergeant said, 'Fuck it, Parley. Let's just get down and get some rest.' And so, D-Day came to an end with both of us sitting back to back in the shallow trench throughout the night."[4]

At Pegasus Bridge, the Ox and Bucks handed over to the Warwickshire Regiment. John Howard led his men through the dark toward Ranville. Jack Bailey found it hard to leave. "You see," he explained, "we had been there a full day and night. We rather felt that this was our bit of territory."[5]

Lt. John Reville of F Company, 5th Ranger Battalion, was on top of the bluff at Omaha. As the light faded, he called his runner, Pvt. Rex Low, pointed out to the 6,000 vessels in the Channel, and said, "Rex, take a look at this. You'll never see a sight like this again in your life."[6]

Pvt. Robert Zafft, a twenty-year-old infantryman in the 115th Regiment, 29th Division, Omaha Beach, put his feelings and experience this way: "I made it up the hill, I made it all the way to where the Germans had stopped us for the night, and I guess I made it up the hill of manhood."[7]

Pvt. Felix Branham was a member of K Company, 116th Infantry, the regiment that took the heaviest casualties of all the

Allied regiments on D-Day. "I have gone through lots of tragedies since D-Day," he concluded his oral history. "But to me, D-Day will live with me till the day I die, and I'll take it to heaven with me. It was the longest, most miserable, horrible day that I or anyone else ever went through.

"I would not take a million dollars for my experiences, but I surely wouldn't want to go through that again for a million dollars."[8]

Sgt. John Ellery, 16th Regiment, 1st Division, Easy Red sector of Omaha, recalled: "The first night in France I spent in a ditch beside a hedgerow wrapped in a damp shelter-half and thoroughly exhausted. But I felt elated. It had been the greatest experience of my life. I was ten feet tall. No matter what happened, I had made it off the beach and reached the high ground. I was king of the hill at least in my own mind, for a moment. My contribution to the heroic tradition of the United States Army might have been the smallest achievement in the history of courage, but at least, for a time, I had walked in the company of very brave men."[9]

Admiral Ramsay ended his June 6 diary with this entry: "We have still to establish ourselves on land. The navy has done its part well. News continued satisfactory throughout the day from E.T.F. [Eastern Task Force, the British beaches] and good progress was made. Very little news was rec[eived] from W.T.F. [the American beaches] & anxiety exists as to the position on shore.

"Still on the whole we have very much to thank God for this day."[10]

One soldier who did not forget to thank God was Lt. Richard Winters, 506th PIR, 101st Airborne. At 0001 on June 6, he had been in a C-47 headed to Normandy. He had prayed the whole way over, prayed to live through the day, prayed that he wouldn't fail.

He didn't fail. He won the DSC that morning.

At 2400 on June 6, before bedding down at Ste.-Marie-du-Mont, Winters (as he later wrote in his diary) "did not forget to get on my knees and thank God for helping me to live through this day and ask for His help on D plus one." And he made a promise to himself: if he lived through the war, he was going to find an isolated farm somewhere and spend the remainder of his life in peace and quiet. In 1951 he got the farm, in south-central Pennsylvania, where he lives today.[11]

• •

"When can their glory fade?" Tennyson asked about the Light Brigade, and so ask I about the men of D-Day.

"O the wild charge they made!
All the world wondered.
Honor the charge they made!"

General Eisenhower, who started it all with his "OK, let's go" order, gets the last word. In 1964, on D-Day plus twenty years, he was interviewed on Omaha Beach by Walter Cronkite.

Looking out at the Channel, Eisenhower said, "You see these people out here swimming and sailing their little pleasure boats and taking advantage of the nice weather and the lovely beach, Walter, and it is almost unreal to look at it today and remember what it was.

"But it's a wonderful thing to remember what those fellows twenty years ago were fighting for and sacrificing for, what they did to preserve our way of life. Not to conquer any territory, not for any ambitions of our own. But to make sure that Hitler could not destroy freedom in the world.

"I think it's just overwhelming. To think of the lives that were given for that principle, paying a terrible price on this beach alone, on that one day, 2,000 casualties. But they did it so that the world could be free. It just shows what free men will do rather than be slaves."[12]

Glossary

AKA	cargo ship, attack
APA	transport ship, attack
BAR	Browning automatic rifle
Belgian Gates	antilanding obstacles
CCS	Combined Chiefs of Staff
CIC	Combat Information Center
CO	commanding officer
COSSAC	Chief of Staff to the Supreme Allied Commander (Designate)
CP	command post
CTF	commander task force
DUKW	2 1/2 ton amphibious truck (Duck)
E-boat	German torpedo boat
ECB	engineer combat battalion
ESB	engineer special brigade
ETO	European Theater of Operations
FUSAG	First United States Army Group
GHQ	general headquarters
JCS	U.S. Joint Chiefs of Staff
LCA	landing craft, assault
LCC	primary control vessel
LCI	landing craft, infantry

LCM	landing craft, medium
LCT	landing craft, tank
LCT(R)	landing craft, tank (rocket)
LCVP	landing craft, vehicle and personnel (Higgins boat)
LST	landing ship, tank
MG-34	a tripod-mounted machine gun with a rate of fire of up to 800 rounds per minute
MG-42	a tripod-mounted machine gun with a rate of fire up to 1,300 rounds per minute
OB West	*Oberbefehlshaber West* (general HQ for the Western Front)
OKH	*Oberkommando des Heeres* (Army High Command)
OKW	*Oberkommando der Wehrmacht* (Armed Forces High Command)
OP	observation post
OSS	Office of Strategic Services
OWI	Office of War Information
Rhino ferry	barge constructed of pontoon units
SAS	Special Air Service
SCR	Signal Corps Radio
SHAEF	Supreme Headquarters Allied Expeditionary Force
SOE	Special Operations Executive
SP	self-propelled guns
SS	*Schutzstaffel*
Sten gun	British 9mm automatic weapon, 30 inches long, weighing 7 pounds
TBS	talk between ships
Tetrahedra	pyramid-shaped steel obstacles
UDT	underwater demolition teams
Waffen-SS	combat arm of the SS
Widerstandsnest	resistance nest

Endnotes

The vast majority of the quotations in this book come from oral histories, written memoirs, letters, action reports and individual and group interviews with the men of D-Day, ranging in rank from the supreme commander to seaman and private, in the Eisenhower Center (EC) at the University of New Orleans. Other depositories that provided similar material include the United States Army Military Institute (AMI) at Carlisle Barracks, Pa.; the Imperial War Museum (IWM), London; the Documentary Center, Battle of Normandy Museum, Caen; the Eisenhower Library (EL), Abilene, Kans.; and the Parachute Museum, Ste.-Mère-Église.

1. THE DEFENDERS

1. It was the looniest of all his crazy decisions. He was not required by the terms of the "Pact of Steel" to come to Japan's aid, as the treaty was for defensive purposes—if one of the partners (Italy, Germany, and Japan) were attacked, the others were pledged to come to her aid. But Japan had not been attacked on December 7, and Japan had not come to Germany's aid in June 1941 when the Germans invaded the Soviet Union.

It was also the loneliest of his lonely decisions. Amazingly, he consulted no one. He threw away his long-range plan for world conquest, in which the final struggle against the United States was left to the next generation, utilizing the resources of the Soviet Union and the rest of Europe. One would have thought he would have at least asked his military leaders what the implications of a declaration of war against the United States were, that he would have at least talked to Goering, Himmler, Goebbels, and his other henchmen about it. But he discussed it with no other person; on December 11, he simply announced it to the Reichstag.

See Sebastian Haffner, *The Meaning of Hitler*, tr. Ewald Osers (Cambridge, Mass.: Harvard University Press, 1979), p. 120.

2. Directive No. 51 is printed in a translated version in Gordon A. Harrison, *Cross-Channel Attack* (Washington, D.C.: Dept. of the Army, 1951), pp. 464–67.

3. Erwin Rommel, *The Rommel Papers*, ed. B. H. Liddell Hart (New York: Harcourt, Brace, 1953), p. 466.

4. Reported in Samuel Mitcham, *Rommel's Last Battle: The Desert Fox and the Normandy Campaign* (New York: Stein & Day, 1983), pp. 44–45.

5. Ralph Williams, "The Short, Unhappy Life of the Messerschmitt ME-262," April 6, 1960, in the Dwight D. Eisenhower Library, Abilene, Kansas.

6. Quoted in John Keegan, *Six Armies in Normandy: From D-Day to the Liberation of Paris* (New York: Penguin Books, 1983), p. 332.

7. Robert Brewer interview, EC.

8. Harrison, *Cross-Channel Attack*, pp. 145–47; U.S. War Department, *Handbook on German Military Forces* (Baton Rouge, La.: L.S.U. Press, 1990), p. 57.

9. U.S. War Department, *Handbook on German Military Forces*, p. 2.

10. Quoted in Mitcham, *Rommel's Last Battle*, p. 26.

11. Directive No. 40 is reprinted in translation in Harrison, *Cross-Channel Attack*, pp. 459–63.

12. *Ibid.*, p. 136.

13. *Ibid.*, pp. 136–37.

14. Heckler interview with Warlimont, July 19–20, 1945, in American Military Institute, Carlisle, Pa.

2. THE ATTACKERS

1. Quoted in Carlo D'Este, *Decision in Normandy* (London: Collins, 1983), p. 21.

2. Samuel Eliot Morison, *The Invasion of France and Germany 1944–1945* (Boston: Little, Brown, 1959), pp. 152–53.

3. For a discussion of landing craft, see Gordon Harrison, *Cross-Channel Attack* (Washington, D.C.: Dept. of the Army, 1951), pp. 59–63.

4. Geoffrey Perret, *There's a War to Be Won: The United States Army in World War II* (New York: Random House, 1992), pp. 110–12.

5. Quoted in Harrison, *Cross-Channel Attack*, p. 64.

6. Jerry Strahan interview, EC.

7. Perret, *There's a War to Be Won*, p. 124.

8. Carl Weast interview, EC.

9. Carwood Lipton interview, EC.

10. Paul Fussell, *Wartime: Understanding and Behavior in the Second World War* (New York, Oxford: Oxford University Press, 1989), p. 282.

11. Charles East interview, EC.

12. Quoted in Max Hastings, *Overlord: D-Day and the Battle for Normandy* (New York: Simon & Schuster, 1984), p. 317.

13. John Howard interview, EC.

14. Quoted in Hastings, *Overlord*, p. 25.

15. *Ibid.*, p. 24.

16. Sidey to Ambrose, 7/9/92, EC.

17. See J. C. Masterman, *The Double-Cross System in the War of 1939–1945* (New Haven: Yale University Press, 1972) and Ronald Lewin, *Ultra Goes to War* (London: Hutchinson, 1978).

18. Gordon Carson interview, EC.

3. THE COMMANDERS

1. For Rommel's early life, see David Irving, *The Trail of the Fox* (New York: Dutton, 1977); for Eisenhower's, see S. E. Ambrose, *Eisenhower: Soldier, General of the Army, President-Elect, 1890–1952* (New York: Simon & Schuster, 1983).

2. Irving, *Trail of the Fox*, pp. 14–15.

3. Ambrose, *Eisenhower*, p. 63.

4. Ed Thayer to his mother, 1/11/18, Eisenhower Library, Abilene, Kansas (hereinafter cited as EL).

5. Irving, *Trail of the Fox*, p. 25.

6. Ambrose, *Eisenhower*, p. 93.

7. Hans von Luck, *Panzer Commander: The Memoirs of Colonel Hans von Luck* (New York: Praeger, 1989), pp. 103–4.

8. Quoted in Stephen E. Ambrose, *Eisenhower: Soldier and President* (New York: Simon & Schuster, 1990), p. 88.

9. From the first draft of Eisenhower's memoirs, in EL. Eisenhower chose not to publish this section.

10. Martin Blumenson, "Rommel," in Thomas Parrish, ed., *The Simon and Schuster Encyclopedia of World War II* (New York: Simon & Schuster, 1978), p. 532.

11. For Eisenhower's letters, see *Letters to Mamie*, ed. John S. D. Eisenhower (Garden City, N.Y.: Doubleday, 1978). For Rommel's, see Irving, *Trail of the Fox*, which quotes from many of them.

12. Irving, *Trail of the Fox*, p. 313.

13. Quoted in Samuel Mitcham, Jr., *Rommel's Last Battle: The Desert Fox and the Normandy Campaign* (New York: Stein & Day, 1983), pp. 18–21.

14. FDR to Stalin, 12/5/43, EL.

15. Bernard Law Montgomery, *Memoirs* (Cleveland: World, 1958), p. 484.

16. Cunningham to Eisenhower, 10/21/43, EL.

17. Dwight D. Eisenhower, *Crusade in Europe* (Garden City, N.Y.: Doubleday, 1948), pp. 206–7.

18. Irving, *Trail of the Fox*, p. 317.

19. Eisenhower, *Crusade in Europe*, p. 220.

20. Irving, *Trail of the Fox*, p. 324.

21. Eisenhower to CCS, 1/23/44, EL.

22. Ambrose, *Eisenhower: Soldier, General of the Army, President-Elect*, pp. 187–88.

4. WHERE AND WHEN?

1. Gordon A. Harrison, *Cross-Channel Attack* (Washington, D.C.: Dept. of the Army, 1951), pp. 48–49.

2. Scott-Bowden interview, Imperial War Museum, London.

3. *Ibid.*

4. *Ibid.*

5. Harrison, *Cross-Channel Attack*, p. 106.

6. Anthony Cave Brown, *Bodyguard of Lies* (New York: Harper & Row, 1975), p. 465.

7. Earl Ziemke, "Operation Kreml: Deception, Strategy, and the Fortunes of War," *Parameters: Journal of the U.S. Army War College* 9 (March 1979): 72–81.

8. The Fortitude story is best told in James Bowman, "Operation Fortitude," a 1,000-page manuscript in EC.

9. Bowman, "Operation Fortitude."

10. Eisenhower to Chiefs of the Belgian, Norwegian, and Dutch Military Missions, 2/23/44, EL.

11. Quoted in Stephen E. Ambrose, *Ike's Spies: Eisenhower and the Espionage Establishment* (Garden City, N.Y.: Doubleday, 1981), p. 90.

12. Eisenhower to Chiefs of Staff Committee, 3/6/44, EL.

13. Eisenhower to Brooke, 4/9/44, EL.

14. Quoted in Ambrose, *Ike's Spies,* p. 91.

15. Forrest Pogue, *The Supreme Command* (Washington, D.C.: Dept. of the Army, 1954), pp. 163–64.

16. Eisenhower to Marshall, 5/21/44, EL.

17. Quoted in Irving, *The Trail of the Fox* (New York: Dutton, 1977), p. 336.

18. Harrison, *Cross-Channel Attack,* p. 259.

19. Quoted in Irving, *Trail of the Fox,* p. 347.

20. Harrison, *Cross-Channel Attack,* p. 259.

21. These weekly summaries are in EL.

22. Quoted in Irving, *Trail of the Fox,* p. 347.

23. *Ibid.,* p. 351.

24. *Ibid.,* p. 354.

25. *Ibid.,* p. 342.

26. Dwight D. Eisenhower, *Letters to Mamie,* ed. John S. D. Eisenhower (Garden City, N.Y.: Doubleday, 1978), pp. 165, 183.

5. UTILIZING ASSETS

1. Marshall to Eisenhower, 2/10/44, EL.

2. Eisenhower to Marshall, 2/19/44, EL.

3. Whiteley to John Kennedy, 9/23/43, EL.

4. Arnold to Eisenhower, 1/21/44, EL.

5. Forrest Pogue, *The Supreme Command* (Washington, D.C.: Dept. of the Army, 1954), p. 127.

6. Stephen E. Ambrose, *Eisenhower: Soldier, General of the Army, President-Elect, 1890–1952* (New York: Simon & Schuster, 1983), p. 287.

7. Pogue, *Supreme Command,* p. 124; Gordon A. Harrison, *Cross-Channel Attack* (Washington, D.C.: Dept. of the Army, 1951), pp. 219–20; Sir Arthur Tedder, *With Prejudice* (London: Cassell, 1966), pp. 510–12.

8. Eisenhower diary, 3/22/44, EL.

9. Tedder, *With Prejudice,* p. 524.

10. Eisenhower to Churchill, 4/5/44, EL.

11. Tedder, *With Prejudice,* pp. 528–33.

12. *Ibid.,* 531–33.

13. Winston S. Churchill, *Closing the Ring* (Boston: Houghton Mifflin, 1952), pp. 529–30.

14. The weekly summaries are in EL.

15. Wesley Frank Craven and James Lea Cate, eds., *Europe: Argument to V-E Day* (Chicago: University of Chicago Press, 1951), p 73.

16. Pogue, *Supreme Command,* p. 132.

17. Hechler interview of Jodl, American Military Institute, Carlisle, Pa.

18. Harrison, *Cross-Channel Attack,* pp. 224, 230.

19. Clement Marie interview, EC.

20. Quoted in Irving, *The Trail of the Fox* (New York: Dutton, 1977), p. 343.

21. André Rougeyron, "Agents for Escape," translated by Marie-Antoinette Verchère-McConnell, manuscript copy in EC.

22. André Heintz interview, EC.

23. Thérèse Gondrée and John Howard interviews, EC.

24. Richard Winters interview, EC.

25. Guillaume Mercader interview, EC.

26. Harrison, *Cross-Channel Attack*, p. 204.

27. *Ibid.*, p. 202.

28. Guillaume Mercader interview, EC.

29. Anthony Brooks interview, EC.

30. *Ibid.* See also M. R. D. Foot, *SOE: The Special Operations Executive 1940–46* (London: BBC, 1984), pp. 226–27.

6. Planning and Preparing

1. Eisenhower interview, EC.

2. Eisenhower to Walter Cronkite on CBS-TV's "D-Day Plus Twenty Years," a documentary shown on June 6, 1964, transcript copy in EC.

3. Smith interview, American Military Institute, Carlisle, Pa.

4. G. Harrison interview with De Guingand, *ibid.*

5. *Ibid.*

6. Friedrich Ruge interview, EC.

7. David Irving, *The Trail of the Fox* (New York: Dutton, 1977), p. 323.

8. Samuel Mitcham, *Rommel's Last Battle* (New York: Stein & Day, 1983), p. 36.

9. *Ibid.*, p. 42.

10. Ruge interview, EC.

11. Irving, *Trail of the Fox*, pp. 344–45.

12. *Ibid.*, p. 345.

13. Hans von Luck, *Panzer Commander* (New York: Praeger, 1989), p. 133.

14. Gordon A. Harrison, *Cross-Channel Attack* (Washington, D.C.: Dept. of the Army, 1951), p. 254.

15. Mitcham, *Rommel's Last Battle*, p. 37.

16. Heydte interview, EC.

17. Hechler interview with Bayerlein, July 12, 1949, American Military Institute, Carlisle, Pa.

18. Detlef Vogel, "Morale and Fighting Power of the *Wehrmacht* in the West on the Eve of the Invasion," paper delivered at the 1992 Military History Institute conference, copy in EC.

19. Paul Carell, *Invasion—They're Coming!*, tr. E. Osers (New York: Dutton, 1963), pp. 26–27.

20. Carlo D'Este, *Decision in Normandy* (London: Collins, 1983), pp. 74–76.

21. Joseph Balkoski, *Beyond the Beachhead: The 29th Infantry Division in Normandy* (Harrisburg, Pa.: Stackpole, 1989), pp. 142–43.

22. John Barnes oral history, EC.

23. Robert Miller oral history, EC.

24. Lord's typewritten account is in American Military Institute, Carlisle, Pa.

25. Russell Miller interview with George Lane, EC.

26. Van Fleet memoir, copy in EC.

27. Samuel Eliot Morison, *The Invasion of France and Germany 1944–1945* (Boston: Little, Brown, 1959), p. 70.

28. D'Este, *Decision in Normandy*, pp. 83–86.

29. Stephen Ambrose, *The Supreme Commander* (Garden City: Doubleday, 1971), pp. 399–400.

7. TRAINING

1. Eisenhower to Marshall, 2/24/43, EL.

2. Van Fleet memoir, copy in EC.

3. John Robert Slaughter manuscript memoir, EC.

4. Robert Walker oral history, EC.

5. Felix Branham oral history, EC.

6. Joseph Balkoski, *Beyond the Beachhead: The 29th Infantry Division in Normandy* (Harrisburg, Pa.: Stackpole, 1989), p. 2.

7. John Robert Slaughter manuscript memoir, EC.

8. Weldon Kratzer letter, EC.

9. Thor Smith interview, EC.

10. Tom Plumb oral history, EC.

11. I am indebted to Billy Arthur's paper, "Pre-Invasion Training: Key to D-Day Success," delivered to the American Historical Institute in Washington, June 1992, for information on Thompson and the Assault Training Center.

12. *Ibid.*

13. Quoted in Warren Tute, John Costello, and Terry Hughes, *D-Day* (London: Pan Books, 1975), p. 83.

14. Eugene Bernstein oral history, EC.

15. R. Younger interview, Imperial War Museum (IWM), copy in EC.

16. David Thomas oral history, EC.

17. Harry Parley oral history, EC.

18. Geoffrey Perret, *There's a War to Be Won* (New York: Random House, 1992), p. 311.

19. Robert Rader oral history, EC.

20. *Currahee!* scrapbook published in Germany in 1945, unpaged.

21. Russell Miller interview with D. Zane Schlemmer, copy in EC.

22. Jim Wallwork interview, EC.

23. James Eikner oral history, EC.

24. John Robert Slaughter manuscript memoir, EC.

25. Henry Glassman, *"Lead the Way, Rangers": A History of the Fifth Ranger Battalion* (printed in Germany, 1945), pp. 12–13.

26. Walter Sidlowski oral history, EC.

27. James Eikner oral history, EC.

28. Script of Paul Thompson talk, EC.

29. Barnett Hoffner oral history, EC.

30. Robert Piauge interview, EC.

31. Peter Masters oral history, EC.

32. Harry Nomburg oral history, EC.

33. Fred Patheiger oral history, EC.

34. Stephen E. Ambrose and James A. Barber, editors, *The Military and American Society: Essays and Readings* (New York: The Free Press, 1972), p. 177

35. Ulysses Lee, *The Employment of Negro Troops* (Washington, D.C.: Office of the Chief of Military History, 1966), pp. 623–24.

36. *Ibid.*, 627.

37. *Ibid.*, 630.

38. Hans von Luck, *Panzer Commander* (New York: Praeger, 1989), p. 134.

39. Detlef Vogel, "Morale and Fighting Power of the *Wehrmacht* in the West on the Eve of the Invasion," paper delivered at the 1992 Military History Institute conference, copy in EC.

40. Peter Masters oral history, EC.

8. MARSHALING AND BRIEFING

1. Eugene Bernstein oral history, EC.

2. John Robert Slaughter oral history, EC.

3. Ralph Eastridge memoir, EC.

4. John Howard oral history, EC.

5. John Robert Slaughter memoir, EC.

6. Edward Jeziorski oral history, EC.

7. John Robert Slaughter oral history, EC.

8. Peter Masters oral history, EC.

9. John Barnes oral history, EC.

10. Edward Jeziorski oral history, EC.

11. Richard Winters oral history, EC.

12. Paul Fussell, *Wartime: Understanding and Behavior in the Second World War* (New York: Oxford University Press, 1989), pp. 240–41.

13. Arthur Schultz oral history, EC. Schultz went on to say "I am one of the characters in Connie Ryan's *The Longest Day*. He had this crap game taking place at the airfield, which is not actually true. It took place at camp. He felt I was a good Catholic boy who shouldn't be betting, so he had me losing the money because of my religious convictions, which was not the case at all. It was because I was trying to humiliate the guy I disliked." For Ryan's version, see *The Longest Day: June 6, 1944* (New York: Popular Library, 1959), pp. 63–64.

14. David Thomas oral history, EC.

15. John Robert Slaughter memoir, EC.

16. Peter Masters oral history, EC.

17. Gerden Johnson, *History of the Twelfth Infantry Regiment in World War II* (Boston: 4th Division Association, 1991), p. 53.

18. Ralph Eastridge letter to his parents, July 27, 1946, EC.

19. Felix Branham oral history, EC.

20. Robert Healey oral history, EC.

21. Merical Dillon oral history, EC.

22. William Dillon oral history, EC.

23. Leroy Jennings oral history, EC.

24. Charles Skidmore oral history, EC.

25. Alan Anderson oral history, EC.

26. Russell Miller interview with Cyril Hendry, copy in EC.

27. Arthur Schultz oral history, EC.

28. David Thomas oral history, EC.

29. John Barnes oral history, EC.

30. Joseph Dragotto oral history, EC.

31. Richard Winters oral history, EC.

32. Alan Anderson oral history, EC.

33. Charles Jarreau interview, EC.

34. Bannerman carried the unfinished letter with him into Normandy. It was captured by the Germans and read by Rommel (David Irving, *Trail of the Fox* [New York: Dutton, 1977], pp. 356–58).

35. Paul Thompson memoir, EC.
36. Richard Freed oral history, EC.
37. John Keegan, *Six Armies in Normandy* (New York: Penguin Books, 1983), p. 331.
38. Copy No. 42 of this "strictly limited" document is in EL.
39. A copy of the document is in EL.
40. Franz Gockel memoir, EC, translated by Derek Zumbro.

9. LOADING

1. Ronald Lewin interview, EC.
2. Clair Galdonik oral history, EC.
3. Charles Jarreau interview, EC.
4. Ralph Eastridge letter, EC.
5. Gen. James Van Fleet memoir, EC.
6. Charles Jarreau interview, EC.
7. Robert Patterson oral history, EC.
8. Ralph Eastridge letter, EC.
9. Samuel Eliot Morison, *The Invasion of France and Germany 1944–1945* (Boston: Little, Brown, 1959), p. 83.
10. All Eisenhower's Orders of the Day are in EL.
11. John Robert Slaughter memoir, EC.
12. Felix Branham oral history, EC.
13. Anthony Duke oral history, EC.
14. Ralph Eastridge letter, EC.
15. Oscar Rich oral history, EC.
16. Clair Galdonik oral history, EC.
17. Walter Sidlowski oral history, EC.
18. Frank Beetle interview, EC.
19. Clyde Kerchner oral history, EC.
20. Robert Walker oral history, EC.
21. Charles Ryan oral history, EC.
22. Michael Foot interview, EC.
23. Dwight D. Eisenhower, *At Ease: Stories I Tell to Friends* (Garden City, N.Y.: Doubleday, 1967), p. 275.
24. David Irving, *The Trail of the Fox* (New York: Dutton, 1977), p. 354; Samuel Mitcham, *Rommel's Last Battle* (New York: Stein & Day, 1983), p. 62.
25. Irving, *Trail of the Fox*, p. 351.
26. *Ibid.*, pp. 354–55.

10. DECISION TO GO

1. Dwight Eisenhower interview, EC.
2. Dwight D. Eisenhower, *Crusade in Europe* (Garden City, N.Y.: Doubleday, 1948), p. 246; Walter Cronkite interview with Eisenhower for CBS-TV, transcript in EC.
3. Eisenhower interview, EC; Eisenhower to Leigh-Mallory, 5/30/44, EL.
4. Cronkite interview with Eisenhower, EC.
5. Dwight Eisenhower interview, EC; the draft of Eisenhower's speech is in EL.
6. Eisenhower diary, 6/3/44, EL.
7. Eisenhower, *Crusade in Europe*, p. 249.
8. Edwin Gale oral history, EC.
9. Dean Rockwell oral history, EC.

10. Homer Carey oral history, EC.
11. Harry Parley oral history, EC.
12. George Roach oral history, EC.
13. Joe Pilck oral history, EC.
14. Robert Miller oral history, EC.
15. Henry Gerald oral history, EC.
16. Eisenhower, *Crusade in Europe*, p. 249.
17. Eisenhower diary entry, 6/3/44, EL.
18. David Irving, *The Trail of the Fox* (New York: Dutton, 1977), p. 354.
19. Benjamin Frans letter, EC.
20. Dean Rockwell oral history, EC.
21. Samuel Grundfast oral history, EC.
22. Felix Branham oral history, EC.
23. Clair Galdonik oral history, EC.
24. John Howard diary, EC.
25. David Wood interview, EC.
26. Edward Jeziorski oral history, EC.
27. Jerry Eades oral history, EC.
28. James Edward oral history, EC.
29. Eugene Bernstein oral history, EC.
30. Gordon A. Harrison, *Cross-Channel Attack* (Washington, D.C.: Dept. of the Army, 1951), p. 276.
31. Kerchner oral history, EC.
32. Kenneth Strong interview, EC.
33. Interviews with Eisenhower, Kenneth Strong, Arthur Tedder, EC; Harry Butcher diary, 6/4–6/44, EL.
34. Samuel Eliot Morison, *The Invasion of France and Germany 1944–45* (Boston: Little, Brown, 1959), p. 83.
35. Walter Cronkite interview with Eisenhower, EC.
36. Kenneth Strong interview, EC.
37. Cronkite interview with Eisenhower, EC.
38. Harry Butcher diary, 6/4–6/44, EL
39. This undated note is in EL. Eisenhower put it into his wallet and forgot about it. A couple of weeks later, he pulled it out, laughed, and commented that thank goodness he had not had to issue it. He threw it into a wastebasket; Butcher retrieved it. Butcher Diary, 6/20/44, EL.
40. Irving, *Trail of the Fox*, p. 364.
41. Heydte interview, EC.
42. Hans von Luck, *Panzer Commander* (New York: Praeger, 1989), p. 135.
43. Walter Warlimont, *Inside Hitler's Headquarters, 1939–1945* (New York: Praeger, 1964), p. 422.
44. Nat Hoskot interview, EC.
45. Sam Gibbons memoir, EC. Gibbons went on to represent the 7th District of Florida in the House of Representatives for many decades.
46. J. Frank Brumbaugh oral history, EC.
47. Edward Jeziorski and Donald Bosworth oral histories, EC.
48. John Delury oral history, EC.
49. Tom Porcella oral history, EC.
50. Carl Cartledge oral history, EC.
51. Charles Shettle oral history, EC.
52. L. Johnson oral history, EC.
53. Dwight Eisenhower interview, EC.
54. Sherman Oyler letter to Mack Teasley, 12/6/83, EL.

55. Wallace Strobble letter, EC.
56. John Richards oral history, EC.
57. Arthur Schultz oral history, EC.
58. *Ibid.*
59. Dwight Eisenhower interview, EC.
60. Kay Summersby Morgan, *Past Forgetting: My Love Affair with Dwight D. Eisenhower* (New York: Simon & Schuster, 1976), p. 216.
61. Professor Robert Love of the Naval Academy history department provided the transcript of Ramsay's entry; Dr. Love is preparing the diary for publication.

11. Cracking the Atlantic Wall

1. James Elmo Jones oral history, EC.
2. For a description of the action, see Stephen E. Ambrose, *Pegasus Bridge: June 6, 1944* (New York: Simon & Schuster, 1985).
3. Matthew Ridgway, *Soldier* (New York: Harper, 1956), p. 4.
4. Eugene Brierre oral history, EC.
5. Dwayne Burns oral history, EC.
6. Ken Russell interview, EC.
7. Clayton Storeby oral history, EC.
8. Harry Reisenleiter oral history, EC.
9. John Keegan, *Six Armies in Normandy: From D-Day to the Liberation of Paris* (New York: Penguin Books, 1983), p. 82.
10. Sidney Ulan oral history, EC.
11. Earl Peters oral history, EC.
12. Charles Ratliff oral history, EC.
13. John Fitzgerald and Carl Cartledge oral histories, EC.
14. William True and Parker Alford oral histories, EC.
15. Tom Porcella oral history, EC.
16. Dwayne Burns oral history, EC.
17. Dan Furlong interview by Russell Miller, EC.
18. Keegan, *Six Armies in Normandy*, p. 85.
19. Arthur DeFilippo oral history, EC.
20. John Taylor oral history, EC.
21. Sherman Oyler letter to Martin Teasley, EL.
22. Len Griffing oral history, EC.
23. *Ibid.*
24. John Fitzgerald oral history, EC.
25. Ray Aeibischer oral history, EC.
26. Richard Winters oral history, EC.
27. Sam Gibbons memoir, EC.
28. Parker Alford oral history, EC.
29. Arthur Schultz oral history, EC.
30. Len Griffing oral history, EC.
31. Clayton Storeby oral history, EC.
32. "Debriefing Conference," 82nd Airborne, held on August 13, 1944 in Leicester, England. Copy in EC.
33. Parker Alford oral history, EC.
34. 82nd Airborne Debriefing Conference, August 13, 1944, copy in EC.
35. Michel de Vallavieille, *D-Day at Utah Beach* (Coutances, Normandy, 1982), p. 22.
36. Ken Russell interview by Ron Drez, EC.
37. Allen Langdon, *"Ready": A World War II History of the 505th Para-*

chute Infantry Regiment (Indianapolis: 82nd Airborne Division Association, 1986), pp. 49–51. This is an indispensable account, highly detailed and accurate.

38. Ken Russell interview by Ron Drez, EC.
39. James Eads oral history, EC.
40. Tom Porcella oral history, EC.
41. David Jones oral history, EC.
42. There is a copy of the report in EC.
43. Beaudin was liberated on July 16 by the 9th Division. Briand Beaudin oral history, EC.
44. *Utah Beach to Cherbourg* (Washington, D.C.: U.S. Army, Center of Military History, 1948), p. 15.
45. Michael Foot interview, EC.
46. Frederick von der Heydte interview, EC.
47. Charles Shettle oral history, EC.
48. Frederick von der Heydte interview, EC.
49. Vallavieille, *D-Day at Utah Beach*, pp. 25–26.
50. S. L.A. Marshall, *Night Drop: The American Airborne Invasion of Normandy* (Boston: Little, Brown, 1962), p. 269.
51. Hans von Luck interview, EC.
52. Zane Schlemmer oral history, EC.
53. James Elmo Jones oral history, EC.
54. Robert Butler oral history, EC.
55. Leonard Lebenson oral history, EC.
56. Charles Skidmore oral history, EC.
57. Harry Reisenleiter oral history, EC.
58. John Fitzgerald oral history, EC.
59. Zane Schlemmer oral history, EC.
60. Carl Cartledge oral history, EC.
61. 82nd Airborne Debriefing Conference, August 13, 1944, copy in EC.

12. "LET'S GET THOSE BASTARDS"

1. 82nd Airborne Debriefing Conference, August 13, 1944, copy in EC.
2. Francis Palys oral history, EC.
3. Quoted in Clay Blair, *Ridgway's Paratroopers: The American Airborne in World War II* (Garden City, N.Y.: Doubleday, 1985), p. 233.
4. Dwayne Burns oral history, EC.
5. Lynn Tomlinson oral history, EC.
6. Dan Furlong interview by Russell Miller, EC.
7. Arthur Schultz oral history, EC.
8. David Howarth, *Dawn of D-Day* (London: Collins, 1959), p. 55.
9. *Ibid.*, pp. 56–60; Napier Crookenden, *Drop Zone Normandy* (New York: Scribners, 1976), pp. 205–9.
10. Major Roseveare and Bill Irving interviews, Imperial War Museum, London.
11. John Kemp interview, EC.
12. Carl Cartledge oral history, EC.
13. John Fitzgerald oral history, EC.
14. Sam Gibbons memoir, EC.
15. Charles Shettle oral history, EC.
16. 505th regimental history, pp. 53–54
17. Gordon A. Harrison, *Cross-Channel Attack* (Washington, D.C.: Dept. of the Army, 1951), p. 288.

13. "The Greatest Show Ever Staged"

1. Charles Shettle oral history, EC.
2. Roger Lovelace oral history, EC.
3. Russell Weigley, *Eisenhower's Lieutenants: The Campaigns of France and Germany, 1944–1945* (Bloomington: Indiana University Press, 1981), p. 70.
4. Roger Lovelace oral history, EC.
5. Carl Carden oral history, EC.
6. John Robinson oral history, EC.
7. Roger Lovelace oral history, EC.
8. John Robinson oral history, EC.
9. J. K. Havener oral history, EC.
10. James Delong oral history, EC.
11. John Meyer oral history, EC.
12. J. K. Havener oral history, EC.
13. A. H. Corry oral history, EC.
14. Charles Harris oral history, EC.
15. Allen Stephens oral history, EC.
16. William Moriarity oral history, EC.
17. A. H. Corry oral history, EC.
18. Carl Carden oral history, EC.
19. John Meyer oral history, EC.
20. Roger Lovelace oral history, EC.
21. J. K. Havener oral history, EC.
22. Ray Sanders oral history, EC.
23. A. H. Corry oral history, EC.
24. Ray Sanders oral history, EC.
25. John Robinson oral history, EC.
26. Arthur Jahnke oral history, copy in EC. Jahnke's story is told in detail in Paul Carell, *Invasion—They're Coming! The German Account of the Allied Landings and the 80 Days' Battle for France* (New York: Dutton, 1963).
27. James Delong oral history, EC.
28. Charles Middleton oral history, EC.
29. Weigley, *Eisenhower's Lieutenants*, p. 94.
30. James Taylor oral history, EC.
31. Jack Barensfeld oral history, EC.
32. James Taylor oral history, EC.
33. Charles Mohrle memoir, EC.
34. Edward Giller oral history, EC.
35. Jack Barensfeld oral history, EC.
36. Peter Moody memoir, EC.
37. William Satterwhite oral history, EC.
38. Donald Porter oral history, EC.
39. Harry Crosby, *A Wing and a Prayer.* (New York: HarperCollins, 1993), pp. 227–28.
40. Charles Shettle oral history, EC.

14. A Long, Endless Column of Ships

1. Samuel Eliot Morison, *The Invasion of France and Germany 1944–1945* (Boston: Little, Brown, 1959), pp. 46–47.
2. *Ibid.,* 79.
3. Dean Rockwell oral history, EC.
4. Morison, *Invasion of France and Germany,* p. 57.
5. John Robert Lewis oral history, EC.

6. Joseph Donlan oral history, EC.
7. Anthony Duke oral history, EC.
8. Morison, *Invasion of France and Germany*, p. 87.
9. Ross Olsen oral history, EC.
10. B. T. Whinney interview, EC.
11. Joseph Balkoski, *Beyond the Beachhead: The 29th Infantry Division in Normandy* (Harrisburg, Pa.: Stackpole, 1989), p. 11.
12. Ronald Seaborne memoir, EC.
13. Ronald Seaborne memoir, EC.
14. Howard Vander Beek memoir, EC.
15. Martin Sommers, "The Longest Hour in History," *Saturday Evening Post*, July 8, 1944.
16. Ross Olsen oral history, EC.
17. James O'Neal oral history, EC.
18. Holdbrook Bradley oral history, EC.
19. Cyrus Aydlett diary entry, June 6, 1944, EC.
20. John Howard interview, EC.
21. Piprel's "Recollection of Events," EC, translated (and given to EC by) M. Michael Clemençon.
22. USS *Harding* Action Report, copy in EC.
23. William Gentry memoir, EC.
24. Romuald Nalecz-Tyminski memoir, EC.
25. Kenneth Wright to his parents, 6/11/44, copy in EC.
26. Grant Guillickson oral history, EC. Guillickson stayed in the Navy thirty years. In 1954 he took a competitive exam and earned a commission as an ensign. Eventually he became chief engineer of the USS *Forrestal*. He retired in 1969 as a commander.
27. Joseph Dolan oral history, EC.
28. A. R. Beyer memoir, EC.
29. Doug Birch oral history, EC.
30. Howard Vander Beek memoir, EC.
31. Warren Tute, John Costello, and Terry Hughes, *D-Day* (London: Pan Books, 1975), p. 188.
32. Morison, *Invasion of France and Germany*, p. 121.
33. Tute, Costello, and Hughes, *D-Day*, p. 188.
34. *Ibid.*, p. 167.
35. *Ibid.*, p. 180.
36. Morison, *Invasion of France and Germany*, pp. 122, 125.
37. Eugene Bernstein oral history, EC.
38. W. N. Solkin oral history, EC.
39. Balkoski, *Beyond the Beachhead*, p. 16.
40. Dean Rockwell oral history, EC.
41. Samuel Grundfast oral history, EC.
42. Martin Waarvick oral history, EC.
43. Dean Rockwell oral history, EC.
44. Franz Gockel memoir, EC, translated by Derek Zumbro.

15. "WE'LL START THE WAR FROM RIGHT HERE"

1. Howard Vander Beek and Sims Gauthier oral histories, EC.
2. Arthur Jahnke oral history, copy in EC; Paul Carell, *Invasion—They're Coming!* (New York: Dutton, 1963), pp. 50–56.
3. Malvin Pike oral history, EC.
4. *Ibid.*

5. Warren Tute, John Costello, and Terry Hughes, *D-Day* (London: Pan Books, 1975), p. 182.

6. There is a copy of Van Fleet's unpublished memoir in EC.

7. Group interview with the 237th ECB by Ron Drez, EC.

8. Orval Wakefield oral history, EC.

9. *Ibid.*

10. Martin Gutekunst oral history, EC.

11. Drez group interview with the 237th ECB, EC.

12. John Ahearn oral history, EC.

13. Elliot Richardson interview, EC.

14. Van Fleet unpublished memoir, copy in EC.

15. Malvin Pike oral history, EC.

16. Van Fleet unpublished memoir, copy in EC.

17. Malvin Pike oral history, EC.

18. Malvin Pike and Eugene Brierre oral histories, EC.

19. Ralph Della-Volpe oral history, EC.

20. Marvin Perrett oral history, EC.

21. John Beck oral history, EC.

22. Morison, *Invasion of France and Germany*, p. 120.

23. Russell Reeder, *Born at Reveille* (New York: Duell, Sloan & Pearce, 1966), pp. 247–48.

24. *Ibid.*, p. 248; Charles Jackson memoir, EC.

25. Clifford Sorenson oral history, EC.

26. Charles Jackson memoir, EC.

27. Ross Olsen oral history, EC.

28. Vincent del Giudice oral history, EC. Del Giudice went on to medical school after the war and became an M.D.

29. Carell, *Invasion—They're Coming!*, pp. 60–61.

30. Orval Wakefield oral history, EC.

31. For an excellent account of one of the 4th's regiments, see Gerden Johnson, *History of the Twelfth Infantry Regiment in World War II* (Boston: Fourth Division Association, 1947).

16. "Nous Restons Ici"

1. Leonard Lebenson oral history, EC.

2. John Delury memoir, EC.

3. D. Zane Schlemmer oral history, EC.

4. Sidney McCallum oral history, EC.

5. L. Johnson oral history, EC.

6. Leland Baker oral history, EC.

7. Summers's story is told in detail in S. L. A. Marshall, *Night Drop: The American Airborne Invasion of Normandy* (Boston: Little, Brown, 1962), pp. 216–22.

8. Leland Baker oral history, EC.

9. Marshall, *Night Drop*, p. 271.

10. Eugene Brierre oral history, EC.

11. Marshall, *Night Drop*, pp. 273–74.

12. Michel de Vallavieille, *D-Day at Utah Beach* (Coutances, 1982), p. 56.

13. Frederick von der Heydte interview, EC.

14. This paragraph is based on interviews by Ken Hechler with Bayerlein, Speidel, Jodl, and other German generals, copies in EC, and on Max Hastings, *Overlord* (New York: Simon & Schuster, 1984), p. 77.

15. Hastings, *Overlord*, p. 76.
16. Carwood Lipton oral history, EC.
17. Richard Winters and Harry Welsh interviews, EC.
18. Sam Gibbons memoir, EC.
19. Heydte memoir, EC.
20. Parker Alford oral history, EC.
21. Charles Shettle oral history, EC.
22. Herbert James oral history, EC.
23. Carl Cartledge oral history, EC.
24. William Sawyer oral history, EC.
25. Jack Issacs oral history, EC.
26. David Thomas oral history, EC.
27. Donald Bosworth memoir, EC.
28. Roy Creek oral history, EC.
29. David Jones oral history, EC.
30. O. B. Hill oral history, EC.
31. Marshall, *Night Drop*, pp. 76–77.
32. Roy Creek oral history, EC. Creek went on: "I would pay particular tribute to Lt. Charlie Ames of E Company 507, Sgt. Asa Ricks, A Company 507, Sgt. Glenn Lapne, A Company 507. They all did everything I asked of them, and much more." Creek went on to become a battalion commander in the 507th.
33. James Coyle memoir, EC.
34. John Fitzgerald oral history, EC.
35. Allen Langdon, *"Ready"* (Indianapolis: 82nd Airborne Division Association, 1986), p. 56.
36. Charles Miller oral history, EC.
37. Langdon, *"Ready,"* pp. 56–57.
38. Otis Sampson oral history, EC. Sampson comes in for high praise in Langdon, *"Ready,"* p. 57. Langdon also points out that the members of the group "have always been more than a little bit indignant that [S.L.A.] Marshall wrote in *Night Drop*, 'Turnbull's men ran all the way to Ste.-Mère-Église.' As several have commented, it wasn't necessary to do so and they didn't. It was practically a physical impossibility besides."
39. Langdon, *"Ready,"* p. 57; Stephen E. Ambrose, *Band of Brothers: E Company, 506th* (New York: Simon & Schuster, 1992), p. 103.
40. John Fitzgerald oral history, EC.
41. *Ibid.*
42. James Coyle memoir, EC.
43. Otis Sampson oral history, EC.
44. Historical Section European Theater of Operations Staff, *Utah Beach to Cherbourg*, p. 31.

17. VISITORS TO HELL

1. Paul Carell, *Invasion—They're Coming!* (New York: Dutton, 1963), p. 76.
2. Robert Walker oral history, EC.
3. A. J. Liebling, "Reporter at Large," *New Yorker*, July 15, 1944, p. 40.
4. Robert Walker oral history, EC.
5. U.S. Army, Historical Section Staff, *Omaha Beachhead*, pp. 28–34.
6. *Ibid.*, pp. 35–41.
7. Carell, *Invasion—They're Coming!*, p. 76.

8. Francis Fane, *Naked Warriors* (New York: Prentice Hall, 1956), pp. 61–62.

9. Joseph Balkoski, *Beyond the Beachhead* (Harrisburg, Pa.: Stackpole, 1989), p. 145.

10. Joe Smith oral history, EC.

11. Charles Jarreau interview, EC.

12. John Barnes oral history, EC.

13. Thomas Valance oral history, EC.

14. S. L. A. Marshall, "First Wave at Omaha Beach," *Atlantic Monthly*, November 1960, p. 68.

15. George Roach oral history, EC.

16. Lee Polek oral history, EC.

17. Harry Bare oral history, EC.

18. John Robertson oral history, EC.

19. Harry Parley oral history, EC.

20. Balkoski, *Beyond the Beachhead*, p. 147.

21. *Ibid.*, p. 149; Marshall, "First Wave at Omaha," p. 69.

22. Benjamin McKinney oral history, EC.

23. Felix Branham oral history, EC.

24. J.T. Shea to Colonel Mason, 6/16/44, copy in EC.

25. Historical Division, War Department, *Omaha Beachhead*, pp. 55–56; Debs Peters oral history, EC.

26. Robert Walker oral history, EC.

27. Sidney Bingham oral history, EC.

28. Quoted in Balkoski, *Beyond the Beachhead*, p. 152.

29. George Kobe oral history, EC.

30. John Robert Slaughter oral history, EC. Slaughter wrote an extended memoir of D-Day for the *Twenty-Niner Newsletter*, November 1990, copy in EC.

31. John Robert Slaughter oral history, EC; Ray Moon memoir, EC.

32. Carl Weast oral history, EC.

33. William Lewis oral history, in an unpublished manuscript put together by John Robert Slaughter, copy in EC.

34. Raymond Howell oral history, EC.

18. Utter Chaos Reigned

1. John MacPhee oral history, EC.

2. Clayton Hanks oral history, EC.

3. Warren Rulien oral history, EC.

4. Charles Thomas oral history, EC.

5. Fred Hall oral history, EC.

6. Forrest Pogue interview with John Spaulding, copy in EC.

7. Kenneth Romanski oral history, EC; U.S. Army, Historical Section Staff, *Omaha Beachhead*, 49.

8. H. W. Shroeder oral history, EC.

9. Albert Mominee oral history, EC.

10. Andy Rooney interview with Joe Dawson, copy in EC.

11. Joe Pilck oral history, EC.

12. Paul Radzom and Warren Rulien oral histories, EC.

13. Andy Rooney interview with Al Smith, copy in EC.

14. Buddy Mazzara oral history, EC.

15. H. W. Shroeder oral history, EC.

16. William Dillon memoir, EC.
17. Ernie Pyle, *Ernie's War: The Best of Ernie Pyle's World War II Dispatches*, ed. David Nichols (New York: Simon & Schuster, 1986), pp. 278–80.
18. John Ellery oral history, EC.

19. TRAFFIC JAM

1. Eisenhower to Lloyd Fredendall, 2/4/43, Eisenhower Library, Abilene, Kansas.
2. Dean Rockwell oral history, EC.
3. F. S. White's handwritten after-action report, supplied to the EC by Dean Rockwell.
4. J. C. Friedman oral history, EC.
5. *Move Out, Verify: The Combat Story of the 743rd Tank Battallion* (Dallas, 1981) p. 27.
6. Paul Radzom and Edward Kelly oral histories, EC.
7. George Ryan oral history, EC.
8. Jerry Eades oral history, EC. He concluded, "Roughly, that's about what I remember of D-Day, June 6, 1944. 'Course, our real trouble didn't start till the next day, and the next and the next."
9. R. J. Lindo oral history, EC.
10. William Otlowski oral history, EC.
11. Charles Sullivan oral history, EC.
12. Warren Tate, John Costello, and Terry Hughes, *D-Day* (London: Pan Books, 1975), p. 131.
13. *Ibid.*, 132–33.
14. Devon Larson oral history, EC.
15. Exum Pike memoir, EC.
16. Don Irwin memoir, EC.
17. James Fudge oral history, EC.
18. Cornelius Ryan, *The Longest Day* (New York: Popular Library, 1959), pp. 271–72. Ryan wrote that this was the only appearance of the Luftwaffe on D-Day, but in fact there was a bombing run by JU-88s. None did any damage.
19. Robert Schober, Ray Howell, and Cecil Powers combined memoir, copy in EC.
20. Robert Miller oral history, EC.
21. Debbs Peters oral history, EC.
22. John Zmudzinski oral history, EC.
23. Allen McMath memoir, EC.
24. Al Littke oral history, EC.
25. John Mather oral history, EC.
26. Barnett Hoffner oral history, EC.
27. Frank Walk interview, EC.
28. Paul Thompson speech, copy in EC.
29. Franz Gockel memoir, EC, translated by Derek Zumbro.

20. "I AM A DESTROYER MAN"

1. Joe Smith oral history, EC.
2. Robert Giguere oral history, EC.
3. William O'Neill oral history, EC.
4. Samuel Eliot Morison, *Invasion of France and Germany 1944–1945* (Boston: Little, Brown, 1959), p. 148.

5. Owen Keeler, "From the Seaward Side," *U.S. Naval Institute Proceedings*, August 1989, p. 126.

6. William Sentry memoir, EC.

7. Ken Shiffer memoir, EC.

8. *Harding* action report, copy in EC.

9. Morison, *Invasion of France and Germany*, p. 144.

10. Ernest Hillberg oral history, EC.

11. Morison, *Invasion of France and Germany*, p. 142.

12. William Sentry memoir, EC.

13. Morison, *Invasion of France and Germany*, p. 143.

14. *Ibid.*, p. 145.

15. Edward Duffy memoir, EC.

16. Keeler, "From the Seaward Side," 126.

17. Morison, *Invasion of France and Germany*, p. 144; Keeler, "From the Seaward Side," p. 126.

18. Morison, *Invasion of France and Germany*, p. 147.

19. Robert Miller oral history, EC.

20. Robert Giguere oral history, EC.

21. William O'Neill oral history, EC.

22. Joe Smith oral history, EC.

23. James Knight, "The DD That Saved the Day," *U.S. Naval Institute Proceedings*, August 1989, pp. 124–26.

24. Morison, *Invasion of France and Germany*, p. 149.

25. *Ibid.*, p. 152.

26. William Bacon oral history, EC.

27. *Ibid.*

28. Pete Martin, "We Shot D-Day on Omaha Beach," *American Legion Magazine*, June 1964, p. 19.

29. William O'Neill oral history, EC.

30. Stanley Borkowski oral history, EC.

31. A. J. Liebling, "Reporter at Large," *New Yorker*, July 8, 1944, p. 40.

32. Ferris Burke oral history, EC.

33. Frank Fedvik oral history, EC.

34. William Sentry oral history, EC; William Carter memoir, EC; *Harding* action report, copy in EC.

35. Charles Jarreau oral history, EC.

36. Capa's account of D-Day, first published in his book *Slightly Out of Focus*, is reprinted in *Robert Capa* (New York: Grossman Publishers, 1974), pp. 68–71; Charles Jarreau oral history, EC.

37. Martin, "We Shot D-Day on Omaha Beach."

21. "Will You Tell Me How We Did This?"

1. Ronald Lane, *Rudder's Rangers* (Manassas, Va.: Ranger Associates, 1979), p. 108.

2. W. C. Heinz, "I Took My Son to Omaha Beach," *Collier's*, June 11, 1954, p. 25.

3. Donald Scribner oral history, EC.

4. Gerald Heaney oral history, EC.

5. Edwin Sorvisto, *Roughing It with Charlie: 2nd Ranger Bn.* (Plzeň, Czechoslovakia, 1945), p. 32.

6. Lane, *Rudder's Rangers*, p. 111.

7. Donald Scribner oral history, EC.

8. Sidney Salomon memoir, EC.
9. Robert Black, *Rangers in World War II* (New York: Ivy Books, 1992), p. 197.
10. Donald Scribner oral history, EC.
11. U.S. Army, Historical Section Staff, *Omaha Beachhead*, p. 75.
12. Sorvisto, *Roughing It with Charlie*, p. 28.
13. Gerald Heaney oral history, EC.
14. Sidney Salomon memoir, EC.
15. Sorvisto, *Roughing It with Charlie*, p. 34.
16. Donald Scribner oral history, EC.
17. Sorvisto, *Roughing It with Charlie*, pp. 35–36. Sorvisto wrote this pamphlet in the summer of 1945. Lieutenant Salomon told him, "Hell, yes, I will take another boat ride, preferably to the coast of Japan!"
18. Heinz, "I Took My Son to Omaha Beach," p. 25.
19. Lane, *Rudder's Rangers*, p. 78.
20. Frank South oral history, EC.
21. James Eikner oral history, EC.
22. George Kerchner oral history, EC.
23. Elmer Vermeer oral history, EC.
24. Heinz, "I Took My Son to Omaha Beach," p. 25; Elmer Vermeer oral history, EC.
25. George Kerchner oral history, EC.
26. Gene Elder oral history, EC.
27. Sigurd Sundby oral history, EC.
28. Frank South oral history, EC.
29. James Eikner oral history, EC.
30. Frank South oral history, EC.
31. George Kerchner oral history, EC.
32. *Ibid.*
33. *Ibid.*
34. James Eikner oral history, EC.
35. Frank South oral history, EC.
36. Elmer Vermeer oral history, EC.
37. James Eikner and Elmer Vermeer oral histories, EC.
38. Elmer Vermeer oral history, EC.
39. Heinz, "I Took My Son to Omaha Beach," p. 26.
40. Black, *Rangers in World War II*, p. 218.
41. Lane, *Rudder's Rangers*, p. 124.
42. *Ibid.*, p. 130.
43. Historical Division, War Department, *Omaha Beachhead*, p. 91.
44. Lane, *Rudder's Rangers*, p. 140.
45. Gene Elder oral history, EC.
46. Salva Maimone oral history, EC.
47. Elmer Vermeer oral history, EC.
48. James Eikner oral history, EC.

22. Up the Bluff at Vierville

1. Joseph Balkoski, *Beyond the Beachhead* (Harrisburg, Pa.: Stackpole, 1989), pp. 153–54.
2. Felix Branham oral history, EC.
3. Robert Walker oral history, EC.
4. 741st action report, Aug. 4, 1944, copy in EC.

5. U.S. Army, Historical Section Staff, *Omaha Beachhead*, p. 81.
6. Cecil Breeden memoir, EC.
7. Balkoski, *Beyond the Beachhead*, p. 156.
8. *Ibid.*, p. 157.
9. Shea to chief of staff, 1st Infantry Division, June 16, 1944, copy in EC.
10. Balkoski, *Beyond the Beachhead*, p. 158.
11. Robert Miller, *Division Commander: A Biography of Major General Norman D. Cota* (Spartanburg, S.C.: Reprint Company, 1989), p. 8.
12. Henry Seitzler oral history, EC.
13. Harry Parley oral history, EC.
14. Memoir to HQ Company, 116th Infantry, copy in EC.
15. Warner Hamlett oral history, EC.
16. John Raaen oral history, EC.
17. Jack Keating oral history, EC.
18. John Raaen oral history, EC.
19. Victor Fast oral history, EC.
20. Francis Dawson oral history, EC.
21. John Raaen oral history, EC.
22. George Kerchner oral history, EC.
23. Jay Mehaffey memoir, EC.
24. John Raaen oral history, EC.
25. Victor Fast oral history, EC.
26. Gale Beccue oral history, EC.
27. John Raaen oral history, EC.
28. John Raaen oral history, EC.
29. Carl Weast oral history, EC.
30. Victor Fast oral history, EC.
31. Carl Weast oral history, EC.
32. Historical Division, War Department, *Omaha Beachhead*, p. 92.

23. CATASTROPHE CONTAINED

1. Omar Bradley and Clay Blair, *A General's Life: An Autobiography* (New York: Simon & Schuster, 1983), p. 249.
2. Max Hastings, *Overlord* (New York: Simon & Schuster, 1984), p. 92.
3. Bradley and Blair, *A General's Life*, p. 251.
4. Eisenhower interview, EC.
5. Gordon A. Harrison, *Cross-Channel Attack* (Washington, D.C.: U.S. Government Printing Office, 1951), p. 320.
6. U.S. Army, Historical Section Staff, *Omaha Beachhead*, p. 87.
7. Chester Wilmot, *The Struggle for Europe* (London: Collins, 1952), p. 259.
8. Chester Hansen diary, June 6, 1944, American Military Institute archives, Carlisle, Pa.
9. Graham Cosmas and Albert Cowdrey, *The Medical Department: Medical Service in the European Theater of Operations* (Washington, D.C.: Center of Military History, U.S. Army, 1992), p. 211.
10. *Ibid.*, pp. 211–12.
11. *Ibid.*, p. 214.
12. U.S. Army, Historical Section Staff, *Omaha Beachhead*, p. 82.
13. *Harding* Action Report, June 6, 1944, copy in EC.
14. Charles Cooke diary, June 4–8, 1944, copy in EC.
15. Hyman Haas oral history, EC.

16. U.S. Army, Historical Section Staff, *Omaha Beachhead*, p. 83.
17. Al Smith lecture transcript on Operation Overlord, copy in EC.
18. U.S. Army, Historical Section Staff, *Omaha Beachhead*, p. 82.
19. *Ibid.*, p. 87.
20. *Ibid.*
21. Forrest Pogue interview with John Spaulding, copy in EC.
22. Andy Rooney interview with Joe Dawson, copy in EC.
23. Forrest Pogue interview with John Spaulding, copy in EC.
24. Al Smith lecture, copy in EC.
25. Fred Hall oral history, EC.
26. Information provided by Maj. Gen. Al Smith in letter to author, EC.
27. John Ellery oral history, EC.
28. Samuel Eliot Morison, *Invasion of France and Germany 1944–1945* (Boston: Little, Brown, 1959), p. 150.
29. Eldon Wiehe oral history, EC.
30. U.S. Army, Historical Section Staff, *Omaha Beachhead*, p. 87.
31. Bradley and Blair, *General's Life*, pp. 251–52.
32. Joseph Balkoski, *Beyond the Beachhead* (Harrisburg, Pa.: Stackpole, 1989), p. 168.

24. Struggle for the High Ground

1. John Raaen oral history, EC.
2. Paul Carell, *Invasion—They're Coming!* (New York: Dutton, 1963), pp. 83–84.
3. Carl Weast oral history, EC.
4. Donald Nelson oral history, EC.
5. William Lewis memoir, in John Robert Slaughter's collection of D-Day stories, copy in EC.
6. Pierre Piprel oral history, EC.
7. Gale Beccue oral history, EC.
8. Harry Parley oral history, EC.
9. Carl Weast oral history, EC.
10. Jay Mehaffey oral history, EC.
11. *Harding* action report, copy in EC.
12. Michel Hardelay oral history, EC.
13. John Robert Slaughter memoir, EC.
14. Historical Division, War Department, *Omaha Beachhead*, p. 95.
15. Francis Dawson oral history, EC.
16. Jay Mehaffey oral history, EC.
17. Paul Calvert memoir, EC.
18. Joseph Balkoski, *Beyond the Beachhead* (Harrisburg, Pa.: Stackpole, 1989), p. 164.
19. John Hooper oral history, EC.
20. Balkoski, *Beyond the Beachhead*, pp. 165–66.
21. Andy Rooney interview with Joe Dawson, copy in EC.
22. *Harding* action report, copy in EC.
23. Charles Ryan oral history, EC.
24. Graham Cosmas and Albert Cowdrey, *The Medical Department* (Washington, D.C.: Center of Military History, U.S. Army, 1992), p. 202.
25. Franz Gockel memoir, EC, translated by Derek Zumbro.
26. U.S. Army, Historical Section Staff, *Omaha Beachhead*, pp. 113–14; Balkoski, *Beyond the Beachhead*, pp. 171–74.

27. U.S. Army, Historical Section Staff, *Omaha Beachhead*, p. 110.
28. Carl Weast oral history, EC.

25. "IT WAS JUST FANTASTIC"

1. Oscar Rich oral history, EC.
2. Charles Cooke oral history, copy in EC.
3. Vince Schlotterbeck letter to "Dear Friends," May 22, 1945, copy in EC.
4. M. C. Marquis oral history, EC.
5. Historical Division, War Department, *Omaha Beachhead*, p. 102.
6. *Ibid.*, p. 104.
7. *Ibid.*; *The "B" Battery Story: The 116th AAA Gun Battalion (Mobile) with the First U.S. Army* (Passaic, N.J.: The B Battery Association, 1990).
8. Dean Rockwell oral history, EC.
9. Ernest Hemingway, "Voyage to Victory," *Collier's*, July 22, 1944.
10. James Roberts oral history, EC.
11. Gordon A. Harrison, *Cross-Channel Attack* (Washington, D.C.: Dept. of the Army, 1951), p. 333.
12. David Irving, *Hitler's War* (New York: Viking, 1977), p. 639.
13. U.S. Army, Historical Section Staff, *Omaha Beachhead*, p. 115.
14. Joseph Goebbels, *The Goebbels Diaries* (Garden City, N.Y.: Doubleday, 1948) p. 620.
15. Irving, *Hitler's War*, p. 640.
16. Eisenhower to Marshall, June 6, 1944, EL.
17. Harry Butcher diary, June 6, 1944, EL.
18. *Newsweek*, June 19, 1944.
19. Henry Seitzler oral history, EC.
20. Robert Healey oral history, EC.

26. THE WORLD HOLDS ITS BREATH

1. Unsigned piece in the *Helena Independent-Record*, June 6, 1944.
2. *New Orleans Times Picayune*, June 7, 1944.
3. Judy Barrett Litoff and David C. Smith, *Since You Went Away: World War II Letters from American Women on the Home Front* (New York: Oxford University Press, 1991), p. 149.
4. *Ibid.*, p. 140.
5. Dwight Eisenhower interview, EC.
6. *New Yorker*, June 10, 1944.
7. From a CBS advertisement quoting letters received on the network's D-Day coverage, in the July 15, 1944, *New Yorker*.
8. *New York Times*, June 7, 1944.
9. *New Yorker*, June 10, 1944.
10. *Ibid.*
11. *New York Times*, June 7, 1944.
12. *Ibid.*
13. *Time*, June 12, 1944.
14. *Wall Street Journal*, June 7, 1944.
15. *New York Times*, June 7, 1944.
16. *New Yorker*, June 14, 1944.
17. *New York Times*, June 7, 1944.

18. *Ibid.*
19. Dwight D. Eisenhower, *Letters to Mamie* (Garden City, N.Y.: Doubleday, 1978), pp. 184–85.
20. *Ibid.*, p. 189; *Time*, June 14, 1944.
21. *Washington Post*, June 7, 1944.
22. *New York Times*, June 7, 1944.
23. *Ibid.*
24. *Time*, June 14, 1944.
25. *Bedford Bulletin*, June 8, July 6, July 20, 1944.
26. *New Orleans Times Picayune*, June 7, 1944.
27. *Ibid.*
28. *New York Times*, June 7, 1944.
29. *Ohio State Journal* (Columbus), June 7, 1944.
30. *Columbus Evening Dispatch*, June 6, 1944; *Columbus Star*, June 7, 1944.
31. *Milwaukee Journal*, June 7, 1944.
32. *Atlanta Constitution*, June 7, 1944.
33. *Missoulian*, June 7, 1944.
34. *Helena Independent Record*, June 7, 1944.
35. *Atlanta Constitution*, June 7, 1944.
36. *Helena Independent Record*, June 7, 1944.
37. *Newsweek*, June 19, 1944.
38. Mollie Panter-Downes, "Letter from London," *New Yorker*, June 10, 1944.
39. "Letter from London," *New Yorker*, June 17, 1944.
40. *The Times* (London), June 7, 1944.
41. *Ibid.*
42. A. M. Sperber, *Murrow: His Life and Times* (New York: Freundlich Books, 1986), p. 241.
43. Warren Tute, John Costell, and Terry Hughes, *D-Day* (London: Pan Books, 1975), p. 225.
44. Anthony Brooks oral history, EC.
45. Gertrude Stein, *Wars I Have Seen* (London: B. T. Batsford, 1945), p. 162.
46. Daniel Lang, "Letter from Rome," *New Yorker*, June 17, 1944.
47. Anne Frank, *The Diary of a Young Girl*, tr. B. M. Mooyaart (New York: Doubleday, 1967), pp. 266–68.
48. *Time*, June 17, 1944.
49. Alexander Werth, *Russia at War, 1941–1945* (New York: Dutton, 1964), pp. 853–55.
50. *The Times* (London), June 7, 1944.

27. Fairly Stuffed with Gadgets

1. Imperial War Museum interview with Hammerton, copy in EC.
2. Imperial War Museum interview with Kenneth Ferguson, copy in EC.
3. Imperial War Museum interview with Cyril Hendry, copy in EC.
4. Imperial War Museum interview with George Honour, copy in EC.
5. Imperial War Museum interview with Kenneth Ferguson, copy in EC.
6. L. F. Ellis, *Victory in the West* (London: H.M. Stationery Office, 1962), 1: 212–13.
7. Stephen E. Ambrose, *Eisenhower: Soldier, General of the Army, President-Elect 1880–1952* (New York: Simon & Schuster, 1983), p. 300.

8. F. H. Hinsley, *British Intelligence in the Second World War* (New York: Cambridge University Press, 1981), pp. 134–35.

9. Paul Carell, *Invasion—They're Coming!* (New York: Dutton, 1963), p. 89.

10. Warren Tute, John Costello, and Terry Hughes, *D-Day* (London: Pan Books, 1975), p. 197.

11. *Ibid.*

28. "EVERYTHING WAS WELL ORDERED"

1. Warren Tute, John Costello, and Terry Hughes, *D-Day* (London: Pan Books, 1975), p. 197.

2. Russell Miller interview with Pat Blamey, copy in EC.

3. Tute, Costello, and Hughes, *D-Day*, p. 174.

4. *Ibid.*, p. 175.

5. Russell Miller interview with Pat Blamey, copy in EC.

6. Ronald Seaborne memoir, EC.

7. Brian T. Whinney oral history, EC.

8. Joseph Barrett memoir, EC.

9. Gordon A. Harrison, *Cross-Channel Attack* (Washington, D.C.: U.S. Government Printing Office, 1951), pp. 330–31.

10. Ronald Seaborne memoir, EC.

11. Tute, Costello, and Hughes, *D-Day*, p. 202.

12. André Heintz interview, EC.

13. Tute, Costello, and Hughes, *D-Day*, p. 202.

14. Brian T. Whinney oral history, EC.

29. PAYBACK

1. John Keegan, *Six Armies in Normandy: From D-Day to the Liberation of Paris* (New York: Penguin Books, 1983), p. 130.

2. IWM interview with Josh Honan, EC.

3. Gerald Henry oral history, EC.

4. Keegan, *Six Armies in Normandy*, pp. 132–33.

5. Gerald Henry oral history, EC.

6. Keegan, *Six Armies in Normandy*, p. 138.

7. IWM interview with John Honan, EC.

8. Imperial War Museum interview with Roland Johnston, copy in EC.

9. Tom Plumb memoir, EC.

10. Russell Miller interview with Sigie Johnson, EC.

11. Warren Tute, John Costello, and Terry Hughes, *D-Day* (London: Pan Books, 1975), p. 207.

12. Reginald Roy, *1944: The Canadians in Normandy* (Ottawa: Canadian War Museum, 1984), p. 13.

13. Tute, Costello, and Hughes, *D-Day*, p. 209.

14. Robert Rogge oral history, EC.

15. G. W. Levers diary, copy in EC.

16. IWM interview with Roland Johnston, copy in EC.

17. Russell Miller interview with Cyril Hendry, EC. See also David Howart, *Dawn of D-Day* (London: Collins, 1959), pp. 218–21.

18. Gerald Henry oral history, EC.

19. Russell Miller interview with Sigie Johnson, EC.

20. Tute, Costello, and Hughes, *D-Day*, p. 209.
21. Keegan, *Six Armies in Normandy*, pp. 137–38.
22. Roy, *1944: The Canadians in Normandy*, pp. 16–17.
23. *Ibid.*, p. 15.
24. Stanley Dudka oral history, EC.
25. Robert Rogge oral history, EC.
26. Stanley Dudka oral history, EC.
27. Gerald Henry oral history, EC.
28. G. W. Levers diary, copy in EC.
29. Roy, *1944: The Canadians in Normandy*, pp. 22–23.
30. Keegan, *Six Armies in Normandy*, p. 142.

30. "An Unforgettable Sight"

1. Rupert Curtis memoir, copy in EC.
2. Russell Miller interview with Kenneth Ferguson, EC.
3. *Slazak* action report, 6/6/44, copy in EC.
4. Russell Miller interview with Etienne Robert Webb, EC.
5. M. R. D. Foot interview, EC.
6. Interview with Robert Piauge, EC.
7. Russell Miller interview with R. Porteous, EC.
8. Kenneth Wright to his parents, 6/11/44, copy in EC.
9. Rupert Curtis memoir, EC.
10. Harold Pickersgill interview, EC.
11. Jacqueline Thornton interview, EC.
12. Harry Nomburg oral history, EC.
13. Peter Masters oral history, EC.
14. Paul Carell, *Invasion—They're Coming!* (New York: Dutton, 1963), pp. 98–101; John Brown oral history, EC.
15. Napier Crookenden, *Drop Zone Normandy* (New York: Scribners, 1976), p. 235.
16. Rupert Curtis memoir, EC.

31. "My God, We've Done It"

1. Jack Bailey oral history, EC.
2. John Howard interview, EC.
3. Richard Todd interview, EC.
4. Todd Sweeney interview, EC.
5. Wally Parr interview, EC.
6. Nigel Taylor interview, EC.
7. Wagger Thornton interview, EC.
8. John Howard interview, EC.
9. Hans von Luck interview, EC.
10. Werner Kortenhaus interview, EC.
11. Peter Masters oral history, EC.
12. *By Air to Battle: The Official Account of the British First and Sixth Airborne Divisions* (London: H.M. Stationery Office, 1945), p. 87.
13. Peter Masters oral history, EC.
14. John Durnford-Slater, *Commando: Memoirs of a Fighting Commando in World War Two* (Annapolis, Md.: Naval Institute Press, 1991), pp. 192–93.
15. Nigel Taylor interview, EC.

16. Wally Parr interview, EC.

17. Huw Wheldon, *Red Berets into Normandy* (Norwich: Jarrold & Sons, 1982), p. 16.

18. Napier Crookenden, *Drop Zone Normandy* (New York: Scribners, 1976), p. 231.

19. Imperial War Museum interview with J. Tillett, EC.

20. Crookenden, *Drop Zone Normandy*, p. 228.

21. Nigel Taylor interview, EC.

32. "When Can Their Glory Fade?"

1. IWM interview with Josh Honan, EC.
2. John Robert Slaughter memoir, EC.
3. John Raaen oral history, EC.
4. Harry Parley oral history, EC.
5. Jack Bailey oral history, EC.
6. John Reville oral history, EC.
7. Robert Zafft oral history, EC.
8. Felix Branham oral history, EC.
9. John Ellery oral history, EC.
10. Ramsay diary entry provided by Bob Love.
11. Richard Winters oral history and diary, EC.
12. Walter Cronkite interview with Eisenhower, copy in EC.

Bibliography

Air Ministry. *By Air to Battle: The Official Account of the British First and Sixth Airborne Divisions.* London: H. M. Stationery Office, 1945.

Ambrose, Stephen E. *Band of Brothers: E Company, 506th Regiment, 101st Airborne: From Normandy to Hitler's Eagle's Nest.* New York: Simon & Schuster, 1992.

———. *Eisenhower: Soldier, General of the Army, President-Elect, 1890–1952.* New York: Simon & Schuster, 1983.

———. *Eisenhower: Soldier and President.* New York: Simon & Schuster, 1990.

———. *Ike's Spies: Eisenhower and the Espionage Establishment.* Garden City, N.Y.: Doubleday, 1981.

———. *Pegasus Bridge: June 6, 1944.* New York: Simon & Schuster, 1985.

———. *The Supreme Commander: The War Years of General Dwight D. Eisenhower.* Garden City: Doubleday, 1971.

Ambrose, Stephen E. and James A. Barber, editors. *The Military and American Society: Essays and Readings.* New York: The Free Press, 1972.

Balkoski, Joseph. *Beyond the Beachhead: The 29th Infantry Division in Normandy.* Harrisburg, Pa.: Stackpole, 1989.

"B" Battery. *The "B" Battery Story: The 116th AAA Gun Battalion with the First U.S. Army.* Passaic, N.J.: The B Battery Association, 1990.

Blair, Clay. *Ridgway's Paratroopers: The American Airborne in World War II*. Garden City, N.Y.: Doubleday, 1985.

Brown, Anthony Cave. *Bodyguard of Lies*. New York: Harper & Row, 1975.

Capa, Robert. *Robert Capa*. New York: Grossman, 1974.

Carell, Paul. *Invasion—They're Coming: The German Account of the Allied Landings and the 80 Days' Battle for France*. New York: Dutton, 1963.

Churchill, Winston S. *Closing the Ring*. (Vol. 5 of *The Second World War*.) Boston: Houghton Mifflin, 1952.

Craven, Wesley Frank, and James Lea Cate, eds. *Europe: Argument to V-E Day, January 1944 to V-E Day*. (Vol. 3 of *The Army Air Forces in World War II*.) Chicago: University of Chicago Press, 1951.

Cosby, Harry. *A Wing and a Prayer*. New York: HarperCollins, 1993.

Cosmas, Graham, and Albert Cowdrey. *The Medical Department: Medical Services in the European Theater of Operations*. Washington, D.C.: Center of Military History, U.S. Army, 1992.

D'Este, Carol. *Decision in Normandy*. London: Collins, 1983.

Durnford-Slater, John. *Commando: Memoirs of a Fighting Commando in World War Two*. Annapolis: Naval Institute Press, 1991.

Eisenhower, Dwight D. *At Ease: Stories I Tell to Friends*. Garden City, N.Y.: Doubleday, 1967.

———. *Crusade in Europe*. Garden City, N.Y.: Doubleday, 1948.

———. *Letters to Mamie*. Edited by John S. D. Eisenhower. Garden City, N.Y.: Doubleday, 1978.

Ellis, L.F. *Victory in the West*, vol. 1, *The Battle of Normandy*. London: H. M. Stationery Office, 1962.

Fane, Francis. *Naked Warriors*. New York: Prentice-Hall, 1956.

Foot, M. R. D. *SOE: The Special Operations Executive 1940–1946*. London: BBC, 1984.

Fussell, Paul. *Wartime: Understanding and Behavior in the Second World War*. New York: Oxford University Press, 1989.

Glassman, Henry. *"Lead the Way, Rangers:" A History of the Fifth Ranger Battalion*. Printed in Germany, 1945.

Goebbels, Joseph. *The Goebbels Diaries: The Last Days*. Edited and translated by Louis Lochner, New York: Doubleday, 1948.

Haffner, Sebastian. *The Meaning of Hitler*. Translated by E. Osers. Cambridge, Mass.: Harvard University Press, 1979.

Harrison, Gordon A. *Cross-Channel Attack*. Washington, D.C.: Office of the Chief of Military History, Department of the Army, 1951.

Hastings, Max. *Overlord: D-Day and the Battle for Normandy*. New York: Simon & Schuster, 1984.

Heinz, W. C. "I Took My Son to Omaha Beach." *Collier's*, June 11, 1954.

Hemingway, Ernest. "Voyage to Victory." *Collier's*, July 22, 1944.

Hinsley, F. H. *British Intelligence in the Second World War: Its Influence on Strategy and Operations*. New York: Cambridge University Press, 1981.

Historical Section European Theater of Operations Staff, eds. *Utah Beach to Cherbourg*. Nashville, Tenn.: Battery Press, 1984.

Howarth, David. *Dawn of D-Day*. London: Collins, 1959.

Irving, David. *Hitler's War*. New York: Viking, 1977.

————. *The Trail of the Fox: The Search for the True Field Marshal Rommel*. New York: Dutton, 1977.

Johnson, Gerden. *History of the Twelfth Infantry Regiment in World War II*. Boston: 4th Division Association, 1947.

Keegan, John. *Six Armies in Normandy: From D-Day to the Liberation of Paris*. New York: Penguin Books, 1983.

Keeler, Owen. "From the Seaward Side." *U. S. Naval Institute Proceedings*, August 1989.

Knight, James. "The DD That Saved the Day." *U.S. Naval Institute Proceedings*, August 1989.

Lane, Ronald. *Rudder's Rangers*. Manassas, Va.: Ranger Associates, 1979.

Lang, Daniel. "Letter from Rome." *New Yorker*. June 17, 1944.

Langdon, Allen. *"Ready:" A World War II History of the 505th Parachute Infantry Regiment*. Indianapolis, Ind.: 82nd Airborne Division Association, 1986.

Lee, Ulysses. *The Employment of Negro Troops*. Washington, D.C.: Office of the Chief of Military History, 1966.

Lewin, Ronald. *Ultra Goes to War*. London: Hutchinson, 1978.

Liebling, A. J. "Reporter at Large." *New Yorker*. July 8 and 15, 1944.

Litoff, Judy Barrett, and David C. Smith, eds. *Since You Went Away: World War II Letters From American Women on the Home Front*. New York: Oxford University Press, 1991.

Luck, Hans von. *Panzer Commander: The Memoirs of Colonel Hans von Luck*. New York: Praeger, 1989.

Marshall, S. L. A. "First Wave at Omaha Beach." *Atlantic Monthly*, November 1960.

————. *Night Drop: The American Airborne Invasion of Normandy*. Boston: Little, Brown, 1962.

Martin, Pete. "We Shot D-Day on Omaha Beach." *American Legon Magazine*, June 1964.

Masterman, J. C. *The Double-Cross System in the War of 1939–1945*. New Haven: Yale University Press, 1972.

Miller, Robert. *Division Commander: A Biography of Major General Norman D. Cota*. Spartanburg, S.C.: The Reprint Co., 1989.

Mitcham, Samuel. *Rommel's Last Battle: The Desert Fox and the Normandy Campaign*. New York: Stein & Day, 1983.

Montgomery, Bernard Law. *Memoirs*. Cleveland: World, 1958.

Morgan, Kay Summersby. *Past Forgetting: My Love Affair with Dwight D. Eisenhower*. New York: Simon & Schuster, 1976.

Morison, Samuel Eliot. *The Invasion of France and Germany, 1944–1945*. (Vol. 11 of *History of United States Naval Operations in World War II*.) Boston: Little, Brown, 1959.

Panter-Downes, Mollie. "Letter from London." *New Yorker*, June 10, 1944.

Parrish, Thomas, ed. *The Simon and Schuster Encyclopedia of World War II*. New York: Simon & Schuster, 1978.

Perret, Geoffrey. *There's A War to Be Won: The United States Army in World War II.* New York: Random House, 1992.

Pogue, Forrest C. *The Supreme Command.* Washington, D.C.: Office of the Chief of Military History, Department of the Army, 1954.

Pyle, Ernie. *Ernie's War: The Best of Ernie Pyle's World War II Dispatches.* Edited by David Nichols. New York: Simon & Schuster, 1986.

Reeder, Russell. *Born at Reveille.* New York: Duell, Sloan & Pearce, 1966.

Rommel, Erwin. *The Rommel Papers.* Edited by B. H. Liddell Hart. New York: Harcourt, Brace, 1953.

Roy, Reginald. *1944: The Canadians in Normandy.* Ottawa: Canadian War Museum, 1984.

Ryan, Cornelius. *The Longest Day: June 6, 1944.* New York: Popular Library, 1959.

Sommers, Martin. "The Longest Hour in History." *Saturday Evening Post,* July 8, 1944.

Sorvisto, Edwin. *Roughing It with Charlie: 2nd Ranger Bn.* Pilzen, Czechoslovakia, 1945.

Sperber, A. M. *Murrow: His Life and Times.* New York: Freundlich, 1986.

Tedder, Sir Arthur. *With Prejudice.* London: Cassell, 1966.

Tute, Warren, John Costello, and Terry Hughes. *D-Day.* London: Pan Books, 1975.

U.S. Army, Historical Section Staff, *Omaha Beachhead: June 6–June 13, 1944.* Nashville, Tenn.: Battery Press, 1984.

U.S. War Department. *Handbook on German Military Forces.* Baton Rouge: Louisiana State University Press, 1990.

Vallavieille, Michel de. *D-Day at Utah Beach.* Coutances, Normandy, 1982.

Warlimont, Walter. *Inside Hitler's Headquarters, 1939–1945.* New York: Praeger, 1964.

Weigley, Russell. *Eisenhower's Lieutenants: The Campaigns of France and Germany, 1944–1945.* Bloomington: Indiana University Press, 1981.

Werth, Alexander. *Russia at War, 1941–1945.* New York: Dutton, 1964.

Wheldon, Huw. *Red Berets into Normandy.* Norwich: Jarrold, 1982.

Wilmot, Chester. *The Struggle for Europe.* London: Collins, 1952.

Ziemke, Earle. "Operation Kreml: Deception, Strategy, and the Fortunes of War." *Parameters: Journal of the U.S. Army War College,* 9 (March 1979): 72–81.

Appendix A

Veterans who contributed oral histories
or written memoirs
to the Eisenhower Center
as of August 13, 1993

Marion H. Adams
Robert Adams
Ray Aebischer
John L. Ahearn
Nicholas Aiavolasiti
Roger L. Airgood
Harold Akridge
Lloyd Alberts
Parker A. Alford *deceased*
Bob Allen *deceased*
Daniel Allen
Weldon J. Allen
Harry C. Allison
Alfred Allred
John S. Allsup
Will Alpern
Al Alvarez
Alan Anderson
Clifford Anderson

Louise S. Armstrong
James E. Arnold *deceased*
Benjamin Arthur, Sr.
Earl Asker *deceased*
Edward A. Askew
William A. Atkins
Carl Atwell
Theo G. Aufort
C. R. Ault
John C. Ausland
Cyrus C. Aydlett

Peter P. Bachmeier
W. Garwood Bacon, Jr. *deceased*
Steve Baehren
Jack Bailey *deceased*
Roderick Bain
Arthur Baker *deceased*
Fred J. Baker

Leland A. Baker *deceased*
Ray Ballard
Charles A. Barbier
Harry C. Bare
Jack R. Barensfeld
Edward Barnes
John J. Barnes
Joseph Barrett
Robert B. Barrix
W. Arthur Barrow
Armond Barth
Farr H. Barto
Eugene H. Barton
James A. Batte
Harold Baumgarten, M.D.
Sherman L. Baxter
Jacques Bayer
Goebel Baynes
James H. Bearden
Sam Walter Bears *deceased*
Briand N. Beaudin
Gale B. Beccue
John A. Beck
Raymond F. Bednar
Howard Beebe
Charles Beecham
Frank Beetle
Daniel R. Beirne
Bryan Bel
Joe Belardo
Leo T. Bement
Donald Bennett
Ronald Bennett
Wilfred Bennett *deceased*
Arden Benthien
Max Berger
William E. Bergmann
Edward Bergstrom
I. R. Berkowitz
Eugene Bernstein
Edwin J. Best
Richard Betts
Bryan Beu
A. R. Beyer

John Biddle
Grandison K. Bienvenu
Ted Billnitzer
Dick Bills
Sidney V. Bingham
Doug Birch
Gordon D. Bishop
Wallace Bishop
John E. Bistrica
John R. Blackburn
Pat Blamey
Joseph S. Blaylock, Sr.
Earl Blocker
Rans Blondo
Edward C. Boccafogli
Jeff Bodenweiser
Robert L. Bogart
Vernal Boline
Calhoun Bond
Letterio R. Bongiorno
Milton Boock
John D. Boone
Everett L. Booth *deceased*
Stan Booth
Stanley Borkowski
Charles Bortzfield
Donald E. Bosworth
Donald G. Botens
Paul Bouchereau
William Boulet
Bill Bowdidge
Ellis C. Boyce
Sgt. Maj. Robert J. Boyda
James C. Boyett
William Boykin
Leo D. Boyle
Bruce D. Bradley
Holdbrook Bradley
Felix P. Branham
James W. Brannen
John Braud
Cecil Breeden
Earle Breeding
Warren R. Breniman

John V. Brennan
William O. Brenner
Robert (Bob) Brewer
Michael A. Brienze
Eugene D. Brierre
Calvin Bright
Mrs. Dorothy Brinkley
Harold E. Brodd
Geoff W. Bromfield
Anthony M. Brooks
John Brooks
Bob Brothers
Sam Broussard
Floyd L. Brown
John G. Brown
Owen L. Brown
Sid Brown
James J. Bruen
Roger L. Brugger
J. Frank Brumbaugh
August Bruno
Phil H. Bucklew   *deceased*
Morris Buckmaster
David Buffalo
Nile Buffington
J. R. Buller
Tom Burgess
Ferris Burke
Ralph R. Burnett
Dwayne T. Burns
Major Thomas V. Burns
Chester Butcher
Robert Butler
Nicholas F. Butrico
Ltc. C. D. Butte
Pat Butters

Tom Cadwallader
Paul Calvert
Joseph L. Camera
Bob Cameron
Donald Campbell
Herbert Campbell   *deceased*

Arthur R. Candelaria
Harold O. Canyon
Robert Capa
John C. Capell
Dr. Aaron Caplan
George Capon
Carl D. Carden
Homer F. Carey
Elmer Carmichael
Jim Carmichael
Harry Carroll
Gordon F. Carson
Donald Carter
Jack Carter
William A. Carter
Carl Cartledge
Kenneth H. Cassens
Richard Cassiday
Joseph Castellano
Coy Chandler
Sidney S. Chapin, Jr.
Eugene Chase
Angelos T. Chatas
N. J. Chelenza
Frank Chesney
Jules Chicoine
Aubrey Childs
Carl Christ
Burton P. Christenson
Burton Christianson
Donald C. Chumley
Arthur Ciechoski
Richard Clancy
Elmer W. Clarey
Asa V. Clark, Jr.
Richard C. Clawson II
William Clayton
Michel M. Clemencon
Nigel Clogstorm
B. A. Coats
Murray Codman
John Colby
Lorell Coleman
John Collins

Richard H. Conley
Henry L. Conner
Ralph E. Cook
Charles M. Cooke, Jr.
Willard F. Coonen
W. R. Copeland
Ed Corbett
Jack Corbett
Tom Corcoran
Kenneth Cordry
Christopher Cornazzani
A. H. Corry
S. Coupe
Milton A. Courtright
Jerry Cowle
Clarence Cox
Joseph Cox
James J. Coyle
Roy E. Creek
Ralph Crenshaw
Theodore Crocker
Dr. Michael Crofoot   deceased
Art Cross
Russell Crossman
Robert Crousore
Jack Crowley
Tom Cruse, Jr.
Jack T. Curtis
Rupert Curtis
Isadore E. Cutler

Lord Dacre of Glanton
Mike Dagner
Joseph A. Dahlia
Carlton Dailey
Robert L. Dains
Edward Daly
Gerald Darr
Charles W. Dauer
Sam P. Daugherty
Dave Davidson
Phillip B. Davidson
Gary S. Davis   deceased
Robert L. Davis
Francis W. Dawson

John R. Dawson
Joseph Dawson
Robert Dawson   deceased
Victor J. Day
William Dean
William J. Decarlton
Arthur Defilippo
Louise Deflon
Arthur Defranco   deceased
Irish Degnan
Kenneth T. Delaney
Robert L. Delashaw
Vincent J. Del Guidice, M.D.
Igor De Lissovoy
Ralph Della-Volpe
Michael Deloney
James M. Delong
John P. Delury
Richard H. Denison
William Denton
Roger Derderian
Morton Descherer
Howard R. Devault
John J. Devink
Ralph E. Deweese   deceased
Antonia R. Didonna
Dominic Diliberto
Gerard M. Dillon
William T. Dillon
David Doehrman
Joseph A. Dolan
Leo Dolan
Joseph Dominguez
Richard Donaghy
Joseph Donlan
"Ike" Dorsey
Joseph Dougherty
Cliff Douglas
Dow L. Dowler
Ralph Dragoo
Joseph A. Dragotto
Ronald J. Drez
James H. Drumwright, Jr.
Stanley Dudka
Edward T. Duffy

Anthony Duke
Lewis Duke
John Dunnigan
Kenneth Dykes

Jerry W. Eades
James Eads
Ted Eaglen
B. Ralph Eastridge
Eugene E. Eckstam
James Edward
Arlo Edwards
Donald K. Edwards
Malcolm G. Edwards
J. Frank Ehrman
Thomas Eichler
James Eikner
Harry Eisen
Dwight D. Eisenhower *deceased*
Gene E. Elder
George Eldridge
John B. Ellery
John S. Elleshope
George Elsey
John Englehart
Donald Ennett
John L. Erexson
Clay Ernest
Frank Ernest, Jr.
Rudi Escher
Joseph H. Esclavon
Don Eutzy
Carl Evans
Robert L. Evans
James M. Everett

Bobby Fachiri
Richard P. Fahey, M.D.
John T. Fanning
Victor H. Fast
William E. Faust
Frank R. Feduik
Jacob A. Feigion
Bernard S. Feinberg
Max Feldman

Andrew A. Fellner
Col Ferguson
Mary Ferrell
Richard Ferris
H. Fielder
Lewis Finkelstein
Martin Finkelstein
James F. Finn
Richard Fiscus
P. L. Fitts
John E. Fitzgerald
Steve Fitzgerald
Barry Fixler
Maro Flagg
Tony Flamio *deceased*
Richard S. Fleming
Rev. K. Fletcher
Arthur Flinner
Robert A. Flory
Hilton M. Floyd
Edward J. Foley
Michael R. D. Foot
George Forteville
George P. Fory
Thomas J. Fournier
Benjamin T. Frana
Geoffrey B. Frank
Benjamin Frans
Richard A. Freed, Sr.
George Freedman
Roger Freeman
Herbert A. Freemark
Alfred L. Freiburger
Max Friedlander
J. C. Friedman
Murray Friedman
James T. Fudge, Ph.D.
Dan Furlong

Steve Gabre
Francis Gabreski
Frank Gaccione
Clair R. Galdonik
Edwin M. Gale
Edward P. Gallogly

Paul Gardiner
Howard C. Gates
Parker Gathings
Ralph Gault
Paul E. Gauthier
Sims S. Gauthier
William Gentry   deceased
Henry Gerald
Edward Gerard
Hon. Sam M. Gibbons
Gerald Gibbs
William D. Gibbs, Jr.
Joseph P. Gibney
Edward S. Giers
Melvin R. Gift
Robert Giguere
Jack Gilfry
Edward B. Giller
Ed Gilleran
James L. Gilligan
Solon B. Gilmore
Thomas J. Gintjee
John Girolamo
Thomas J. Glennon
Emanuel E. Gluck
Edward J. Gnatowski
Franz Gockel
Russell C. Goddard
Harry Goldberg
Glen Golden
Henry L. Goldsmith
Lawrence Goldstein
Bryan L. Good
George W. Goodspeed
Ralph E. Goranson
Walter Gordon
Victor Gore
Harry D. Graham
Dick Granet
Dennis G. Gray
Jack Gray
Leslie B. Gray
Elmer R. Green
Joseph L. Green
David Greenberg

John Montgomery Greene
Gordon Emerson Greenlaw
Gabriel N. Greenwood
John Greenwood
Richard Gresso
Bill Grey
Leslie Grice
Len Griffing
O. T. Grimes
Maxwell Grimm
R. K. Grondin
Lyle Groundwater.
Samuel N. Grundfast
Charlie Guarino
William Guarnere
Stanley Guess
Carroll Guidry
Grant G. Gullickson
Martin Gutekunst
Forrest Guth
Mariano Guy

Hyman Haas
George R. Hackett
Tim Hackney
Harry T. Hagaman
William J. Hahn
Earl Hale
Fred W. Hall, Jr.
Raymond Hall
Robert A. Hall
Patricia Hamas
J. H. Hamilton
Warner H. Hamlett
Dorr Hampton
Clayton E. Hanks
Curtis Hansen
Michel Hardelay
Randy Hardy
Herman Hareland
John Hargesheimer
David Harmon
William E. Harness
Charles E. Harris
Fred Harris

Leslie Harris
Clarence Hart
William Hart
Rainer Hartmetz
George E. Hartshorn
C. G. Hasselfeldt
J. K. Havener
Douglas Hawkins
Wallace B. Hawkins
Robert L. Hayes, III
Robert L. Healey
Gerald W. Heaney
Bennie L. Heathman
Charles W. Heins
André Heintz
Beatrice Heller
B. P. Henderson
Ted Henderson
Cyril Hendry
Gerald M. Henry
Leonard F. Herb
Paul Hernandez
Leo Heroux
Andrew Hertz
R. Hesketh
Clarence Hester
James W. Hewitt
Frederick von der Heydte
Victor Hicken
Howard W. Hicks
Lindley R. Higgins
Henry J. Hill
Howard Hill
James Hill
O. B. Hill
Ernest Hillberg
John D. Hinton
Herman Frank Hinze
Newal Hobbs
Robert A. Hobbs
G. K. Hodenfield
Jack L. Hodgkinson
Marion C. Hoffman
Ted Hoffmeister
Barnett Hoffner

James F. Hogan
David Holbrook
James G. Holland
Penny Gooch Holloway
Major Donald Holman
Bill Holmes
Frank Holmes
Bob Holsher
John Honan
Josh Honan
Ed H. Honnen
George Honour
John Hooper
Thomas A. Horne
Merwin H. Horner, Jr.
A. W. Horton
Nathaniel R. Hoskot
Warren Hotard
Colin Howard
E. D. Howard
Frank O. Howard
John Howard
Raymond Howell
Charles M. Huber
Tony Hubert
Jerry Hudson
Charles Huff
Dan Hugger
R. R. Hughart
A. H. Hultman
Harry Hunt
Albert W. Huntley
Ernie Husted
George Hutnick
Bernard F. Hydo

Jack Ihle
Jack Ilfrey
Bill Irving
Don Irwin
Jack R. Isaacs
Orville Iverson

Sam Jacks
Col. C. L. Jackson

Quiles R. Jacobs
Jack Jacobsen
Arthur Jahnke
Alma Jakobson
Herbert M. James   deceased
Charles Jarreau
Ralph Jenkins
Steve Jenkins
Henry D. Jennings
James Jennings
Leroy Jennings
Edward J. Jeziorski
Harry Johnson
Lagrande K. Johnson
Russell Johnson
Steve Johnson
George H. Johnston
Roland Johnston
David M. Jones
Edward G. Jones, Jr.
George A. Jones
J. Elmo Jones
J. W. Jones
James A. Jones
Oscar W. Jones
William E. Jones
William H. Jones
Captain Jordan
Erik M. Juleen

John Kaheny
Albert Kamento
Chris Kanaras
Robert Karwoski
Thomas S. Kattar
M. B. Kauffman
Robert E. Kaufman   deceased
Jack Keating
Elbert Keel
Ned F. Kegler
Steve Kellman
Dr. Edward J. Kelly
Robert Kelly
John Kemp
Edward Kempton

Frank J. Kennedy
Harry Kennedy   deceased
George Kerchner
Ester Kesler
Leslie W. Kick
Maurice Kiddler   deceased
William C. Kiessel
R. H. Kilburn
William Kilgore   deceased
Jack D. Kill
Jerry R. Kimball   deceased
John T. King, III
Russell King
William L. King
Lorin D. Kinsel
Trenton L. Knack
George Kobe
Harvey W. Koenig
Vincent A. Kordack
Werner Kortenhaus
Walter T. Kozack
David Koziczkowski
Chester Kozik
Weldon L. Kratzer
Herb Krauss
E. Krieger
Raymond Kristoff
James A. Krucas
M. G. Kruglinski
L. M. Kuenzi
Major Frank J. Kuhn, Jr.
Clemens Kujawa
Peter Kukurba
William Kupp
A. W. Kuppers
Bob Kurtz
James Q. Kurz
R. Ben Kuykendall

Ivan Ladany
Richard G. Laine, Jr.
George Lane
Gilbert H. Lane
Devon G. Larson
Lance Larson

John L. Latham
Wood Lathrop Lawrence
George Lawson
Howard A. Lawson
Reverend Bill Layton
Ken Lease
Leonard Lebenson
Thomas Lee
Wesley T. Leeper
William H. Lefevre
Elbert E. Legg
George Leidenheimer
Paul Lello
G. W. Levers *deceased*
Ronald Lewin
John R. Lewis, Jr.
Robert L. Lewis
William Lewis
Leo K. Lick
Elinor Lilley
R. J. Lindo
Ruth S. Linley
C. Carwood Lipton
Lou Lisko
Al Littke *deceased*
John Livingston
Warren R. Lloyd
Bill Lodge
Ralph Logan
Donald E. Loker
Joe Lola
Noah F. Lomax
Leonard Lomell
James A. Long
William R. Long, Sr.
Paul Longrigg
Kenneth P. Lord
Roger V. Lovelace
David Lownds
Hans von Luck
Walter Lukasavage, Jr.
Ewell B. Lunsford *deceased*
George Luz
Lou Lyle
Edward Lynch, Jr.

Thomas Lynch

Frederick Macdonald
Edward P. Mackenzie
John Mackenzie
John H. MacPhee
George W. Madison
Donald J. Magilligan *deceased*
Salva P. Maimone
Lou Mais
Frederick C. Maisel, Jr.
Don Malarkey
Edith Manford
Ray A. Mann *deceased*
Moses Defriese Manning
Bob Maras
Jim Marine
Maynard C. Marquis
John Marshall
Paul M. Marshall
Billy Martin
Herbert F. Martin
Homer Martin
John Martin
Peter Martin
Russell Martin
Thomas Martin
Walter Martini
Alexander Marzenoski
Stan Mason
Peter Masters
John Mather
Captain Russ Mathers
S. H. Matheson
Robert Mathias *deceased*
Robert Mattingly
William W. Maves
John G. Mayer
Craig Mays
Buddy Mazzara
Herbert E. McAdoo
Sidney McCallum
Joseph E. McCann, Jr.
Donald McCarthy
Dick McCauley

William H. McChesney
Earl E. McClung
Billy McCoy
Robert McCrory
Francis H. McFarland
Leroy D. McFarland
John S. McGee
Daniel A. McGovern
George McGovern
Rieman McIntosh
Frank E. McKee
Clarence McKelvey
Anthony W. McKenzie
Benjamin F. McKinney
Erenest J. McKnight
Colin H. McLaurin
John McLean
John W. McLean
Stephen J. McLeod
G. F. McMahon
Allen M. McMath *deceased*
Howard McMillen
Raleigh L. McMullen
Robert McMurray
Neil McQuarrie
G. V. McQueen
Jack A. McQuiston
Joe Meckoll
Mac Meconis
Stan Medland
J. Medusky
Jay H. Mehaffey
Kenneth G. Meierhoefer
Anthony J. Mennella
Guillaume Mercader
Don Mercier
Douglas Meredith
Dillon H. Merical
James G. Merola
Kenneth J. Merritt
Frank Mertzel
John E. Meyer
Bruce F. Meyers
Larry J. Micka

Charles Middleton
John R. Midkiff
Jim Mildenberger
George E. Miles
Charles H. Miller
Robert H. Miller
Robert M. Miller
Robert V. Miller
Victor J. Miller
Stanley E. Mills *deceased*
Woodrow W. Millsaps
William J. Milne
James L. Milton
Leslie D. Minchew
Wallace E. Minnick
Peronneau Mitchell
Michael Mitroff
Woodrow R. Mock, Jr.
Jack Modesett
Joseph S. Moelich, Sr.
John Moench
Charles D. Mohrle
Albert Mominee
David E. Mondt
John Montgomery
William C. Montgomery
John Montrose
Peter R. Moody
Raymond E. Moon
Ferdinand Morello
Rocco J. Moretto
Aubrey Morgan
William J. Moriarity
Jesse Morrow
John R. G. Morschel
Dan J. Morse
Richard Mote
Captain Andre Mouton
Armin Mruck
Bert Mullins
Placido Munnia
Gilbert E. Murdock
James Murphy
Claude Murray

Frank Murray
F. L. Mutter

Romuald Nalecz-Tyminski
E. Ray Nance
Roger D. Nedry
William S. Nehez
Charles Neighbor
Don Nelson
Donald T. Nelson
Albert Nendza
Cliff Neumann
Kenneth C. Newberg
George K. Newhall
Arthur L. Nichols, Jr.   *deceased*
Roy W. Nickrent
R. J. Nieblas
Julius R. Noble
Harry Nomburg
Francis M. Norr
Frank J. Nowacki
Alfred Nuesser
Ralph J. Nunley
Donald W. Nuttall

William Oatman
Edward Obert
Ralph G. Oehmcke
Lou Offenberg
Harold J. O'Leary
Ingvald G. Olesrud
Ross Olsen
James C. O'Neal, Jr.
William T. O'Neill
John B. O'Rourke
Lawrence Orr
William Otlowski
James Ousley
William T. Owens
Sherman J. Oyler
Jim Oyster

Joseph J. Palladino
Clifford Palliser

N. L. Palmer, Jr.   *deceased*
Francis A. Palys
Ellison W. Parfitt
Bill Parish
Darel C. Parker
Richard Parker
W. E. Parker
William Parker
John Parkins
Harry Parley
Wally Parr
Tony B. Parrino
Harold L. Parris
Philip J. Parrott
Clifton Parshall
Tom Parsons
Fred C. Patheiger   *deceased*
Mario Patruno
J. Robert Patterson
Ralph Patton
Michael C. Paul
Vernon L. Paul   *deceased*
Anthony J. Paulino
Joe Pavlick
John M. Peck, M.D.
James O. Peek
Al Pekasiewicz
John Pellegren
Aaron D. Pendleton
Ken Penn
Juluis Perlinski   *deceased*
Marvin Perrett
John A. Perry
Gene Person
Debs H. Peters   *deceased*
Earl W. Peters
H. B. Peterson
Jerry Peterson
Lt. Col. Jerry Peterson
Joseph L. Petry
Elvin W. Phelps
Woodrow W. Phelps
Jack Phillips
James Phillips

Jerry L. Phillips
Robert M. Phillips
Paul Phinney
Robert Piauge
Harold Pickersgill
Gregory Pidhorecki
Dewey Pierce
Exum L. Pike, Sr.
Malvin R. Pike
Joe Pilck
Kenneth Pipes
Pierre Piprel
Sidney S. Platt
Leonard Ploeckelman
Edward Plona
Tom Plumb
Felix C. Podalok
George T. Poe
Forrest Pogue
Lee Polek
Sgt. John Polyniak
Tom Porcella
Mario Porcellini
Angelo Porta
Pat Porteous
Donald Porter
Dennis Pott
Vincent Powell
Cecil Powers
Darrell Powers
Ralph Powers
Lee Pozek
Orvis C. Preston
Walter Preston
L. A. Prewritt
John Price
Virgil T. Price
Walter Pridmore
Jack B. Prince

Richard H. Quigley
Tom Quigley
Louis F. Quirk, Jr.

John C. Raaen, Jr.

Duwaine Raatz
Robert J. Rader
Paul Q. Radzom
Emerald M. Ralston *deceased*
John Ramano
Oswaldo V. Ramirez
Bill Ramsey
Denver Randleman
Louis Rann
Glen Rappold
Charles Ratliff
Bill Ray
Larry Raygor
Samuel Reali
Paul Ream
Quinton F. Reams
William C. Reckord
Robert E. Reed
Russell P. Reeder, Jr.
Richard Reese
Sandy Reid
Joe D. Reilly
Harry L. Reisenleiter
Bill Rellstab
John J. Reville
K. B. Reynolds
Oscar Rich
John R. Richards
John W. Richards
Elliot Richardson
Robert Richardson
Samuel Richardson
Wilbur Richardson
Samuel Ricker, Sr.
Clinton E. Riddle
James R. Rider
Ross Riggs
John W. Ripley
Jason Rivet
George V. Roach
Arthur E. Roberts
Douglas Roberts
Elvy B. Roberts
James M. Roberts
Javis Roberts

John W. Robertson
Robert T. Robertson
William S. Robilliard
John H. Robinson
Dean Rockwell
Charles W. Rodekuhr
Edward K. Roger
Paul Rogers
Robert E. Rogge
Edgar M. Rolland
Nick Romanetz
Kenneth L. Romanski
Edward L. Ronczy
Bob Rooney
James M. Roos
Theodore Roosevelt
Robert Rose
Zolman Rosenfield *deceased*
George Rosie
William Rosz
Wayne Roten
William J. Roulette
Frank Rowe
G. Royster
Mike Rudanovich, Jr.
David W. Ruditz
Thomas R. Rudolf
Eugene W. Rule *deceased*
Warren Rulien
Mel I. Rush
Charles P. Rushforth, III
Carlton P. Russell
Ken Russell
James A. Russo, Jr.
Peter N. Russo
H. A. Rutherford
Ron Rutland
George Ryal
Bob Ryan
Charles J. Ryan
George Ryan
William F. Ryan

Werner Saenger *deceased*
Edwin Safford

Harvey Safford
Robert L. Sales
Robert Salley
Sidney A. Salomon
Lawrence F. Salva
Charles E. Sammon
James Sammons
Otis Sampson
Raymond Sanders
Archie Sanderson
Hector J. Santa Anna
Alfred J. Sapa
Joseph E. Sardo, III
Jack R. Sargeant
William E. Satterwhite
Cliff Saul
Robert Saveland
Jeff Savelkoul
William M. Sawyer
Michael Sayers
Dennis Scanlan
Franklin J. Schaffner *deceased*
Irl C. Schahrer
Leonard Schallehn
Eldon Schinning
D. Zane Schlemmer
Vincent H. Schlotterbeck
Roy F. Schmoyer
Rudy Schneider
Robert Schober
Donald P. Schoo
Edgar A. Schroeder *deceased*
Herbert W. Schroeder
Oliver A. Schuh
William G. Schuler
Everett P. Schultheis
Arthur B. Schultz
Edward R. Schwartz
William F. Schwerin, M.D.
John Scilliere
W. Murphy Scott
Donald L. Scribner
Richard Scudder
Ronald Seaborne
Larry J. Seavy-Cioffi

Elmer Seech
Irvin W. Seelye
John Seitz
Henry E. Seitzler
Cletus Sellner
William Sentry
Jack R. Sergeant
Roy G. Settle
Ohmer D. Shade
Edward Shames
Don Shanley
Fred Shaver
Horace G. Shaw
James Shaw
Robert Shaw
Walter P. Shawd
J. T. Shea
Brian Shelley
Joseph Shelly
Charles G. Shettle
K. F. Shiffer
Alex Shisko
Tom Shockley
C. Richard Shoemaker
Ron Shuff
Walter Sidlowski
Stan Silva
Frank L. Simeone
Thomas A. Simms
Walter Simon
W. A. Simpkins
Louis Simpson
Ralph H. Sims
Clifford H. Sinnet
Wayne Sisk
Charles E. Skidmore, Jr.
C. B. Jack Skipper
Paul L. Skogsberg
John R. Slaughter
John K. Slingluff
Albert H. Smith, Jr.
Allen T. Smith *deceased*
Anthony M. Smith
David M. Smith

George A. Smith
Helen Smith
Jim Smith
Joe G. Smith
John F. Smith
Lewis C. Smith
Ronald E. Smith
Thor Smith
W. B. Smith
William C. Smith
Bob Smittle
Irving Smolens
Harry Smyle
Ernie Snow
Ronald Snyder
Dr. William N. Solkin
Clifford R. Sorenson
John Souch
Joe J. Sousa
Frank E. South
John Spaulding
Doug Spitler
Albert Spoheimer, Jr.
Floyd Stanard
Edward H. Stanton
William D. Steel
Ralph V. Steele
David Steinberg
Tom Steinhardt
Ralph Steinway
Allen Stephens
Roy O. Stevens
Charles W. Stockell
Clayton E. Storeby
John J. Storm
Raymond Stott
Joshwil Straub *deceased*
Bob Strayer
Francis H. Strickler
Robert F. Stringer
Raymond L. Strischek
Wallace C. Strobel
Rod Strohe
Kenneth Strong

Clyde D. Strosnider, Sr.
Ray Stubbe
John C. Studt
Lewis Sturdovon
Phillip Sturgeon, M.D.
Jon Sturm
Stanley Stypulkowski
Charles R. Sullivan
Sigurd Sundby
S. S. Suntag
Frank Swann
J. Leslie Sweetnam
Oscar F. Swenson
Fred Swets
William L. Swisher
Edward Szaniawski

Ralph Tancordo
Fred R. Tannery
Vernon W. Tart
Wayne Tate
Manuel Tavis
Amos Taylor
Frank Taylor
James R. Taylor
John R. Taylor *deceased*
Nigel Taylor *deceased*
Ron Taylor
W. B. Taylor
Captain Alan Tequseay
Joseph Terebessy, Sr.
Terry Terrebonne
Charles H. Thomas
David E. Thomas
Paul Thompson
James M. Thomson
Charles C. Thornton, Jr.
Jacqueline Thornton
John Thornton
Wagger Thornton
J. Tilleh
J. Tillett
Jack L. Tipton

Richard Todd
Lynn C. Tomlinson
Joseph Toughill
Benno V. Tourdelille
Arthur W. Tower
Joe Toye
Charles R. Trail
    Travett
Dewey O. Tredway *deceased*
Frank A. Tremblay
Raymond A. Trittler
K. A. J. Trott
John F. Troy
William True
William H. Tucker
Arthur W. Tupper
Thomas B. Turner
William A. Turner
Robert S. Tweed

Alexander Uhlig
Sidney M. Ulan
Matthew Urban
Willis L. Ure

Thomas Valance
Norman Vance
Howard Vander Beek
James Van Fleet
Elmer Vermeer *deceased*
Sarifino R. Visco
Raymond Voight
Walter Vollrath, Jr.
Walter Voss
Willis L. Vowell
Martin Waarvick
Orville Wade
Orval Wakefield
Frank Walk
Robert E. Walker
Sir Patrick Wall
James Wallwork
Martin Walsh

George R. Walter
Marion G. Wamsley
William Wangaman
Dr. Simon V. Ward, Jr.
Lawrence Waring
Adolph Warnecke
Lloyd Warren
Rev. Wilfred Washington
Homer E. Wassam
John Watkins
Orville Watkins
Col. James H. Watts
James L. Watts
Carl Weast
E. R. Webb
Glover Webb
David K. Webster
Fritz Weinschenk
Dean Weisert
James Weller
Harry Welsh
Wendell E. Wendt
Floyd West
Henry F. West
Albert Nash Whatley
Elmer M. Wheeler
Brian T. Whinney
Harry T. Whitby
F. S. White
George White
James A. White
Don Whitehead
J. J. Whitmeyer, Jr.
Frank Whitney
Don T. Whitsitt
Eldon Wiehe
Arthur B. Wieqk
Herbert H. Wiggins
Felix P. Wilkerson
Robert A. Wilkins
James Wilkinson
George Williams
Joe B. Williams
Thomas E. Williams

George E. Williamson   *deceased*
Harvey Williamson
Kenneth R. Williamson
Robert J. Williamson
Richard Willstatter
Leonard Wilmont
William Wilps
Alan R. Wilson
J. E. Wilson
Seth Wilson
William Wingett
Edgar R. Winters
Richard D. Winters
William R. Winters
Tom Winterton
Walter F. Wintsch
Gene Wirwahn
J. J. Witmeyer
C. L. Witt
Willie B. Wolfe
David Wood
George R. Woodbridge
Julian R. Woods
Carroll Wright
Joseph N. Wright
Kenneth Wright
Richard Wright
Ted Wright
Brony Wronoski

Edward L. Yarberry   *deceased*
Willie Yates
Dick Young
Edwin P. Young
Samuel Young

Robert Zafft
Walter F. Zagol
Charles Zalewski
Charles Zeccola
Lester Zick
John Zink
Sam Zittrer
John Zmudzinski

Index

The National D-Day Museum

**THE NATIONAL
D-DAY MUSEUM
NEW ORLEANS**

In 1992, the U.S. Congress authorized the building of the National D-Day Museum in New Orleans, on the site where the Higgins boats were constructed and tested. The Museum's mission is to remind the American people of the day when the fury of an aroused democracy was hurled against Nazi-occupied Europe, and to inspire future generations by showing that there is nothing this Republic cannot do when everyone gets on the team. In addition to hands-on displays, a photographic gallery, weapons, uniforms, and other artifacts, the Museum will house an Archives that will hold all printed work on D-Day, plus the oral and written memoirs from participants in the battle that the Eisenhower Center at the University of New Orleans has been gathering since 1983. This is the largest collection of eyewitness accounts of a single battle in the world. For information on how to become a Friend of the Museum, or to donate artifacts, please write the National D-Day Museum, 1600 Canal Street, Suite 501, New Orleans, La. 70112.

The author is donating his royalties from this paperback edition of *D-Day* to the National D-Day Museum.

POCKET
BOOKS

BAND OF BROTHERS

Stephen E. Ambrose

The *Sunday Times* #1 bestseller and a major BBC series produced by Tom Hanks and Steven Spielberg.

In BAND OF BROTHERS, Stephen E. Ambrose pays tribute to the men of Easy Company, a crack rifle company in the US Army. From their rigorous training in Georgia in 1942 to the dangerous parachute landings on D-Day and their triumphant capture of Hitler's 'Eagle's Nest' in Berchtesgarden, Ambrose tells the story of this remarkable company. Repeatedly sent on the toughest missions, these brave men fought, went hungry, froze and died in the service of their country.

'Superb . . . his scholarly writing style seems to know that heroism needs no cheap embellishment. Gripping and humbling'
GLASGOW HERALD

PRICE £6.99
ISBN 0 7434 2990 7

**POCKET
BOOKS**

CITIZEN SOLDIERS
THE US ARMY FROM THE NORMANDY
BEACHES TO THE SURRENDER OF
GERMANY
Stephen E. Ambrose

The *Sunday Times* #1 bestselling author.

This sequel to D-DAY opens at 00:01 hours, June 7, 1944 on the Normandy Beaches and ends at 02:45 hours, May 7, 1945 with the overrunning of Germany. From the enlisted men and junior officers, Ambrose draws on hundreds of interviews from those on both sides of the war. The experience of these citizen soldiers reveals the ordinary sufferings and hardships of war.

'History boldly told and elegantly written . . . Gripping' *Wall Street Journal*

'*Citizen Soldiers* is about the most gripping account of the Second World War that I have ever read' Joseph Heller

'*Citizen Soldiers* is an unforgettable testament to the World War II generation' *The New York Times*.

**PRICE £8.99
ISBN 0 7434 5015 9**